Minimum Wages in Canada:
A Statistical Portrait With Policy Implications

by

Ken Battle

January 2003

Copyright © 2003 by The Caledon Institute of Social Policy

ISBN 1-55382-035-5

Published by:

The Caledon Institute of Social Policy
1600 Scott Street, Suite 620
Ottawa, Ontario, Canada
K1Y 4N7
Phone: (613) 729-3340
Fax: (613) 729-3896
E-mail: caledon@caledoninst.org
Website: *www.caledoninst.org*

Caledon publications are available on our website and from:

Renouf Publishing Company Limited
5369 Canotek Road
Ottawa, Ontario, Canada
K1J 9J3
Phone: (613) 745-2665
Fax: (613) 745-7660

Contents

INTRODUCTION	1
CANADA	
a. Minimum Wages in Canada	3
b. Minimum Wage Workers in Canada	32
NEWFOUNDLAND AND LABRADOR	
a. Minimum Wages in Newfoundland and Labrador	48
b. Minimum Wage Workers in Newfoundland and Labrador	57
PRINCE EDWARD ISLAND	
a. Minimum Wages in Prince Edward Island	67
b. Minimum Wage Workers in Prince Edward Island	75
NOVA SCOTIA	
a. Minimum Wages in Nova Scotia	83
b. Minimum Wage Workers in Nova Scotia	91
NEW BRUNSWICK	
a. Minimum Wages in New Brunswick	102
b. Minimum Wage Workers in New Brunswick	111
QUEBEC	
a. Minimum Wages in Quebec	121
b. Minimum Wage Workers in Quebec	130
ONTARIO	
a. Minimum Wages in Ontario	140
b. Minimum Wage Workers in Ontario	149
MANITOBA	
a. Minimum Wages in Manitoba	159
b. Minimum Wage Workers in Manitoba	167
SASKATCHEWAN	
a. Minimum Wages in Saskatchewan	177
b. Minimum Wage Workers in Saskatchewan	185

ALBERTA
a. Minimum Wages in Alberta   195
b. Minimum Wage Workers in Alberta   204

BRITISH COLUMBIA
a. Minimum Wages in British Columbia   214
b. Minimum Wage Workers in British Columbia   223

YUKON   233

NORTHWEST TERRITORIES   239

NUNAVUT   245

HOW CANADIAN MINIMUM WAGES COMPARE INTERNATIONALLY
Canada and the US   250
Canada and other countries   251

POLICY IMPLICATIONS   252

ENDNOTES   263

REFERENCES   271

APPENDICES
1. Summary of key findings   272
2. Tables   282

INTRODUCTION

The minimum wage sets a floor below which employers cannot pay their workers, subject both to statutory enforcement by government and civil action on the part of employees. The minimum wage is unusual in that it is among the few direct state interventions in the free market economy. Also one of the oldest social policies – originating in New Zealand in 1894 and spreading to Canada in the early part of the 20th century – the minimum wage remains controversial, as explained in the final section of this report.

The debate on minimum wages in Canada takes place in an empirical void. Despite a couple of important studies of minimum wages in some provinces,[1] there is no comprehensive, up-to-date source of essential data, information and analysis on minimum wages and minimum wage workers throughout the country.

This study helps fill that void by charting trends and rankings of minimum wages in Canada's ten provinces and three territories, as well as in the form of a national weighted average. The report traces the changing value of minimum wages from 1965 to the present and compares them to before-tax and after-tax poverty lines, average earnings and welfare incomes. It also investigates the size and key characteristics of the minimum wage workforce nationally and in each province. The report compares Canadian minimum wages to those in the US and a number of advanced industrialized nations. The final section discusses the policy debate on the minimum wage in light of the findings of this research.

This study has a forward-looking and longer-term purpose. It establishes a set of baseline indicators that will be updated regularly to provide an invaluable time series on minimum wages and minimum wage workers in Canada. Researchers will be able to analyze in depth trends and patterns in minimum wages and minimum wage workers both nationally and from one jurisdiction to another across the country. Policy makers, administrators and researchers will have a unique source of comprehensive information from which to cull evidence that can help inform and test their arguments.

This report presents a massive array of statistics. To help guide the reader, the text is illustrated with a series of graphs, and in most cases the underlying data are shown. The appendix gives the same (and additional) data in tabular form, and also provides a summary of the major findings of the study.

The organization is modular. The first section looks at trends in the national average minimum wage and analyzes the characteristics of Canada's minimum wage workforce. Equivalent data where available, using the same set of headings and graphs, are then presented and discussed individually for each of the ten provinces and three territories.

Data on minimum wage rates are from the author's compilation over many years from Labour Canada, now available online from Human Resources Development Canada's Labour Program website [Human Resources Development Canada, 2002]. The Caledon Institute of Social Policy calculated annual minimum wage earnings in each province and territory and converted the results to constant dollars, which we then compared to before-tax and after-tax poverty lines and to average earnings. We also calculated national minimum wage statistics, using a weighted average of provincial, territorial and federal rates. Estimates of the minimum wage workforce in Canada and the ten provinces (no data are available for the three territories) in 2000 were provided to Caledon through special runs undertaken by Statistics Canada. Caledon is grateful to the officials who supplied these data, though of course the presentation and analysis of the statistics are ours alone and are not the responsibility of Statistics Canada.

The data on after-tax and disposable minimum wage incomes and child benefits were calculated by the Caledon Institute using its model of the federal income tax system and 13 provincial/territorial income tax regimes. Welfare income estimates – to which minimum wage disposable income is compared – are from the National Council of Welfare [National Council of Welfare 2002].

Dollar trends and changes are always given in constant (inflation-adjusted) figures. Percentages sometimes do not add to 100 due to rounding.

CANADA

a. Minimum Wages in Canada

Fourteen minimum wage jurisdictions

Every provincial and territorial government in Canada sets minimum wages through employment standards legislation, though the rate varies from one jurisdiction to another. The federal government also administers its own minimum wage – since July 17, 1996 set equal to the provincial/territorial rate for federally-protected workers in each jurisdiction– under the Canada Labour Code to cover private sector industries that are interprovincial or international in scope, including air, marine, rail and road transportation, telecommunications, banks and some federal Crown corporations. Ottawa also in practice applies the federal minimum wage to federal government employees.[2] In total, 14 governments – the federal government, the ten provinces and the three territories – set and enforce minimum wages. The self-employed are not covered by minimum wage legislation.

Most Canadian employees are covered by the general 'adult' minimum wage rate, though some jurisdictions set different rates for certain industries, occupations or classes of workers – or exclude them from minimum wage protection.[3] Historically, lower minimum wage rates applied to very young workers and to women. Domestic and farm workers either had a lower rate or were excluded altogether from minimum wage protection. Salespersons, construction workers, hairdressers and restaurant workers also received differential treatment, as did workers with disabilities. However, the trend in recent years has been to remove such exclusions and thus effectively to extend coverage of the adult minimum wage rate.

Most jurisdictions have dropped the practice of setting lower minimum wage rates for very young employees, though Ontario, the Northwest Territories and Nunavut continue to do so. Ontario's minimum wage rate for students under 18 employed up to 28 hours a week, or during a school holiday, is $6.60 an hour or 25 cents below the $6.85 adult rate; the Northwest Territories and Nunavut pay $6.00 an hour for employees under age 16 as opposed to $6.50 for the adult rate.[4] Nova Scotia sets a lower minimum wage for inexperienced workers (for the first three months' work) – currently $5.35 an hour or 45 cents less than the $5.80 adult rate. British Columbia recently followed suit with a 'first-job' or 'training' minimum wage of $6.00 an hour ($2.00 below the adult rate of $8.00) that applies to first-time workers' initial 500 hours of employment. Newfoundland and Yukon exclude young workers (16 and 17 years old, respectively) from coverage, though Yukon covers young workers in certain occupations.

Alberta, Saskatchewan and Manitoba still allow employers to pay below-adult minimum wages to persons with disabilities, but these provisions are rarely used today. Quebec excludes trainees in vocational integration programs from minimum wage coverage.

While Alberta, Saskatchewan, Manitoba and Ontario still do not cover most farm workers under minimum wage legislation, Saskatchewan covers certain kinds of work (egg hatcheries, greenhouses and nurseries, and bush clearing) and Ontario includes workers who harvest fruit, vegetables or tobacco for marketing or storage. Several other jurisdictions have improved coverage of farm labourers, though certain conditions apply (e.g., PEI covers farm labourers in commercial operations and Quebec covers farm workers in operations with at least four employees). Newfoundland, the Northwest Territories, Nunavut and Yukon include farm workers under their general minimum wage.

New Brunswick excludes domestic workers from minimum wage protection. Prince Edward Island, Quebec and Manitoba do not cover employees who provide care for children or for infirm, ill or aged persons in private homes. Home workers (e.g., teleworkers and pieceworkers in the clothing and textiles industry) are not regulated in all jurisdictions; they receive varying forms of protection in Ontario, Manitoba, Saskatchewan and British Columbia.[5]

Some jurisdictions set special minimum wage rates for certain categories of workers. These special categories include live-in camp leaders and camp counsellors, residential caretakers in apartment buildings, employees serving alcohol in licensed establishments, employees who receive tips, loggers and forestry workers. Most jurisdictions exclude from minimum wage coverage supervisory and managerial employees, students working in training programs, participants in work experience and rehabilitation programs, registered apprentices and salespersons on commission. Some jurisdictions exclude counsellors and instructors at non-profit educational or recreational camps and playgrounds, film and video extras, workers on fishing vessels, teachers, offenders performing community services, and residential caretakers.

Interprovincial rank: dollar value of minimum wages (Figure A1)

Minimum wages in Canada range widely across the ten provinces and three territories, from a low of $5.90 an hour in Alberta to a high of $8.00 in BC, as of December 2002. (Remember that the federal minimum wage is set at the provincial and territorial rate, so provincial/territorial trends include workers in each province and territory covered by the federal minimum wage). Jurisdictions can be divided into two broad groups. The lower group, within 10 cents of one another, is made up of Alberta ($5.90), Newfoundland, Nova Scotia, New Brunswick and Prince Edward Island ($6.00 each). The higher group consists of Manitoba, the Northwest Territories and Nunavut ($6.50 each), Saskatchewan ($6.65), Ontario ($6.85), Quebec and Yukon ($7.20 each) and British Columbia ($8.00).

Minimum wage rates can change during the course of a year, and 2002 is no exception. Newfoundland increased its minimum wage from $5.50 to $5.75 an hour on May 1, 2002 and again to $6.00 on November 1; Nova Scotia from $5.80 to $6.00 on October 1; New Brunswick from $5.90 to $6.00 on April 1; Quebec from $7.00 to $7.20 on October 1; Manitoba from $6.25 to $6.50 effective April 1; and Saskatchewan from $6.00 to $6.35 on May 1 and $6.65 on November 1, 2002. To take into account these within-year changes, Figure A1 shows the average hourly minimum wage in 2002 in each province and territory, assuming the maximum full-time (40 hours a week) year-long (52 weeks) employment.

Minimum Wages in Canada: A Statistical Portrait With Policy Implications

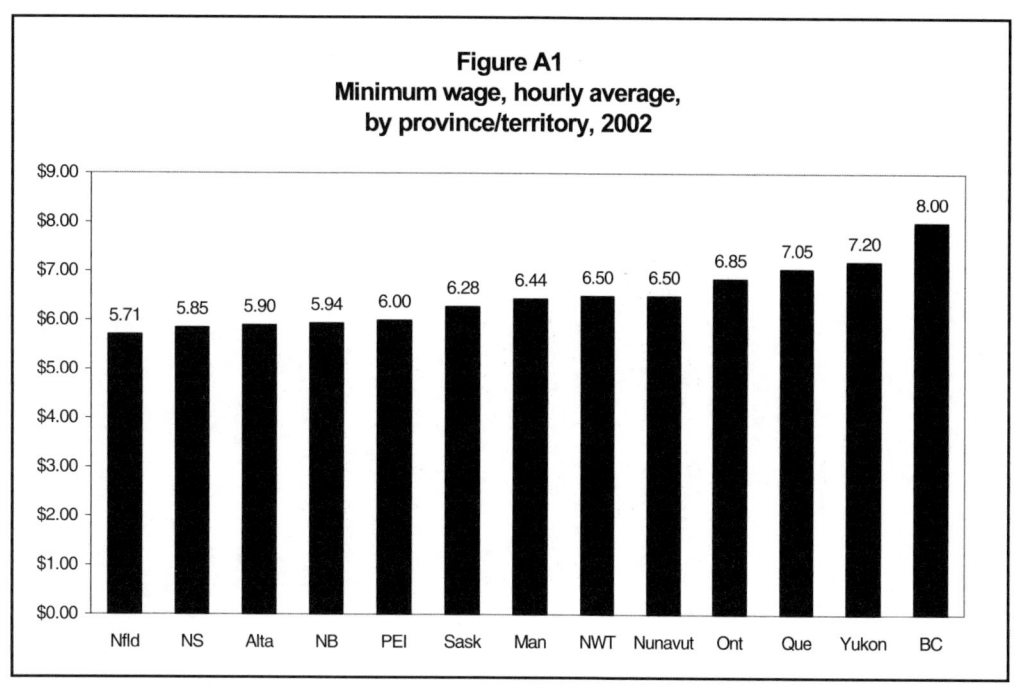

Average hourly minimum wages in 2002 range from $5.71 in Newfoundland to $5.85 in Nova Scotia, $5.90 in Alberta, $5.94 in New Brunswick, $6.00 in Prince Edward Island, $6.28 in Saskatchewan, $6.44 in Manitoba, $6.50 in the Northwest Territories and Nunavut,[6] $6.85 in Ontario, $7.05 in Quebec, $7.20 in Yukon and $8.00 in British Columbia.

Trend in dollar value of national average minimum wage (Figure A2)

Because minimum wages are not indexed (i.e., are not regularly adjusted to take into account changes in basic economic indicators such as the cost of living or wages), their value fluctuates over time depending on the frequency and amount of changes in rates compared to the rate of inflation or wage growth. Figure A2 shows the trend in the average minimum wage for Canada (i.e., the weighted average for federal, provincial and territorial jurisdictions) from 1965 through 2001 (the most recent year for which a weighted average can be calculated); each year's average minimum wage has been converted to inflation-adjusted (i.e., constant) 2001 dollars to show the real trend, after factoring out the impact of inflation on the dollar. The purpose of this measure is to show the national trend in minimum wages, blended according to each province's relative weight in the workforce; actual trends vary from one province and territory to another, as we show later.

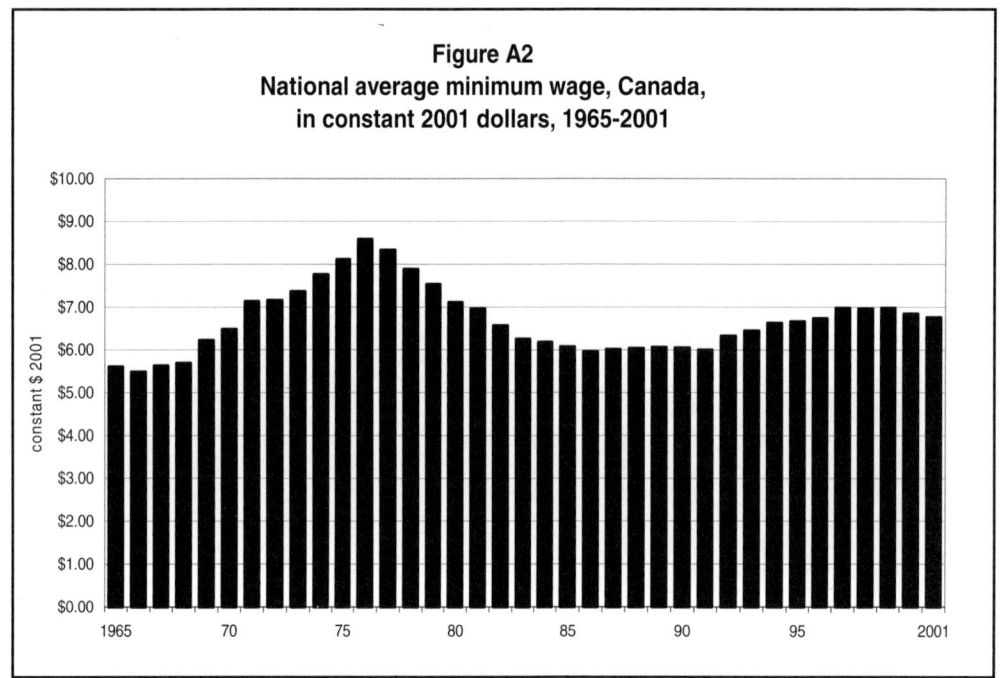

Figure A2
National average minimum wage, Canada,
in constant 2001 dollars, 1965-2001

Contrary to conventional wisdom, minimum wages in Canada are not on a steady decline: The reality is – as is usually the case in public policy – more complex and less apocalyptic. The average minimum wage rose substantially between 1965 and 1976, fell (but not all the way back) in the late 1970s and first half of the 1980s, levelled off in the second half of the 1980s, gradually recovered somewhat in the first part of the 1990s, flattened between 1997 and 1999, and then fell slightly in 2000 and 2001.

The national average minimum wage (expressed in inflation-adjusted 2001 dollars) increased from $5.60 in 1965 to $8.58 in 1976, declined to $5.96 by 1986, rose to $6.98 in 1997 and slipped a bit to $6.76 in 2001. In 2001, the Canadian average minimum wage remained significantly below its 1976 peak – $1.82 an hour less or 21.2 percent smaller in real terms. However, in 2001 the national average minimum wage was $1.16 or 20.7 percent higher than in 1965.

The national trend does not, of course, paint precisely the same picture for each province and territory. This report later examines each jurisdiction's individual trend in detail. However, the plateau-like pattern of the national average minimum wage is similar in almost all provinces and territories, as subsequent analysis will show: A sharp increase in the value of the minimum wage between 1965 and the peak in the mid-1970s was followed by a similar or smaller decrease until the mid-1980s or early 1990s, then one of three trends throughout the rest of the 1990s and into the first decade of the new century – modest improvements (PEI, Manitoba, Alberta and BC), flattening out (Newfoundland, Nova Scotia, New Brunswick, Saskatchewan and Yukon) or decline (Quebec, Ontario, the Northwest Territories and Nunavut).[7]

The two main drivers of the national trend are Ontario and Quebec, which between them make up 65.9 percent of Canada's minimum wage workforce. Ontario, with the largest (38.5 percent) share of minimum wage workers, has seen a steady decline in the value of its minimum wage from 1995 through 2002. Quebec's decline has been shorter (1997 through 2002) and smaller than Ontario's.

Interprovincial rank: minimum wages as percentage of average earnings (Figure A3)

A more instructive measure of minimum wages is how they compare to average wages, since that provides a gauge of how the lowest-paid worker compares to the average worker and since both minimum wages and average wages vary from one province and territory to another. The range from one part of Canada to another is very broad indeed. In 2001 (the most recent year for which data on average earnings are available), the jurisdiction whose minimum wage represented the lowest percentage of its average earnings was the Northwest Territories, at 30.2 percent. British Columbia ranked highest, with a minimum wage amounting to 46.2 percent of average earnings.

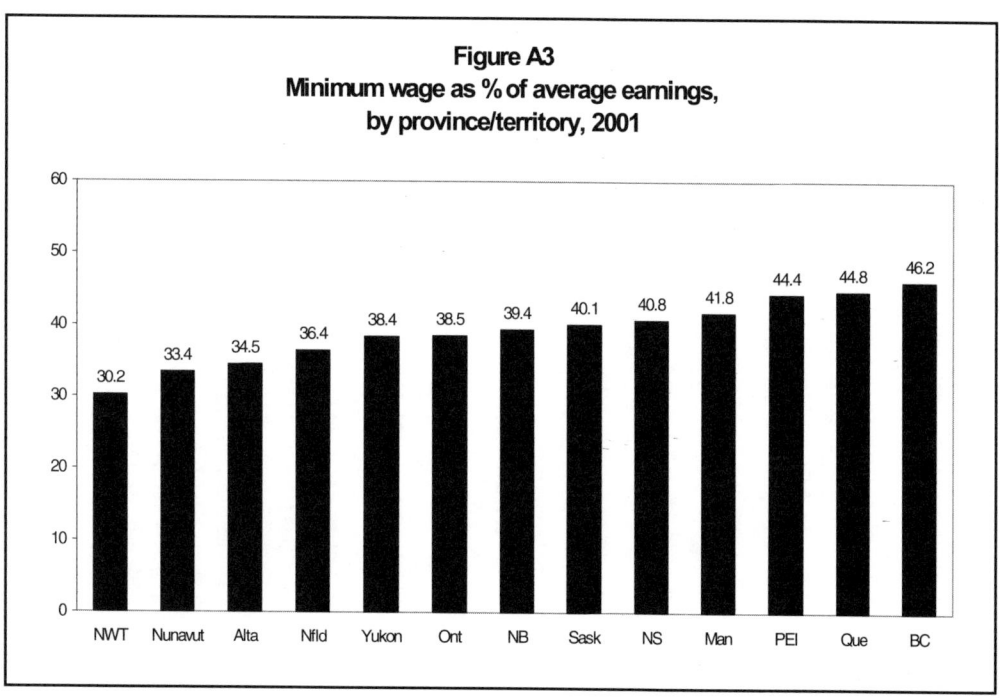

Minimum Wages in Canada: A Statistical Portrait With Policy Implications

From lowest to highest in terms of the ratio of the minimum wage to average earnings, the rankings for 2001 were: the Northwest Territories (30.2 percent), Nunavut (33.4 percent), Alberta (34.5 percent), Newfoundland (36.4 percent), Yukon (38.4 percent), Ontario (38.5 percent), New Brunswick (39.4 percent), Saskatchewan (40.1 percent), Nova Scotia (40.8 percent), Manitoba (41.8 percent), Prince Edward Island (44.4 percent), Quebec (44.8 percent) and British Columbia (46.2 percent). Figure A3 gives the rankings.

Trends in national average minimum wage and average earnings (Figure A4)

The black line in Figure A4 shows the trend in the average Canadian minimum wage, the gray line the trend in average earnings and the vertical bars the trend in the minimum wage as a percentage of average earnings. Read the left-hand axis for the minimum wage and average earnings and the right-hand axis for the minimum wage as a percentage of earnings.

The overall pattern is similar to that for the value of the minimum wage over time. The average minimum wage rose as a percentage of average earnings between 1965 (44.5 percent) and 1976 (50.3 percent), declined slowly until the mid-1980s when it levelled off for the rest of the decade at around 38

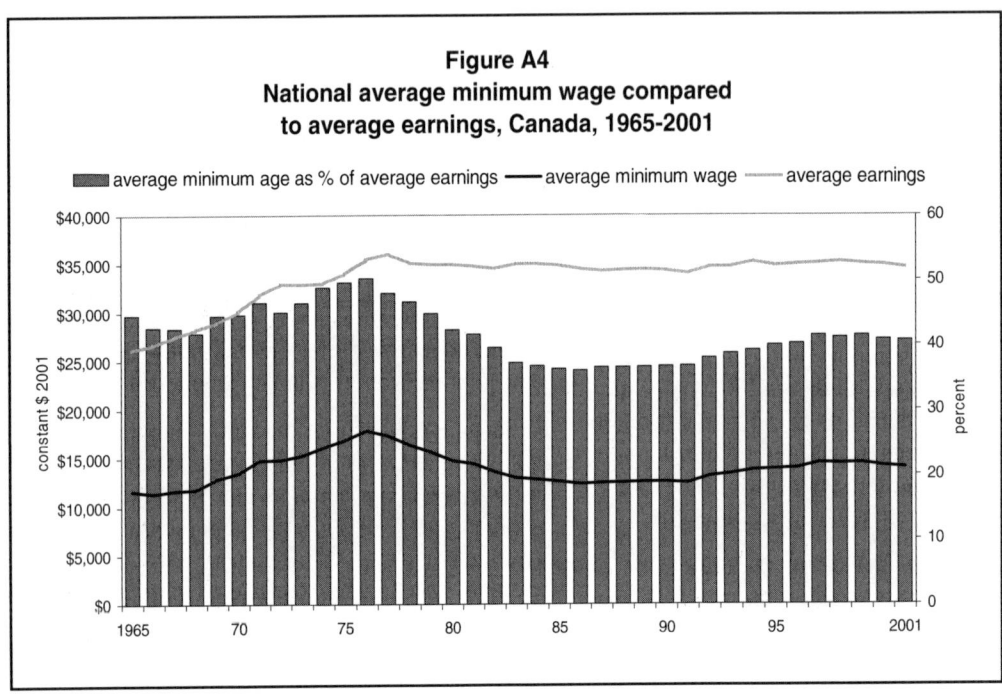

percent, increased in the early 1990s (to 41.4 percent in 1997 and 1999) and then slipped slightly to 40.8 percent in 2000 and 40.7 percent in 2001.

Average earnings increased from $26,158 in 1965 to $36,045 in 1977 and then more or less levelled off, with some small fluctuations, standing at $34,576 in 2001. On an annual (full-time, all-year) basis, the average minimum wage went from $11,651 in 1965 to $17,836 in 1976, slid to $12,399 in 1986 and regained ground to stand at $14,057 in 2001.

Ontario's falling minimum wage

Ontario, with Canada's largest (38.5 percent) share of minimum wage workers, has seen a steady decline in the value of its minimum wage from 1995 through 2002 because the rate has been frozen at $6.85 for seven long years.

In 1995, Ontario had Canada's highest minimum wage – $7.74 expressed in inflation-adjusted 2002 dollars. By 2002, Ontario had slipped from first to fourth place, trailing Quebec ($7.20 as of October, $7.05 annual average), Yukon ($7.20) and British Columbia ($8.00).

In 1995, Ontario's minimum wage amounted to 43.2 percent of its average earnings, ranking the province top in Canada on that measure. By 2001, Ontario's minimum wage had plummeted to 38.5 percent of average earnings, placing the province in sixth-lowest place among the 13 jurisdictions, ahead of only the Northwest Territories, Nunavut, Alberta, Newfoundland and Yukon – and far behind its neighbour Quebec, which took second place with 44.8 percent, and British Columbia at 46.2 percent.

National average minimum wage compared to before-tax poverty lines (Figure A5)

Statistics Canada publishes two sets of 'low income cut-offs,' popularly known as poverty lines or low income lines. The 'before-tax low income cut-offs' are based on gross, pre-tax income (i.e., income from employment, investments, private pensions and other private sources plus income from government programs such as public pensions, Employment Insurance, child benefits and welfare). In recent years, the agency has added a second version of the low income cut-offs, the 'after-tax low income cut-offs,' which factor into the picture the federal and provincial/territorial income taxes that Canadians pay.

Statistics Canada sees two advantages of the after-tax low income cut-offs over the traditional before-tax lines: First, while the before-tax lines take account of government income programs, they do not measure the impact of income taxes – another powerful mechanism for redistributing incomes. Second, people live on after-tax, not gross, income so "it is logical to use people's after-tax income to draw conclusions about their overall economic well-being." [Statistics Canada 2001: 89]. However, while the after-tax low income lines factor in income taxes, they do not take into consideration the payroll taxes (i.e.,

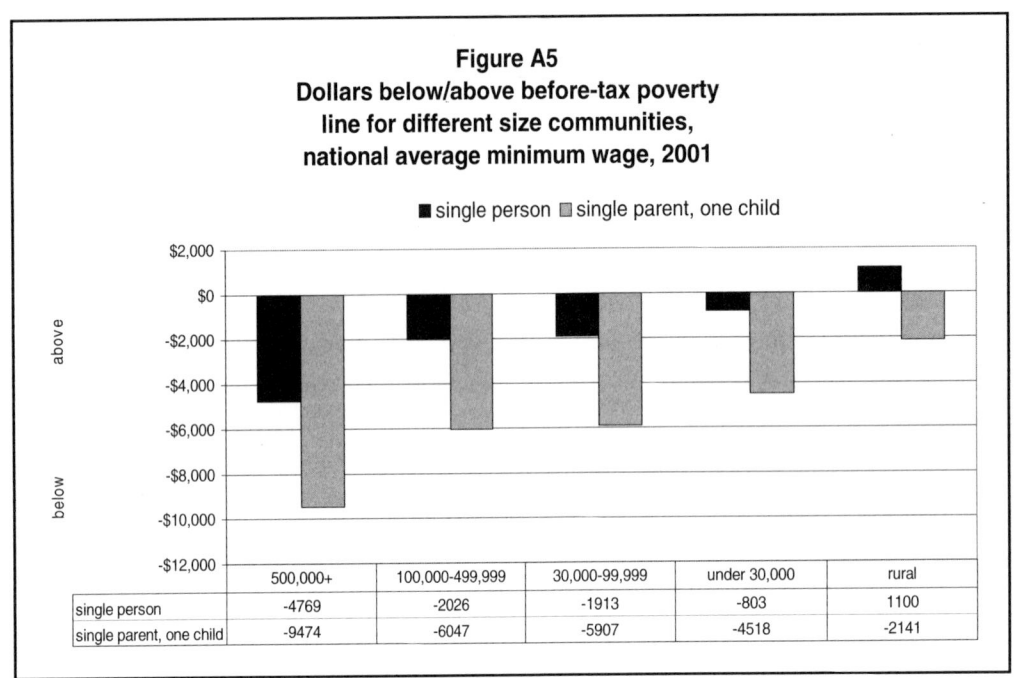

Canada or Quebec Pension Plan contributions and Employment Insurance premiums) that also reduce Canadians' take-home pay.

Statistics Canada's low income cut-offs (both pre-tax and after-tax) vary according to five sizes of community (500,000 or more, 100,000-499,999, 30,000-99,999, under 30,000 and rural) and seven sizes of household (from one person to seven or more). Because the low income lines are lower for smaller communities and households, the minimum wage represents a larger proportion of the lines in smaller communities and households. Here we compare minimum wages to the before-tax low income cut-offs for two households – a single person and a family of two (e.g., a single parent with one child) – and all five community sizes.

In 2001 (the most recent year for which estimates are available), the national average minimum wage ranged from 74.7 percent of the before-tax low income cut-off for one person in metropolitan centers of 500,000 or larger to 87.4 percent for large cities in the 100,000-499,999 category, 88.0 percent for smaller cities between 30,000 and 99,999, 94.6 percent for towns under 30,000 and 108.5 percent for rural areas.

In dollar terms, the average Canadian minimum wage in 2001 fell $4,769 below the low income line for one person in metropolitan centers, $2,026 under for communities between 100,000 and 499,999 inhabitants, $1,913 beneath the line for small cities between 30,000 and 99,999, and $803 below for communities under 30,000 – but $1,100 above the poverty line for rural areas. Figure A5 shows the dollar gap between the average minimum wage and the before-tax poverty line for one person in different size communities.

Because the poverty line varies by family size, minimum wages – which do not vary by family size – fall farther below the poverty line for families than for single workers. We look at the poverty gap for a single parent with one child, which falls in the two-person family size category. (Note that the low income cut-offs do not vary by type of family; for example, a childless couple and single parent with one child are treated the same.)

In 2001, the average minimum wage in Canada ranged from 59.7 percent of the low income line for a two-person family in metropolitan centers of 500,000 or larger to 69.9 percent for large cities (in the 100,000-499,999 size category), 70.4 percent for communities between 30,000 and 99,999 inhabitants, 75.7 percent for towns under 30,000 and 86.8 percent for rural areas. The national average minimum wage fell $9,474 below the low income line for a family of two in metropolitan areas, $6,047 beneath the line for cities in the 100,000-499,999 category, $5,907 under for communities between 30,000 and 99,999 inhabitants, $4,518 below for towns under 30,000 and $2,141 under the poverty line for rural areas.

Trend in national average minimum wage as percentage of before-tax poverty lines (Figure A6)

The long-term picture when we compare the average minimum wage to the before-tax poverty line is the same as the trend in dollar value.

Canada's average minimum wage rose from 61.9 percent of the before-tax low income cut-off for one person in a metropolitan center in 1965 to 94.7 percent of the poverty line in 1976, falling to 65.8 percent in 1986. However, the ratio of the minimum wage to the poverty line increased somewhat in the 1990s, rising to 77.1 percent of the poverty line in 1997 though slipping to 74.7 percent by 2001.

For a two-person family (e.g., a single parent with one child), the minimum wage went from 49.5 percent of the low income line in 1965 to a peak of 75.8 percent in 1976, declining to a low of 52.7 percent in 1986, rising by 1997 to 61.7 percent of the poverty line and then easing to 59.7 percent in 2001. (In 2001, the estimated low income cut-off for the largest community size – 500,000-plus – was $18,289 for one person and $23,535 for a family of two.)

Minimum wages compared to after-tax poverty lines (Figures A7-A11)

The above analysis compared the national average minimum wage to Statistics Canada's before-tax low income cut-offs, which are based on gross, pre-tax income (i.e., income from employment,

Minimum Wages in Canada: A Statistical Portrait With Policy Implications

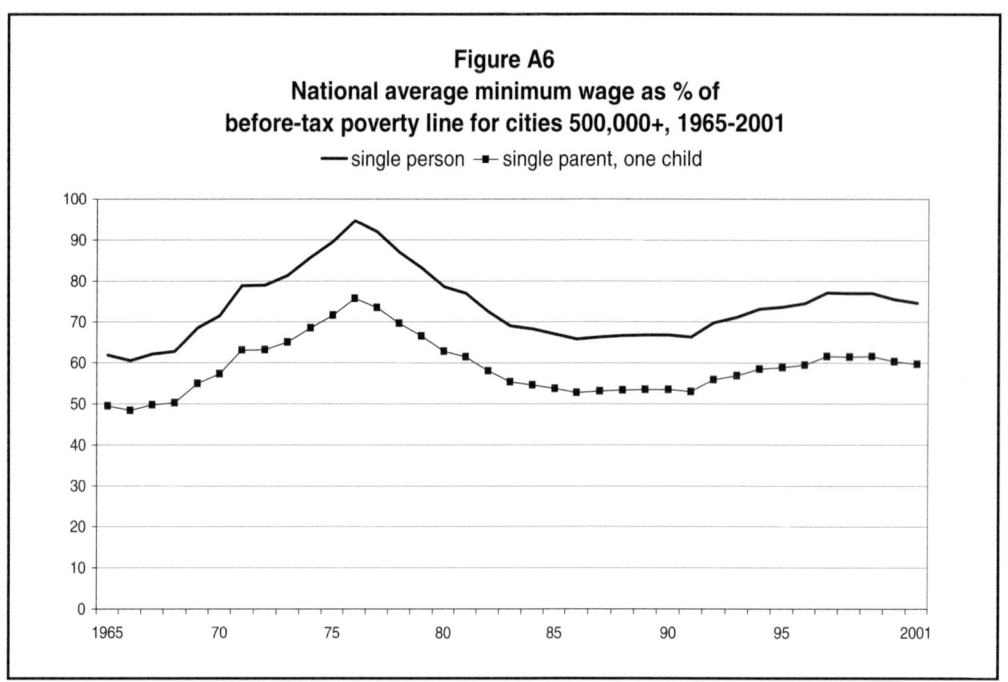

investments, private pensions and other private sources plus income from government programs such as public pensions, Employment Insurance, child benefits and welfare). The following analysis examines the after-tax income of five types of household working for minimum wages – a single person, a single parent with one child age 2, a one-earner couple with two children aged 10 and 15, a two-earner couple supporting two children (10 and 15) on one-and-a-half minimum wages, and a two-earner couple with two children (10 and 15) and two full minimum wages. We subtract after-tax minimum wage incomes from the after-tax low income cut-off for the largest city in each province; negative results means that minimum wage incomes fall short of the poverty line, while positive figures mean that minimum wage incomes are above the poverty line.

After-tax income includes not just minimum wage earnings but also government programs such as the federal GST (Goods and Services Tax) credit, federal and provincial child benefits and various provincial refundable tax credits, and then deducts federal and provincial income taxes (but not payroll taxes). Note that the discussion does not include Yukon, the Northwest Territories and Nunavut because the low income cut-offs do not apply to these jurisdictions. Here and in the provincial and territorial income data provided later, we assume that households receive all income benefits for which they are eligible; in reality, some people do not apply for certain programs – such as earnings supplements – for various reasons (e.g., they do not know the benefit exists or that they might be eligible for it, or they do not want the hassle of dealing with government any more than they have to already).

12   Caledon Institute of Social Policy

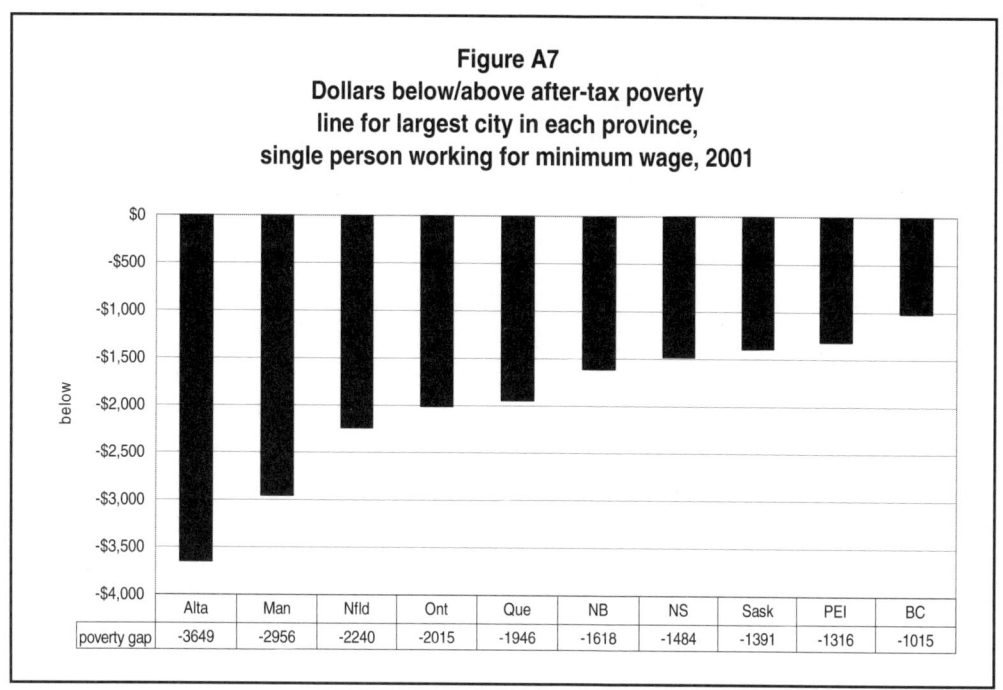

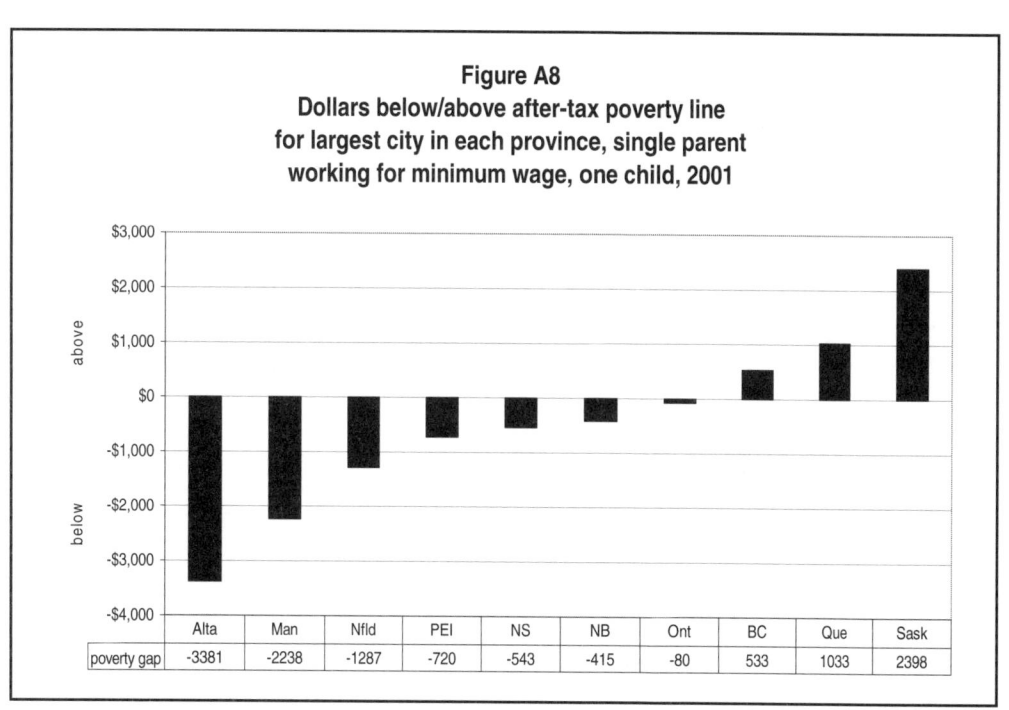

After-tax income from minimum wages and other government benefits for single minimum wage workers falls short of the after-tax poverty line for the largest city in every province. Figure A7 illustrates the results. The shortfall (i.e., the distance below the after-tax poverty line) ranges from $3,649 in Alberta (the largest poverty gap) to $1,015 in neighbouring British Columbia (the smallest poverty gap).

The picture is different for minimum wage single parents with one young child, depicted in Figure A8. While after-tax minimum wage incomes are below the after-tax poverty line for the largest city in most provinces – ranging from $3,381 below the poverty line in Alberta to $80 under in Ontario – the gap is not as deep as for single people because single parents pay little or no income tax and receive the federal Canada Child Tax Benefit and, in virtually all provinces and territories (Prince Edward Island excepted), provincial child benefits. In British Columbia, Quebec and Saskatchewan, single parents with one child manage to rise above the poverty line – by $533 in British Columbia, $1,033 in Quebec and $2,398 in Saskatchewan – thanks in large part to relatively generous provincial child benefits and earnings supplements that bolster the incomes of working poor families. British Columbia also has Canada's highest minimum wage.

The poverty gap is deep for couples with two children that rely upon one parent's minimum wage, as illustrated in Figure A9. Such families receive income from the various federal and provincial child benefits, earnings supplements and assorted federal and provincial refundable credits. They also pay little

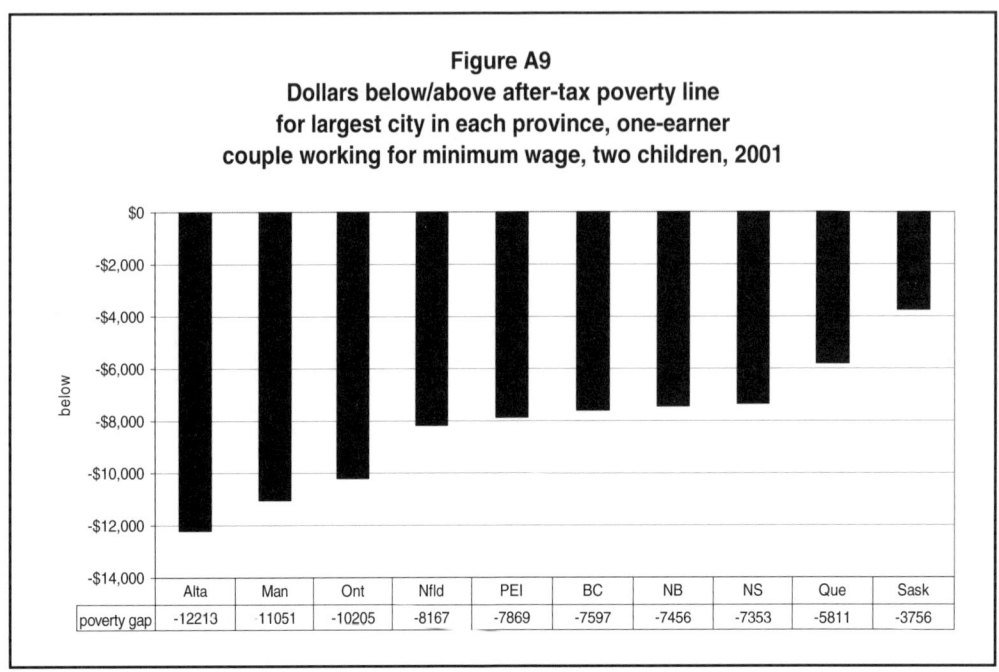

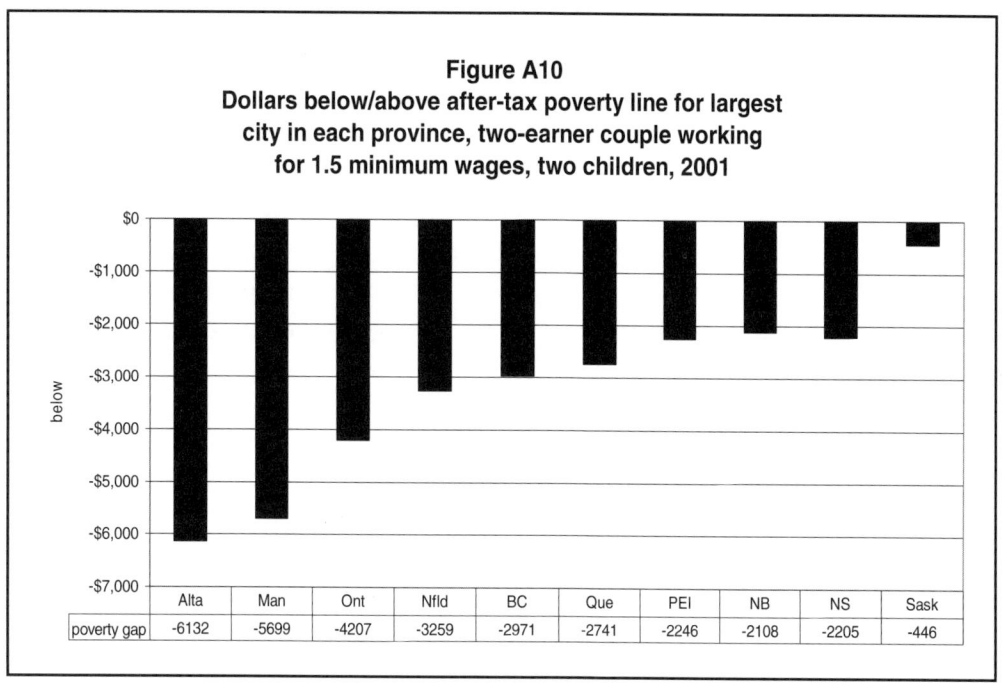

or no income tax. However, these positives are nowhere near strong enough to overcome the fact that four people struggling to live upon one minimum wage income are substantially below the poverty line. The poverty gap ranges from $12,213 in Alberta to $3,756 in Saskatchewan. The labour market pays wages (minimum and otherwise) and salaries to individuals in their capacity as workers, not family heads or spouses, whereas poverty lines (as a gauge of need) take family size into account.

We also examine the case of a two-earner couple with two children in which one parent works full time, all year at the minimum wage and the other parent earns half this amount (i.e., works part time and/or part year at the minimum wage) – for a total of 1.5 minimum wages. We do not assume that both parents work for the maximum (i.e., 40 hours a week, 52 weeks a year) minimum wage since many low-paid workers face difficulties finding enough hours or weeks of work and because parents often need to juggle work with child care responsibilities. Even with the contribution of the lower-earning parent, this family's income still falls below the after-tax poverty line for the largest city in every province. Figure A10 shows the poverty gap, which ranges from $6,132 in Alberta's largest cities (Calgary and Edmonton) to $446 in Saskatchewan's largest cities (Regina and Saskatoon).

Our fifth and final example is a two-earner couple with two children in which both parents work full time, year round for the minimum wage. In other words, this case assumes the maximum earnings from the minimum wage. The picture improves considerably, as shown in Figure A11, since these families manage to place above the after-tax poverty line in seven of the ten provinces (from $180 over the poverty line in Quebec to $2,836 above in Saskatchewan). On the other hand, families with two full-time minimum wage workers have a modest income indeed – those in Saskatchewan fare best, but are only $2,836 above the poverty line for the largest city – and families in Manitoba, Alberta and Ontario still end up below the poverty line (by $1,556, $771 and $231, respectively).

In summary, minimum wages fail to lift single workers, most single-parent families with one child and all one-earner couples with two children above the after-tax poverty line for the largest cities throughout Canada. Two-earner couples with two children, in which one parent works full time, year round at the minimum wage and the other parent earns half this amount, still fall short of the poverty line. Two-child two-earner couples in which both parents work full time, all year for the minimum wage manage to climb over the poverty line in seven of the ten provinces (though not by much) – but still remain below the poverty line in Manitoba, Alberta and Ontario.

Contribution of child benefits (Figures A12-A19)

As part of the ongoing National Child Benefit reform, the federal government is boosting the Canada Child Tax Benefit for low-income families and most provinces and territories are replacing (partially or wholly) their welfare payments on behalf of children with income-tested child benefits.[8] The purpose and impact of the reform involves real increases in child benefits for working poor families (including those at the minimum wage) to bring them up to the level of child benefits paid to welfare families. In most provinces,

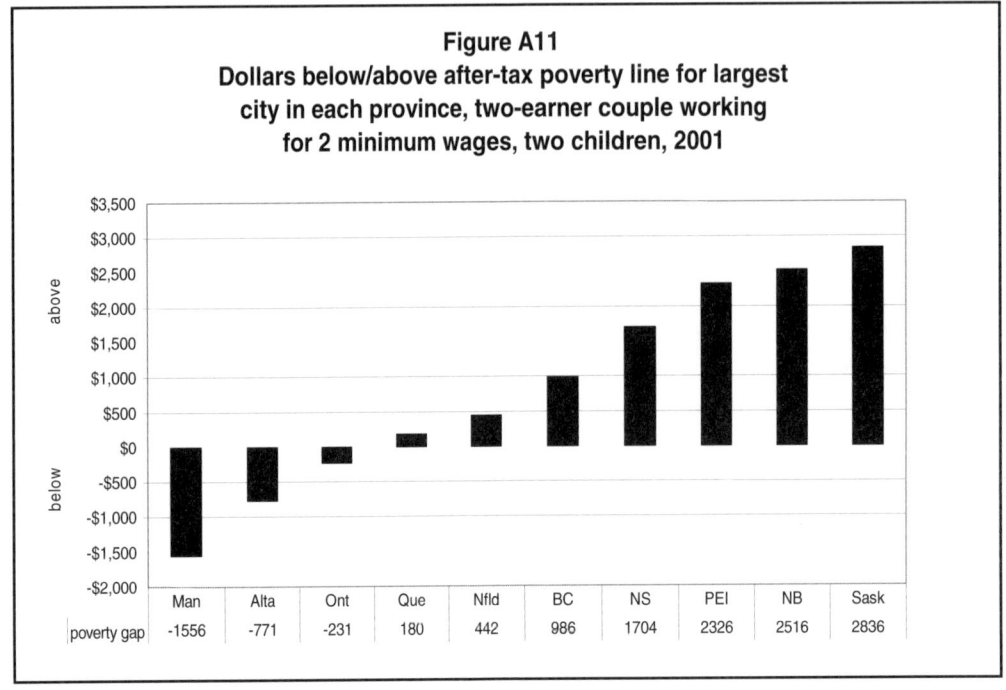

families on social assistance (welfare) are seeing no net increase in their child benefits. Before the reform, welfare families received about twice as much child benefits as working poor families, so provinces and territories are reducing welfare child benefits as Ottawa increases the Canada Child Tax Benefit (though these savings are being channeled to other programs and services for poor families with children). The National Child Benefit seeks to provide the same level of child benefits to all low-income families, regardless of their sources of income (welfare or the workforce), through a common income-tested system replacing the previous uncoordinated and inequitable mix of provincial needs-tested social assistance and federal income-tested child benefits [Battle and Mendelson 2001; Department of Finance Canada 1997; Federal/provincial/territorial governments 2002].

When the new Canada Child Tax Benefit began in July 1998, it paid a maximum $1,625 for families with one child and $1,425 for each additional child, with a $213 supplement for each child six and under for whom the child care expense deduction is not claimed, as well as $75 more for the third and each additional child. Currently (for the July 2002-June 2003 pay period) the maximum Canada Child Tax Benefit amounts to $2,444 for one child, $2,238 for a second child and $2,240 for each additional child, plus a $226 supplement for each child six and under for whom the child care expense deduction is not claimed, as well as $80 more for the third and each additional child. By July of 2004, maximum benefits are projected to reach $2,520 for one child, $2,308 for a second child and $2,311 for each additional child, with a $235 young child supplement and another $83 for the third and each additional child. For a

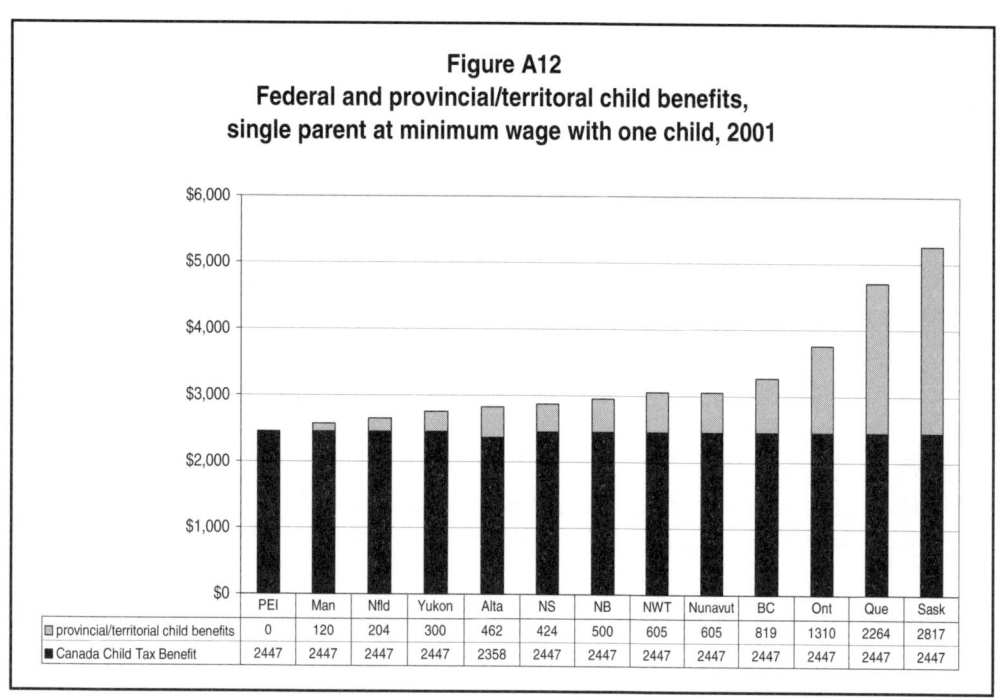

Figure A12
Federal and provincial/territorial child benefits, single parent at minimum wage with one child, 2001

	PEI	Man	Nfld	Yukon	Alta	NS	NB	NWT	Nunavut	BC	Ont	Que	Sask
provincial/territorial child benefits	0	120	204	300	462	424	500	605	605	819	1310	2264	2817
Canada Child Tax Benefit	2447	2447	2447	2447	2358	2447	2447	2447	2447	2447	2447	2447	2447

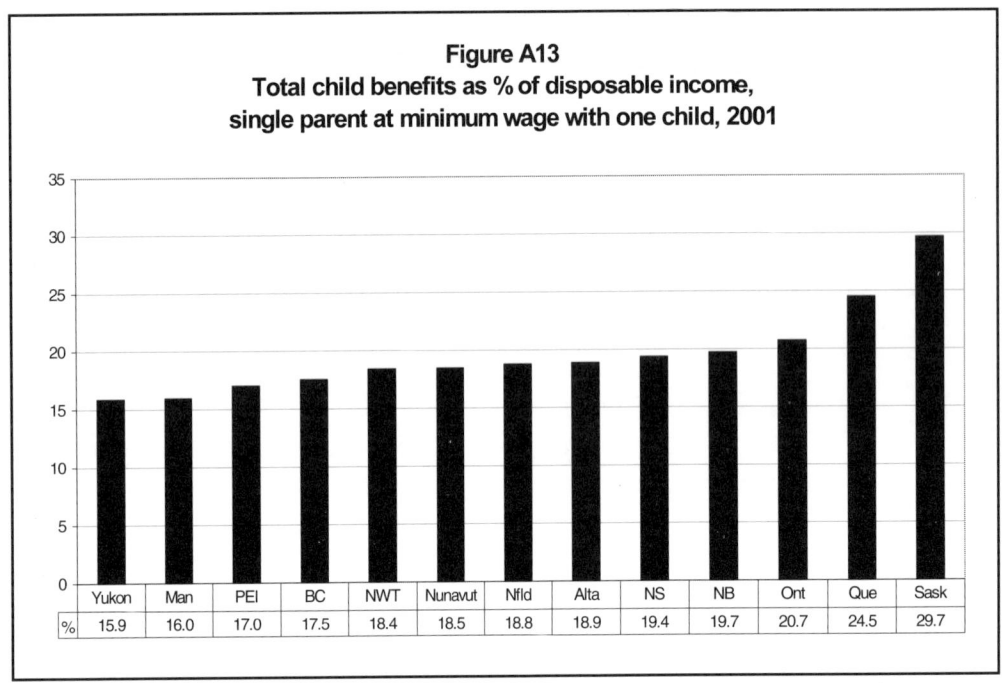

family with one child under and one child over 7, the maximum Canada Child Tax Benefit came to $3,263 as of July 1998 and will reach a projected $5,063 in July 2004. Moreover, the 2002 Speech From the Throne indicated that Ottawa plans significant increases to the Canada Child Tax Benefit, so hopefully the maximum rates will be boosted over the next several years.

Federal and provincial child benefits are contributing substantially to the incomes of minimum wage and other working poor families. Figure A12 shows federal and provincial/territorial child benefits received in 2001 for a minimum wage worker who is a single parent and has one child age 2. The federal Canada Child Tax Benefit paid $2,447 everywhere except for Alberta's $2,358, since that province varies the rate according to children's age. Among the 12 jurisdictions which have child-related benefits (Prince Edward Island alone does not provide such a program), payments ranged from $120 in Manitoba to $204 in Newfoundland, $300 in Yukon, $424 in Nova Scotia, $462 in Alberta, $500 in New Brunswick, $605 in the Northwest Territories and Nunavut, $819 in British Columbia, $1,310 in Ontario and a substantial $2,264 in Quebec and $2,817 in Saskatchewan.

Combined federal-provincial/territorial child benefits for these one-parent families with one young child ranged from ranged from $2,447 in Prince Edward Island to $2,567 in Manitoba, $2,651 in Newfoundland, $2,747 in Yukon, $2,820 in Alberta, $2,871 in Nova Scotia, $2,947 in New Brunswick, $3,052 in the Northwest Territories and Nunavut, $3,266 in British Columbia, $3,757 in Ontario, $4,711 in

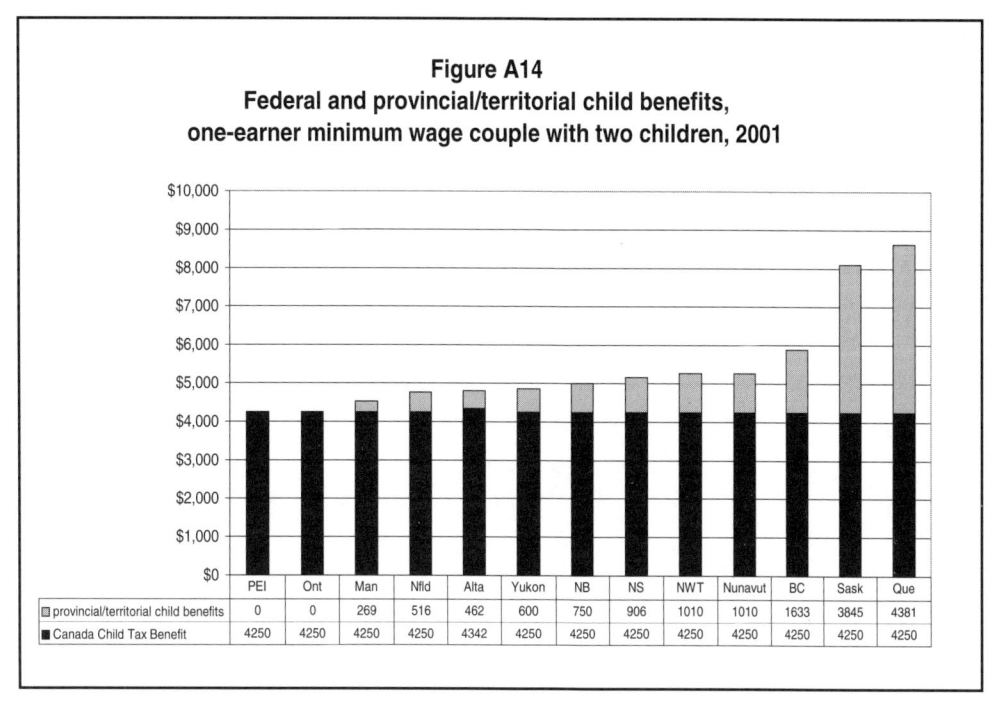

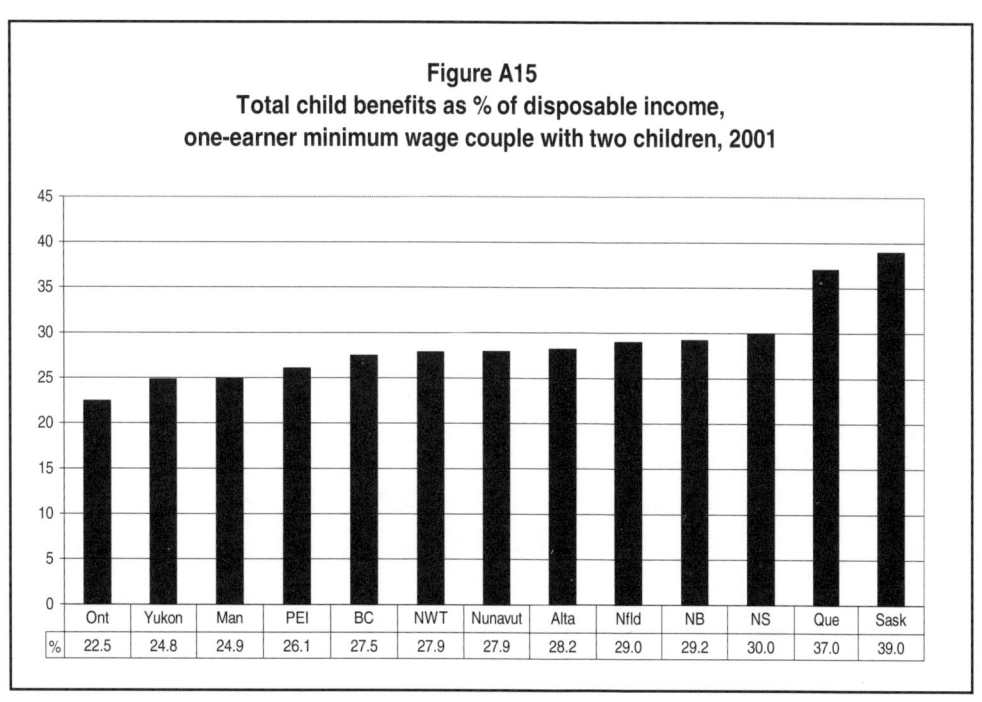

Minimum Wages in Canada: A Statistical Portrait With Policy Implications

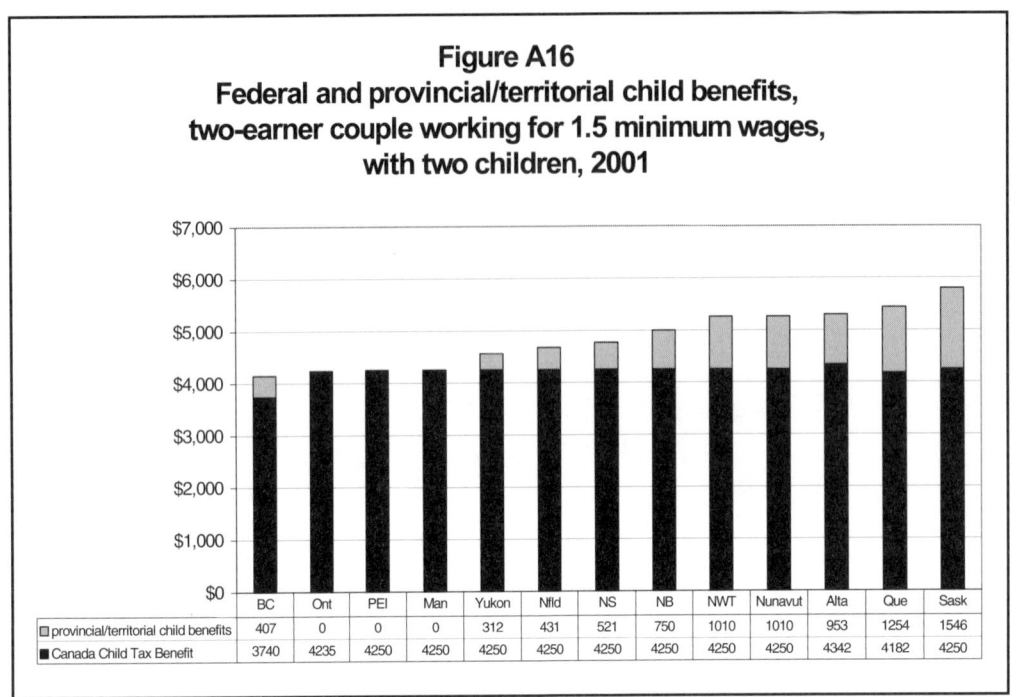

Quebec and $5,264 in Saskatchewan. As a percentage of disposable income, shown in Figure A13, child benefits for these families ranged from 15.9 percent in Yukon to 16.0 percent in Manitoba, 17.0 percent in Prince Edward Island, 17.5 percent in British Columbia, 18.4 percent in the Northwest Territories, 18.5 percent in Nunavut, 18.8 percent in Newfoundland, 18.9 percent in Alberta, 19.4 percent in Nova Scotia, 19.7 percent in New Brunswick, 20.7 percent in Ontario, 24.5 percent in Quebec and a high of 29.7 percent in Saskatchewan.

Figure A14 illustrates federal and provincial/territorial child benefits paid in 2001 to a minimum wage worker who has a spouse working in the home and two children aged 10 and 15. The federal Canada Child Tax Benefit came to $4,250 in every province except for Alberta's $4,342, whose rates vary according to children's age groups. Provincial/territorial child benefits ranged from $269 in Manitoba to $462 in Alberta, $516 in Newfoundland, $600 in Yukon, $750 in New Brunswick, $906 in Nova Scotia, $1,010 in the Northwest Territories and Nunavut, $1,633 in British Columbia, $3,845 in Saskatchewan and a high of $4,381 in Quebec. Prince Edward Island has no provincial child benefit. Ontario's program is targeted to children under seven, so provides no benefits to the family in this example, whose children are aged 10 and 15.

Combined federal-provincial/territorial child benefits for this one-earner low-income couple with two children went from $4,250 in Prince Edward Island and Ontario to $4,519 in Manitoba, $4,766 in Newfoundland, $4,519 in Manitoba, $4,804 in Alberta, $4,850 in Yukon, $5,000 in New Brunswick,

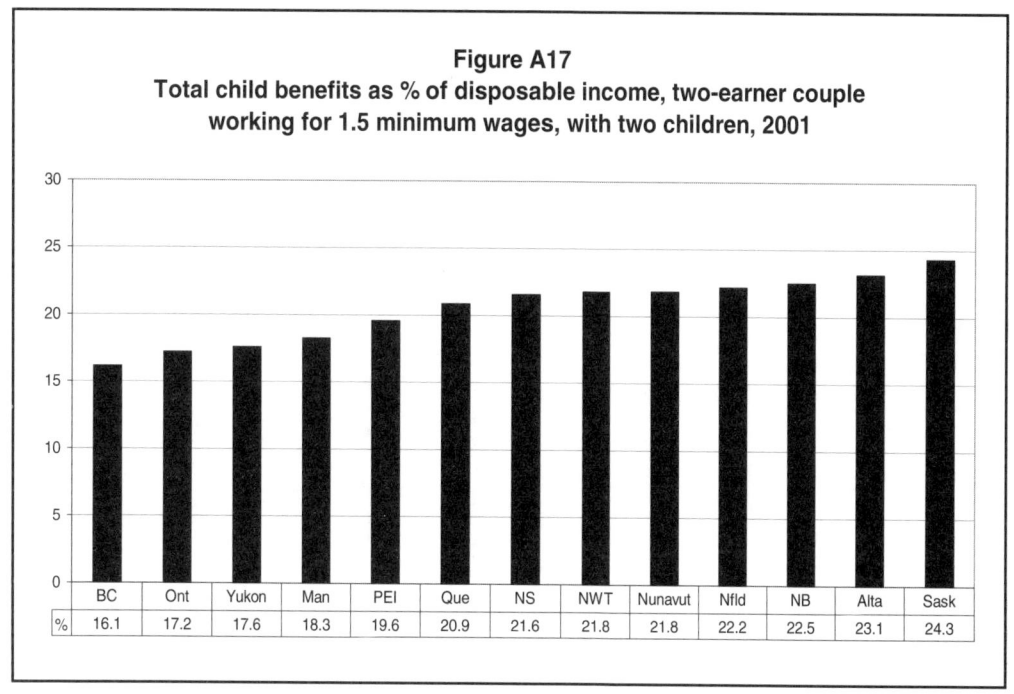

Figure A17
Total child benefits as % of disposable income, two-earner couple working for 1.5 minimum wages, with two children, 2001

%	BC	Ont	Yukon	Man	PEI	Que	NS	NWT	Nunavut	Nfld	NB	Alta	Sask
	16.1	17.2	17.6	18.3	19.6	20.9	21.6	21.8	21.8	22.2	22.5	23.1	24.3

$5,156 in Nova Scotia, $5,260 in the Northwest Territories and Nunavut, $5,883 in British Columbia, $8,105 in Saskatchewan and a high of $8,631 in Quebec. As a percentage of disposable income, illustrated in Figure A15, child benefits for these families varied from 22.5 percent in Ontario to 24.8 percent in Yukon, 24.9 percent in Manitoba, 26.1 percent in Prince Edward Island, 27.5 percent in British Columbia, 27.9 percent in the Northwest Territories and Nunavut, 28.2 percent in Alberta, 29.0 percent in Newfoundland, 29.2 percent in New Brunswick, 30.0 percent in Nova Scotia, 37.0 percent in Quebec and a high of 39.0 percent in Saskatchewan.

Figure A16 shows federal and provincial/territorial child benefits received in 2001 for a two-earner couple in which one parent works full time, year round for the minimum wage and the other parent works half time at the minimum wage, supporting two children aged 10 and 15. The federal Canada Child Tax Benefit came to the maximum $4,250 in most provinces and territories except for those whose minimum wage is high enough to bring the family over the maximum payment for the federal child benefit (net income in 2001 of $30,004 for January-June and $32,000 for July-December). In the latter jurisdictions, the Canada Child Tax Benefit came to $3,740 in British Columbia (with Canada's highest minimum wage), $4,182 in Quebec and $4,235 in Ontario. The Canada Child Tax Benefit paid $4,342 for the family in Alberta, whose rates vary according to children's age. Provincial/territorial child benefits ranged from $312 in Yukon to $407 in British Columbia, $431 in Newfoundland, $521 in Nova Scotia, $750 in New Brunswick, $953 in Alberta, $1,010 in the Northwest Territories and Nunavut, $1,254 in Quebec and a

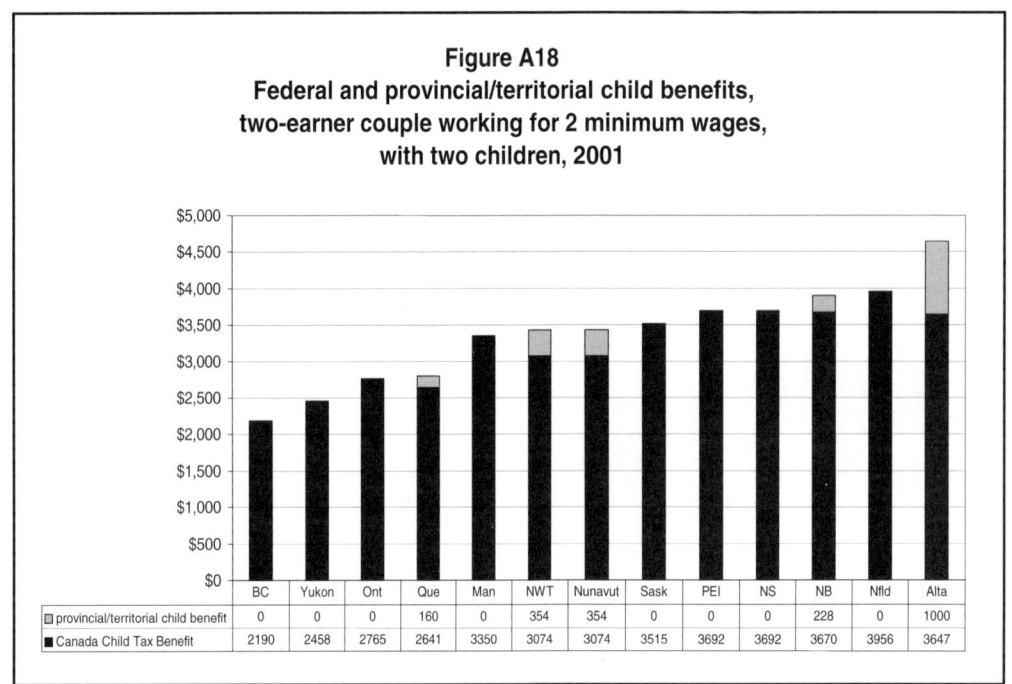

high of $1,546 in Saskatchewan. Prince Edward Island has no provincial child benefit. Ontario's program is targeted to children under 7 years old, so provides no benefits to the family in this example, whose children are aged 10 and 15. The Manitoba family's income was high enough that it did not qualify for provincial child benefits.

Combined federal-provincial/territorial child benefits for this two-earner low-income couple with two children went from $4,147 in British Columbia to $4,235 in Ontario, $4,250 in Prince Edward Island and Manitoba, $4,357 in Yukon, $4,681 in Newfoundland, $4,771 in Nova Scotia, $5,000 in New Brunswick, $5,260 in the Northwest Territories and Nunavut, $5,295 in Alberta, $5,436 in Quebec and a high of $5,796 in Saskatchewan. Figure A17 shows that child benefits for these families varied from 16.1 percent of disposable income in British Columbia to 17.2 percent in Ontario, 17.6 percent in Yukon, 18.3 percent in Manitoba, 19.6 percent in Prince Edward Island, 20.9 percent in Quebec, 21.6 percent in Nova Scotia, 21.8 percent in the Northwest Territories and Nunavut, 22.2 percent in Newfoundland, 22.5 percent in New Brunswick, 23.1 percent in Alberta and a high of 24.3 percent in Saskatchewan.

In our second illustrative two-earner family, both parents work full time, all year for the minimum wage. Their combined earnings are high enough that they do not qualify for the maximum Canada Child Tax Benefit but instead receive a smaller amount, since the program is geared to the amount of family

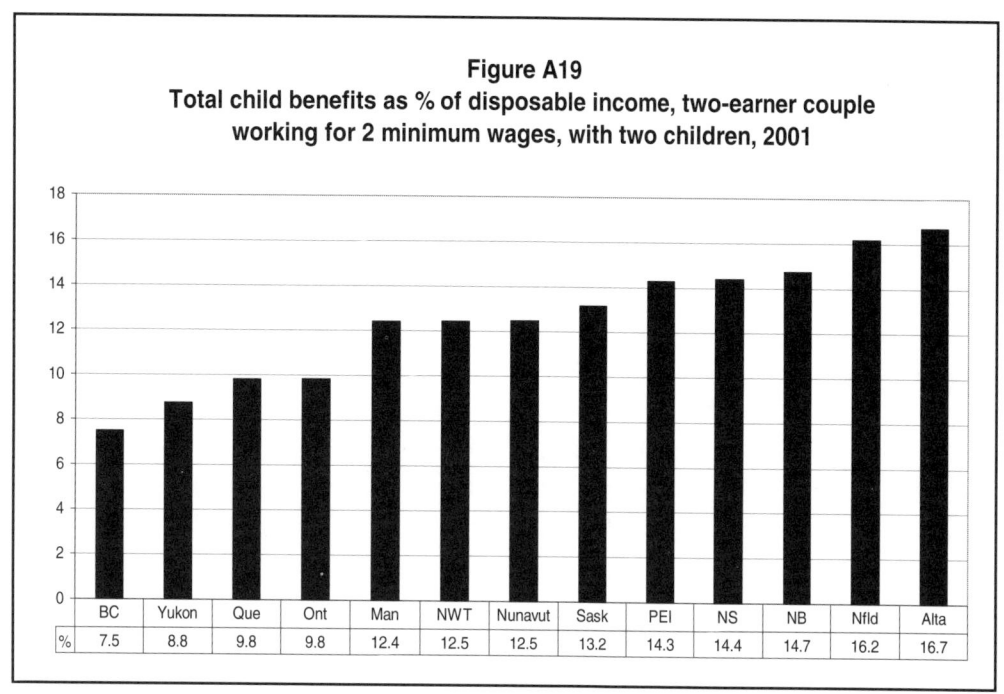

income. The family's Canada Child Tax Benefit in 2001 ranged from $2,190 in British Columbia to $2,458 in Yukon, $2,641 in Quebec, $2,765 in Ontario, $3,074 in the Northwest Territories and Nunavut, $3,350 in Manitoba, $3,515 in Saskatchewan, $3,647 in Alberta, $3,670 in New Brunswick, $3,692 in Prince Edward Island and Nova Scotia, and $3,956 in Newfoundland. Provincial/territorial child benefits range from $160 in Quebec to $228 in New Brunswick, $354 in the Northwest Territories and Nunavut, and $1,000 in Alberta. Figure A18 illustrates the results.

Total federal-provincial/territorial child benefits in 2001 for this two-minimum wage family with two children were $2,190 in British Columbia, $2,458 in Yukon, $2,765 in Ontario, $2,801 in Quebec, $3,350 in Manitoba, $3,428 in the Northwest Territories and Nunavut, $3,515 in Saskatchewan, $3,692 in Prince Edward Island and Nova Scotia, $3,898 in New Brunswick, $3,956 in Newfoundland and a high of $4,647 in Alberta. Figure A19 shows that child benefits ranged from 7.5 percent of disposable income in British Columbia to 8.8 percent in Yukon, 9.8 percent in Quebec and Ontario, 12.4 percent in Manitoba, 12.5 percent in the Northwest Territories and Nunavut, 13.2 percent in Saskatchewan, 14.3 percent in Prince Edward Island, 14.4 percent in Nova Scotia, 14.7 percent in New Brunswick, 16.2 percent in Newfoundland and 16.7 percent in Alberta.

Minimum Wages in Canada: A Statistical Portrait With Policy Implications

Minimum wages versus welfare (Figures A20-A29)

Are Canadians better off working for minimum wage or going on welfare? The answer varies according to the number of people in the household and where they live. Note that by "better off" we are using the term in the narrow sense of a straight cash calculus: Some observers would argue that people are better off working at minimum wage even if their income is lower than welfare because the latter – especially if it is a long-lasting or recurrent source of income – can atrophy recipients' labour force skills and motivation and marginalize them both economically and socially.

Figure A20 compares income from social assistance ('welfare') and other government income programs[9] for single employable recipients to disposable income from minimum wages (i.e., minimum wages plus available refundable tax credits minus federal and provincial income taxes, Canada or Quebec Pension Plan contributions and Employment Insurance premiums) for single Canadians working full time all year for the minimum wage in each jurisdiction in 2001 (the latest year for which welfare estimates are available). The grey bars indicate total income from social assistance and other cash benefits, while the black bars show disposable income from minimum wages.

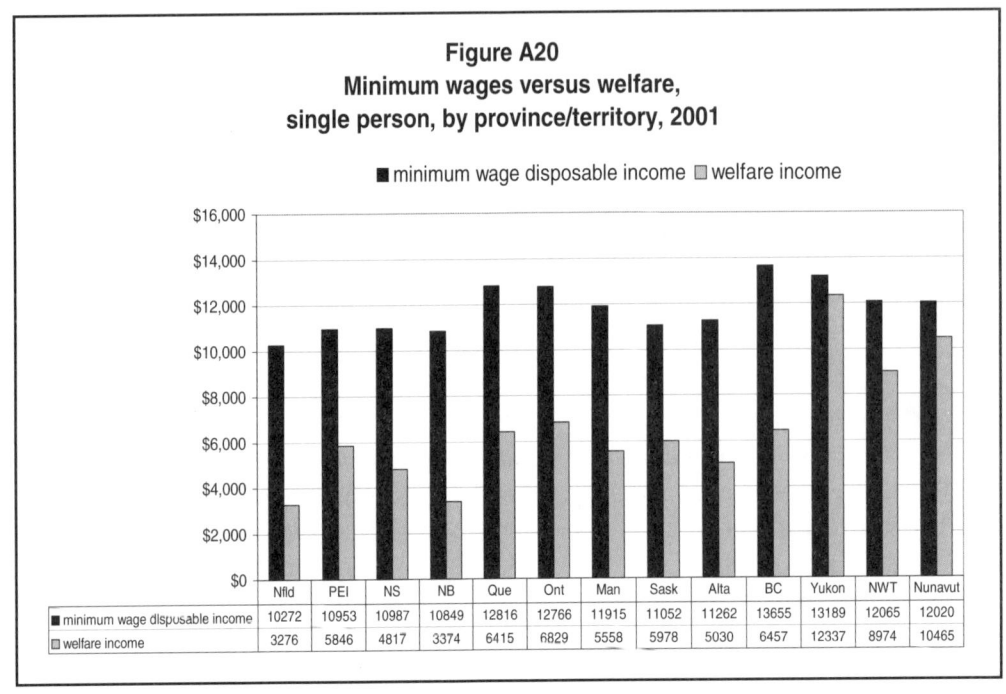

24   *Caledon Institute of Social Policy*

Minimum Wages in Canada: A Statistical Portrait With Policy Implications

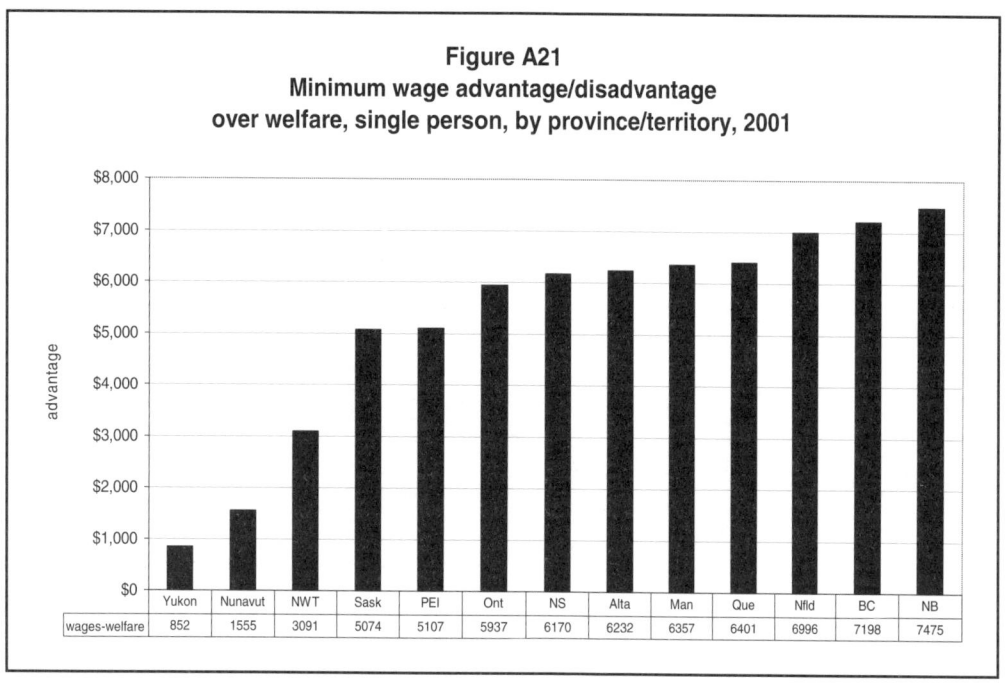

In every province and territory in Canada, single people are better off working for the minimum wage (even after subtracting income and payroll taxes) than on welfare. The 'minimum wage advantage' is largest in provinces paying low social assistance benefits. For example, single employable welfare recipients in Newfoundland got only $3,276 at last estimate (2001), the lowest in Canada and fully $6,996 below the $10,272 disposable income from the province's minimum wage which, while low, is not as low as welfare. At the other end of the spectrum, minimum wage disposable income and welfare incomes are much closer together in the three territories because their welfare rates are much higher than in other jurisdictions (to a significant extent reflecting their higher cost of living).

The minimum wage advantage over welfare for single Canadians varies considerably across the country, as indicated in Figure A21. It ranges from just $852 in Yukon, which has a relatively high minimum wage but even higher welfare benefits (the highest in Canada), to $7,475 in New Brunswick, which has a relatively low minimum wage but even lower welfare benefits. In between these extremes, the minimum wage advantage amounted to $1,555 in Nunavut, $3,091 in the Northwest Territories, $5,074 in Saskatchewan, $5,107 in Prince Edward Island, $5,937 in Ontario, $6,170 in Nova Scotia, $6,232 in Alberta, $6,357 in Manitoba, $6,401 in Quebec, $6,996 in Newfoundland and $7,198 in British Columbia.

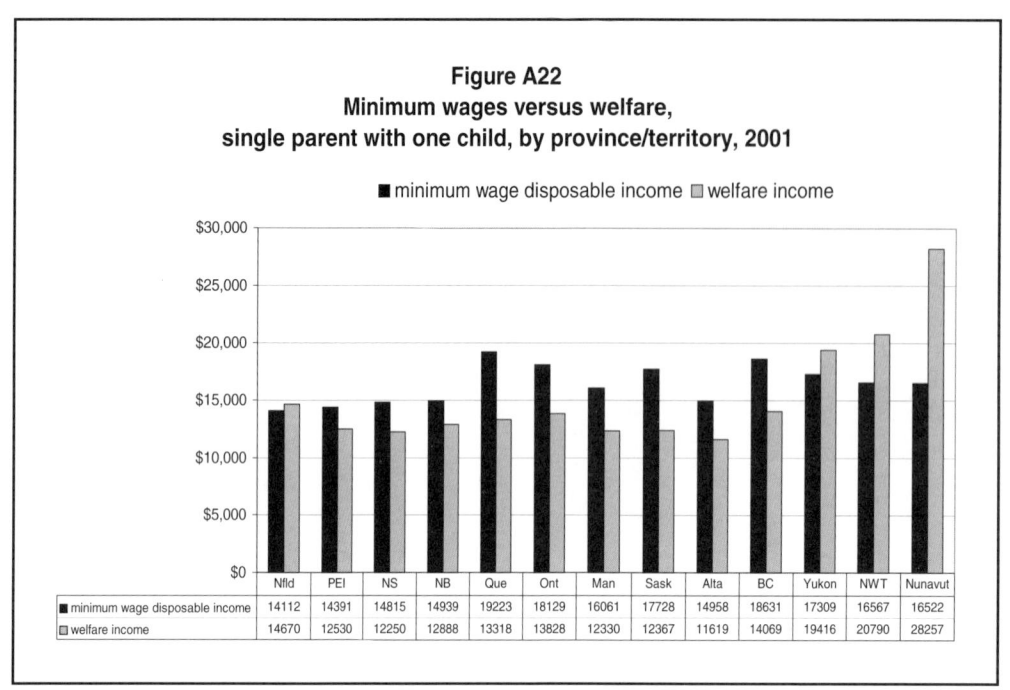

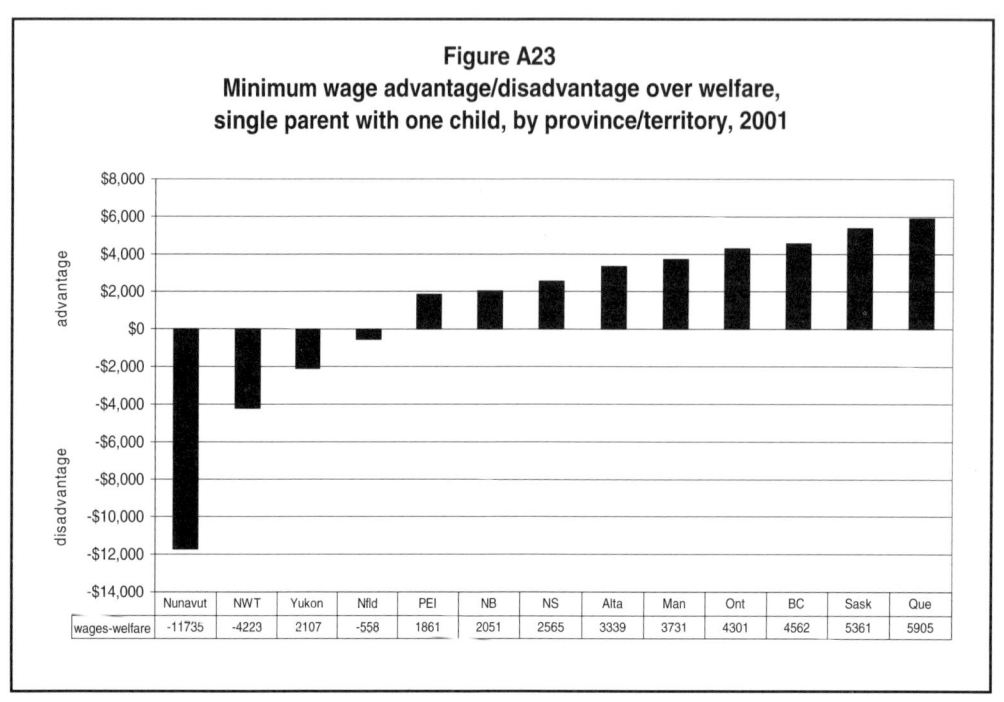

All welfare systems throughout Canada allow recipients to supplement their benefits with some outside employment earnings, though above a specified amount (established as a dollar maximum and, sometimes, also a percentage of outside income) their benefits are reduced dollar-for-dollar of wages. However, there are no national estimates as to how common this practice is; moreover, reliable estimates cannot be provided for the seven of the 13 jurisdictions that include in their calculations a percentage of outside income (usually net of work-related expenses).

The important point is that the minimum wage advantage over welfare is reduced if the latter is supplemented by outside earnings. For example, Newfoundland's welfare income of $3,276 for a single employable recipient can be boosted by up to $900 a year in exempt earnings, to $4,176 – reducing the minimum wage advantage from $6,996 compared to welfare only to $6,096 for welfare-*cum*-exempt earnings. Maximum exempt earnings vary considerably across the country. For the provinces with dollar maximums only, they range for a single employable welfare recipient from $600 in Nova Scotia to $900 in Newfoundland, $1,800 in the Northwest Territories and Nunavut, $2,300 in New Brunswick and $2,400 in Quebec. Minimum wages still pay better than welfare-with-exempt earnings – except in Nunavut, where a single welfare recipient's income from social assistance and exempt earnings came to $245 more than disposable income from the territory's minimum wage in 2001.

The picture changes once minimum wage earners have dependants to support. Figures A22 and A23 look at the case of a single parent with one child age 2. The gap between take-home pay from the

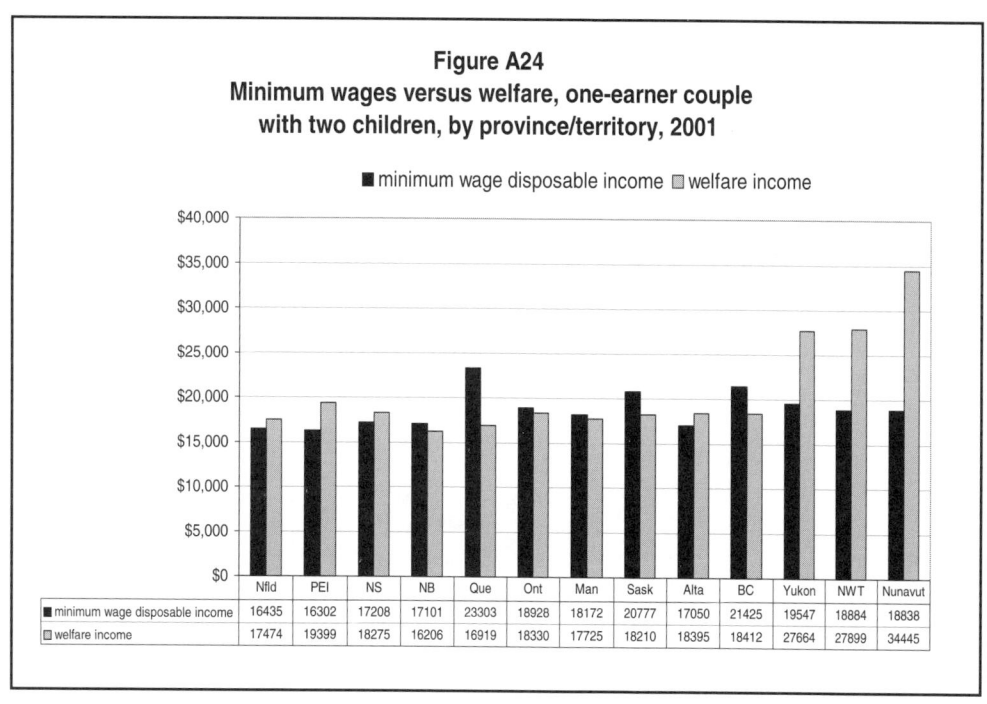

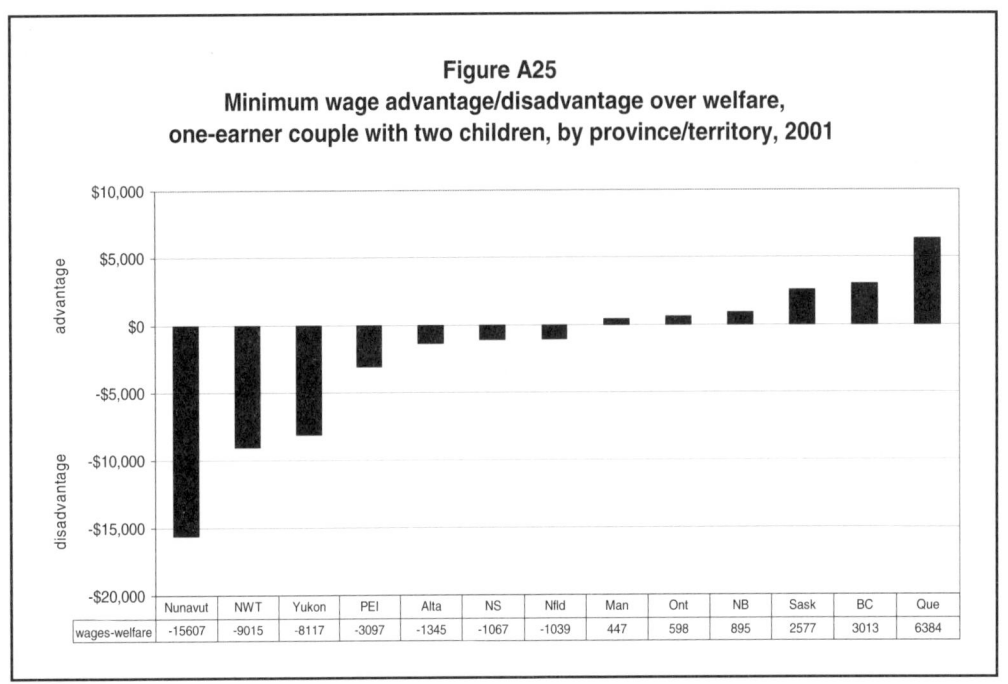

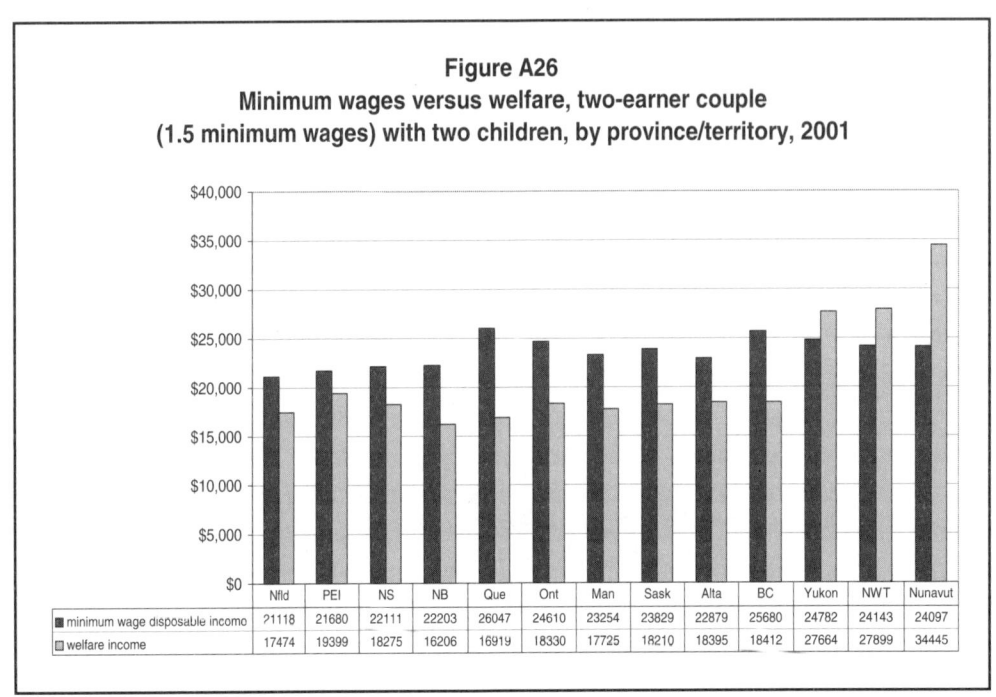

minimum wage and income from welfare is smaller than it is for single people because welfare pays benefits for other family members (including children), whereas minimum wages do not adjust for family size.

Minimum wage income exceeds welfare income in nine jurisdictions for a single parent with a child age 2: by $1,861 in Prince Edward Island, $2,051 in New Brunswick, $2,565 in Nova Scotia, $3,339 in Alberta, $3,731 in Manitoba, $4,301 in Ontario, $4,562 in British Columbia, $5,361 in Saskatchewan and $5,905 in Quebec. But in four of the 13 jurisdictions – Nunavut, the Northwest Territories, Yukon and Newfoundland — a single mother with a young child gets more from welfare than from working for minimum wage: $11,735 more in Nunavut, $4,223 more in the Northwest Territories, $2,107 more in Yukon and $558 more in Newfoundland. The minimum wage disadvantage is most striking in Nunavut, where a single mother with a young child would be $11,735 worse off working for minimum wage than on welfare.

The welfare-versus-minimum wage calculus tilts further towards welfare when the latter is supplemented with outside earnings. In Quebec, for example, a single parent with one young child can supplement her welfare benefits by up to $2,400, raising total income from $13,318 to $15,718 and thus reducing the minimum wage advantage from $5,905 to $3,505.

Our third illustrative household is a one-earner couple with two children aged 10 and 15; in other words, four people rely on one minimum wage. Figure A24 compares minimum wages and welfare, while

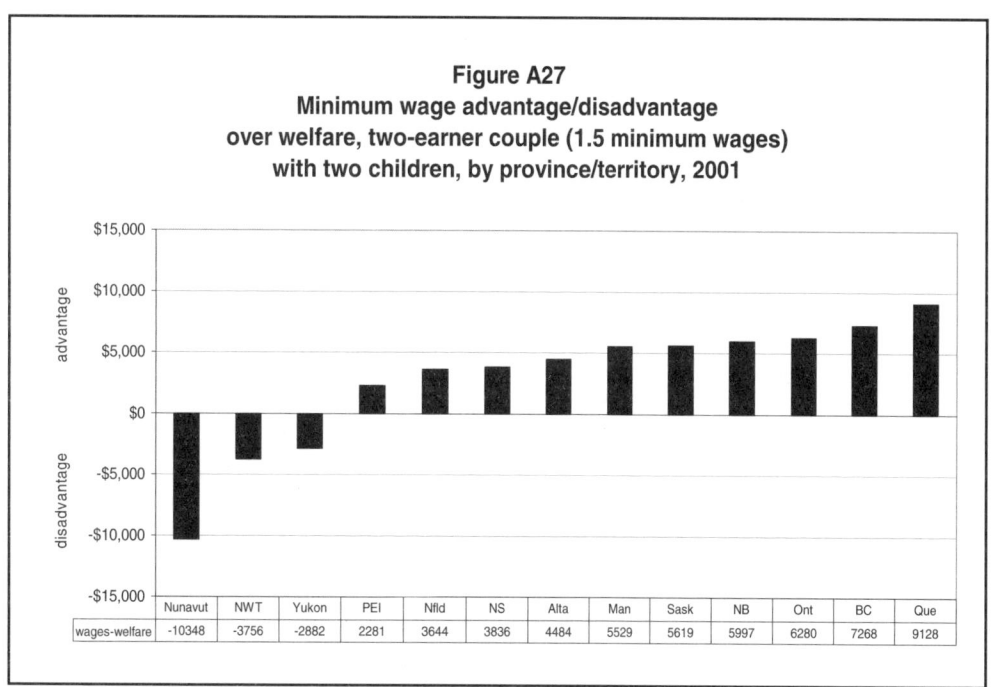

Figure A25 shows the dollar difference. In only six of the 13 jurisdictions – Manitoba, Ontario, New Brunswick, Saskatchewan, British Columbia and Quebec – could a one-earner couple with two children get more income from the minimum wage than welfare. In some jurisdictions, the minimum wage advantage is substantial – $2,577 in Saskatchewan, $3,013 in British Columbia and $6,384 in Quebec. But in other cases, the minimum wage advantage is modest – $447 in Manitoba, $598 in Ontario and $895 in New Brunswick. In four provinces, welfare paid only a few thousand dollars more than minimum wage work – $1,039 in Newfoundland, $1,067 in Nova Scotia, $1,345 in Alberta and $3,097 in Prince Edward Island. In the three territories, the 'welfare advantage' is extreme – $8,117 in Yukon, $9,015 in the Northwest Territories and $15,607 in Nunavut.

If welfare is supplemented by exempt earnings, then of course the minimum wage advantage is reduced. In Nunavut, for example, this family's $34,445 in welfare income can be raised by exempt earnings to $38,045 – $19,207 more than the $18,838 disposable income from minimum wage.

Our fourth family type is a two-earner couple with two children 10 and 15 in which one parent works full time, all year for minimum wage while the other parent works part time (half the annual maximum) for minimum wage. Figures A26 and A27 show that families earning one-and-a-half minimum wages fare better than those on welfare in all ten provinces, though the minimum wage advantage varies greatly from one province to another – ranging from just $2,281 in Prince Edward Island to a substantial

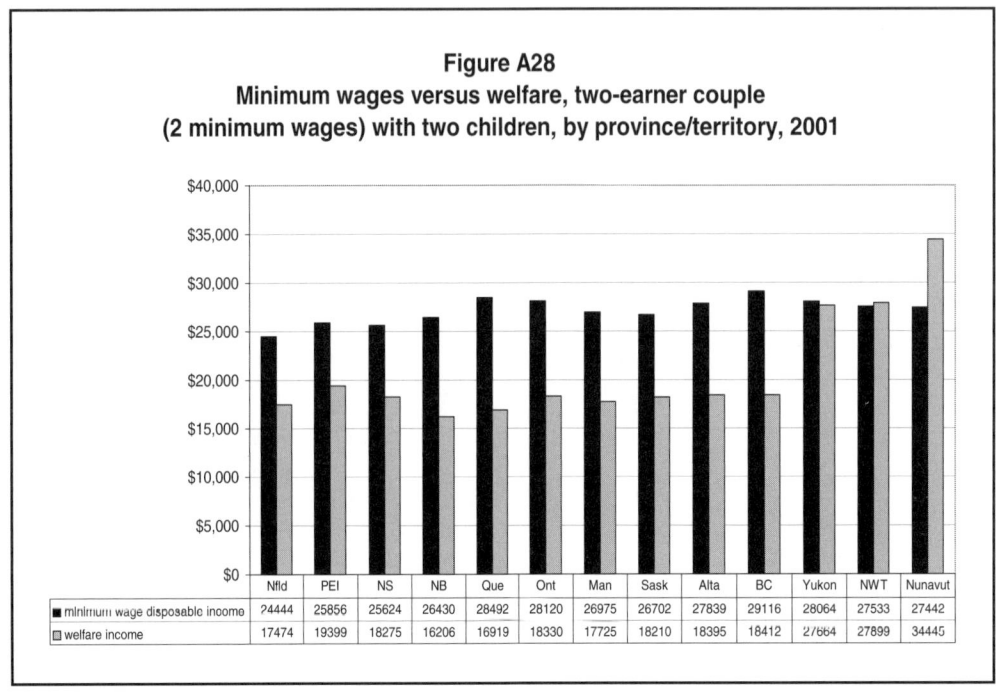

$9,128 in Quebec, which has both a higher minimum wage than PEI (the Quebec family earns $21,816 as opposed to the PEI family's $18,096) and pays $1,254 in provincial child benefits whereas PEI has no provincial child benefit. Despite the fact that the territories' minimum wages are on the higher end of the scale (family earnings from 1.5 minimum wages come to $22,464 in Yukon and $20,280 in the Northwest Territories and Nunavut), their welfare rates are relatively high ($27,664 in Yukon, $27,899 in the Northwest Territories and $34,445 in Nunavut). In the end, then, welfare still pays better than minimum wages in the three territories: $10,348 more in Nunavut, $3,756 more in the Northwest Territories and $2,882 more in Yukon.

Our fifth and final family type is a two-earner couple with two children 10 and 15 in which each parent works full time, all year for the minimum wage. Figure A28 compares disposable income from the minimum wage with income from welfare and other government sources, while Figure A29 subtracts the latter from the former. The minimum wage advantage is substantial in all ten provinces, ranging from $6,457 in Prince Edward Island to $6,970 in Newfoundland, $7,349 in Nova Scotia, $8,492 in Saskatchewan, $9,250 in Manitoba, $9,444 in Alberta, $9,790 in Ontario, $10,224 in New Brunswick, $10,704 in British Columbia and a high of $11,573 in Quebec. However, two-minimum wage families in Yukon and the Northwest Territories earn about as much from working full time for the minimum wage as they would get from welfare; minimum wages pay $400 more than welfare in Yukon and $366 less than welfare in the

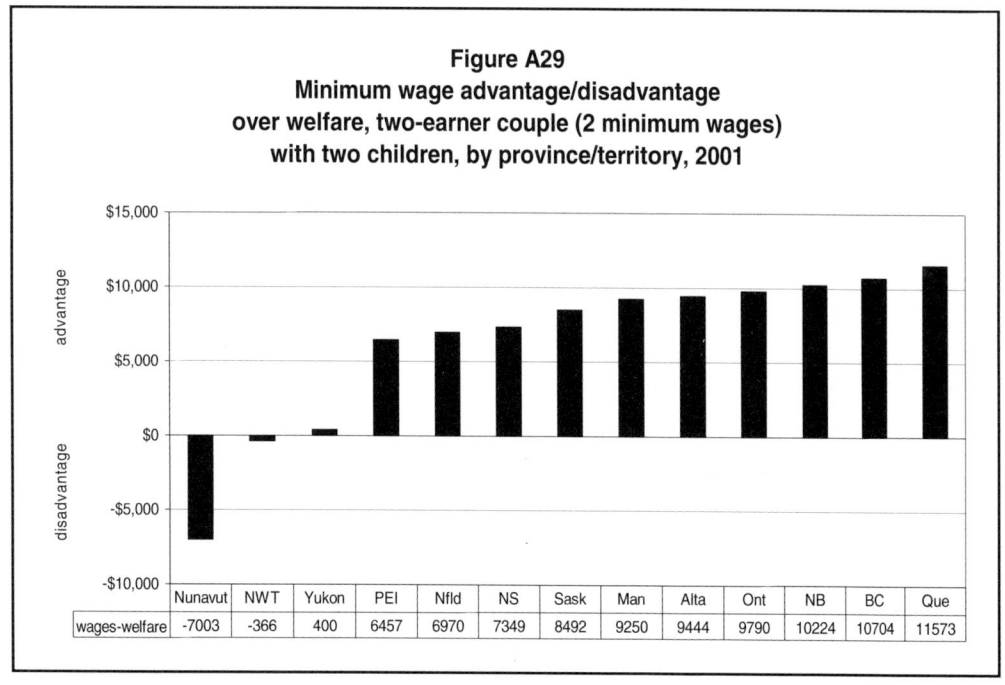

Northwest Territories. In Nunavut, a family with two children would get $7,003 more from welfare than if both parents worked full-time for the minimum wage.

Clearly, a worker earning the minimum wage cannot provide a living wage for a family, and both parents must work full time, year round at the minimum wage to earn more than welfare. Even single workers earning the minimum wage must struggle to get by, though welfare benefits for employable single people are so low that even the minimum wage – while anything but generous – offers more.

b. Minimum Wage Workers in Canada

In 2000, an estimated 580,000 workers – 4.6 percent of the total 12.5 million employees – worked for minimum wages.[10] Note that these figures underestimate the size of Canada's minimum wage workforce because the Statistics Canada survey that collects labour force information does not cover the three territories – Yukon, the Northwest Territories and Nunavut.

The following text with illustrative graphs analyzes key characteristics of minimum wage workers in Canada. Appendix 2 (pages 312-314) provides detailed statistics in tabular form.

Province (Figures A30 and A31)

While 4.6 percent of Canadian employees worked for minimum wages in 2000, the percentage varies significantly from one province to another. Figure A30 gives the results.

Newfoundland has the largest proportion of its employees working for the minimum wage – 8.7 percent – followed by New Brunswick (6.0 percent), Saskatchewan (5.9 percent), Quebec (5.4 percent), Manitoba (5.2 percent), Nova Scotia (5.0 percent), British Columbia (4.6 percent), Ontario (4.5 percent), Prince Edward Island (3.6 percent) and, last, Alberta (just 2.0 percent). The percentage of workers at the minimum wage is also known as the 'incidence' of minimum wage workers in the employed labour force. The province with the highest incidence of minimum wage workers – Newfoundland – has more than four times as large an incidence of minimum wage workers as the province with the smallest percentage of minimum wage workers, Alberta.

Six provinces – Newfoundland, New Brunswick, Saskatchewan, Quebec, Manitoba and Nova Scotia – have an above-average incidence of minimum wage workers while Ontario, Prince Edward Island and Alberta have a below-average rate. British Columbia's 4.6 percent minimum wage incidence is identical to the national rate.

Another way of ranking provinces is to compare their share of all minimum wage workers with their share of all employees. Some provinces have a larger percentage of minimum wage workers than they do of all employees, and vice versa. Figure A31 illustrates the findings.

By dividing a province's share of all minimum wage workers by its share of all employees, we can construct a simple index of proportionality: The higher the number is above 1, the more minimum wage workers are overrepresented in a province; the lower the result is below 1, the more underrepresented they are.

Minimum wage workers are most overrepresented in Newfoundland, which has 2.7 percent of all minimum wage workers but only 1.4 percent of all employees (producing an index of 1.93), followed by New Brunswick (1.30), Saskatchewan (1.27), Quebec (1.17), Manitoba (1.14) and Nova Scotia (1.07). Results under 1.0 indicate that minimum wage workers are underrepresented in a province. Minimum wage workers are slightly underrepresented in British Columbia (0.98) and Ontario (0.97) and more underrepresented in Prince Edward Island (0.75). They are most underrepresented in Alberta, which accounted for 4.5 percent of all minimum wage workers but 10.4 percent of all employees (producing an index of 0.43).

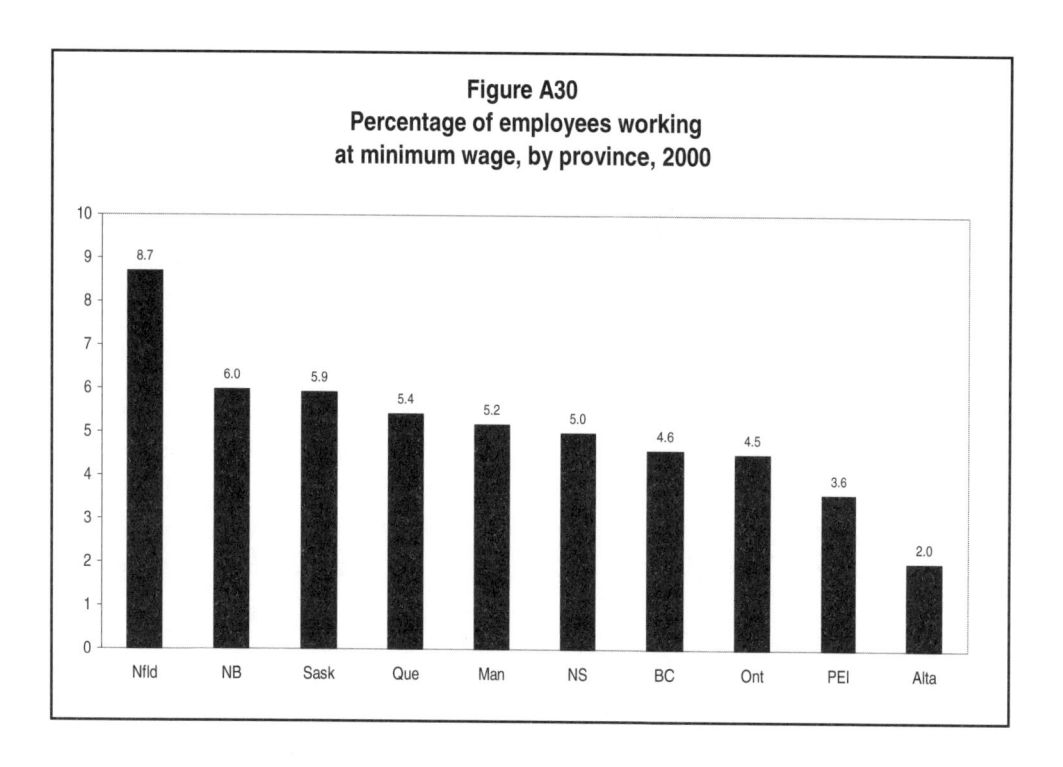

**Figure A30
Percentage of employees working
at minimum wage, by province, 2000**

Province	Percentage
Nfld	8.7
NB	6.0
Sask	5.9
Que	5.4
Man	5.2
NS	5.0
BC	4.6
Ont	4.5
PEI	3.6
Alta	2.0

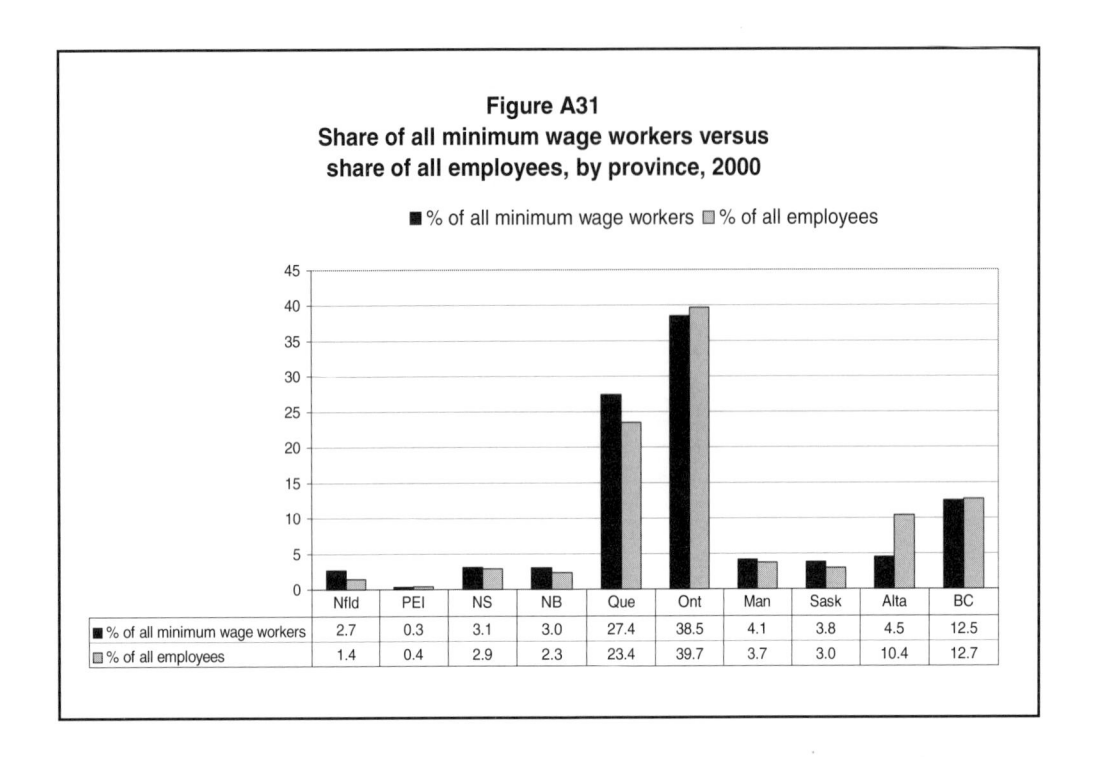

Figure A31
Share of all minimum wage workers versus share of all employees, by province, 2000

	Nfld	PEI	NS	NB	Que	Ont	Man	Sask	Alta	BC
% of all minimum wage workers	2.7	0.3	3.1	3.0	27.4	38.5	4.1	3.8	4.5	12.5
% of all employees	1.4	0.4	2.9	2.3	23.4	39.7	3.7	3.0	10.4	12.7

While the incidence of minimum wage workers in each province – i.e., the percentage of its employees who work for the minimum wage – is a key indicator, so too is each province's share of all minimum wage workers. Incidence results tell us the risk of working for the minimum wage in each province, whereas shares show how minimum wage workers are distributed across the country. A province can have a relatively high rate of minimum wage workers yet, if its overall workforce is small, can account for a small percentage of all minimum wage workers.

Newfoundland is a good example. While it has the highest percentage of minimum wage workers amongst its total employed workforce of all provinces (8.7 percent), it has only 2.7 percent of all minimum wage workers. On the other hand, only 4.5 percent of Ontario employees worked at the minimum wage in 2000, but they represent the largest share of all minimum wage workers in Canada (38.5 percent). This result is not surprising, since Ontario also has the largest share of all employees in the country – 39.7 percent.

Ontario had 38.5 percent of all minimum wage earners in 2000, followed by Quebec at 27.4 percent and British Columbia at 12.5 percent. Thus the large majority of minimum wage employees – 78.4 percent or close to eight in ten – work in Ontario, Quebec or British Columbia, the three largest provinces that together had three-quarters (75.8 percent) of all employees in 2000. By contrast, the three provinces with the highest incidence of minimum wage workers – Newfoundland first, New Brunswick second and Saskatchewan third – ranked only ninth, eighth and sixth, respectively, in their share of all minimum wage workers in Canada and together accounted for only 9.5 percent of the nation's minimum wage workforce.

Gender (Figures A32-A34)

Women run a higher risk of working for minimum wages than men, and women also constitute the majority of the minimum wage workforce.

In 2000, 6.0 percent of female employees worked for minimum wages compared to only 3.7 percent of male workers. Of the total 580,000 minimum wage workforce, 360,400 – 62.1 percent – were women and 219,600 – 37.9 percent – were men. Figure A32 pictures the results.

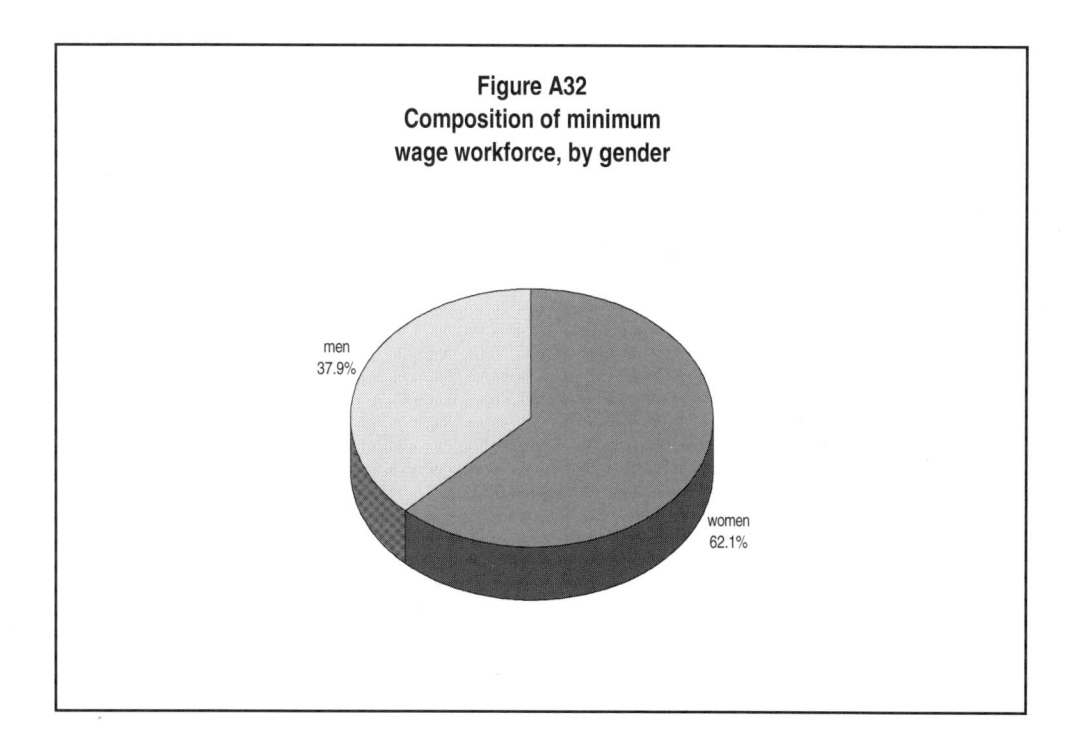

**Figure A32
Composition of minimum wage workforce, by gender**

men 37.9%
women 62.1%

Women are significantly overrepresented in the minimum wage workforce. They made up 62.1 percent of minimum wage workers but only 48.1 percent of all employees in 2000. Men are underrepresented because they constituted only 37.9 percent of minimum wage workers as opposed to 51.9 percent of all employees.

The gender bias among minimum wage workers holds when we control for major age categories. While younger workers of both sexes run a higher risk of working for minimum wages, women still fare worse than men within each age category. Figure A33 shows the results.

Among workers aged 15 to 19, 39.6 percent of women worked for minimum wages in 2000 compared to 26.8 percent of male workers. In the 20-24 age group, 8.4 percent of women as opposed to 5.7 percent of men worked for minimum wages. Among workers 25-44, 2.9 percent of women but just 1.3 percent of men worked at the bottom of the wage ladder. Among employees 45-64, 2.8 percent of women and 1.1 percent of men worked for minimum wages, while 9.8 percent of women 65 and older as opposed to 7.1 percent of elderly men were in the minimum wage workforce.

The gap between the sexes widens with increasing age among workers under 65. Women in the 15-19 and 20-24 age groups are 1.5 times more likely to work for minimum wages than men in those age groups, but the ratio increases to 2.3 times for those aged 25-44 and 2.6 times for those in the 45-64 age group. Among elderly workers, women are 1.6 times more likely than men to work for minimum wages.

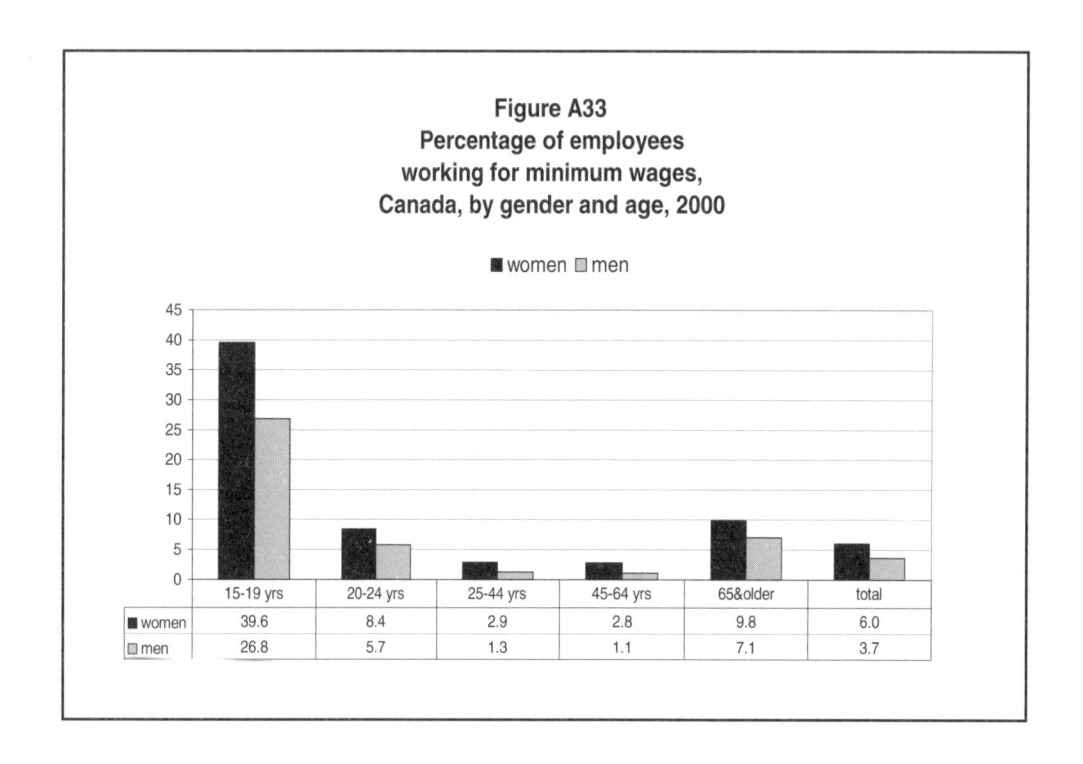

**Figure A33
Percentage of employees working for minimum wages, Canada, by gender and age, 2000**

	15-19 yrs	20-24 yrs	25-44 yrs	45-64 yrs	65&older	total
women	39.6	8.4	2.9	2.8	9.8	6.0
men	26.8	5.7	1.3	1.1	7.1	3.7

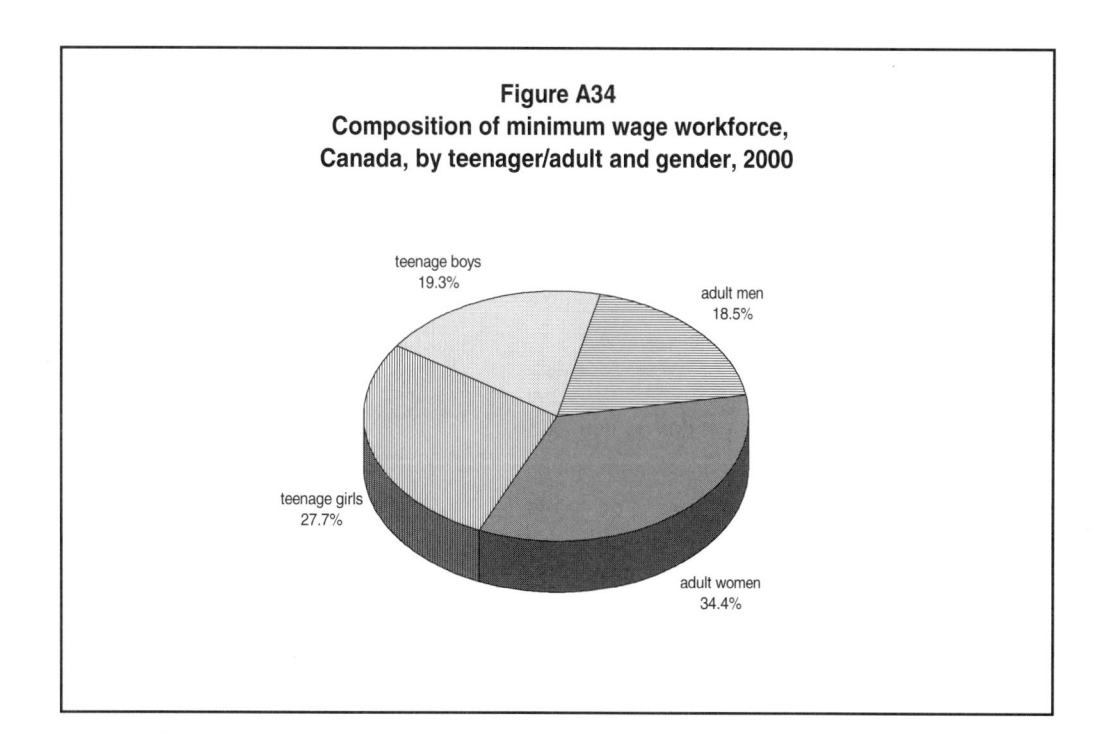

Figure A34
Composition of minimum wage workforce, Canada, by teenager/adult and gender, 2000

- teenage boys 19.3%
- adult men 18.5%
- adult women 34.4%
- teenage girls 27.7%

Figure A34 divides the minimum wage workforce into teenage girls and boys and adult women and men. Adult women are the largest group, at 199,600 (34.4 percent of the total), followed by teenage girls (160,800 or 27.7 percent), teenage boys (112,200 or 19.3 percent) and adult men (107,300 or 18.5 percent).

Age (Figures A35-A37)

The odds of working for minimum wage are highest for young employees and decrease sharply and steadily as workers get older, though the risk begins to rise again among those 55 and older.

Figure A35 illustrates the relationship between age and incidence of minimum wage work. The percentage of employees working for minimum wages falls from 43.7 percent for workers aged 15-16 to 29.9 percent for those 17-19, 7.0 percent for workers aged 20-24, 2.6 percent for those 25-29, 2.1 percent for those 30-34, 1.8 percent for those 35-44 and 1.7 percent for the 45-54 age group. The risk then rises to 2.6 percent for those aged 55-64 and 8.2 percent for the 65-and-over age category.

Figure A35
Percentage of employees working for minimum wages, Canada, by age, 2000

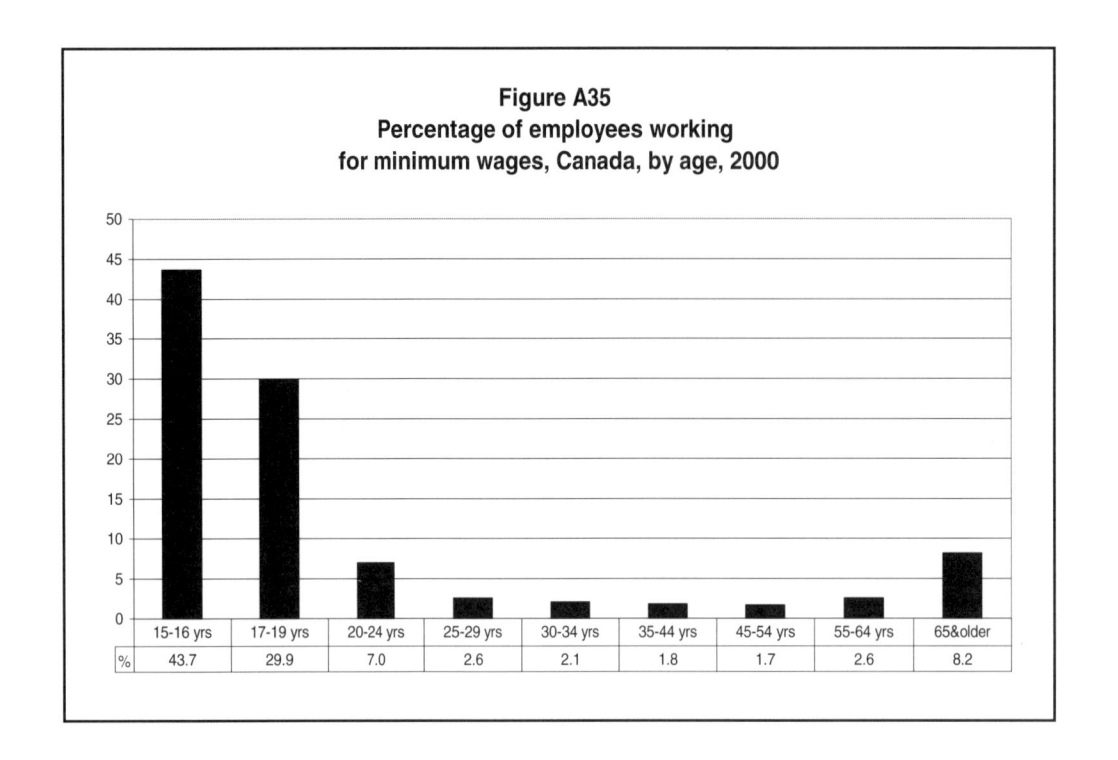

	15-16 yrs	17-19 yrs	20-24 yrs	25-29 yrs	30-34 yrs	35-44 yrs	45-54 yrs	55-64 yrs	65&older
%	43.7	29.9	7.0	2.6	2.1	1.8	1.7	2.6	8.2

Figure A36
Share of minimum wage workers versus share of all employees, Canada, by age group, 2000

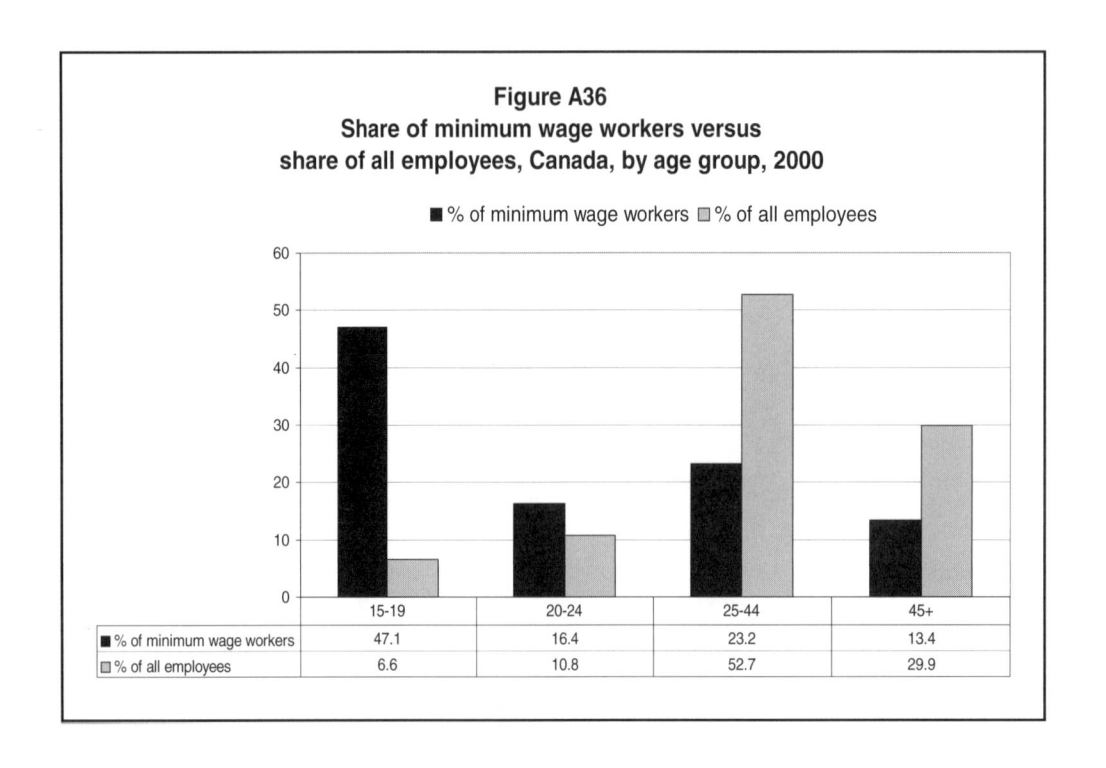

■ % of minimum wage workers ☐ % of all employees

	15-19	20-24	25-44	45+
% of minimum wage workers	47.1	16.4	23.2	13.4
% of all employees	6.6	10.8	52.7	29.9

Young people not only are more likely to work for minimum wage than other employees, but the young also make up a large proportion of the minimum wage workforce. Figure A36 compares the age makeup of minimum wage workers and all employees. Almost half (47.1 percent) of minimum wage workers are in the 15-19 age group, as opposed to only 6.6 percent of all employees. The 20-24 age group represents 16.4 percent of minimum wage workers compared to 10.8 percent of all workers. Thus six in ten minimum wage workers (63.5 percent) are under 25 years of age.

While a significant proportion – 23.2 percent – of minimum wage workers are in the 'prime age' 25-44 category, that group constitutes a much larger proportion – 52.7 percent or more than half – of all employees. Workers aged 45 and older make up 13.4 percent of minimum wage employees but 29.9 percent all employees.

Figure A37 divides Canada's minimum wage workforce into four broad age groups. Teenagers (15-19) constitute 47.1 percent of minimum wage workers. Prime age workers (25-44) make up 23.2 percent, followed by young adults (aged 20-24) at 16.4 percent and older workers (45 and older) at 13.4 percent. While teenagers are the largest of the four groups, nonetheless adults aged 20 and older form the majority (52.9 percent) of minimum wage workers.

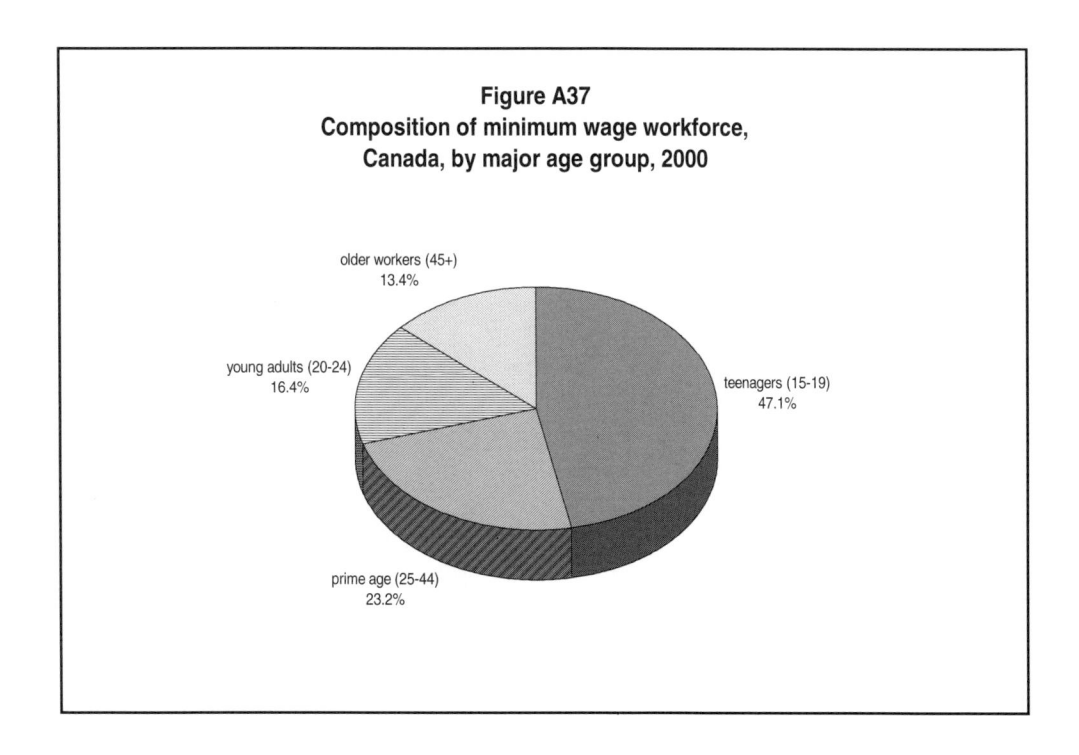

**Figure A37
Composition of minimum wage workforce,
Canada, by major age group, 2000**

- older workers (45+) 13.4%
- young adults (20-24) 16.4%
- teenagers (15-19) 47.1%
- prime age (25-44) 23.2%

Education (Figures A38 and A39)

Figure A38 shows the risk of working for minimum wage among workers with varying levels of education.

At first glance, the relationship between level of education and incidence of minimum wage employment does not seem to correspond to common sense: Workers in the lowest educational group (elementary education only) are less likely to work for minimum wage (7.7 percent do) than those with some high school (13.4 percent), while those with some postsecondary education run a higher risk (7.1 percent) than high school graduates (4.4 percent). However, as one would expect, the chances of working for minimum wages are lowest for the two highest education categories – just 2.2 percent for employees with a postsecondary certificate or diploma (e.g., from a community college or vocational institute) and a mere 1.3 percent for those with a university degree.

Once we look at the education-minimum wage link for different age groups, the reasons for the apparently inconsistent relationship comes clear: Young people working at part-time or seasonal (i.e., summer) jobs – typically paying the minimum or a low wage – figure prominently in the 'some high school' and 'some postsecondary education' categories; they are still at high school, community college or university, whereas workers in the other educational categories have completed their education.

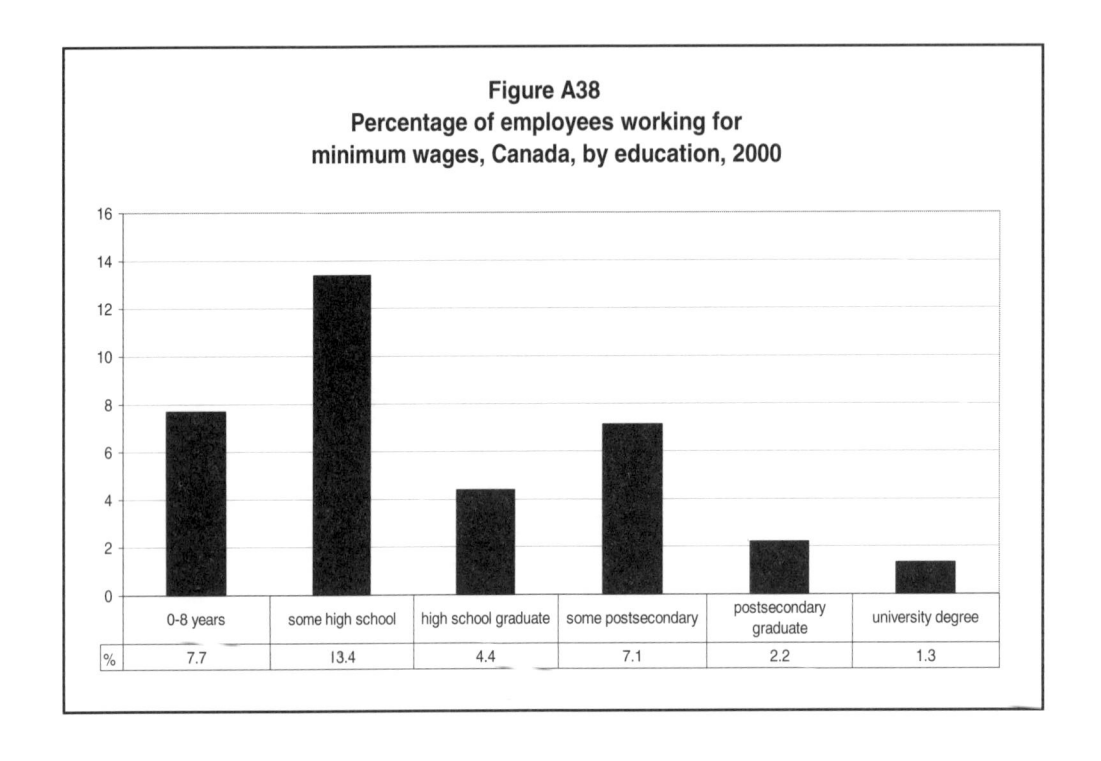

Figure A38
Percentage of employees working for minimum wages, Canada, by education, 2000

	0-8 years	some high school	high school graduate	some postsecondary	postsecondary graduate	university degree
%	7.7	13.4	4.4	7.1	2.2	1.3

The majority (63.4 percent) of minimum wage workers are in the 15-24 age group. Among these young workers, the odds of working for minimum wages are 29.2 percent for those with 0-8 years of schooling, 31.0 percent for those with some high school, 12.7 percent for high school graduates, 15.3 percent for those with some postsecondary education, 7.7 percent for postsecondary graduates and 4.5 percent for university graduates.

But for other age groups, there is the expected inverse and linear relationship between educational attainment and incidence of minimum wage work. Among the 23.2 percent of minimum wage workers aged 25-44, the odds of working for minimum wages are 5.9 percent for those with 0-8 years of education, 4.1 percent for those with some high school, 2.6 percent for high school graduates, 2.2 percent for those with some postsecondary education, 1.5 percent for postsecondary graduates and 1.2 percent for university graduates. Among the 13.4 percent of minimum wage workers aged 45 and older, the incidence of minimum wage work ranges from 5.5 percent for those with 0-8 years of education to 3.3 percent for those with some high school, 2.1 percent for high school graduates, 2.2 percent for those with some postsecondary education, 1.5 percent for postsecondary graduates and just 1.1 percent for university graduates.

Figure A39 shows each educational group's share of Canada's minimum wage workforce in 2000. The largest group of minimum wage workers (37.8 percent) are those with some high school education,

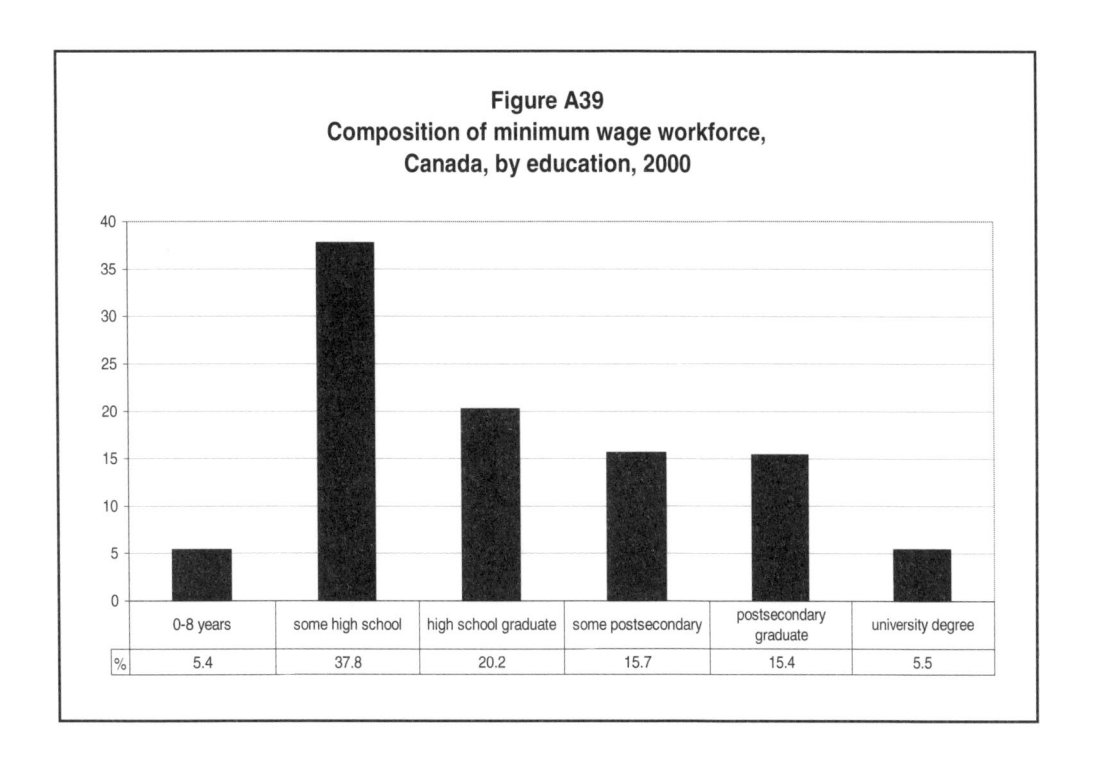

Figure A39
Composition of minimum wage workforce, Canada, by education, 2000

	0-8 years	some high school	high school graduate	some postsecondary	postsecondary graduate	university degree
%	5.4	37.8	20.2	15.7	15.4	5.5

followed by high school graduates (20.2 percent), those with some postsecondary education (15.7 percent), postsecondary graduates (15.4 percent), those with university degrees (5.5 percent) and workers with only 0-8 years of education (5.4 percent). Many minimum wage workers are students (high school or postsecondary) pursuing their education. A sizeable group of minimum wage workers (36.6 percent or more than a third) have some form of postsecondary education.

Summer students

During the summer months of 2000 (May through August), 405,400 or 17.0 percent of the total 2,386,7000 employees aged 15-25 worked for minimum wages. Most of these young minimum wage workers (295,900 or 73.0 percent) were full-time students planning to return to school in September. Another 20,700 were full-time students not planning to go back to school, while 7,800 had not made up their minds. Minimum wage work clearly is an important source of employment income for Canadian students furthering their education.

The remaining 80,900 minimum wage workers in the 15-24 age group were not full-time students, and their incidence of minimum wage work was substantially lower. Only 7.3 percent of young employees who were not students (80,900 out of the total 1,109,200) worked for the base wage as opposed to 17.0 percent of full-time students.

Full-time and part-time workers (Figures A40 and A41)

As suggested above, the fact that young people are more likely to work part time helps explain why workers still pursuing their education tend to face a higher risk of minimum wages than those who have completed their schooling and are working full time. Figure A40 indicates that 15.3 percent of part-time workers are paid minimum wages compared to only 2.4 percent of those employed full time.

Gender somewhat complicates the relationship between full-time and part-time work and the minimum wage. Women who work part time are less likely than men who work part time to earn minimum wages (13.7 and 19.2 percent, respectively), whereas women employed full time run a higher risk of working for minimum wages than their male counterparts (3.3 and 1.6 percent, respectively).

The majority of minimum wage workers (58.1 percent) work part time, while 41.9 percent are employed full time, as pictured in Figure A41. Women make up the majority of minimum wage employees working both full time (60.5 percent are women) and part time (63.3 percent are women). Among all employees, though, women constitute a minority of full-time workers (43.2 percent) but the majority of part-time workers (70.8 percent).

Figure A40
Percentage of employees working for minimum wages, Canada, by full-time/part-time and gender, 2000

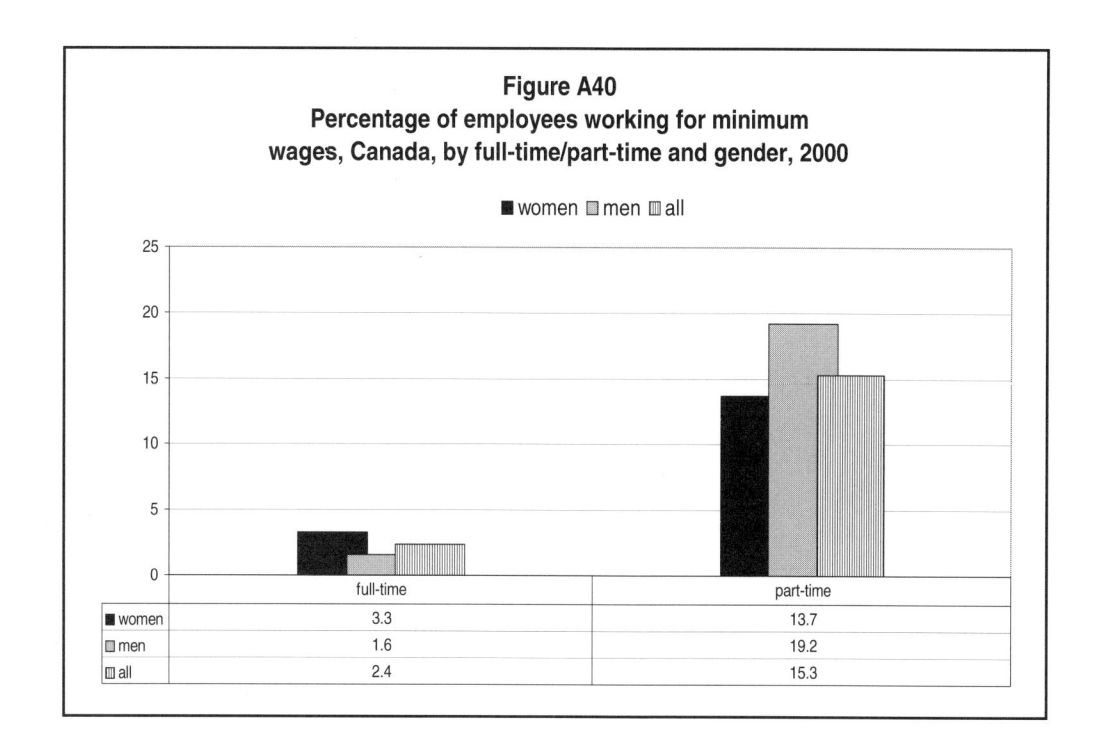

	full-time	part-time
women	3.3	13.7
men	1.6	19.2
all	2.4	15.3

Figure A41
Composition of minimum wage workforce, Canada, full-time and part-time workers, 2000

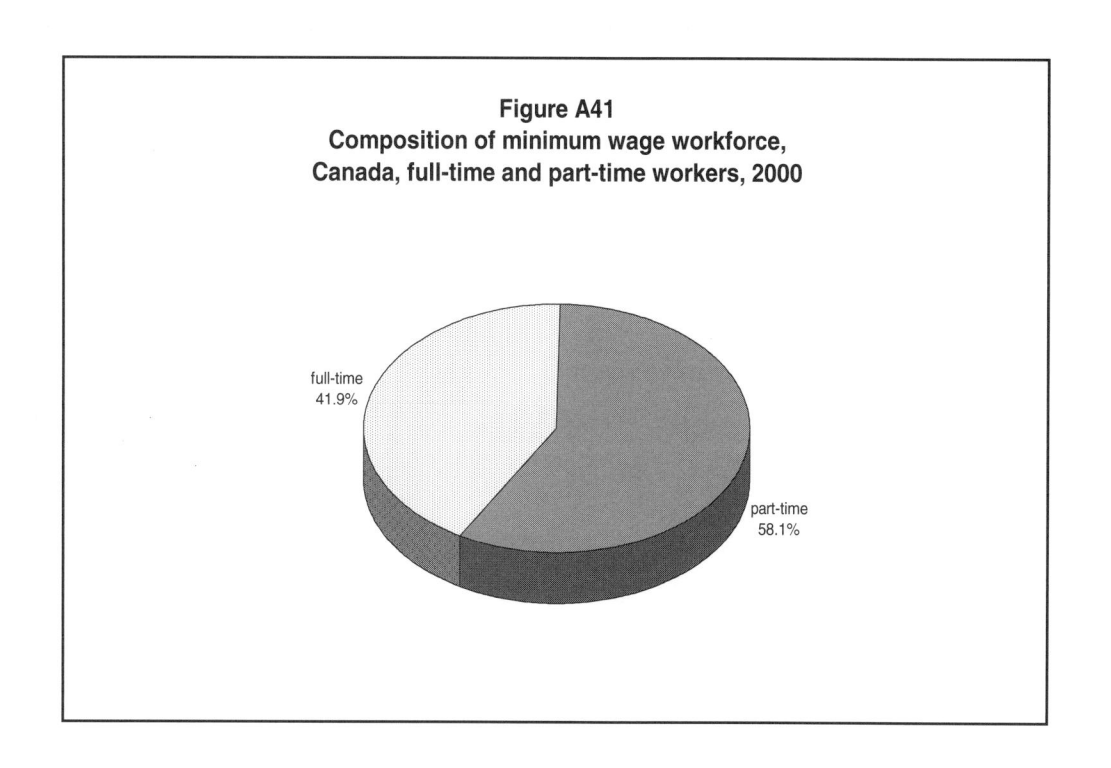

full-time 41.9%
part-time 58.1%

Family status (Figure A42)

We noted earlier that six in ten minimum wage workers are under 25. This finding is reflected in information on family status, illustrated by Figure A42. The largest group of minimum wage workers – 60.2 percent or 349,300 out of the total 580,000 – are older children living with their parents (or relatives with relatives, as in the case of a niece or nephew living with an aunt and uncle, or grandchildren with grandparents). Of this category of older children living with their parents or relatives, 258,400 or 74.0 percent are aged 15-19, 62,700 or 18.0 percent are 20-24 and the remaining 28,300 or 8.0 percent are 25 or older. More than half (199,000 or 57.0 percent) are in school and working part time or part year (e.g., in summer).

The next largest group of minimum wage workers (144,800 or 25.0 percent of the total) are members of couples (married or living together). In most cases (108,000 or 74.6 percent of this category), the minimum wage worker's spouse is employed, usually at more than the minimum wage. A typical example in this category would be mothers combining (unpaid) childrearing work with part-time minimum wage work. Another 36,800 of minimum wage workers living in couples have a spouse who is not employed (most of them are not in the labour force).

An estimated 62,000 or 10.7 percent of minimum wage workers are what Statistics Canada calls 'unattached individuals' (i.e., living alone or with non-relatives). Half (31,400) live alone; most of this group

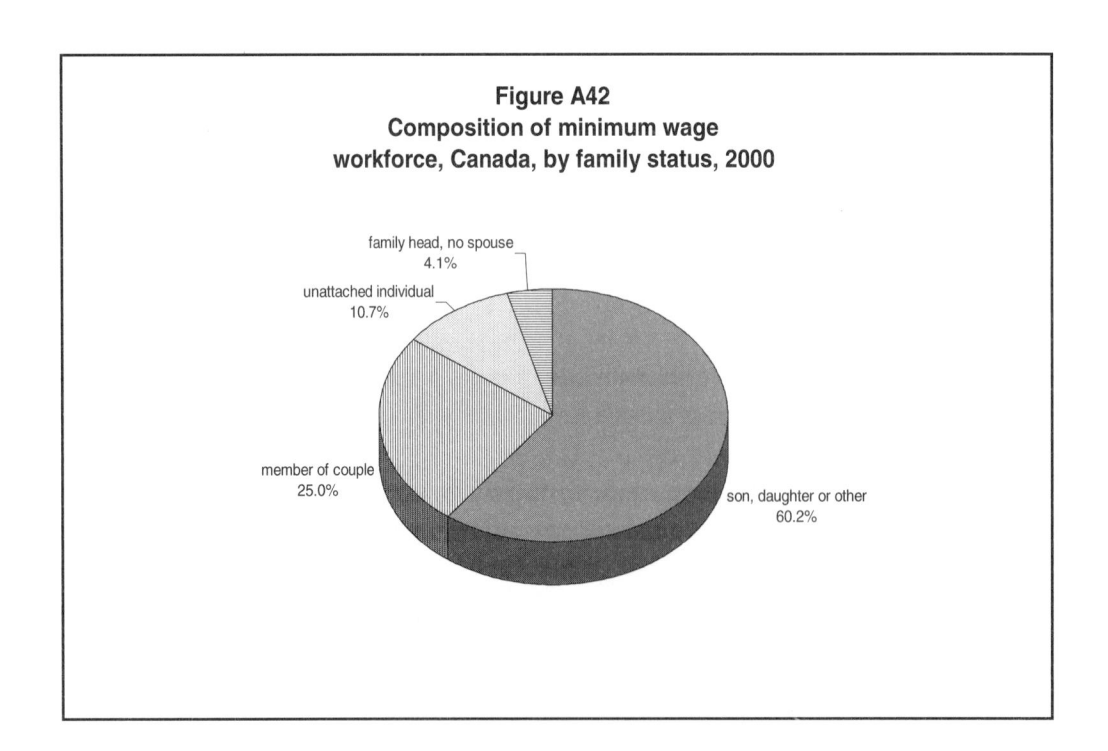

**Figure A42
Composition of minimum wage workforce, Canada, by family status, 2000**

- family head, no spouse 4.1%
- unattached individual 10.7%
- member of couple 25.0%
- son, daughter or other 60.2%

(16,900) are aged 25-54, while 8,000 are 15-24 and the remaining 6,500 are 55 or older. The other half (30,500) live with non-relatives; the largest group (16,600) are young people 15-24 living with friends or roommates, while 12,700 are 25-54 and 1,200 are 55 or older.

Finally, 23,800 or just 4.1 percent of the minimum wage workforce are heads of families with no spouse present. Most of them (21,600) are single parents with children under 18.

Industry (Figures A43 and A44)

There are significant differences among industries in the percentage of their workforce paid the minimum wage. Figure A43 ranks industries from highest to lowest according to the percentage of their workers who are at the minimum wage. (Note that estimates are not available for the category of utilities because of insufficient sample size).

The top five are accommodation and food services (19.4 percent of employees work for minimum wage), agriculture (15.4 percent), trade (8.8 percent), other services (7.7 percent) and information, culture and recreation (6.2 percent). Next come management, administrative and other support (5.1 percent), finance, insurance, real estate and leasing (2.5 percent), transportation and warehousing (2.2 percent) and health care and social assistance (2.0 percent). Industries with relatively few jobs (under 2 percent) that pay minimum wage include educational services (1.7 percent), forestry, fishing, mining, oil and gas (1.5 percent), manufacturing (1.4 percent), public administration (1.1 percent), professional, scientific and technical services (1.0 percent) and construction (1.0 percent).

The picture is somewhat different in terms of the distribution of minimum wage workers among the various industries, shown in Figure A44. The two largest minimum wage employers are trade (with 30.2 percent of all minimum wage workers in Canada) and accommodation and food services (28.9 percent) – for a combined total of 59.1 percent of the minimum wage workforce. Next come other services (6.1 percent), information, culture and recreation (6.1 percent), manufacturing (5.2 percent), health care and social assistance (4.5 percent) and the remaining industry categories.

Four industries rank in the top five both in terms of incidence and share of minimum wage workers – accommodation and food services (ranked first in incidence and second in share), trade (third in incidence and first in share), other services (fourth in incidence and third in share) and information, culture and recreation (ranked fifth in incidence and fourth in share).

The proportionality index indicates industries in which minimum wage workers are overrepresented or underrepresented. Scores of more than 1.0 indicate overrepresentation and scores under 1.0 measure the degree of underrepresentation.

Minimum wage workers are most overrepresented in accommodation and food services (an index of 4.18), followed by agriculture (3.31), trade (1.89), other services (1.65), information, culture and

Figure A43
Percentage of employees working for minimum wages, by industry, 2000

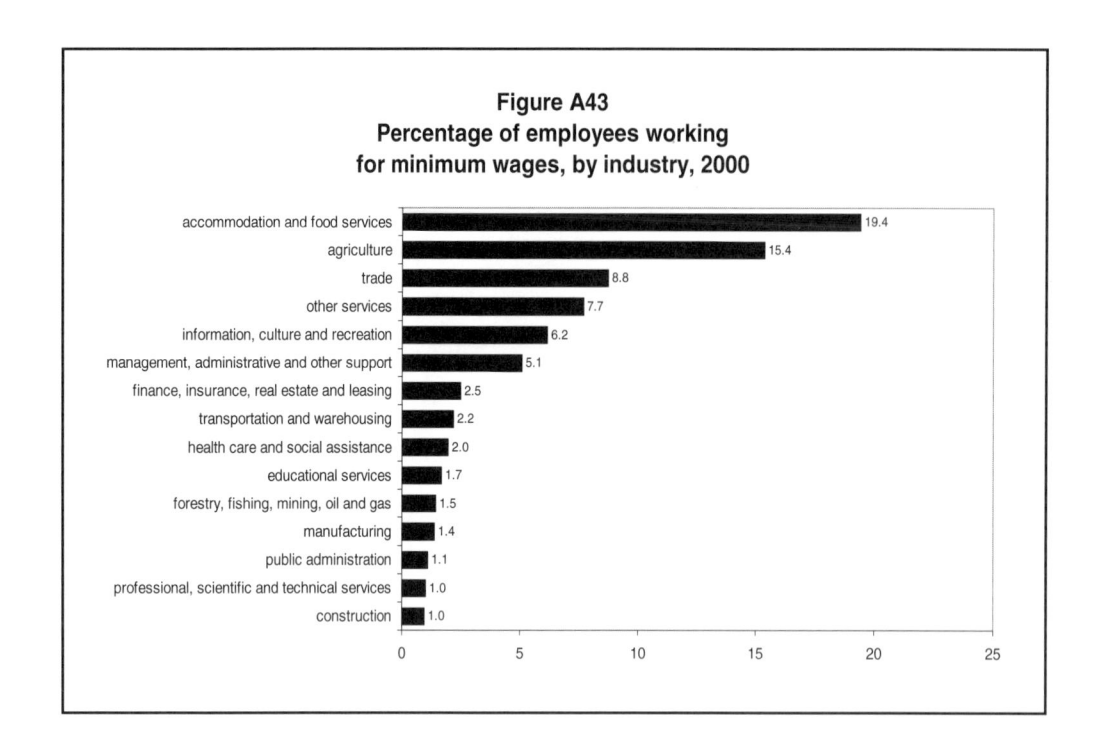

Industry	%
accommodation and food services	19.4
agriculture	15.4
trade	8.8
other services	7.7
information, culture and recreation	6.2
management, administrative and other support	5.1
finance, insurance, real estate and leasing	2.5
transportation and warehousing	2.2
health care and social assistance	2.0
educational services	1.7
forestry, fishing, mining, oil and gas	1.5
manufacturing	1.4
public administration	1.1
professional, scientific and technical services	1.0
construction	1.0

Figure A44
Composition of minimum wage workforce, by industry, 2000

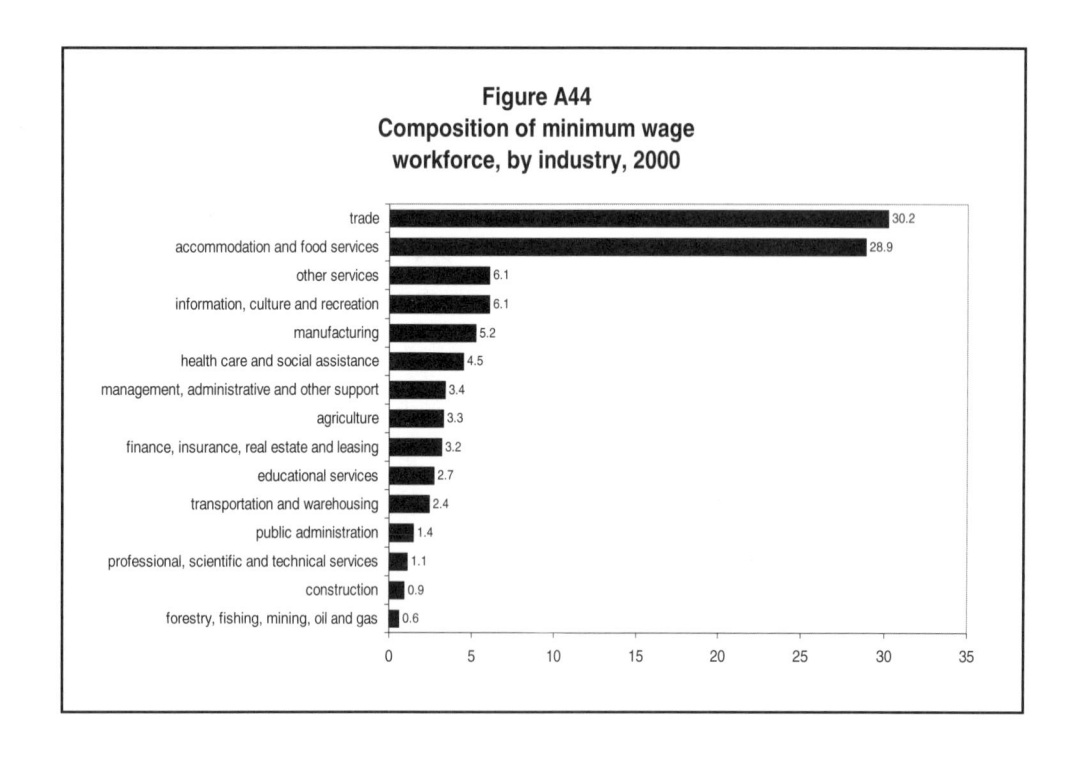

Industry	%
trade	30.2
accommodation and food services	28.9
other services	6.1
information, culture and recreation	6.1
manufacturing	5.2
health care and social assistance	4.5
management, administrative and other support	3.4
agriculture	3.3
finance, insurance, real estate and leasing	3.2
educational services	2.7
transportation and warehousing	2.4
public administration	1.4
professional, scientific and technical services	1.1
construction	0.9
forestry, fishing, mining, oil and gas	0.6

recreation (1.33) and management, administration and other support (1.09). They are most underrepresented in construction (0.21), followed by professional, scientific and technical services (0.22), public administration (0.24), manufacturing (0.30), forestry, fishing, mining, oil and gas (0.31), educational services (0.36), health care and social assistance (0.42), transportation and warehousing (0.47) and finance, insurance, real estate and leasing (0.54).

NEWFOUNDLAND AND LABRADOR

a. Minimum Wages in Newfoundland and Labrador

Interprovincial rank: dollar value of minimum wages (Figure B1)

In 2002, the government of Newfoundland and Labrador raised the province's minimum wage from $5.50 an hour to $5.75 in May and again to $6.00 in November – placing it ahead of Alberta, at $5.90. Even with these increases, however, Newfoundland's average hourly minimum wage for 2002 – $5.71 – still ranked it lowest among Canada's ten provinces and three territories. At $8.00 an hour, British Columbia's minimum wage is Canada's highest. Figure B1 gives the rankings.

Trend in dollar value of minimum wage (Figure B2)

Because minimum wages are not indexed, their value changes over time. Figure B2 shows the trend in Newfoundland's minimum wage from 1965 to 2002; each year's average minimum wage has been converted to inflation-adjusted (i.e., constant) 2002 dollars to show the real trend, after taking into account the impact of inflation on the dollar.

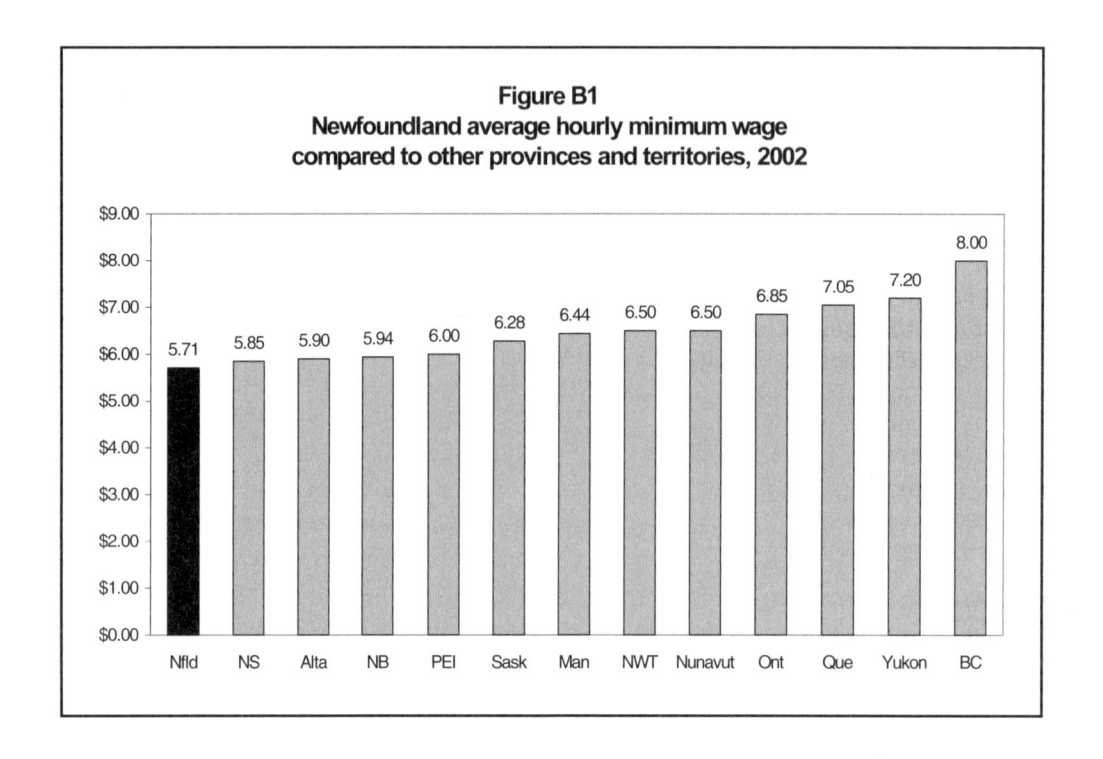

Figure B1
Newfoundland average hourly minimum wage compared to other provinces and territories, 2002

Nfld	5.71
NS	5.85
Alta	5.90
NB	5.94
PEI	6.00
Sask	6.28
Man	6.44
NWT	6.50
Nunavut	6.50
Ont	6.85
Que	7.05
Yukon	7.20
BC	8.00

**Figure B2
Newfoundland minimum wage,
in constant 2002 dollars, 1965-2002**

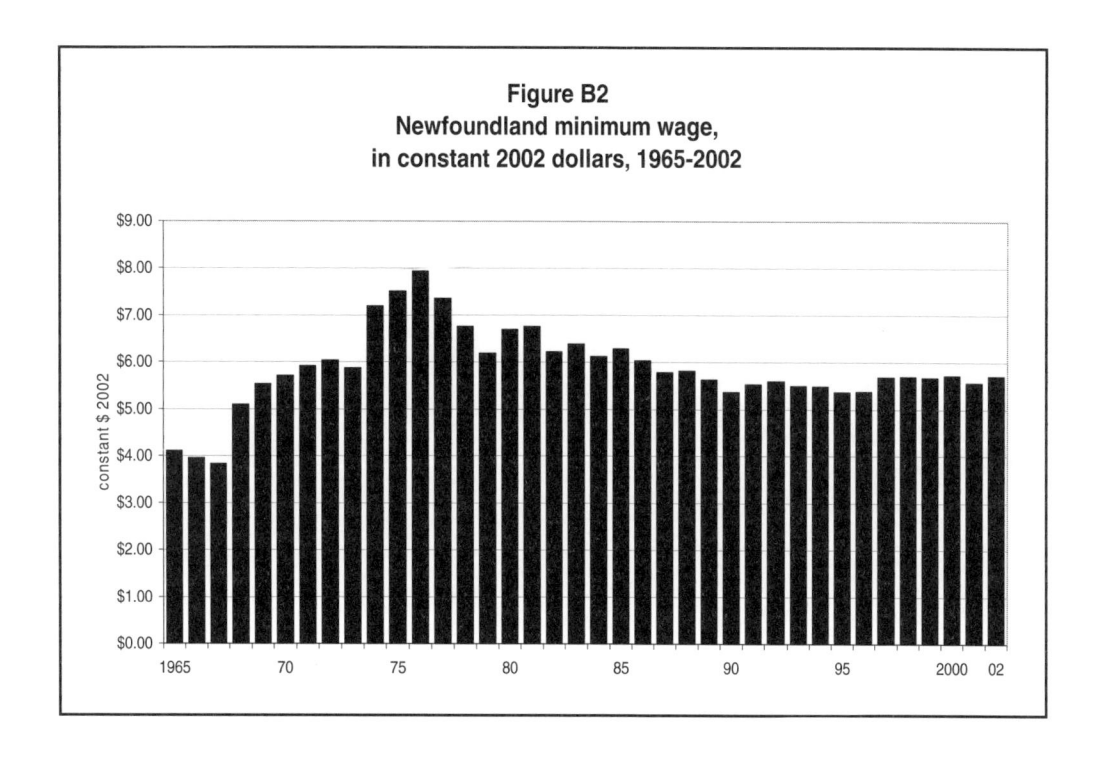

Newfoundland's minimum wage increased substantially overall between 1965 and its 1976 peak, almost doubling in value from $4.11 to $7.94. It then declined slowly though fairly steadily until 1990 ($5.37), remained more or less flat between 1990 and 1996, increased somewhat to $5.68 in 1997 and plateaued again, standing at an annual average of $5.71 for 2002. In short, Newfoundland's minimum wage increased sharply from the mid-60s to the mid-70s, fell considerably in the late 1970s and 1980s, and levelled off overall in the 1990s.

In 2002, Newfoundland's minimum wage ($5.71 an hour average) remained significantly below its 1976 peak ($7.94) – $2.23 less or 28.1 percent lower in real terms. However, in 2002 the minimum wage was $1.60 or 39.0 percent higher than in 1965 ($4.11).

Interprovincial rank: minimum wages as percentage of average earnings (Figure B3)

A more informative gauge of the minimum wage is how it compares to the average wage in each jurisdiction. Newfoundland does somewhat better on this measure.

In 2001 (the most recent year for which data on average earnings are available), Newfoundland's average minimum wage ($5.50 that year) represented 36.4 percent of the province's $15.09 hourly

Figure B3
Newfoundland minimum wage as % of average earnings, compared to other provinces and territories, 2001

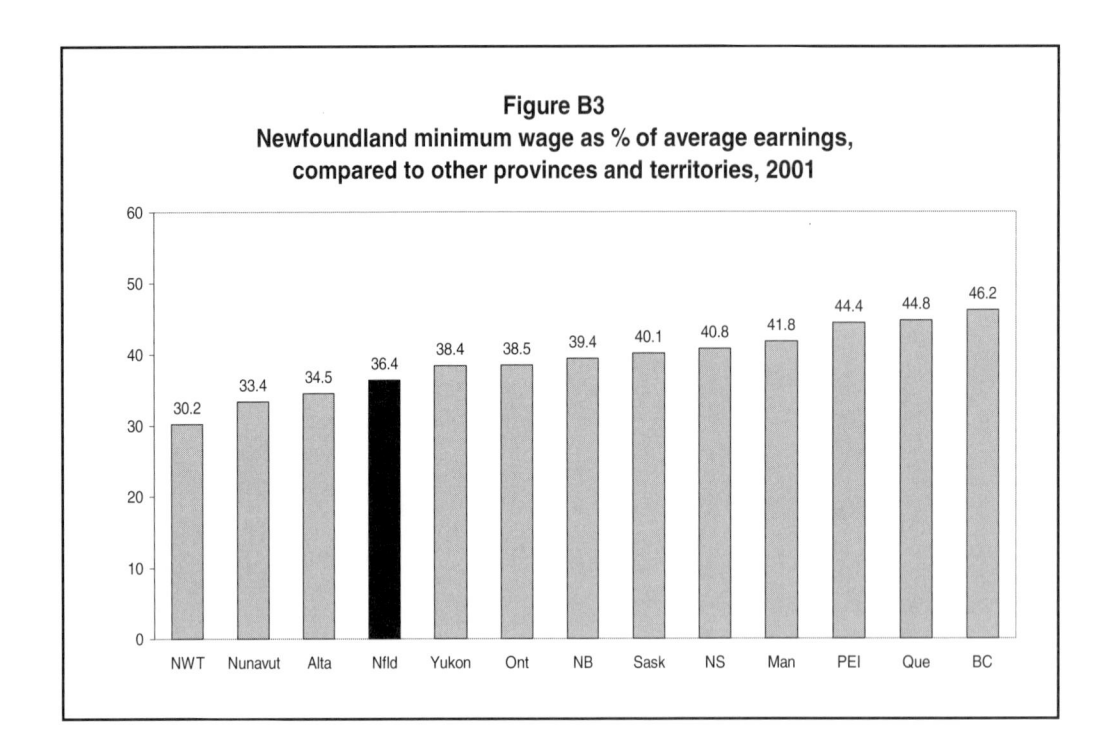

Jurisdiction	%
NWT	30.2
Nunavut	33.4
Alta	34.5
Nfld	36.4
Yukon	38.4
Ont	38.5
NB	39.4
Sask	40.1
NS	40.8
Man	41.8
PEI	44.4
Que	44.8
BC	46.2

average earnings, ranking it fourth-lowest among the 13 jurisdictions (i.e., ten provinces and three territories), ahead of the Northwest Territories (30.2 percent, the lowest), Nunavut (33.4 percent) and Alberta (34.5 percent). British Columbia, at 46.2 percent, placed first.

Trends in minimum wage and average earnings (Figure B4)

The black line in Figure B4 shows the trend in the minimum wage, the gray line the trend in average earnings and the vertical bars the trend in the minimum wage as a percentage of average earnings. Read the left-hand axis for the minimum wage and average earnings and the right-hand axis for the minimum wage as a percentage of earnings.

The overall pattern is similar to the trend in the value of the minimum wage over time. Newfoundland's minimum wage as a percentage of average earnings rose between 1965 (34.4 percent) and 1976 (44.5 percent), declined slowly until the 1990s when it levelled off for the first half of the decade at around 35 percent, and increased somewhat in the latter half to 37.2 percent in 1997, though it has since slipped to 36.4 percent in 2001.

**Figure B4
Newfoundland minimum wage
compared to average earnings, 1965-2001**

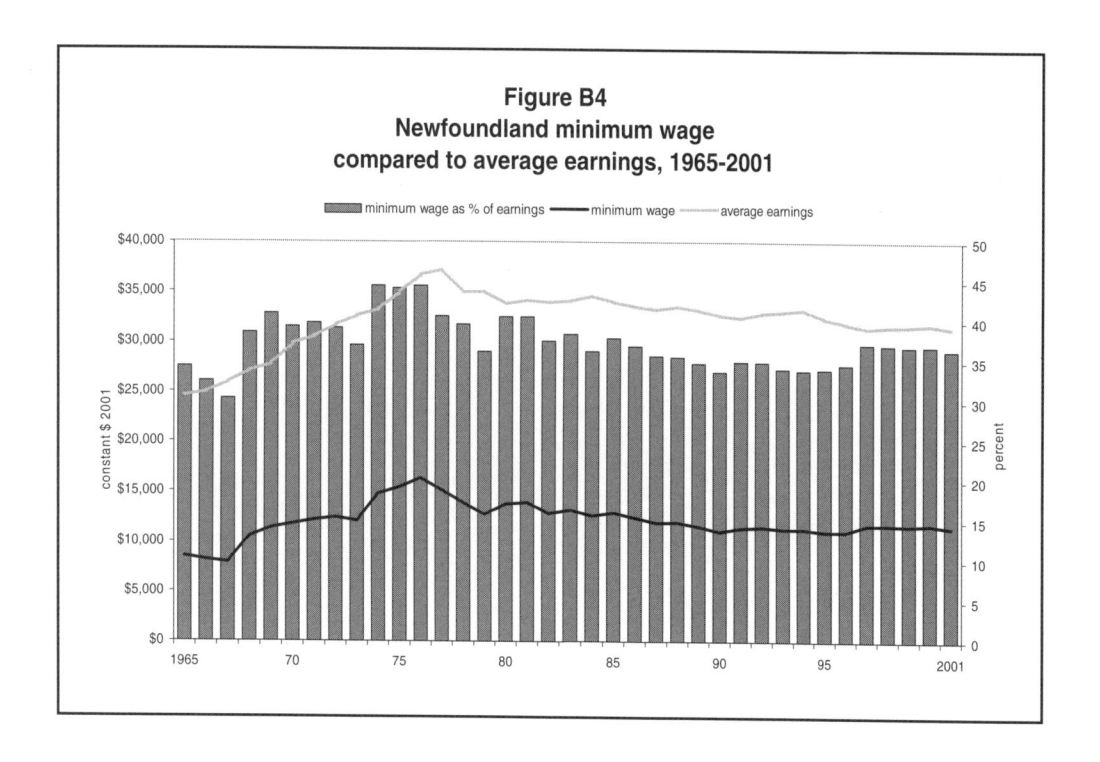

Average earnings (expressed in constant 2001 dollars) increased from $24,528 in 1965 to $37,191 in 1977, but then declined overall to reach $31,387 in 2001. On an annual (full-time, all-year) basis, the minimum wage went from $8,438 in 1965 to $16,301 in 1976, slid to $11,025 in 1990 and stood at $11,440 in 2001.

Minimum wage compared to before-tax poverty lines (Figure B5)

Statistics Canada publishes two sets of low income cut-offs. The before-tax low income cut-offs are based on gross, pre-tax income (i.e., income from employment, investments, private pensions and other private sources plus income from government programs such as public pensions, Employment Insurance, child benefits and welfare). The after-tax low income cut-offs use the same definition of income but factor into the picture the federal and provincial income taxes that Canadians pay. We first compare the minimum wage to the before-tax poverty lines.

Because the poverty line is lower for smaller communities, the minimum wage represents a larger proportion of the poverty line in smaller communities. In 2002, Newfoundland's minimum wage ranged from 72.9 percent of the before-tax low income cut-off for one person in St. John's (which lies in the

Figure B5
Dollars below before-tax poverty line for different size communities, Newfoundand minimum wage, 2002

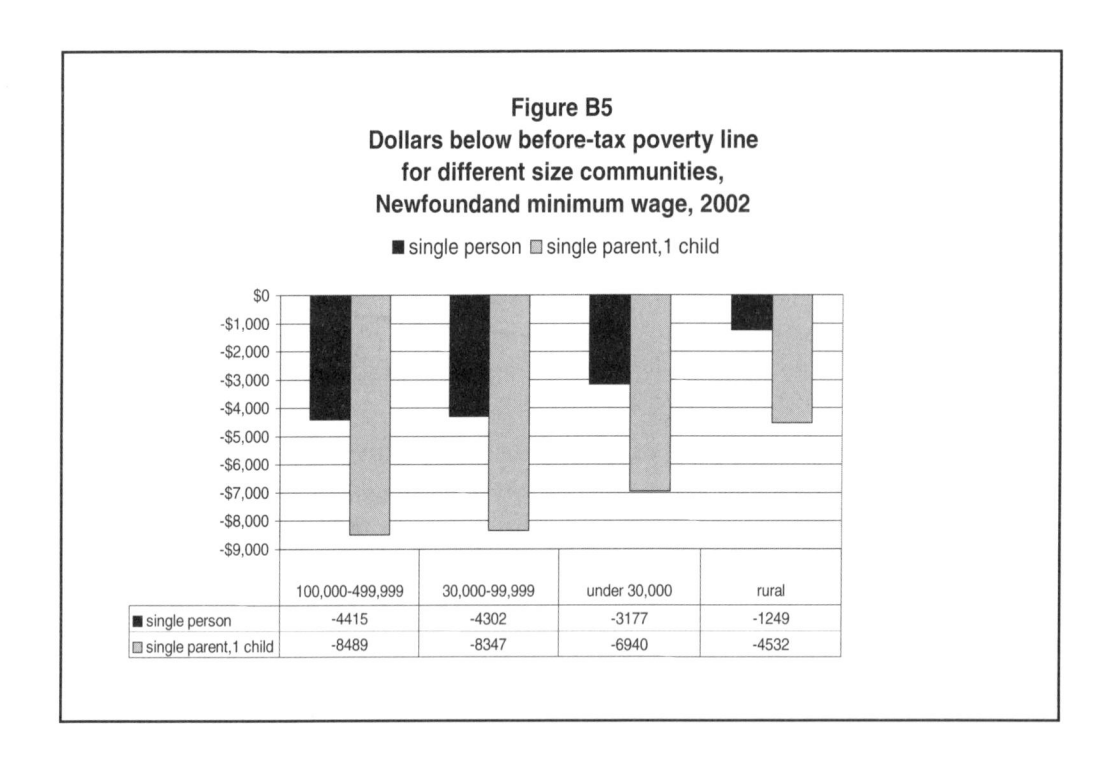

	100,000-499,999	30,000-99,999	under 30,000	rural
single person	-4415	-4302	-3177	-1249
single parent,1 child	-8489	-8347	-6940	-4532

100,000-499,999 community size category) to 73.4 percent for communities between 30,000 and 99,999, 78.9 percent for towns under 30,000 and 90.5 percent for rural areas.

In dollar terms, Newfoundland's minimum wage in 2002 fell $4,415 below the before-tax poverty line for one person in St. John's, $4,302 below for communities with 30,000 to 99,999 inhabitants, $3,177 below for towns under 30,000 and $1,249 below the poverty line for rural areas. Figure B5 shows the dollar gap between the minimum wage and the before-tax poverty line for one person in different size communities throughout the province.

Because the poverty line varies by family size, minimum wages (which do not vary by family size) fall farther below the poverty line for families than for single workers. We look next at the poverty gap for a single parent with one child, which falls in the two-person family size category. (Note that the low income cut-offs do not vary by type of family; for example, a childless couple and single parent with one child are treated the same.)

In 2002, Newfoundland's minimum wage varied from 58.3 percent of the before-tax poverty line for a two-person family in St. John's (in the 100,000-499,999 size category) to 58.7 percent for communities between 30,000 and 99,999, 63.1 percent for towns under 30,000 and 72.4 percent for rural areas. The minimum wage fell $8,489 below the low income line for a family of two in St. John's, $8,347 under for communities with 30,000 to 99,999 inhabitants, $6,940 under towns under 30,000 and $4,532 below the poverty line for rural areas.

Trend in minimum wage as percentage of before-tax poverty lines (Figure B6)

The long-term trend when we compare the minimum wage to the poverty line (as measured by Statistics Canada's before-tax low income cut-offs, which vary by size of family and of community) is the same as the trend in dollar value. In 2002, the estimated before-tax poverty line for the largest city in the province (St. John's, which falls in the 100,000-499,999 category) was $16,295 for one person and $20,369 for a family of two.

Newfoundland's minimum wage rose from 52.5 percent of the before-tax poverty line for one person in St. John's in 1965 to 101.3 percent of the poverty line in 1976, falling to 68.5 percent in 1990 and more or less levelling off for the first half of the 1990s. However, the trend improved somewhat in the latter half of the 1990s, rising to 73.0 percent of the poverty line in 2000, dipping slightly to 71.1 percent in 2001 but then recovering to 72.9 percent in 2002. For a two-person family (e.g., a single parent with one child), the minimum wage went from 42.0 percent of the low income line in 1965 to a peak of 81.1 percent

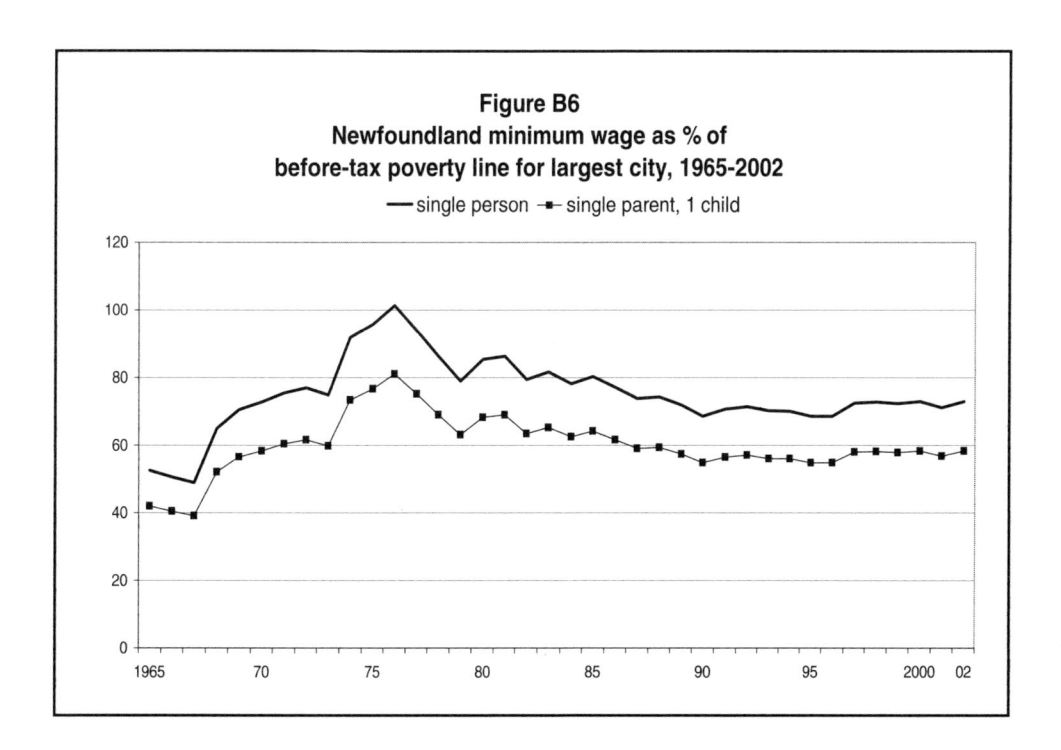

**Figure B6
Newfoundland minimum wage as % of
before-tax poverty line for largest city, 1965-2002**

Minimum Wages in Canada: A Statistical Portrait With Policy Implications

in 1976, declining to a low of 54.8 percent in 1990 and 1995 but rising again to 58.3 percent in 2002. Figure B6 shows the trends.

Minimum wage compared to after-tax poverty lines (Figure B7)

Statistics Canada publishes after-tax low income cut-offs as well as before-tax low income cut-offs. We look here at how after-tax minimum wage incomes in Newfoundland for five types of household – single persons, single parents with one child, one-earner couples with two children, two-earner couples supporting two children on one-and-a-half minimum wages, and two-earner couples with two children and two full minimum wages – compare to the after-tax poverty lines for different size communities. 'After-tax minimum wage incomes' means incomes from the minimum wage and available federal and provincial income programs, minus federal and provincial income taxes.

For a single person earning the minimum wage, after-tax income came to $10,870,[11] which is $2,240 below the after-tax poverty line for St. John's, $2,038 below for centres of 30,000-99,999, $925 less for towns under 30,000 but $666 above the poverty line for rural residents. A single parent with one child received $14,710[12] in after-tax income from minimum wage earnings and federal and provincial child benefits and tax credits, which came to $1,287 below the after-tax poverty line for St. John's and $1,040

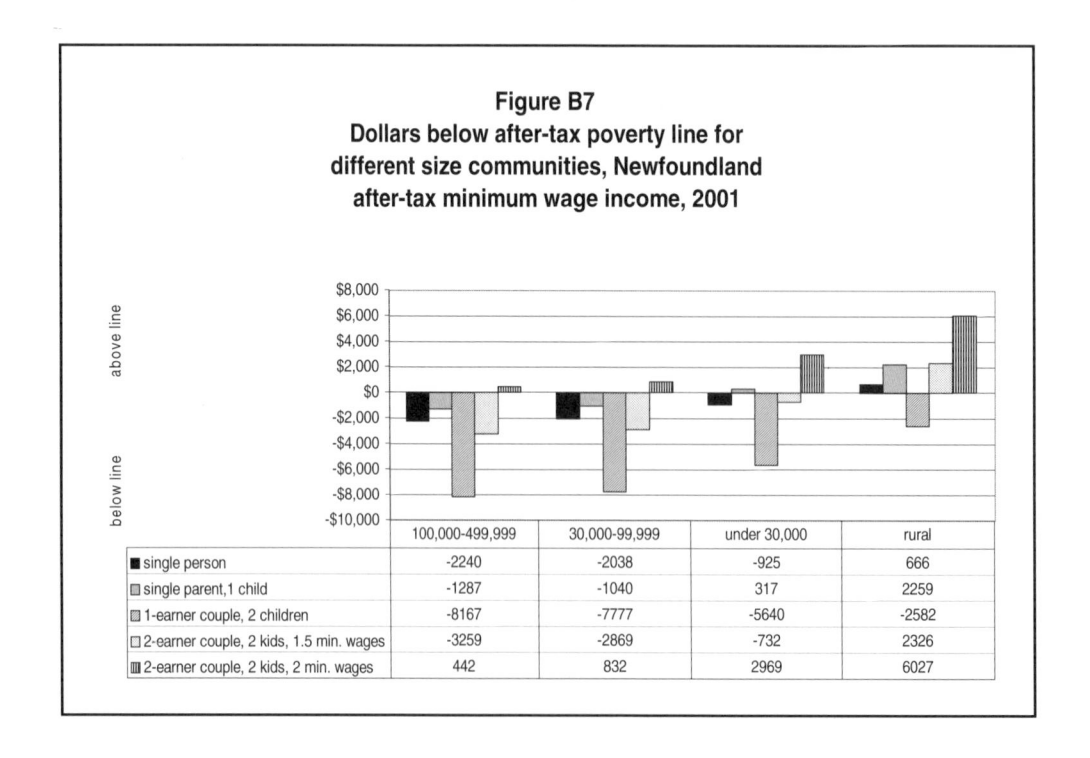

**Figure B7
Dollars below after-tax poverty line for different size communities, Newfoundland after-tax minimum wage income, 2001**

	100,000-499,999	30,000-99,999	under 30,000	rural
single person	-2240	-2038	-925	666
single parent, 1 child	-1287	-1040	317	2259
1-earner couple, 2 children	-8167	-7777	-5640	-2582
2-earner couple, 2 kids, 1.5 min. wages	-3259	-2869	-732	2326
2-earner couple, 2 kids, 2 min. wages	442	832	2969	6027

under for centres of 30,000-99,999, but $317 above the line for towns under 30,000 and $2,259 above the poverty line for rural residents.

For a one-earner couple with two children, after-tax minimum wage income amounted to $17,033[13] – $8,167 below the after-tax poverty line for St. John's, $7,777 under for centres of 30,000-99,999, $5,640 below for towns under 30,000 and $2,582 below the line for rural residents. In the case of a two-earner couple earning 1.5 times the minimum wage and supporting two children, after-tax minimum wage income amounted to $21,941[14] – $3,259 below the after-tax poverty line for St. John's, $2,869 under for centres of 30,000-99,999, $732 below for towns under 30,000 but $2,326 above the after-tax poverty line for rural residents. For a two-earner couple in which both parents worked full time, year round for the minimum wage and supported two children, after-tax minimum wage income was $25,642[15] – $442 above the after-tax poverty line for St. John's, $832 over the line for centres of 30,000-99,999, $2,969 over for towns under 30,000 and $6,027 above the after-tax poverty line for rural residents.

Contribution of child benefits

Child benefits supplement the incomes of the large majority of Canadian families and are most important to low- and modest-income families. Improvements to the federal Canada Child Tax Benefit, and the creation of the Newfoundland and Labrador Child Benefit, are contributing significantly to the incomes of minimum wage and other working poor families.

The single parent supporting one child on minimum wage earnings got total child benefits of $2,651 in 2001 – $2,447 from the Canada Child Tax Benefit and $204 from the Newfoundland and Labrador Child Benefit – which amounted to 18.8 percent of disposable income. The one-earner couple with two children received $4,766 worth of child benefits – $4,250 from the Canada Child Tax Benefit and $516 from the Newfoundland and Labrador Child Benefit – worth a substantial 29.0 percent of disposable income.

The two-earner family in which one parent works full time, all year at the minimum wage and the other parent half that time child got benefits worth a total of $4,681 or 22.2 percent of disposable income – $4,250 from the federal Canada Child Tax Benefit and $431 from the provincial Newfoundland and Labrador Child Benefit. The two-earner family in which both parents work full time, all year at the minimum wage received $3,956 from the Canada Child Tax Benefit (its income was too high to qualify for the Newfoundland and Labrador Child Benefit), which comes to 16.2 percent of disposable income.

Minimum wage versus welfare (Figure B8)

For a single person earning the minimum wage in Newfoundland, disposable income – i.e., minimum wage earnings plus refundable tax credits minus income and payroll taxes – amounted to $10,272

Figure B8
Minimum wage versus welfare, by household type, Newfoundland, 2001

	single person	single parent, 1 child	one-earner couple, 2 children	couple, 2 kids, 1.5 min. wages	couple, 2 kids, 2 min. wages
minimum wage disposable income	10272	14112	16435	21118	24444
welfare income	3276	14670	17474	17474	17474

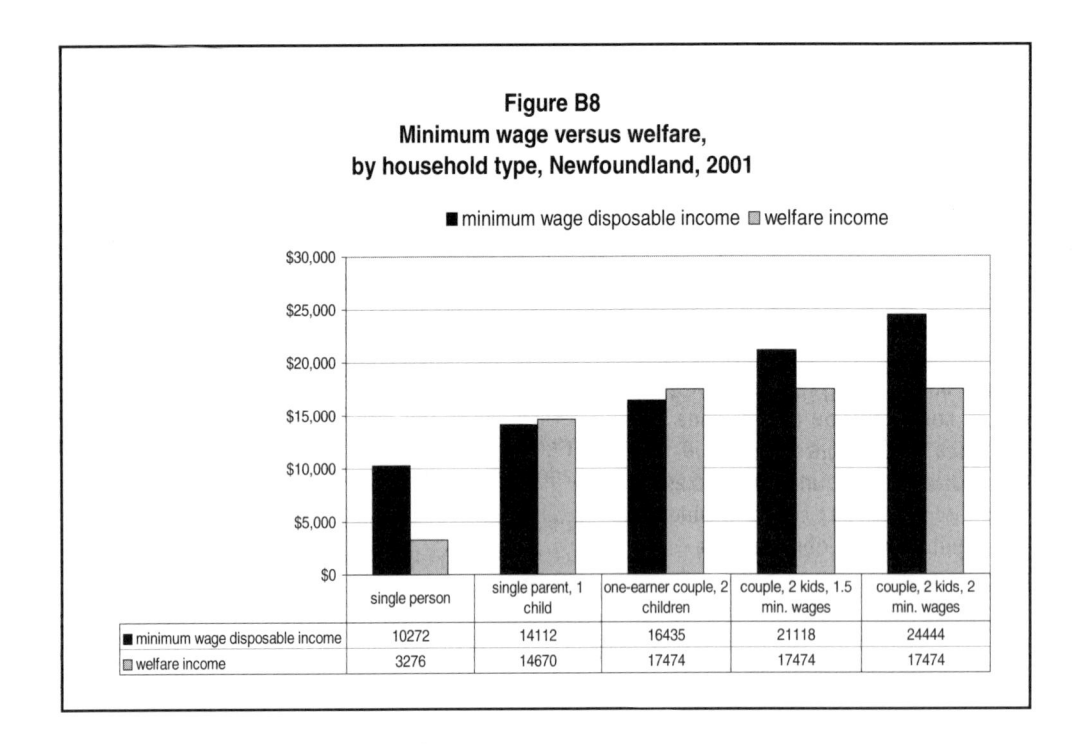

in 2001, which is a sizeable $6,996 more than the very low $3,276 from welfare. Figure B8 shows the comparison.

But welfare pays better than minimum wages for a single parent with one child age 2. Total income from welfare and available child benefits and refundable tax credits came to $14,670, or $558 more than the $14,112 from after-tax minimum wage earnings, child benefits and refundable tax credits.

Welfare also offers more than the minimum wage for the one-earner couple in our example. A one-earner couple earning the minimum wage and supporting two children aged 10 and 15 got $17,474 from welfare, child benefits and tax credits as opposed to $16,435 ($1,039 less) from minimum wage disposable income.

For two-parent families to earn more than welfare, both parents must work. We look at two examples of two-earner families.

In the first, one parent works full time, year round at the minimum wage while the other earns half this amount (i.e., works part time and/or part year); as with the one-earner family, there are two children aged 10 and 15. The family's disposable income from one-and-a-half minimum wages came to $21,118 in 2001 or $3,644 more than the $17,474 from welfare, child benefits and refundable tax credits.

The other two-earner family earns double the minimum wage since we assume that both parents work full time, year round at the minimum wage. Total disposable income was $24,444 or $6,970 more than the $17,474 from welfare and other government income benefits.

b. Minimum Wage Workers in Newfoundland and Labrador

The following text with illustrative graphs analyzes key characteristics of minimum wage workers in Newfoundland and Labrador. Appendix 2 provides detailed statistics in tabular form (pages 282-284).

Interprovincial rank: incidence of minimum wage workers (Figure B9)

In 2000, an estimated 15,500 Newfoundlanders – 8.7 percent of the total 178,300 employees – worked for the minimum wage. Newfoundland's 8.7 percent figure means that it has the highest incidence of minimum wage workers in Canada – almost double the overall national rate of 4.6 percent. Alberta, with only 2.0 percent of its workforce at the minimum wage, ranks lowest. Figure B9 shows the results

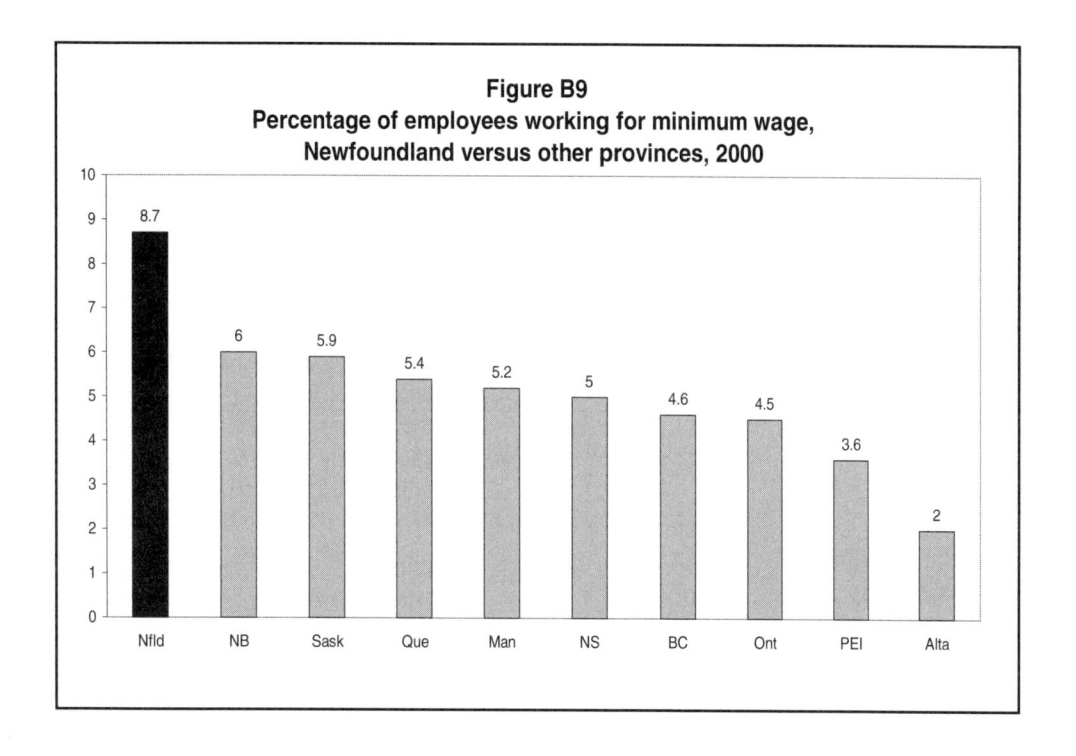

Figure B9
Percentage of employees working for minimum wage, Newfoundland versus other provinces, 2000

Province	Percentage
Nfld	8.7
NB	6
Sask	5.9
Que	5.4
Man	5.2
NS	5
BC	4.6
Ont	4.5
PEI	3.6
Alta	2

Moreover, minimum wage workers are most overrepresented in Newfoundland. While the province accounts for only 2.7 percent of all minimum wage workers in the country, it has an even smaller share of Canadian employees (1.4 percent), producing an index of 1.87 (the higher the result above 1.00, the more overrepresented are minimum wage workers).

Gender and age (Figures B10-B13)

In Newfoundland as in the rest of Canada, women run a higher risk of working for minimum wage than men, and women also make up the majority of the minimum wage workforce.

In 2000, 12.1 percent of Newfoundland female employees worked for minimum wage compared to only 5.4 percent of male workers. Of the total 15,500 minimum wage workers, 10,600 – 68.4 percent – were women and 4,900 – 31.6 percent – were men. Figure B10 gives the gender breakdown.

Women are overrepresented in Newfoundland's minimum wage workforce. They constituted 68.4 percent of minimum wage workers but only 49.0 percent of all the province's employees in 2000. Men are underrepresented. They accounted for less one-third (31.6 percent) of minimum wage workers in Newfoundland but slightly more than half (51.0 percent) of all employees.

The gender bias among minimum wage workers holds when we control for major age categories. While younger workers of both sexes run a higher risk of working for minimum wage, women still fare worse than men within each age category.

Figure B11 shows the results. Among female workers aged 15 to 19, 61.0 percent worked for the minimum wage in 2000 in contrast to 48.6 percent of male workers in the same age group. Among those aged 20-24, 34.0 percent of women compared to 19.1 percent of men worked for the minimum wage. Among workers 25-44, 6.5 percent of women as opposed to 2.1 percent of men were at the bottom of the wage ladder. Among employees 45 and older, 6.9 percent of women but only 1.0 percent of men worked for the minimum wage.

The minimum wage risk gap between the sexes is wider for older workers. Women in the 15-19 age group are 1.3 times more likely than men in the same age group to work for the minimum wage, and the ratio is similar – 1.8 times – for those aged 20-24. However, the gap between the sexes increases to 3.1 for those aged 25-44 and 6.9 for those over 45.

Young people not only are more likely to work for minimum wage than other employees, but the young also make up a large proportion of the minimum wage workforce. Figure B12 compares the age makeup of minimum wage workers and all employees in Newfoundland. More than one-quarter (27.6 percent) of minimum wage workers are in the 15-19 age group, compared to just 4.4 percent of all employees. Employees aged 20-24 represent 32.1 percent of minimum wage workers as opposed to only

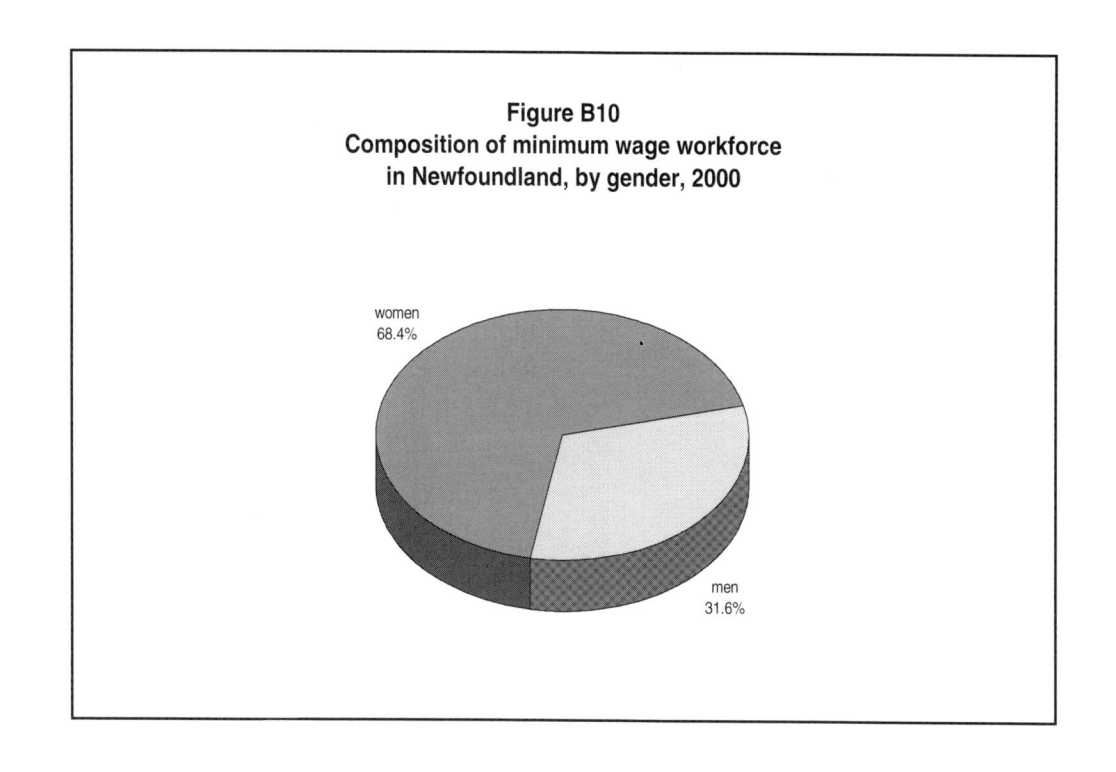

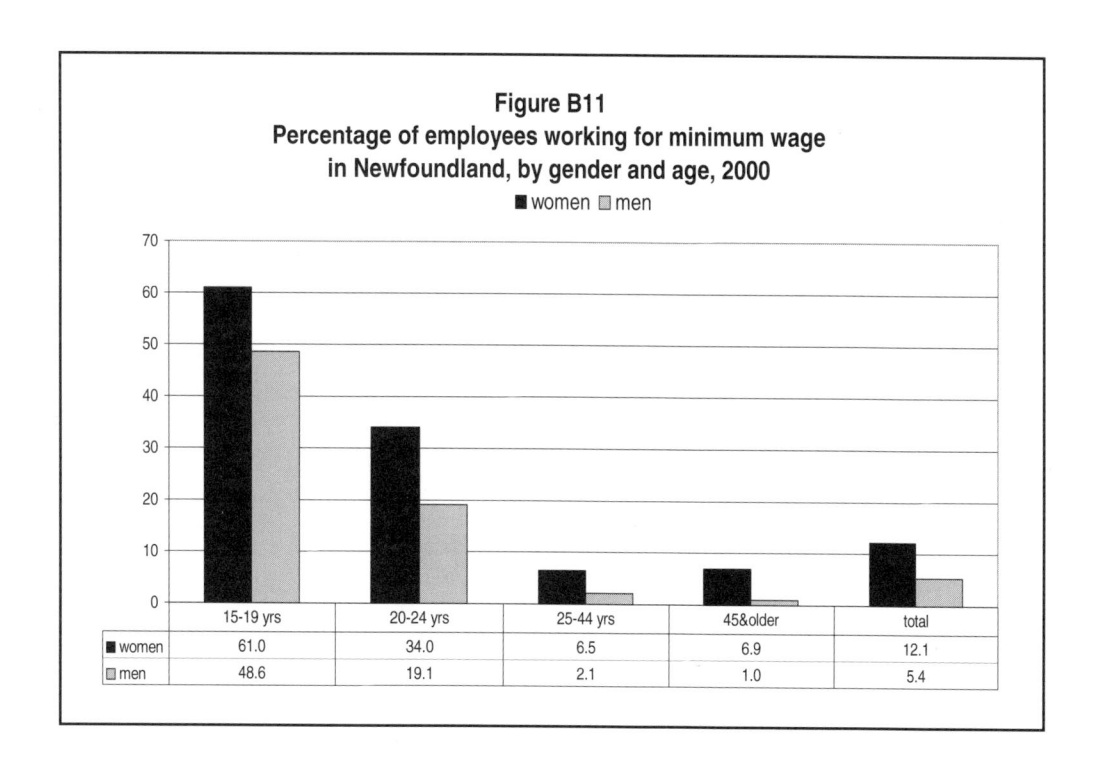

**Figure B10
Composition of minimum wage workforce
in Newfoundland, by gender, 2000**

women 68.4%
men 31.6%

**Figure B11
Percentage of employees working for minimum wage
in Newfoundland, by gender and age, 2000**

	15-19 yrs	20-24 yrs	25-44 yrs	45&older	total
women	61.0	34.0	6.5	6.9	12.1
men	48.6	19.1	2.1	1.0	5.4

Minimum Wages in Canada: A Statistical Portrait With Policy Implications

Figure B12
Share of minimum wage workers versus share of all employees in Newfoundland, by age group, 2000

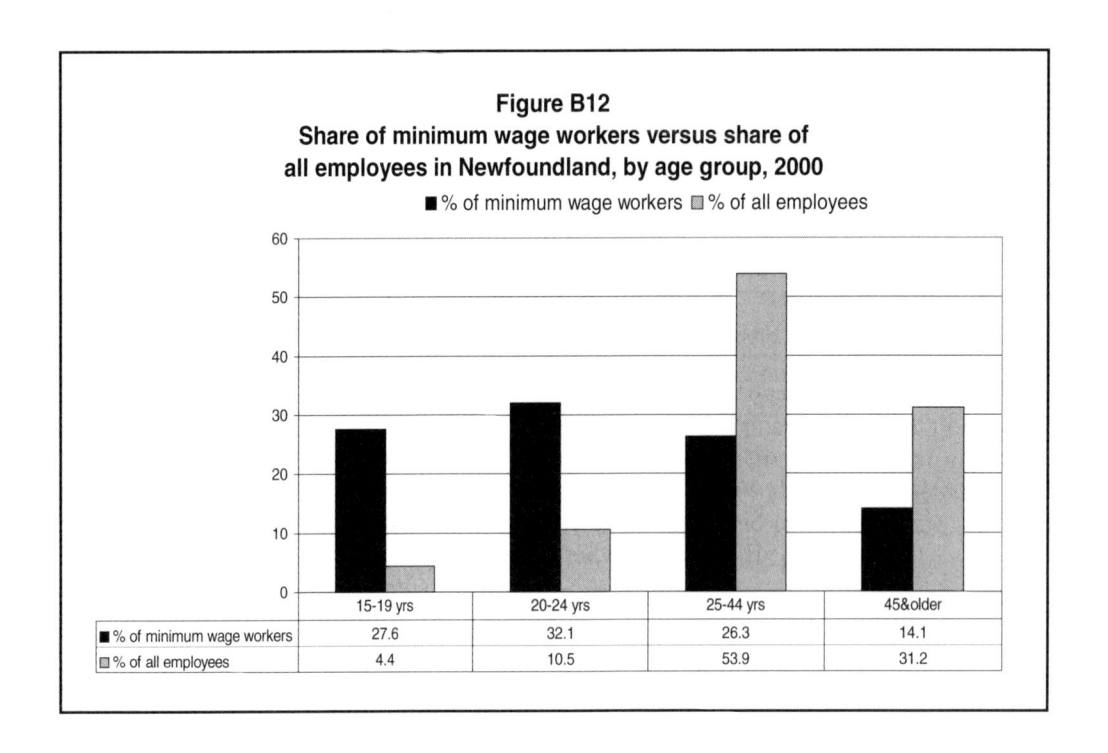

	15-19 yrs	20-24 yrs	25-44 yrs	45&older
% of minimum wage workers	27.6	32.1	26.3	14.1
% of all employees	4.4	10.5	53.9	31.2

Figure B13
Composition of minimum wage workforce in Newfoundland, by teenager/adult and gender, 2000

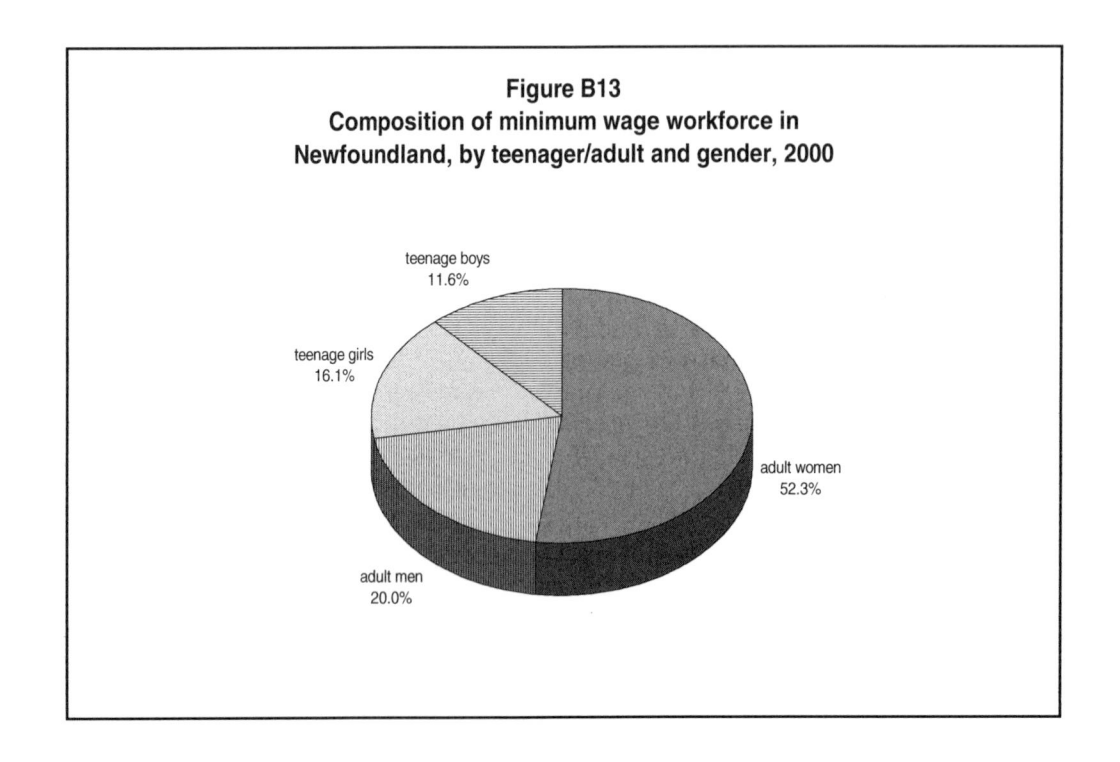

- teenage boys: 11.6%
- teenage girls: 16.1%
- adult women: 52.3%
- adult men: 20.0%

10.5 percent of all workers. All told, six in ten minimum wage workers (59.7 percent) are under 25 years of age.

The opposite holds for older workers in Newfoundland. While a sizeable proportion – 26.3 percent – of minimum wage workers are between 25 and 44, that age group constitutes a much larger proportion – 53.9 percent or more than half – of all employees. Workers aged 45 and older make up just 14.1 percent of minimum wage employees but 31.2 percent of all employees.

Figure B13 divides the minimum wage workforce in Newfoundland into teenage girls and boys and adult women and men. Adult women are the largest group, at 8,100 or 52.3 percent of the total, followed by adult men (3,100 or 20.0 percent), teenage girls (2,500 or 16.1 percent) and teenage boys (1,800 or 11.5 percent). The large majority (72.3 percent) of Newfoundland's minimum wage workers are adults; the national average is much lower (52.9 percent).

Education (Figures B14 and B15)

Figure B14 shows the percentage of minimum wage workers in Newfoundland according to level of education.

At first glance, the relationship between level of education and incidence of minimum wage employment does not seem to correspond to common sense: Workers in the lowest educational group (elementary education only) are less likely to work for minimum wage (9.6 percent do) than those with some high school (17.8 percent), while those with some postsecondary education run a higher risk (18.8 percent) than high school graduates (11.4 percent). However, as one would expect, the chances of working for minimum wage are lowest for the two highest education categories – 5.2 percent for those with a postsecondary certificate or diploma (e.g., from a community college or vocational institute) and only 2.0 percent for those with a university degree.

Once we look at the education-minimum wage link for different age groups, the reasons for the apparently inconsistent relationship comes clear: Young people working at part-time or seasonal (i.e., summer) jobs – typically paying the minimum or a low wage – figure prominently in the 'some high school' and 'some postsecondary education' categories; they are still at high school, community college or university, whereas workers in the other educational categories have completed their education.

Figure B15 shows each educational group's share of Newfoundland's minimum wage workforce in 2000. The largest group of minimum wage workers (26.5 percent) are postsecondary graduates, followed by those with some high school (25.8 percent), high school graduates (20.6 percent), those with some postsecondary education (19.4 percent), workers with only 0-8 years of education (4.5 percent) and university graduates (3.2 percent). Many minimum wage workers are students (high school or

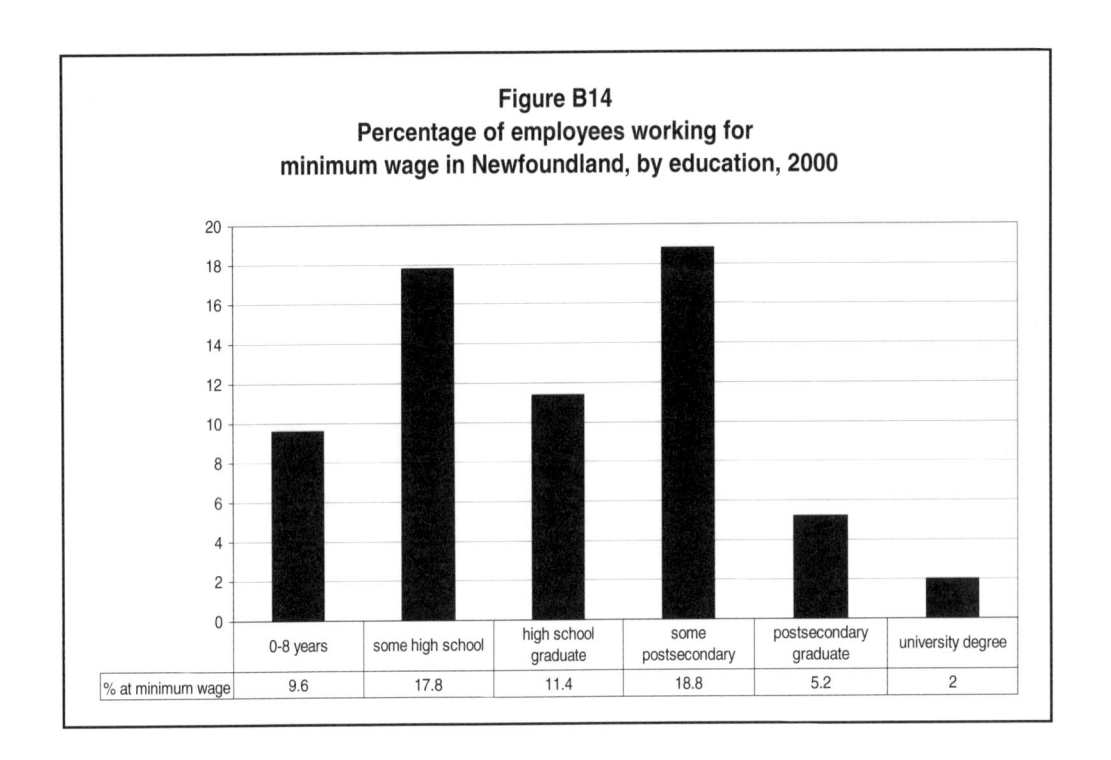

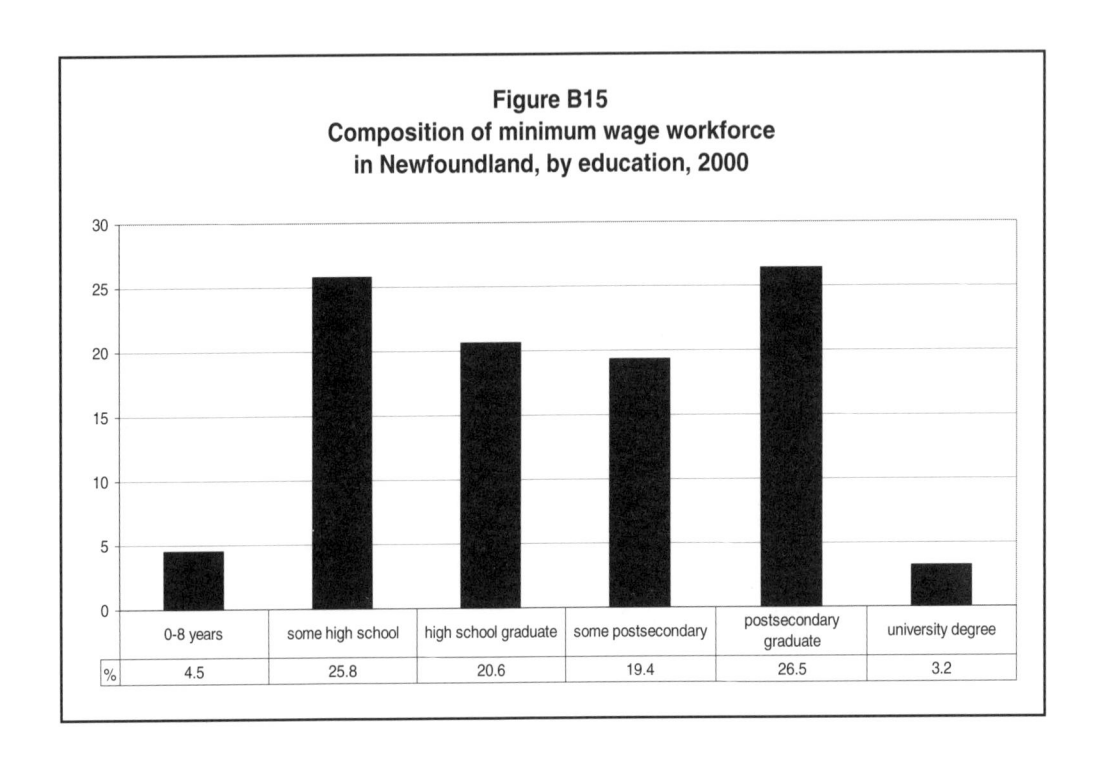

Figure B14
Percentage of employees working for minimum wage in Newfoundland, by education, 2000

	0-8 years	some high school	high school graduate	some postsecondary	postsecondary graduate	university degree
% at minimum wage	9.6	17.8	11.4	18.8	5.2	2

Figure B15
Composition of minimum wage workforce in Newfoundland, by education, 2000

	0-8 years	some high school	high school graduate	some postsecondary	postsecondary graduate	university degree
%	4.5	25.8	20.6	19.4	26.5	3.2

postsecondary) pursuing their education. A sizeable group of minimum wage workers (49.1 percent or close to half) have some form of postsecondary education.

Full-time and part-time work (Figures B16 and B17)

The fact that young people are more likely to work part time helps explain why workers still pursuing their education tend to face a higher risk of minimum wage work than those who have completed their schooling and are working full time. Figure B16 indicates that 24.5 percent of part-time workers are at the minimum wage compared to only 5.9 percent of those employed full time. Nevertheless, the majority of minimum wage workers in Newfoundland (58.1 percent) work full time, while 41.9 percent are employed part time, as illustrated in Figure B17.

Gender alters the relationship between full-time and part-time work and the minimum wage. Women who work part time in Newfoundland run a lesser risk of being at the bottom of the wage ladder than do men who work part time (23.8 and 28.2 percent, respectively). However, women employed full time are more likely than men to work for the minimum wage (9.0 and 3.5 percent, respectively).

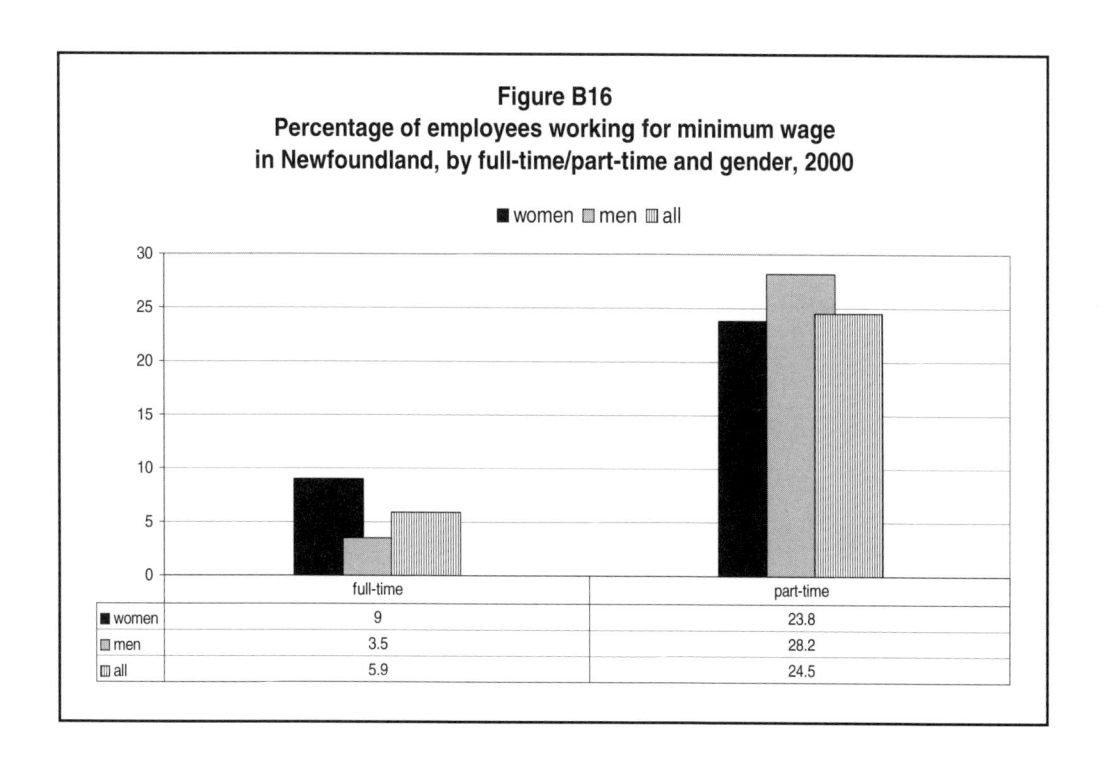

Figure B16
Percentage of employees working for minimum wage in Newfoundland, by full-time/part-time and gender, 2000

	full-time	part-time
women	9	23.8
men	3.5	28.2
all	5.9	24.5

Women make up the majority of minimum wage employees in the province working both full time (67.8 percent are women) and part time (70.8 percent are women). Among all employees, though, women constitute a minority of full-time workers (44.8 percent) but the bulk of part-time workers (72.8 percent).

Family status (Figure B18)

We noted above that six in ten of Newfoundland's minimum wage workers are under 25 years of age. Light on this fundamental fact of the minimum wage workforce is shed by information on family status, depicted in Figure B18, which shows that the largest group of minimum wage workers – 8,100 or 52.3 percent of the total 15,500 – are older children living with their parents (or relatives with relatives, as in the case of a niece or nephew living with an aunt and uncle, or grandchildren with grandparents). Of this category, 4,100 or 50.6 percent are aged 15-19, 3,300 or 40.7 percent are 20-24 and the remaining 700 or 8.7 percent are 25 or older. Just over one-third (2,800 or 34.6 percent) are still in school and working part time or part year (e.g., in summer).

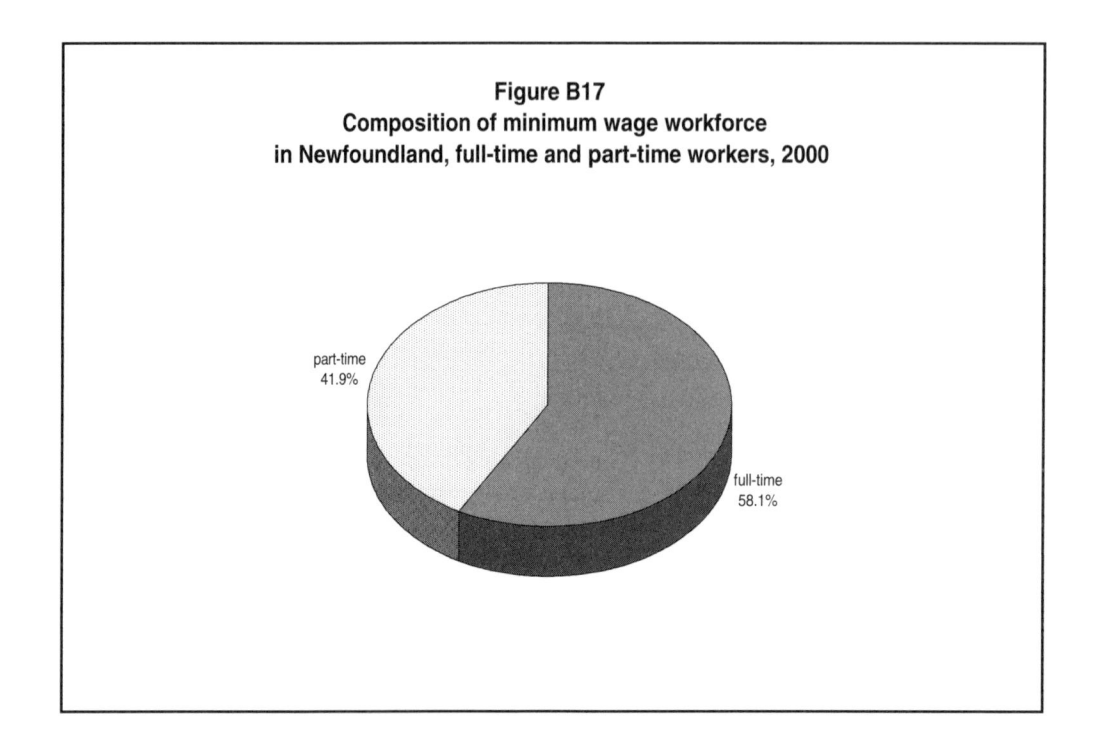

**Figure B17
Composition of minimum wage workforce
in Newfoundland, full-time and part-time workers, 2000**

part-time 41.9%

full-time 58.1%

The next largest group of minimum wage workers in Newfoundland – 5,600 or 36.1 percent of the total – are members of couples (married or living together). In most cases (3,600 or 64.3 percent of the category total of 5,600), the minimum wage worker's spouse is employed, typically earning more than the minimum wage. A typical example in this category would be mothers combining (unpaid) childrearing work with part-time minimum wage work. Another 2,000 minimum wage workers living in couples have a spouse who is not employed (most of the latter are not in the labour force).

An estimated 1,400 or 9.0 percent of minimum wage workers are unattached individuals. More than half of this category (800 or 57.1 percent) live alone; of this group, 400 are 15-24, 200 are aged 25-54 and 200 are 55 or older. An estimated 500 of the province's unattached minimum wage workers are young people aged 15-24 living with friends or roommates.

Finally, an estimated 400 workers or just 2.6 percent of the minimum wage workforce are heads of families with no spouse present. Half of these people are single parents with children under 18.

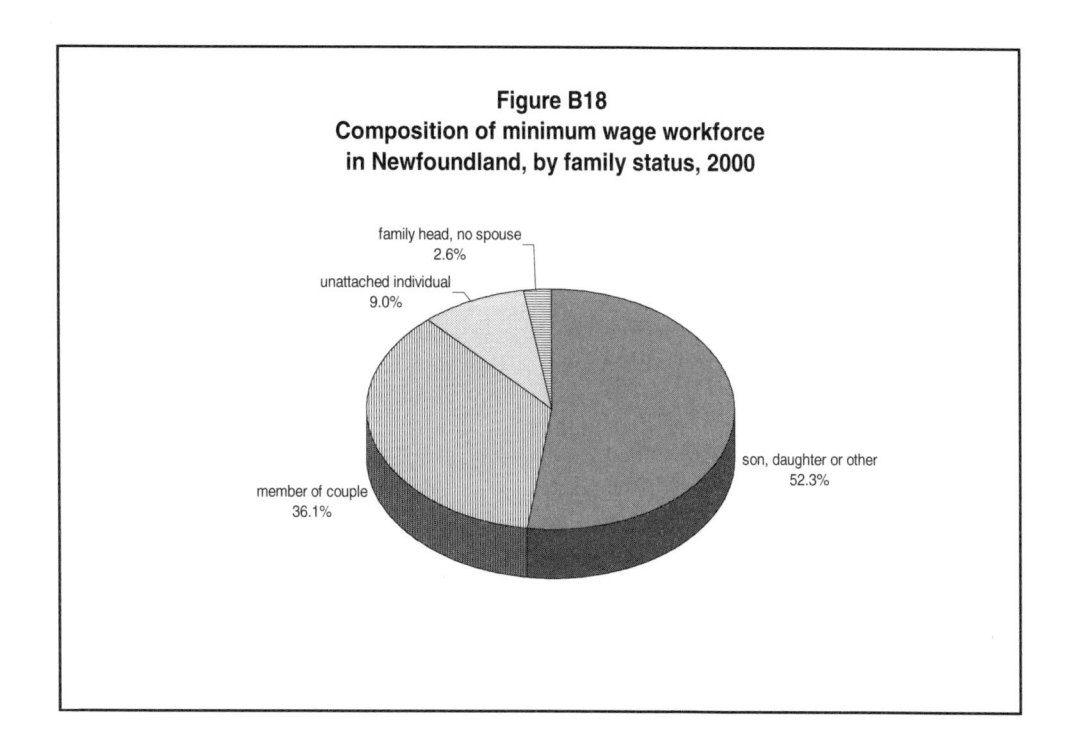

Figure B18
Composition of minimum wage workforce in Newfoundland, by family status, 2000

- family head, no spouse 2.6%
- unattached individual 9.0%
- member of couple 36.1%
- son, daughter or other 52.3%

Industry

National data show that the incidence and distribution of minimum wage workers varies significantly according to industries. The same applies to Newfoundland, though sample size constraints permit estimates for only six of 16 industrial categories. Among the industrial categories for which estimates are available, accommodation and food services tops the list (33.0 percent of employees work for minimum wage), followed by other services (19.2 percent), trade (18.4 percent), management, administrative and other support (14.3), information, culture and recreation (12.7 percent) and health care and social assistance jobs (4.0 percent).

Estimates are available for the industrial composition of the whole employed workforce in Newfoundland. Trade tops the list, at an estimated 32,100 or 18.0 percent of all employees. Next comes health care and social assistance, at 27,600 or 15.5 percent of all employees, followed by public administration (16,100 or 9.0 percent), educational services (15,800 or 8.9 percent), manufacturing (15,400 or 8.6 percent), accommodation and food services (10,900 or 6.1 percent), transportation and warehousing (10,000 or 5.6 percent), construction (9,100 or 5.1 percent), forestry, fishing, mining, oil and gas (8,600 or 4.8 percent), other services (7,800 or 4.4 percent), finance, insurance, real estate and leasing (6,400 or 3.6 percent), information, culture and recreation (6,300 or 3.5 percent), professional, scientific and technical services (5,300 or 3.0 percent), management, administrative and other support (4,200 or 2.4 percent), utilities (1,800 or 1.0 percent) and agriculture (900 or 0.5 percent).

PRINCE EDWARD ISLAND

a. Minimum Wages in Prince Edward Island

Interprovincial rank: dollar value of minimum wages (Figure C1)

Prince Edward Island's minimum wage rose from $5.60 to $6.00 an hour on January 1, 2002.[16] Prince Edward Island ranked fifth-lowest among Canada's ten provinces and three territories in 2002, ahead of New Brunswick ($5.94), Alberta ($5.90), Nova Scotia ($5.85) and Newfoundland (which averaged $5.71 an hour). Prince Edward Island's $6.00 minimum wage was $2.00 an hour below highest-ranked British Columbia's $8.00 rate in 2002.

Trend in dollar value of minimum wage (Figure C2)

Minimum wages are not indexed, so their value changes over time. Figure C2 shows the trend in Prince Edward Island's minimum wage from 1965 to 2002; each year's average minimum wage has been converted to inflation-adjusted (i.e., constant) 2002 dollars to show the real trend, after taking into account the impact of inflation on the dollar.

Figure C1
Prince Edward Island minimum wage compared to other provinces and territories, 2002

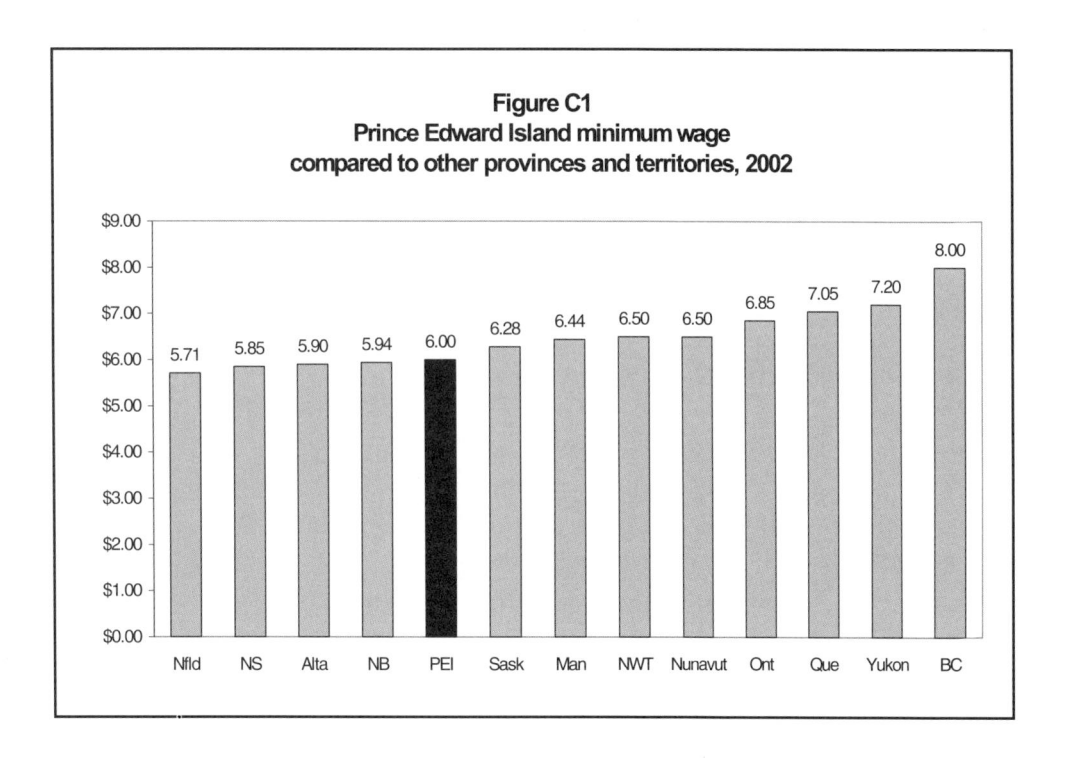

Province/Territory	Minimum Wage
Nfld	5.71
NS	5.85
Alta	5.90
NB	5.94
PEI	6.00
Sask	6.28
Man	6.44
NWT	6.50
Nunavut	6.50
Ont	6.85
Que	7.05
Yukon	7.20
BC	8.00

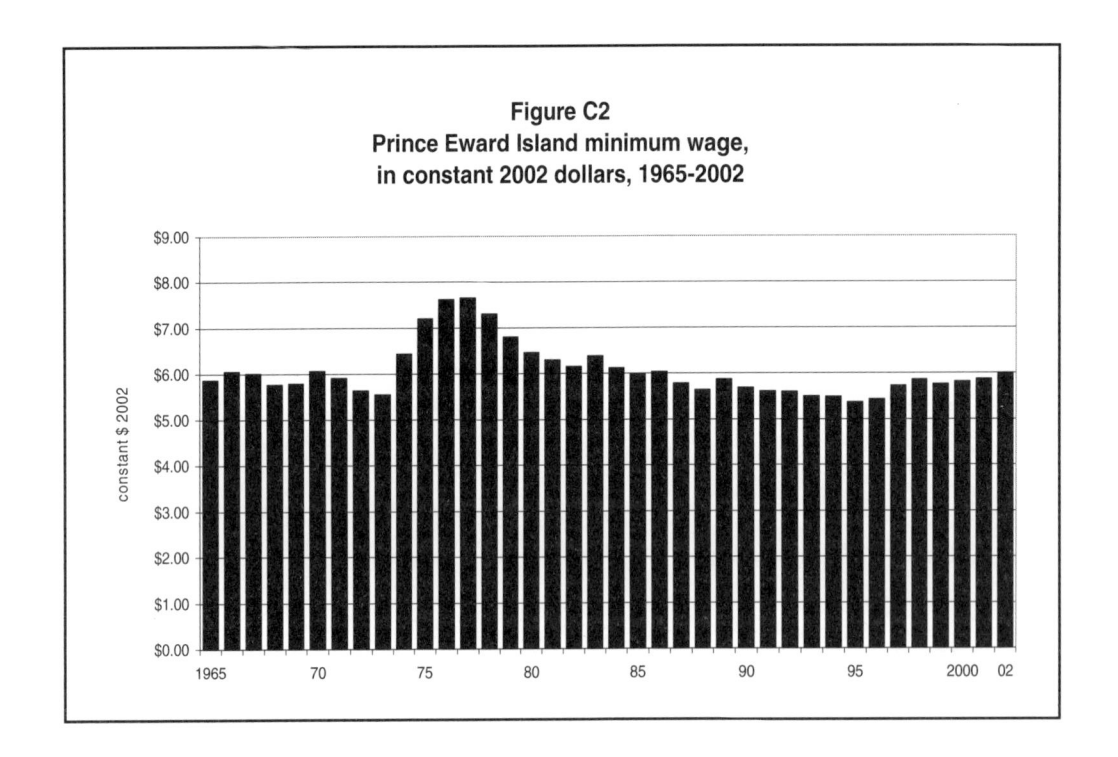

**Figure C2
Prince Eward Island minimum wage,
in constant 2002 dollars, 1965-2002**

Prince Edward Island's minimum wage was $5.87 in 1965 and remained more or less flat until 1970 (in the $5.80-$6.00 range), fell to $6.44 in 1974, rose to a peak of $7.66 in 1977, declined gradually to $5.37 in 1995 and recovered somewhat to $6.00 in 2002. Over the long term, with the exception of the sharp increase between 1974 and 1976, Prince Edward Island's minimum wage has remained more or less the same. Its 2002 rate, $6.00, was not far above the 1965 rate of $5.87. However, its 2002 level was $1.66 an hour or 21.7 percent below its $7.66 peak in 1977.

Interprovincial rank: minimum wages as percentage of average earnings (Figure C3)

While Prince Edward Island ranks fifth-lowest among the 13 jurisdictions according to its dollar value, a strikingly different ranking results when we compare the province's minimum wage to its average wage. At last count (2001 for earnings data), Prince Edward Island's minimum wage ($5.80 that year) amounted to 44.4 percent of the $13.05 hourly average earnings, placing the province third-highest among all jurisdictions, behind only Quebec (44.8 percent) and British Columbia (46.2 percent).

Figure C3
Prince Edward Island minimum wage as % of average earnings, compared to other provinces and territories, 2001

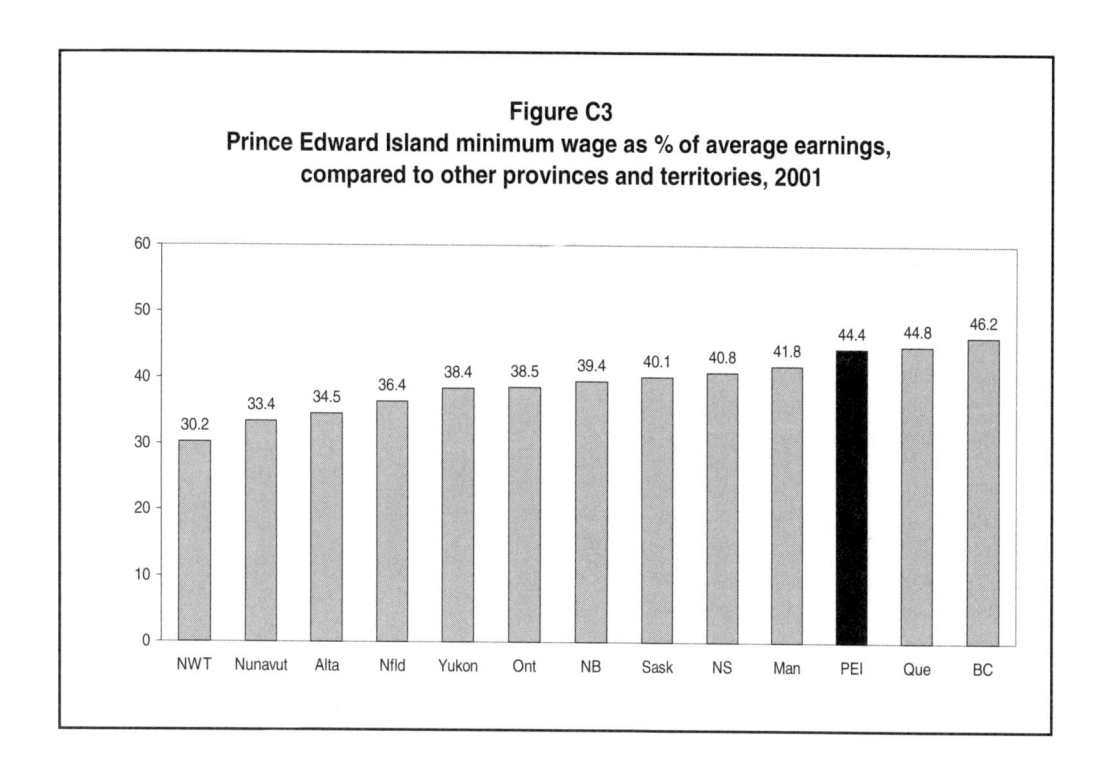

NWT	Nunavut	Alta	Nfld	Yukon	Ont	NB	Sask	NS	Man	PEI	Que	BC
30.2	33.4	34.5	36.4	38.4	38.5	39.4	40.1	40.8	41.8	44.4	44.8	46.2

Trends in minimum wage and average earnings (Figure C4)

The black line in Figure C4 shows the trend in the minimum wage, the gray line the trend in average earnings and the vertical bars the trend in the minimum wage as a percentage of average earnings. Read the left-hand axis for the minimum wage and average earnings and the right-hand axis for the minimum wage as a percentage of earnings.

Over time, Prince Edward Island's minimum wage has fallen as a percentage of average earnings, from a peak of 57.3 percent in 1966 to a low of 37.9 percent in 1996. It since has recovered some of the lost ground, reaching 44.4 percent in 2001.

Average earnings (in constant 2001 dollars) increased from $21,684 in 1965 to $32,692 in 1977 and declined to the $28,000-$30,000 range for most of the 1980s and 1990s; they have fallen steadily since 1996 to reach $27,141 by 2001. On an annual (full-time, all-year) basis, the minimum wage went from $12,055 in 1965 to $15,726 in 1977, slid to $11,027 in 1995 and stood at $12,064 in 2001.

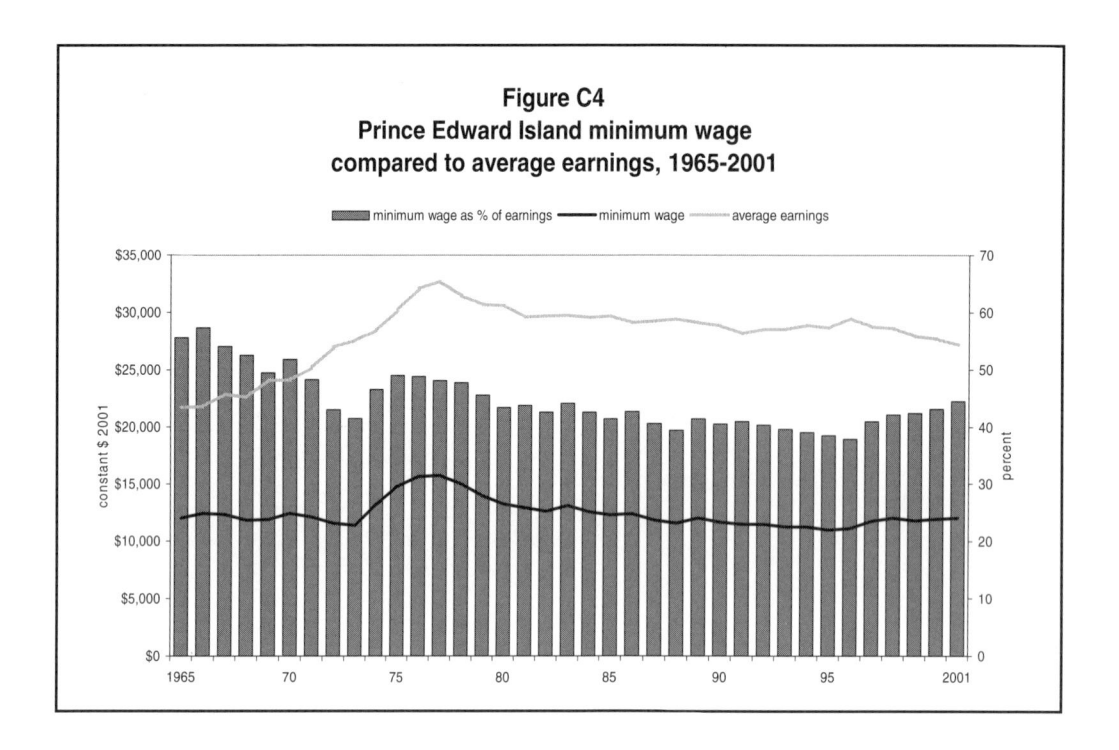

**Figure C4
Prince Edward Island minimum wage
compared to average earnings, 1965-2001**

Minimum wage compared to before-tax poverty lines (Figure C5)

Statistics Canada publishes two sets of low income cut-offs. The before-tax low income cut-offs are based on gross, pre-tax income (i.e., income from employment, investments, private pensions and other private sources plus income from government programs such as public pensions, Employment Insurance, child benefits and welfare). The after-tax low income cut-offs use the same definition of income but also factor into the picture the federal and provincial income taxes that Canadians pay. We first compare the minimum wage to the before-tax poverty lines.

Because the poverty line is lower for smaller communities, the minimum wage represents a larger proportion of the poverty line in smaller communities. In 2002, Prince Edward Island's minimum wage ranged from 77.1 percent of the before-tax low income cut-off for one person in Charlottetown (which is in the 30,000-99,999 size category) to 82.9 percent for communities under 30,000 and 95.1 percent for rural areas.

In dollar terms, PEI's minimum wage in 2002 was $3,702 below the before-tax poverty line for one person in Charlottetown, $2,577 below for towns under 30,000 and $649 below the poverty line for rural residents. Figure C5 shows the dollar gap between the minimum wage and the before-tax poverty line for one person in different size communities throughout the province.

Figure C5
Dollars below before-tax poverty line for different size communities, Prince Edward Island minimum wage, 2002

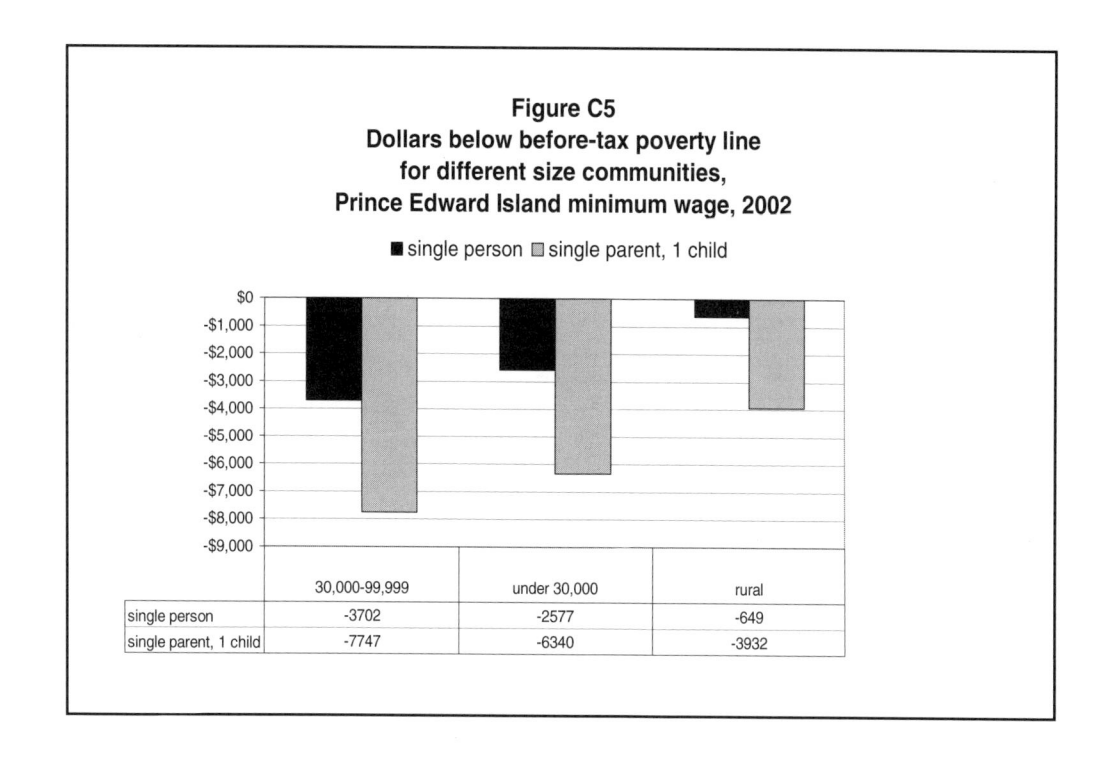

	30,000-99,999	under 30,000	rural
single person	-3702	-2577	-649
single parent, 1 child	-7747	-6340	-3932

Because the poverty line varies by family size, minimum wages (which do not vary by family size) are deeper below the poverty line for families than for single workers. We also look at the poverty gap for a single parent with one child, which is in the two-person family size category. In 2002, the minimum wage in Prince Edward Island varied from 61.7 percent of the before-tax low income line for a family of two in Charlottetown (in the 30,000-99,999 group) to 66.3 percent for towns under 30,000 and 76.0 percent for rural areas. The minimum wage fell $7,747 under the before-tax poverty line for a two-person family in Charlottetown, $6,340 below for communities under 30,000 and $3,932 under for rural residents.

Trend in minimum wage as percentage of before-tax poverty lines (Figure C6)

The long-term trend when we compare the minimum wage to Statistics Canada's low income cut-offs mirrors the trend in its dollar value. In 2002, the estimated before-tax low income line for the largest centre in the province (Charlottetown, which falls in the 30,000-99,999 category) was $16,182 for one person and $20,227 for a family of two.

Prince Edward Island's minimum wage rose from 75.5 percent of the before-tax poverty line for one person in Charlottetown in 1965 to 98.4 percent in 1977, falling to a low of 69.0 percent in 1995. However, the trend improved somewhat in the latter half of the 1990s, rising to 77.1 percent of the poverty

**Figure C6
Prince Edward Island minimum wage as % of
before-tax poverty line for largest city, 1965-2002**

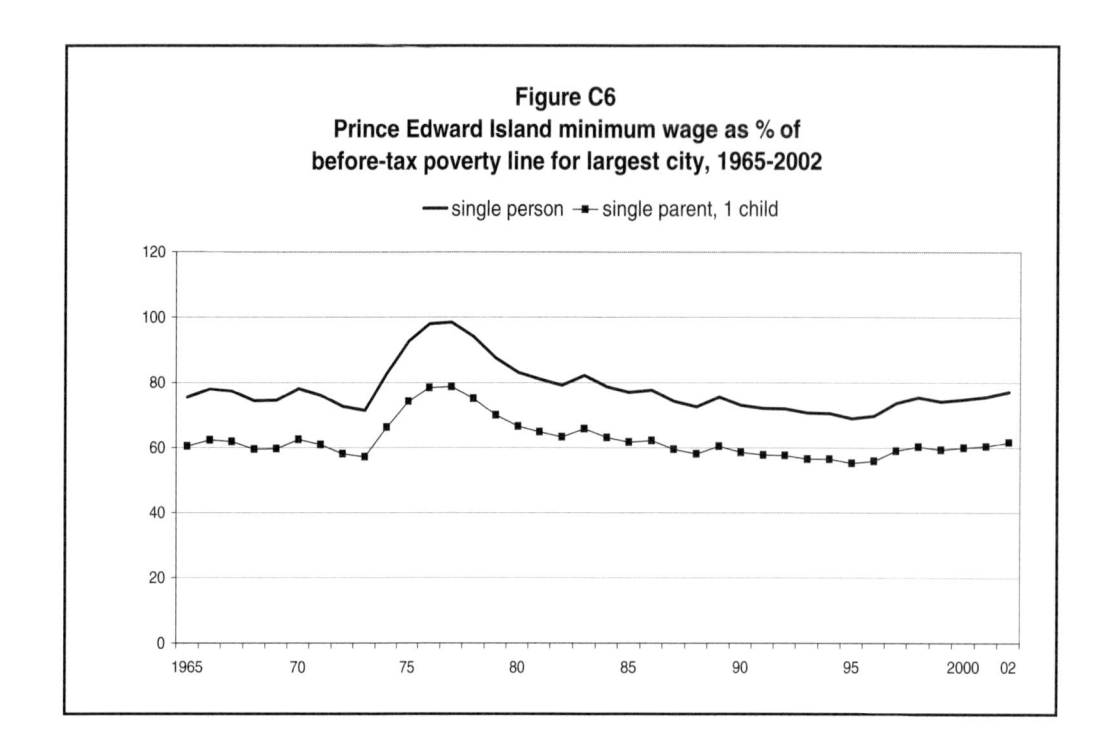

line in 2002. For a two-person family (e.g., a single parent with one child), the minimum wage went from 60.4 percent of the before-tax low income cut-off in 1965 to a peak of 78.8 percent in 1977, declining to a low of 55.2 percent in 1995 but recovering to 61.7 percent of the low income cut-off in 2002. Figure C6 shows the trends.

Minimum wage compared to after-tax poverty lines (Figure C7)

Statistics Canada publishes after-tax low income cut-offs as well as before-tax low income cut-offs. We focus here on how after-tax minimum wage incomes in Prince Edward Island for five types of household – single persons, single parents with one child, one-earner couples with two children, two-earner couples supporting two children on one-and-a-half minimum wages, and two-earner couples with two children and two full minimum wages – compare to the after-tax poverty lines for different size communities. 'After-tax minimum wage incomes' means incomes from the minimum wage and available federal and provincial income programs minus federal and provincial income taxes.

For a single person earning the minimum wage, after-tax income came to $11,592,[17] which is $1,316 below the after-tax poverty line for Charlottetown (in the 30,000-99,999 category), $203 below for towns under 30,000 but $1,388 above the poverty line for rural residents. A single parent with one child received $15,030[18] in after-tax income from minimum wage earnings and federal and provincial child

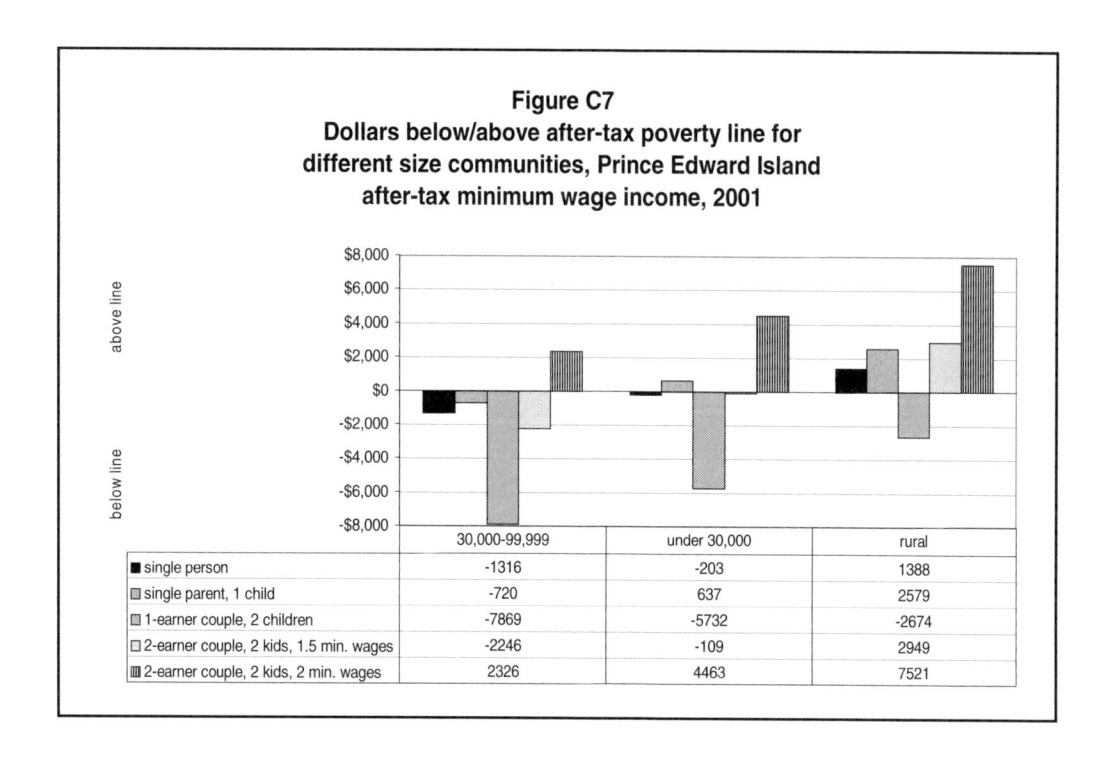

Figure C7
Dollars below/above after-tax poverty line for different size communities, Prince Edward Island after-tax minimum wage income, 2001

	30,000-99,999	under 30,000	rural
single person	-1316	-203	1388
single parent, 1 child	-720	637	2579
1-earner couple, 2 children	-7869	-5732	-2674
2-earner couple, 2 kids, 1.5 min. wages	-2246	-109	2949
2-earner couple, 2 kids, 2 min. wages	2326	4463	7521

benefits and tax credits, which came to $720 below the after-tax poverty line for Charlottetown but $637 above the line for towns under 30,000 and $2,579 above the poverty line for rural residents.

For a one-earner couple with two children, after-tax minimum wage income amounted to $16,941[19] – $7,869 below the after-tax poverty line for Charlottetown, $5,732 under for towns smaller than 30,000 and $2,674 beneath the line for rural residents. In the case of a two-earner couple earning 1.5 times the minimum wage and supporting two children, after-tax minimum wage income amounted to $22,564[20] – $2,246 below the after-tax poverty line for Charlottetown, $109 under for towns under 30,000 but $2,949 above the after-tax poverty line for rural residents. For a two-earner couple in which both parents worked full time, year round for the minimum wage and supported two children, after-tax minimum wage income was $27,136[21] – $2,326 above the after-tax poverty line for Charlottetown, $4,463 over for towns under 30,000 and $7,521 above the after-tax poverty line for rural residents.

Contribution of child benefits

Child benefits supplement the incomes of the large majority of Canadian families and are particularly important to low- and modest-income families. Improvements to the federal Canada Child Tax Benefit are benefiting minimum wage and other working poor families. However, Prince Edward Island is alone in Canada in not providing a provincial child benefit.

Minimum Wages in Canada: A Statistical Portrait With Policy Implications

A single parent supporting one child on minimum wage earnings got $2,447 from the Canada Child Tax Benefit, which amounted to 17.0 percent of disposable income. A one-earner couple with two children received $4,250 from the Canada Child Tax Benefit, which contributed 26.1 percent of disposable income.

A two-earner family in which one parent works full time, all year at the minimum wage and the other parent half that time got child benefits worth a total of $4,250 from the Canada Child Tax Benefit or 19.6 percent of disposable income. A two-earner family in which both parents work full time, all year at the minimum wage received $3,692 from the Canada Child Tax Benefit, which comes to 14.3 percent of disposable income.

Minimum wage versus welfare (Figure C8)

For a single person earning the minimum wage in Prince Edward Island, disposable income – i.e., minimum wage earnings plus the refundable GST credit minus income and payroll taxes – amounted to $10,953 in 2001, which is a sizeable $5,107 more than the $5,846 payable from welfare. Figure C8 pictures the results.

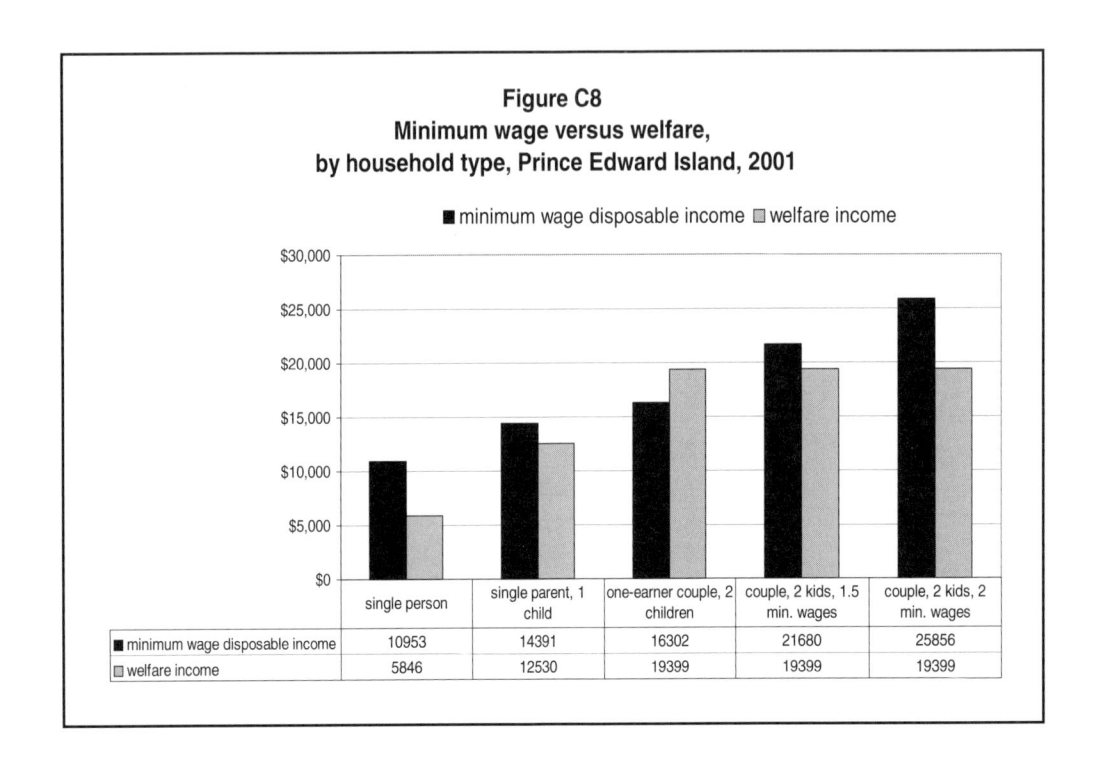

Figure C8
Minimum wage versus welfare, by household type, Prince Edward Island, 2001

	single person	single parent, 1 child	one-earner couple, 2 children	couple, 2 kids, 1.5 min. wages	couple, 2 kids, 2 min. wages
minimum wage disposable income	10953	14391	16302	21680	25856
welfare income	5846	12530	19399	19399	19399

74   Caledon Institute of Social Policy

Minimum wages also pay better than welfare for a single parent with one child age 2, though the advantage over welfare is smaller than for single people. Disposable income from after-tax minimum wage earnings, child benefits and the refundable GST credit amounted to $14,391 in 2001, or $1,861 more than the $12,530 from welfare, child benefits and the refundable GST credit.

However, a one-earner couple earning the minimum wage and supporting two children aged 10 and 15 fared better on welfare than minimum wage. Total income from welfare, child benefits and the GST credit amounted to $19,399 – a substantial $3,097 more than the $16,302 disposable income from minimum wages, child benefits and the GST credit.

For two-parent families to earn more than welfare, both parents must work. We look at two examples.

In the first case, one parent works full time, year round at the minimum wage while the other earns half this amount (i.e., works part time and/or part year); as above, there are two children aged 10 and 15. The family's disposable income from one-and-a-half minimum wages came to $21,680 in 2001 or $2,281 more than the $19,399 from welfare, child benefits and the refundable GST credit.

The other two-earner family earns double the minimum wage since we assume that both parents work full time, year round at the minimum wage. Total disposable income was $25,856 or $6,457 more than the $19,399 from welfare and other government income benefits.

b. Minimum Wage Workers in Prince Edward Island

The following text with illustrative graphs analyzes key characteristics of minimum wage workers in Prince Edward Island. Appendix 2 provides detailed statistics in tabular form (pages 285-287).

Interprovincial rank: incidence of minimum wage workers (Figure C9)

In 2000, an estimated 1,900 Prince Edward Islanders – 3.6 percent of the province's total 53,100 employees – worked for the minimum wage. PEI's 3.6 percent figure ranks it second-lowest in Canada, the lowest being Alberta with only 2.0 percent of its workforce at the minimum wage. Figure C9 shows the results. The national minimum wage incidence was 4.6 percent.

Minimum wage workers are underrepresented in Prince Edward Island: The province accounts for 0.3 percent of Canada's minimum wage workers but 0.4 percent of all employees, producing an index of .77 (the lower the result below 1.0, the more underrepresented are minimum wage workers).

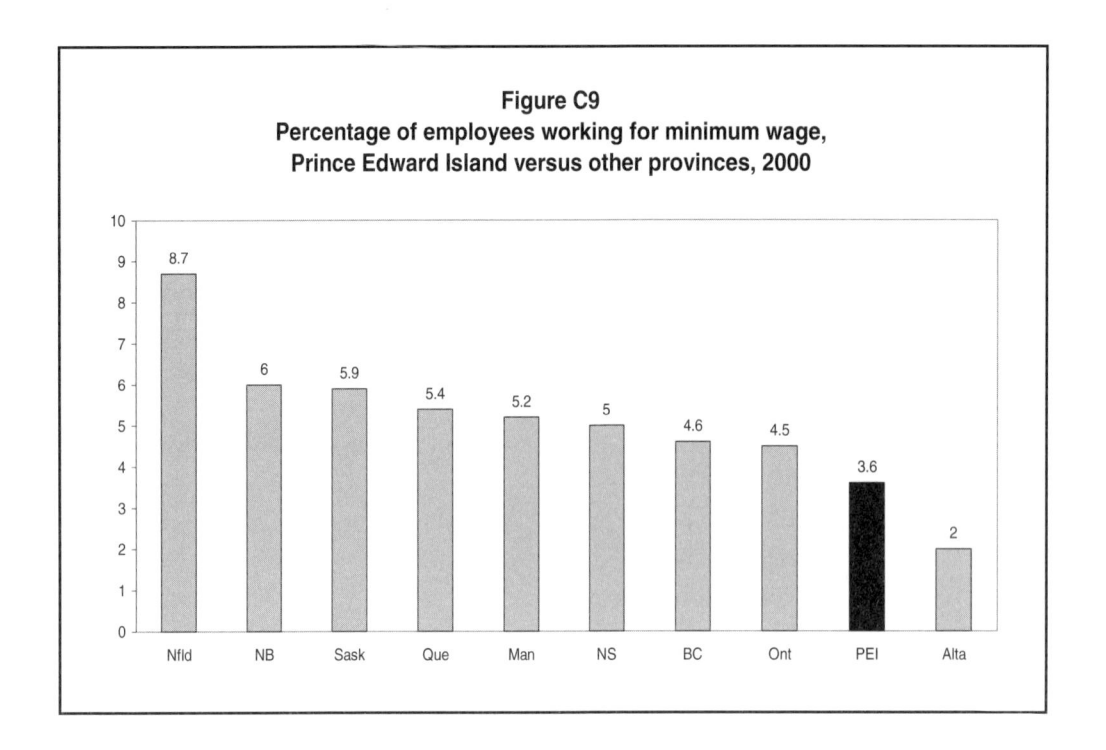

Figure C9
Percentage of employees working for minimum wage, Prince Edward Island versus other provinces, 2000

Province	Percentage
Nfld	8.7
NB	6
Sask	5.9
Que	5.4
Man	5.2
NS	5
BC	4.6
Ont	4.5
PEI	3.6
Alta	2

Gender and age (Figures C10-C12)

Throughout Canada, women run a higher risk of working for minimum wage than men, and women make up the majority of the minimum wage workforce. Prince Edward Island is unusual because the differences between the sexes are much smaller than in other provinces.

In 2000, 3.6 percent of female employees worked for the PEI minimum wage, which is just a tad more than the 3.5 percent of male workers. Of the total 1,900 minimum wage workers, an estimated 1,000 – 52.6 percent – were women while 900 – 47.4 percent – were men, as depicted in Figure C10.

Unlike other provinces, women and men share similar proportions of the minimum wage and total workforces. Women are only fractionally overrepresented in PEI's minimum wage workforce, accounting for 52.6 percent of minimum wage workers and 52.2 percent of all the province's employees in 2000. Men are slightly underrepresented, with 47.4 percent of minimum wage workers and 47.8 percent of all employees.

While younger workers of both sexes run a higher risk of working for minimum wage, young men fare worse than women in Prince Edward Island. Figure C11 illustrates the differences. Among female

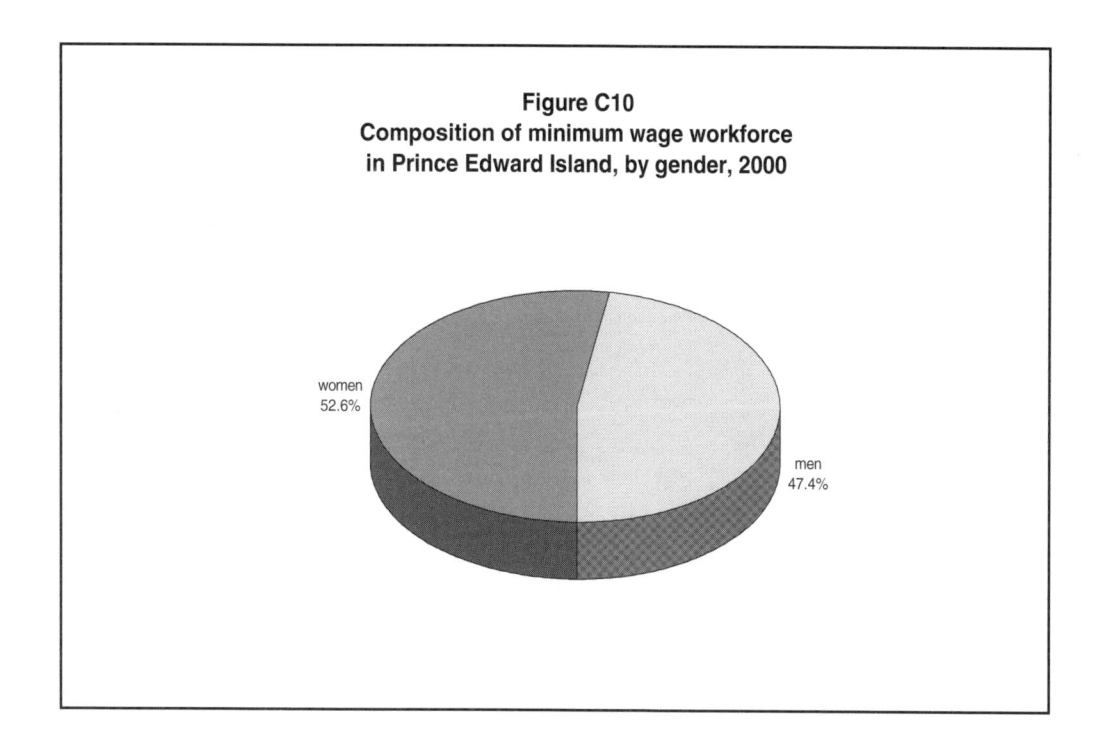

**Figure C10
Composition of minimum wage workforce
in Prince Edward Island, by gender, 2000**

women 52.6%
men 47.4%

workers aged 15 to 19, 21.7 percent worked for the minimum wage in 2000 compared to 29.2 percent of male workers in the same age group. (Sample size limitations preclude estimates for men aged 20-24, so the graph shows 0.0 for men.) Women have a slightly higher incidence of minimum wage work than men among the broader 15-24 age group (14.8 and 14.5 percent, respectively). Among older age groups, women run a higher risk of working for minimum wage than men. Among workers 25-44, 1.4 percent of women as opposed to just 0.8 percent of men were at the bottom of the wage ladder. Among employees 45 and older, 1.2 percent of women but no men worked for the minimum wage.

Young people not only are more likely to work for minimum wage than other employees, but the young also make up a large proportion of the minimum wage workforce. Figure C12 compares the age makeup of minimum wage workers and all employees in Prince Edward Island. Six in ten (63.2 percent) of minimum wage workers are in the 15-19 age group, as opposed to just 8.9 percent of all employees. Employees aged 20-24 represent 15.8 percent of minimum wage workers as opposed to 11.9 percent of all workers. All told, eight in ten minimum wage workers (79.0 percent) are under 25 years of age.

The opposite holds for older workers in Prince Edward Island. Only 15.8 percent of minimum wage workers are between 25 and 44, as opposed to 49.5 percent of all employees. Workers aged 45 and older make up just 5.3 percent of minimum wage employees but 29.8 percent of all employees.

Figure C11
Percentage of employees working for minimum wage in Prince Edward Island, by gender and age, 2000

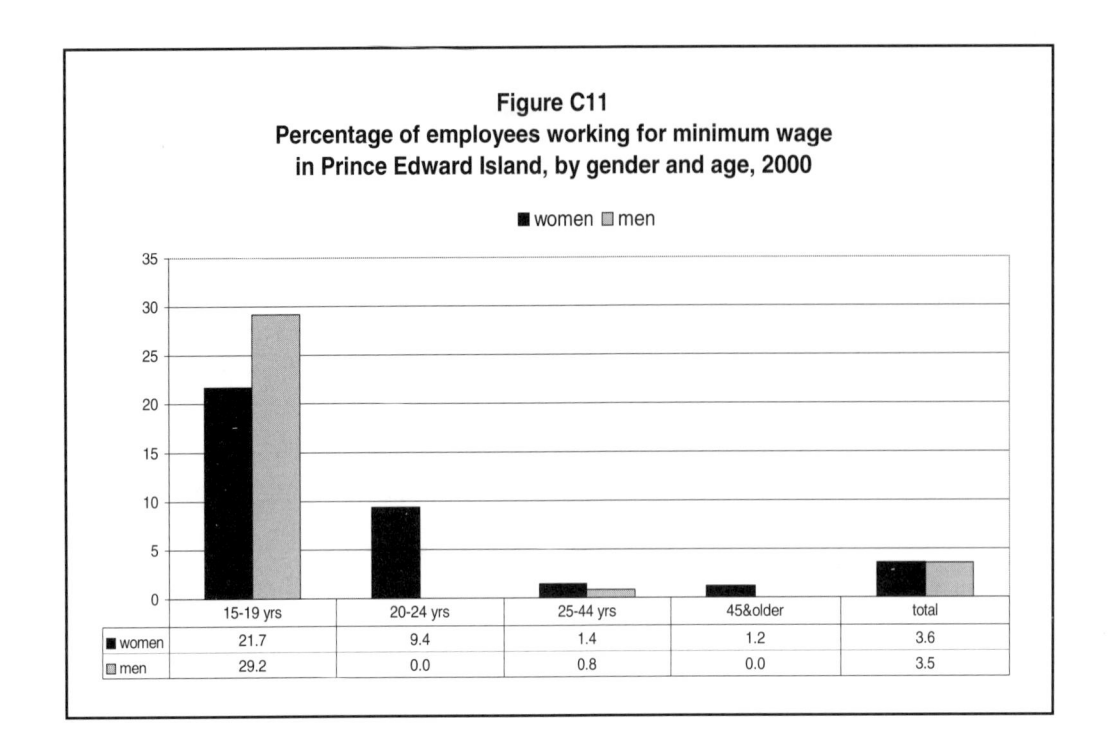

	15-19 yrs	20-24 yrs	25-44 yrs	45&older	total
women	21.7	9.4	1.4	1.2	3.6
men	29.2	0.0	0.8	0.0	3.5

Figure C12
Share of minimum wage workers versus share of all employees in Prince Edward Island, by age group, 2000

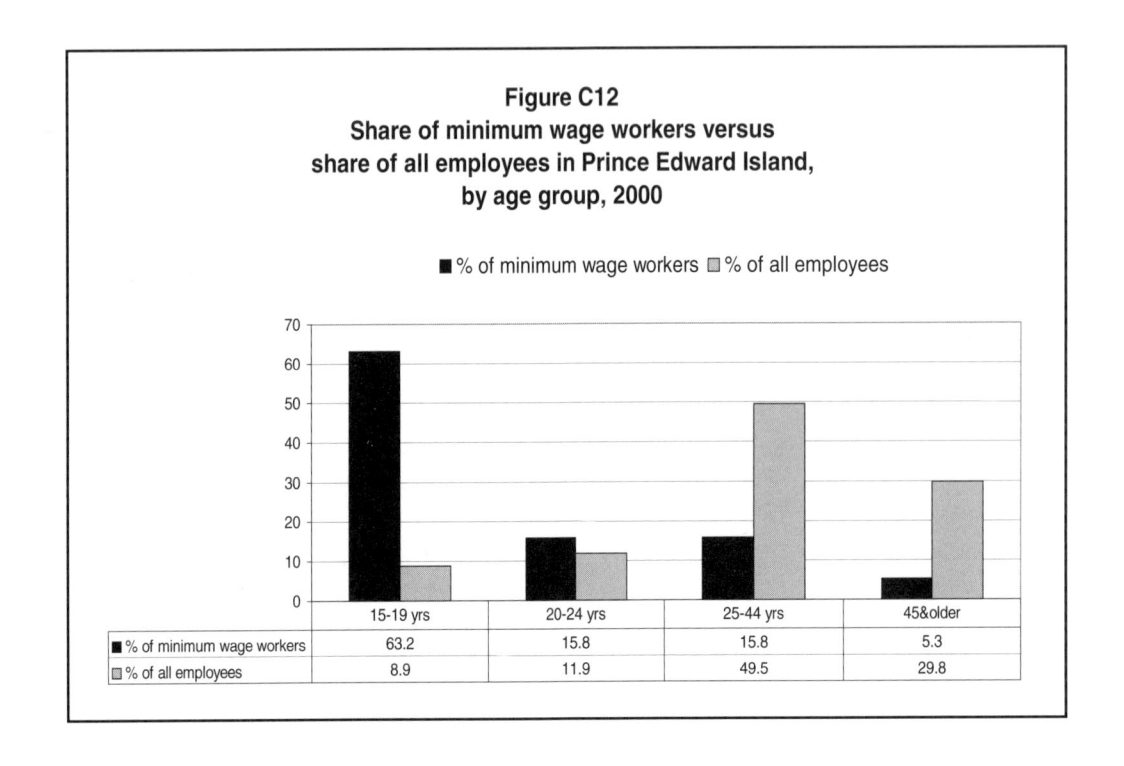

	15-19 yrs	20-24 yrs	25-44 yrs	45&older
% of minimum wage workers	63.2	15.8	15.8	5.3
% of all employees	8.9	11.9	49.5	29.8

Education

We computed the incidence of minimum wage workers in Prince Edward Island according to level of education. Unfortunately, sample size limitations preclude estimates for the elementary and university graduate categories.

At first glance, the relationship between level of education and incidence of minimum wage employment does not seem to correspond to common sense: Workers in the lowest educational group for which estimates can be made (those with some high school) are less likely to work for minimum wage (1.1 percent do) than those who graduated high school (4.0 percent), while those with some postsecondary education run the highest risk of all (6.4 percent). However, those with a postsecondary certificate or diploma run a smaller risk (1.0 percent) than those with just some postsecondary education (6.4 percent), as one would expect.

Incomplete data make conjectures risky. However, a possible partial explanation for the relatively high incidence of minimum wage work among those with some postsecondary education is that young people working at part-time or seasonal (i.e., summer) jobs – typically paying the minimum or a low wage – figure prominently in this educational category.

Full-time and part-time work (Figures C13 and C14)

Part-time workers in PEI run a much greater risk of working for minimum wage than do full-time employees. Figure C13 indicates that 13.3 percent of part-time workers are at the minimum wage compared to only 1.8 percent of those employed full time. The majority of minimum wage workers on the island (60 percent) work part time, while only 40 percent work full time (see Figure C14).

The relationship between full-time and part-time work and the minimum wage is different for women and men. Women who work part time in PEI run half the risk of tooling at the bottom of the wage ladder than do men who work part time (10.0 and 20.0 percent, respectively). However, women employed full time are more likely than men to work for the minimum wage (2.3 and 1.3 percent, respectively).

Women make up the majority (62.5 percent) of minimum wage workers employed on a full-time basis, though women and men each constitute half of minimum wage workers in the province working part time. Among all employees, women constitute 49.4 percent of full-time workers and two-thirds (66.7 percent) of part-time workers.

Figure C13
Percentage of employees working for minimum wage in Prince Edward Island, by full-time/part-time and gender, 2000

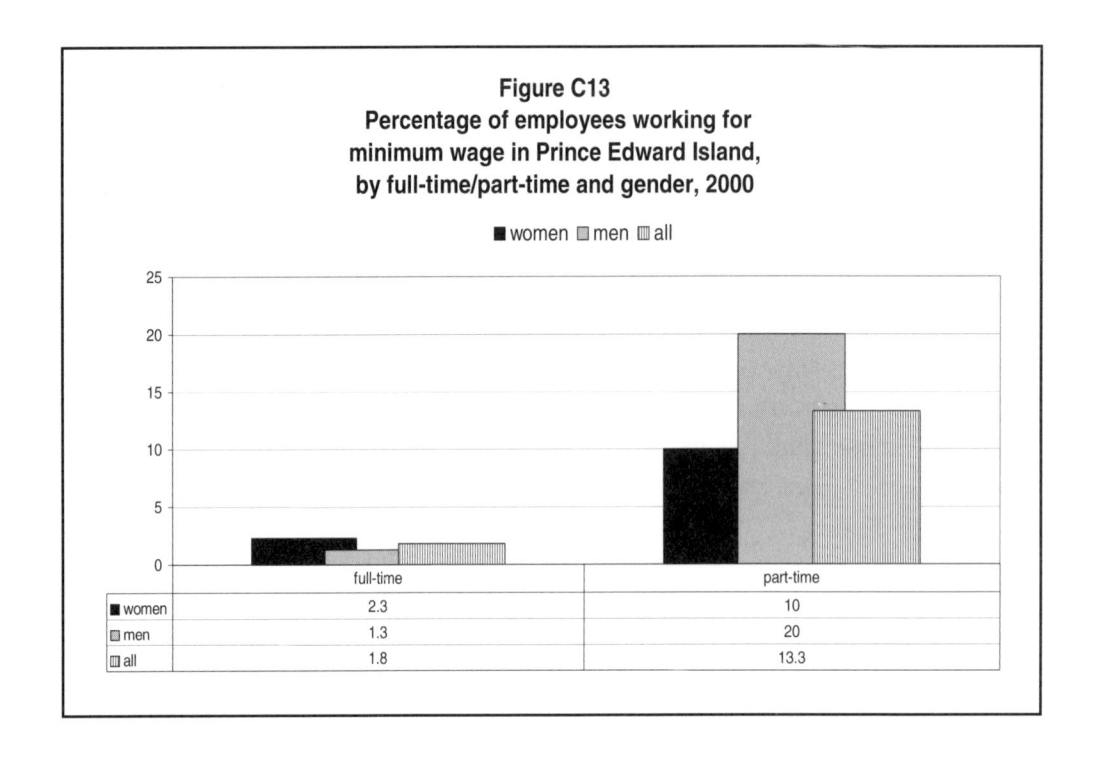

	full-time	part-time
women	2.3	10
men	1.3	20
all	1.8	13.3

Figure C14
Composition of minimum wage workforce in Prince Edward Island, full-time and part-time workers, 2000

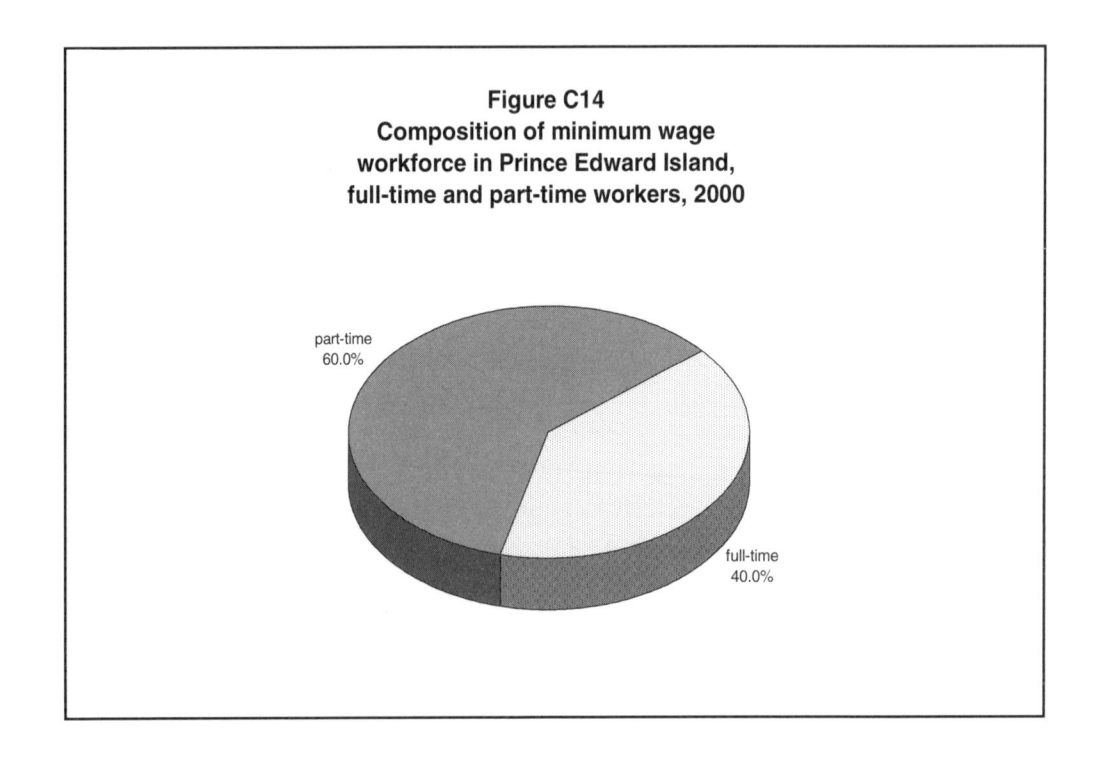

- part-time: 60.0%
- full-time: 40.0%

Family status (Figure C15)

Figure C15 illustrates the family status of minimum wage workers on Prince Edward Island. Sample size limitations preclude estimates for single-parent families.

We noted above that the large majority – 84.2 percent – of PEI's minimum wage workers are under 25 years of age. Information on family status underscores this essential characteristic: The largest group of minimum wage workers – an estimated 1,400 or 73.7 percent of the total 1,900 – are older children living with their parents (or relatives with relatives, as in the case of a niece or nephew living with an aunt and uncle, or grandchildren with grandparents). Of this category, 1,200 or 85.7 percent are aged 15-19 and the remaining 200 or 14.3 percent are 20-24. Over half (800 or 57.1 percent) are still in school and working part time or part year (e.g., in summer).

The next largest group of minimum wage workers in Prince Edward Island – 300 or 15.8 percent of the total – are members of couples (married or living together). In most cases (200 or two-thirds of the category), the minimum wage worker's spouse is employed and earns more than the minimum wage. A typical example in this category would be mothers combining (unpaid) childrearing work with part-time minimum wage work. The other 100 minimum wage workers living in couples have a spouse who is not employed and not in the labour force.

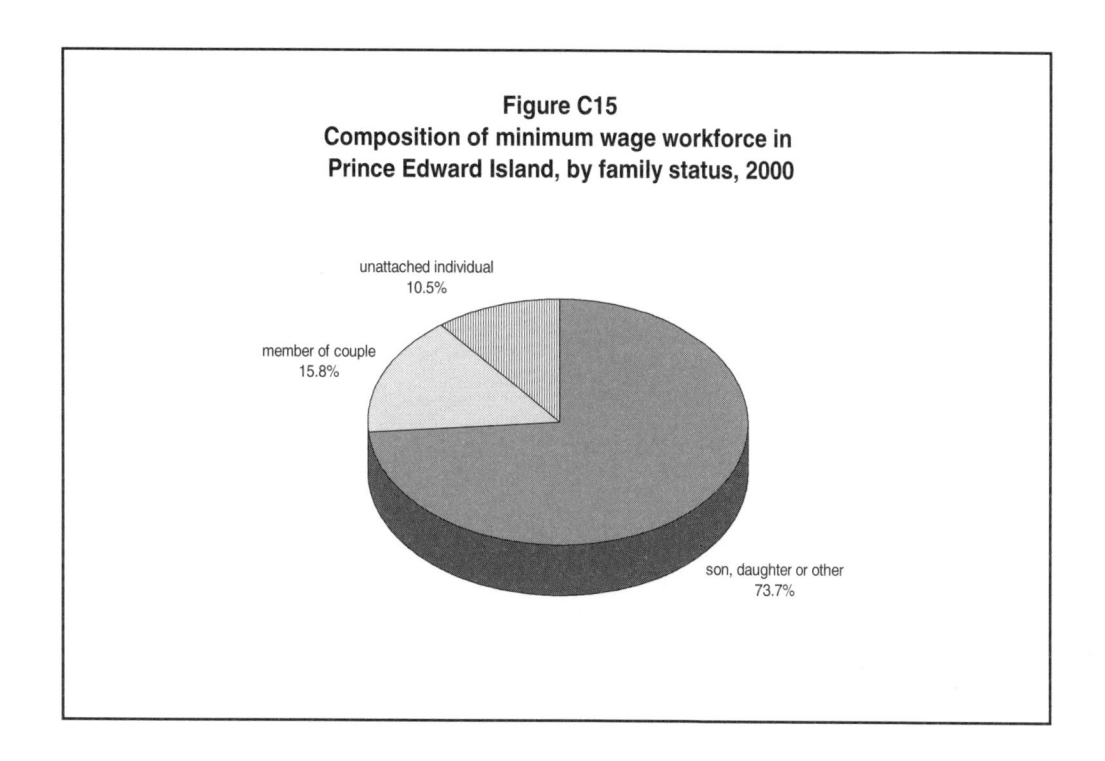

**Figure C15
Composition of minimum wage workforce in
Prince Edward Island, by family status, 2000**

- unattached individual 10.5%
- member of couple 15.8%
- son, daughter or other 73.7%

Another 200 or 10.5 percent of PEI's minimum wage workers are unattached individuals, of whom 100 live alone and 100 with non-relatives (e.g., friends or roommates).

Industry

National data show that the incidence and distribution of minimum wage workers varies significantly according to industries. While doubtless the same applies to Prince Edward Island, sample size constraints permit estimates for only two of 16 industrial categories. Among the estimated 4,500 workers in accommodation and food services, about 300 or 6.7 percent work for minimum wage, as opposed to just 3.6 percent for the entire workforce. Workers in the trade category have the same incidence of minimum wage work: An estimated 600 or 6.7 percent of the total 8,900 trade workers earn minimum wage.

However, estimates are available for the industrial composition of the whole employed workforce in Prince Edward Island (with the exception of utilities). Trade tops the list, at 8,900 or 16.8 percent of all employees. Next comes health care and social assistance, at 6,500 or 12.2 percent of the all employees, followed by manufacturing (6,000 or 11.3 percent), public administration (5,600 or 10.5 percent), accommodation and food services (4,500 or 8.5 percent), educational services (4,100 or 7.7 percent), construction (3,000 or 5.6 percent), agriculture (2,500 or 4.7 percent), information, culture and recreation (2,200 or 4.1 percent), other services (2,100 or 4.0 percent), transportation and warehousing (1,900 or 3.6 percent), finance, insurance, real estate and leasing (1,900 or 3.6 percent), management, administrative and other support (1,600 or 3.0 percent), professional, scientific and technical services (1,500 or 2.8 percent) and forestry, fishing, mining, oil and gas (800 or 1.5 percent).

NOVA SCOTIA

a. Minimum Wages in Nova Scotia

Interprovincial rank: dollar value of minimum wages (Figure D1)

Nova Scotia's minimum wage averaged $5.85 in 2002 (rising from $5.80 to $6.00 on October 1), ranking the province second-lowest among Canada's ten provinces and three territories, after Newfoundland (which averaged $5.71 in 2002, taking into account two within-year increases). British Columbia's $8.00 hourly minimum wage – Canada's highest – is $2.20 above Nova Scotia's.

Trend in dollar value of minimum wage (Figure D2)

Because minimum wages are not indexed, their value changes over time. Figure D2 shows the trend in Nova Scotia's minimum wage from 1965 to 2002; each year's average minimum wage has been converted to inflation-adjusted (i.e., constant) 2002 dollars to show the real trend, after taking into account the impact of inflation on the dollar.

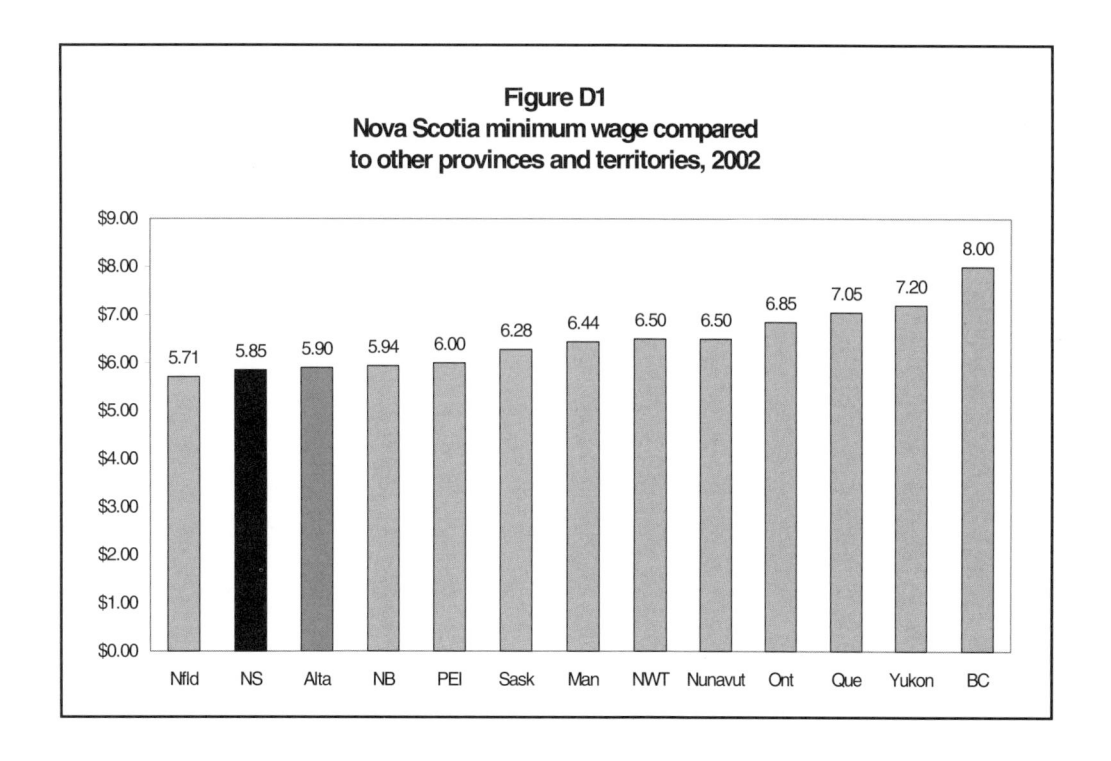

**Figure D1
Nova Scotia minimum wage compared to other provinces and territories, 2002**

Nfld	5.71
NS	5.85
Alta	5.90
NB	5.94
PEI	6.00
Sask	6.28
Man	6.44
NWT	6.50
Nunavut	6.50
Ont	6.85
Que	7.05
Yukon	7.20
BC	8.00

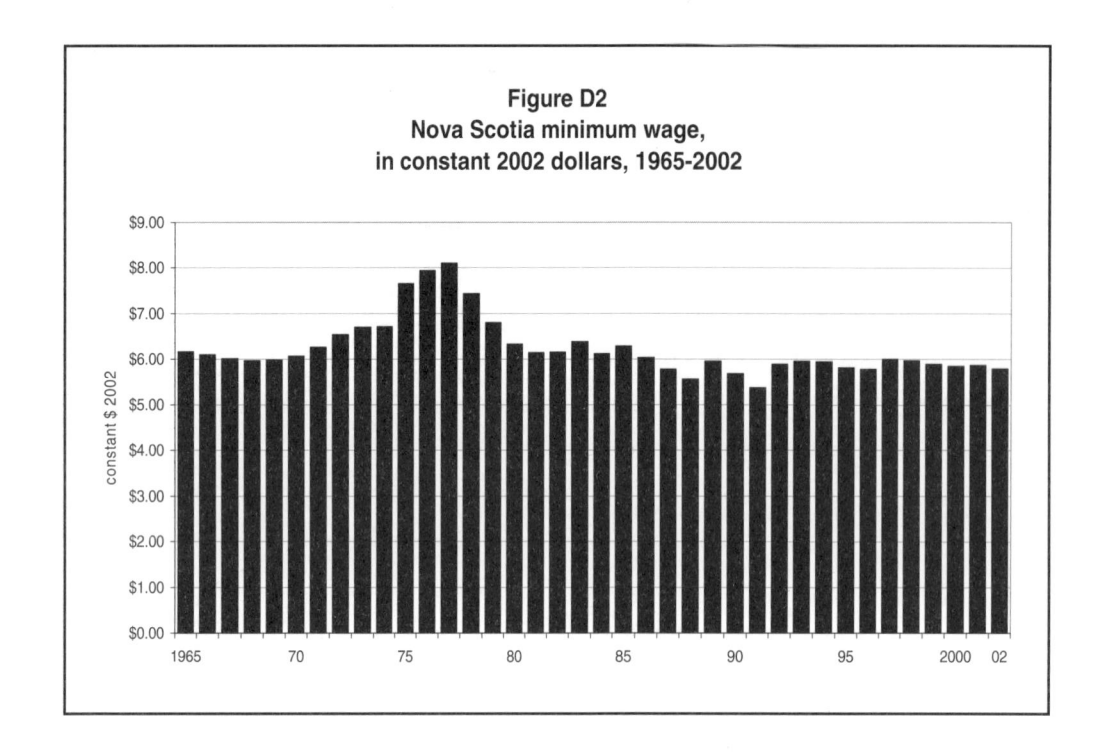

**Figure D2
Nova Scotia minimum wage,
in constant 2002 dollars, 1965-2002**

With the exception of an upward blip in the second half of the 1970s, Nova Scotia's minimum wage has remained relatively constant over the years, for the most part around $6.00. It has slipped somewhat in recent years, from $6.01 in 1997 to $5.85 in 2002. Its $5.85 level in 2002 is $2.25 or 27.8 percent below its 1977 peak of $8.10 an hour, though closer to the $6.16 level of 1965.

Interprovincial rank: minimum wages as percentage of average earnings (Figure D3)

Nova Scotia fares far better when it comes to how its minimum wage compares to its average wage. In 2001 (the most recent year for which data on average earnings are available), Nova Scotia's $5.80 minimum wage represented 40.8 percent of its $14.23 hourly average earnings, ranking the province fifth-highest and ahead of all jurisdictions except Manitoba, Prince Edward Island, Quebec and British Columbia. Figure D3 illustrates the results.

Trends in minimum wage and average earnings (Figure D4)

The black line in Figure D4 shows the trend in the minimum wage, the gray line the trend in average earnings and the vertical bars the trend in the minimum wage as a percentage of average earnings. Read the

**Figure D3
Nova Scotia minimum wage as % of average earnings,
compared to other provinces and territories, 2001**

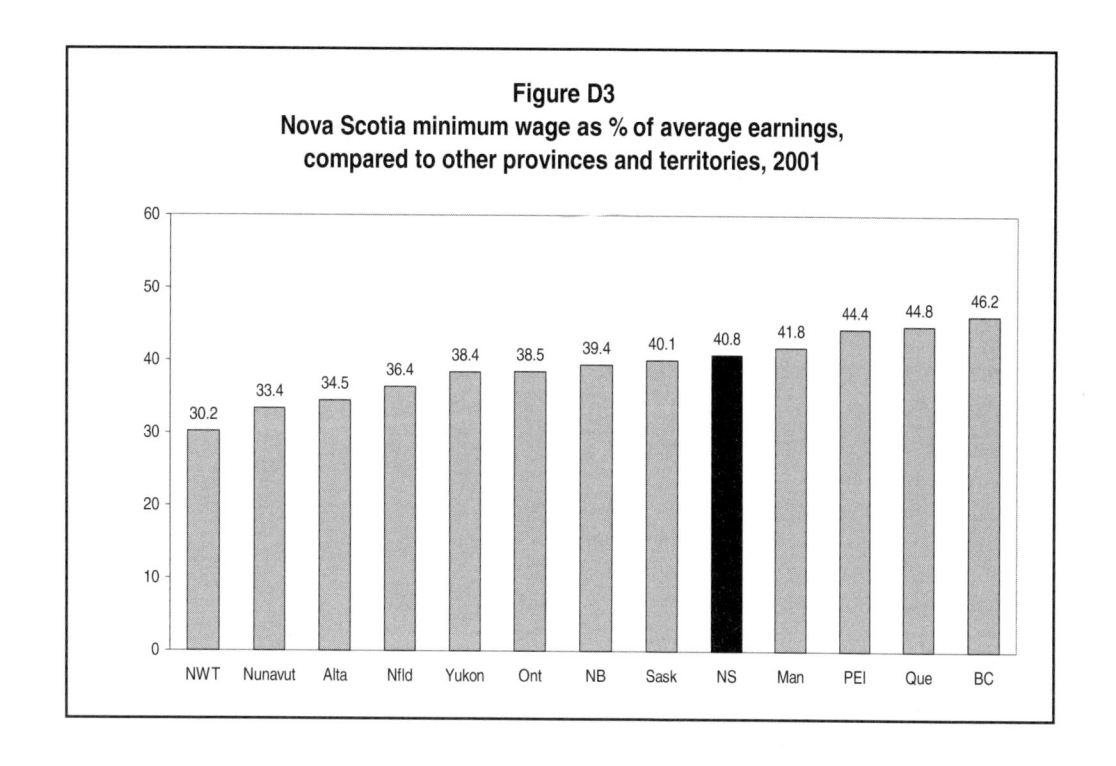

Province/Territory	%
NWT	30.2
Nunavut	33.4
Alta	34.5
Nfld	36.4
Yukon	38.4
Ont	38.5
NB	39.4
Sask	40.1
NS	40.8
Man	41.8
PEI	44.4
Que	44.8
BC	46.2

**Figure D4
Nova Scotia minimum wage
compared to average earnings, 1965-2001**

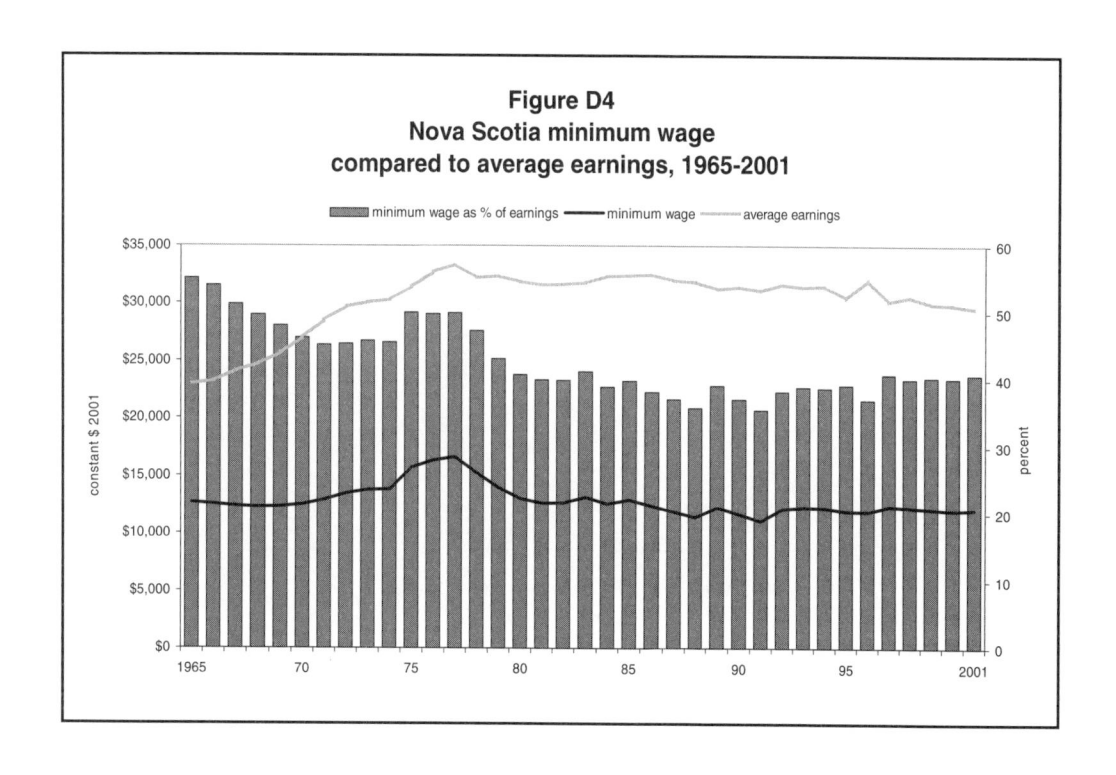

left-hand axis for the minimum wage and average earnings and the right-hand axis for the minimum wage as a percentage of earnings.

Nova Scotia's minimum wage has fallen relative to average earnings over the years, though it rebounded somewhat in the 1990s and the start of the new century. It declined from 55.1 percent in 1965 to a low of 35.5 percent in 1991, though recovering somewhat in the latter part of the 1990s to stand at 40.8 percent in 2001.

Average earnings (in constant 2001 dollars) increased from $22,988 in 1965 to a peak of $33,315 in 1977 and have slipped slowly overall since, standing at $29,592 in 2001. On an annual (full-time, all-year) basis, the minimum wage went from $12,658 in 1965 to $16,633 in 1977, slid to $11,054 in 1991 and stood at $12,064 in 2001.

Minimum wage compared to before-tax poverty lines (Figure D5)

Statistics Canada publishes two sets of low income cut-offs. The before-tax low income cut-offs are based on gross, pre-tax income (i.e., income from employment, investments, private pensions and other private sources plus income from government programs such as public pensions, Employment Insurance,

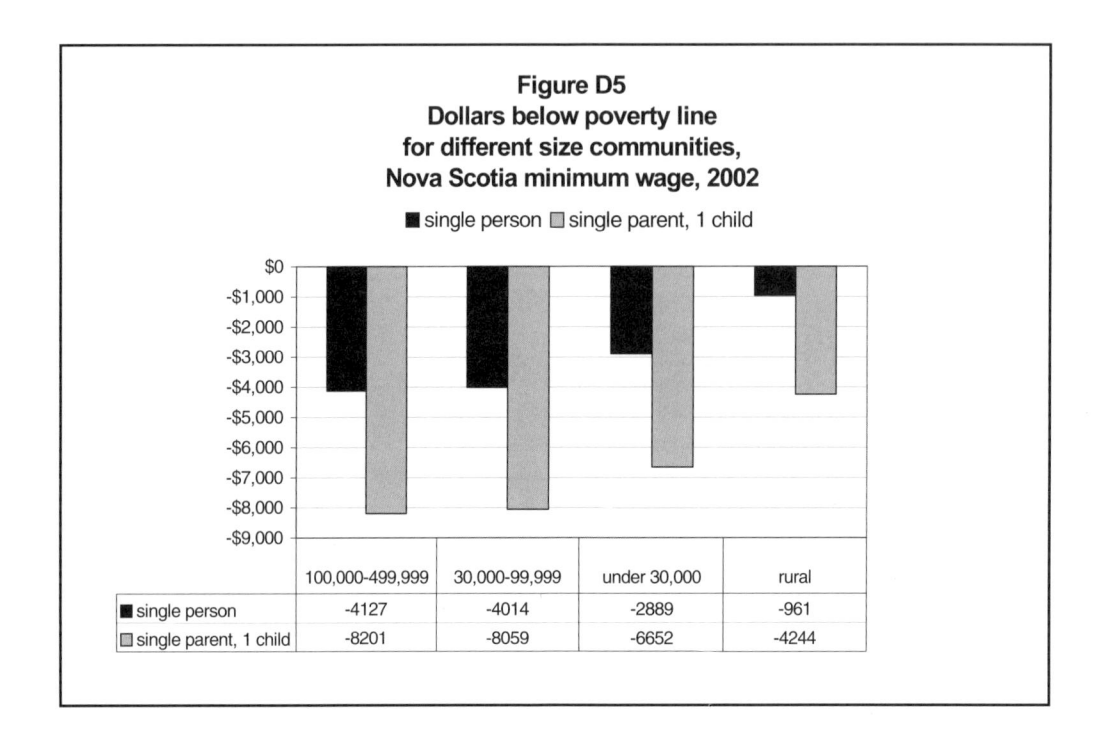

**Figure D5
Dollars below poverty line
for different size communities,
Nova Scotia minimum wage, 2002**

	100,000-499,999	30,000-99,999	under 30,000	rural
single person	-4127	-4014	-2889	-961
single parent, 1 child	-8201	-8059	-6652	-4244

child benefits and welfare). The after-tax low income cut-offs use the same definition of income but also factor into the picture the federal and provincial income taxes that Canadians pay. We first compare the minimum wage to the before-tax poverty lines.

Because the poverty line is lower for smaller communities, the minimum wage represents a larger proportion of the poverty line in smaller communities. In 2002, Nova Scotia's minimum wage ranged from 74.7 percent of the before-tax poverty line for one person in Halifax (which is in the 100,000-499,999 size category) to 75.2 percent for communities between 30,000 and 99,999 inhabitants, 80.8 percent for towns under 30,000 and 92.7 percent for rural areas.

In dollar terms, Nova Scotia's minimum wage in 2002 fell $4,127 short of the before-tax low income cut-off for one person in Halifax, $4,014 below for communities between 30,000 and 99,999, $2,889 below for towns under 30,000 and $961 below the poverty line for rural areas. Figure D5 shows the dollar gap between the minimum wage and the before-tax poverty line for one person in different size communities throughout the province.

Because the poverty line varies by family size, minimum wages (which do not vary by family size) fall farther below the poverty line for families than for single workers. We look at the poverty gap for a single parent with one child, which falls in the two-person family size category. In 2002, Nova Scotia's minimum wage varied from 59.7 percent of the before-tax low income line for a two-person family in Halifax (which is in the 100,000-499,999 category) to 60.2 percent for communities between 30,000 and 99,999, 64.7 percent for towns under 30,000 and 74.1 percent for rural areas. The minimum wage was $8,201 below the before-tax poverty line for a family of two in Halifax, $8,059 under the line for communities between 30,000 and 99,999, $6,652 below in towns under 30,000 and $4,244 under the line for rural residents.

Trend in minimum wage as percentage of before-tax poverty lines (Figure D6)

The long-term trend when we compare the minimum wage to the poverty line (as measured by Statistics Canada's low income cut-offs, which vary by size of family and of community) is the same as the trend in dollar value. In 2002, the estimated before-tax low income line for the largest city in the province – Halifax, which falls in the 100,000-499,999 category – was $16,295 for one person and $20,369 for a family of two.

Nova Scotia's minimum wage rose from 78.7 percent of the before-tax poverty line for one person in Halifax in 1965 to 103.4 percent in 1977, falling to a low of 68.7 percent in 1991. However, the trend improved slightly in the 1990s and stood at 74.7 percent of the poverty line for one person in Halifax in 2002. For a two-person family (e.g., a single parent with one child), the minimum wage went from 63.0 percent of the before-tax low income cut-off for Halifax in 1965 to a peak of 82.7 percent in 1977, declined to a low of 55.0 percent in 1991 and then recovered a bit, standing at 59.7 percent of the poverty line in 2002. Figure D6 shows the trends.

Figure D6
Nova Scotia minimum wage as % of before-tax poverty line for largest city, 1965-2002

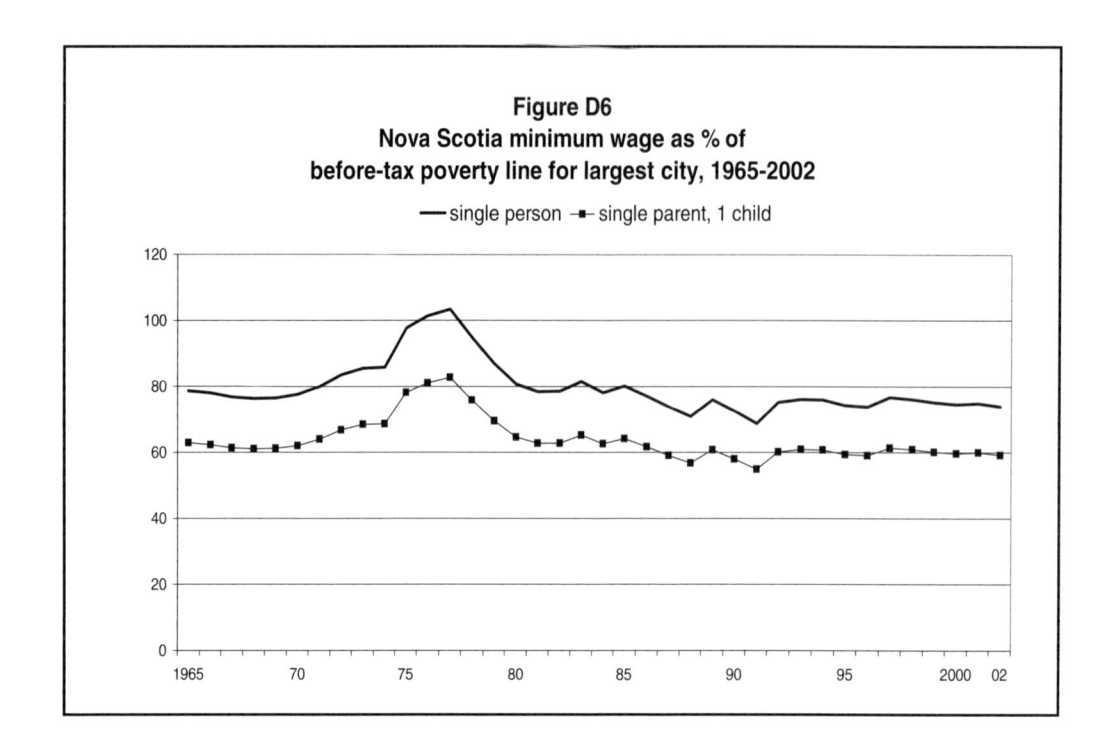

Minimum wage compared to after-tax poverty lines (Figure D7)

Statistics Canada publishes after-tax low income cut-offs as well as before-tax low income cut-offs. We look here at how after-tax minimum wage incomes in Nova Scotia for five types of household – single persons, single parents with one child, one-earner couples with two children, two-earner couples supporting two children on one-and-a-half minimum wages, and two-earner couples with two children and two full minimum wages – compare to the after-tax poverty lines for different size communities. 'After-tax minimum wage incomes' means incomes from the minimum wage and available federal and provincial income programs minus federal and provincial income taxes.

For a single person earning the minimum wage, after-tax income came to $11,626,[22] which is $1,484 below the after-tax poverty line for Halifax, $1,282 under for centres of 30,000-99,999 and $169 beneath the line for towns under 30,000, but $1,422 above the poverty line for rural residents. A single parent with one child received $15,454[23] in after-tax income from minimum wage earnings and federal and provincial child benefits and tax credits, which came to $543 below the after-tax poverty line for Halifax and $296 under for centres of 30,000-99,999, but $1,061 above the line for towns under 30,000 and $3,003 over the line for rural residents. For a one-earner couple with two children, after-tax minimum wage income amounted to $17,847[24] – $7,353 below the after-tax poverty line for Halifax, $6,963 under

Figure D7
Dollars below/above after-tax poverty line for different size communities, Nova Scotia after-tax minimum wage income, 2001

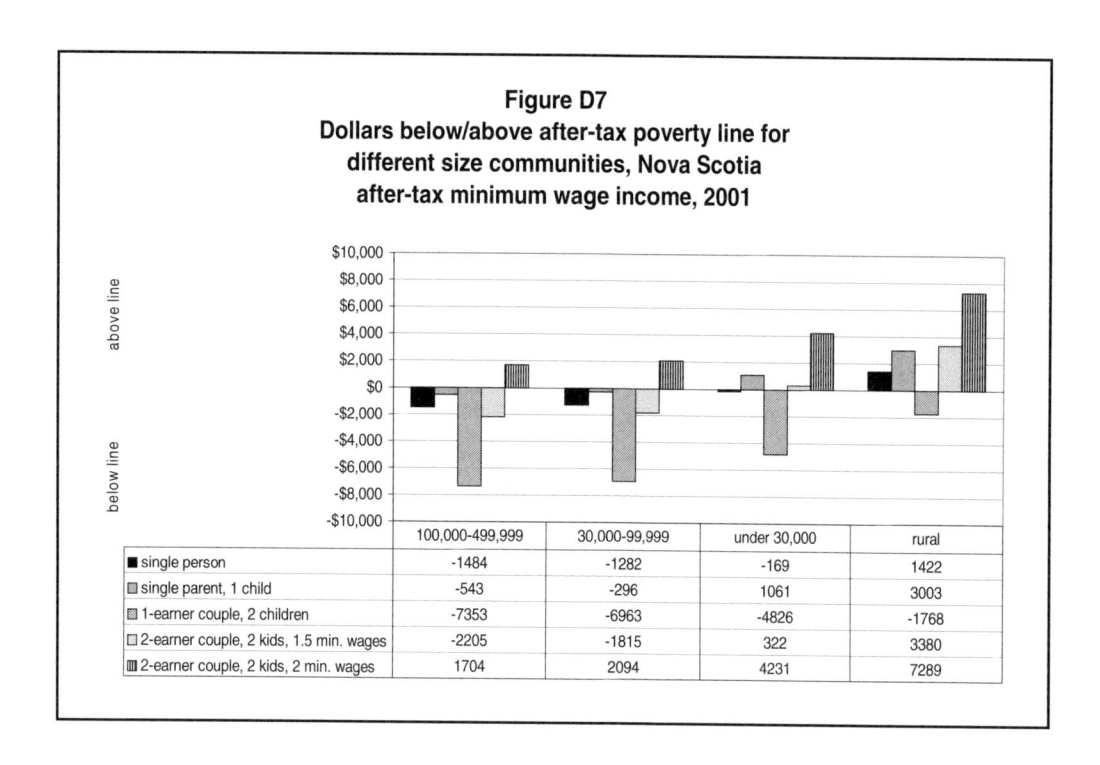

	100,000-499,999	30,000-99,999	under 30,000	rural
single person	-1484	-1282	-169	1422
single parent, 1 child	-543	-296	1061	3003
1-earner couple, 2 children	-7353	-6963	-4826	-1768
2-earner couple, 2 kids, 1.5 min. wages	-2205	-1815	322	3380
2-earner couple, 2 kids, 2 min. wages	1704	2094	4231	7289

for centres 30,000-99,999, $4,826 below for towns smaller than 30,000 and $1,768 beneath the line for rural residents.

We look at two kinds of two-earner families, both with two children aged 10 and 15 as above for the one-earner family. In the first example, we assume that one parent works full time, year round for the minimum wage and the other earned half that amount. That family's after-tax minimum wage income amounted to $22,995[25] – $2,205 below the after-tax poverty line for Halifax and $1,185 under for centres 30,000-99,999 but $322 above the line for towns smaller than 30,000 and $3,380 over the line for rural residents.

In the other case, we assume that both parents work full time, year round for the minimum wage. After-tax minimum wage income amounted to $26,904[26] – $1,704 above the after-tax poverty line for Halifax, $2,094 above for centres 30,000-99,999, $4,231 over the line for towns smaller than 30,000 and $7,289 above the line for rural residents.

Contribution of child benefits

Child benefits supplement the incomes of the large majority of Canadian families and are particularly important to low- and modest-income families. Improvements to the federal Canada Child Tax Benefit and Nova Scotia's creation of a provincial child benefit program are providing significant income supplements to minimum wage and other working poor families with children.

The single parent supporting one child on minimum wage earnings got $2,447 from the Canada Child Tax Benefit and $424 from the Nova Scotia Child Benefit, for a total of $2,871 – 19.4 percent of disposable income. The one-earner couple with two children received $4,250 from the Canada Child Tax Benefit and $906 from the Nova Scotia Child Benefit, for a combined child benefit of $5,156 or a sizeable 30.0 percent of disposable income.

The two-earner family in which one parent works full time, all year at the minimum wage and the other parent half that time got child benefits worth a total of $4,771 ($4,250 from the Canada Child Tax Benefit and $521 from the Nova Scotia Child Benefit) or 21.6 percent of disposable income. The two-earner family in which both parents work full time, all year at the minimum wage received $3,692 from the Canada Child Tax Benefit, which comes to 14.4 percent of disposable income.

Minimum wage versus welfare (Figure D8)

For a single person earning the minimum wage in Nova Scotia, disposable income – i.e., minimum wage earnings plus the refundable GST credit minus income and payroll taxes – amounted to $10,987 in 2001, which is a sizeable $6,170 more than the meagre $4,817 from welfare and the GST credit. Figure D8 shows the comparison.

Minimum wages also pay better than welfare for a single parent with one child age 2, though the advantage is smaller than for single people. Disposable income from after-tax minimum wage earnings, child benefits and the refundable GST credit amounted to $14,815 in 2001, or $2,565 more than the $12,250 from welfare, child benefits and the GST credit.

However, a one-earner couple earning the minimum wage and supporting two children aged 10 and 15 did better on welfare than working at the minimum wage. Total disposable income from minimum wages, child benefits and the GST credit amounted to $17,208 – $1,067 less than the $18,275 total income from welfare, child benefits and the GST credit.

For two-parent families to earn more than welfare, both parents must work. We look at two examples.

**Figure D8
Minimum wage versus welfare in
Nova Scotia, by household type, 2001**

	single person	single parent, 1 child	one-earner couple, 2 children	couple, 2 kids, 1.5 min. wages	couple, 2 kids, 2 min. wages
minimum wage disposable income	10987	14815	17208	22111	25624
welfare income	4817	12250	18275	18275	18275

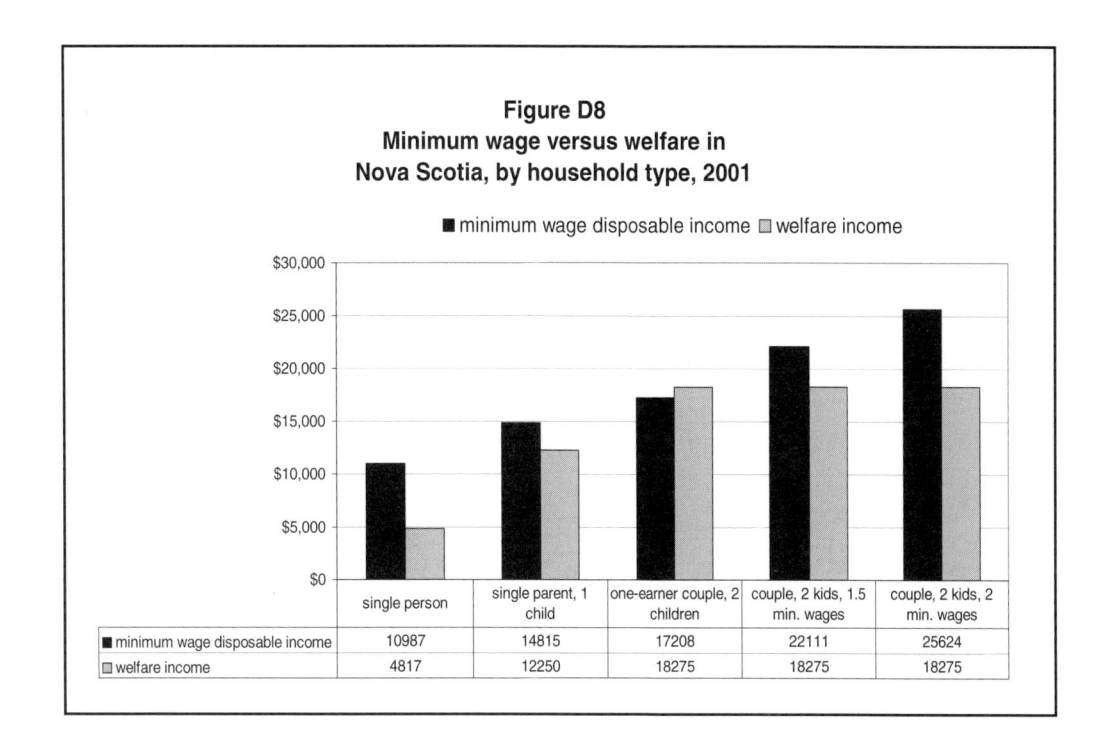

In the first, one parent works full time, year round at the minimum wage while the other earns half this amount (i.e., works part time and/or part year); as above, there are two children aged 10 and 15. The family's disposable income from one-and-a-half minimum wages came to $22,111 in 2001 or $3,836 more than the $18,275 from welfare, child benefits and the refundable GST credit

The other two-earner family earns double the minimum wage since both parents work full time, year round at the minimum wage. Total disposable income was $25,624 or $7,349 more than the $18,275 from welfare and other government income benefits.

b. Minimum Wage Workers in Nova Scotia

The following text with illustrative graphs analyzes key characteristics of minimum wage workers in Nova Scotia. Appendix 2 provides detailed statistics in tabular form (pages 288-290).

Interprovincial rank: incidence of minimum wage workers (Figure D9)

In 2000, an estimated 17,900 Nova Scotians – 5.0 percent of the province's 361,100 employees – worked for the minimum wage. That places Nova Scotia in the lower half of the pack, the lowest incidence of minimum wage workers being Alberta (2.0 percent) and the highest Newfoundland (8.7 percent). Figure D9 illustrates the rankings. With 5.0 percent of its workers at the minimum wage, Nova Scotia is just slightly above the 4.6 percent national figure.

Minimum wage workers are slightly overrepresented in Nova Scotia. While the province accounts for 3.1 percent of all minimum wage workers in the country, it has a smaller share of all Canadian employees (2.9 percent), producing an index of 1.07 (the higher the result above 1.00, the more overrepresented are minimum wage workers).

Gender and age (Figures D10-D13)

In Nova Scotia as in the rest of Canada, women run a higher risk of working for minimum wage than men, and women also make up the majority of the minimum wage workforce.

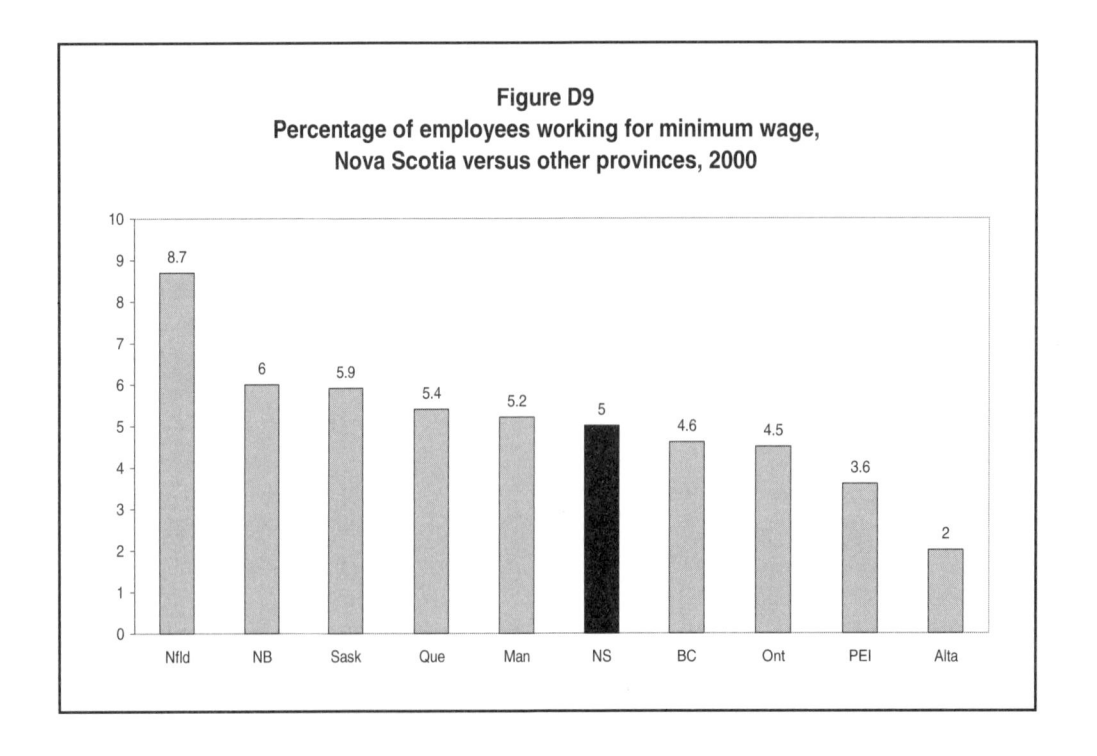

Figure D9
Percentage of employees working for minimum wage, Nova Scotia versus other provinces, 2000

Province	Percentage
Nfld	8.7
NB	6
Sask	5.9
Que	5.4
Man	5.2
NS	5
BC	4.6
Ont	4.5
PEI	3.6
Alta	2

**Figure D10
Composition of minimum wage workforce
in Nova Scotia, by gender, 2000**

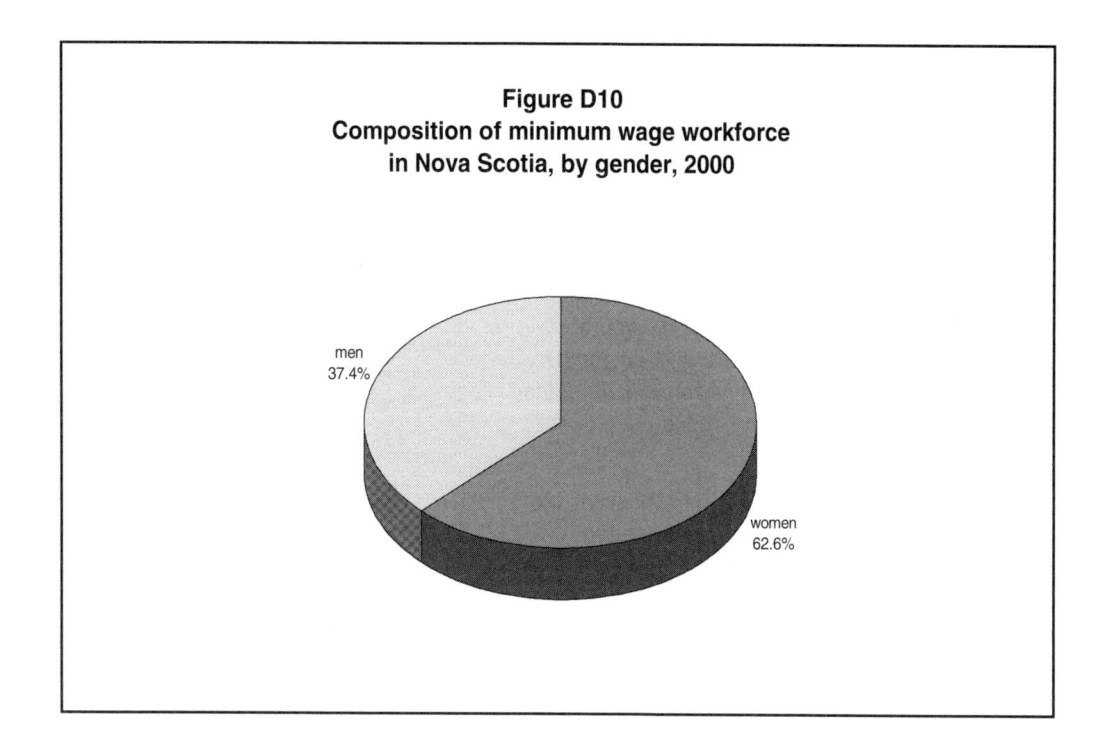

men 37.4%
women 62.6%

In 2000, 6.3 percent of female employees in Nova Scotia worked for the minimum wage compared to only 3.7 percent of male workers. Of the province's total 17,900 minimum wage workers, 11,200 – 62.6 percent – were women and 6,700 – 37.4 percent – were men. Figure D10 shows the results.

Women are overrepresented in Nova Scotia's minimum wage workforce. They constituted 62.6 percent of minimum wage workers but only 49.3 percent of all the province's employees in 2000. Men are underrepresented. They accounted for only 37.4 percent of minimum wage workers in Newfoundland but slightly more than half (50.7 percent) of all employees.

The gender bias among minimum wage workers holds when we control for major age categories. While younger workers of both sexes run a higher risk of working for minimum wage, women still fare worse than men within each age category with but one exception (the 20-24 age group). Figure D11 shows the pattern.

Among female workers in Nova Scotia aged 15 to 19, 39.7 percent worked for the minimum wage in 2000 in contrast to 30.7 percent of male workers in the same age group. Among workers aged 20-24, though, 8.2 percent of women but a slightly larger proportion of men (8.7 percent) worked for the

Figure D11
Percentage of employees working for minimum wage in Nova Scotia, by gender and age, 2000

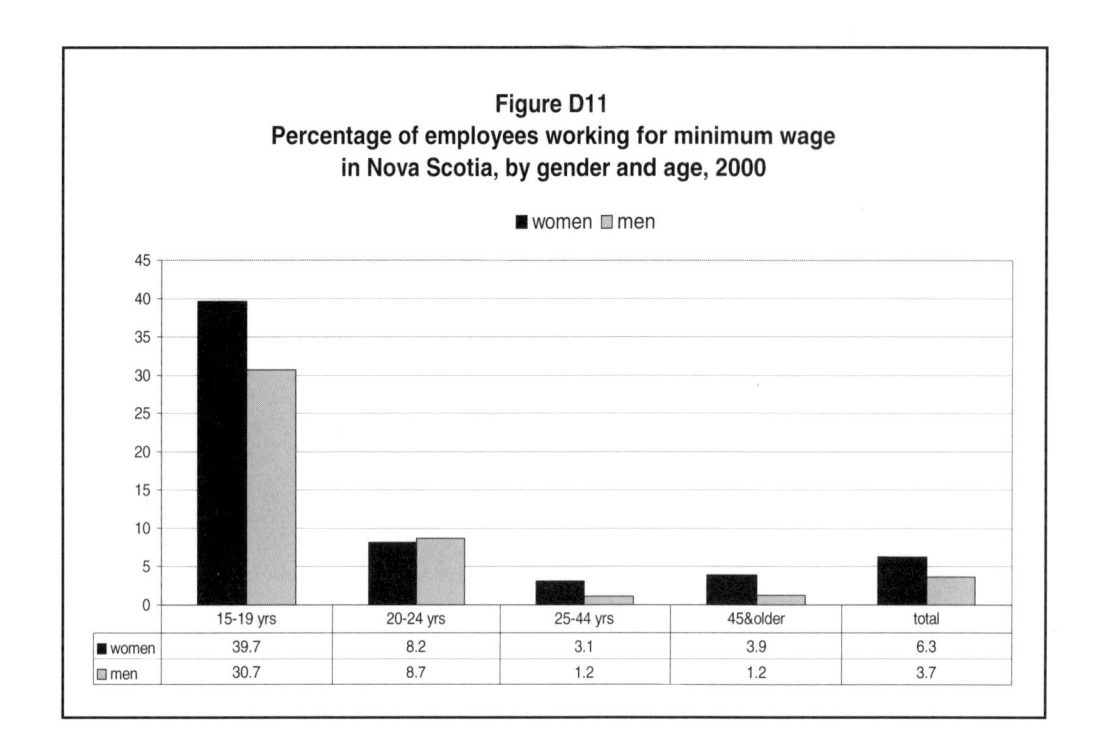

	15-19 yrs	20-24 yrs	25-44 yrs	45&older	total
women	39.7	8.2	3.1	3.9	6.3
men	30.7	8.7	1.2	1.2	3.7

Figure D12
Share of minimum wage workers versus share of all employees in Nova Scotia, by age group, 2000

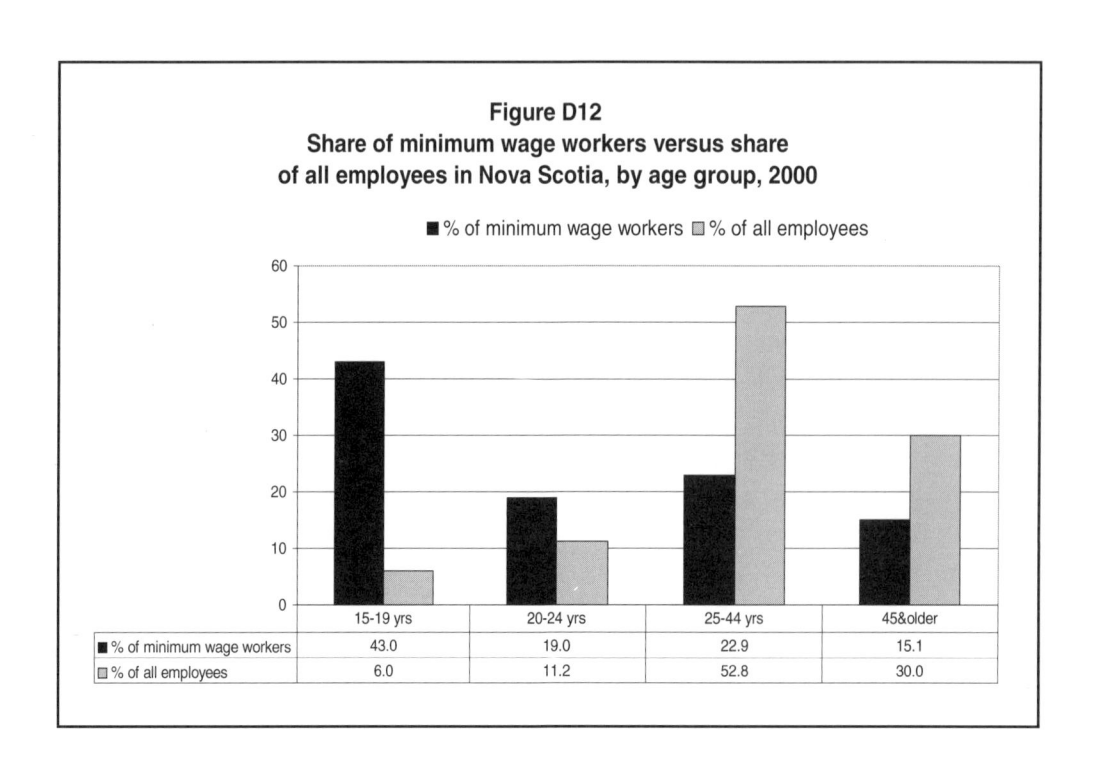

	15-19 yrs	20-24 yrs	25-44 yrs	45&older
% of minimum wage workers	43.0	19.0	22.9	15.1
% of all employees	6.0	11.2	52.8	30.0

**Figure D13
Composition of minimum wage workforce
in Nova Scotia, by teenager/adult and gender, 2000**

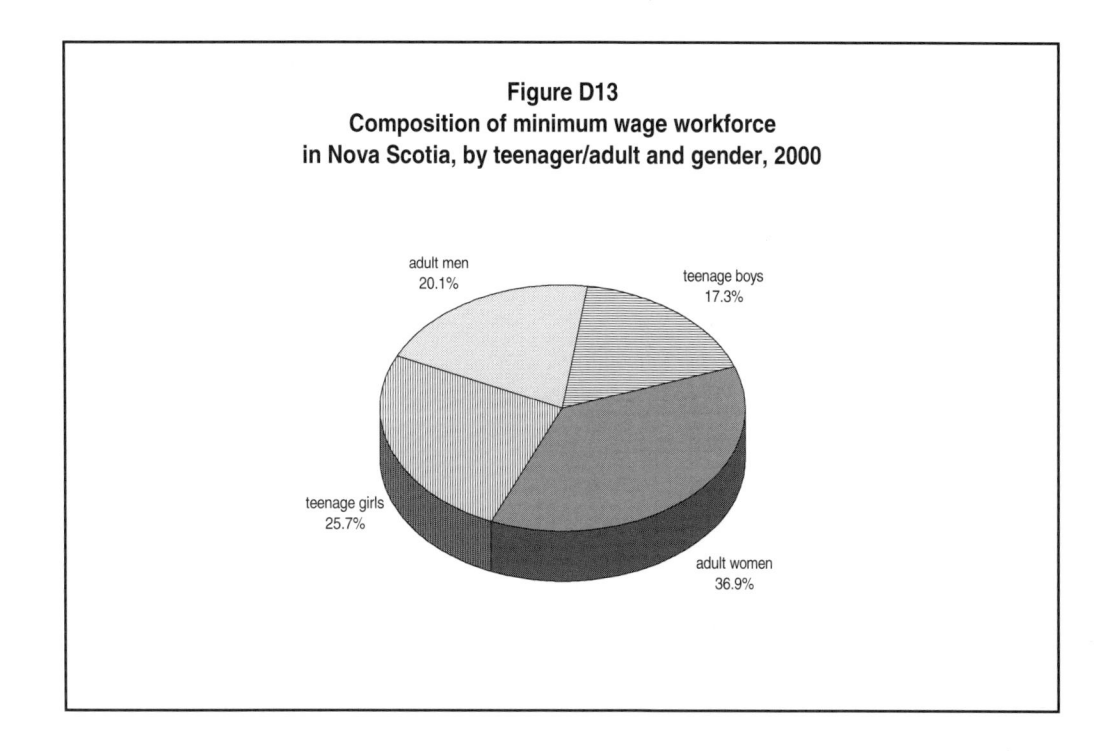

- adult men 20.1%
- teenage boys 17.3%
- adult women 36.9%
- teenage girls 25.7%

minimum wage. Among workers 25-44, 3.1 percent of women as opposed to 1.2 percent of men were at the bottom of the wage ladder. Among employees 45 and older, 3.9 percent of women but only 1.2 percent of men worked for the minimum wage.

The minimum wage risk gap between the sexes is wider for older workers. Women in the 15-24 age group are 1.2 times more likely than men to work for the minimum wage. The gap between the sexes widens to 2.6 for those aged 25-44 and 3.3 for those over 45.

Young people not only are more likely to work for minimum wage than other employees, but the young also make up a large proportion of the minimum wage workforce. Figure D12 compares the age makeup of minimum wage workers and all employees in Nova Scotia. Forty-three percent of minimum wage workers are in the 15-19 age group, as opposed to just 6.0 percent of all employees. Employees aged 20-24 represent 19.0 percent of minimum wage workers as opposed to 11.2 percent of all workers. All told, six in ten minimum wage workers (62.0 percent) are under 25 years of age.

The opposite holds for older workers. While a sizeable proportion – 22.9 percent – of minimum wage workers are between 25 and 44, that age group constitutes a much larger proportion – 52.8 percent or more than half – of all employees. Workers aged 45 and older make up just 15.1 percent of minimum wage employees but 30.0 percent – twice the share – of all employees.

Figure D13 divides the minimum wage workforce in Nova Scotia into teenage girls and boys and adult women and men. Adult women are the largest group, at 6,600 or 36.9 percent of the total, followed by teenage girls (4,600 or 25.7 percent), adult men (3,600 or 20.1 percent) and teenage boys (3,100 or 17.3 percent). The majority (57.0 percent) of Nova Scotia's minimum wage workers are adults; the national average is a bit lower (52.9 percent).

Education (Figures D14 and D15)

Figure D14 shows the incidence of minimum wage workers in Nova Scotia according to level of education.

At first glance, the relationship between level of education and incidence of minimum wage employment does not seem to correspond to common sense: Workers in the lowest educational group (elementary education only) are less likely to work for minimum wage (5.0 percent do) than those with some high school (12.9 percent), while those with some postsecondary education run a higher risk (8.3 percent) than high school graduates (5.8 percent). However, as one would expect, the chances of working for minimum wage are lowest for the two highest education categories – 2.3 percent for those with a

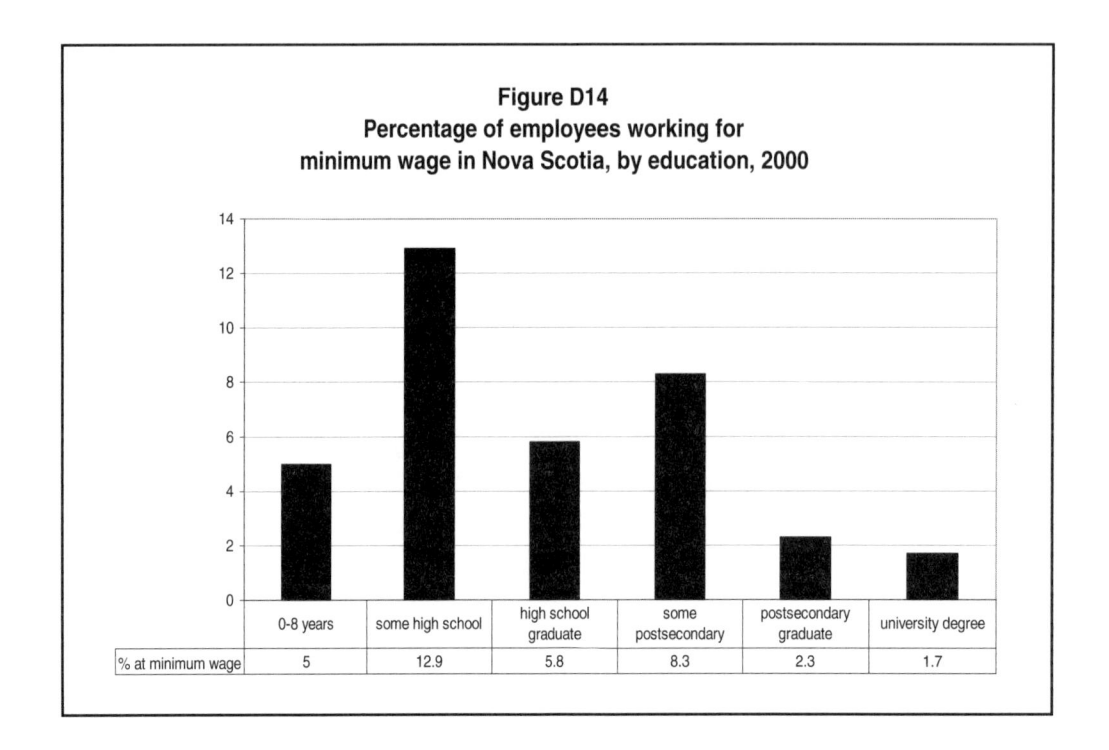

**Figure D14
Percentage of employees working for minimum wage in Nova Scotia, by education, 2000**

	0-8 years	some high school	high school graduate	some postsecondary	postsecondary graduate	university degree
% at minimum wage	5	12.9	5.8	8.3	2.3	1.7

Figure D15
Composition of minimum wage workforce in Nova Scotia, by education, 2000

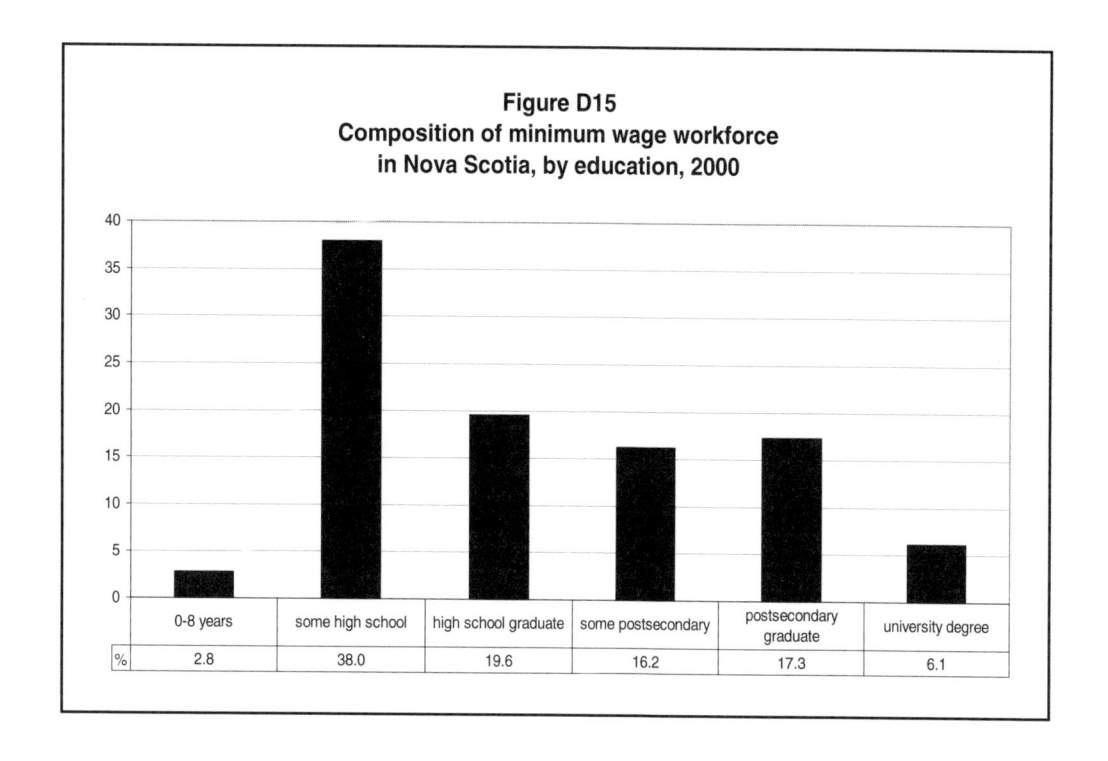

%	0-8 years	some high school	high school graduate	some postsecondary	postsecondary graduate	university degree
	2.8	38.0	19.6	16.2	17.3	6.1

postsecondary certificate or diploma (e.g., from a community college or vocational institute) and just 1.7 percent for those with a university degree.

Once we look at the education-minimum wage link for different age groups, the reasons for the apparently inconsistent relationship comes clear: Young people working at part-time or seasonal (i.e., summer) jobs – typically paying the minimum or a low wage – figure prominently in the 'some high school' and 'some postsecondary education' categories; they are still at high school, community college or university, whereas workers in the other educational categories have completed their education.

Figure D15 shows each educational group's share of Nova Scotia's minimum wage workforce in 2000. The largest group of minimum wage workers are those with some high school (38.0 percent), followed by high school graduates (19.6 percent), postsecondary graduates (17.3 percent), those with some postsecondary education (16.2 percent), university graduates (6.1 percent) and workers with only 0-8 years of education (2.8 percent). Many minimum wage workers are students (high school or postsecondary) pursuing their education. A sizeable group of minimum wage workers (39.6 percent) have some form of postsecondary education.

Full-time and part-time work (Figures D16 and D17)

The fact that young people are more likely to work part time helps explain why workers still pursuing their education tend to face a higher risk of minimum wage work than those who have completed their schooling and are working full time. Figure D16 indicates that 15.7 percent of part-time workers in Nova Scotia are at the minimum wage compared to only 2.6 percent of those employed full time. Nevertheless, a substantial group of minimum wage workers in the province (42.8 percent) work full time, while 57.2 percent are employed part time, as shown in Figure D17.

Gender alters the relationship between full-time and part-time work and the minimum wage. Figure D16 shows that women who work part time in Nova Scotia run a lesser risk of being at the bottom of the wage ladder than do men who work part time (14.3 and 18.9 percent, respectively). However, women employed full time are more likely than men working full time to earn the minimum wage (3.4 and 1.9 percent, respectively).

Women make up the majority of minimum wage employees in the province working both full time (58.4 percent are women) and part time (65.0 percent are women). Among all employees, though, women

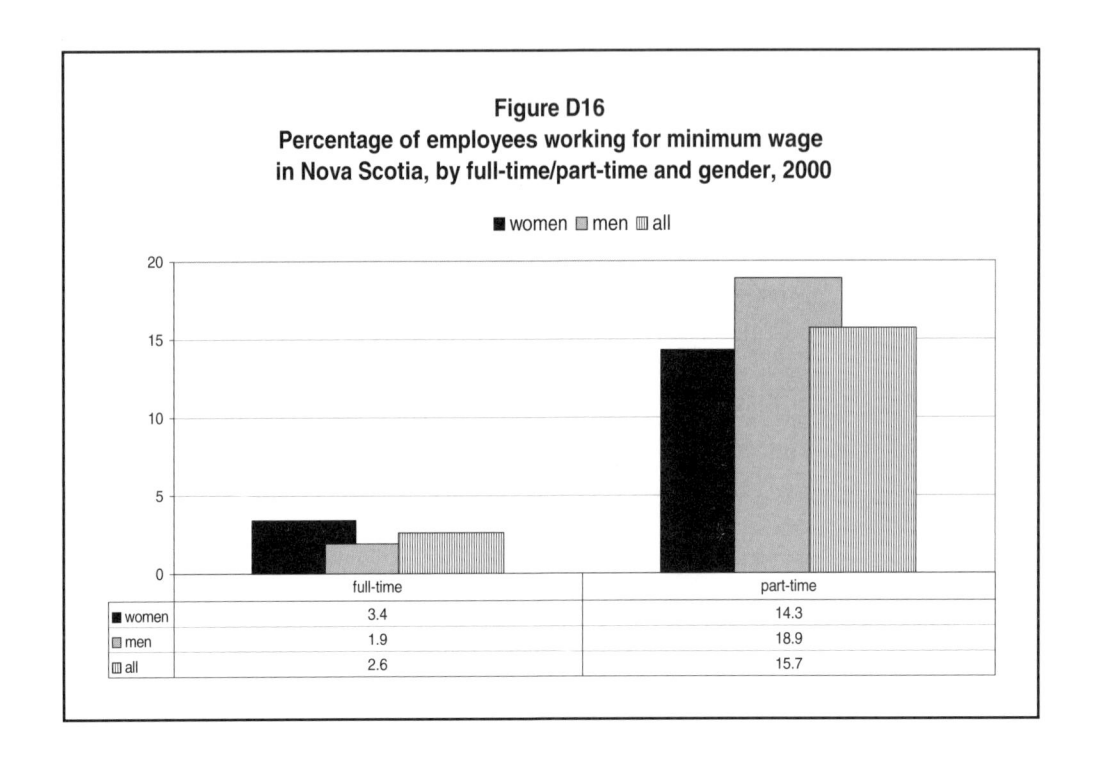

Figure D16
Percentage of employees working for minimum wage in Nova Scotia, by full-time/part-time and gender, 2000

	full-time	part-time
women	3.4	14.3
men	1.9	18.9
all	2.6	15.7

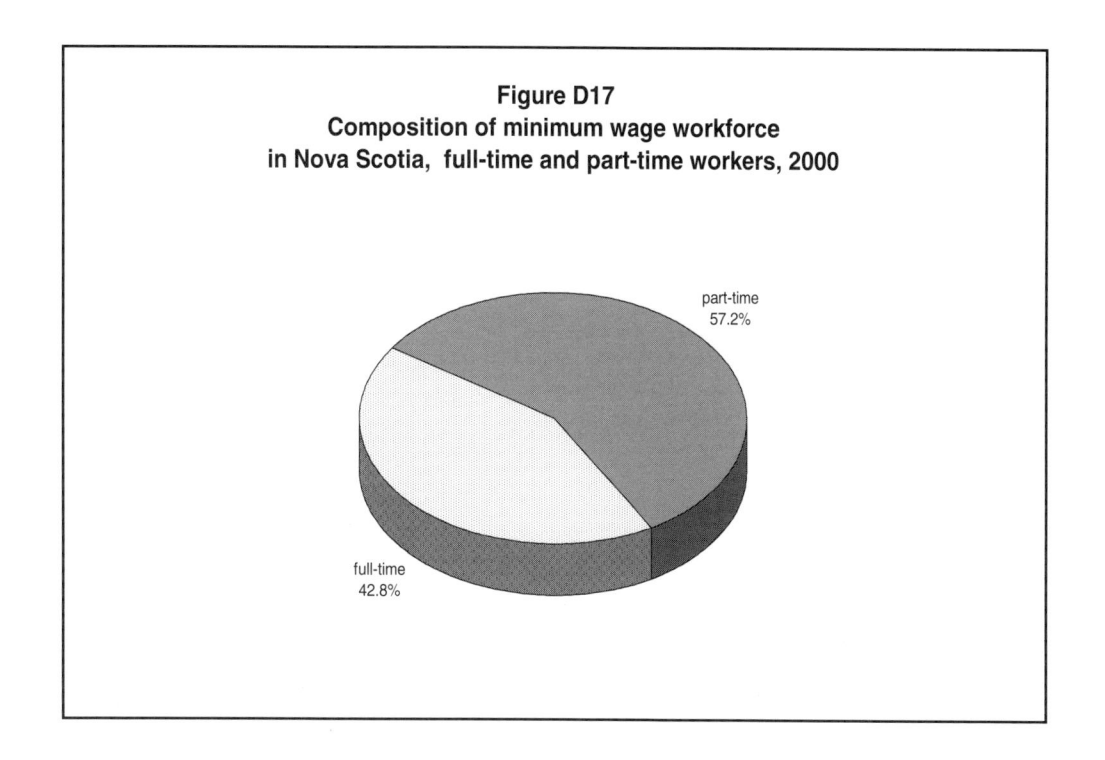

**Figure D17
Composition of minimum wage workforce
in Nova Scotia, full-time and part-time workers, 2000**

part-time 57.2%
full-time 42.8%

constitute a minority of full-time workers (44.4 percent) but the majority of part-time workers (71.2 percent).

Family status (Figure D18)

We noted above that six in ten of Nova Scotia's minimum wage workers are under 25 years of age. This fundamental fact of the minimum wage workforce is underscored by information on family status, as illustrated by Figure D18.

The largest group of minimum wage workers – an estimated 10,800 or 60.3 percent of the total 17,900 – are older children living with their parents (or relatives with relatives, as in the case of a niece or nephew living with an aunt and uncle, or grandchildren with grandparents). Of this category, 7,400 or 68.5 percent are aged 15-19, 2,300 or 21.3 percent are 20-24 and the remaining 900 or 8.2 percent are 25 or older (percentages do not add to 100 because of rounding). More than half (5,900 or 54.6 percent) are still in school and working part time or part year (e.g., in summer).

The next largest group of minimum wage workers in Nova Scotia – 4,800 or 26.8 percent of the total – are members of couples (married or living together). In most cases (3,600 or 75.0 percent of the

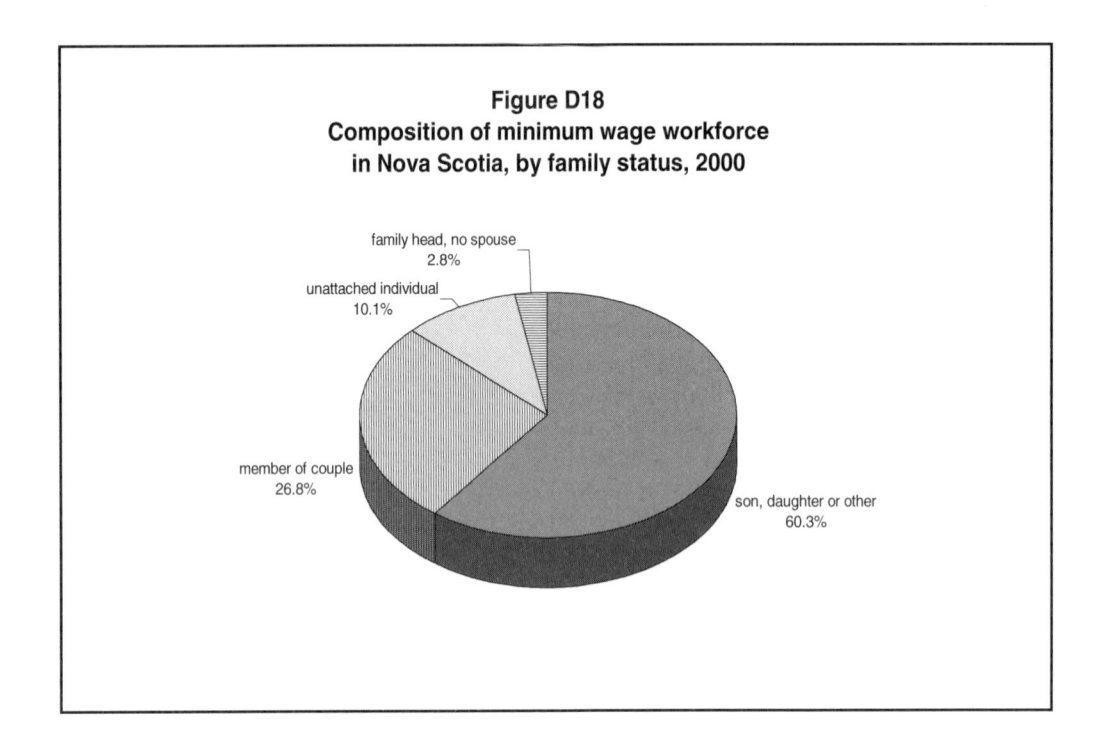

Figure D18
Composition of minimum wage workforce in Nova Scotia, by family status, 2000

- family head, no spouse: 2.8%
- unattached individual: 10.1%
- member of couple: 26.8%
- son, daughter or other: 60.3%

category total of 4,800), the minimum wage worker's spouse is employed, typically earning more than the minimum wage. A typical example in this category would be mothers combining (unpaid) childrearing work with part-time minimum wage work. Another 1,200 or 25.0 percent of married minimum wage workers are in couples whose spouse is not employed (most of then are not in the labour force).

An estimated 1,800 or 10.1 percent of minimum wage workers are unattached individuals. Half of this category (900 workers) live alone; of this group, around 100 are 15-24, 600 are aged 25-54 and 200 are 55 or older. About 900 of the province's unattached minimum wage workers live with friends or roommates; most (600) are young (15-24) and 300 are aged 25-54.

Finally, some 500 or just 2.8 percent of the minimum wage workforce are heads of families with no spouse present. Most (400 or 80.0 percent) of these workers are single parents with children under 18.

Industry

National data show that the incidence and distribution of minimum wage workers varies significantly according to industries. The same applies to Nova Scotia, though sample size constraints permit estimates for only nine of 16 industrial categories. Among the industrial categories for which estimates are available, accommodation and food services tops the list (16.3 percent of employees in this classification work for the minimum wage), followed by trade (9.2 percent), other services (8.1 percent), management, administrative and other support (6.5 percent), information, culture and recreation (6.2 percent), finance, insurance, real estate and leasing (5.8 percent), educational services (2.3 percent), health care and social assistance jobs (1.8 percent) and manufacturing (1.4 percent).

Estimates are available for the industrial composition of the whole employed workforce in Nova Scotia. Trade tops the list, at an estimated 67,400 or 18.7 percent of all employees. Next comes health care and social assistance, at 45,500 or 12.6 percent of all employees, followed by manufacturing (41,500 or 11.5 percent), educational services (31,100 or 8.6 percent), public administration (25,400 or 7.0 percent), accommodation and food services (24,600 or 6.8 percent), finance, insurance, real estate and leasing (18,900 or 5.2 percent), construction (18,400 or 5.1 percent), transportation and warehousing (17,500 or 4.8 percent), information, culture and recreation (14,600 or 4.0 percent), management, administrative and other support (13,900 or 3.8 percent), other services (13,500 or 3.7 percent), professional, scientific and technical services (12,200 or 3.4 percent), forestry, fishing, mining, oil and gas (9,400 or 2.6 percent), agriculture (4,400 or 1.2 percent) and utilities (2,800 or 0.8 percent).

NEW BRUNSWICK

a. Minimum Wages in New Brunswick

Interprovincial rank: dollar value of minimum wage (Figure E1)

New Brunswick's minimum wage increased from $5.90 to $6.00 an hour on August 1, 2002, so its annual average for 2002 amounted to $5.94 an hour. New Brunswick's minimum wage ranked fourth-lowest among Canada's ten provinces and three territories in 2002, after Newfoundland, Nova Scotia and Alberta. British Columbia's $8.00 hourly minimum wage is Canada's highest.

Trend in dollar value of minimum wage (Figure E2)

Because minimum wages are not indexed, their value changes over time. Figure E2 shows the trend in New Brunswick's minimum wage from 1965 to 2002; each year's average minimum wage has been converted to inflation-adjusted (i.e., constant) 2002 dollars to show the real trend, after taking into account the impact of inflation on the value of the dollar.

Figure E1
New Brunswick average hourly minimum wage compared to other provinces and territories, 2002

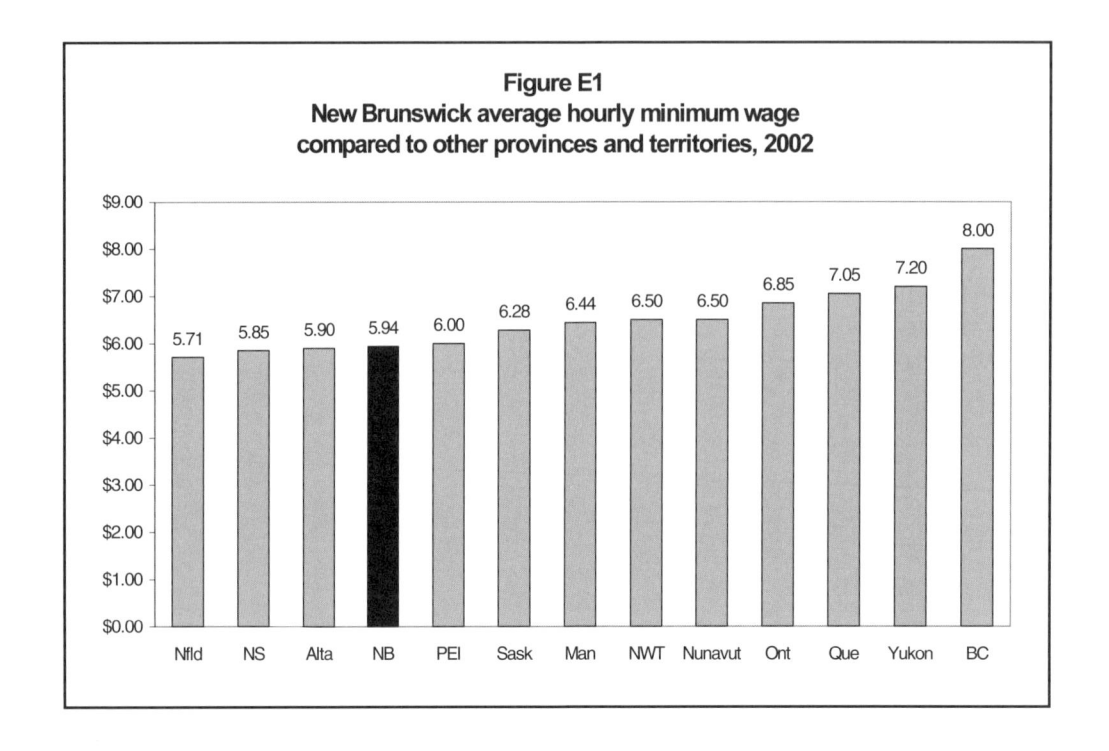

Province/Territory	Minimum Wage
Nfld	5.71
NS	5.85
Alta	5.90
NB	5.94
PEI	6.00
Sask	6.28
Man	6.44
NWT	6.50
Nunavut	6.50
Ont	6.85
Que	7.05
Yukon	7.20
BC	8.00

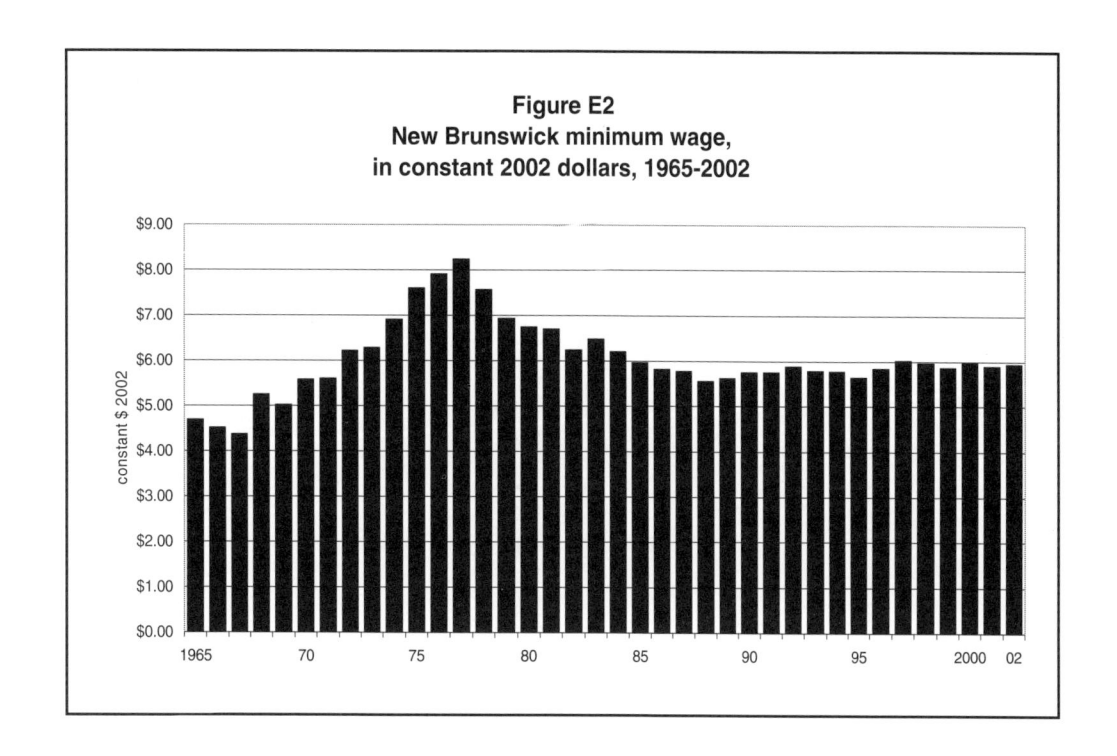

**Figure E2
New Brunswick minimum wage,
in constant 2002 dollars, 1965-2002**

New Brunswick's minimum wage increased substantially overall between 1965 ($4.70) and its 1977 peak ($8.25), declined slowly though quite steadily until 1988 ($5.56) and then saw a modest increase in the second half of the 1990s to stand at $5.94 by 2002. Its 2002 value was $2.31 or 28.0 percent below the 1977 high point, though $1.24 or 26.5 percent higher than the 1965 level.

Interprovincial rank: minimum wage as percentage of average earnings (Figure E3)

New Brunswick ranks somewhat higher – about mid-pack – in terms of how its minimum wage compares to its average earnings. In 2001 (the most recent year for which data on average earnings are available), New Brunswick's $5.83 minimum wage came to 39.4 percent of the province's $14.78 hourly average earnings. Lowest was the Northwest Territories, at 30.2 percent, while the highest was British Columbia, at 46.2 percent. Figure E3 gives the results.

Figure E3
New Brunswick minimum wage as % of average earnings, compared to other provinces and territories, 2001

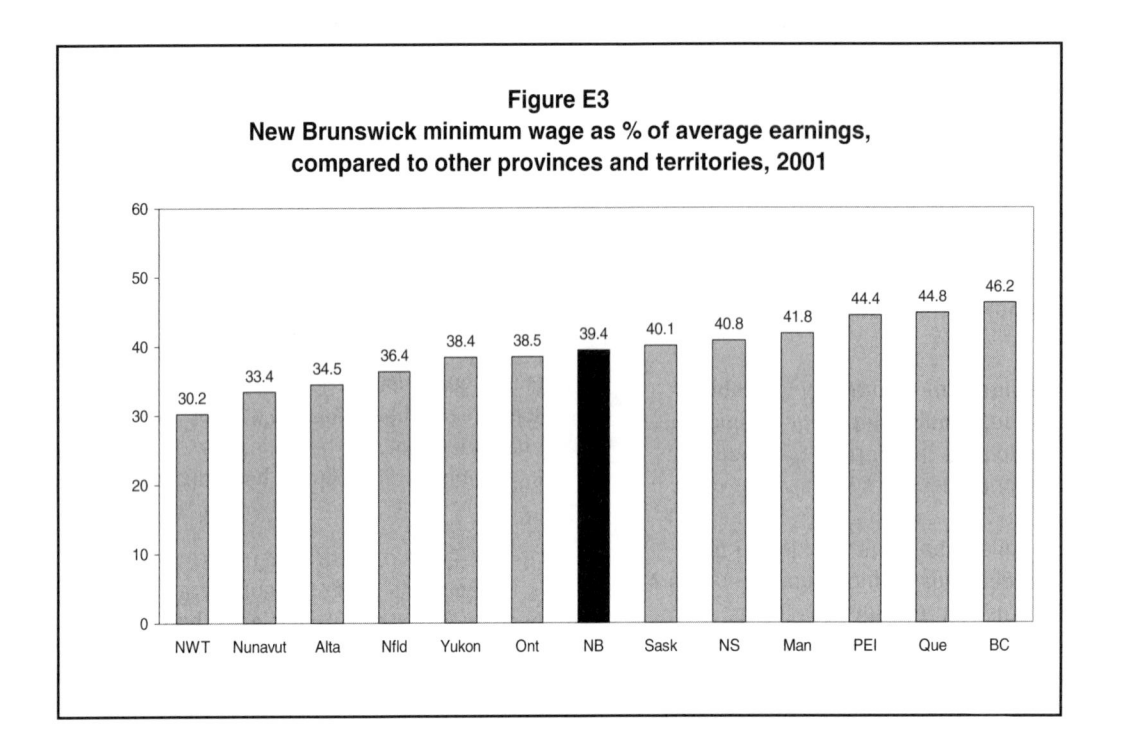

Province/Territory	%
NWT	30.2
Nunavut	33.4
Alta	34.5
Nfld	36.4
Yukon	38.4
Ont	38.5
NB	39.4
Sask	40.1
NS	40.8
Man	41.8
PEI	44.4
Que	44.8
BC	46.2

Trends in minimum wage and average earnings (Figure E4)

The black line in Figure E4 shows the trend in the minimum wage, the gray line the trend in average earnings and the vertical bars the trend in the minimum wage as a percentage of average earnings. Read the left-hand axis for the minimum wage and average earnings and the right-hand axis for the minimum wage as a percentage of earnings.

New Brunswick's minimum wage rose relative to average earnings between 1965 and 1977 and then, with some small ups and downs, declined until the late 1980s and recovered somewhat in the late 1990s and first two years of the new century. The minimum wage increased from 42.9 percent of average earnings in 1965 to 50.2 percent in 1977, fell to a low of 36.5 percent in 1988 and amounted to 39.4 percent of average earnings in 2001.

Average earnings (in constant 2001 dollars) increased from $22,493 in 1965 to a peak of $33,756 in 1977 and then drifted down to $30,744 in 2001. On an annual (full-time, all-year) basis, the minimum wage went from $9,644 in 1965 to $16,936 in 1977, fell to $11,418 in 1988 and stood at $12,116 in 2001.

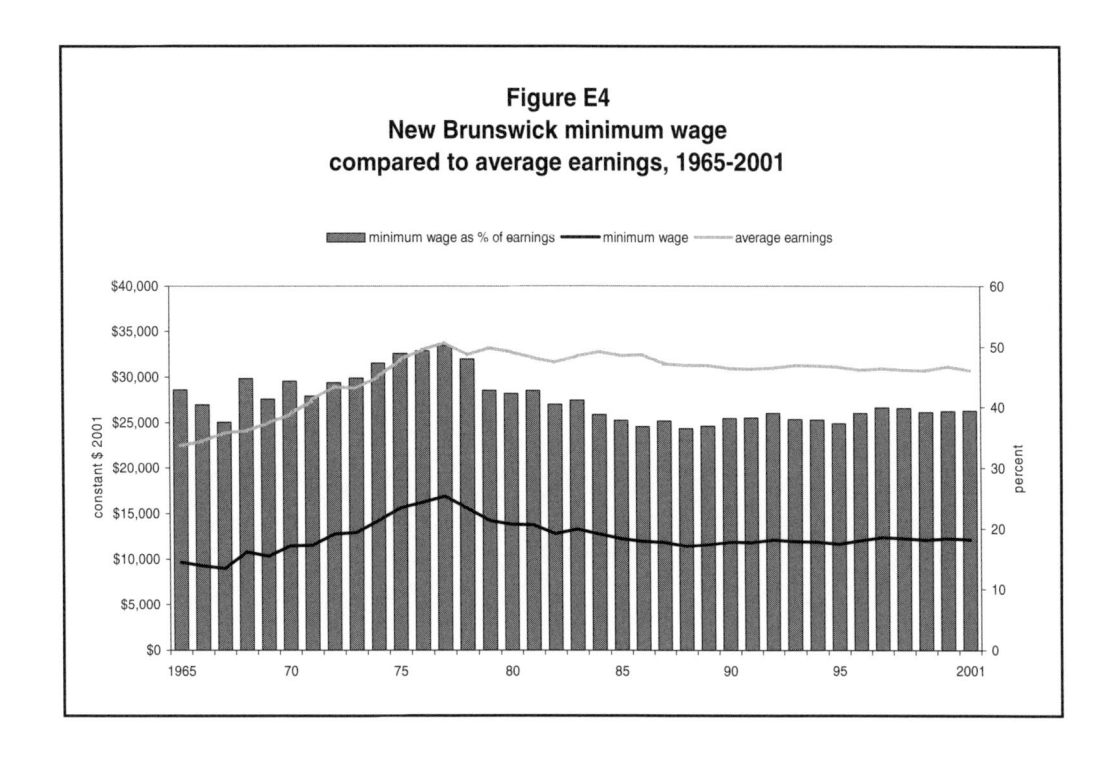

**Figure E4
New Brunswick minimum wage
compared to average earnings, 1965-2001**

Minimum wage compared to before-tax poverty lines (Figure E5)

Statistics Canada publishes two sets of low income cut-offs. The before-tax low income cut-offs are based on gross, pre-tax income (i.e., income from employment, investments, private pensions and other private sources plus income from government programs such as public pensions, Employment Insurance, child benefits and welfare). The after-tax low income cut-offs use the same definition of income but also factor into the picture the federal and provincial income taxes that Canadians pay. We first compare the minimum wage to the before-tax poverty lines.

Because the poverty line is lower for smaller communities, the minimum wage represents a larger proportion of the before-tax poverty line in smaller communities. In 2002, New Brunswick's minimum wage ranged from 75.8 percent of the before-tax low income line for one person in Saint John (which lies in the 100,000-499,999 community size category) to 76.4 percent for communities with 30,000 to 99,999 inhabitants, 82.1 percent for towns under 30,000 and 94.1 percent for rural areas.

New Brunswick's minimum wage in 2002 fell $3,939 short of the before-tax low income cut-off for one person in Saint John, $3,826 below for communities between 30,000 and 99,999, $2,701 under for towns under 30,000 and $773 below the poverty line for rural residents. Figure E5 shows the dollar gap

Figure E5
Dollars below before-tax poverty line for different size communities, New Brunswick minimum wage, 2002

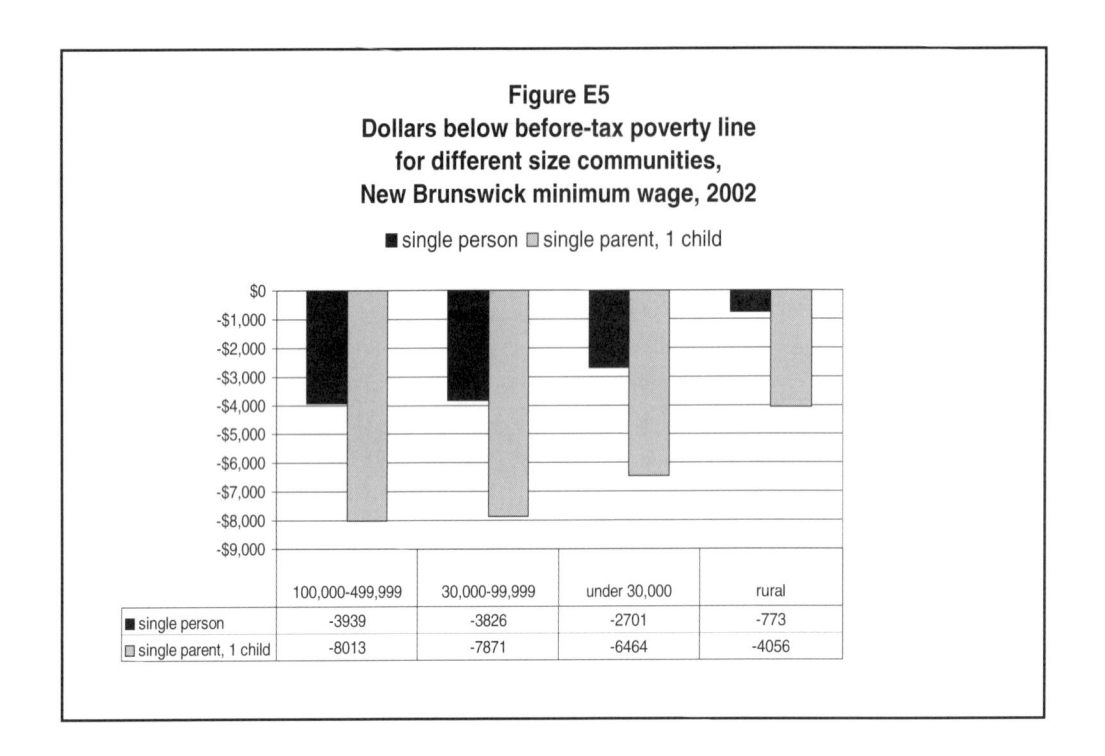

	100,000-499,999	30,000-99,999	under 30,000	rural
single person	-3939	-3826	-2701	-773
single parent, 1 child	-8013	-7871	-6464	-4056

between the minimum wage and the poverty line for one person in different size communities throughout the province.

Because the poverty line varies by family size, minimum wages (which do not vary by family size) fall farther below the poverty line for families than for single workers. We look at the poverty gap for a single parent with one child, which falls in the two-person family size category. In 2002, New Brunswick's minimum wage varied from 60.7 percent of the before-tax low income line for a two-person family in Saint John (in the 100,000-499,999 size category) to 61.1 percent for communities between 30,000 and 99,999, 65.7 percent for towns under 30,000 and 75.3 percent for rural areas. The minimum wage was $8,013 below the before-tax poverty line for a family of two in Saint John, $7,871 under for communities between 30,000 and 99,999, $6,464 below for towns under 30,000 and $4,056 beneath the poverty line for rural residents.

Trend in minimum wage as percentage of before-tax poverty lines (Figure E6)

The long-term trend when we compare the minimum wage to the poverty line (as measured by Statistics Canada's before-tax low income cut-offs, which vary by size of family and of community) mirrors

Figure E6
New Brunswick minimum wage as % of before-tax poverty line for largest city, 1965-2002

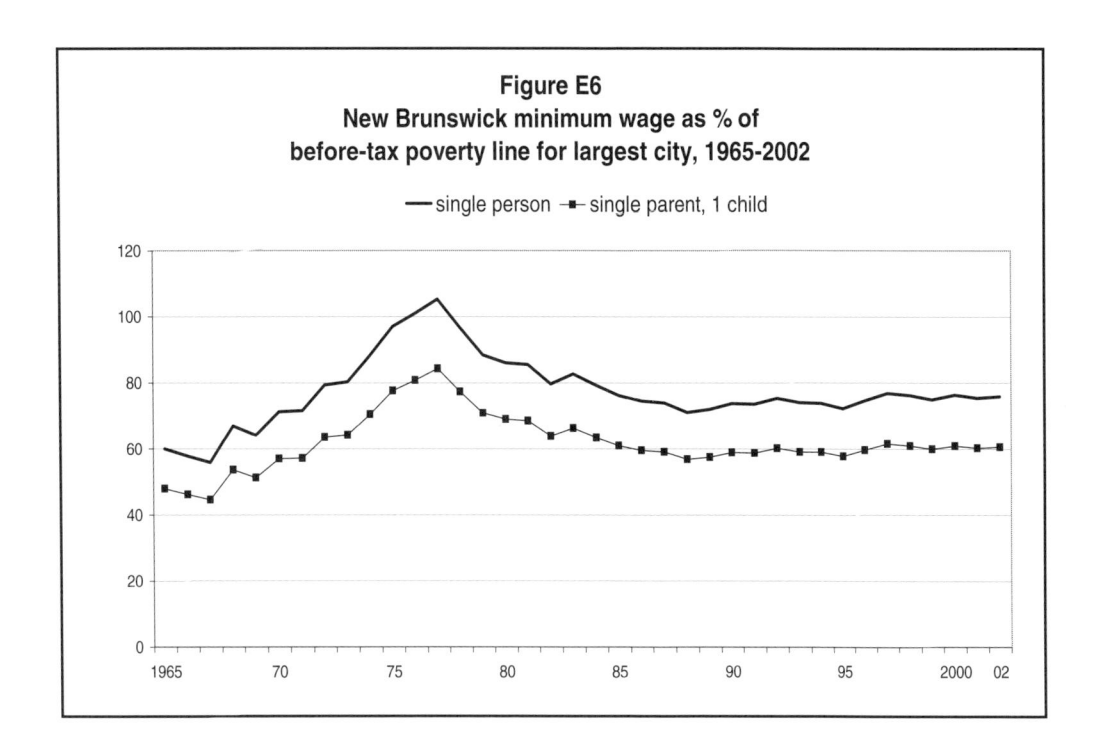

the trend in its dollar value. In 2002, the estimated before-tax poverty line for the largest city in the province (Saint John) was $16,295 for one person and $20,369 for a family of two.

New Brunswick's minimum wage rose from 60.0 percent of the before-tax poverty line for one person living in Saint John in 1965 to 105.3 percent in 1977, falling to 71.0 percent in 1988. However, the trend improved slightly in the 1990s and stood at 75.8 percent of the before-tax low income cut-off for one person in Saint John in 2002. For a two-person family (e.g., a single parent with one child), the minimum wage went from 48.0 percent of the before-tax poverty line in 1965 to a peak of 84.2 percent in 1977, declining to 56.8 percent in 1988 but rising to 60.7 percent of the poverty line in 2002. Figure E6 shows the trends.

Minimum wage compared to after-tax poverty lines (Figure E7)

Statistics Canada publishes after-tax low income cut-offs as well as before-tax low income cut-offs. Here we compare after-tax minimum wage incomes in New Brunswick for five types of household – single persons, single parents with one child, one-earner couples with two children, two-earner couples supporting two children on one-and-a-half minimum wages, and two-earner couples with two children and two full minimum wages – to the after-tax poverty lines for different size communities. 'After-tax minimum

Minimum Wages in Canada: A Statistical Portrait With Policy Implications

Figure E7
Dollars below/above after-tax poverty line
for different size communities, New Brunswick
after-tax minimum wage income, 2001

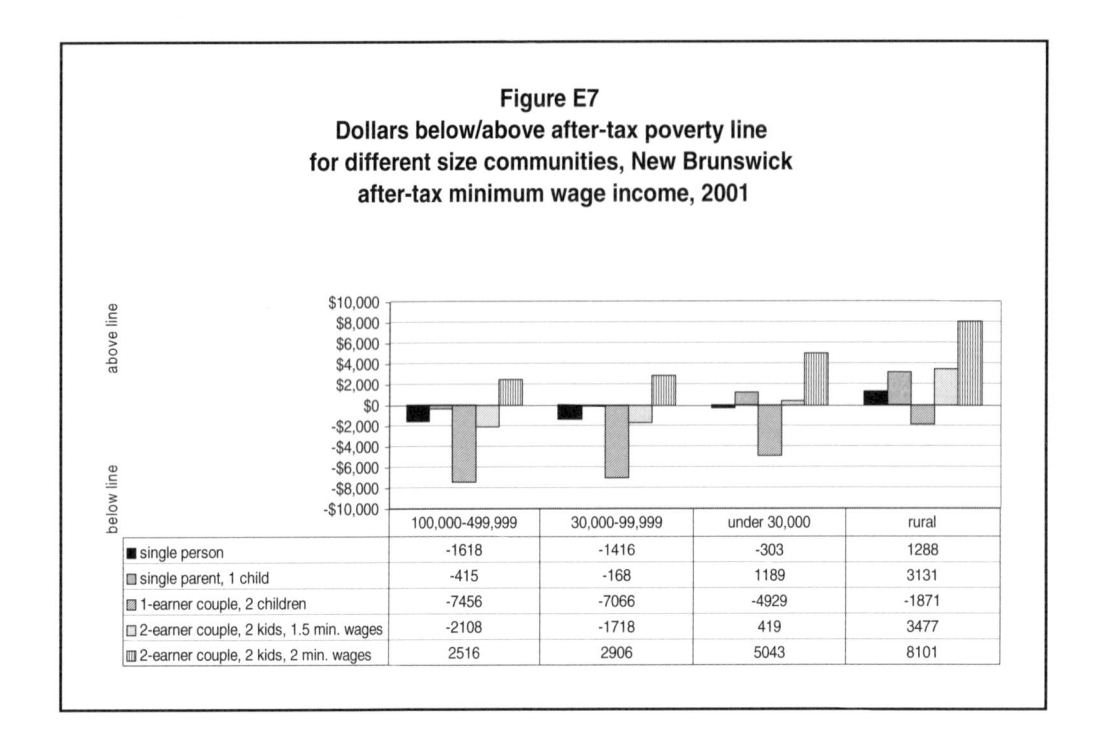

	100,000-499,999	30,000-99,999	under 30,000	rural
single person	-1618	-1416	-303	1288
single parent, 1 child	-415	-168	1189	3131
1-earner couple, 2 children	-7456	-7066	-4929	-1871
2-earner couple, 2 kids, 1.5 min. wages	-2108	-1718	419	3477
2-earner couple, 2 kids, 2 min. wages	2516	2906	5043	8101

wage incomes' means incomes from the minimum wage and available federal and provincial income programs minus federal and provincial income taxes.

For a single person earning the minimum wage, after-tax income came to $11,492,[27] which is $1,618 below the after-tax poverty line for Saint John, $1,416 below for centres of 30,000-99,999, $303 below for towns under 30,000 but $1,288 above the poverty line for rural residents. A single parent with one child received $15,582[28] in after-tax income from minimum wage earnings and federal and provincial child benefits and tax credits, which came to $415 below the after-tax poverty line for Saint John and $168 under for centers between of 30,000 and 99,999 but $1,189 above the line for towns under 30,000 and $3,131 above the poverty line for rural residents.

For a one-earner couple with two children, after-tax minimum wage income amounted to $17,744[29] – $7,456 below the after-tax poverty line for Saint John, $7,066 under for centres between 30,000 and 99,999, $4,929 below for towns smaller than 30,000 and $1,871 beneath the line for rural residents. The two-earner couple supporting two children on one-and-a-half minimum wages had after-tax minimum wage income of $23,092[30] – $2,108 below the after-tax poverty line for Saint John and $1,718 under for centres between 30,000 and 99,000 but $419 above the line for towns smaller than 30,000 and $3,477 over for rural residents. Disposable income for the two-earner couple in which both parents worked full time, year round at the minimum wage amounted to $27,715[31] – $2,516 over the after-tax poverty line for Saint John, $2,906 above the line for centres between 30,000 and 99,999, $5,043 over for towns smaller than 30,000 and $8,101 above the line for rural residents.

Contribution of child benefits

Child benefits supplement the incomes of the large majority of Canadian families and are especially important to low- and modest-income families. Improvements to the federal Canada Child Tax Benefit, and New Brunswick's creation of child benefit and earnings supplement programs, are boosting the incomes of minimum wage families and other working poor families.

The single-parent minimum wage worker with one child got $2,447 from the Canada Child Tax Benefit, $250 from the New Brunswick Child Tax Benefit and $250 from the New Brunswick Working Income Supplement, for a total of $2,947 – 19.7 percent of disposable income. The one-earner couple with two children received $4,250 from the Canada Child Tax Benefit, $500 from the New Brunswick Child Tax Benefit and $250 from the New Brunswick Working Income Supplement, for a combined child benefit of $5,000 worth 29.2 percent of disposable income.

The two-earner family in which one parent works full time, all year at the minimum wage and the other parent half that time got child benefits of $4,250 from the Canada Child Tax Benefit, $500 from the New Brunswick Child Benefit and $250 from the New Brunswick Working Income Supplement, totaling $5,000 or 22.5 percent of disposable income. The two-earner family in which both parents work full time, all year at the minimum wage received $3,670 from the Canada Child Tax Benefit, $144 from the New Brunswick Child Tax Benefit and $84 from the New Brunswick Working Income Supplement, for a combined child benefit of $3,898 or 14.7 percent of disposable income.

Minimum wage versus welfare (Figure E8)

For a single person earning the minimum wage in New Brunswick, disposable income – i.e., minimum wage earnings plus the refundable GST credit minus income and payroll taxes – amounted to $10,849 in 2001, which is a sizeable $7,475 more than the meagre $3,374 from welfare. Figure E8 gives the results.

Minimum wages also pay better than welfare for a single parent with one child age 2, though the advantage is not as great as for single people. Disposable income from after-tax minimum wage earnings,

Figure E8
Minimum wage versus welfare in New Brunswick, by household type

	single person	single parent, 1 child	one-earner couple, 2 children	couple, 2 kids, 1.5 min. wages	couple, 2 kids, 2 min. wages
minimum wage disposable income	10849	14939	17101	22203	26430
welfare income	3374	12888	16206	16206	16206

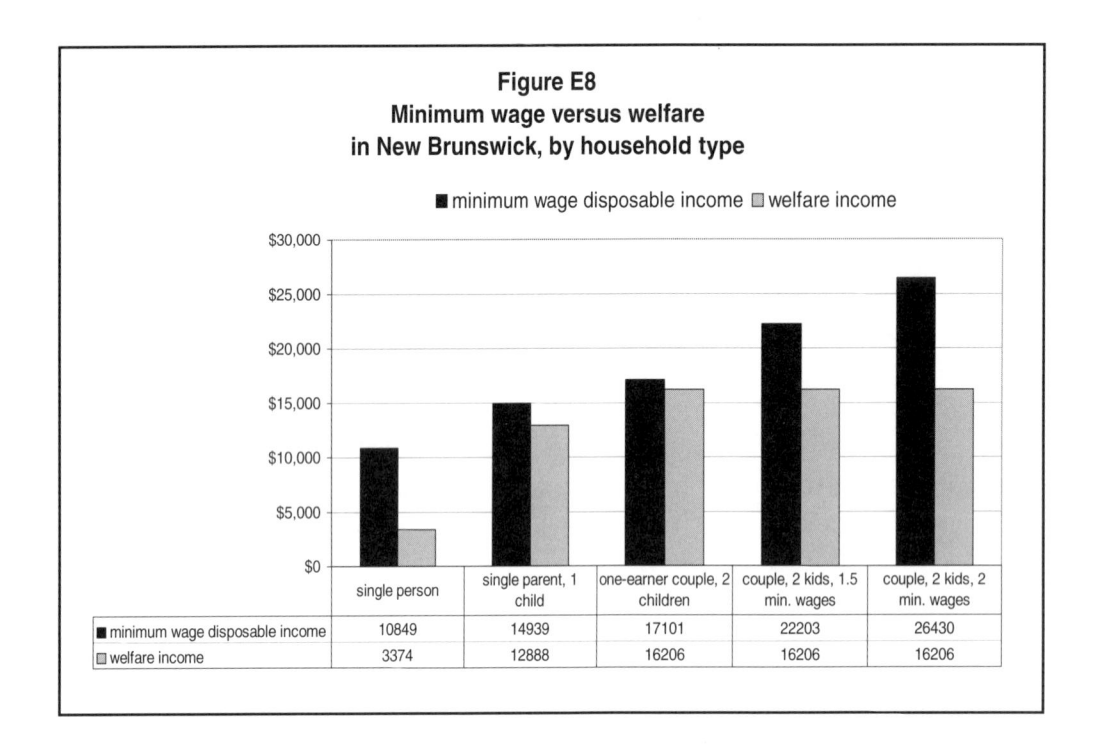

child benefits and the refundable GST credit amounted to $14,939 in 2001, or $2,051 more than the $12,888 from welfare, child benefits and the GST credit.

However, the minimum wage advantage is much smaller for a one-earner couple earning the minimum wage and supporting two children aged 10 and 15. Total disposable income from minimum wages, child benefits and the refundable GST credit came to $17,101, or just $895 more than the $16,206 from welfare, child benefits and the GST tax credit.

For two-parent families to earn more than welfare, both parents must work. We look at two examples.

In the first family, one parent works full time, year round at the minimum wage while the other earns half this amount (i.e., works part-time and/or part-year); as above, there are two children aged 10 and 15. This family's disposable income from one-and-a-half minimum wages came to $22,203 in 2001 or $5,997 more than the $16,206 from welfare, child benefits and the refundable GST credit.

The other two-earner family earns double the minimum wage since we assume that both parents work full time, year round at the minimum wage. Total disposable income was $26,430 or a hefty $10,224 more than the $16,206 from welfare and other government income benefits.

b. Minimum Wage Workers in New Brunswick

The following text with illustrative graphs analyzes key characteristics of minimum wage workers in New Brunswick. Appendix 2 provides detailed statistics in tabular form (pages 291-293).

Interprovincial rank: incidence of minimum wage workers (Figure E9)

In 2000, an estimated 17,500 New Brunswickers – 6.0 percent of the total 293,100 employees – worked for the minimum wage. New Brunswick's 6.0 percent figure means that it has the second-highest incidence of minimum wage workers in Canada, after Newfoundland (8.7 percent). Alberta, with only 2.0 percent of its workforce at the minimum wage, ranks lowest. Figure E9 shows the results. The national minimum wage incidence was 4.6 percent.

Moreover, minimum wage workers are overrepresented in New Brunswick. While the province accounts for 3.0 percent of all minimum wage workers in the country, it has a smaller share of all employees (2.3 percent), producing an index of 1.29 (the higher the result above 1.00, the more overrepresented are minimum wage workers).

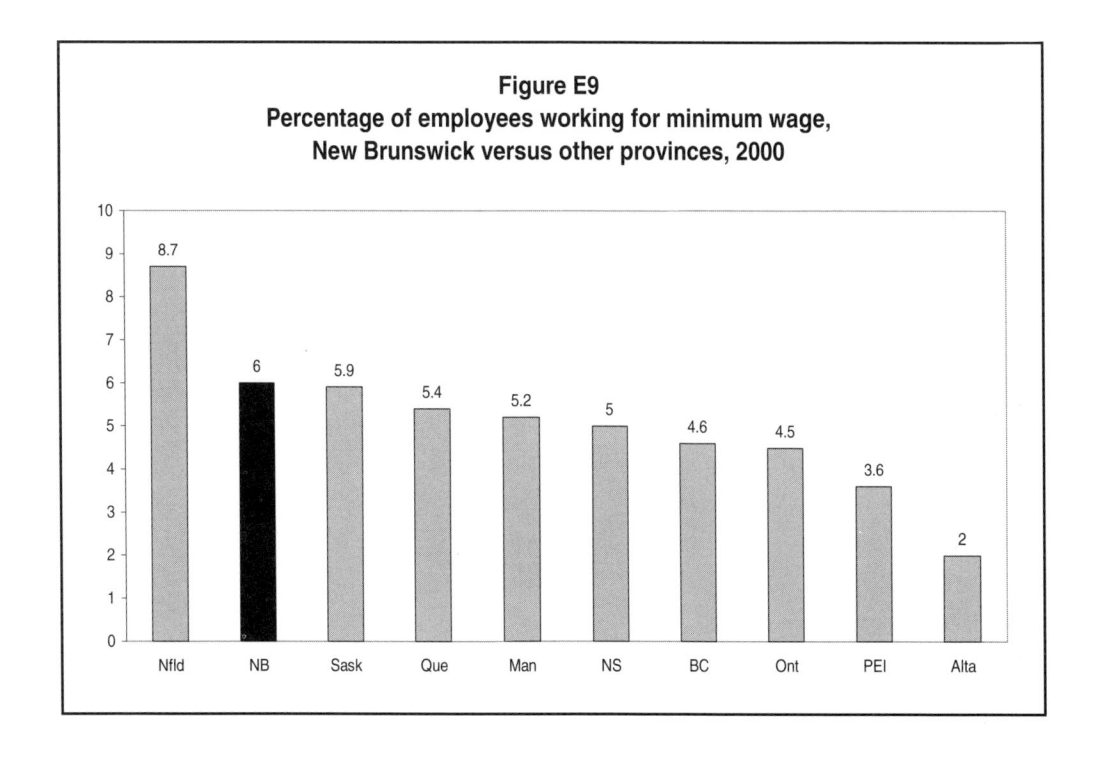

Figure E9
Percentage of employees working for minimum wage, New Brunswick versus other provinces, 2000

Province	Percentage
Nfld	8.7
NB	6
Sask	5.9
Que	5.4
Man	5.2
NS	5
BC	4.6
Ont	4.5
PEI	3.6
Alta	2

Gender and age (Figures E10-E13)

In New Brunswick as in the rest of Canada, women run a higher risk of working for minimum wage than men, and women also make up the majority of the minimum wage workforce.

In 2000, 8.4 percent of New Brunswick female employees worked for minimum wage compared to only 3.8 percent of male workers. Of the total 17,500 minimum wage workers, 11,800 – 67.4 percent – were women and 5,700 – 32.6 percent – were men, as shown in Figure E10.

Women are overrepresented in New Brunswick's minimum wage workforce. They constituted 67.4 percent of minimum wage workers but only 48.2 percent of all the province's employees in 2000. Men are underrepresented. They accounted for less than one-third (32.6 percent) of minimum wage workers but slightly more than half (51.8 percent) of all employees.

The gender bias among minimum wage workers holds when we control for major age categories, as seen in Figure E11. While younger workers of both sexes run a higher risk of working for minimum wage, women still fare worse than men within each age category.

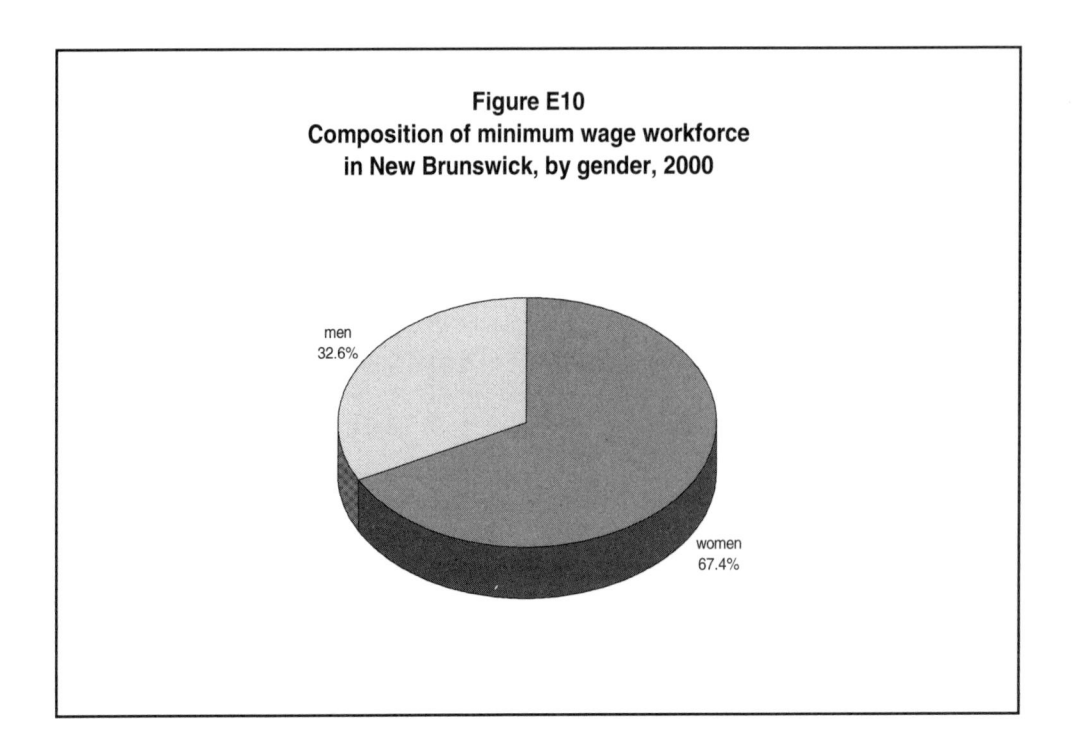

Figure E10
Composition of minimum wage workforce in New Brunswick, by gender, 2000

men 32.6%
women 67.4%

Figure E11
Percentage of employees working for minimum wage in New Brunswick, by gender and age, 2000

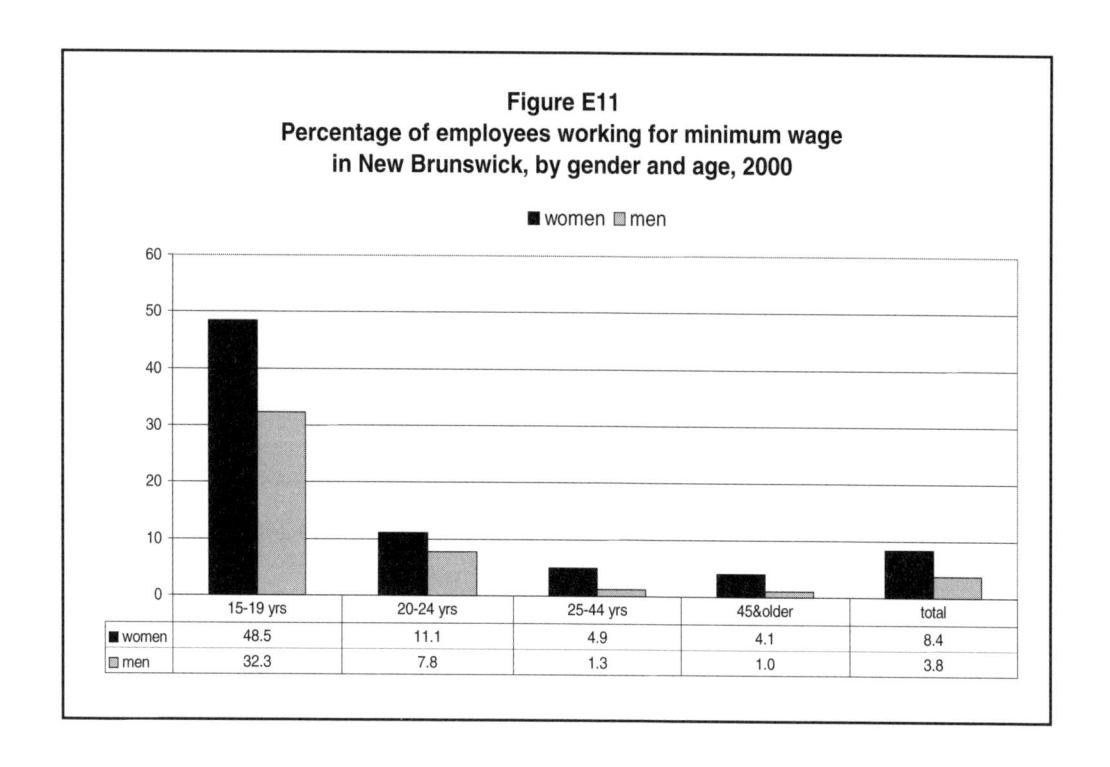

	15-19 yrs	20-24 yrs	25-44 yrs	45&older	total
women	48.5	11.1	4.9	4.1	8.4
men	32.3	7.8	1.3	1.0	3.8

Figure E12
Share of minimum wage workers versus share of all employees in New Brunswick, by age group, 2000

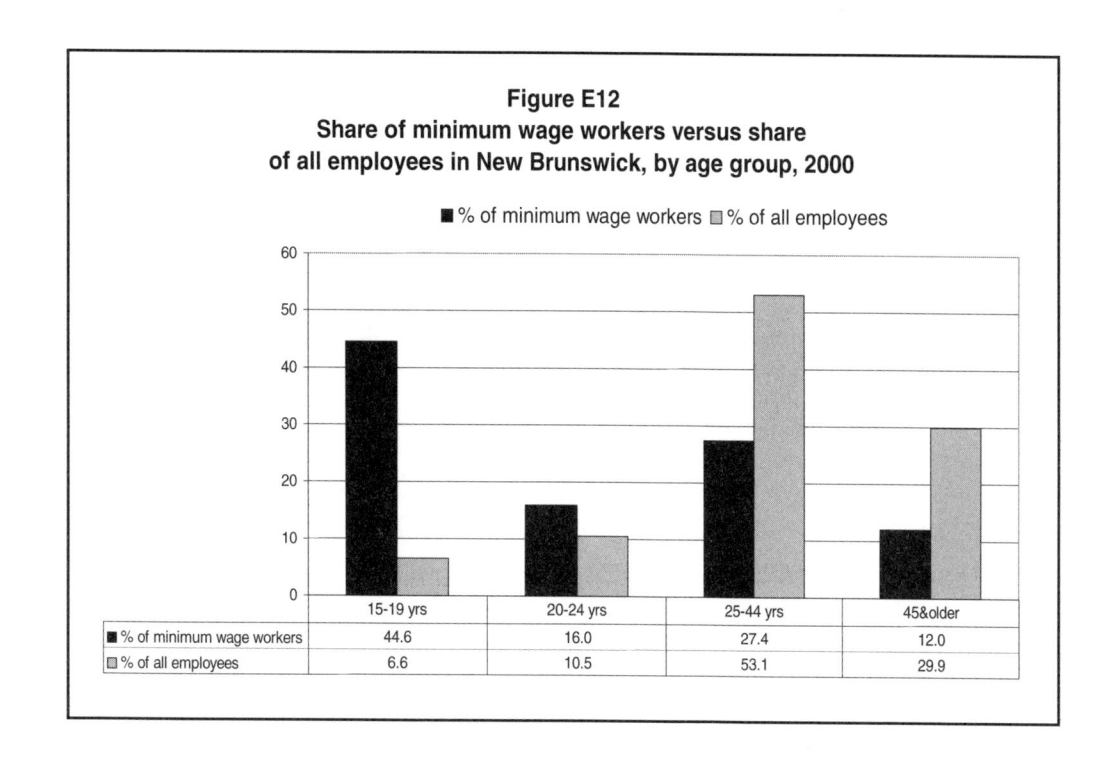

	15-19 yrs	20-24 yrs	25-44 yrs	45&older
% of minimum wage workers	44.6	16.0	27.4	12.0
% of all employees	6.6	10.5	53.1	29.9

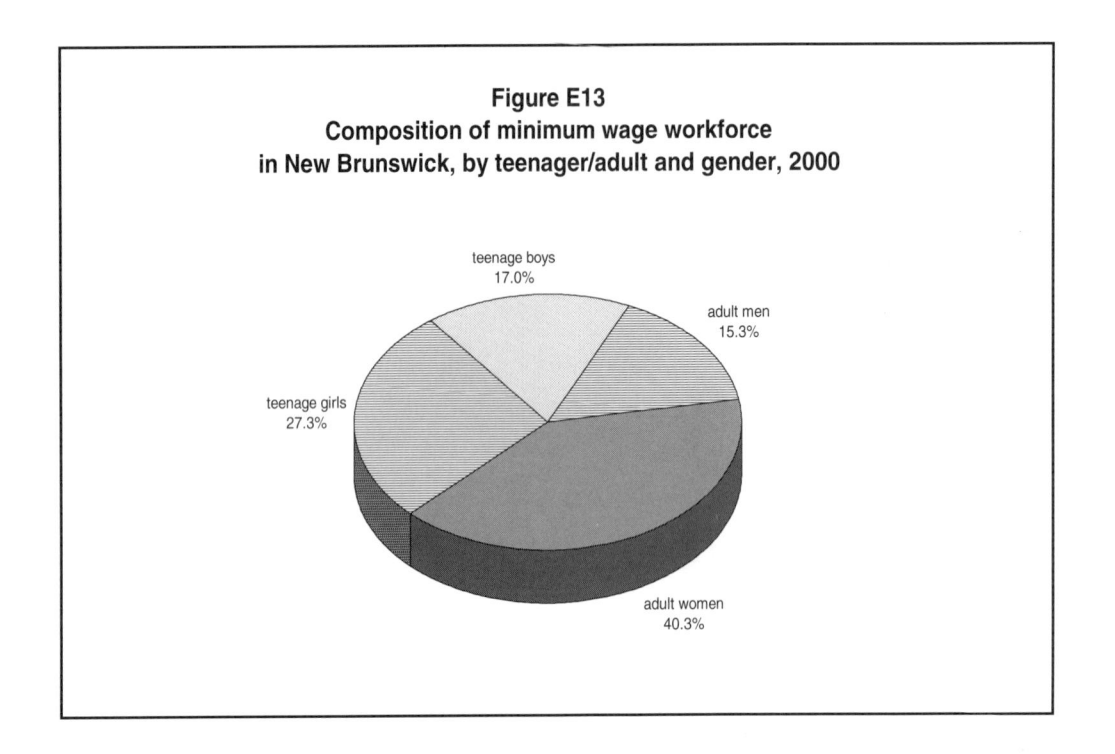

**Figure E13
Composition of minimum wage workforce
in New Brunswick, by teenager/adult and gender, 2000**

- teenage boys: 17.0%
- adult men: 15.3%
- adult women: 40.3%
- teenage girls: 27.3%

Among female workers aged 15 to 19, 48.5 percent worked for the minimum wage in 2000 in contrast to 32.3 percent of male workers in the same age group. Among workers 20-24, 11.1 percent of women compared to 7.8 percent of men worked for the minimum wage. Among workers 25-44, 4.9 percent of women as opposed to 1.3 percent of men were at the bottom of the wage ladder. Among employees 45 and older, 4.1 percent of women but only 1.0 percent of men worked for the minimum wage in New Brunswick.

The minimum wage risk gap between the sexes is wider for older workers. Women in the 15-24 age group are 1.5 times more likely to work for the minimum wage than men in that age group, but the ratio increases to 3.7 for those aged 25-44 and 4.1 for those over 45.

Young people not only are more likely to work for minimum wage than other employees, but the young also make up a large proportion of the minimum wage workforce. Figure E12 compares the age makeup of minimum wage workers and all employees in New Brunswick. A sizeable proportion (44.6 percent) of minimum wage workers are in the 15-19 age group, as opposed to just 6.6 percent of all employees. Employees aged 20-24 represent 16.0 percent of minimum wage workers as opposed to 10.5 percent of all workers. All told, six in ten minimum wage workers in the province (60.6 percent) are under 25 years of age.

The opposite holds for older workers in New Brunswick. While a sizeable proportion – 27.4 percent – of minimum wage workers are between 25 and 44, that age group constitutes a much larger proportion – 53.1 percent or more than half – of all employees. Workers aged 45 and older make up just 12.0 percent of minimum wage employees but 29.9 percent all employees.

Figure E13 divides the minimum wage workforce in New Brunswick into teenage girls and boys and adult women and men. Adult women are the largest group, at 7,100 or 40.3 percent of the total, followed by teenage girls (4,800 or 27.3 percent), teenage boys (3,000 or 17.0 percent) and adult men (2,700 or 15.3 percent). The majority (55.6 percent) of New Brunswick's minimum wage workers are adults; the national average is a bit lower (52.9 percent).

Education (Figures E14 and E15)

Figure E14 shows the incidence of minimum wage workers in New Brunswick according to level of education.

At first glance, the relationship between level of education and incidence of minimum wage employment does not seem to correspond to common sense: Workers in the lowest educational group

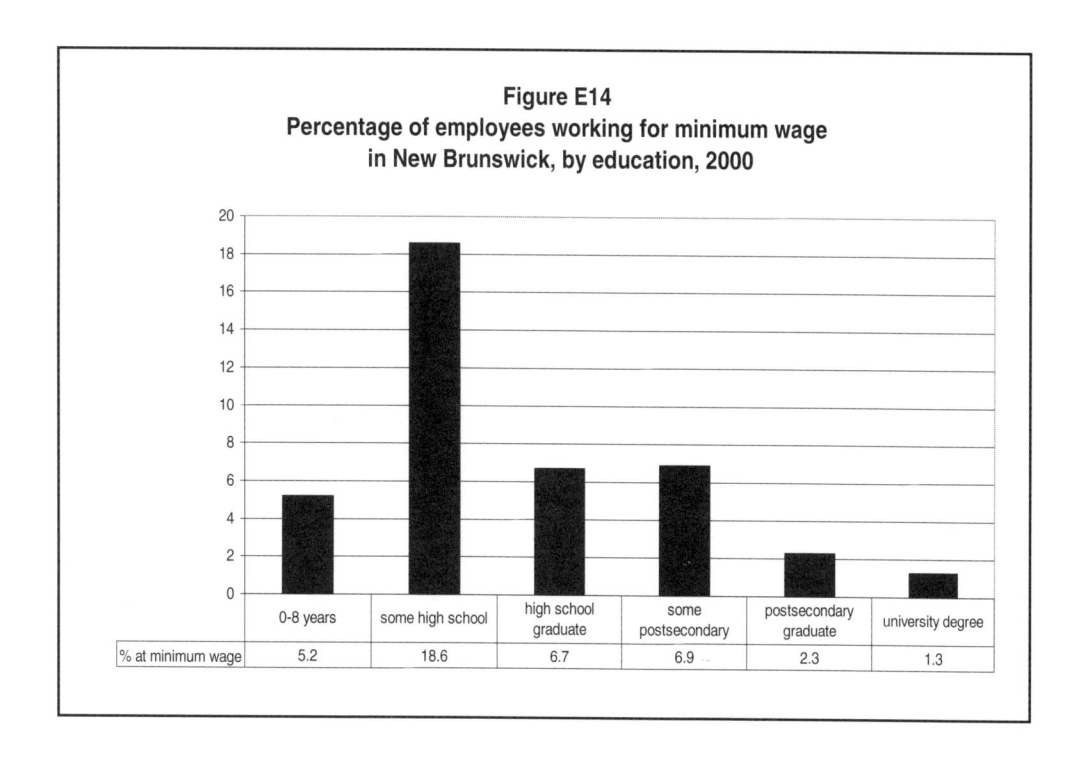

Figure E14
Percentage of employees working for minimum wage in New Brunswick, by education, 2000

	0-8 years	some high school	high school graduate	some postsecondary	postsecondary graduate	university degree
% at minimum wage	5.2	18.6	6.7	6.9	2.3	1.3

Figure E15
Composition of minimum wage workforce in New Brunswick, by education, 2000

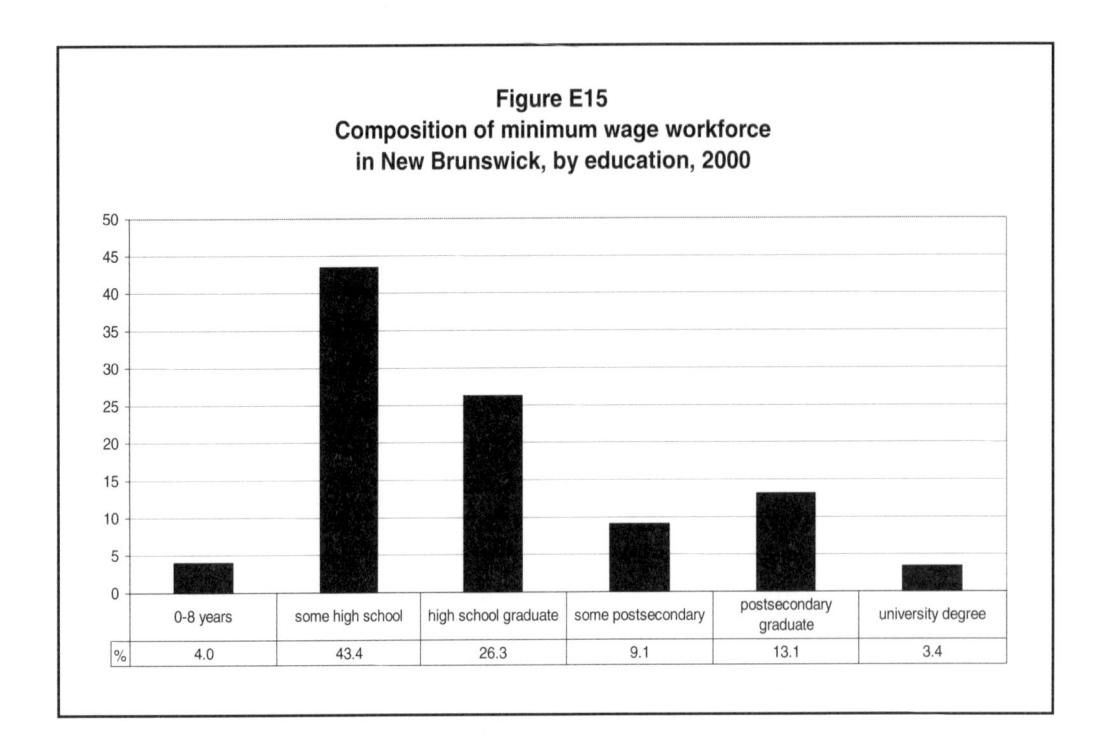

	0-8 years	some high school	high school graduate	some postsecondary	postsecondary graduate	university degree
%	4.0	43.4	26.3	9.1	13.1	3.4

(elementary education only) are less likely to work for minimum wage (5.2 percent do) than those with some high school (18.6 percent), while those with some postsecondary education run a slightly higher risk (6.9) than high school graduates (6.7 percent). However, as one would expect, the chances of working for minimum wage are lowest for the two highest education categories – 2.3 percent for those with a postsecondary certificate or diploma (e.g., from a community college or vocational institute) and only 1.3 percent for those with a university degree.

Once we look at the education-minimum wage link for different age groups, the reasons for the apparently inconsistent relationship comes clear: Young people working at part-time or seasonal (i.e., summer) jobs – typically paying the minimum or a low wage – figure prominently in the 'some high school' and 'some postsecondary education' categories; they are still at high school, community college or university, whereas workers in the other educational categories have completed their education.

Figure E15 shows each educational group's share of New Brunswick's minimum wage workforce in 2000. The largest group of minimum wage workers are those with some high school (43.4 percent), followed by high school graduates (26.3 percent), postsecondary graduates (13.1 percent), those with some postsecondary education (9.1 percent), workers with only 0-8 years of education (4.0 percent) and university graduates (3.4 percent). Many minimum wage workers are students (high school or postsecondary) pursuing their education. A sizeable group of minimum wage workers (25.6 percent) have some form of postsecondary education.

Full-time and part-time work (Figure E16 and E17)

The fact that young people are more likely to work part time helps explain why workers still pursuing their education tend to face a higher risk of minimum wage work than those who have completed their schooling and are working full time. Figure E16 indicates that 21.8 percent of part-time workers are at the minimum wage compared to only 3.3 percent of those employed full time. While the majority of minimum wage workers in New Brunswick (52.6 percent) work part time, a sizeable group (47.4 percent) are employed part time, as indicated in Figure E17.

Gender alters the relationship between full-time and part-time work and the minimum wage. Women who work part time in New Brunswick run a lesser risk of being at the bottom of the wage ladder than do men who work part time (20.4 and 25.0 percent, respectively). However, women employed full time are more likely than men in that group to earn the minimum wage (4.9 and 2.1 percent, respectively).

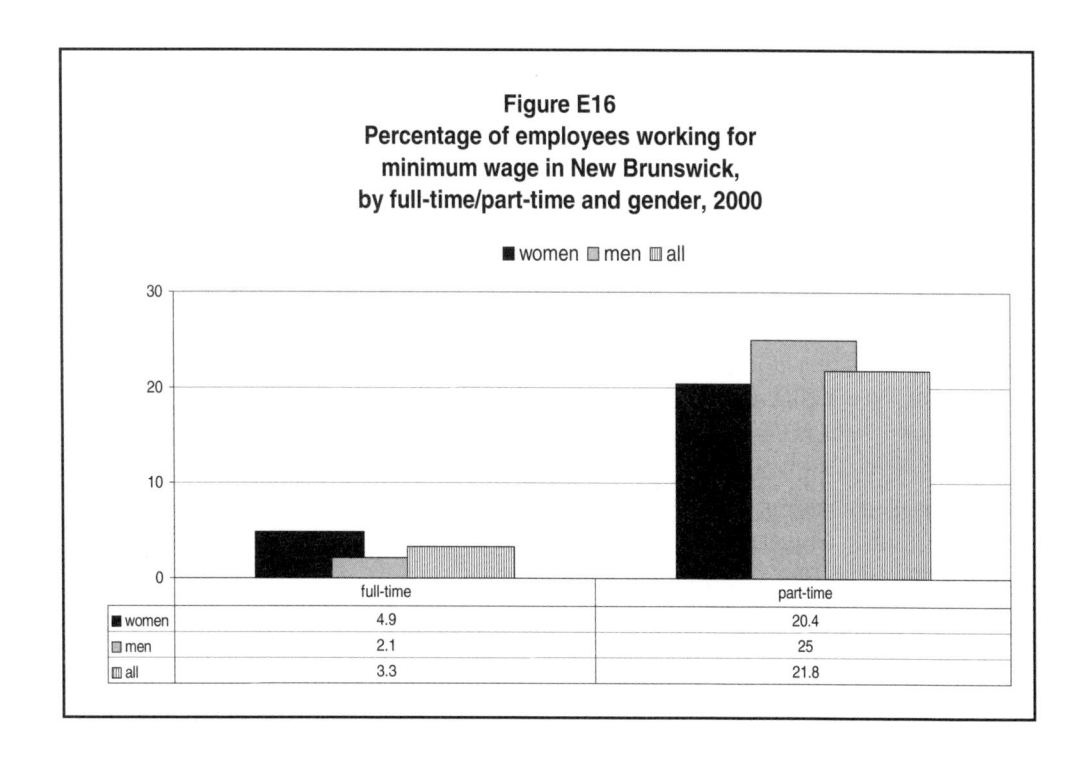

Figure E16
Percentage of employees working for minimum wage in New Brunswick, by full-time/part-time and gender, 2000

	full-time	part-time
women	4.9	20.4
men	2.1	25
all	3.3	21.8

**Figure E17
Composition of minimum wage workforce in
New Brunswick, full-time and part-time workers, 2000**

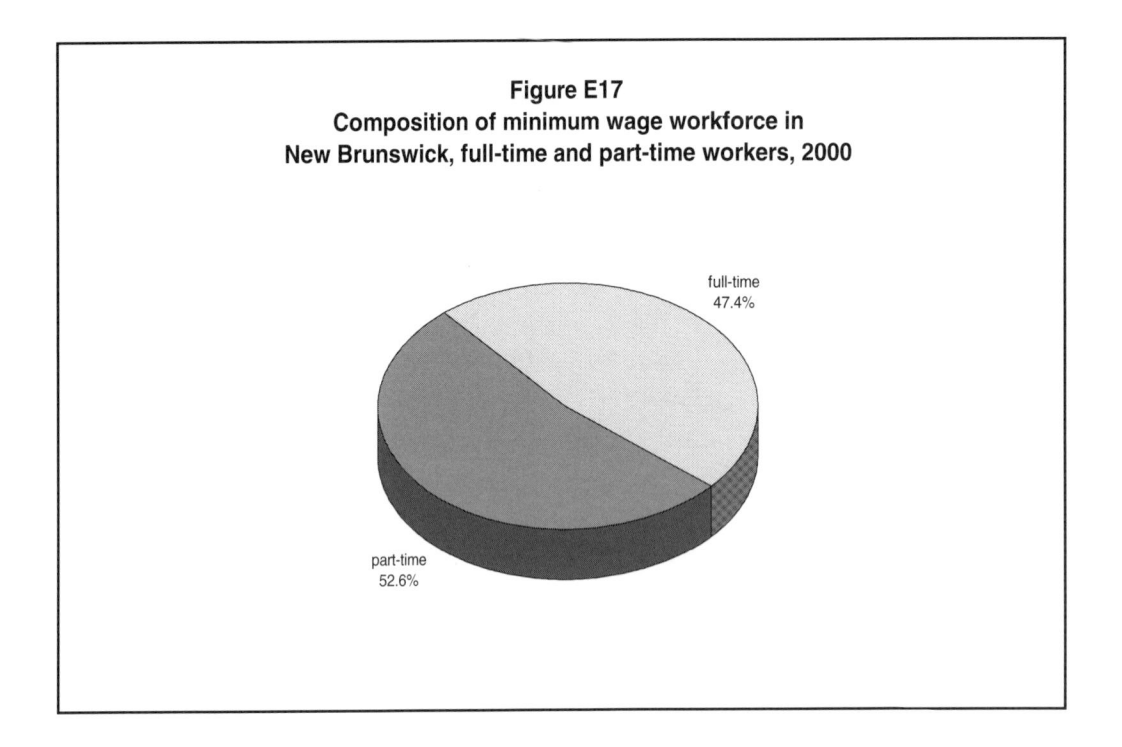

full-time 47.4%
part-time 52.6%

Women make up the majority of minimum wage employees in the province working both full time (65.1 percent are women) and part time (69.6 percent are women). Among all employees, though, women constitute a minority of full-time workers (43.8 percent) but the bulk of part-time workers (74.4 percent).

Family status (Figure E18)

We noted above that six in ten of New Brunswick's minimum wage workers are under 25 years of age. Light on this fundamental fact of the minimum wage workforce is shed by information on family status, illustrated by Figure E18, which shows that the largest group of minimum wage workers – 10,300 or 59.5 percent of the total – are older children living with their parents (or relatives with relatives, as in the case of a niece or nephew living with an aunt and uncle, or grandchildren with grandparents). Of this category, 7,500 or 72.8 percent are aged 15-19, 1,900 or 18.4 percent are 20-24 and the remaining 800 or 7.8 percent are 25 or older. Close to half (5,000 or 48.5 percent) are still in school and working part-time or part-year (e.g., in summer).

The next largest group of minimum wage workers in New Brunswick – 5,300 or 30.6 percent of the total – are members of couples (married or living together). In most cases (4,100 or 77.4 percent of

QUEBEC

a. Minimum Wages in Quebec

Interprovincial rank: dollar value of minimum wages (Figure F1)

Quebec's minimum wage went from $7.00 to $7.20 an hour on October 1, 2002, for an hourly average of $7.05 in 2002. In 2002, Quebec ranked third-highest among Canada's ten provinces and three territories, ahead of Ontario ($6.85) and behind only Yukon ($7.20) and British Columbia ($8.00). Figure F1 shows the results.

Trend in dollar value of minimum wage (Figure F2)

Because minimum wages are not indexed, their value changes over time. Figure F2 shows the trend in Quebec's minimum wage from 1965 to 2002; each year's average minimum wage has been converted to inflation-adjusted (i.e., constant) 2002 dollars to show the real trend, after taking into account the impact of inflation on the dollar.

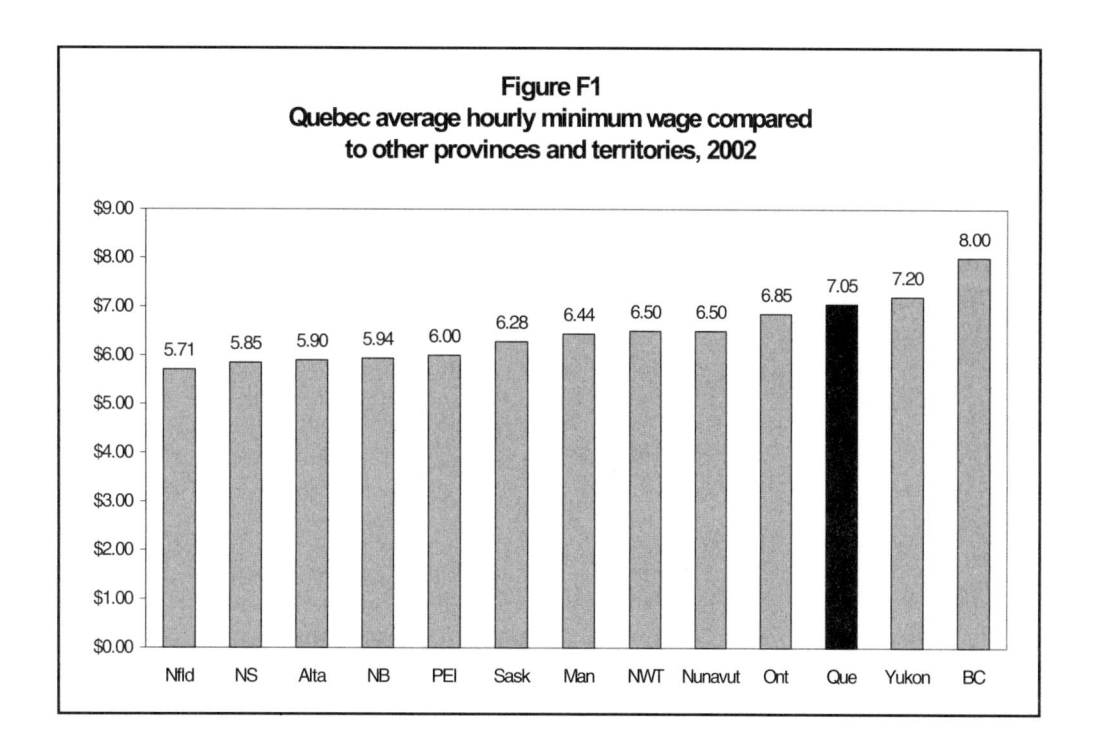

Figure F1
Quebec average hourly minimum wage compared to other provinces and territories, 2002

Nfld	NS	Alta	NB	PEI	Sask	Man	NWT	Nunavut	Ont	Que	Yukon	BC
5.71	5.85	5.90	5.94	6.00	6.28	6.44	6.50	6.50	6.85	7.05	7.20	8.00

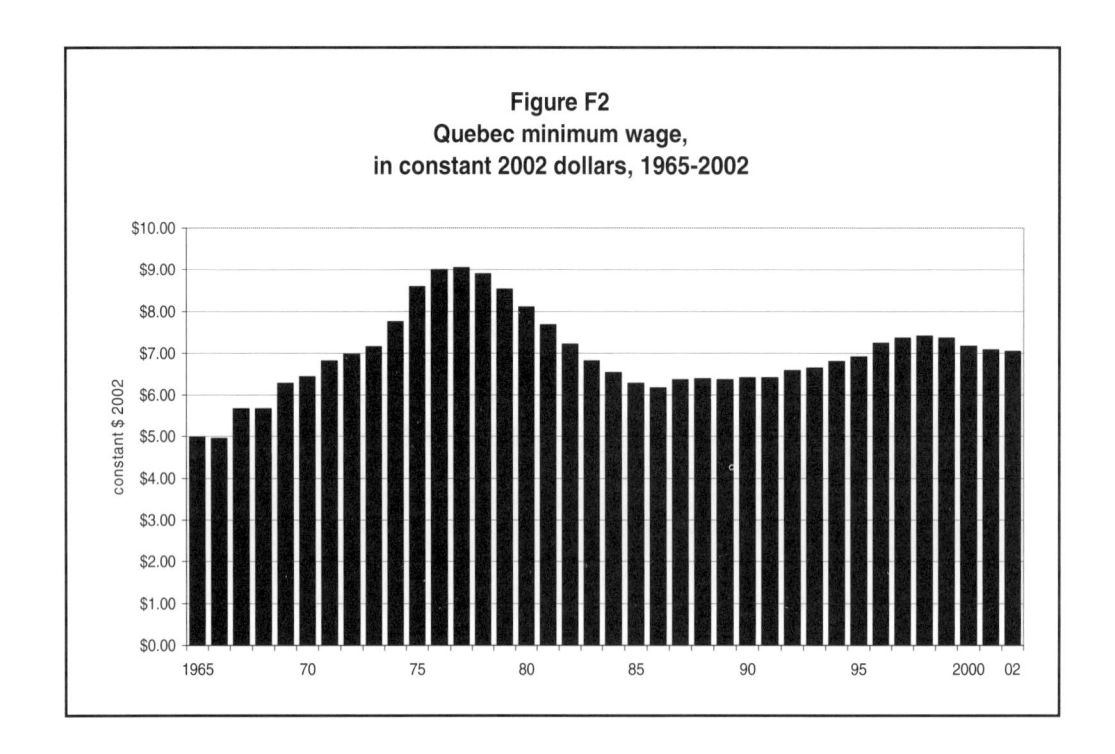

**Figure F2
Quebec minimum wage,
in constant 2002 dollars, 1965-2002**

Quebec's minimum wage increased substantially overall between 1965 ($4.99) and its 1977 peak ($9.06), declined considerably in the early 1980s (to $6.17 in 1986), recovered gradually in the 1990s to reach $7.41 in 1998 and then slipped steadily to $7.05 by 2002. Its 2002 value was $2.01 or 22.2 percent less than the 1977 high point, though a substantial $2.06 or 41.3 percent more than in 1965.

Interprovincial rank: minimum wages as percentage of average earnings (Figure F3)

Quebec ranks second-highest in Canada in terms of how its minimum wage compares to its average wage. In 2001 (the most recent year for which data on average earnings are available), Quebec's $6.99 minimum wage represented 44.8 percent of its $15.59 hourly average earnings. Only British Columbia, at 46.2 percent, was higher than Quebec. Figure F3 shows the rankings.

Trends in minimum wage and average earnings (Figure F4)

The black line in Figure F4 shows the trend in the minimum wage, the gray line the trend in average earnings and the vertical bars the trend in the minimum wage as a percentage of average earnings. Read the

**Figure F3
Quebec minimum wage as % of average earnings,
compared to other provinces and territories, 2001**

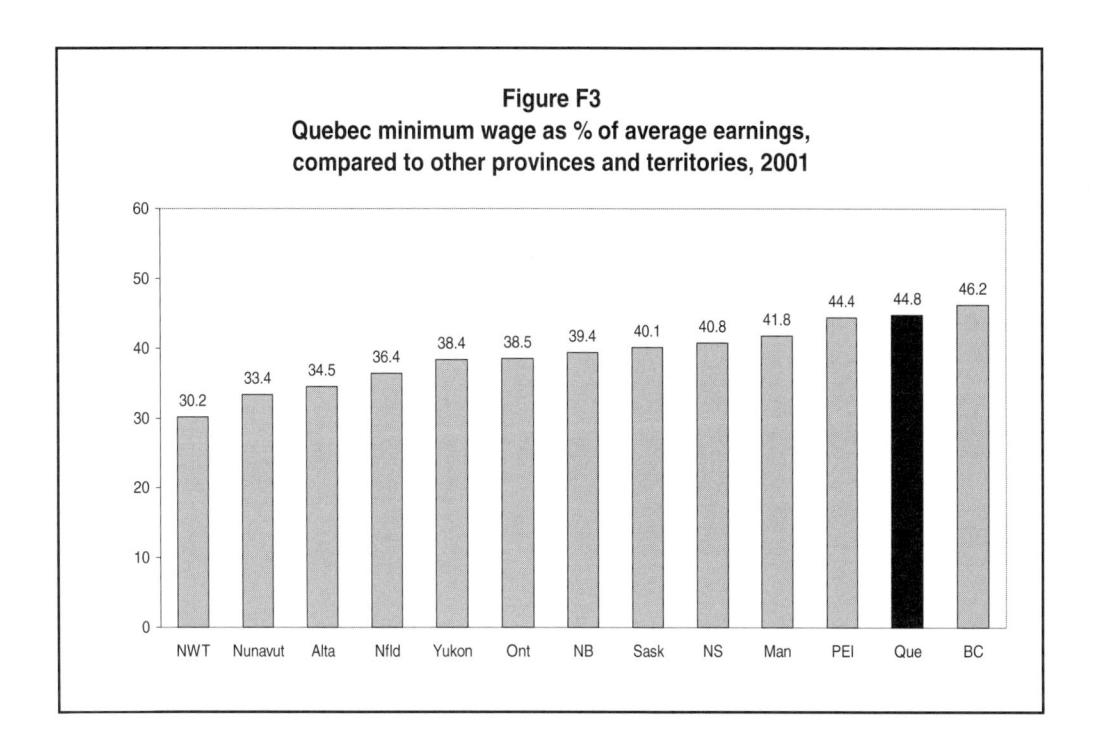

NWT	Nunavut	Alta	Nfld	Yukon	Ont	NB	Sask	NS	Man	PEI	Que	BC
30.2	33.4	34.5	36.4	38.4	38.5	39.4	40.1	40.8	41.8	44.4	44.8	46.2

**Figure F4
Quebec minimum wage compared
to average earnings, 1965-2001**

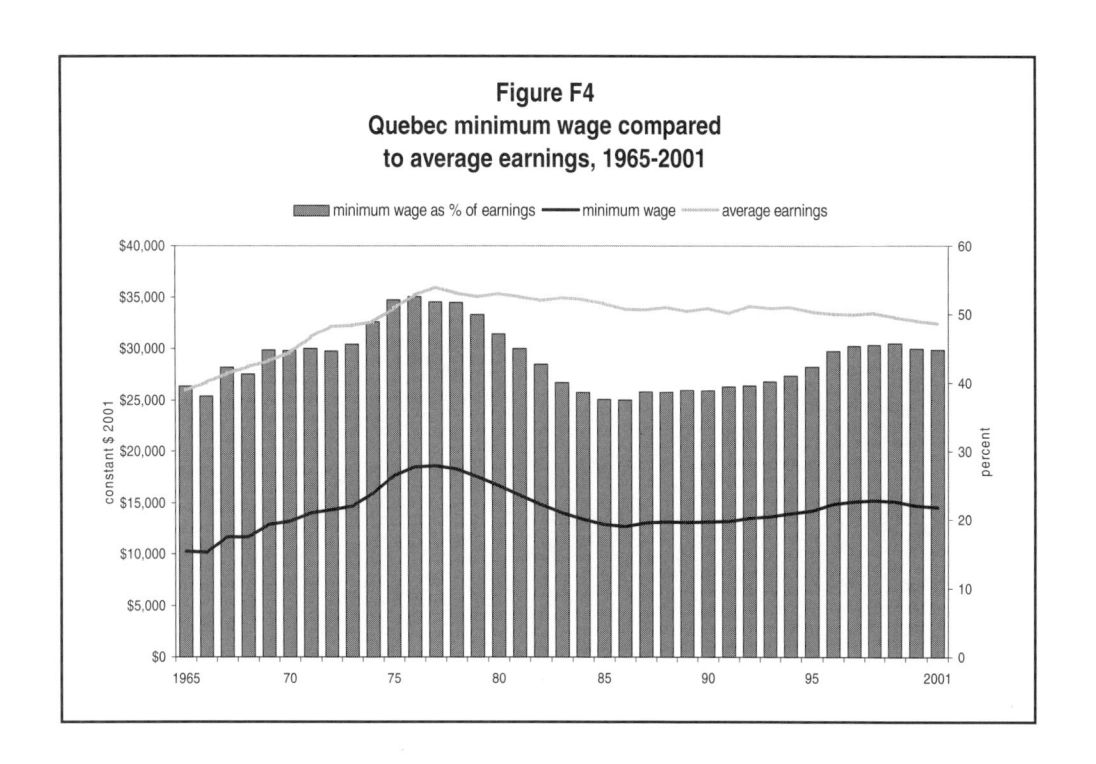

left-hand axis for the minimum wage and average earnings and the right-hand axis for the minimum wage as a percentage of earnings.

Quebec's minimum wage rose relative to average earnings between 1965 and 1976, declined until 1985 and then recovered some of its lost ground, though not fully back to its mid-1970s level. The minimum wage increased from 39.5 percent of average earnings in 1965 to 52.5 percent in 1976, fell to a low of 37.5 percent in 1985 and then recovered to 45.8 percent by 1999, though it has slipped a bit to 44.8 percent in 2001.

Average earnings (expressed in constant 2001 dollars) went from $25,917 in 1965 to a peak of $35,920 in 1977 and then drifted slowly down to reach $32,434 in 2001. On an annual (full-time, all-year) basis, the minimum wage went from $10,247 in 1965 to $18,599 in 1977, fell to $12,668 in 1986 and recovered to $15,213 in 1998, though it slipped to $14,544 by 2001.

Minimum wage compared to before-tax poverty lines (Figure F5)

Statistics Canada publishes two sets of low income cut-offs. The before-tax low income cut-offs are based on gross, pre-tax income (i.e., income from employment, investments, private pensions and other

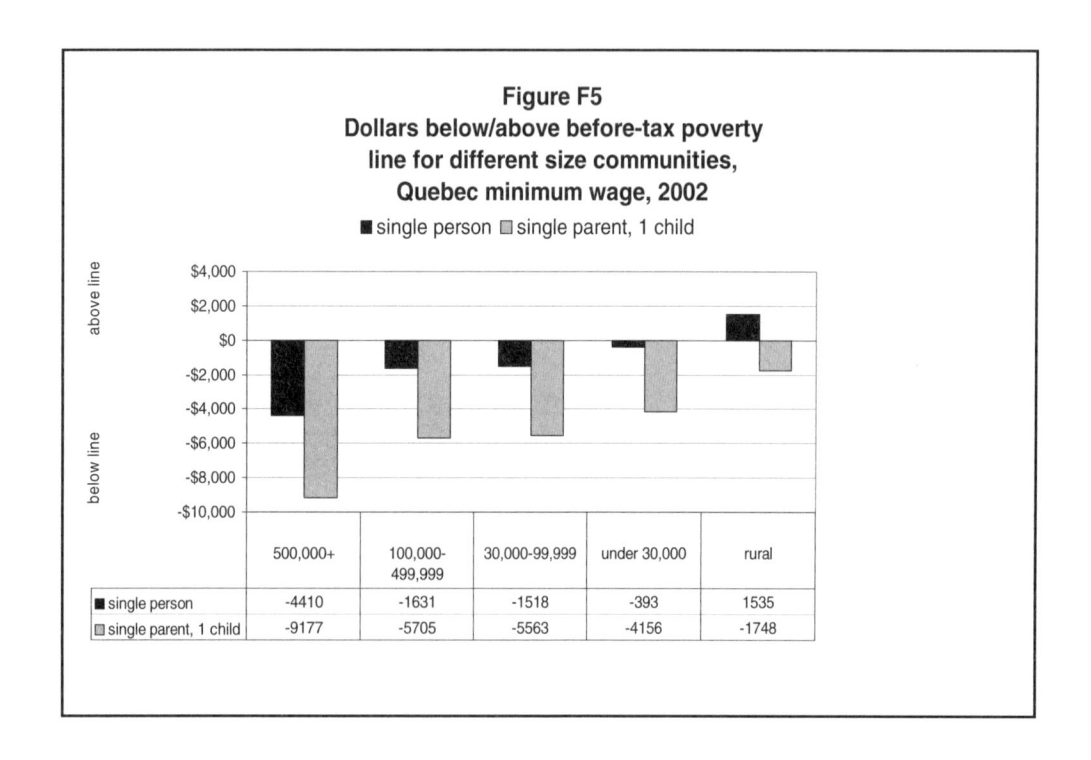

**Figure F5
Dollars below/above before-tax poverty line for different size communities, Quebec minimum wage, 2002**

	500,000+	100,000-499,999	30,000-99,999	under 30,000	rural
single person	-4410	-1631	-1518	-393	1535
single parent, 1 child	-9177	-5705	-5563	-4156	-1748

private sources plus income from government programs such as public pensions, Employment Insurance, child benefits and welfare). The after-tax low income cut-offs use the same definition of income but also factor into the picture the federal and provincial income taxes that Canadians pay. We first compare the minimum wage to the before-tax poverty lines.

Because the poverty line is lower for smaller communities, the minimum wage represents a larger proportion of the poverty line in smaller communities. In 2002, Quebec's minimum wage ranged from 76.9 percent of the before-tax low income line for one person in metropolitan centres with more than 500,000 residents (Montreal and Quebec City) to 90.0 percent for cities between 100,000 and 499,999 (Chicoutimi-Jonquière, Sherbrooke and Trois-Rivières), 90.6 percent for small urban areas between 30,000 and 99,999, 97.4 percent for towns under 30,000 and 111.7 percent for rural residents.

Quebec's minimum wage in 2002 fell $4,410 short of the before-tax low income line for one person in metropolitan centers (Montreal and Quebec City), $1,631 below the line in cities between 100,000 and 499,999, $1,518 below the line for communities between 30,000 and 99,999 inhabitants and $393 below for towns under 30,000, though it was $1,535 above the poverty line for rural areas. Figure F5 shows the dollar gap between the minimum wage and the poverty line for one person in different size communities throughout Quebec.

Because the poverty line varies by family size, minimum wages (which do not vary by family size) fall farther below the poverty line for families than for single workers. We look at the poverty gap for a single parent with one child, which falls in the two-person family size category. In 2002, Quebec's minimum wage varied from 61.5 percent of the low income line for a two-person family in cities of 500,000 or larger (Montreal and Quebec City) to 72.0 percent for cities between 100,000 and 499,999, 72.5 percent for communities between 30,000 and 99,999 inhabitants, 77.9 percent for towns under 30,000 and 89.3 percent for rural residents. Quebec's minimum wage was $9,177 below the before-tax low income cut-off for a family of two living in cities with more than 500,000 inhabitants (Montreal and Quebec City), $5,705 below the line for cities in the 100,000 to 499,999 category, $5,563 beneath the line for communities between 30,000 and 99,999 inhabitants, $4,156 below for towns under 30,000 and $1,748 under the poverty line for rural areas.

Trend in minimum wage as percentage of before-tax poverty lines (Figure F6)

The long-term trend when we compare the minimum wage to the poverty line (as measured by Statistics Canada's low income cut-offs, which vary by size of family and of community) is the same as the trend in dollar value. In 2002, the estimated before-tax low income line for the largest cities in Quebec (Montreal and Quebec City, with populations over 500,000) was $19,074 for one person and $23,841 for a family of two.

**Figure F6
Quebec minimum wage as % of before-tax
poverty line for largest cities, 1965-2002**

— single person   -■- single parent with one child

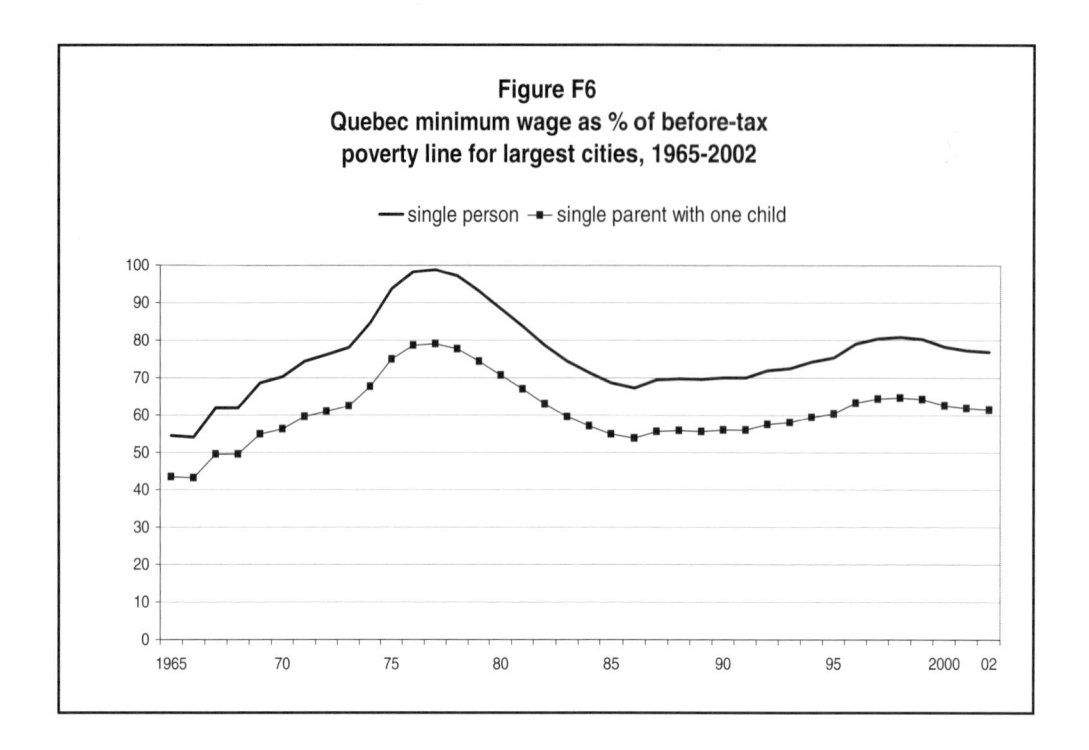

Quebec's minimum wage rose from 54.4 percent of the before-tax poverty line for one person in 1965 to 98.8 percent in 1977, falling back down to 67.3 percent in 1986. The trend then improved throughout the second half of the 1980s and most of the 1990s and hit 80.8 percent of the poverty line for one person in Montreal or Quebec City in 1998, though it has since slid to 76.9 percent in 2002. For a two-person family (e.g., a single parent with one child), the minimum wage went from 43.5 percent of the before-tax poverty line in 1965 to a peak of 79.0 percent in 1977, declined to 53.8 percent in 1986, rose to 64.6 percent in 1998 and lost ground again to reach 61.5 percent in 2002. Figure F6 shows the trends.

Minimum wage compared to after-tax poverty lines (Figure F7)

Statistics Canada publishes after-tax low income cut-offs as well as before-tax low income cut-offs. Here we compare after-tax minimum wage incomes in Quebec for five types of household – single persons, single parents with one child, one-earner couples with two children, two-earner couples supporting two children on one-and-a-half minimum wages, and two-earner couples with two children and two full minimum wages – to the after-tax poverty lines for different size communities. 'After-tax minimum wage incomes' means incomes from the minimum wage and available federal and Quebec income programs minus federal and Quebec income taxes.

For a single person earning the minimum wage, after-tax income came to $13,618,[32] which is $1,946 below the after-tax poverty line for metropolitan centers over 500,000 (Montreal and Quebec City) but $508 above the line for cities between 100,000 and 499,999, $710 above the line for centres of 30,000-99,999, $1,823 above for towns under 30,000 and $3,414 over the poverty line for rural residents. A single parent with one child received $20,025[33] in after-tax income from minimum wage earnings and federal and provincial child benefits and tax credits, which came to $1,033 above the after-tax poverty line for Montreal and Quebec City, $4,028 above the line for cities between 100,000 and 499,999, $4,275 over the line for centres between 30,000 and 99,999, $5,632 above for towns under 30,000 and $7,574 above the poverty line for rural residents.

For a one-earner couple with two children, after-tax minimum wage income amounted to $24,105[34] – $5,811 below the after-tax poverty line for Montreal and Quebec City, $1,095 under the line for cities between 100,000 and 499,999, $705 below for centres between 30,000 and 99,999 but $1,432 above the line for towns smaller than 30,000 and $4,490 over the after-tax poverty line for rural residents. For a two-earner couple supporting two children on one-and-a-half minimum wages, after-tax minimum wage income amounted to $27,107[35] – $2,741 below the after-tax poverty line for Montreal and Quebec City but $1,975 over the line for cities between 100,000 and 499,999, $2,365 above the line for centres between 30,000 and 99,999, $4,502 over for towns smaller than 30,000 and $7,560 above the after-tax poverty line for rural residents. Disposable income for a two-earner couple supporting two children on two

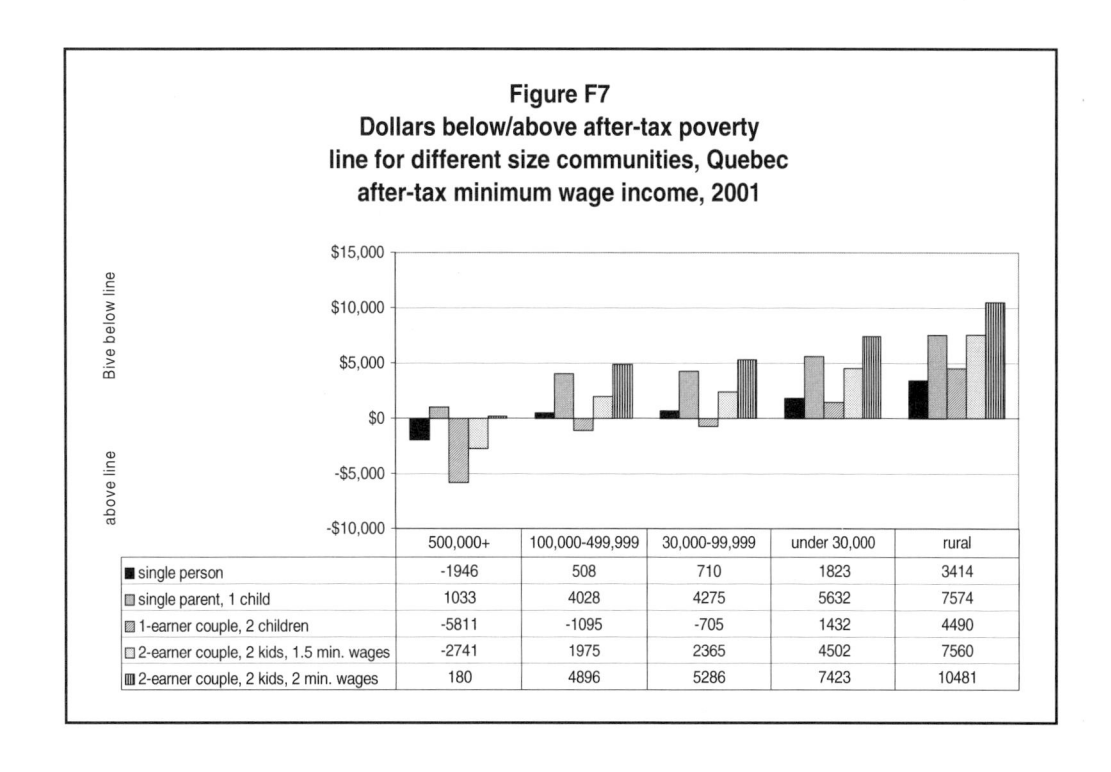

Figure F7
Dollars below/above after-tax poverty line for different size communities, Quebec after-tax minimum wage income, 2001

	500,000+	100,000-499,999	30,000-99,999	under 30,000	rural
single person	-1946	508	710	1823	3414
single parent, 1 child	1033	4028	4275	5632	7574
1-earner couple, 2 children	-5811	-1095	-705	1432	4490
2-earner couple, 2 kids, 1.5 min. wages	-2741	1975	2365	4502	7560
2-earner couple, 2 kids, 2 min. wages	180	4896	5286	7423	10481

minimum wages was $30,096[36] – $180 above the after-tax poverty line for Montreal and Quebec City, $4,896 over the line for cities between 100,000 and 499,999, $5,286 above the line for centres between 30,000 and 99,999, $7,423 over for towns smaller than 30,000 and $10,481 above the after-tax poverty line for rural residents.

Contribution of child benefits

Child benefits supplement the incomes of the large majority of Canadian families and are especially important to low- and modest-income families. Improvements to the federal Canada Child Tax Benefit, along with Quebec's relatively generous family allowances and earnings supplement programs, are boosting the incomes of minimum wage and other working poor families with children.

The single-parent minimum wage worker with one child got $2,447 from the Canada Child Tax Benefit, $1,925 from Quebec family allowances and $339 from the Quebec Parental Wage Assistance Program – for a total of $4,711 or 24.5 percent of disposable income. The one-earner couple with two children received $4,250 from the Canada Child Tax Benefit, $1,250 from Quebec family allowances and $3,131 from the Quebec Parental Wage Assistance Program – totalling $8,631 or 37.0 percent of disposable income.

The two-earner family in which one parent works full time, all year at the minimum wage and the other parent half that time got child benefits worth a total of $4,182 from the Canada Child Tax Benefit and $1,254 in Quebec child benefits, totaling $5,436 or 20.9 percent of disposable income. The two-earner family in which both parents work full time, all year at the minimum wage received $2,641 from the Canada Child Tax Benefit and $160 in Quebec child benefits, for a combined child benefit of $2,801 or 9.8 percent of disposable income.

Minimum wage versus welfare (Figure F8)

For a single person earning the minimum wage in Quebec, disposable income – i.e., minimum wage earnings plus refundable tax credits minus income and payroll taxes – amounted to $12,816 in 2001, which is a sizeable $6,401 more than the $6,415 from welfare and the GST credit. Figure F8 illustrates the findings.

Minimum wages also pay better than welfare for a single parent with one child age 2, though the advantage is not as great as for single people. Disposable income from after-tax minimum wage earnings, child benefits, earnings supplements and refundable tax credits amounted to $19,223 in 2001, or $5,905 more than the $13,318 from welfare, child benefits and the GST tax credit.

Figure F8
Minimum wage versus welfare in Quebec, by household type, 2001

	single person	single parent, 1 child	one-earner couple, 2 children	couple, 2 kids, 1.5 min. wages	couple, 2 kids, 2 min. wages
minimum wage disposable income	12816	19223	23303	26047	28492
welfare income	6415	13318	16919	16919	16919

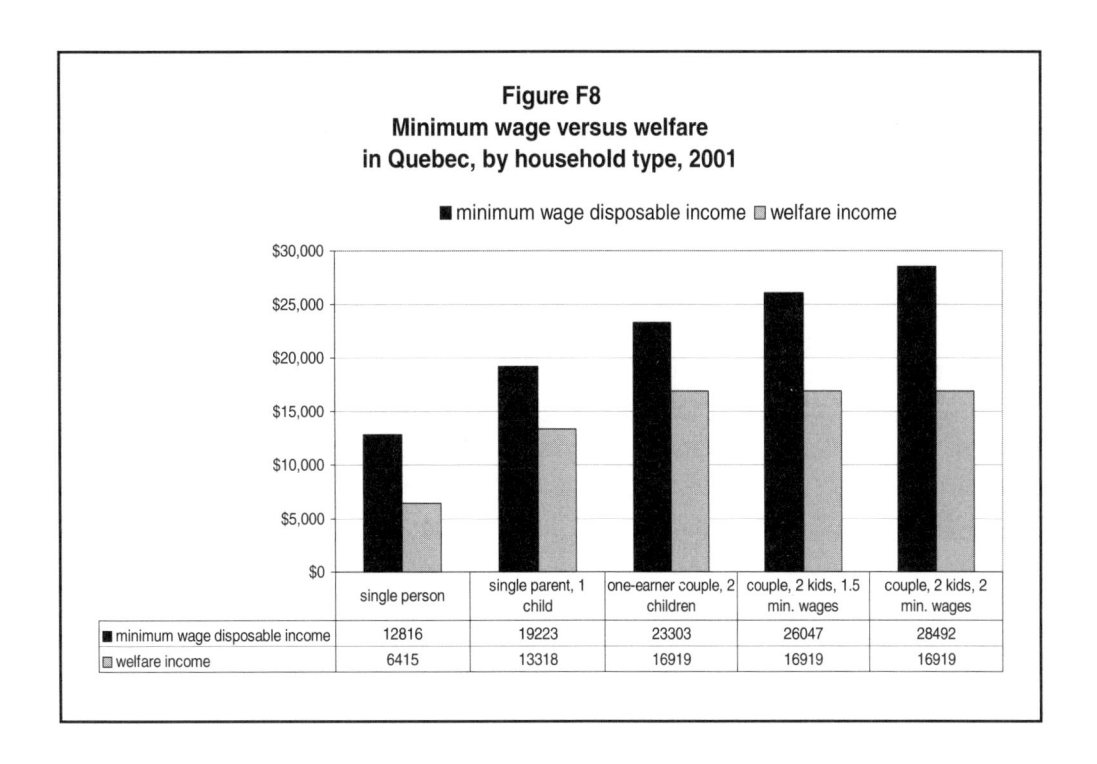

Minimum wages also provide a significant advantage over welfare for a one-earner couple earning the minimum wage and supporting two children aged 10 and 15, in part because of Quebec's earnings supplementation program available to working poor families. Total disposable income from minimum wages, child benefits, earnings supplements and tax credits came to $23,303, or $6,384 more than the $16,919 from welfare, child benefits and the GST credit. Quebec's earnings supplementation program, Parental Wage Assistance, contributed a substantial $3,131 to the minimum wage family's income in 2001.

Naturally, the minimum wage advantage is greater in the case of two-earner families. We look at two examples.

In the first case, one parent works full time, year round at the minimum wage while the other earns half this amount (i.e., works part-time and/or part-year); as above, there are two children aged 10 and 15. This family's disposable income from one-and-a-half minimum wages came to $26,047 in 2001 or $9,128 more than the $16,919 from welfare, child benefits and the refundable GST credit. Quebec child benefits contributed $1,254 to the minimum wage family's income.

The other two-earner family earns double the minimum wage since we assume that both parents work full time, year round at the minimum wage. Total disposable income was $28,492 or a substantial $11,573 more than the $16,919 from welfare and other government income programs.

b. Minimum Wage Workers in Quebec

The following text with illustrative graphs analyzes key characteristics of minimum wage workers in Quebec. Appendix 2 provides detailed statistics in tabular form (pages 294-296).

Interprovincial rank: incidence of minimum wage workers (Figure F9)

In 2000, an estimated 158,800 workers in Quebec – 5.4 percent of the total 2,926,400 employees – worked for the minimum wage. Figure F9 shows Quebec's ranking. Quebec's 5.4 percent figure means that it has the fourth-highest incidence of minimum wage workers in Canada, after Saskatchewan (5.9 percent), New Brunswick (6.0 percent) and Newfoundland (8.7 percent). Alberta, with only 2.0 percent of its workforce at the minimum wage, ranks lowest. The national minimum wage incidence was 4.6 percent in 2000.

Minimum wage workers are overrepresented in Quebec. While it accounts for 27.4 percent of all minimum wage workers in the country, Quebec has a smaller share of all employees (23.4 percent), producing an index of 1.17 (the higher the result above 1.00, the more overrepresented are minimum wage workers).

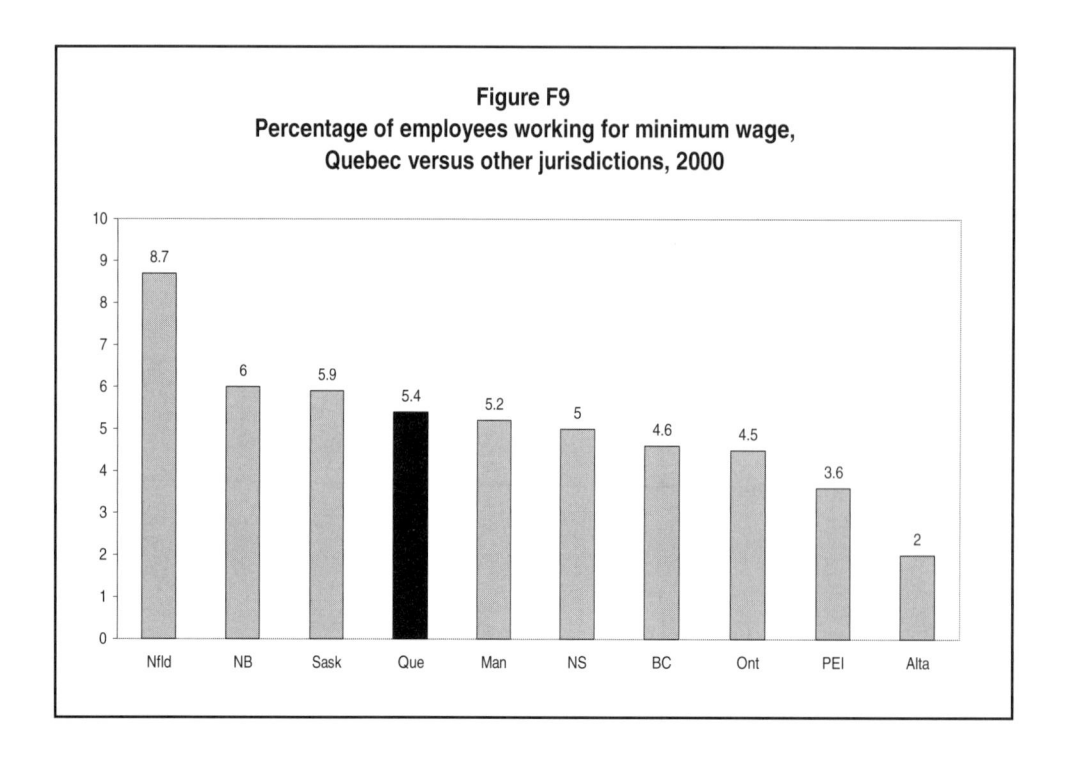

Figure F9
Percentage of employees working for minimum wage, Quebec versus other jurisdictions, 2000

Nfld	NB	Sask	Que	Man	NS	BC	Ont	PEI	Alta
8.7	6	5.9	5.4	5.2	5	4.6	4.5	3.6	2

Gender and age (Figures F10-F13)

In Quebec as in the rest of Canada, women run a higher risk of working for minimum wage than men, and women also make up the majority of the minimum wage workforce.

In 2000, 7.2 percent of Quebec's female employees worked for minimum wage compared to only 3.9 percent of male workers. Of the total 158,800 minimum wage workers, 98,800 – 62.3 percent – were women and 59,900 – 37.7 percent – were men, as seen in Figure F10.

Women are overrepresented in Quebec's minimum wage workforce. They constituted 62.2 percent of minimum wage workers but only 47.1 percent of all the province's employees in 2000. Men are underrepresented. They accounted for only 37.7 percent of minimum wage workers but more than half (52.9 percent) of all employees.

The gender bias among minimum wage workers holds when we control for major age categories. Figure F11 illustrates the pattern. While younger workers of both sexes run a higher risk of working for minimum wage, women still fare worse than men within each age category.

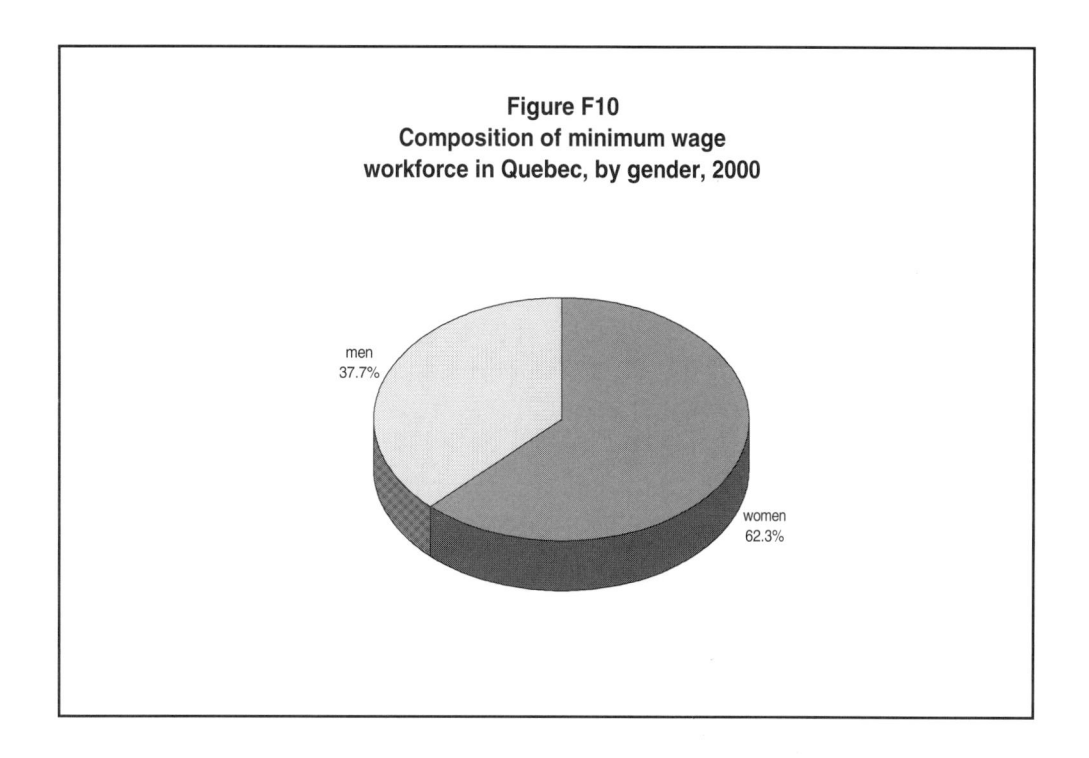

Figure F10
Composition of minimum wage workforce in Quebec, by gender, 2000

men 37.7%
women 62.3%

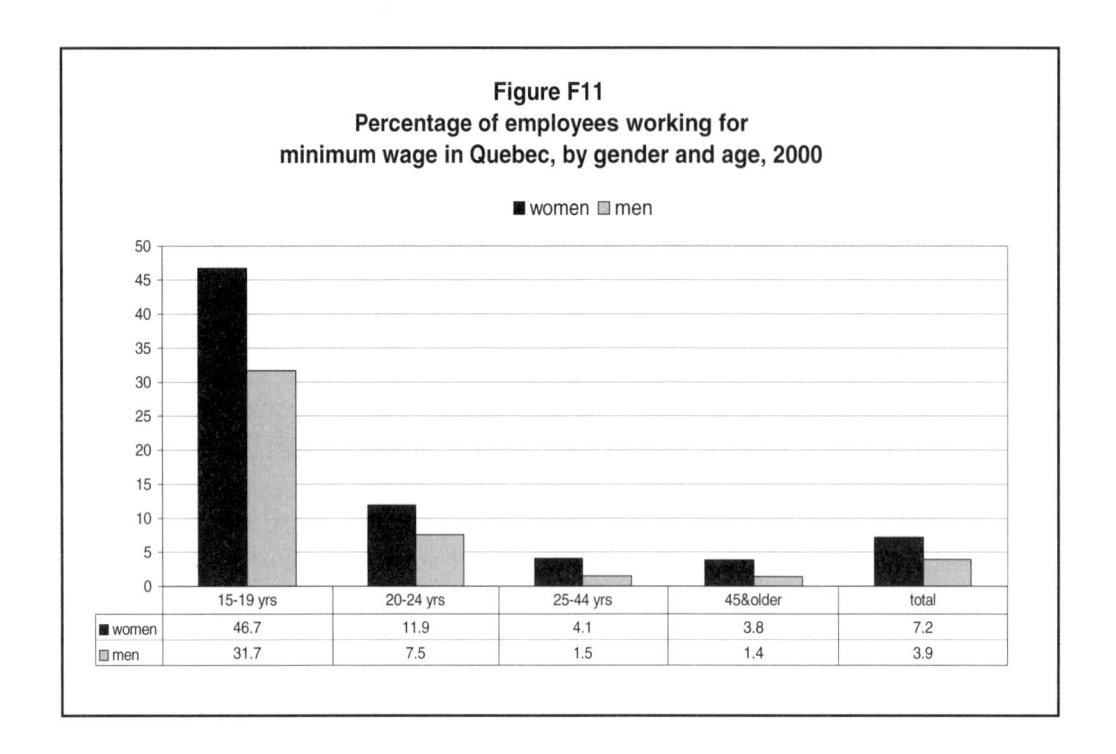

**Figure F11
Percentage of employees working for
minimum wage in Quebec, by gender and age, 2000**

	15-19 yrs	20-24 yrs	25-44 yrs	45&older	total
women	46.7	11.9	4.1	3.8	7.2
men	31.7	7.5	1.5	1.4	3.9

Among female workers aged 15 to 19, 46.7 percent worked for the minimum wage in 2000 in contrast to 31.7 percent of male workers in the same age group. Among those 20-24, 11.9 percent of women compared to 7.5 percent of men worked for the minimum wage. Among workers 25-44, 4.1 percent of women as opposed to 1.5 percent of men were at the bottom of the wage ladder. Among employees 45 and older, 3.8 percent of women but only 1.4 percent of men worked for the minimum wage in Quebec.

The minimum wage risk gap between the sexes is wider for older workers. Women in the 15-24 age group are 1.5 times more likely to work for the minimum wage than men in that age group, but the ratio increases to 2.7 for those aged 25-44 and those over 45.

Young people not only are more likely to work for minimum wage than other employees, but the young also make up a large proportion of the minimum wage workforce. Figure F12 compares the age makeup of minimum wage workers and all employees in Quebec. A sizeable proportion (39.9 percent) of minimum wage workers are in the 15-19 age group, as opposed to just 5.6 percent of all employees. Employees aged 20-24 represent 19.7 percent of minimum wage workers as opposed to only 11.1 percent of all workers. All told, six in ten minimum wage workers in Quebec (59.6) are under 25 years of age.

Figure F12
Share of minimum wage workers versus share of all employees in Quebec, by age group, 2000

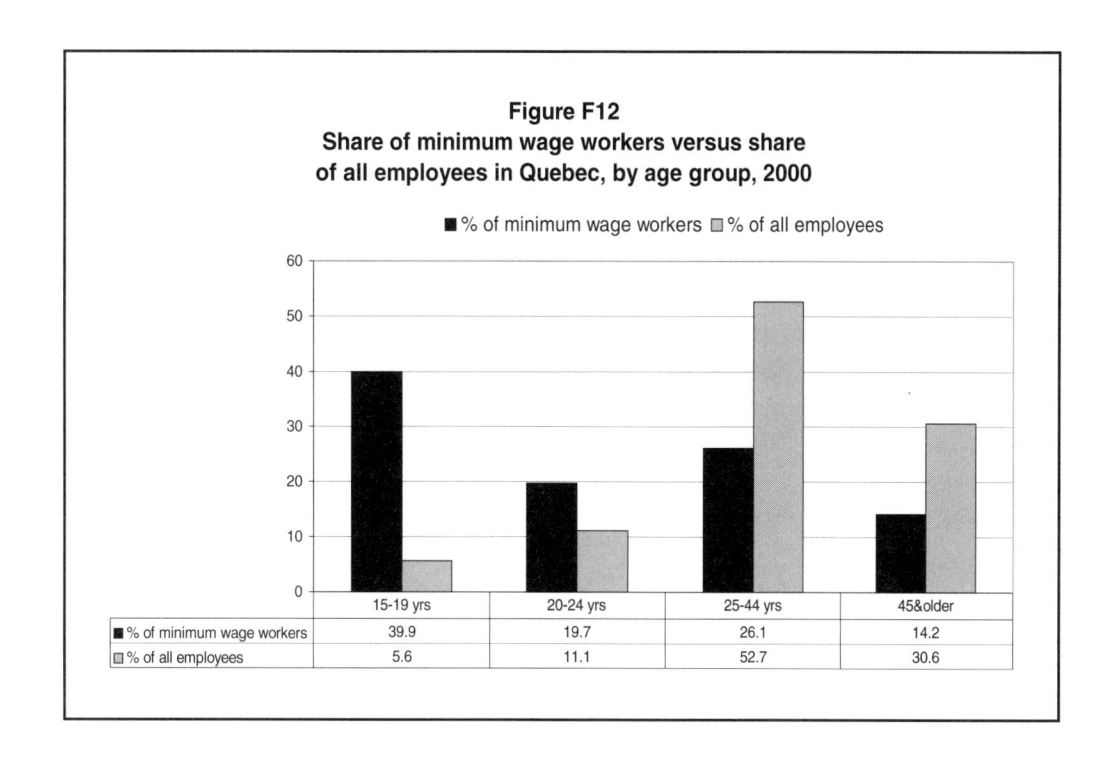

	15-19 yrs	20-24 yrs	25-44 yrs	45&older
% of minimum wage workers	39.9	19.7	26.1	14.2
% of all employees	5.6	11.1	52.7	30.6

Figure F13
Composition of minimum wage workforce in Quebec, by teenager/adult and gender, 2000

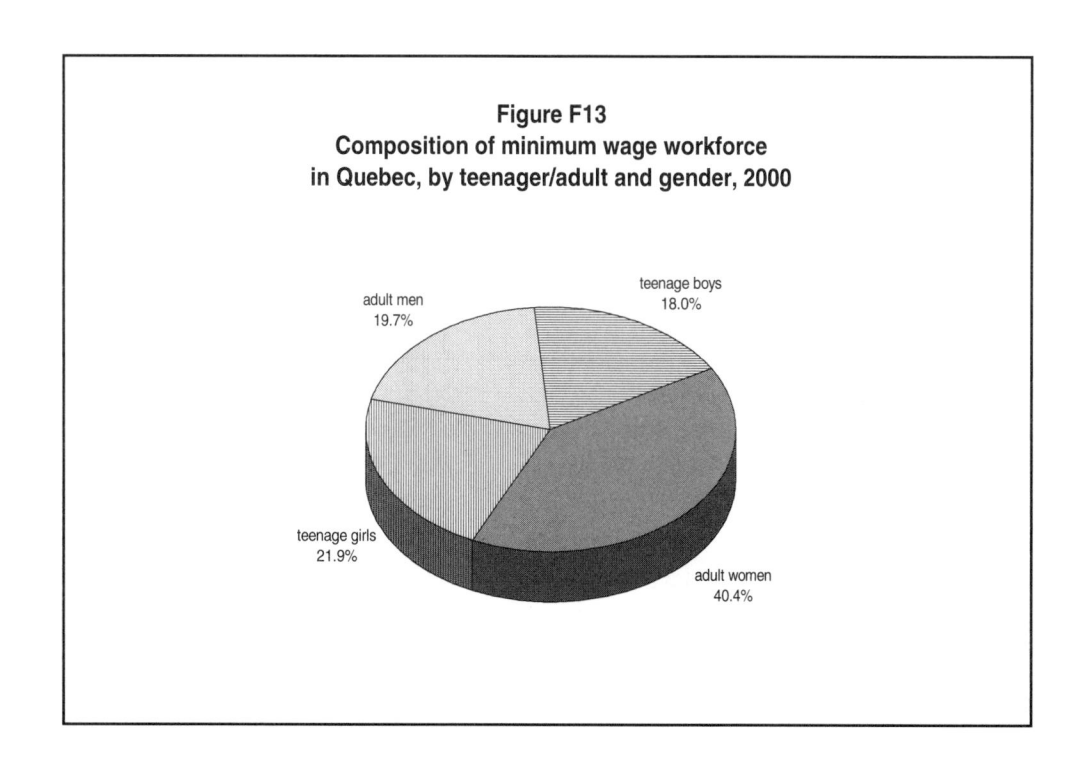

- adult men: 19.7%
- teenage boys: 18.0%
- adult women: 40.4%
- teenage girls: 21.9%

The opposite holds for older workers. While a sizeable proportion – 26.1 percent – of minimum wage workers in Quebec are between 25 and 44, that age group constitutes a much larger proportion – 52.7 percent or more than half – of all employees. Workers aged 45 and older make up just 14.2 percent of minimum wage employees but 30.6 percent all employees.

Figure F13 divides the minimum wage workforce in Quebec into teenage girls and boys and adult women and men. Adult women are the largest group, at 64,100 or 40.4 percent of the total, followed by teenage girls (34,800 or 21.9 percent), adult men (31,300 or 19.7 percent) and teenage boys (28,600 or 18.0 percent). The majority (60.1 percent) of Quebec's minimum wage workers are adults; the national average is somewhat lower (52.9 percent).

Education (Figures F14 and F15)

Figure F14 shows the incidence of minimum wage workers in Quebec according to level of education.

At first glance, the relationship between level of education and incidence of minimum wage employment does not seem to correspond to common sense: Workers in the lowest educational group (elementary education only) are less likely to work for minimum wage (8.2 percent do) than those with

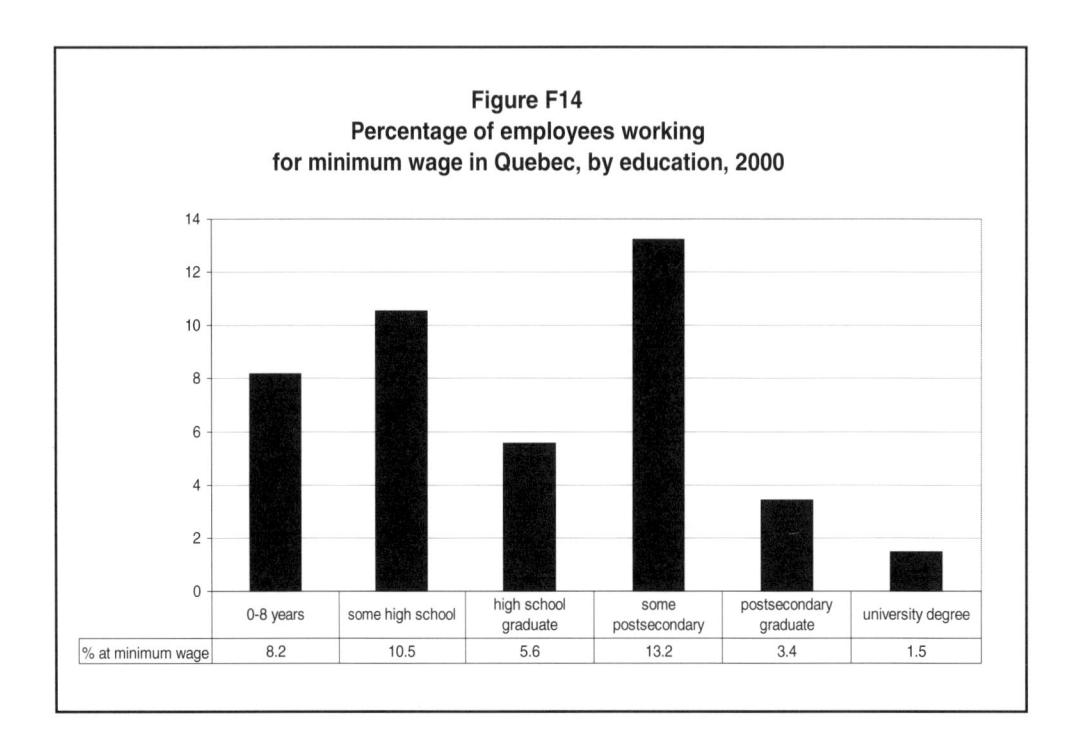

Figure F14
Percentage of employees working for minimum wage in Quebec, by education, 2000

	0-8 years	some high school	high school graduate	some postsecondary	postsecondary graduate	university degree
% at minimum wage	8.2	10.5	5.6	13.2	3.4	1.5

**Figure F15
Composition of minimum wage workforce
in Quebec, by education, 2000**

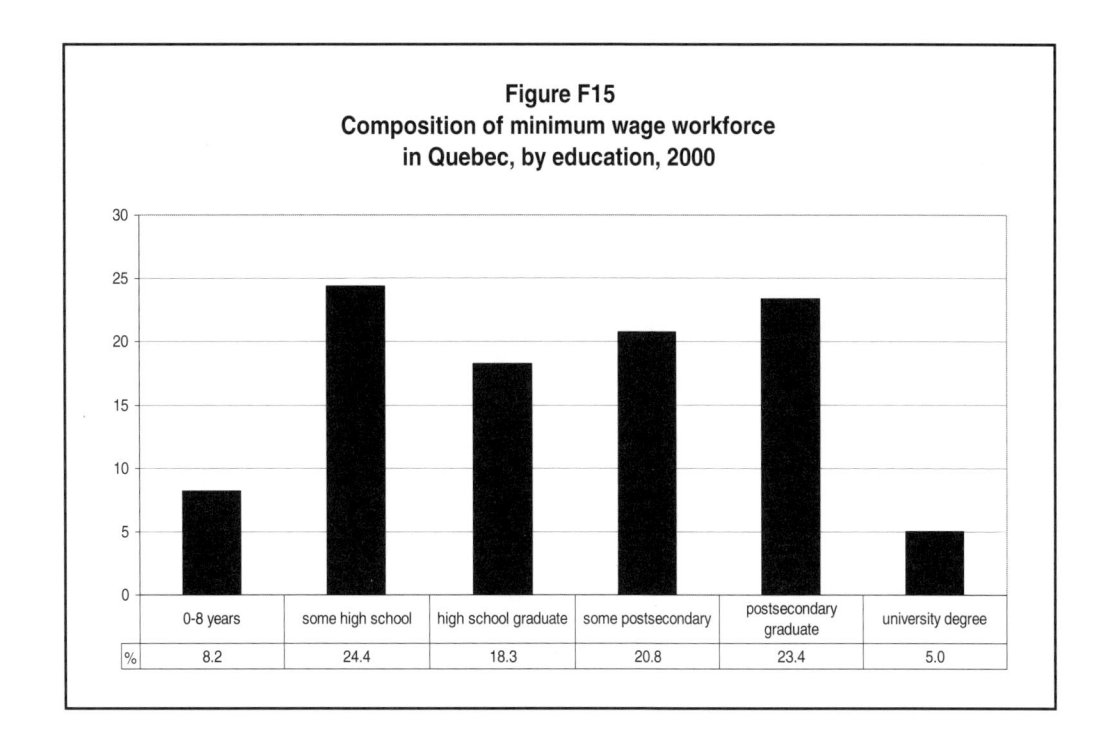

	0-8 years	some high school	high school graduate	some postsecondary	postsecondary graduate	university degree
%	8.2	24.4	18.3	20.8	23.4	5.0

some high school (10.5 percent), while those with some postsecondary education run a higher risk (13.2 percent) than high school graduates (5.6 percent). However, as one would expect, the chances of working for minimum wage are lowest for the two highest education categories – 3.4 percent for those with a postsecondary certificate or diploma (e.g., from a community college or vocational institute) and only 1.5 percent for those with a university degree.

Once we look at the education-minimum wage link for different age groups, the reasons for the apparently inconsistent relationship comes clear: Young people working at part-time or seasonal (i.e., summer) jobs – typically paying the minimum or a low wage – figure prominently in the 'some high school' and 'some postsecondary education' categories; they are still at high school, community college or university, whereas workers in the other educational categories have completed their education.

Figure F15 shows each educational group's share of Quebec's minimum wage workforce in 2000. The largest group of minimum wage workers are those with some high school (24.4 percent), followed by postsecondary graduates (23.4 percent), those with some postsecondary education (20.8 percent), high school graduates (18.3 percent), workers with only 0-8 years of education (8.2 percent) and university graduates (5.0 percent). Many minimum wage workers are students (high school or postsecondary) pursuing their education. A sizeable group of minimum wage workers (49.2 percent or close to half) have some form of postsecondary education.

Full-time and part-time work (Figures F16 and F17)

The fact that young people are more likely to work part time helps explain why workers still pursuing their education tend to face a higher risk of minimum wage work than those who have completed their schooling and are working full time. Figure F16 indicates that 16.8 percent of part-time workers are at the minimum wage compared to only 3.1 percent of those employed full time.

While the majority of minimum wage workers in Quebec (52.6 percent) work part time, a sizeable group (47.4 percent) are employed full time. Figure F17 shows the results.

Gender alters the relationship between full-time and part-time work and the minimum wage. Women who work part time in Quebec run a lesser risk of being at the bottom of the wage ladder than do men who work part time (15.3 and 20.2 percent, respectively). However, women employed full time are more likely than men in that group to earn the minimum wage (4.5 and 2.1 percent, respectively).

Women make up the majority of minimum wage employees in the province working both full time (61.6 percent are women) and part time (62.9 percent are women). Among all employees, though, women constitute a minority of full-time workers (42.5 percent) but the bulk of part-time workers (69.0 percent).

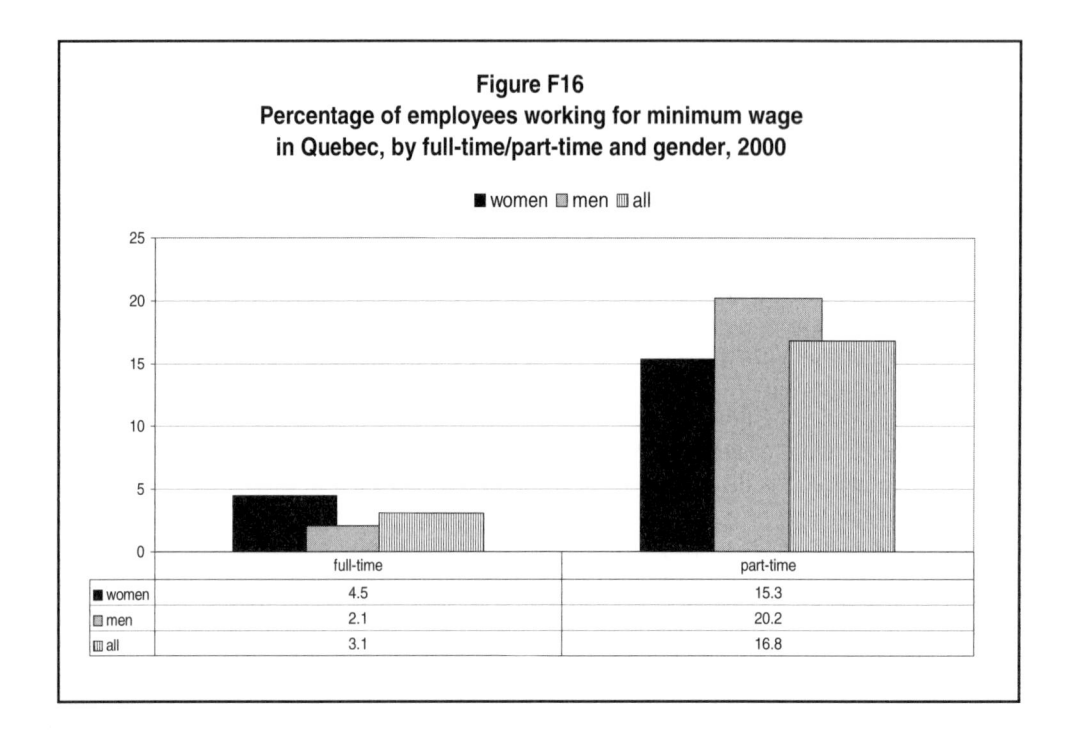

Figure F16
Percentage of employees working for minimum wage in Quebec, by full-time/part-time and gender, 2000

	full-time	part-time
women	4.5	15.3
men	2.1	20.2
all	3.1	16.8

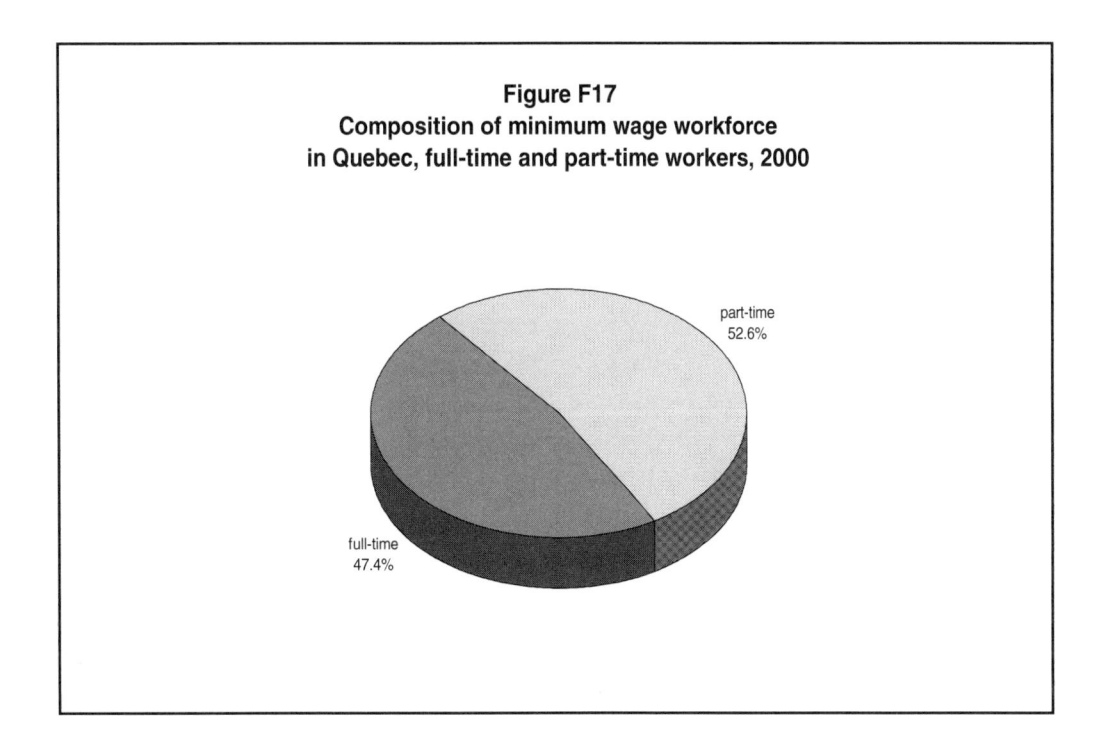

**Figure F17
Composition of minimum wage workforce
in Quebec, full-time and part-time workers, 2000**

part-time 52.6%
full-time 47.4%

Family status (Figure F18)

We noted above that six in ten of Quebec's minimum wage workers are under 25 years of age. Light on this fundamental fact of the minimum wage workforce is shed by information on family status, illustrated in Figure F18.

The largest group of minimum wage workers – 83,500 or 52.7 percent of the total 158,800 – are older children living with their parents (or relatives with relatives, as in the case of a niece or nephew living with an aunt and uncle, or grandchildren with grandparents). Of this category, 58,800 or 70.4 percent are aged 15-19, 18,700 or 22.4 percent are 20-24 and the remaining 6,000 or 7.2 percent are 25 or older. More than half (43,900 or 52.6 percent) are still in school and working part-time or part-year (e.g., in summer).

The next largest group of minimum wage workers in Quebec – 46,200 or 29.1 percent of the total – are members of couples (married or living together). In most cases (34,500 or 74.7 percent of the category total of 46,200), the minimum wage worker's spouse is employed, typically at more than the minimum wage. A typical example in this category would be mothers combining (unpaid) childrearing work

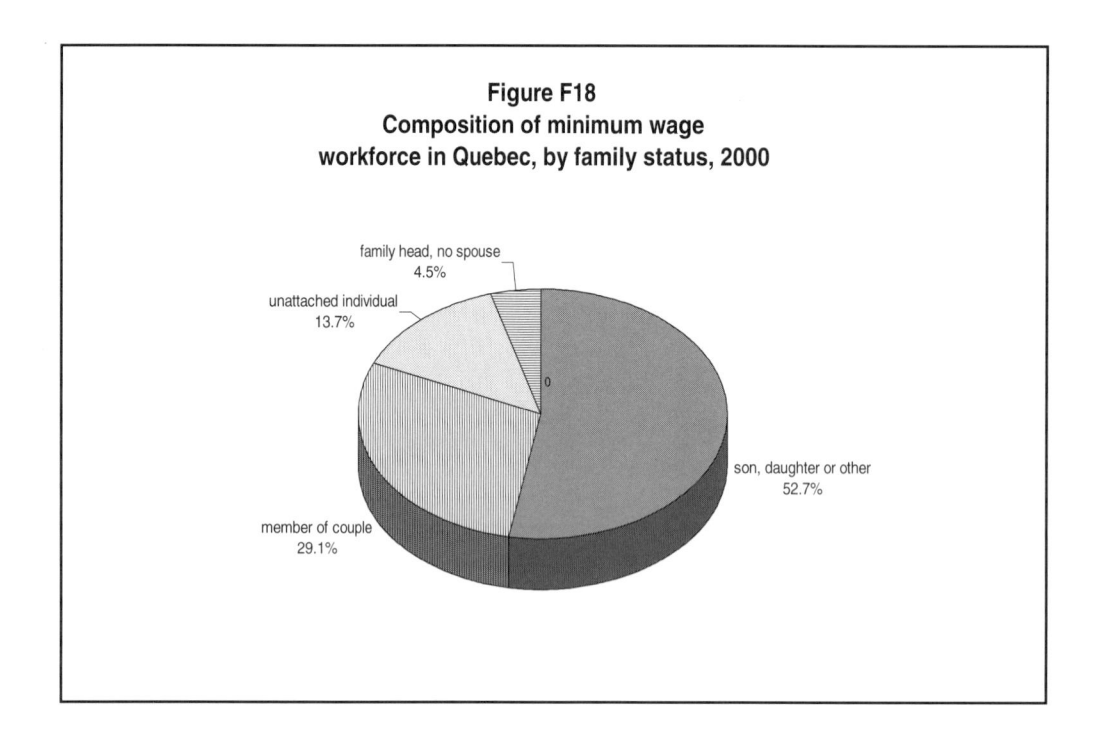

Minimum Wages in Canada: A Statistical Portrait With Policy Implications

**Figure F18
Composition of minimum wage
workforce in Quebec, by family status, 2000**

- family head, no spouse 4.5%
- unattached individual 13.7%
- member of couple 29.1%
- son, daughter or other 52.7%

with part-time minimum wage work. Another 11,700 or 25.3 percent of minimum wage workers living in couples have a spouse who is not employed (most of the latter are not in the labour force).

An estimated 21,700 or 13.7 percent of minimum wage workers are unattached individuals. The majority of this category (12,100 or 55.8 percent) live alone; of this group, 3,900 are 15-24, 6,300 are aged 25-54 and 1,800 are 55 or older. About 9,600 of the province's unattached minimum wage workers are living with friends or roommates; 6,500 are 15-24, 3,100 are 25-54 and 100 are 55 or older.

Finally, some 7,200 or 4.5 percent of Quebec's minimum wage workers head families with no spouse present; most (6,700) are single parents with children under 18.

Industry

National data show that the incidence and distribution of minimum wage workers varies significantly according to industries. The same applies to Quebec, though sample size constraints preclude estimates for four of the 16 industrial categories (forestry, fishing, mining, oil and gas; utilities; construction; and professional, scientific and technical services). Among the industrial categories for which estimates are available, accommodation and food services top the list (23.6 percent of employees work for minimum wage), followed by agriculture (20.3 percent), trade (9.8 percent), other services (9.1 percent), information, culture and recreation (7.5 percent), management, administrative and other support (6.1 percent), health care and social assistance (2.9 percent), transportation and warehousing (2.8 percent), manufacturing (2.3 percent), finance, insurance, real estate and leasing (2.3 percent), public administration (1.5 percent) and educational services (1.4 percent).

Estimates are available for the industrial composition of the whole employed workforce in Quebec. Manufacturing tops the list, at an estimated 600,700 or 20.5 percent of all employees. Next comes trade (478,800 or 16.4 percent), followed by health care and social assistance (326,300 or 11.2 percent of all employees), educational services (214,900 or 7.3 percent), public administration (206,200 or 7.0 percent), accommodation and food services (180,800 or 6.2 percent), finance, insurance, real estate and leasing (154,300 or 5.3 percent), transportation and warehousing (144,900 or 5.0 percent), professional, scientific and technical services (133,200 or 4.6 percent), information, culture and recreation (122,000 or 4.2 percent), other services (109,000 or 3.7 percent), construction (94,900 or 3.2 percent), management, administrative and other support (76,700 or 2.6 percent), forestry, fishing, mining, oil and gas (34,100 or 1.2 percent), utilities (26,800 or 0.9 percent) and agriculture (22,700 or 0.8 percent).

ONTARIO

a. Minimum wages in Ontario

Interprovincial rank: dollar value of minimum wages (Figure G1)

Ontario's minimum wage has been frozen at $6.85 since 1995 – a very long seven years. In 1995, Ontario had Canada's highest minimum wage – $7.74 expressed in inflation-adjusted 2002 dollars. By 2002, Ontario had slipped from first to fourth place, trailing Quebec ($7.20 as of October 1, $7.05 annual average), Yukon ($7.20) and British Columbia ($8.00). Figure G1 illustrates the rankings.

Trend in dollar value of minimum wage (Figure G2)

Because minimum wages are not indexed, their value changes over time. Figure G2 shows the trend in Ontario's minimum wage from 1965 to 2002; each year's average minimum wage has been converted to inflation-adjusted (i.e., constant) 2002 dollars to show the real trend, after taking into account the impact of inflation on the dollar.

Ontario's minimum wage increased rapidly between 1965 ($5.87 an hour) and its 1976 peak ($8.26), declined considerably in the first half of the 1980s (to $5.97 in 1983), then rose gradually in the 1990s to reach $7.74 in 1994 and 1995. It has declined steadily since 1995 – to $6.85 in 2002 – due to the freeze, which has eroded its value by a considerable 11.5 percent. Its 2002 level was $1.41 or 17.1 percent lower than the 1976 high point, though still $.98 or 16.7 percent more than in 1965.

Interprovincial rank: minimum wages as percentage of average earnings (Figure G3)

In 1995, Ontario's minimum wage amounted to 43.2 percent of its average earnings, ranking the province highest in Canada on that measure. By 2001, Ontario's minimum wage had plummeted to 38.5 percent of average earnings, placing the province sixth-lowest of the 13 jurisdictions, ahead of only the Northwest Territories, Nunavut, Alberta, Newfoundland and Yukon – and far behind its neighbour Quebec, which took second place with 44.8 percent. Figure G3 ranks the jurisdictions.

Trends in minimum wage and average earnings (Figure G4)

The black line in Figure G4 shows the trend in the minimum wage, the gray line the trend in average earnings and the vertical bars the trend in the minimum wage as a percentage of average earnings. Read the left-hand axis for the minimum wage and average earnings and the right-hand axis for the minimum wage as a percentage of earnings.

Figure G1
Ontario minimum wage compared to other provinces and territories, 2002

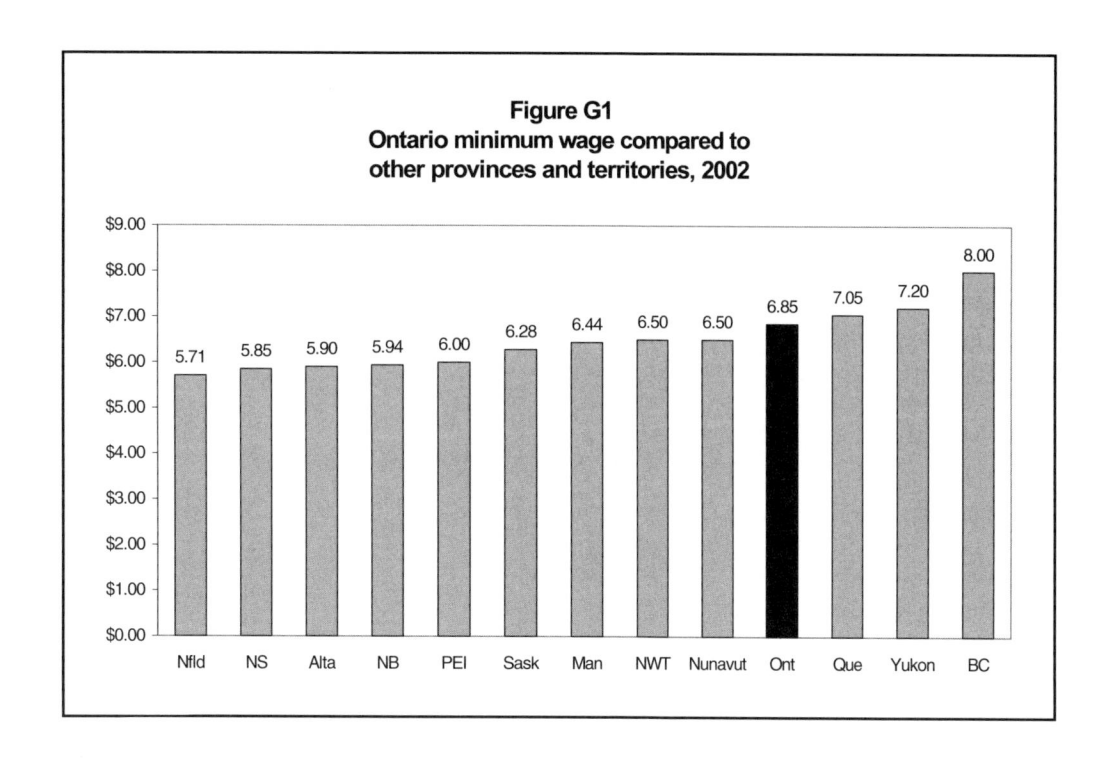

Province/Territory	Minimum Wage
Nfld	5.71
NS	5.85
Alta	5.90
NB	5.94
PEI	6.00
Sask	6.28
Man	6.44
NWT	6.50
Nunavut	6.50
Ont	6.85
Que	7.05
Yukon	7.20
BC	8.00

Figure G2
Ontario minimum wage, in constant 2002 dollars, 1965-2002

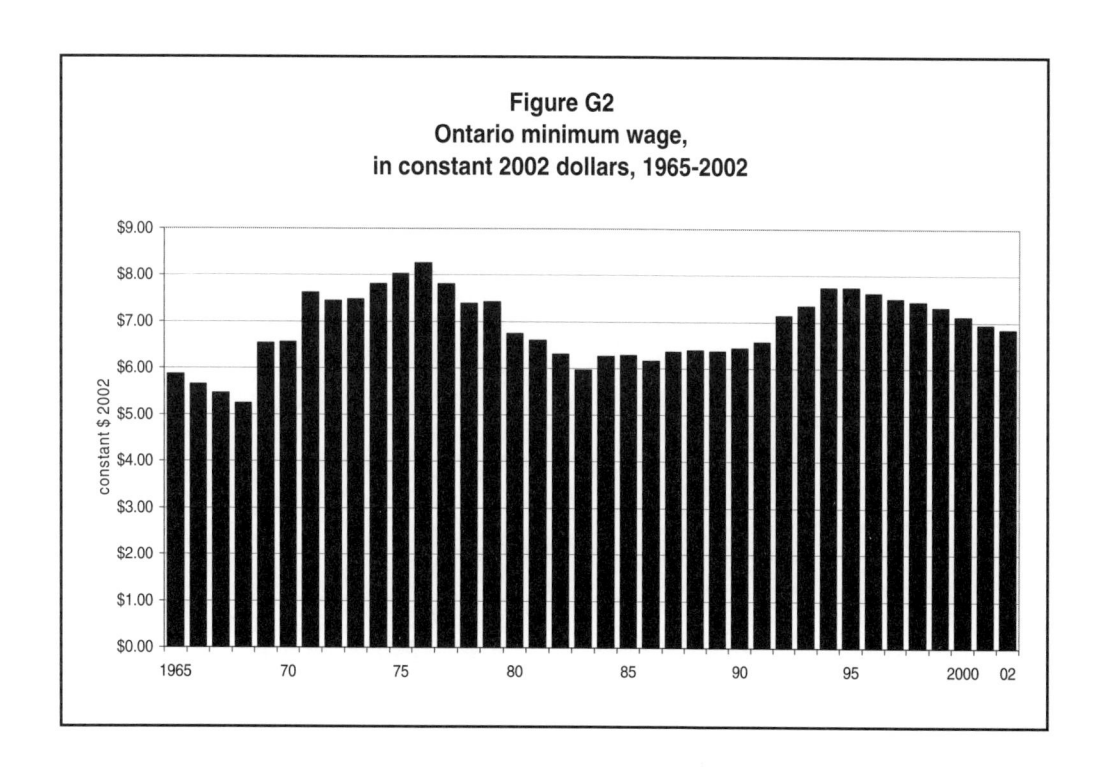

Minimum Wages in Canada: A Statistical Portrait With Policy Implications

**Figure G3
Ontario minimum wage as % of average earnings,
compared to other provinces and territories, 2001**

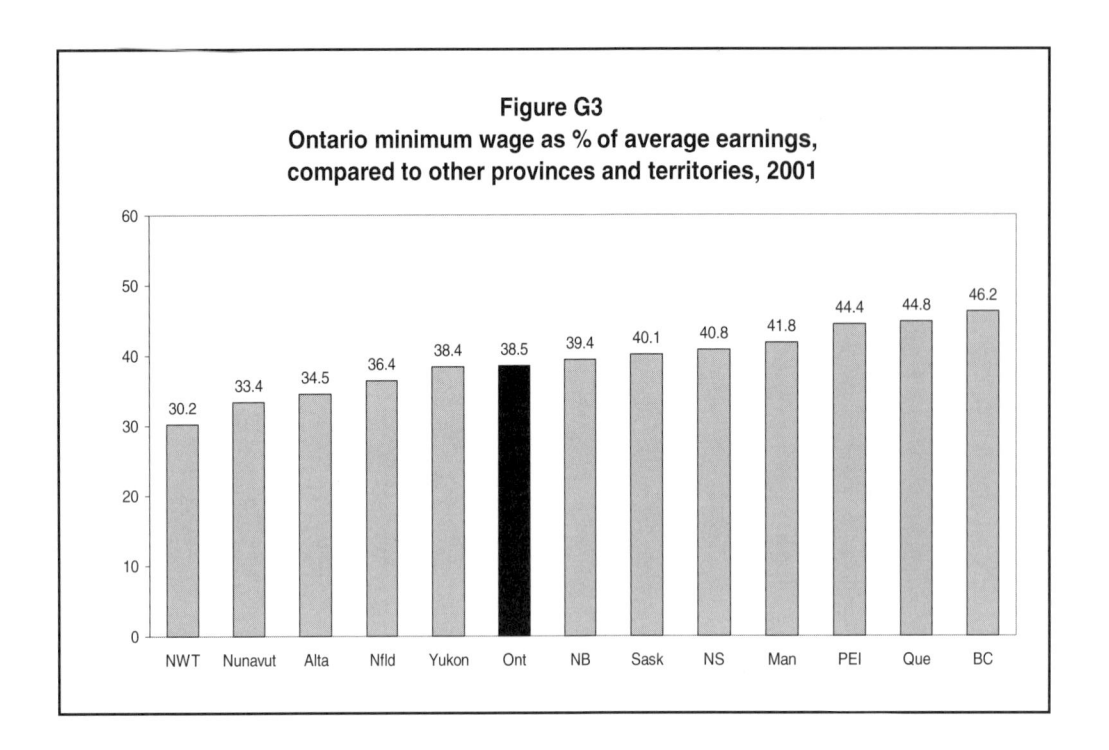

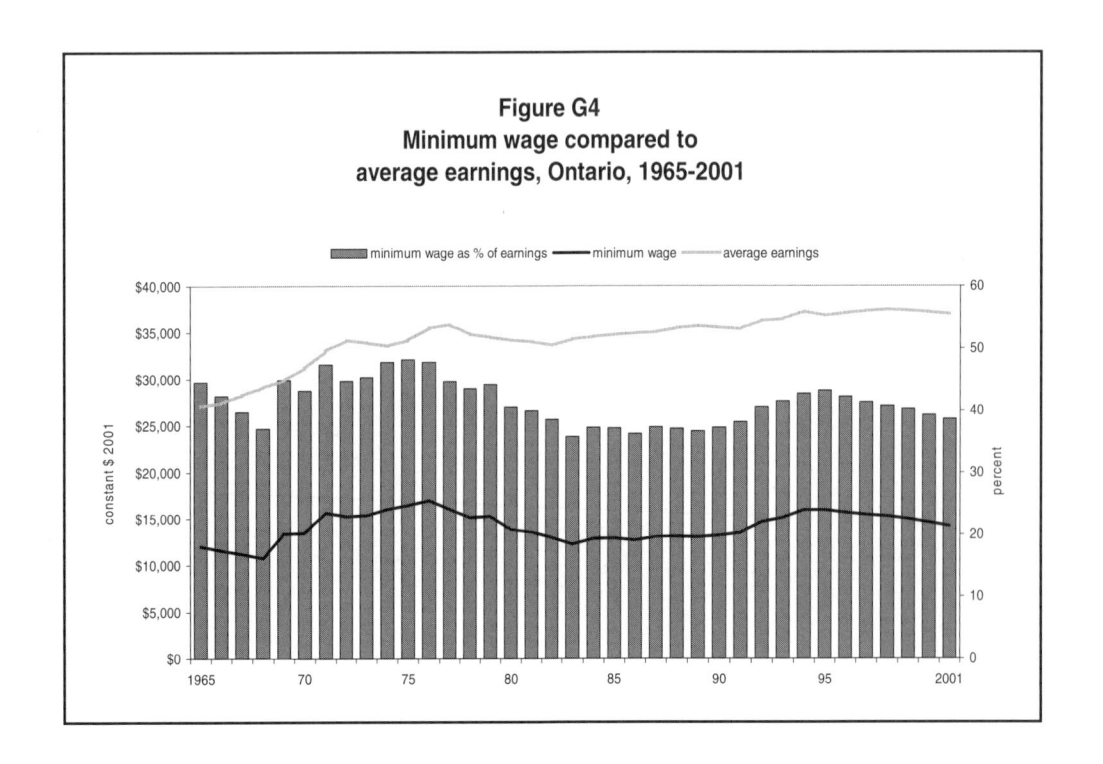

Province/Territory	%
NWT	30.2
Nunavut	33.4
Alta	34.5
Nfld	36.4
Yukon	38.4
Ont	38.5
NB	39.4
Sask	40.1
NS	40.8
Man	41.8
PEI	44.4
Que	44.8
BC	46.2

**Figure G4
Minimum wage compared to
average earnings, Ontario, 1965-2001**

142   *Caledon Institute of Social Policy*

The graph indicates an undulating pattern with several ups and downs over the years, though the minimum wage represented a smaller percentage of average earnings in the 1980s and 1990s than in the 1970s. In 1965, Ontario's minimum wage represented 44.5 percent of the province's average earnings. The ratio of minimum wage to average earnings peaked at 48.2 percent in 1975, fell to a low of 35.7 percent in 1983, rose again to 43.2 percent by 1995 but since has slipped steadily to 38.5 percent in 2001.

Average earnings in Ontario have increased pretty much steadily over the years, from $27,092 in 1965 to a peak of $37,467 in 1998 though they have since slipped a bit to $36,967 in 2001. By contrast, the province's minimum wage has seen ups and downs over the years, which accounts for the ups and downs but overall decline in its value relative to (steadily rising) average earnings. On an annual (full-time, all-year) basis, Ontario's minimum wage went from $12,055 in 1965 to $16,965 in 1976, fell to $12,249 in 1983, rose to $15,903 in 1995 but have lost ground since to stand at $14,298 in 2001.

Minimum wage compared to before-tax poverty lines (Figure G5)

Statistics Canada publishes two sets of low income cut-offs. The before-tax low income cut-offs are based on gross, pre-tax income (i.e., income from employment, investments, private pensions and other private sources plus income from government programs such as public pensions, Employment Insurance, child benefits and welfare). The after-tax low income cut-offs use the same definition of income but also factor into the picture the federal and provincial income taxes that Canadians pay. We first compare the minimum wage to the before-tax poverty lines.

Because the poverty line is lower for smaller communities, the minimum wage represents a larger proportion of the poverty line in smaller communities. In 2002, Ontario's minimum wage ranged from 74.7 percent of the before-tax low income line for one person in cities of 500,000 or more (Toronto, Ottawa and Hamilton) to 87.4 percent for cities with 100,000 to 499,999 inhabitants (London, Kitchener, St.Catherines-Niagara, Windsor, Oshawa, Sudbury and Thunder Bay), 88.0 percent for small urban areas between 30,000 and 99,999 inhabitants, 94.6 percent for towns under 30,000 and 108.5 percent for rural residents.

Ontario's minimum wage in 2002 fell $4,826 short of the before-tax low income line for one person in metropolitan areas of 500,000 or more, $2,047 below the line in cities between 100,000 and 499,999, $1,934 below the line for communities between 30,000 and 99,999 and $809 below for towns under 30,000, though it was $1,119 above the poverty line for rural residents. Figure G5 shows the dollar gap between the minimum wage and the before-tax poverty line for one person in different size communities throughout Ontario.

Because the poverty line varies by family size, minimum wages (which do not vary by family size) fall farther below the poverty line for families than for single workers. We look at the poverty gap for a single parent with one child, which falls in the two-person family size category. In 2002, Ontario's minimum

Minimum Wages in Canada: A Statistical Portrait With Policy Implications

**Figure G5
Dollars below/above before-tax poverty line
for different size communities,
Ontario minimum wage, 2002**

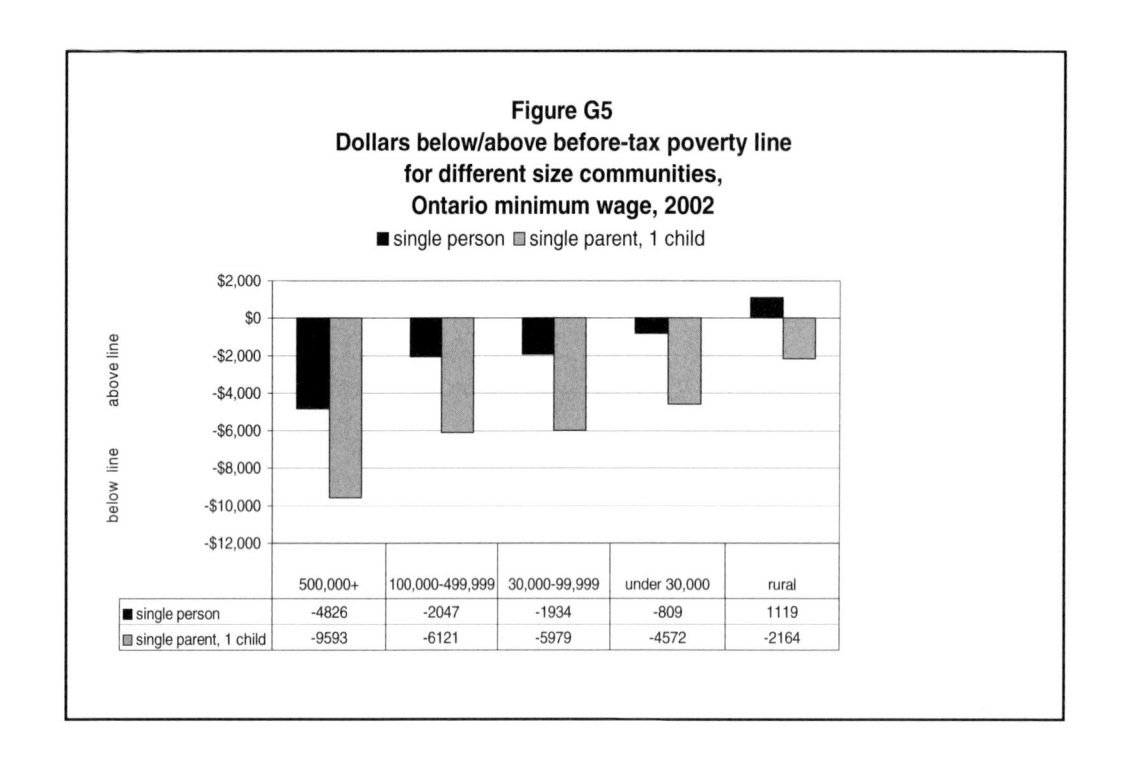

	500,000+	100,000-499,999	30,000-99,999	under 30,000	rural
single person	-4826	-2047	-1934	-809	1119
single parent, 1 child	-9593	-6121	-5979	-4572	-2164

wage varied from 59.8 percent of the before-tax low income line for a two-person family in metropolitan centres to 70.0 percent for cities between 100,000 and 499,999, 70.4 percent for communities between 30,000, and 99,999, 75.7 percent for towns under 30,000 and 86.8 percent for rural areas. Ontario's minimum wage was $9,593 below the before-tax low income line for a family of two in metropolitan centres over 500,000, $6,121 beneath the line for cities in the 100,000 to 499,999 category, $5,979 under for communities between 30,000 and 99,999 inhabitants, $4,572 below for towns under 30,000 and $2,164 under for rural residents. Figure G5 gives the results.

Trend in minimum wage as percentage of before-tax poverty lines (Figure G6)

The long-term trend when we compare the minimum wage to the poverty line (as measured by Statistics Canada's low income cut-offs, which vary by size of family and of community) is the same as the trend in dollar value. In 2002, the estimated before-tax poverty line for metropolitan centres (500,000 inhabitants and larger) was $19,074 for one person and $23,841 for a family of two.

Ontario's minimum wage rose from 64.0 percent of the before-tax poverty line for one person in 1965 to 90.1 percent of the poverty line in 1976, falling to 65.1 percent in 1983. The trend improved in the latter half of the 1980s and into the 1990s, reaching 84.5 percent in 1995, but since has declined to

**Figure G6
Ontario minimum wage as % of before-tax poverty line for largest cities, 1965-2002**

— single person -■- single parent, 1 child

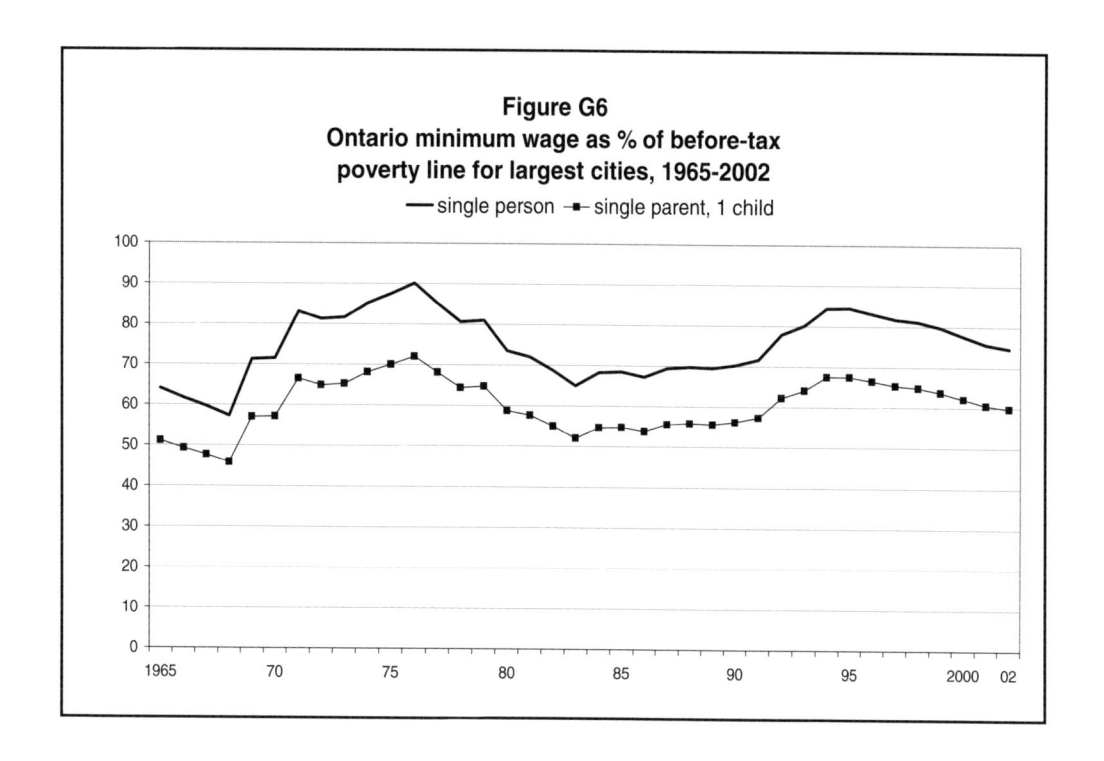

74.7 percent of the poverty line for one person in a city of 500,000 or more in 2002. For a two-person family (e.g., a single parent with one child), the minimum wage went from 51.2 percent of the low income line in 1965 to a peak of 72.1 percent in 1976, declined to 52.0 percent in 1983, rose again to 67.6 percent in 1995 but fell to 59.8 percent by 2001. Figure G6 shows the trends.

Minimum wage compared to after-tax poverty lines (Figure G7)

Statistics Canada publishes after-tax low income cut-offs as well as before-tax low income cut-offs. We compare here after-tax minimum wage incomes in Ontario for five types of household – single persons, single parents with one child, one-earner couples with two children, two-earner couples supporting two children on one-and-a-half minimum wages, and two-earner couples with two children and two full minimum wages – to the after-tax poverty lines for different size communities. 'After-tax minimum wage incomes' means incomes from the minimum wage and available federal and provincial income programs minus federal and provincial income taxes. Figure G7 illustrates the findings.

For a single person earning the minimum wage, after-tax income came to $13,549,[37] which is $2,015 below the after-tax poverty line for metropolitan centres (500,000 and over) but $439 above the line for cities between 100,000 and 499,999, $641 over for centres of 30,000-99,999, $1,754 above for

**Figure G7
Dollars below/above after-tax poverty line
for different size communities, Ontario
after-tax minimum wage income, 2001**

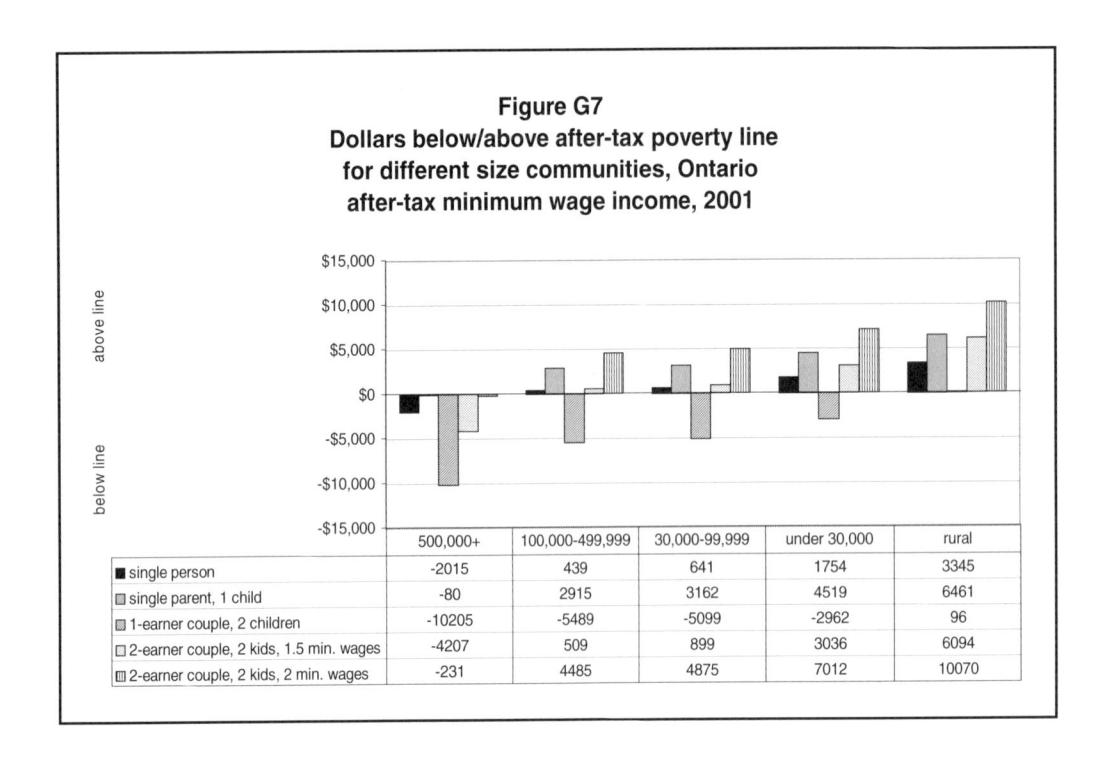

	500,000+	100,000-499,999	30,000-99,999	under 30,000	rural
single person	-2015	439	641	1754	3345
single parent, 1 child	-80	2915	3162	4519	6461
1-earner couple, 2 children	-10205	-5489	-5099	-2962	96
2-earner couple, 2 kids, 1.5 min. wages	-4207	509	899	3036	6094
2-earner couple, 2 kids, 2 min. wages	-231	4485	4875	7012	10070

towns under 30,000 and $3,345 over the poverty line for rural residents. A single parent with one child received $18,912[38] in after-tax income from minimum wage earnings and federal and provincial child benefits and refundable tax credits, which came to just $80 below the after-tax poverty line for metropolitan centers but $2,915 above the line for cities between 100,000 and 499,999, $3,162 over the line for centres between 30,000 and 99,999, $4,519 above for towns under 30,000 and $6,461 above the poverty line for rural residents.

For a one-earner couple with two children, after-tax minimum wage income amounted to $19,711[39] – $10,205 below the after-tax poverty line for metropolitan areas, $5,489 beneath the poverty line for cities between 100,000 and 499,999, $5,099 under for centres between 30,000 and 99,999, $2,962 below for towns smaller than 30,000 but $96 above the after-tax poverty line for rural residents. For a two-earner couple with two children and a total of 1.5 minimum wages between the two parents, after-tax minimum wage income amounted to $25,709[40] – $4,207 below the after-tax poverty line for metropolitan areas but $509 above the poverty line for cities between 100,000 and 499,999, $899 over for centres between 30,000 and 99,999, $3,036 above for towns smaller than 30,000 and $6,094 over the after-tax poverty line for rural residents. For a two-earner couple with two children and earnings totalling two minimum wages, after-tax minimum wage income was $29,685[41] – only $231 below the after-tax poverty line for metropolitan areas and $4,485 over the poverty line for cities between 100,000 and 499,999,

$4,875 above for centres between 30,000 and 99,999, $7,012 above for towns smaller than 30,000 and $10,070 more than the after-tax poverty line for rural residents.

Contribution of child benefits

Child benefits supplement the incomes of the large majority of Canadian families and are especially important to low- and modest-income families. Improvements to the federal Canada Child Tax Benefit, along with Ontario's new Ontario Child Care Supplement for Working Families with preschool children, are providing significant income supplements to minimum wage and other working poor families with children.

The single-parent minimum wage worker with one child got $2,447 from the Canada Child Tax Benefit and $1,310 from the Ontario Child Care Supplement for Working Families in 2001, for a total of $3,757 or 20.7 percent of disposable income. The one-earner couple with two children received $4,250 from the Canada Child Tax Benefit – worth 22.5 percent of disposable income – but did not qualify for the Ontario Child Care Supplement for Working Families because this family's children were above the age limit (six years old) for that program.

Quebec's child-related benefits and earnings supplement are much more generous than Ontario's. In 2001, Quebec paid the single parent with one young child in our example $2,264 as opposed to Ontario's $1,310. Quebec child benefits for the one-income couple with two children 10 and 15 amounted to $4,381; Ontario provided no benefits to this family.

The two-earner family in which one parent works full time, all year at the minimum wage and the other parent half that time got child benefits worth $4,235 from the Canada Child Tax Benefit, which represents 17.2 percent of disposable income. The two-earner family in which both parents work full time, all year at the minimum wage received $2,765 from the Canada Child Tax Benefit or 9.8 percent of disposable income.

Minimum wage versus welfare (Figure G8)

For a single person earning the minimum wage in Ontario, disposable income – i.e., minimum wage earnings plus refundable tax credits minus income and payroll taxes – amounted to $12,766 in 2001, which is a sizeable $5,937 more than the $6,829 from welfare and refundable tax credits. Figure G8 shows the comparison.

Minimum wages also pay better than welfare for a single parent with one child age 2, though the advantage is not as great as for single people. Disposable income from after-tax minimum wage earnings, child benefits and refundable tax credits amounted to $18,129 in 2001, or $4,301 more than the $13,828 from welfare, child benefits and refundable tax credits.

Figure G8
Minimum wage versus welfare in Ontario, by household type, 2001

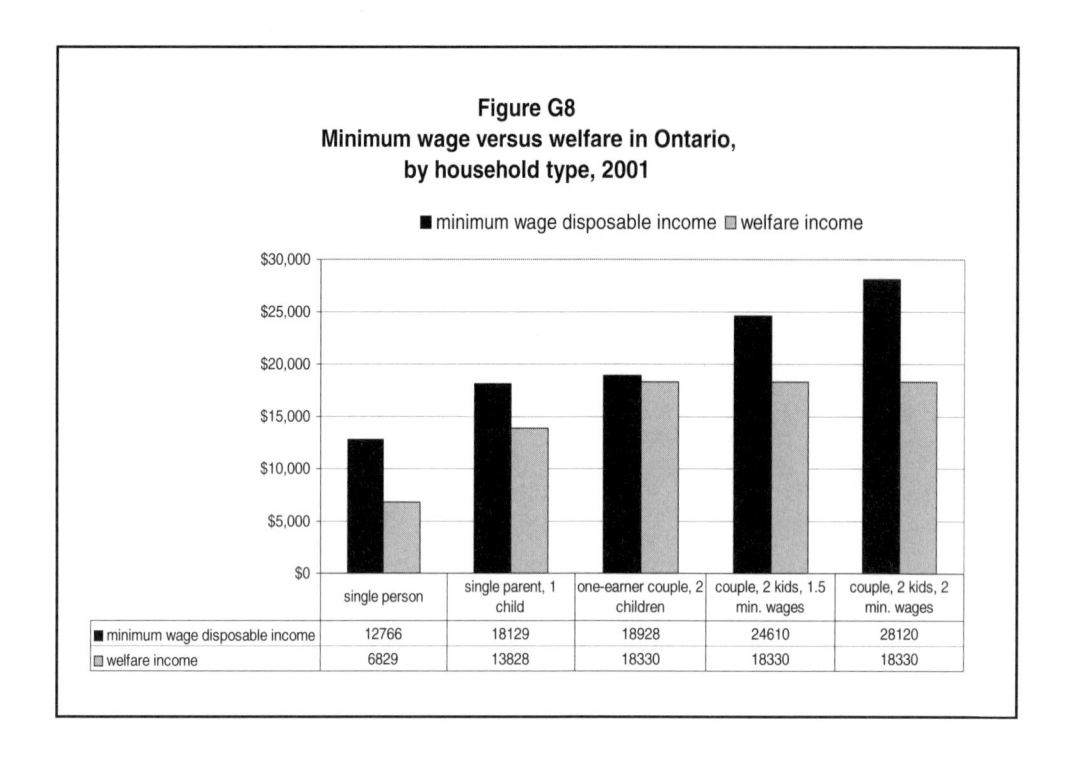

	single person	single parent, 1 child	one-earner couple, 2 children	couple, 2 kids, 1.5 min. wages	couple, 2 kids, 2 min. wages
minimum wage disposable income	12766	18129	18928	24610	28120
welfare income	6829	13828	18330	18330	18330

However, the minimum wage advantage virtually disappears for a one-earner couple earning the minimum wage and supporting two children aged 10 and 15. Total disposable income from minimum wages, child benefits and tax credits came to $18,928, or just $598 more than the $18,330 from welfare, child benefits and refundable tax credits.

Naturally, the minimum wage advantage is greater in the case of two-earner families. We look at two examples.

In the first case, one parent works full time, year round at the minimum wage while the other earns half this amount (i.e., works part-time and/or part-year); as above, there are two children aged 10 and 15. This family's disposable income from one-and-a-half minimum wages came to $24,610 in 2001 or $6,280 more than the $18,330 from welfare, child benefits and the refundable GST credit.

The other two-earner family earns double the minimum wage since we assume that both parents work full time, year round at the minimum wage. Total disposable income was $28,120 or a substantial $9,790 more than the $18,330 from welfare and other government income programs.

148   Caledon Institute of Social Policy

b. Minimum Wage Workers in Ontario

The following text with illustrative graphs analyzes key characteristics of minimum wage workers in Ontario. Appendix 2 provides detailed statistics in tabular form (pages 297-299).

Interprovincial rank: incidence of minimum wage workers (Figure G9)

In 2000, an estimated 223,500 workers in Ontario – 4.5 percent of the total 4,959,500 employees – worked for the minimum wage. Ontario's 4.5 percent figure means that it has the third-lowest incidence of minimum wage workers in Canada, after Prince Edward Island (3.6 percent) and Alberta (2.0 percent). Figure G9 shows the ranking. Ontario's minimum wage incidence is virtually the same as the national average of 4.6 percent.

Minimum wage workers are slightly underrepresented in Ontario While the province accounts for 38.5 percent of all minimum wage workers in the country – the largest share of any province – it has a larger share of all employees (39.7 percent), producing an index of 0.97 (the lower the result below 1.00, the more underrepresented are minimum wage workers). Not surprisingly, Ontario – Canada's largest province – accounts for the largest share of both the minimum wage workforce and the total workforce.

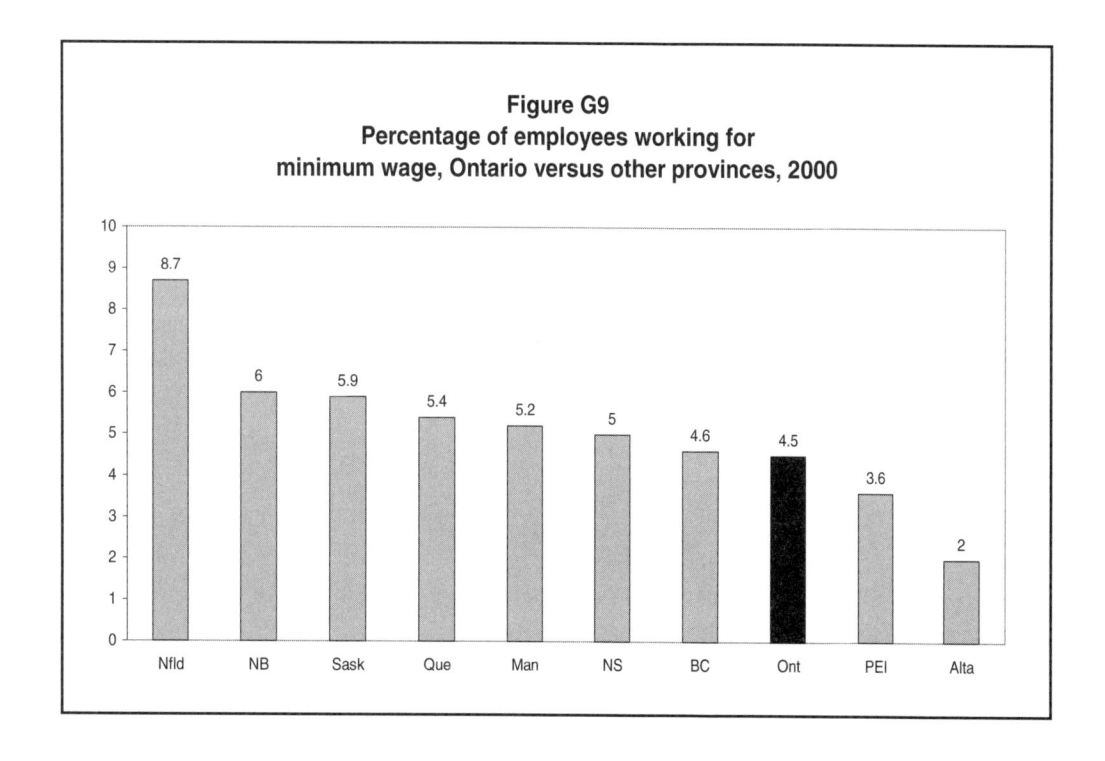

Figure G9
Percentage of employees working for minimum wage, Ontario versus other provinces, 2000

Province	Percentage
Nfld	8.7
NB	6
Sask	5.9
Que	5.4
Man	5.2
NS	5
BC	4.6
Ont	4.5
PEI	3.6
Alta	2

Gender and age (Figures G10-G13)

In Ontario as in the rest of Canada, women run a higher risk of working for minimum wage than men, and women also make up the majority of the minimum wage workforce.

In 2000, 5.8 percent of Ontario's female employees worked for minimum wage compared to only 3.3 percent of male workers. Of the total 223,500 minimum wage workers, 139,800 – 62.6 percent – were women and 83,700 – 37.4 percent – were men, as illustrated in Figure G10.

Women are overrepresented in Ontario's minimum wage workforce. They constituted 62.6 percent of minimum wage workers but only 48.5 percent of all the province's employees in 2000. Men are underrepresented. They accounted for only 37.4 percent of minimum wage workers but more than half (51.5 percent) of all employees.

The gender bias among minimum wage workers holds when we control for major age categories. Figure G11 shows that, while younger workers of both sexes run a higher risk of working for minimum wage, women still fare worse than men within each age category.

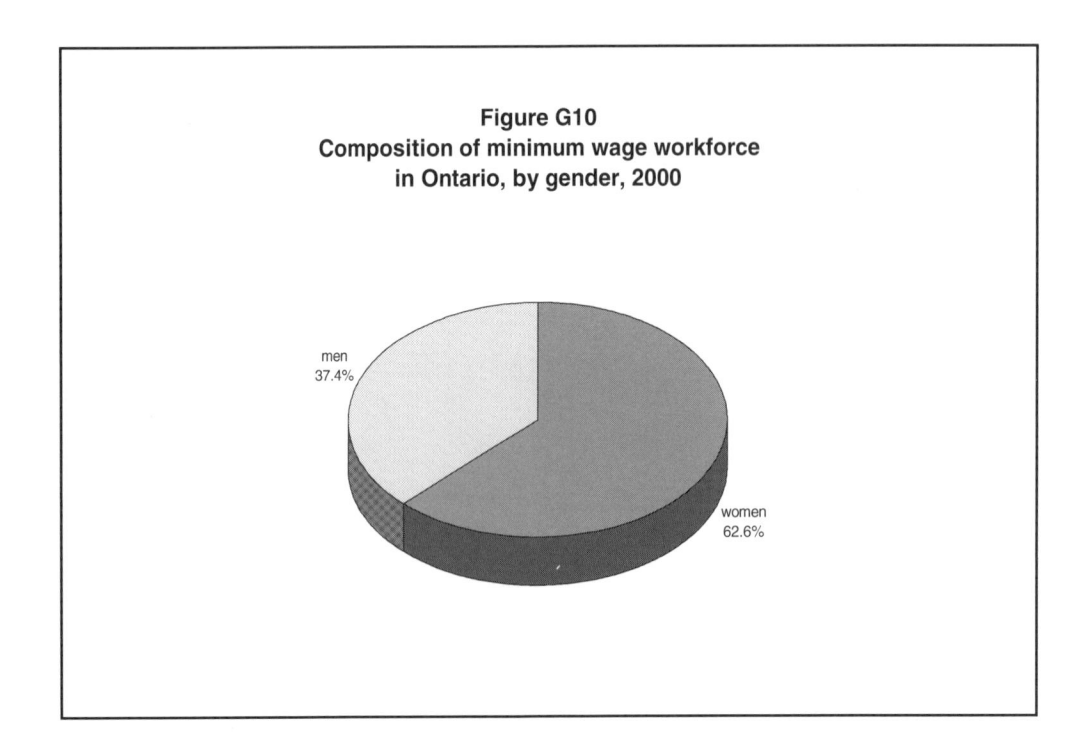

**Figure G10
Composition of minimum wage workforce
in Ontario, by gender, 2000**

men 37.4%

women 62.6%

Figure G11
Percentage of employees working for minimum wage in Ontario, by gender and age, 2000

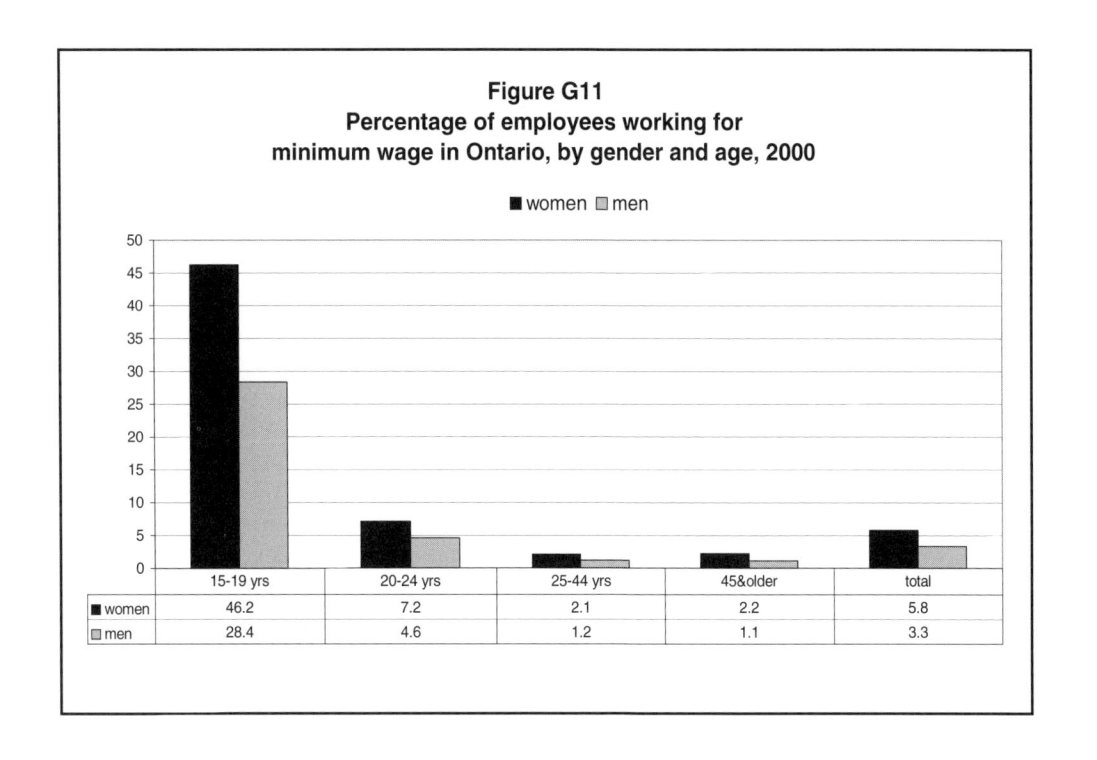

	15-19 yrs	20-24 yrs	25-44 yrs	45&older	total
women	46.2	7.2	2.1	2.2	5.8
men	28.4	4.6	1.2	1.1	3.3

Figure G12
Share of minimum wage workers versus share of all employees in Ontario, by age group, 2000

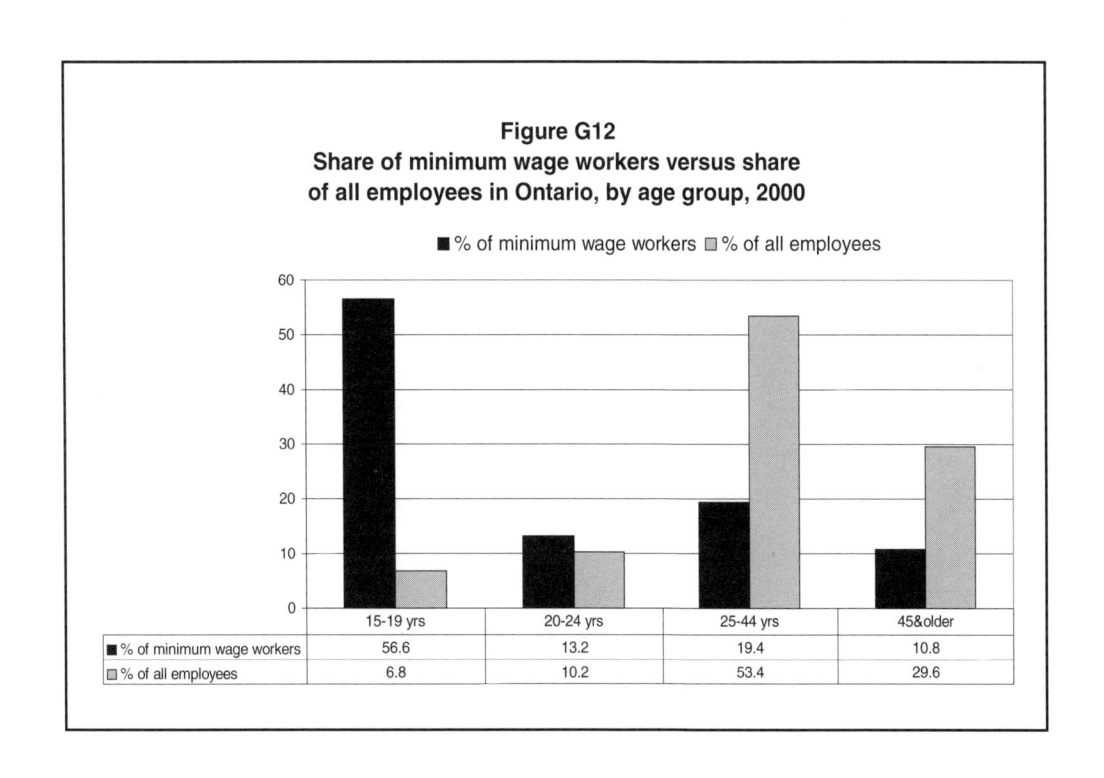

	15-19 yrs	20-24 yrs	25-44 yrs	45&older
% of minimum wage workers	56.6	13.2	19.4	10.8
% of all employees	6.8	10.2	53.4	29.6

Among female workers aged 15 to 19, 46.2 percent worked for the minimum wage in 2000 in contrast to 28.4 percent of male workers in the same age group. Among employees aged 20-24, 7.2 percent of women compared to 4.6 percent of men worked for the minimum wage. Among workers 25-44, 2.1 percent of women as opposed to 1.2 percent of men were at the bottom of the wage ladder. Among employees 45 and older, 2.2 percent of women but only 1.1 percent of men worked for the minimum wage in Ontario.

The minimum wage risk gap between the sexes is wider for older workers. Women in the 15-24 age group are 1.2 times more likely to work for the minimum wage than men in that age group, but the ratio increases to 1.8 for those aged 25-44 and 2.0 for those over 45.

Young people not only are more likely to work for minimum wage than other employees, but the young also make up a large proportion of the minimum wage workforce. Figure G12 compares the age makeup of minimum wage workers and all employees in Ontario. More than half (56.6 percent) of minimum wage workers are in the 15-19 age group, as opposed to just 6.8 percent of all employees. Employees aged 20-24 represent 13.2 percent of minimum wage workers as opposed to 10.2 percent of all workers. All told, seven in ten minimum wage workers in Ontario (69.8) are under 25 years of age.

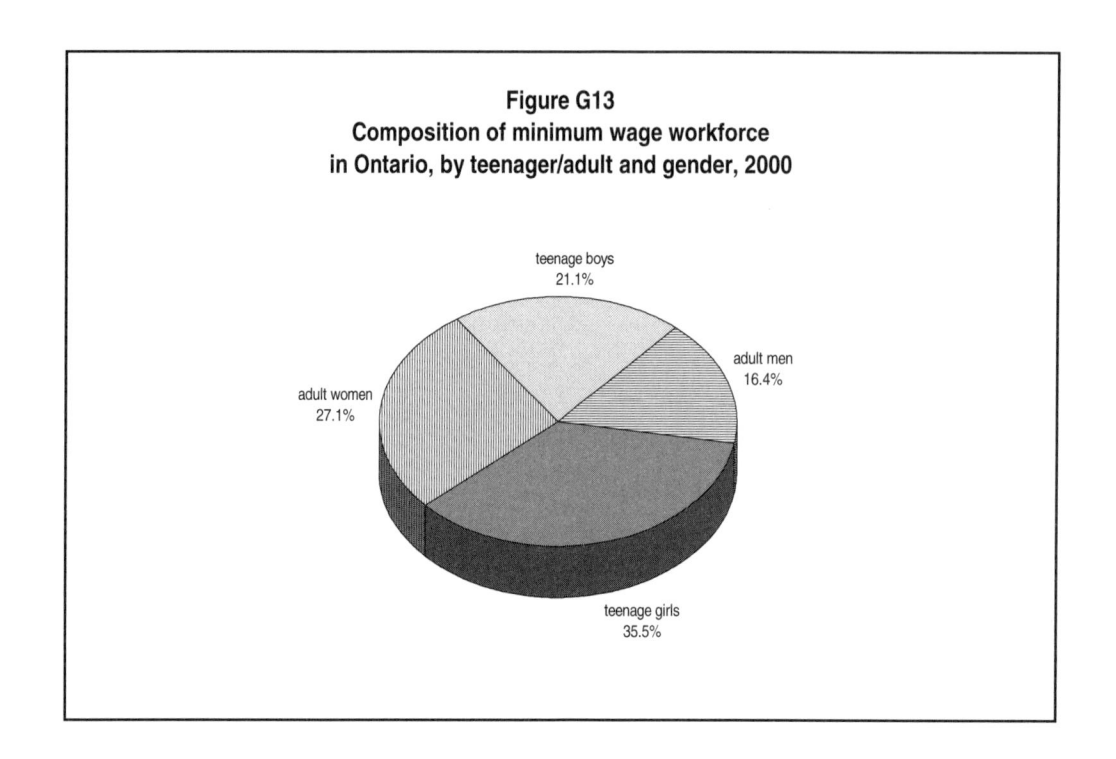

Figure G13
Composition of minimum wage workforce in Ontario, by teenager/adult and gender, 2000

- teenage boys 21.1%
- adult men 16.4%
- teenage girls 35.5%
- adult women 27.1%

The opposite holds for older workers. While a sizeable proportion – 19.4 percent – of minimum wage workers in Ontario are between 25 and 44, that age group constitutes a much larger proportion – 53.4 percent or more than half – of all employees. Workers aged 45 and older make up just 10.8 percent of minimum wage employees but 29.6 percent all employees.

Figure G13 divides the minimum wage workforce in Ontario into teenage girls and boys and adult women and men. Teenage girls are the largest group, at 79,300 or 35.5 percent of the total, followed by adult women (60,500 or 27.1 percent), teenage boys (47,100 or 21.1 percent) and adult men (36,600 or 16.4 percent). The majority (56.6 percent) of Ontario's minimum wage workers are teenagers, whereas on a national basis (and in most other jurisdictions) adults form the majority (at 52.9 percent nationally).

Education (Figures G14 and G15)

Figure G14 shows the incidence of minimum wage workers in Ontario according to level of education.

At first glance, the relationship between level of education and incidence of minimum wage employment does not seem to correspond to common sense: Workers in the lowest educational group

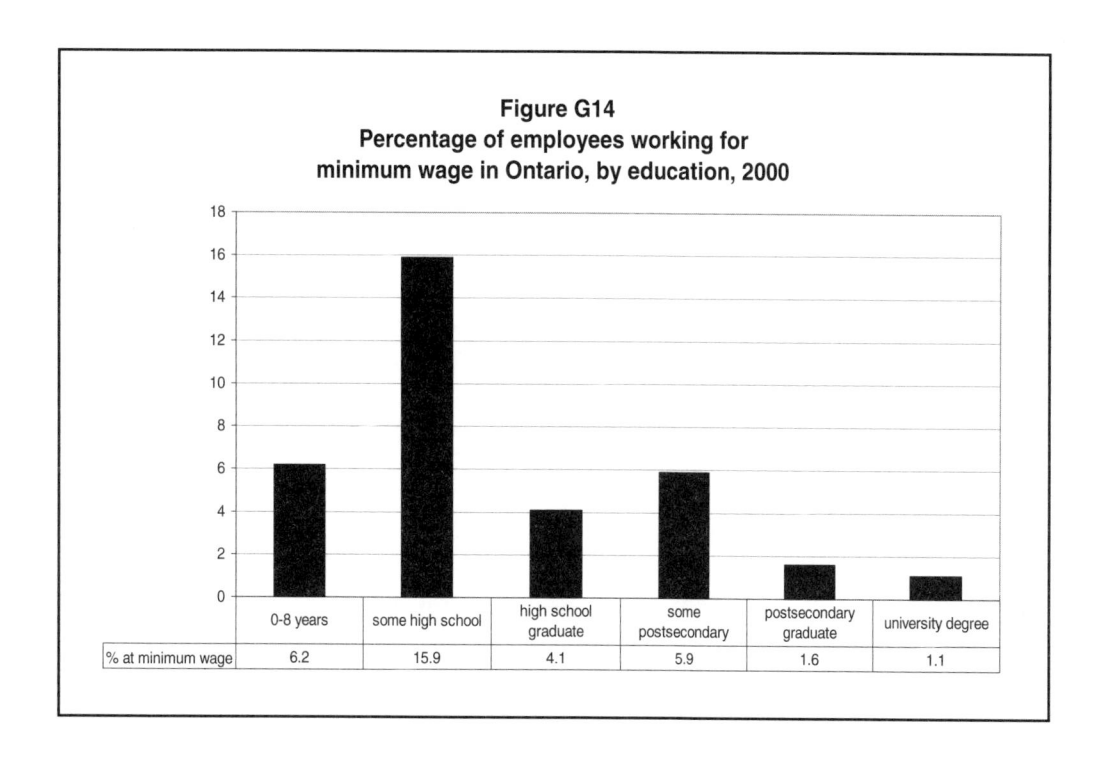

Figure G14
Percentage of employees working for minimum wage in Ontario, by education, 2000

	0-8 years	some high school	high school graduate	some postsecondary	postsecondary graduate	university degree
% at minimum wage	6.2	15.9	4.1	5.9	1.6	1.1

**Figure G15
Composition of minimum wage workforce
in Ontario, by education, 2000**

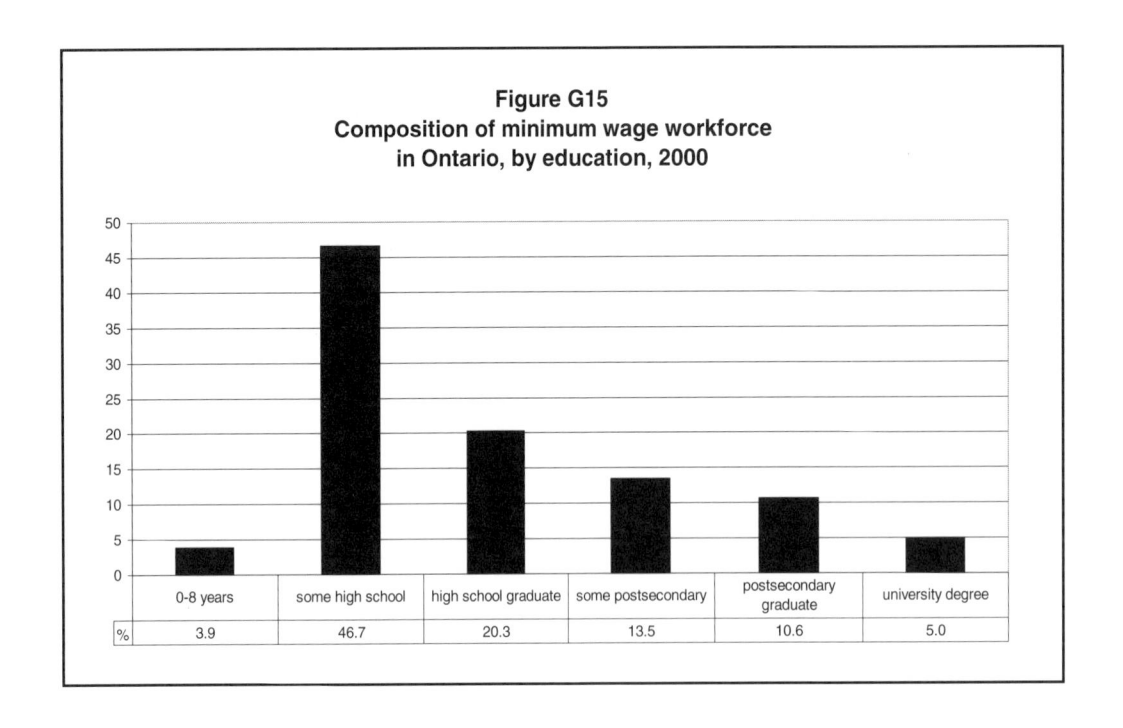

	0-8 years	some high school	high school graduate	some postsecondary	postsecondary graduate	university degree
%	3.9	46.7	20.3	13.5	10.6	5.0

(elementary education only) are less likely to work for minimum wage (6.2 percent do) than those with some high school (15.9 percent), while those with some postsecondary education run a higher risk (5.9 percent) than high school graduates (4.1 percent). However, as one would expect, the chances of working for minimum wage are lowest for the two highest education categories – 1.6 percent for those with a postsecondary certificate or diploma (e.g., from community college) and only 1.1 percent for those with a university degree.

Once we look at the education-minimum wage link for different age groups, the reasons for the apparently inconsistent relationship comes clear: Young people working at part-time or seasonal (i.e., summer) jobs – typically paying the minimum or a low wage – figure prominently in the 'some high school' and 'some postsecondary education' categories; they are still at high school, community college or university, whereas workers in the other educational categories have completed their education.

Figure G15 shows each educational group's share of Ontario's minimum wage workforce in 2000. The largest group of minimum wage workers are those with some high school (46.7 percent), followed by high school graduates (20.3 percent), those with some postsecondary education (13.5 percent), postsecondary graduates (10.6 percent), university graduates (5.0 percent) and those with 0-8 years of education (3.9 percent). Many minimum wage workers are students (high school or postsecondary) pursuing their education. A significant group of minimum wage workers (29.1 percent) have some form of postsecondary education.

Full-time and part-time work (Figures G16 and G17)

The fact that young people are more likely to work part time helps explain why workers still pursuing their education tend to face a higher risk of minimum wage work than those who have completed their schooling and are working full time. Figure G16 indicates that 17.2 percent of part-time workers are at the minimum wage compared to only 1.8 percent of those employed full time.

While the majority of minimum wage workers in Ontario (66.1 percent) work part time, a sizeable group (33.9 percent) are employed full time. Figure G17 pictures the results.

Gender alters the relationship between full-time and part-time work and the minimum wage. Women who work part time in Ontario run a lesser risk of being at the bottom of the wage ladder than do men who work part time (15.8 and 20.4 percent, respectively). However, women employed full time are more likely than men in that group to earn the minimum wage (2.5 and 1.3 percent, respectively).

Women make up the majority of minimum wage employees in the province working both full time (59.4 percent are women) and part time (64.2 percent are women). Among all employees, though, women constitute a minority of full-time workers (44.0 percent) but the bulk of part-time workers (69.8 percent).

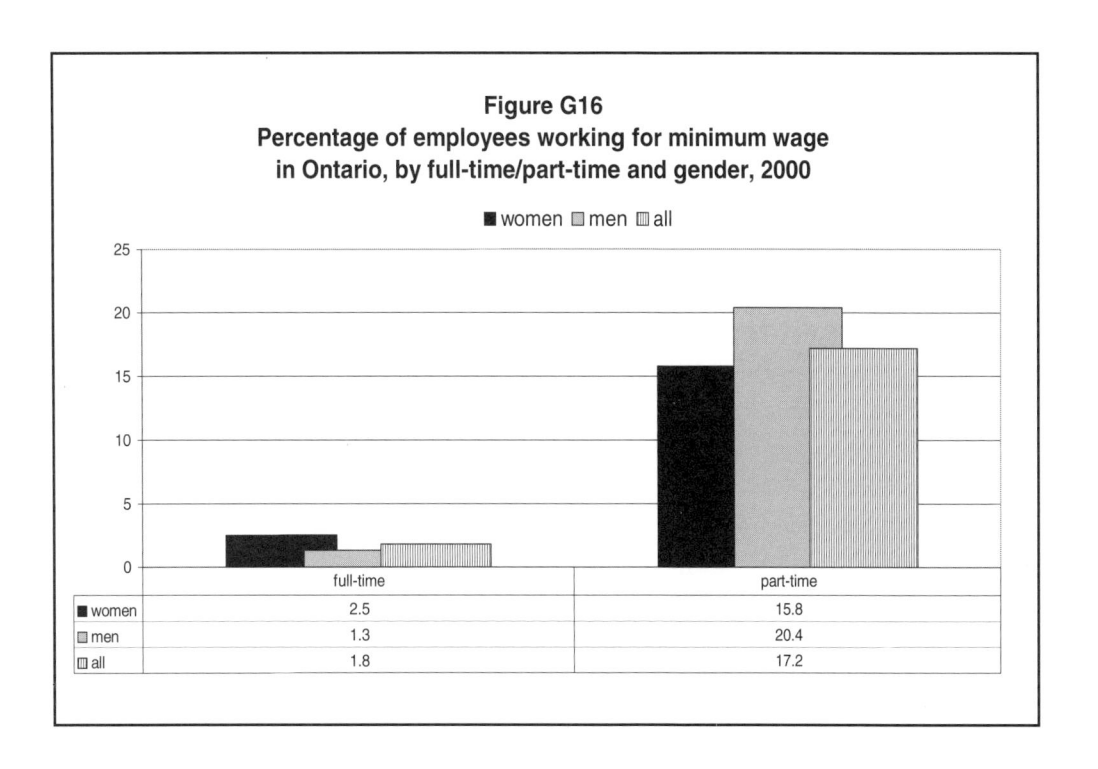

Figure G16
Percentage of employees working for minimum wage in Ontario, by full-time/part-time and gender, 2000

	full-time	part-time
women	2.5	15.8
men	1.3	20.4
all	1.8	17.2

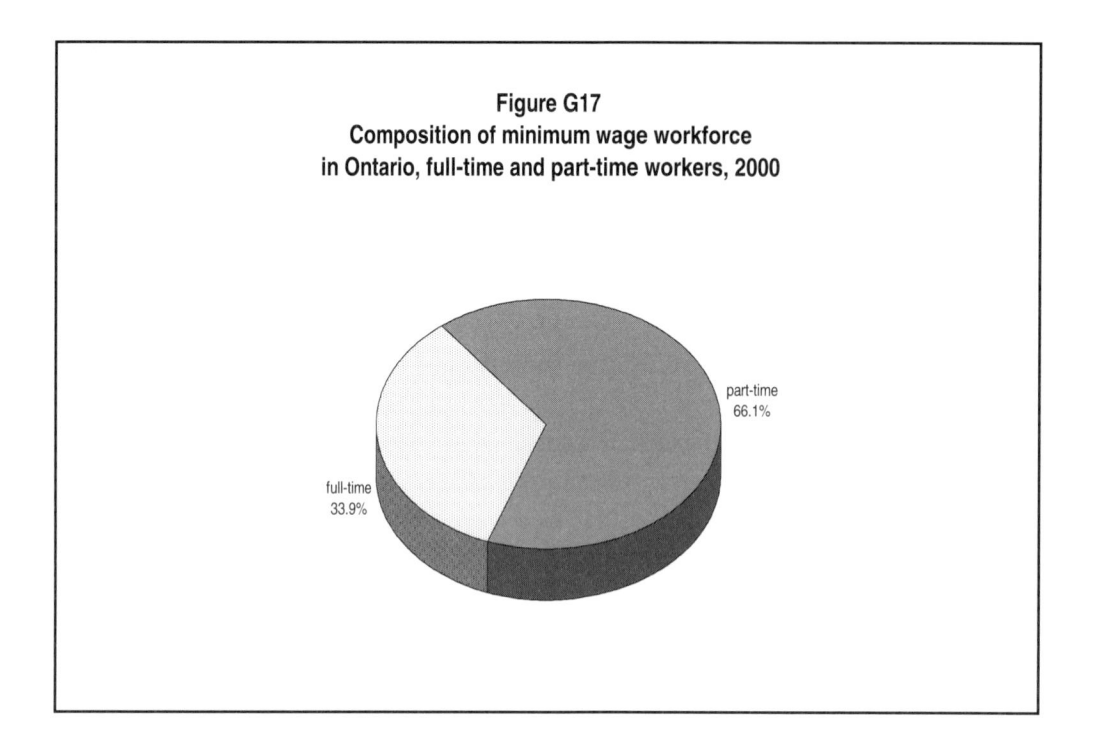

**Figure G17
Composition of minimum wage workforce
in Ontario, full-time and part-time workers, 2000**

part-time 66.1%
full-time 33.9%

Family status (Figure G18)

We noted above that seven in ten of Ontario's minimum wage workers are under 25 years of age. Light on this fundamental fact of the minimum wage workforce is shed by information on family status, illustrated in Figure G18.

The largest group of minimum wage workers – 153,500 or 68.8 percent of the total 223,500 – are older children living with their parents (or relatives with relatives, as in the case of a niece or nephew living with an aunt and uncle, or grandchildren with grandparents). Of this category, 121,000 or 78.8 percent are aged 15-19, 22,000 or 14.3 percent are 20-24 and the remaining 10,600 or 6.9 percent are 25 or older. Six in ten (96,300 or 62.7 percent) are still in school and working part-time or part-year (e.g., in summer).

The next largest group of minimum wage workers in Ontario – 41,800 or 18.7 percent of the total – are members of couples (married or living together). In most cases (31,000 or 74.2 percent of the category total of 41,800), the minimum wage worker's spouse is employed, typically at more than the minimum wage. A typical example in this category would be mothers combining (unpaid) childrearing work with part-time minimum wage work. Another 10,800 or 25.8 percent of minimum wage workers living in couples have a spouse who is not employed (most of the latter are not in the labour force).

An estimated 19,100 or 8.5 percent of minimum wage workers are unattached individuals. Just under half of this category (9,300 or 48.7 percent) live alone; of this group, 1,700 are 15-24, 4,800 are aged 25-54 and 2,800 are 55 or older. About 9,900 of the province's unattached minimum wage workers live with friends or roommates; in this category, 4,400 are under 24, 4,800 are 25-44 and 600 are 55 or older.

Finally, some 9,000 or 4.0 percent of Ontario's minimum wage workers head families with no spouse present; most (8,100) are single parents with children under 18.

Industry

National data show that the incidence and distribution of minimum wage workers varies significantly according to industries. The same applies to Ontario, though sample size constraints preclude estimates for two of the 16 industrial categories (forestry, fishing, mining, oil and gas; utilities). Among the industrial categories for which estimates are available, accommodation and food services top the list (22.1 percent of employees work for minimum wage), followed by agriculture (17.4 percent), trade (9.6 percent), other

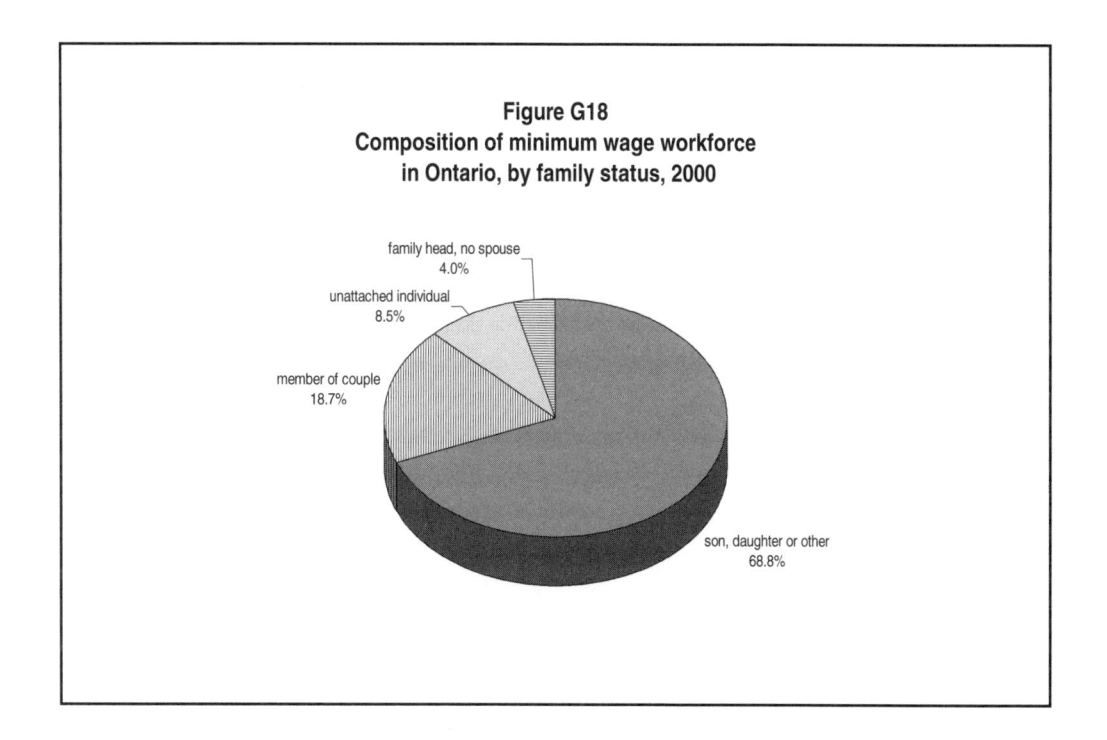

Figure G18
Composition of minimum wage workforce
in Ontario, by family status, 2000

- family head, no spouse 4.0%
- unattached individual 8.5%
- member of couple 18.7%
- son, daughter or other 68.8%

services (6.5 percent), information, culture and recreation (6.0 percent), management, administrative and other support (3.7 percent), finance, insurance, real estate and leasing (2.4 percent), transportation and warehousing (2.3 percent), educational services (2.1 percent), health care and social assistance (1.7 percent), public administration (1.0 percent) and, finally, construction and manufacturing at a tiny 0.8 percent each.

Estimates are available for the industrial composition of the whole employed workforce in Ontario. Manufacturing tops the list, at an estimated 1,066,100 or 21.5 percent of all employees. Next comes trade (750,600 or 15.1 percent) followed by health care and social assistance (472,100 or 9.5 percent of all employees), educational services (349,000 or 7.0 percent), finance, insurance, real estate and leasing (331,700 or 6.7 percent), accommodation and food services (308,200 or 6.2 percent), professional, scientific and technical services (279,000 or 5.6 percent), public administration (274,000 or 5.5 percent), information, culture and recreation (239,800 or 4.8 percent), transportation and warehousing (221,700 or 4.5 percent), construction (205,600 or 4.1 percent), management, administrative and other support (177,800 or 3.6 percent), other services (167,300 or 3.4 percent), utilities (46,300 or 0.9 percent), agriculture (39,100 or 0.8 percent) and forestry, fishing, mining, oil and gas (31,400 or 0.6 percent).

MANITOBA

a. Minimum Wages in Manitoba

Interprovincial rank: dollar value of minimum wage (Figure H1)

Manitoba's minimum wage increased from $6.00 to $6.25 on April 1, 2001 and again on April 1, 2002 to $6.60 an hour, producing an hourly average of $6.44 for 2002. In 2002, Manitoba's $6.44 average hourly minimum wage ranked the province about mid-pack (seventh-highest) among Canada's ten provinces and three territories, the lowest being Newfoundland ($5.71) and the highest British Columbia ($8.00).

Trend in dollar value of minimum wage (Figure H2)

Because minimum wages are not indexed, their value changes over time. Figure H2 shows the trend in Manitoba's minimum wage from 1965 to 2002; each year's average minimum wage has been converted to inflation-adjusted (i.e., constant) 2002 dollars to show the real trend, after taking into account the impact of inflation on the dollar.

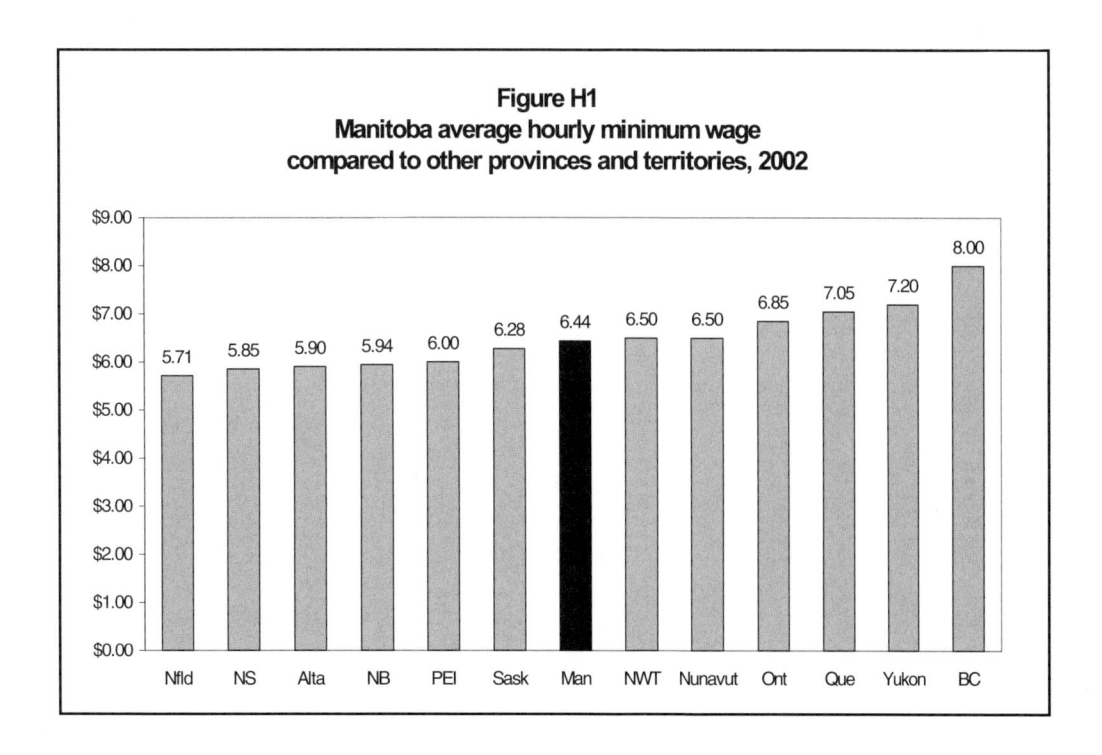

Figure H1
Manitoba average hourly minimum wage compared to other provinces and territories, 2002

Nfld	5.71
NS	5.85
Alta	5.90
NB	5.94
PEI	6.00
Sask	6.28
Man	6.44
NWT	6.50
Nunavut	6.50
Ont	6.85
Que	7.05
Yukon	7.20
BC	8.00

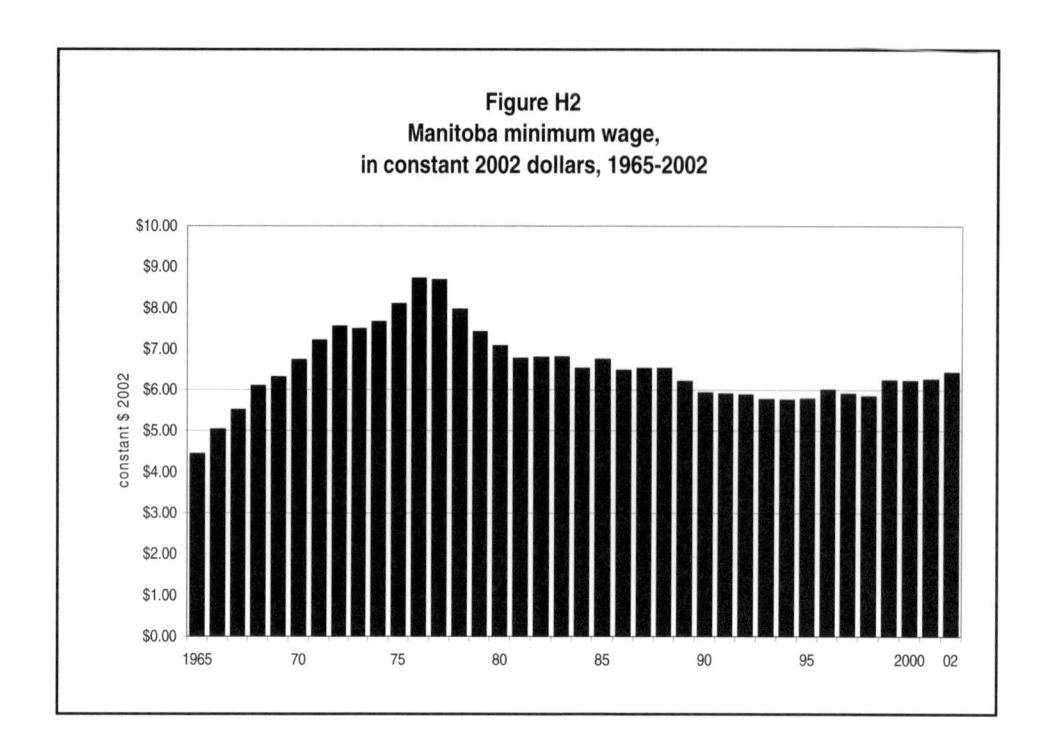

**Figure H2
Manitoba minimum wage,
in constant 2002 dollars, 1965-2002**

Manitoba's minimum wage almost doubled between 1965 ($4.45 an hour) and its 1976 peak ($8.73), declined in several step-like stages until the mid-1990s ($5.78 in 1994) and then increased a bit in the latter part of the 1990s and into the next decade to reach $6.44 in 2002. Its value in 2002 was a sizeable $2.29 or 26.2 percent lower than the 1976 high point, though $1.99 or 44.6 percent higher than in 1965.

Interprovincial rank: minimum wages as percentage of average earnings (Figure H3)

Manitoba ranks higher in terms of how its minimum wage compares to its average wage. In 2001 (the most recent year for which data on average earnings are available), Manitoba's $6.19 minimum wage represented 41.8 percent of its $14.81 hourly average earnings, placing the province fourth-highest among 13 jurisdictions that range from the Northwest Territories at 30.2 percent to British Columbia at 46.2 percent. Figure H3 shows the ranking.

Trends in minimum wage and average earnings (Figure H4)

The black line in Figure H4 shows the trend in the minimum wage, the gray line the trend in average earnings and the vertical bars the trend in the minimum wage as a percentage of average earnings. Read the

Figure H3
Manitoba minimum wage as % of average earnings, compared to other provinces and territories, 2001

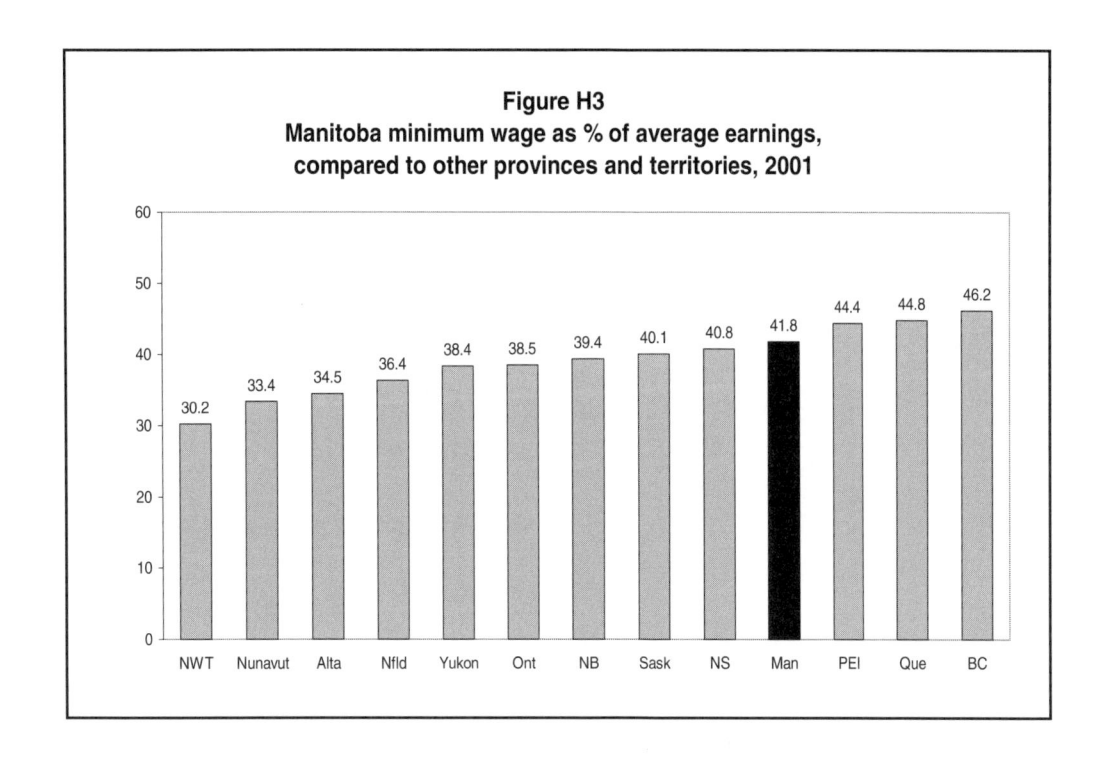

Region	%
NWT	30.2
Nunavut	33.4
Alta	34.5
Nfld	36.4
Yukon	38.4
Ont	38.5
NB	39.4
Sask	40.1
NS	40.8
Man	41.8
PEI	44.4
Que	44.8
BC	46.2

Figure H4
Manitoba minimum wage compared to average earnings, 1965-2001

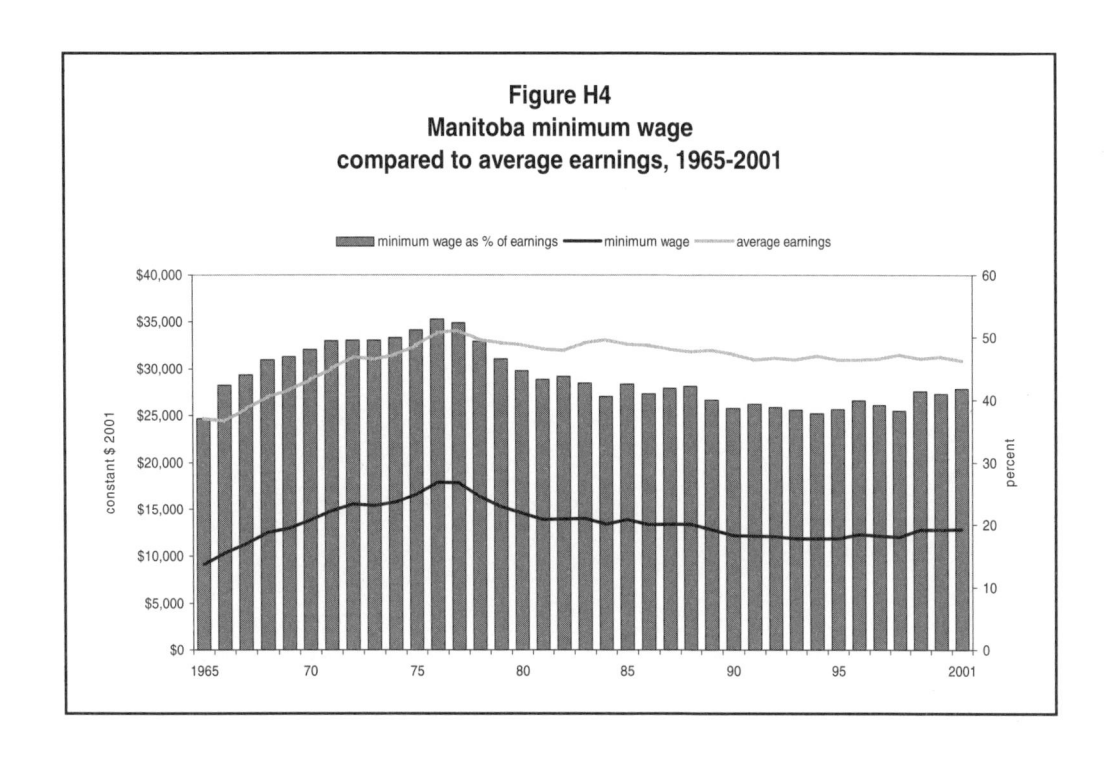

left-hand axis for the minimum wage and average earnings and the right-hand axis for the minimum wage as a percentage of earnings.

The long-term trend indicates that Manitoba's minimum wage increased from 37.0 percent of average earnings in 1965 to 52.9 percent in 1976, fell to 37.9 percent in 1994 and climbed back up to 41.8 percent in 2001. The up-down-slightly up trend is similar to that for the dollar value of the minimum wage.

Average earnings in Manitoba went from $24,704 in 1965 to $34,090 in 1977 and then saw a slow overall decline to $30,814 in 2001. The province's minimum wage also increased between 1965 and the mid-1970s but then declined overall thereafter, which explains why it also fell as a percentage of average wages. On an annual (full-time, all-year) basis, Manitoba's minimum wage went from $9,140 in 1965 to $17,918 in 1976, declined to $11,863 in 1994 and stood at $12,870 in 2001.

Minimum wage compared to before-tax poverty lines (Figure H5)

Statistics Canada publishes two sets of low income cut-offs. The before-tax low income cut-offs are based on gross, pre-tax income (i.e., income from employment, investments, private pensions and other private sources plus income from government programs such as public pensions, Employment Insurance, child benefits and welfare). The after-tax low income cut-offs use the same definition of income but also factor into the picture the federal and provincial income taxes that Canadians pay. We first compare the minimum wage to the before-tax poverty lines, illustrated in Figure H5.

Because the poverty line is lower for smaller communities, the minimum wage represents a larger proportion of the poverty line in smaller communities. In 2002, Manitoba's minimum wage ranged from 70.2 percent of the before-tax low income line for one person in Winnipeg (which falls in the 500,000-plus category) to 82.7 percent for small urban areas between 30,000 and 99,999 inhabitants, 88.9 percent for towns under 30,000 and 102.0 percent for rural areas. Note that Manitoba has no cities in the 100,000-499,999 category, the second-largest population size in the low income cut-offs.

Manitoba's minimum wage in 2002 fell $5,684 short of the before-tax low income line for one person in Winnipeg, $2,792 under the line for communities between 30,000 and 99,999 inhabitants, $1,667 beneath for towns under 30,000 but $261 above the poverty line for rural residents. Figure H5 shows the dollar gap between the minimum wage and the before-tax poverty line for one person in different size communities throughout Manitoba.

Because the poverty line varies by family size, minimum wages (which do not vary by family size) fall farther below the poverty line for families than for single workers. We look at the poverty gap for a single parent with one child, which falls in the two-person family size category. In 2002, Manitoba's minimum wage varied from 56.2 percent of the before-tax low income line for a two-person family in

**Figure H5
Dollars below before-tax poverty line
for different size communities,
Manitoba minimum wage, 2002**

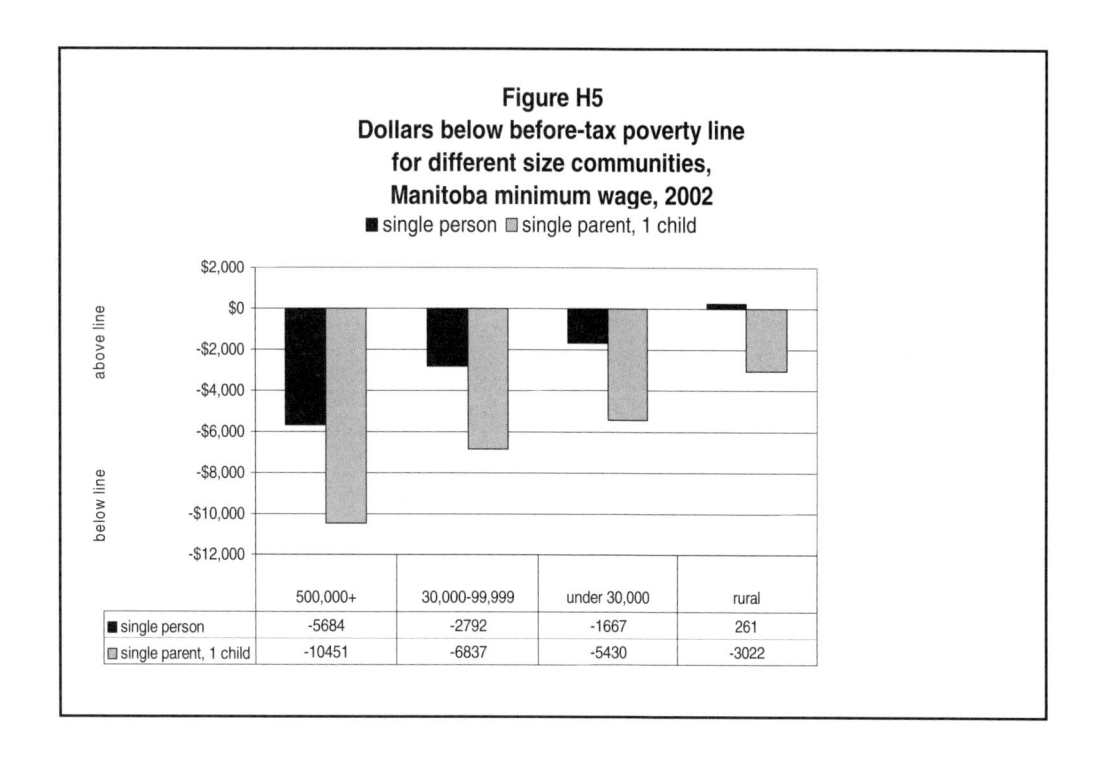

	500,000+	30,000-99,999	under 30,000	rural
single person	-5684	-2792	-1667	261
single parent, 1 child	-10451	-6837	-5430	-3022

Winnipeg to 66.2 percent for communities between 30,000 and 99,999 inhabitants, 71.7 percent for towns under 30,000 and 81.6 percent for rural residents. Manitoba's minimum wage fell $10,451 below the before-tax low income line for a family of two in Winnipeg, $6,837 beneath for communities between 30,000 and 99,999 inhabitants, $5,430 below for towns under 30,000 and $3,022 under the line for rural residents.

Trend in minimum wage as percentage of before-tax poverty lines (Figure H6)

The long-term trend when we compare the minimum wage to the poverty line (as measured by Statistics Canada's before-tax low income cut-offs, which vary by size of family and of community), is the same as the trend in dollar value. In 2002, the estimated before-tax low income line for a city the size of Winnipeg was $19,074 for one person and $23,841 for a family of two.

Manitoba's minimum wage rose from 48.5 percent of the poverty line for one person living in Winnipeg in 1965 to 95.2 percent in 1976, falling to 63.0 percent by 1994 but climbing back to 70.2 percent in 2002. For a two-person family (e.g., a single parent with one child), the minimum wage went from 38.8 percent of the before-tax low income cut-off for Winnipeg in 1965 to a peak of 76.1 percent in 1976, declined to 50.4 percent by 1994 but rose to 56.2 percent in 2002. Figure H6 shows the trends.

**Figure H6
Manitoba minimum wage as % of before-tax poverty line for largest city, 1965-2002**

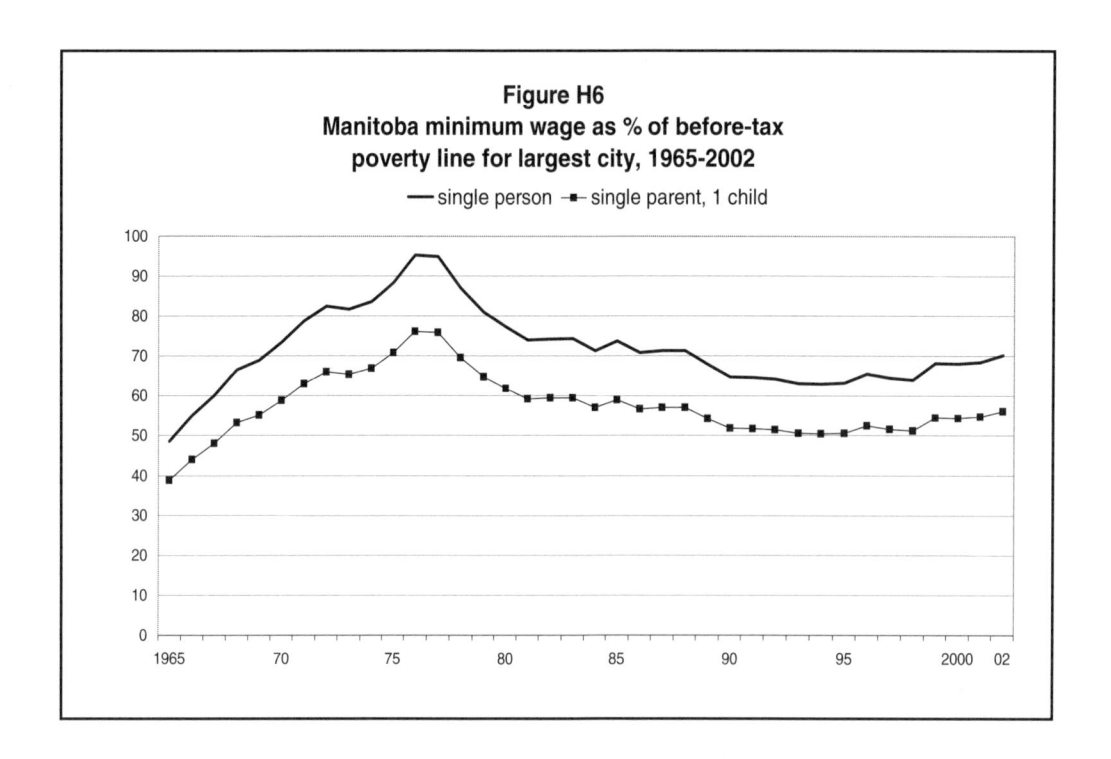

Minimum wage compared to after-tax poverty lines (Figure H7)

Statistics Canada publishes after-tax low income cut-offs as well as before-tax low income cut-offs. We look here at how after-tax minimum wage incomes in Manitoba for five types of household – single persons, single parents with one child, one-earner couples with two children, two-earner couples supporting two children on one-and-a-half minimum wages, and two-earner couples with two children and two full minimum wages – compare to the after-tax poverty lines for different size communities. 'After-tax minimum wage incomes' means incomes from the minimum wage and available federal and provincial income programs minus federal and provincial income taxes. Figure H7 gives the results.

For a single person earning the minimum wage, after-tax income came to $12,608,[42] which is $2,956 below the after-tax poverty line for Winnipeg (a metropolitan centre with over 500,000 residents) and $300 below for centres of 30,000-99,999, though $813 above the line for towns under 30,000 and $2,404 above the poverty line for rural residents. A single parent with one child received $16,754[43] in after-tax income from minimum wage earnings and federal and provincial child benefits and tax credits, which came to $2,238 below the after-tax poverty line for Winnipeg but $1,004 over the line for centres between 30,000 and 99,999, $2,361 above for towns under 30,000 and $4,303 above the poverty line for rural residents.

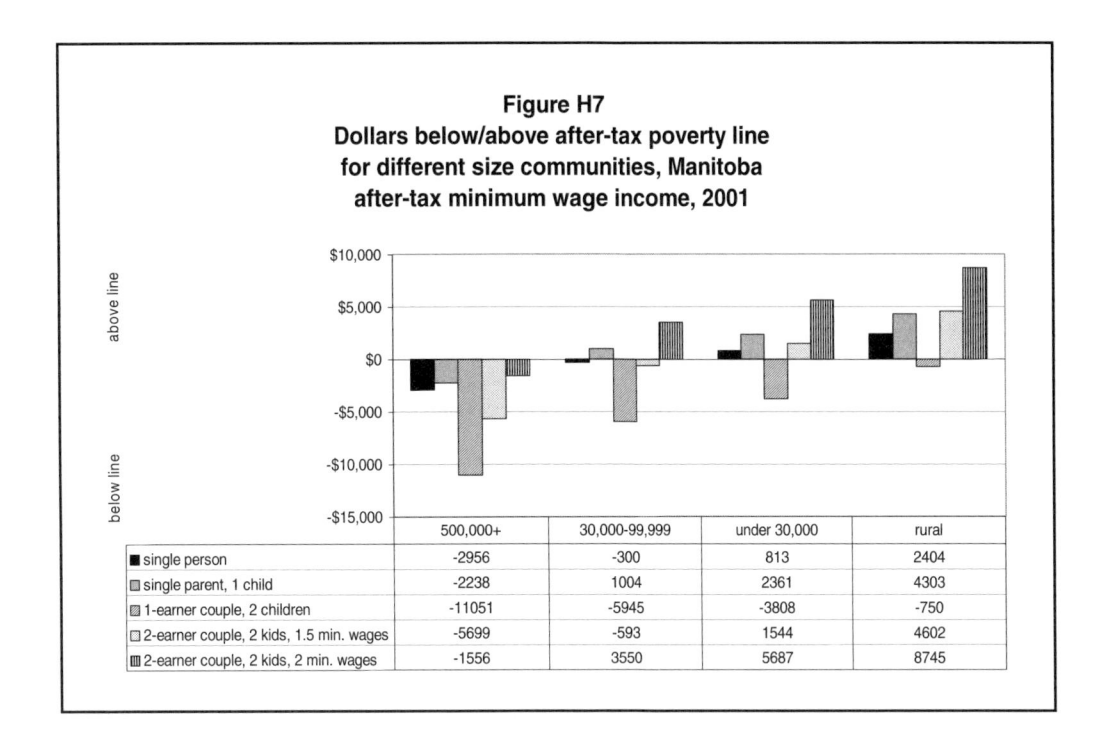

Figure H7
Dollars below/above after-tax poverty line for different size communities, Manitoba after-tax minimum wage income, 2001

	500,000+	30,000-99,999	under 30,000	rural
single person	-2956	-300	813	2404
single parent, 1 child	-2238	1004	2361	4303
1-earner couple, 2 children	-11051	-5945	-3808	-750
2-earner couple, 2 kids, 1.5 min. wages	-5699	-593	1544	4602
2-earner couple, 2 kids, 2 min. wages	-1556	3550	5687	8745

For a one-earner couple with two children, after-tax minimum wage income amounted to $18,865[44] – $11,051 below the after-tax poverty line for Winnipeg, $5,945 under for centres between 30,000 and 99,999, $3,808 below for towns smaller than 30,000 and $750 under the after-tax poverty line for rural residents. (No results are given for the 100,000-499,999 size since Manitoba has no cities in that category). For a two-earner couple supporting two children on combined parents' earnings of one-and-a-half minimum wages, after-tax minimum wage income amounted to $24,217[45] – $5,699 below the after-tax poverty line for Winnipeg and $593 under for centres between 30,000 and 99,999, though $1,544 above the line for towns smaller than 30,000 and $4,602 over the after-tax poverty line for rural residents. For a two-earner couple with two children and both parents working full time, year round for the minimum wage, after-tax minimum wage income was $28,360[46] – $1,556 below the after-tax poverty line for Winnipeg but $3,550 above the line for centres between 30,000 and 99,999, $5,687 over for towns smaller than 30,000 and $8,745 above the after-tax poverty line for rural residents.

Contribution of child benefits

Child benefits supplement the incomes of the large majority of Canadian families and are especially important to low- and modest-income families. Improvements to the federal Canada Child Tax Benefit are boosting the incomes of minimum wage and other working poor families.

The single-parent minimum wage worker with one child got $2,447 from the Canada Child Tax Benefit and $120 from the Manitoba Child Related Income Support Program (CRISP) – for a total of $2,567 or 16.0 percent of disposable income. The one-earner couple with two children received $4,250 from the Canada Child Tax Benefit and $269 from the Child Related Income Support Program for a total child benefit of $4,519, worth 24.9 percent of disposable income.

The two-earner family in which one parent works full time, all year at the minimum wage and the other parent half that time got child benefits of $4,250 from the Canada Child Tax Benefit, which represents 18.3 percent of disposable income. The two-earner family in which both parents work full time, all year at the minimum wage received $3,350 from the Canada Child Tax Benefit or 12.4 percent of disposable income.

Minimum wage versus welfare (Figure H8)

For a single person earning the minimum wage in Manitoba, disposable income – i.e., minimum wage earnings plus refundable tax credits minus income and payroll taxes – amounted to $11,915 in 2001, which is a sizeable $6,357 more than the $5,558 from welfare and refundable tax credits. Figure H8 illustrates the comparison.

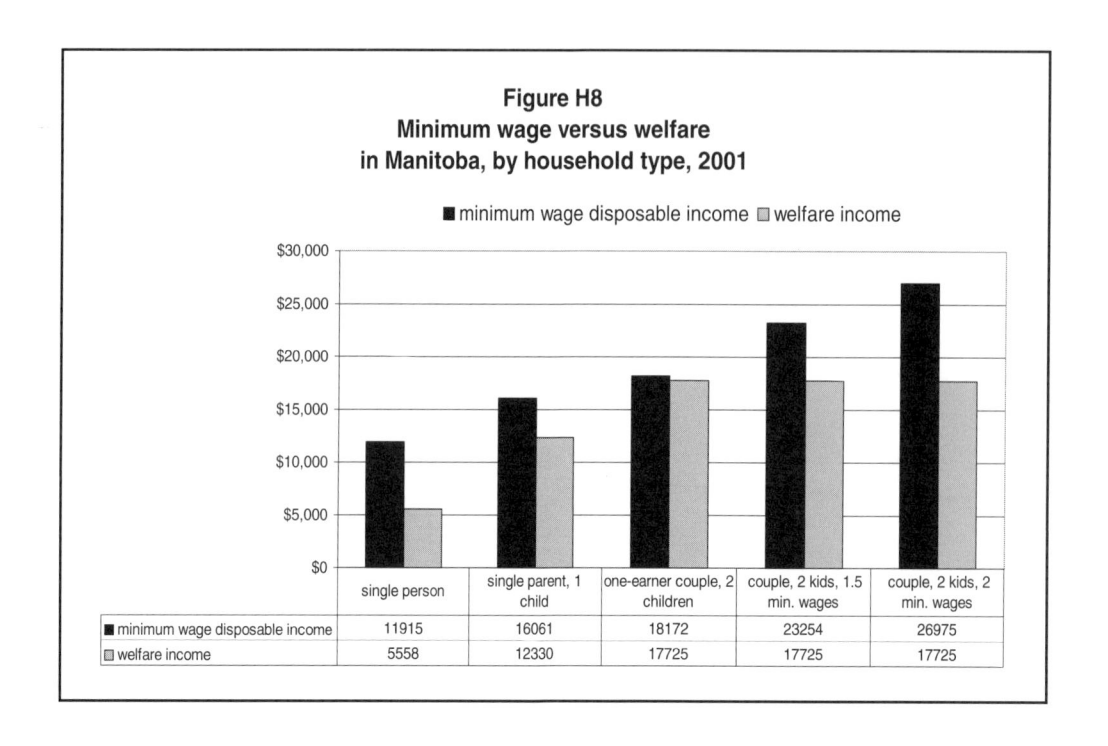

Figure H8
Minimum wage versus welfare in Manitoba, by household type, 2001

	single person	single parent, 1 child	one-earner couple, 2 children	couple, 2 kids, 1.5 min. wages	couple, 2 kids, 2 min. wages
minimum wage disposable income	11915	16061	18172	23254	26975
welfare income	5558	12330	17725	17725	17725

Minimum wages also pay better than welfare for a single parent with one child age 2, though the advantage is not as great as for single people. Disposable income from after-tax minimum wage earnings, child benefits and refundable tax credits amounted to $16,061 in 2001, or $3,731 more than the $12,330 from welfare, child benefits and refundable tax credits.

However, the minimum wage advantage virtually disappears for a one-earner couple earning the minimum wage and supporting two children aged 10 and 15. Total disposable income from minimum wages, child benefits and tax credits came to $18,172, or just $447 more than the $17,725 from welfare, child benefits and refundable tax credits.

Naturally, the minimum wage advantage is greater in the case of two-earner families. We look at two examples.

In the first case, one parent works full time, year round at the minimum wage while the other earns half this amount (i.e., works part-time and/or part-year); as above, there are two children aged 10 and 15. This family's disposable income from one-and-a-half minimum wages came to $23,254 in 2001 or $5,529 more than the $17,725 from welfare, child benefits and the refundable GST credit.

The other two-earner family earns double the minimum wage since we assume that both parents work full time, year round at the minimum wage. Total disposable income was $26,975 or a substantial $9,250 more than the $17,725 from welfare and other government income programs.

b. Minimum Wage Workers in Manitoba

The following text with illustrative graphs analyzes key characteristics of minimum wage workers in Manitoba. Appendix 2 provides detailed statistics in tabular form (pages 300-302).

Interprovincial rank: incidence of minimum wage workers (Figure H9)

In 2000, an estimated 24,000 workers in Manitoba – 5.2 percent of the total 462,800 employees – worked for the minimum wage. Manitoba's 5.2 percent figure ranks it about mid-pack among the provinces, which range from 2.0 percent in Alberta to 8.7 percent in Newfoundland. Figure H9 shows the results. The national average is 4.6 percent.

Minimum wage workers are somewhat overrepresented in Manitoba. The province accounts for 4.1 percent of all minimum wage workers in the country but only 3.7 percent of all employees, producing an index of 1.12 (the higher the result above 1.00, the more overrepresented are minimum wage workers).

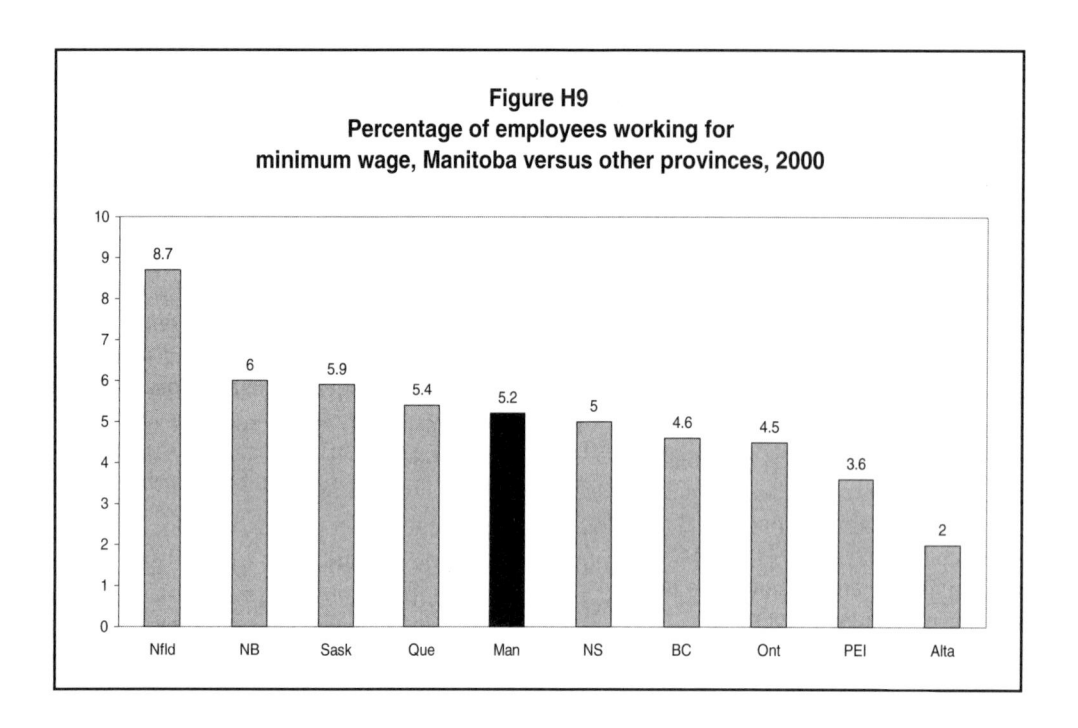

Figure H9
Percentage of employees working for minimum wage, Manitoba versus other provinces, 2000

Province	Percentage
Nfld	8.7
NB	6
Sask	5.9
Que	5.4
Man	5.2
NS	5
BC	4.6
Ont	4.5
PEI	3.6
Alta	2

Gender and age (Figures H10-H13)

In Manitoba as in the rest of Canada, women run a higher risk of working for minimum wage than men, and women also make up the majority of the minimum wage workforce.

In 2000, 6.3 percent of Manitoba's female employees worked for minimum wage compared to only 4.1 percent of male workers. Of the total 24,000 minimum wage workers, 14,200 – 59.2 percent – were women and 9,800 – 40.8 percent – were men, as shown in Figure H10.

Women are overrepresented in Manitoba's minimum wage workforce. They constituted 59.2 percent of minimum wage workers but only 48.8 percent of all the province's employees in 2000. Men are underrepresented. They accounted for only 40.8 percent of minimum wage workers but 51.2 percent of all employees.

The gender bias among minimum wage workers holds when we control for major age categories, as illustrated in Figure H11. While younger workers of both sexes run a higher risk of working for minimum wage, women still fare worse than men within each age category.

**Figure H10
Composition of minimum wage workforce
in Manitoba, by gender, 2000**

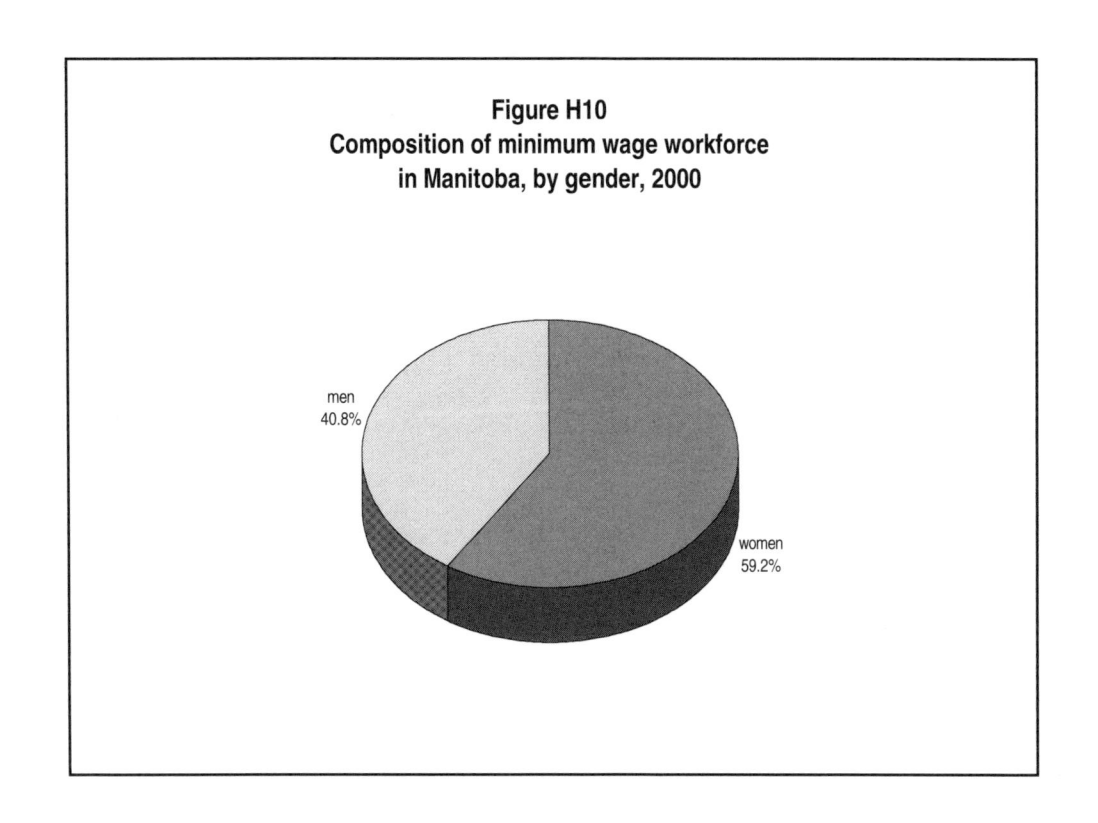

men 40.8%
women 59.2%

**Figure H11
Percentage of employees working for
minimum wage in Manitoba, by gender and age, 2000**

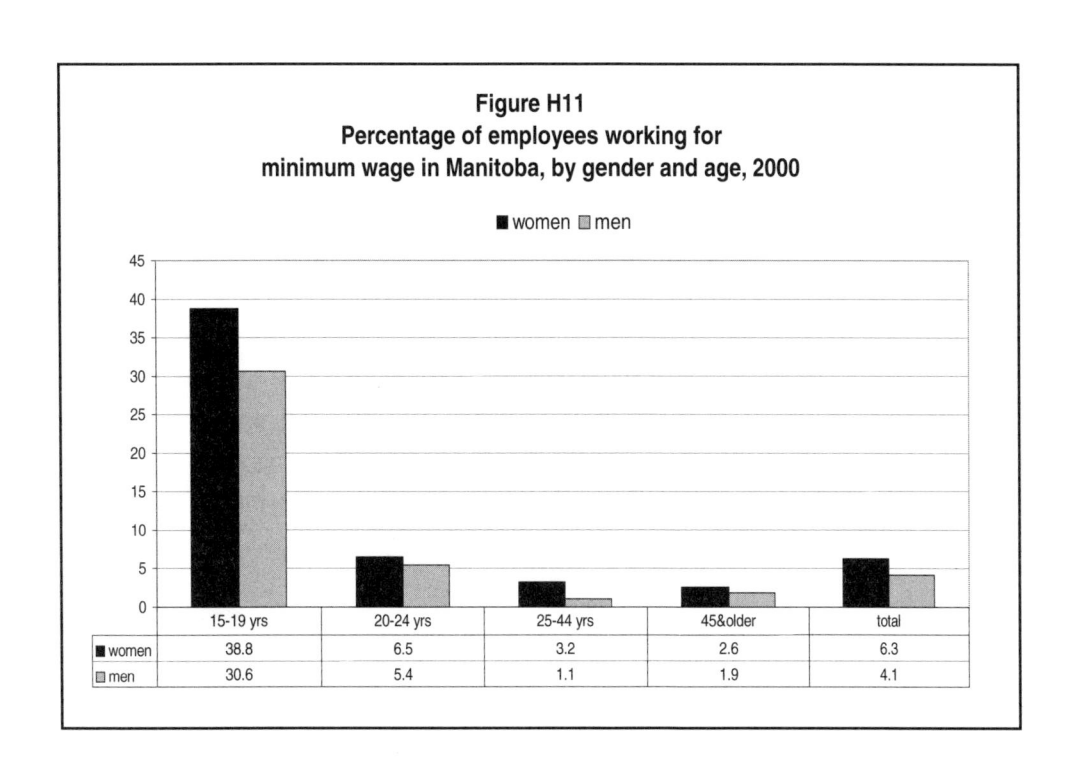

■ women ☐ men

	15-19 yrs	20-24 yrs	25-44 yrs	45&older	total
women	38.8	6.5	3.2	2.6	6.3
men	30.6	5.4	1.1	1.9	4.1

Minimum Wages in Canada: A Statistical Portrait With Policy Implications

**Figure H12
Share of minimum wage workers versus share
of all employees in Manitoba, by age group, 2000**

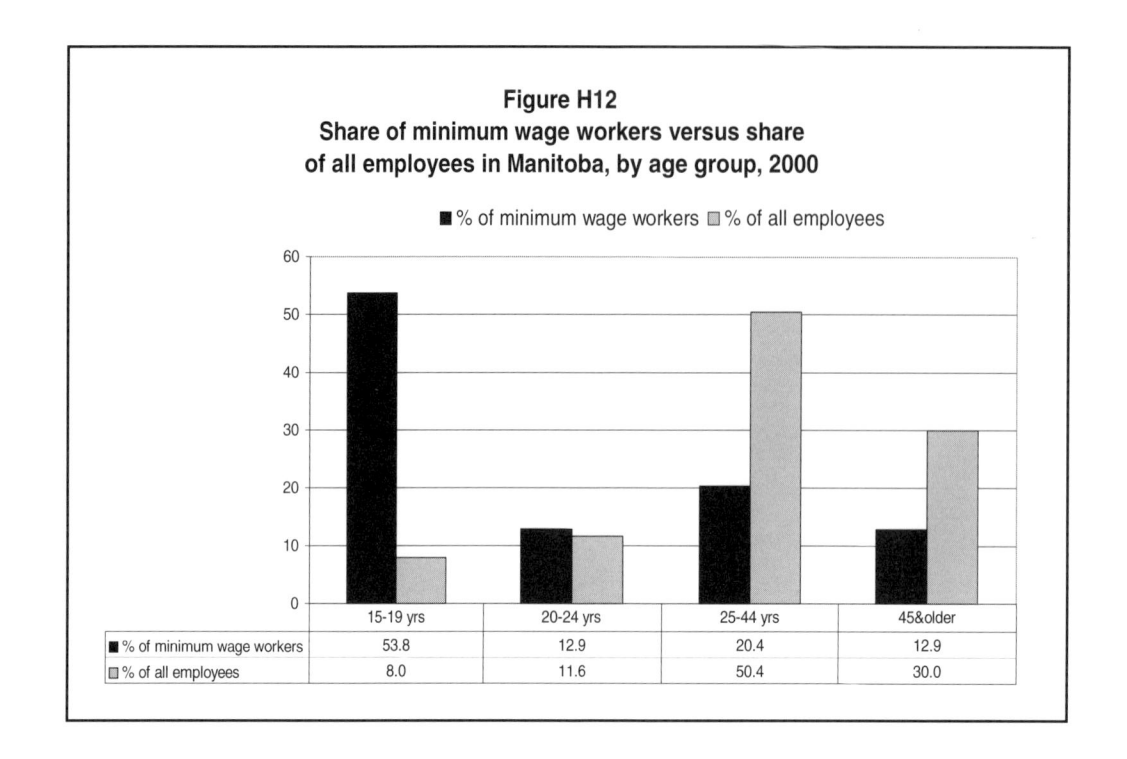

	15-19 yrs	20-24 yrs	25-44 yrs	45&older
% of minimum wage workers	53.8	12.9	20.4	12.9
% of all employees	8.0	11.6	50.4	30.0

**Figure H13
Composition of minimum wage workforce
in Manitoba, by teenagers/adults and gender**

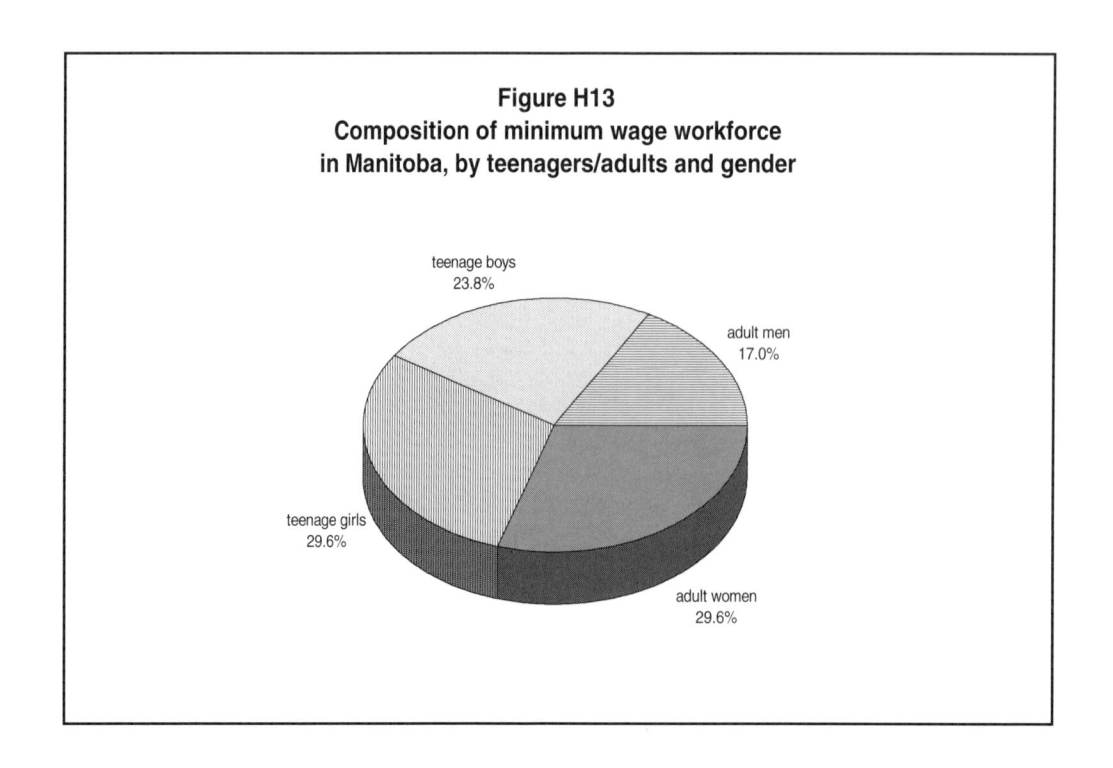

- teenage boys 23.8%
- adult men 17.0%
- adult women 29.6%
- teenage girls 29.6%

Among female workers aged 15 to 19, 38.8 percent worked for the minimum wage in 2000 in contrast to 30.6 percent of male workers in the same age group. Among those 20-24, 6.5 percent of women compared to 5.4 percent of men worked for the minimum wage. Among workers 25-44, 3.2 percent of women as opposed to just 1.1 percent of men were at the bottom of the wage ladder. Among employees 45 and older, 2.6 percent of women but only 1.9 percent of men worked for the minimum wage in Manitoba.

Young people not only are more likely to work for minimum wage than other employees, but the young also make up a large proportion of the minimum wage workforce. Figure H12 compares the age makeup of minimum wage workers and all employees in Manitoba. More than half (53.8 percent) of minimum wage workers are in the 15-19 age group, as opposed to just 8.0 percent of all employees. Employees aged 20-24 represent 12.9 percent of minimum wage workers as opposed to 11.6 percent of all workers. All told, two in three minimum wage workers in Manitoba (66.7) are under 25 years of age.

The opposite holds for older workers. While a sizeable proportion – 20.4 percent – of minimum wage workers in Manitoba are between 25 and 44, that age group constitutes a much larger proportion – 50.4 percent – of all employees. Workers aged 45 and older make up just 12.9 percent of minimum wage employees but 30.0 percent all employees.

Figure H13 divides the minimum wage workforce in Manitoba into teenage girls and boys and adult women and men. Adult women and teenage girls tie for the largest groups, each at 71,000 or 29.6 percent of the total, followed by teenage boys (5,700 or 23.8 percent) and adult men (4,100 or 17.0 percent). The majority (53.4 percent) of Manitoba's minimum wage workers are teenagers, whereas on a national basis (and in most other jurisdictions) adults form the majority (at 52.9 percent nationally).

Education (Figures H14 and H15)

Figure H14 shows the incidence of minimum wage workers in Manitoba according to level of education.

At first glance, the relationship between level of education and incidence of minimum wage employment does not seem to correspond to common sense: Workers in the lowest educational group (elementary education only) are less likely to work for minimum wage (10.0 percent do) than those with some high school (15.3 percent), while those with some postsecondary education run a higher risk (4.8 percent) than high school graduates (4.4 percent). However, as one would expect, the chances of working for minimum wage are lowest for the two highest education categories – 1.7 percent for those with a postsecondary certificate or diploma (e.g., from community college) and 1.8 percent for those with a university degree.

Once we look at the education-minimum wage link for different age groups, the reasons for the apparently inconsistent relationship comes clear: Young people working at part-time or seasonal (i.e.,

Minimum Wages in Canada: A Statistical Portrait With Policy Implications

**Figure H14
Percentage of employees working for
minimum wage in Manitoba, by education, 2000**

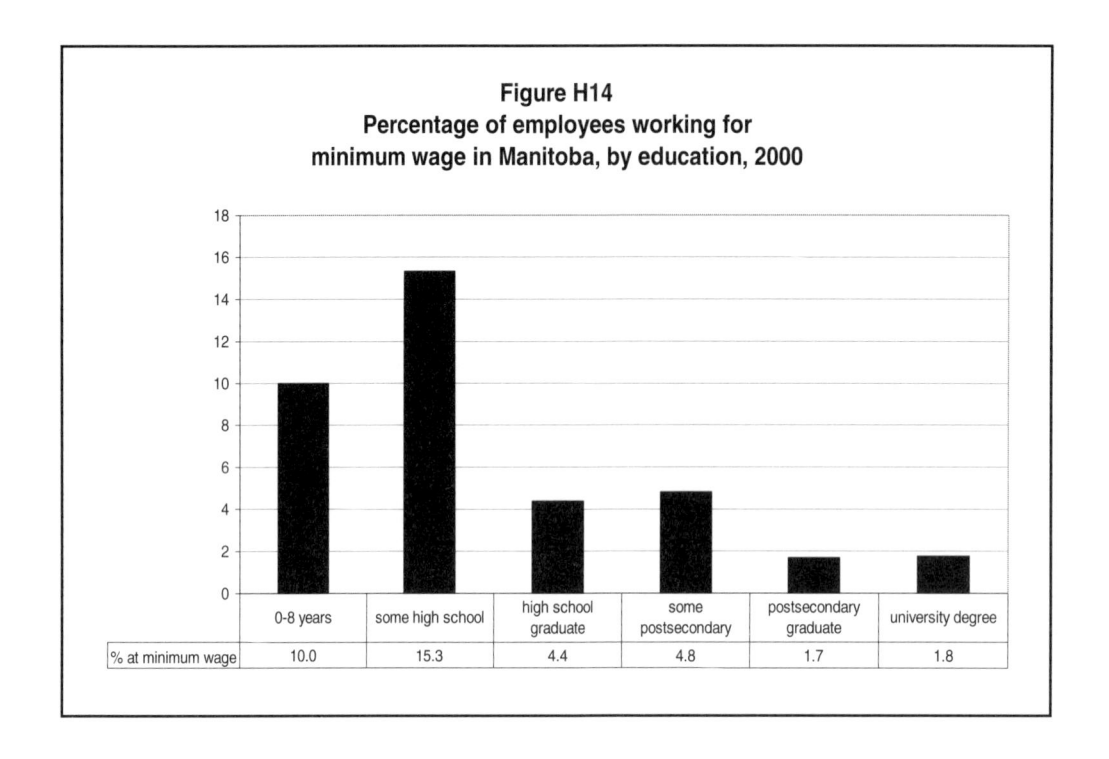

	0-8 years	some high school	high school graduate	some postsecondary	postsecondary graduate	university degree
% at minimum wage	10.0	15.3	4.4	4.8	1.7	1.8

**Figure H15
Composition of minimum wage workforce
in Manitoba, by education, 2000**

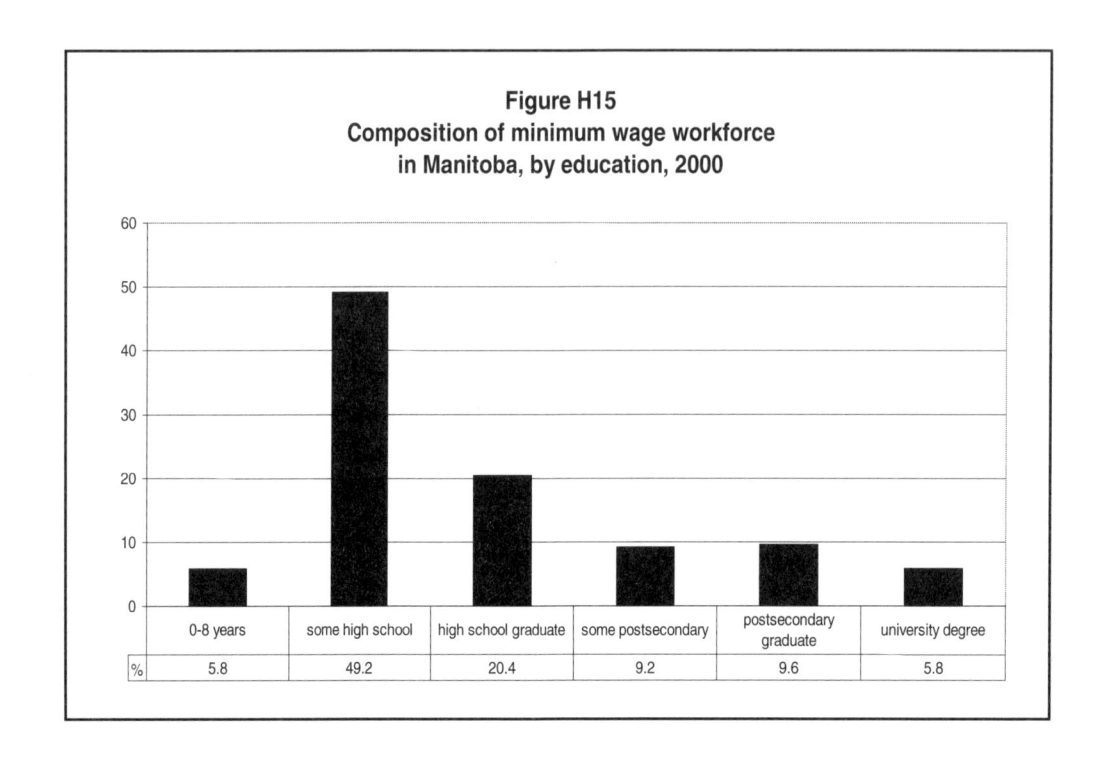

	0-8 years	some high school	high school graduate	some postsecondary	postsecondary graduate	university degree
%	5.8	49.2	20.4	9.2	9.6	5.8

summer) jobs – typically paying the minimum or a low wage – figure prominently in the 'some high school' and 'some postsecondary education' categories; they are still at high school, community college or university, whereas workers in the other educational categories have completed their education.

Figure H15 shows each educational group's share of Manitoba's minimum wage workforce in 2000. The largest group of minimum wage workers are those with some high school (49.2 percent), followed by high school graduates (20.4 percent), postsecondary graduates (9.6 percent) and those with some postsecondary education (9.2 percent); tied – at 5.8 percent each – are university graduates and those with 0-8 years of education. Many minimum wage workers are students (high school and postsecondary) pursuing their education. A significant group of minimum wage workers (24.6 percent) have some form of postsecondary education.

Full-time and part-time work (Figures H16 and H17)

The fact that young people are more likely to work part time helps explain why workers still pursuing their education tend to face a higher risk of minimum wage work than those who have completed their schooling and are working full time. Figure H16 indicates that 16.5 percent of part-time workers are at the minimum wage compared to only 2.6 percent of those employed full time.

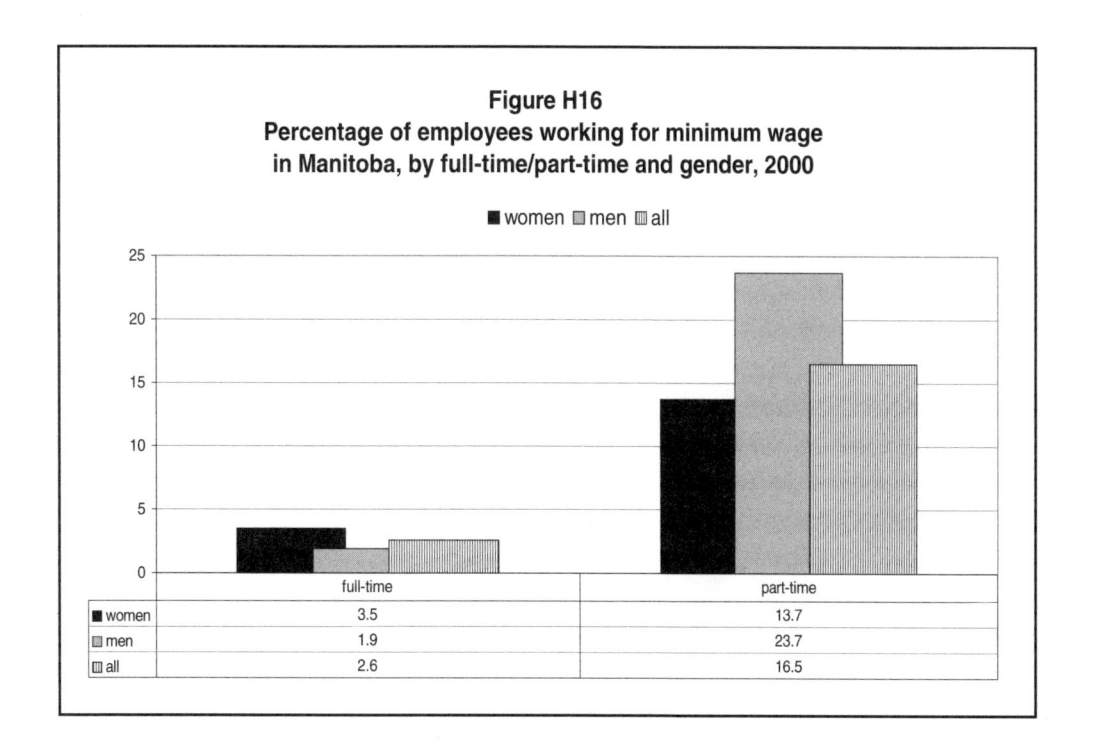

Figure H16
Percentage of employees working for minimum wage in Manitoba, by full-time/part-time and gender, 2000

	full-time	part-time
women	3.5	13.7
men	1.9	23.7
all	2.6	16.5

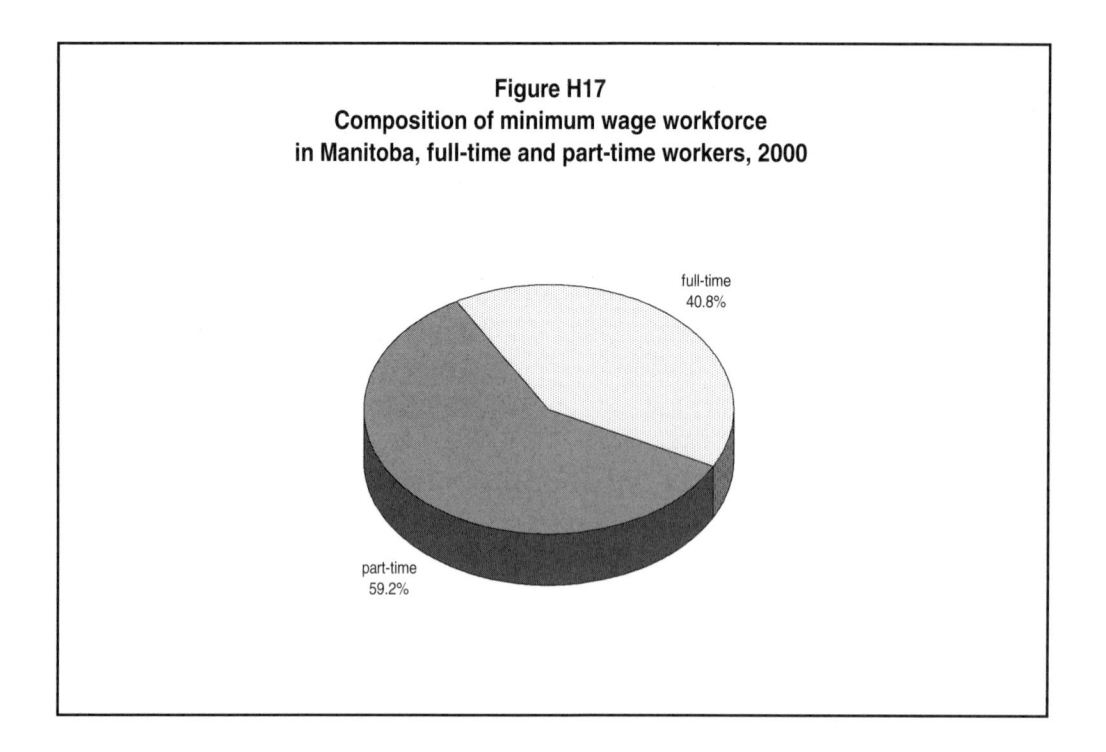

**Figure H17
Composition of minimum wage workforce
in Manitoba, full-time and part-time workers, 2000**

full-time
40.8%

part-time
59.2%

While the majority of minimum wage workers in Manitoba (59.2 percent) work part time, a sizeable group (40.8 percent) are employed full time. Figure H17 shows the comparison.

Gender alters the relationship between full-time and part-time work and the minimum wage. Women who work part time in Manitoba run a lesser risk of being at the bottom of the wage ladder than do men who work part time (13.7 and 23.7 percent, respectively). However, women employed full time are more likely than men in that group to earn the minimum wage (3.5 and 1.9 percent, respectively).

Women make up the majority of minimum wage employees in the province working both full time (58.2 percent are women) and part time (59.9 percent are women). Among all employees, though, women constitute a minority of full-time workers (43.5 percent) but the bulk of part-time workers (72.0 percent).

Family status (Figure H18)

We noted above that two-thirds of Manitoba's minimum wage workforce is under 25 years of age. Light on this fundamental fact of the minimum wage workforce is shed by information on family status, depicted in Figure H18, which shows that the largest group of minimum wage workers – 15,000 or 62.2

**Figure H18
Composition of minimum wage workforce
in Manitoba, by family status, 2000**

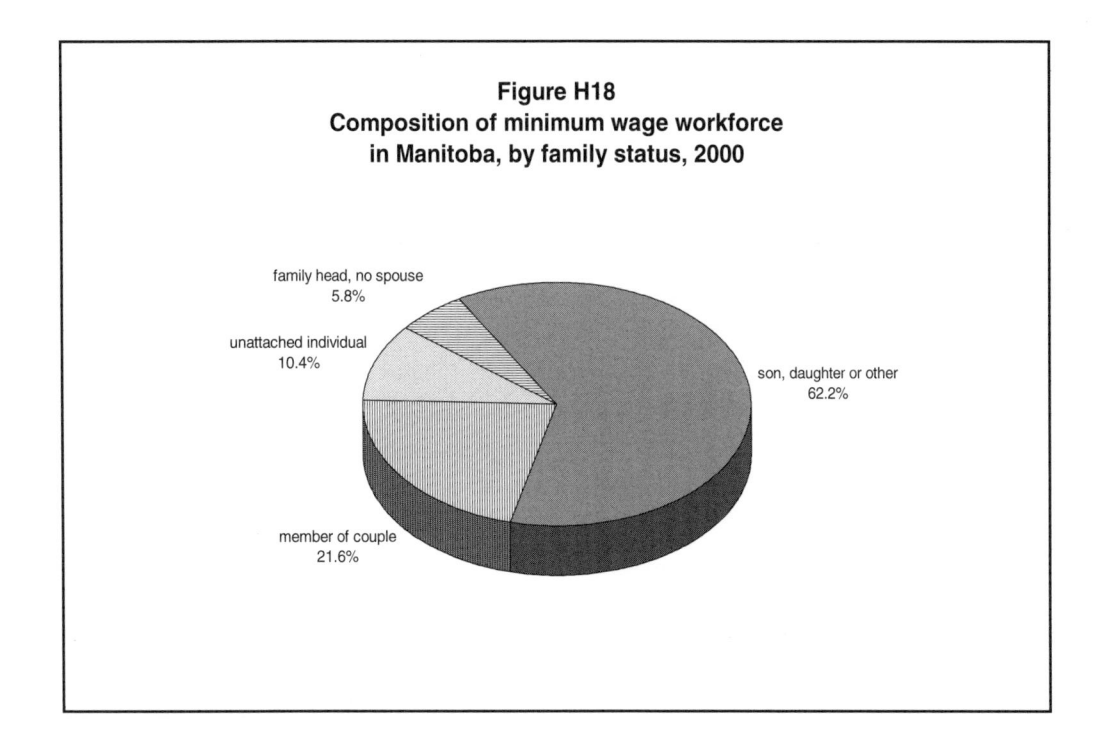

- family head, no spouse 5.8%
- unattached individual 10.4%
- son, daughter or other 62.2%
- member of couple 21.6%

percent of the total 24,000 – are older children living with their parents (or relatives with relatives, as in the case of a niece or nephew living with an aunt and uncle, or grandchildren with grandparents). Of this category, 12,000 or 80.0 percent are aged 15-19, 1,900 or 12.6 percent are 20-24 and the remaining 1,100 or 7.3 percent are 25 or older. More than half (8,300 or 55.3 percent) are still in school and working part-time or part-year (e.g., in summer).

The next largest group of minimum wage workers in Manitoba – 5,200 or 21.6 percent of the total – are members of couples (married or living together). In most cases (4,200 or 80.8 percent of the category total of 5,200), the minimum wage worker's spouse is employed, earning more than the minimum wage. A typical example in this category would be mothers combining (unpaid) childrearing work with part-time minimum wage work. Another 1,000 or 19.2 percent of minimum wage workers living in couples have a spouse who is not employed (most of the latter are not in the labour force).

An estimated 2,500 or 10.4 percent of minimum wage workers in Manitoba are unattached individuals. More than half of this category (1,400 or 56.0 percent) live alone; of this group, 300 are 15-24, 700 are aged 25-54 and 400 are 55 or older. About 1,100 of the province's unattached minimum wage workers live with friends or roommates; in this category, 600 are under 24, 400 are 25-44 and 100 are 55 or older.

Finally, some 1,400 or 5.8 percent of Manitoba's minimum wage workers head families with no spouse present; most (1,200) are single parents with children under 18.

Industry

National data show that the incidence and distribution of minimum wage workers varies significantly according to industries. The same applies to Manitoba, though sample size constraints preclude estimates for five of the 16 industrial categories (forestry, fishing, mining, oil and gas; utilities; construction; professional, scientific and technical services; and public administration). Among the industrial categories for which estimates are available, accommodation and food services top the list (23.9 percent of employees work for minimum wage), followed by agriculture (14.5 percent), management, administrative and other support (10.8 percent), trade (8.8 percent), information, culture and recreation (7.7 percent), other services (7.3 percent), educational services (2.4 percent), finance, insurance, real estate and leasing (2.3 percent), manufacturing (1.9 percent), transportation and warehousing (1.7 percent) and health care and social assistance (1.4 percent).

Estimates are available for the industrial composition of the whole employed workforce in Manitoba. Trade tops the list, at an estimated 71,500 or 15.4 percent of all employees. Next comes manufacturing (68,600 or 14.8 percent), followed by health care and social assistance (63,100 or 13.6 percent of all employees), educational services (37,600 or 8.1 percent), public administration (33,100 or 7.2 percent), accommodation and food services (32,600 or 7.0 percent), transportation and warehousing (29,200 or 6.3 percent), finance, insurance, real estate and leasing (25,700 or 5.6 percent), construction (18,700 or 4.0 percent), information, culture and recreation (18,200 or 3.9 percent), other services (16,500 or 3.6 percent), professional, scientific and technical services (14,900 or 3.2 percent), management, administrative and other support (12,000 or 2.6 percent), agriculture (8,300 or 1.8 percent), utilities (6,800 or 1.5 percent) and forestry, fishing, mining, oil and gas (5,900 or 1.3 percent).

SASKATCHEWAN

a. Minimum Wages in Saskatchewan

Interprovincial rank: dollar value of minimum wage (Figure I1)

Saskatchewan's minimum wage increased twice in 2002 – from $6.00 to $6.35 on May 1 and to $6.65 on November 1, resulting in an annual average hourly rate of $6.28. In 2002, Saskatchewan's $6.28 average minimum wage ranked about mid-pack (sixth-lowest) among Canada's ten provinces and three territories, the lowest being Newfoundland ($5.71 hourly average) and the highest British Columbia ($8.00). Figure I1 shows the rankings.

Trend in dollar value of minimum wage (Figure I2)

Because minimum wages are not indexed, their value changes over time. Figure I2 shows the trend in Saskatchewan's minimum wage from 1965 to 2002; each year's average minimum wage has been converted to inflation-adjusted (i.e., constant) 2002 dollars to show the real trend, after taking into account the impact of inflation on the dollar.

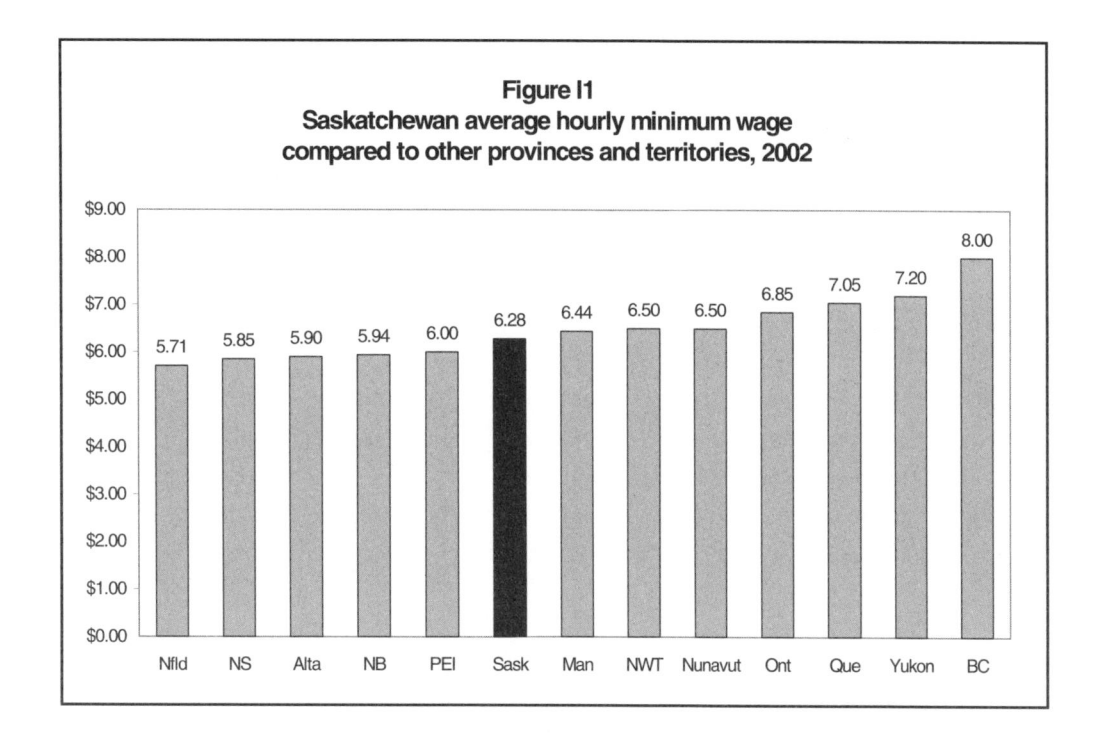

Figure I1
Saskatchewan average hourly minimum wage compared to other provinces and territories, 2002

Nfld	5.71
NS	5.85
Alta	5.90
NB	5.94
PEI	6.00
Sask	6.28
Man	6.44
NWT	6.50
Nunavut	6.50
Ont	6.85
Que	7.05
Yukon	7.20
BC	8.00

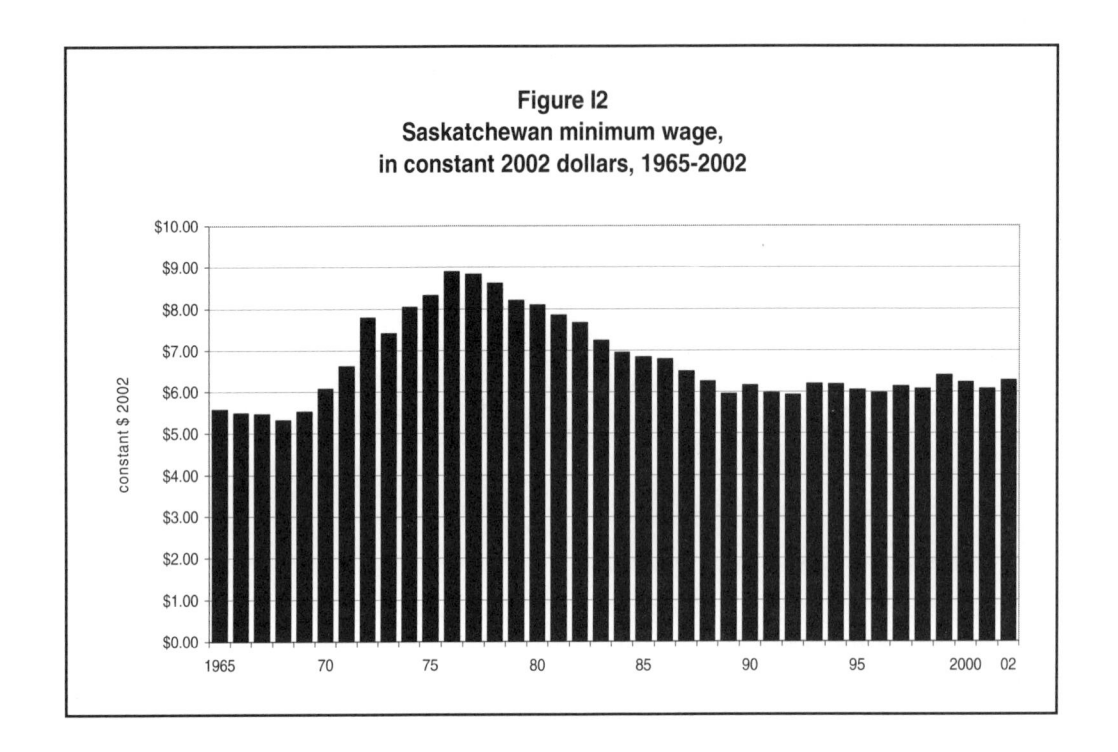

**Figure I2
Saskatchewan minimum wage,
in constant 2002 dollars, 1965-2002**

Saskatchewan's minimum wage shows an up-down-flat, plateau-like pattern. It rose substantially between 1965 ($5.58 an hour) and its 1976 peak ($8.89), declined pretty much steadily until 1993 ($5.93) and then leveled off around $6.00 for most of the 1990s, though it stood a bit higher ($6.28) in 2002. Its $6.28 value in 2002 was a sizeable $2.61 or 29.4 percent lower than the 1976 high point, and was only 70 cents or 12.6 percent more than in 1965.

Interprovincial rank: minimum wages as percentage of average earnings (Figure I3)

Saskatchewan ranks somewhat higher in terms of how its minimum wage compares to its average wage. In 2001 (the most recent year for which data on average earnings are available), Saskatchewan's minimum wage ($6.00 an hour) represented 40.1 percent of its $14.95 hourly average earnings, placing the province sixth-highest among 13 jurisdictions that range from the Northwest Territories at 30.2 percent to British Columbia at 46.2 percent. Figure I3 shows the results.

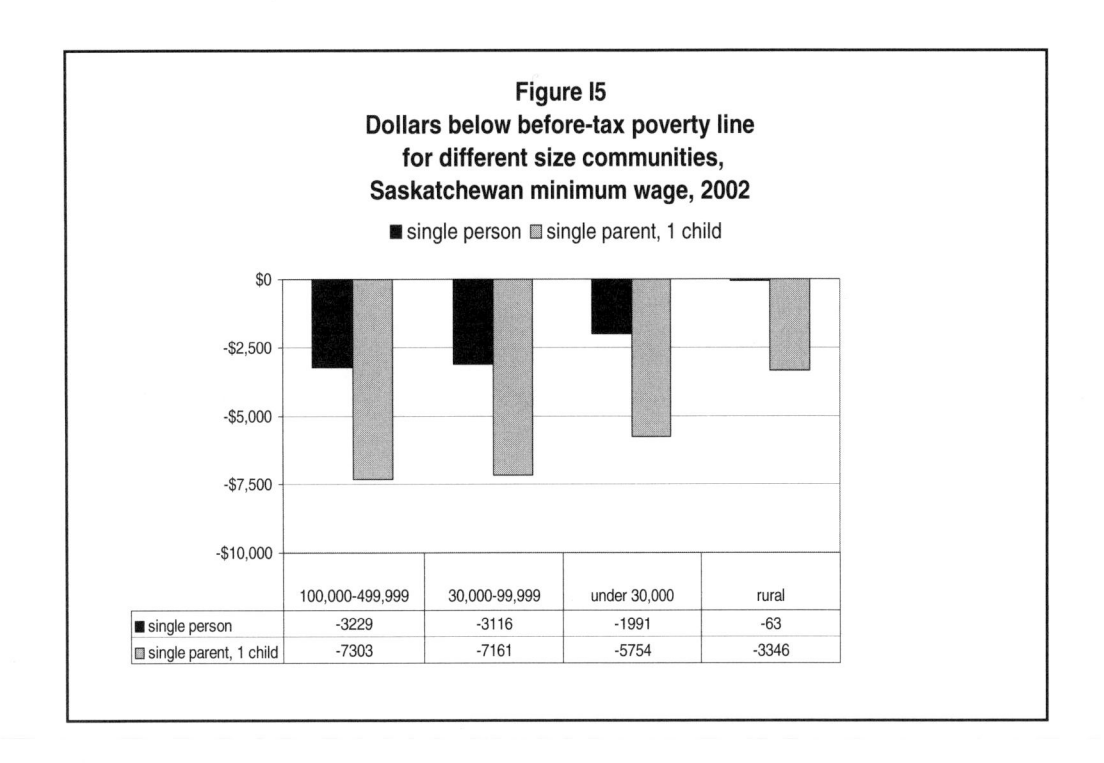

Figure I5
Dollars below before-tax poverty line for different size communities, Saskatchewan minimum wage, 2002

	100,000-499,999	30,000-99,999	under 30,000	rural
single person	-3229	-3116	-1991	-63
single parent, 1 child	-7303	-7161	-5754	-3346

I5 shows the dollar gap between the minimum wage and the poverty line for one person in different size communities throughout Saskatchewan.

Because the poverty line varies by family size, minimum wages (which do not vary by family size) fall farther below the poverty line for families than for single workers. We look at the poverty gap for a single parent with one child, which falls in the two-person family size category. In 2002, Saskatchewan's minimum wage varied from 64.1 percent of the low income line for a two-person family in Regina or Saskatoon to 64.6 percent for communities between 30,000 and 99,999, 69.4 percent for towns under 30,000 and 79.6 percent for rural areas. Saskatchewan's minimum wage was $7,303 below the low income line for a family of two in Regina or Saskatoon, $7,161 under for communities between 30,000 and 99,999 inhabitants, $5,754 beneath the line for towns under 30,000 and $3,346 under for rural residents.

Trend in minimum wage as percentage of before-tax poverty lines (Figure I6)

The long-term trend when we compare the minimum wage to the poverty line (as measured by Statistics Canada's before-tax low income cut-offs, which vary by size of family and of community) is the same as the trend in dollar value. In 2002, the estimated low income line for a city the size of Regina or Saskatoon was $16,295 for one person and $20,369 for a family of two.

**Figure I6
Saskatchewan minimum wage as % of
before-tax poverty line for largest cities, 1965-2002**

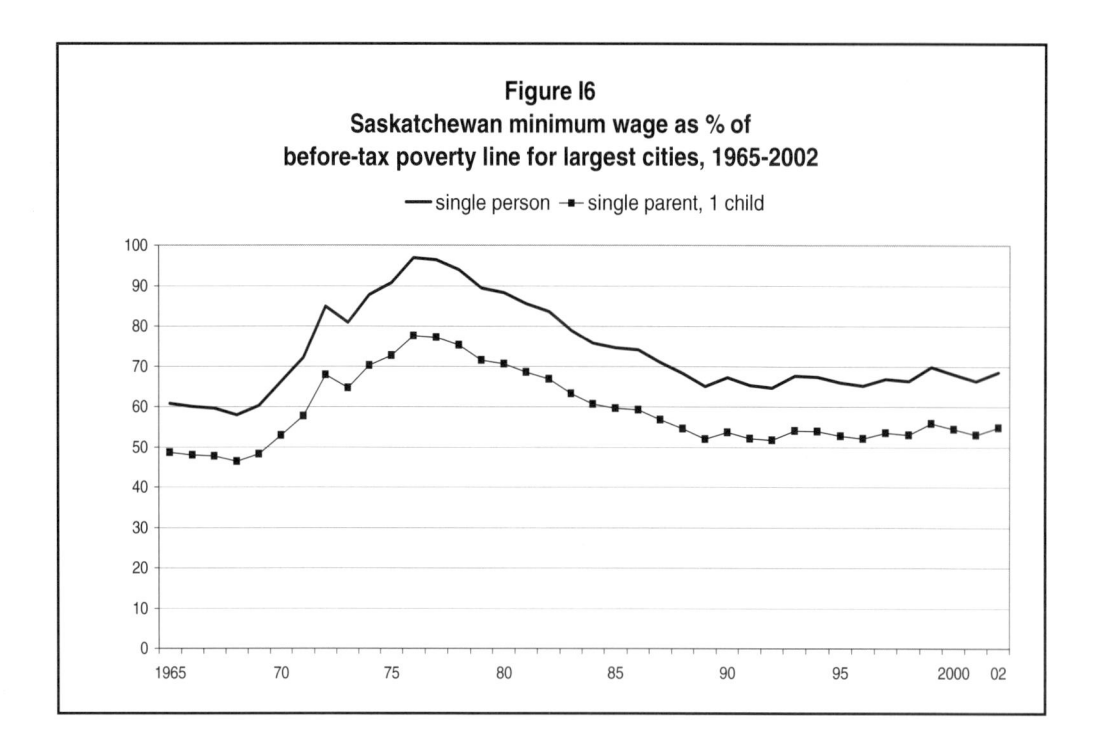

Saskatchewan's minimum wage rose from 60.8 percent of the before-tax poverty line for one person living in Regina or Saskatoon in 1965 to 97.0 percent of the poverty line in 1976, fell to around 66 percent in the early 1990s and stood at 68.5 percent in 2002. For a two-person family (e.g., a single parent with one child), the minimum wage went from 48.7 percent of the low income line for Regina or Saskatoon in 1965 to a peak of 77.6 percent in 1976, declined to around 53 percent in the early 1990s and hovered around that mark, amounting to 54.8 percent in 2002. Figure I6 shows the trends.

Minimum wage compared to after-tax poverty lines (Figure I7)

Statistics Canada publishes after-tax low income cut-offs as well as before-tax low income cut-offs. We look here at how after-tax minimum wage incomes in Saskatchewan for five types of household – single persons, single parents with one child, one-earner couples with two children, two-earner couples supporting two children on one-and-a-half minimum wages, and two-earner couples with two children and two full minimum wages – compare to the after-tax poverty lines for different size communities. 'After-tax minimum wage incomes' means incomes from the minimum wage and available federal and provincial income programs minus federal and provincial income taxes.

For a single person earning the minimum wage, after-tax income came to $11,719,[47] which is $1,391 below the after-tax poverty line for cities between 100,000 and 499,999, $1,189 under the line for centres of 30,000-99,999 and $76 below for towns under 30,000, though $1,515 above the poverty line for rural residents. A single parent with one child received $18,395[48] in after-tax income from minimum wage earnings and federal and provincial child benefits and tax credits, which came to $2,398 above the poverty line for Regina and Saskatoon (in the 100,000 to 499,999 category), $2,645 over the line for centres between 30,000 and 99,999, $4,002 above for towns under 30,000 and $5,944 above the after-tax poverty line for rural residents.

For a one-earner couple with two children, after-tax minimum wage income amounted to $21,444[49] – $3,756 below the after-tax poverty line for Saskatoon and Regina, $3,336 under for centres between 30,000 and 99,999, $1,229 below for towns smaller than 30,000 but $1,829 above the after-tax poverty line for rural residents. For a two-earner couple with two children and one-and-a-half minimum wages, after-tax income came to $24,754[50] – $446 below the after-tax poverty line for Saskatoon and Regina and $56 under for centres between 30,000 and 99,999, but $2,081 above the line for towns smaller than 30,000 and $5,139 above the after-tax poverty line for rural residents. A two-earner couple with two children and earning two full time, year round minimum wages had after-tax minimum wage income of $28,036[51] – $2,836 above the after-tax poverty line for Saskatoon and Regina, $3,226 over for centres between 30,000 and 99,999, $5,363 above the line for towns smaller than 30,000 and $8,421 above the after-tax poverty line for rural residents.

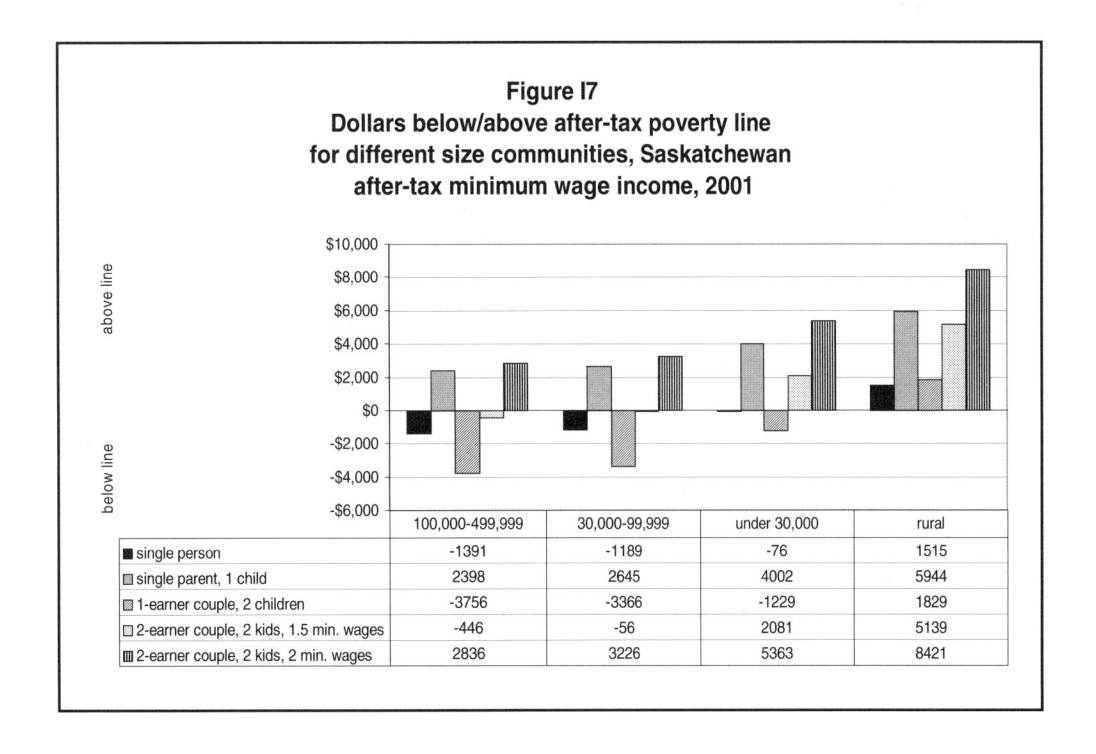

Figure I7
Dollars below/above after-tax poverty line for different size communities, Saskatchewan after-tax minimum wage income, 2001

	100,000-499,999	30,000-99,999	under 30,000	rural
single person	-1391	-1189	-76	1515
single parent, 1 child	2398	2645	4002	5944
1-earner couple, 2 children	-3756	-3366	-1229	1829
2-earner couple, 2 kids, 1.5 min. wages	-446	-56	2081	5139
2-earner couple, 2 kids, 2 min. wages	2836	3226	5363	8421

Contribution of child benefits

Child benefits supplement the incomes of the large majority of Canadian families and are especially important to low- and modest-income families. Improvements to the federal Canada Child Tax Benefit, along with Saskatchewan's new child benefits – the most generous of all the provinces and territories – are boosting the incomes of minimum wage and other working poor families.

The single-parent minimum wage worker with one child got $2,447 from the federal Canada Child Tax Benefit and $2,817 from provincial child-related benefits ($389 from the Saskatchewan Child Benefit and $2,428 from the Saskatchewan Employment Supplement) – for a substantial total of $5,264 or 29.7 percent of disposable income. The one-earner couple with two children received $4,250 from the Canada Child Tax Benefit and $3,845 in provincial child benefits ($985 from the Saskatchewan Child Benefit and $2,870 from the Saskatchewan Employment Supplement) for a combined federal-provincial child benefit of $8,095, worth 39.0 percent of disposable income.

The two-earner family in which one parent works full time, all year at the minimum wage and the other parent half that time got child benefits worth a total of $4,250 from the Canada Child Tax Benefit and $1,546 from Saskatchewan child benefits ($211 from the Saskatchewan Child Benefit and $1,335 from the Saskatchewan Employment Supplement), which comes to $5,796 or 24.3 percent of disposable income. The two-earner family in which both parents work full time, all year at the minimum wage received $3,515 from the Canada Child Tax Benefit or 13.2 percent of disposable income.

Minimum wage versus welfare (Figure I8)

For a single person earning the minimum wage in Saskatchewan, disposable income – i.e., minimum wage earnings plus federal and provincial refundable tax credits minus income and payroll taxes – amounted to $11,052 in 2001, which is a sizeable $5,074 more than the $5,978 from welfare and refundable tax credits. Figure I8 shows the comparison.

Minimum wages also pay better than welfare for a single parent with one child age 2, though the advantage is not as great as for single people. Disposable income from after-tax minimum wage earnings, child benefits and federal and provincial refundable tax credits amounted to $17,728 in 2001, or $5,361 more than the $12,367 from welfare, child benefits and refundable tax credits.

However, the minimum wage advantage is much smaller for a one-earner couple earning the minimum wage and supporting two children aged 10 and 15. Total disposable income from minimum wages, child benefits and federal and provincial refundable tax credits came to $20,777, or $2,567 more than the $18,210 from welfare, child benefits and refundable tax credits.

**Figure I8
Minimum wage versus welfare in Saskatchewan, by household type, 2001**

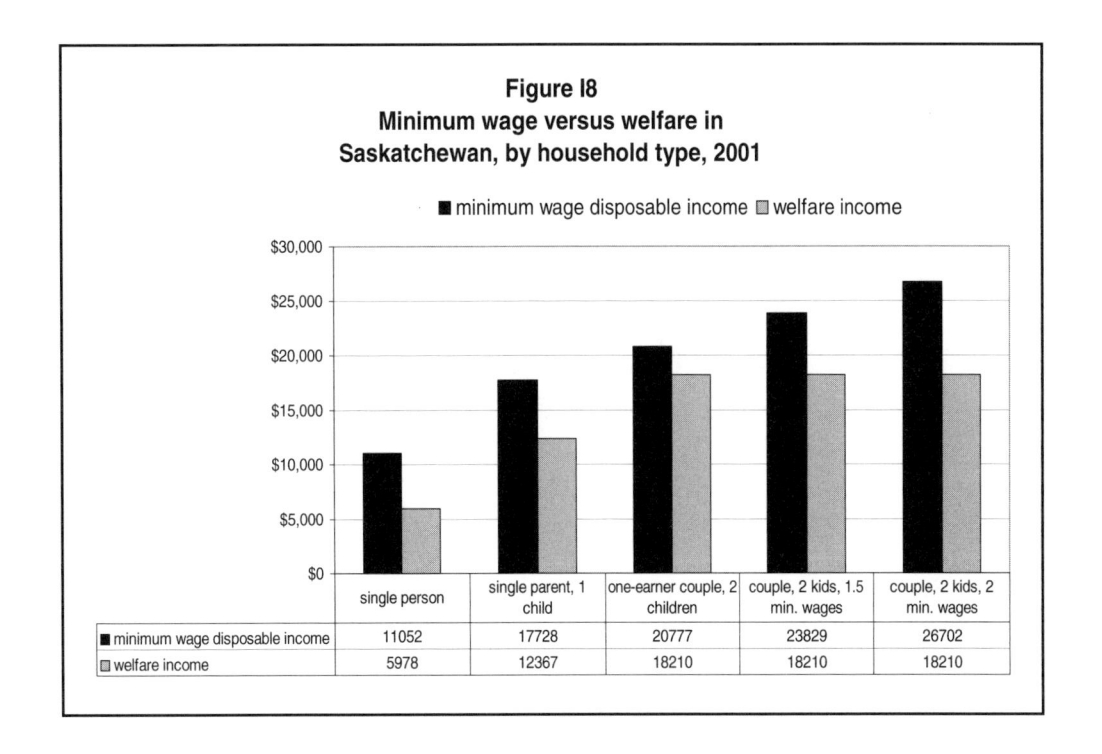

	single person	single parent, 1 child	one-earner couple, 2 children	couple, 2 kids, 1.5 min. wages	couple, 2 kids, 2 min. wages
minimum wage disposable income	11052	17728	20777	23829	26702
welfare income	5978	12367	18210	18210	18210

Naturally, the minimum wage advantage is greater in the case of two-earner families. We look at two examples.

In the first case, one parent works full time, year round at the minimum wage while the other earns half this amount (i.e., works part-time and/or part-year); as above, there are two children aged 10 and 15. This family's disposable income from one-and-a-half minimum wages came to $23,829 in 2001 or $5,619 more than the $18,210 from welfare, child benefits and the refundable GST credit.

The other two-earner family earns double the minimum wage since we assume that both parents work full time, year round at the minimum wage. Total disposable income in 2001 was $26,702 or $8,492 more than the $18,210 from welfare and other government income programs.

b. Minimum Wage Workers in Saskatchewan

The following text with illustrative graphs analyzes key characteristics of minimum wage workers in Saskatchewan. Appendix 2 provides detailed statistics in tabular form (pages 303-305).

Interprovincial rank: incidence of minimum wage workers (Figure I9)

In 2000, an estimated 22,000 workers in Saskatchewan – 5.9 percent of the total 371,700 employees – worked for the minimum wage. Saskatchewan's 5.9 percent figure ranks it third-highest among the provinces, which range from 2.0 percent in Alberta to 8.7 percent in Newfoundland. Figure I9 shows the rankings. The national average was 4.6 percent in 2000.

Minimum wage workers are overrepresented in Saskatchewan. The province accounts for 3.8 percent of all minimum wage workers in the country but only 3.0 percent of all employees, producing an index of 1.27 (the higher the result above 1.00, the more overrepresented are minimum wage workers).

Gender and age (Figure I10-I13)

In Saskatchewan as in the rest of Canada, women run a higher risk of working for minimum wage than men, and women also make up the majority of the minimum wage workforce.

In 2000, 6.6 percent of Saskatchewan's female employees worked for minimum wage compared to 5.2 percent of male workers. Of the total 22,000 minimum wage workers, 12,300 – 55.9 percent – were women and 9,700 – 44.1 percent – were men, as indicated in Figure I10.

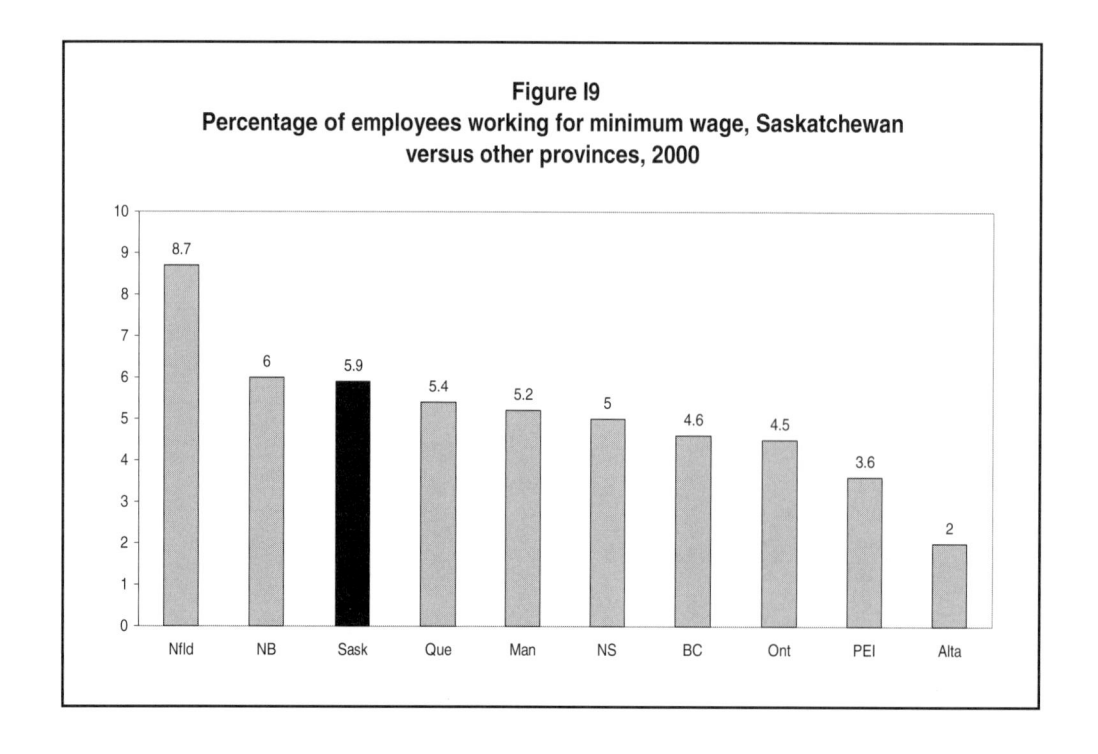

Figure I9
Percentage of employees working for minimum wage, Saskatchewan versus other provinces, 2000

Province	Percentage
Nfld	8.7
NB	6
Sask	5.9
Que	5.4
Man	5.2
NS	5
BC	4.6
Ont	4.5
PEI	3.6
Alta	2

**Figure I10
Composition of minimum wage workforce
in Saskatchewan, by gender, 2000**

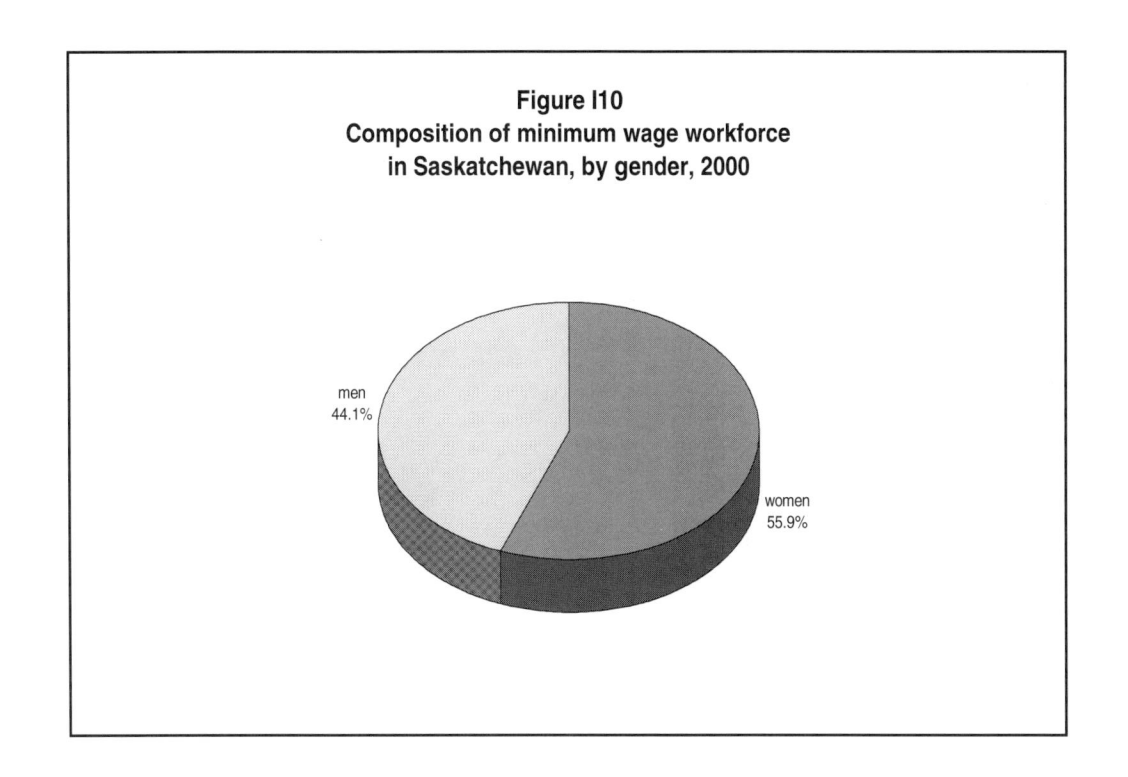

men 44.1%
women 55.9%

**Figure I11
Percentage of employees working for minimum wage
in Saskatchewan, by gender and age, 2000**

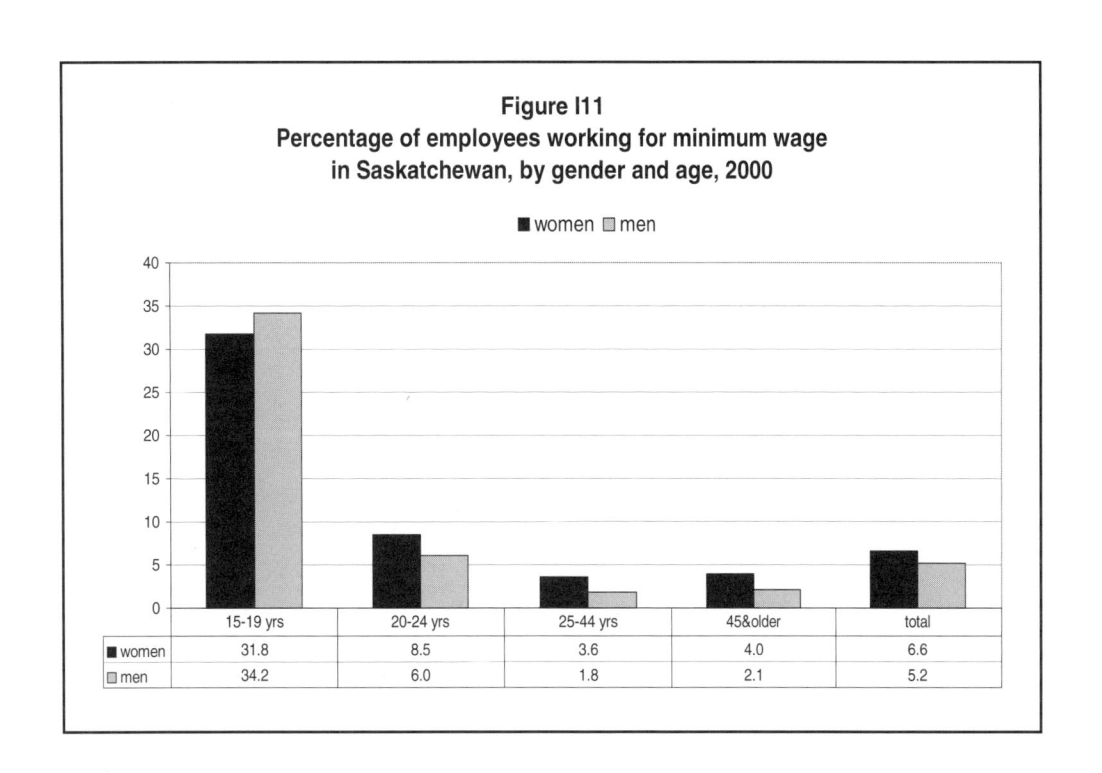

	15-19 yrs	20-24 yrs	25-44 yrs	45&older	total
women	31.8	8.5	3.6	4.0	6.6
men	34.2	6.0	1.8	2.1	5.2

Figure I12
Share of minimum wage workers versus share of all employees in Saskatchewan, by age group, 2002

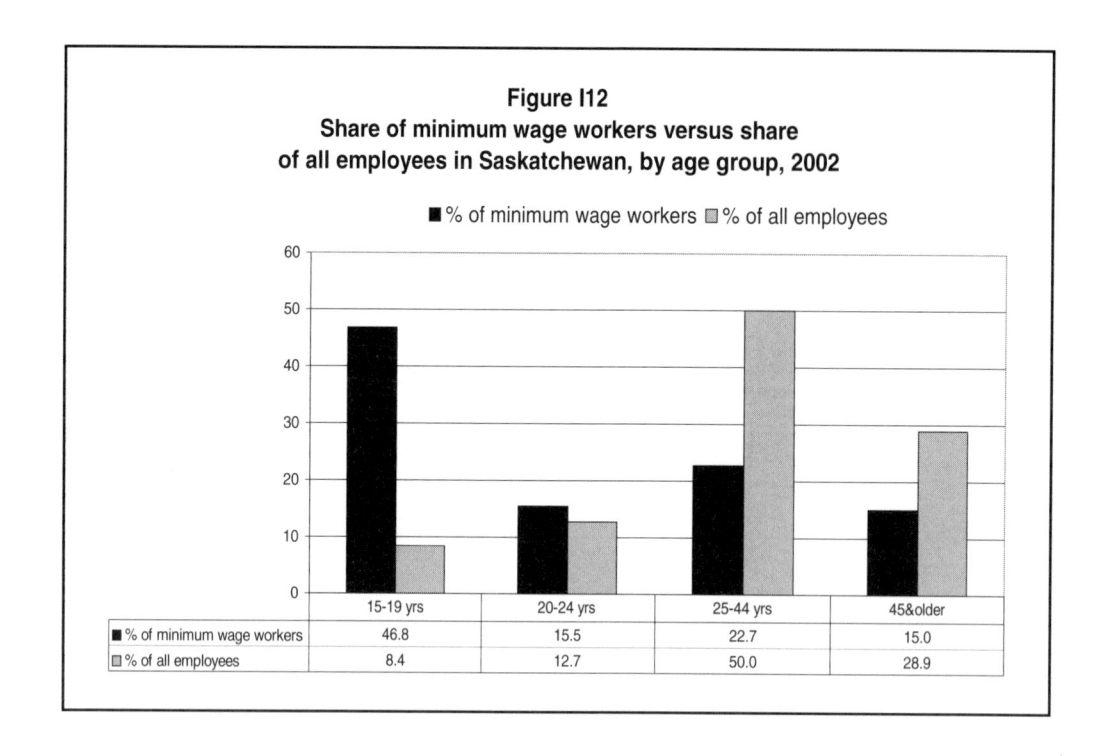

	15-19 yrs	20-24 yrs	25-44 yrs	45&older
% of minimum wage workers	46.8	15.5	22.7	15.0
% of all employees	8.4	12.7	50.0	28.9

Women are overrepresented in Saskatchewan's minimum wage workforce. They constituted 55.9 percent of minimum wage workers but 49.8 percent of all the province's employees in 2000. Men are underrepresented. They accounted for only 44.1 percent of minimum wage workers but 50.2 percent of all employees.

The gender bias among minimum wage workers holds when we control for major age categories, as indicated in Figure I11. While younger workers of both sexes run a higher risk of working for minimum wage, women still fare worse than men within each age category save one (15-19).

Among female workers aged 15 to 19, 31.8 percent worked for the minimum wage in 2000, but the incidence was higher (34.2 percent) among male workers in the same age group. But in all other age categories, women run a higher risk of working for minimum wage than do men. Among those 20-24, 8.5 percent of women compared to 6.0 percent of men worked for the minimum wage. Among workers 25-44, 3.6 percent of women as opposed to just 1.8 percent of men were at the bottom of the wage ladder. Among employees 45 and older, 4.0 percent of women but only 2.1 percent of men worked for the minimum wage in Saskatchewan.

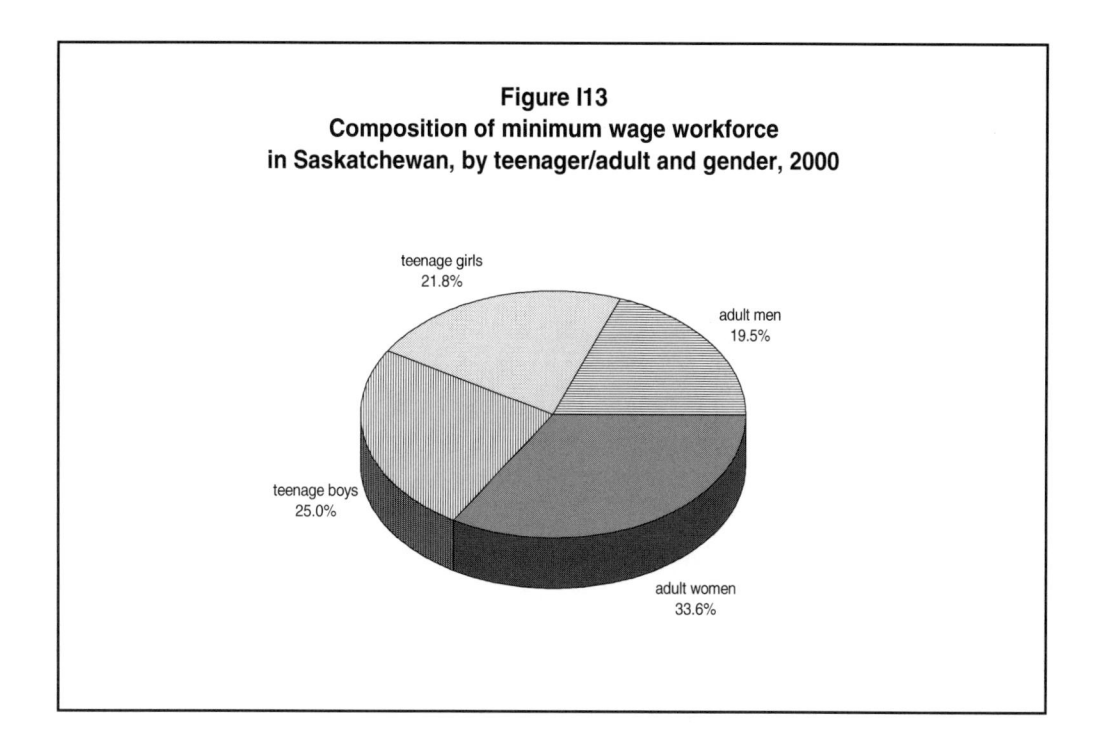

**Figure I13
Composition of minimum wage workforce
in Saskatchewan, by teenager/adult and gender, 2000**

- teenage girls: 21.8%
- adult men: 19.5%
- adult women: 33.6%
- teenage boys: 25.0%

Young people not only are more likely to work for minimum wage than other employees, but the young also make up a large proportion of the minimum wage workforce. Figure I12 compares the age makeup of minimum wage workers and all employees in Saskatchewan. Close to half (46.8 percent) of minimum wage workers are in the 15-19 age group, as opposed to just 8.4 percent of all employees. Employees aged 20-24 represent 15.5 percent of minimum wage workers but 12.7 percent of all workers. All told, six in ten minimum wage workers in Saskatchewan (62.3) are under 25 years of age.

The opposite holds for older workers. While a sizeable proportion – 22.7 percent – of minimum wage workers in Saskatchewan are between 25 and 44, that age group constitutes a much larger proportion – 50.0 percent – of all employees. Workers aged 45 and older make up 15.0 percent of minimum wage employees but 28.9 percent all employees.

Figure I13 divides the minimum wage workforce in Saskatchewan into teenage girls and boys and adult women and men. Adult women are the largest group, at 7,400 or 33.6 percent of the total, followed by teenage boys (5,500 or 25.0 percent), teenage girls (4,800 or 21.8 percent) and adult men (4,300 or 19.5 percent). The majority (53.1 percent) of Saskatchewan's minimum wage workers are adults, which is the case in most provinces (the national average is 52.9 percent).

Education (Figures I14 and I15)

Figure I14 shows the incidence of minimum wage workers in Saskatchewan according to level of education.

At first glance, the relationship between level of education and incidence of minimum wage employment does not seem to correspond to common sense: Workers in the lowest educational group (elementary education only) are less likely to work for minimum wage (15.7 percent do) than those with some high school (16.6 percent), while those with some postsecondary education run a higher risk (6.9 percent) than high school graduates (5.1 percent). However, as one would expect, the chances of working for minimum wage are lowest for the two highest education categories – 2.5 percent for those with a postsecondary certificate or diploma (e.g., from community college) and 1.9 percent for those with a university degree.

Once we look at the education-minimum wage link for different age groups, the reasons for the apparently inconsistent relationship comes clear: Young people working at part-time or seasonal (i.e., summer) jobs – typically paying the minimum or a low wage – figure prominently in the 'some high school' and 'some postsecondary education' categories; they are still at high school, community college or university, whereas workers in the other educational categories have completed their education.

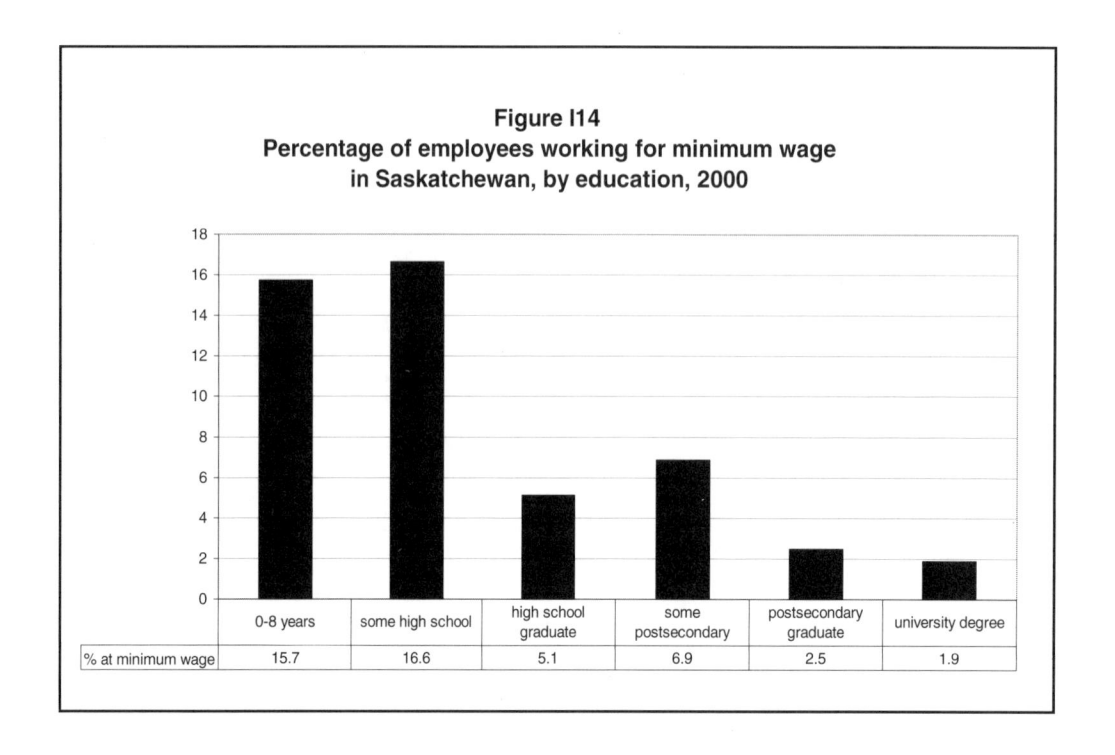

Figure I14
Percentage of employees working for minimum wage in Saskatchewan, by education, 2000

	0-8 years	some high school	high school graduate	some postsecondary	postsecondary graduate	university degree
% at minimum wage	15.7	16.6	5.1	6.9	2.5	1.9

**Figure I15
Composition of minimum wage workforce
in Saskatchewan, by education, 2000**

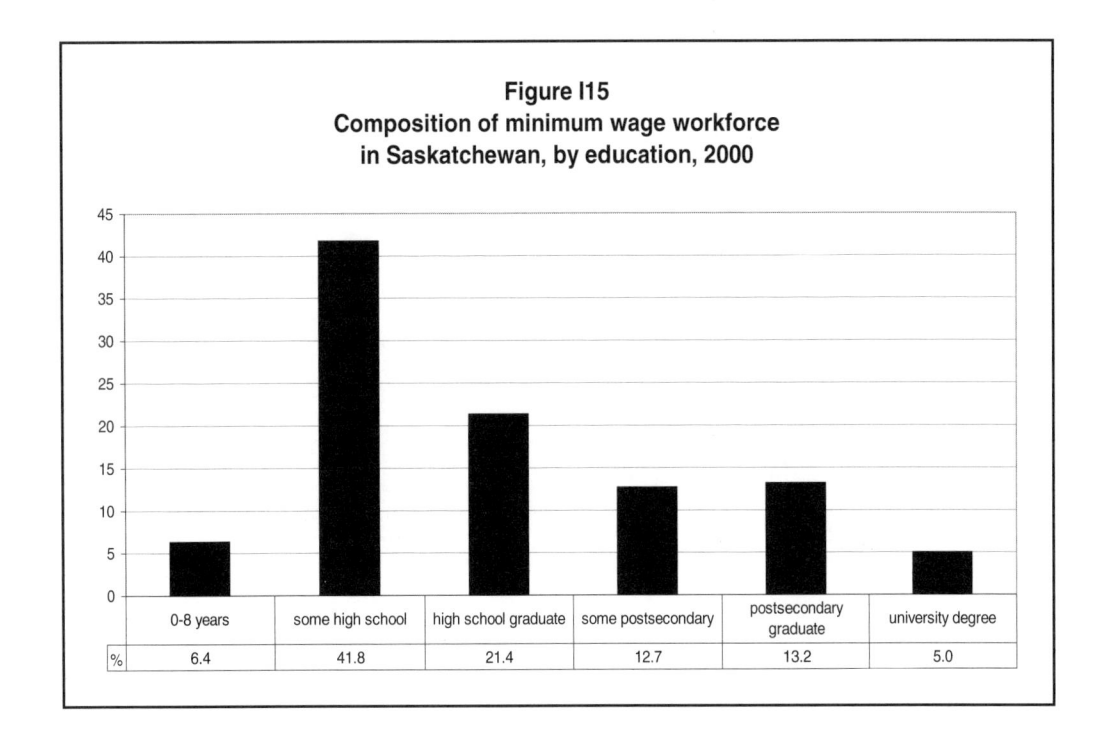

	0-8 years	some high school	high school graduate	some postsecondary	postsecondary graduate	university degree
%	6.4	41.8	21.4	12.7	13.2	5.0

Figure I15 shows each educational group's share of Saskatchewan's minimum wage workforce in 2000. The largest group of minimum wage workers are those with some high school (41.8 percent), followed by high school graduates (21.4 percent), postsecondary graduates (13.2 percent), those with some postsecondary education (12.7 percent), workers with 0-8 years of education (6.4 percent) and university graduates (5.0 percent). Many minimum wage workers are students (high school or postsecondary) pursuing their education. A significant group of minimum wage workers (30.9 percent) have some form of postsecondary education.

Full-time and part-time work (Figures I16 and I17)

The fact that young people are more likely to work part time helps explain why workers still pursuing their education tend to face a higher risk of minimum wage work than those who have completed their schooling and are working full time. Figure I16 shows that 16.7 percent of part-time workers are at the minimum wage compared to only 3.3 percent of those employed full time.

While the majority of minimum wage workers in Saskatchewan (55.5 percent) work part time, a sizeable group (44.5 percent) are employed full time. Figure I17 illustrates the proportions.

**Figure I16
Percentage of employees working for minimum wage in Saskatchewan, by full-time/part-time and gender, 2000**

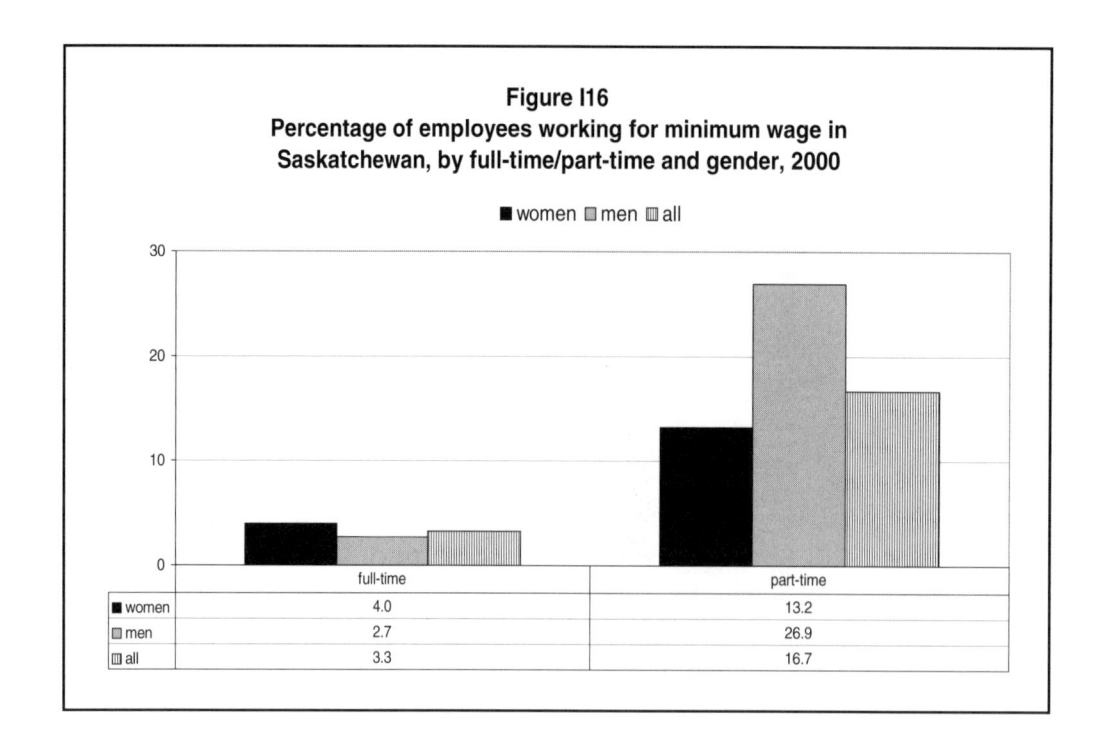

	full-time	part-time
women	4.0	13.2
men	2.7	26.9
all	3.3	16.7

**Figure I17
Composition of minimum wage workforce in Saskatchewan, full-time and part-time workers, 2000**

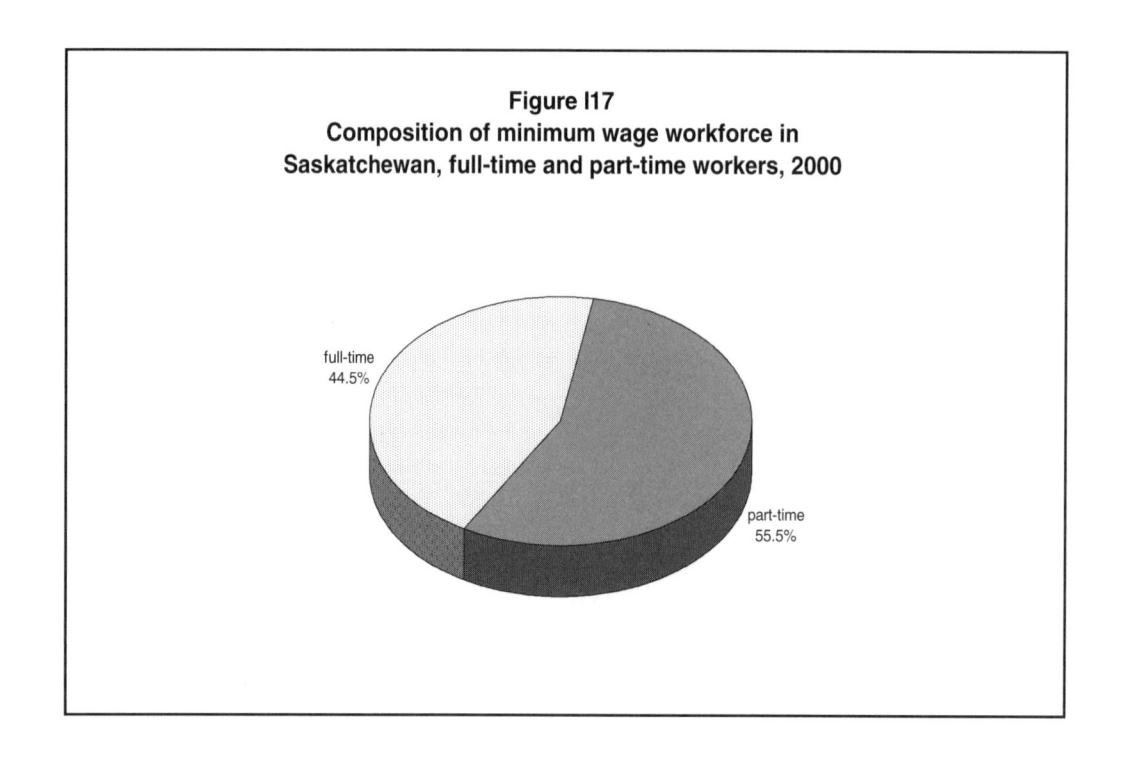

full-time 44.5%
part-time 55.5%

Gender alters the relationship between full-time and part-time work and the minimum wage. Women who work part time in Saskatchewan run a lesser risk of being at the bottom of the wage ladder than do men who work part time (13.2 and 26.9 percent, respectively). However, women employed full time are more likely than men in that group to earn the minimum wage (4.0 and 2.7 percent, respectively).

Women make up the majority of minimum wage employees in the province working both full time (53.1 percent are women) and part time (58.2 percent are women). Among all employees, though, women constitute a minority of full-time workers (44.0 percent) but the bulk of part-time workers (73.7 percent).

Family status (Figure I18)

We noted above that six in ten of Saskatchewan's minimum wage workers are under 25 years of age. Light on this fundamental fact of the minimum wage workforce is shed by information on family status in Figure I18, which shows that the largest group of minimum wage workers – 12,200 or 56.0 percent of the total 22,000 – are older children living with their parents (or relatives with relatives, as in the case of a niece or nephew living with an aunt and uncle, or grandchildren with grandparents). Of this category, 9,700 or 79.5 percent are aged 15-19, 1,700 or 13.9 percent are 20-24 and the remaining 800 or 6.6 percent are 25 or older. More than half (7,000 or 57.4 percent) are still in school and working part-time or part-year (e.g., in summer).

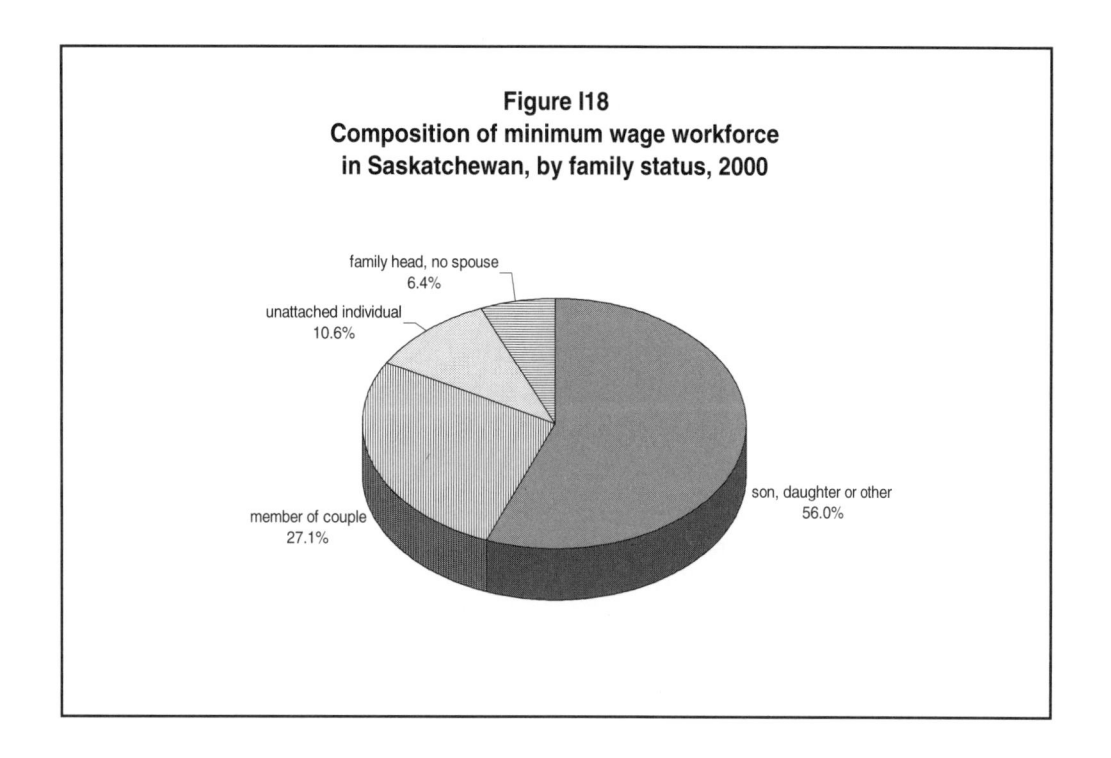

Figure I18
Composition of minimum wage workforce in Saskatchewan, by family status, 2000

- family head, no spouse 6.4%
- unattached individual 10.6%
- member of couple 27.1%
- son, daughter or other 56.0%

The next largest group of minimum wage workers in Saskatchewan – 5,900 or 27.1 percent of the total – are members of couples (married or living together). In most cases (4,600 or 78.0 percent of the category total of 5,900), the minimum wage worker's spouse is employed, earning more than the minimum wage. A typical example in this category would be mothers combining (unpaid) childrearing work with part-time minimum wage work. Another 1,300 or 22.0 percent of minimum wage workers living in couples have a spouse who is not employed (most of the latter are not in the labour force).

An estimated 2,300 or 10.6 percent of minimum wage workers in Saskatchewan are unattached individuals. Just under half of this category (1,100 or 48.8 percent) live alone; of this group, 300 are 15-24, 600 are aged 25-54 and 200 are 55 or older. About 1,200 of the province's unattached minimum wage workers live with friends or roommates; in this category, 900 are under 24, 300 are 25-44 and 100 are 55 or older.

Finally, some 1,400 or 6.4 percent of Saskatchewan's minimum wage workers head families with no spouse present; most (1,100) are single parents with children under 18.

Industry

National data show that the incidence and distribution of minimum wage workers varies significantly according to industries. The same applies to Saskatchewan, though sample size constraints preclude estimates for seven of the 16 industrial categories (forestry, fishing, mining, oil and gas; utilities; construction; transportation and warehousing; finance, insurance, real estate and leasing; professional, scientific and technical services; and public administration). Among the industrial categories for which estimates are available, accommodation and food services top the list (22.7 percent of employees work for minimum wage), followed by agriculture (13.3 percent), management, administrative and other support (12.7 percent), trade (9.8 percent), information, culture and recreation (9.7 percent), other services (8.1 percent), educational services (2.0 percent), health care and social assistance (1.9 percent) and manufacturing (1.8 percent).

Estimates are available for the industrial composition of the whole employed workforce in Saskatchewan. Trade tops the list, at an estimated 66,300 or 17.8 percent of all employees. Next comes health care and social assistance (47,900 or 12.9 percent of all employees), followed by educational services (34,500 or 9.3 percent), accommodation and food services (29,500 or 7.9 percent), manufacturing (27,600 or 7.4 percent), public administration (26,700 or 7.2 percent), finance, insurance, real estate and leasing (23,100 or 6.2 percent), transportation and warehousing (22,800 or 6.1 percent), information, culture and recreation (16,500 or 4.4 percent), other services (16,000 or 4.3 percent), construction (15,300 or 4.1 percent), forestry, fishing, mining, oil and gas (14,400 or 3.9 percent), professional, scientific and technical services (11,300 or 3.0 percent), agriculture (9,800 or 2.6 percent), management, administrative and other support (6,300 or 1.7 percent) and utilities (3,600 or 1.0 percent).

ALBERTA

a. Minimum Wages in Alberta

Interprovincial rank: dollar value of minimum wages (Figure J1)

Alberta's minimum wage last increased from $5.65 to $5.90 on October 1, 1999. In 2002, Alberta's $5.90 minimum wage ranked the province third-lowest among Canada's ten provinces and three territories, the lowest being Newfoundland ($5.71 annual average) and the highest British Columbia ($8.00). Figure J1 illustrates the rankings.

Trend in dollar value of minimum wage (Figure J2)

Because minimum wages are not indexed, their value changes over time. Figure J2 shows the trend in Alberta's minimum wage from 1965 to 2002; each year's average minimum wage has been converted to inflation-adjusted (i.e., constant) 2002 dollars to show the real trend, after taking into account the impact of inflation on the dollar.

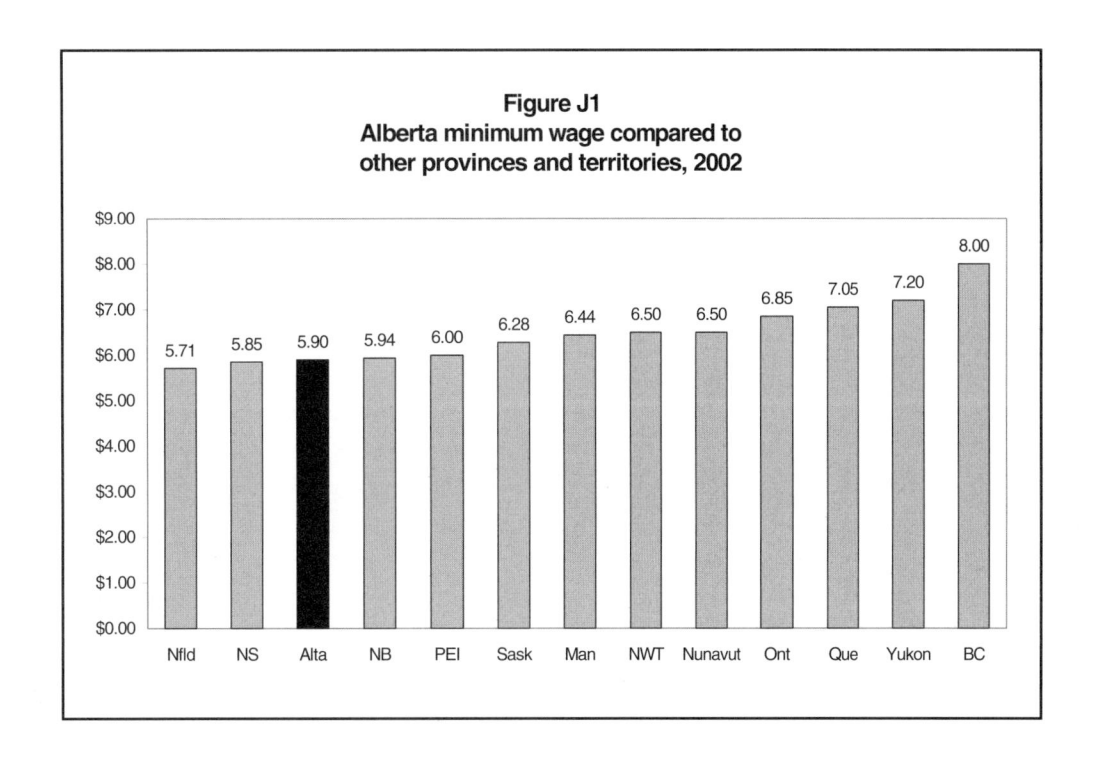

Figure J1
Alberta minimum wage compared to other provinces and territories, 2002

Nfld	5.71
NS	5.85
Alta	5.90
NB	5.94
PEI	6.00
Sask	6.28
Man	6.44
NWT	6.50
Nunavut	6.50
Ont	6.85
Que	7.05
Yukon	7.20
BC	8.00

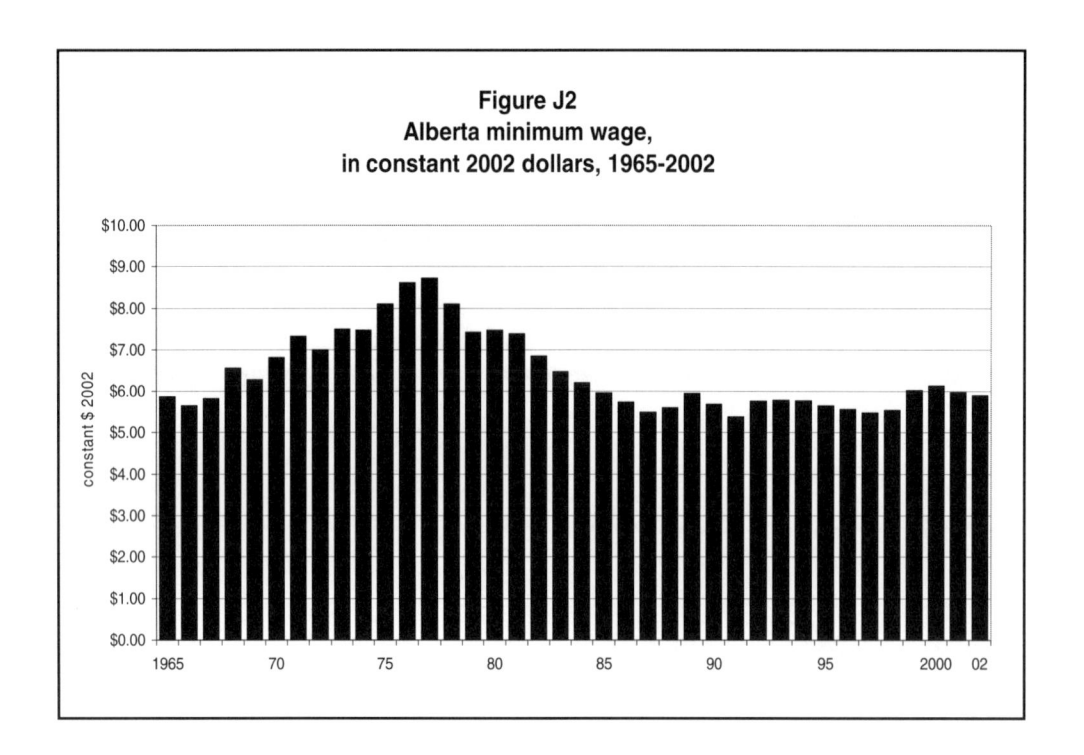

**Figure J2
Alberta minimum wage,
in constant 2002 dollars, 1965-2002**

Alberta's minimum wage shows an up-down-level plateau-like pattern over the years. It increased substantially between 1965 ($5.87 an hour) and its 1977 peak ($8.72), declined to $5.38 in 1991 and then more or less flattened out during the 1990s; it rose at the start of the new century to $6.13 in 2000 but has slipped a bit to $5.90 in 2002. Its value in 2002 was a sizeable $2.82 or 32.4 percent lower than the 1977 high point though virtually the same (just 3 cents more) as its 1965 level.

Interprovincial rank: minimum wages as percentage of average earnings (Figure J3)

Alberta also ranks third-from-the-bottom in terms of how its minimum wage compares to its average wage. In 2001 (the most recent year for which data on average earnings are available), Alberta's $5.90 minimum wage represented only 34.5 percent of its $17.10 hourly average earnings. The Northwest Territories were last at 30.2 percent, while British Columbia came first at 46.2 percent. Figure J3 shows the results.

Trends in minimum wage and average earnings (Figure J4)

The black line in Figure J4 shows the trend in the minimum wage, the gray line the trend in average earnings and the vertical bars the trend in the minimum wage as a percentage of average earnings. Read the

**Figure J3
Alberta minimum wage as % of average earnings,
compared to other provinces and territories, 2001**

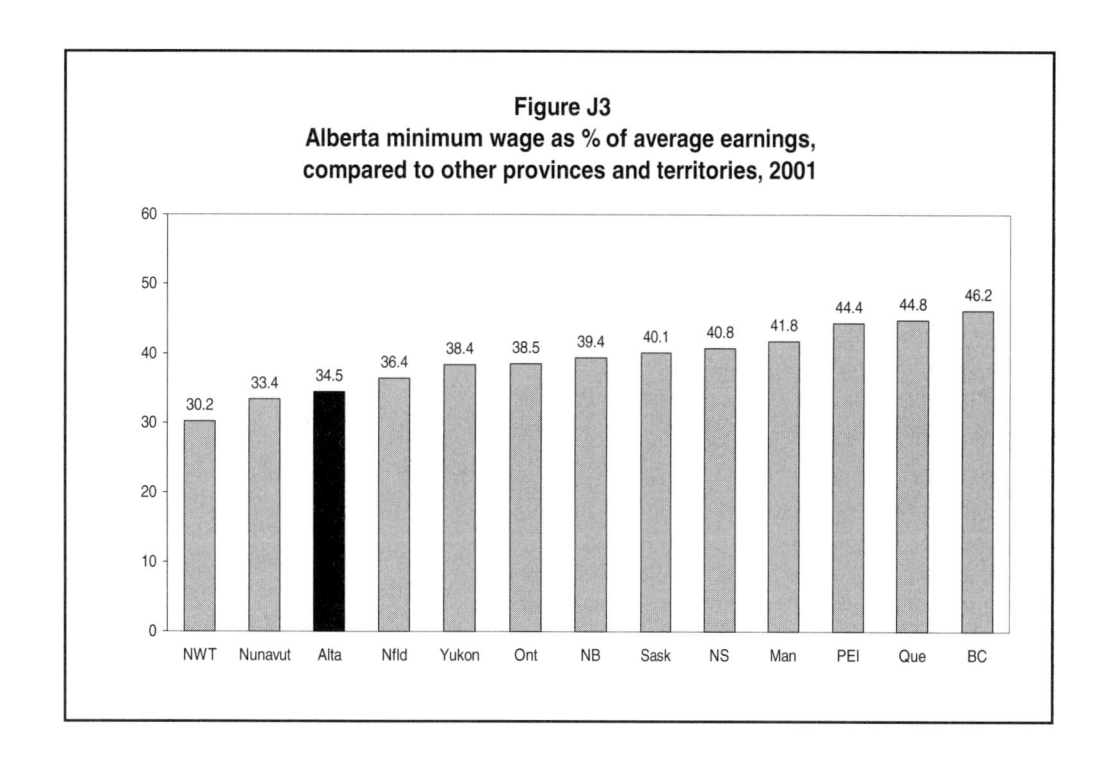

NWT	Nunavut	Alta	Nfld	Yukon	Ont	NB	Sask	NS	Man	PEI	Que	BC
30.2	33.4	34.5	36.4	38.4	38.5	39.4	40.1	40.8	41.8	44.4	44.8	46.2

**Figure J4
Alberta minimum wage
compared to average earnings, 1965-2001**

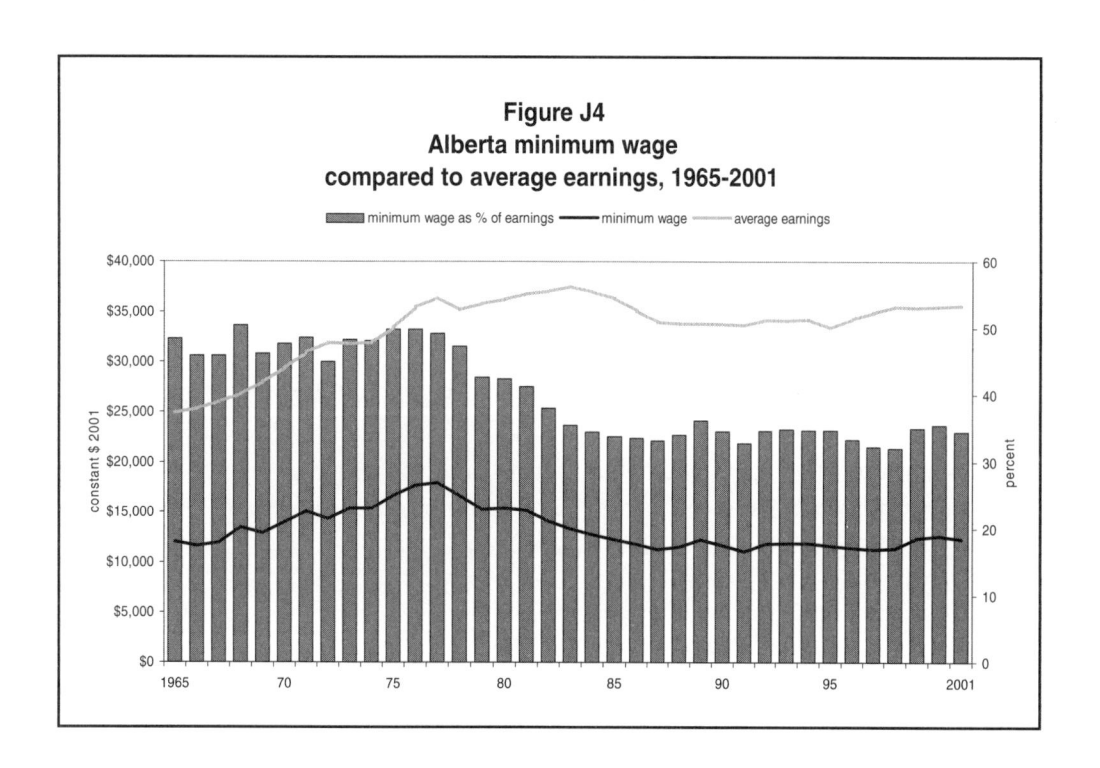

left-hand axis for the minimum wage and average earnings and the right-hand axis for the minimum wage as a percentage of earnings.

The long-term trend indicates that Alberta's minimum wage has declined substantially relative to average earnings. The minimum wage ranged between 45 and 50 percent of average earnings in the 1965-1978 period and then fell considerably to the 33-34 percent level by the mid-1980s, remaining around that mark in the latter half of the 1980s and throughout most of the 1990s to stand at 34.5 percent in 2001.

Average earnings in Alberta increased from $24,870 in 1965 to $37,485 in 1983, declined to $33,392 in 1995 but recovered somewhat to reach $35,571 in 2001. The province's minimum wage also increased between 1965 and the mid-1970s but fell overall thereafter, which explains why its percentage of the average wage also declined until a small recovery at the end of the 1990s. On an annual (full-time, all-year) basis, Alberta's minimum wage went from $12,055 in 1965 to $17,913 in 1977, fell to $11,054 in 1991 but recovered somewhat to stand at $12,272 in 2001.

Minimum wage compared to before-tax poverty lines (Figure J5)

Statistics Canada publishes two sets of low income cut-offs. The before-tax low income cut-offs are based on gross, pre-tax income (i.e., income from employment, investments, private pensions and other private sources plus income from government programs such as public pensions, Employment Insurance, child benefits and welfare). The after-tax low income cut-offs use the same definition of income but also factor into the picture the federal and provincial income taxes that Canadians pay. We first compare the minimum wage to the before-tax poverty lines, as shown in Figure J5.

Because the poverty line is lower for smaller communities, the minimum wage represents a larger proportion of the poverty line in smaller communities. In 2002, Alberta's minimum wage ranged from 64.3 percent of the before-tax low income line for one person in Edmonton and Calgary (which are in the 500,000-plus category) to 75.8 percent for small urban areas with between 30,000 and 99,999 inhabitants, 81.5 percent for towns under 30,000 and 93.5 percent for rural residents. Note that there are no Alberta cities in the second-largest size category, 100,000-499,999 (as is also the case for Manitoba), so that category is not included in the analysis of before-tax and after-tax poverty gaps.

Alberta's minimum wage in 2002 fell $6,802 short of the before-tax low income line for one person in Calgary or Edmonton, $3,910 below the line for communities between 30,000 and 99,999, $2,785 beneath for towns under 30,000 and $857 below the poverty line for rural residents. Figure J5 shows the dollar gap between the minimum wage and the poverty line for one person in different size communities throughout the province.

Because the poverty line varies by family size, minimum wages (which do not vary by family size) fall farther below the poverty line for families than for single workers. We look at the poverty gap for a

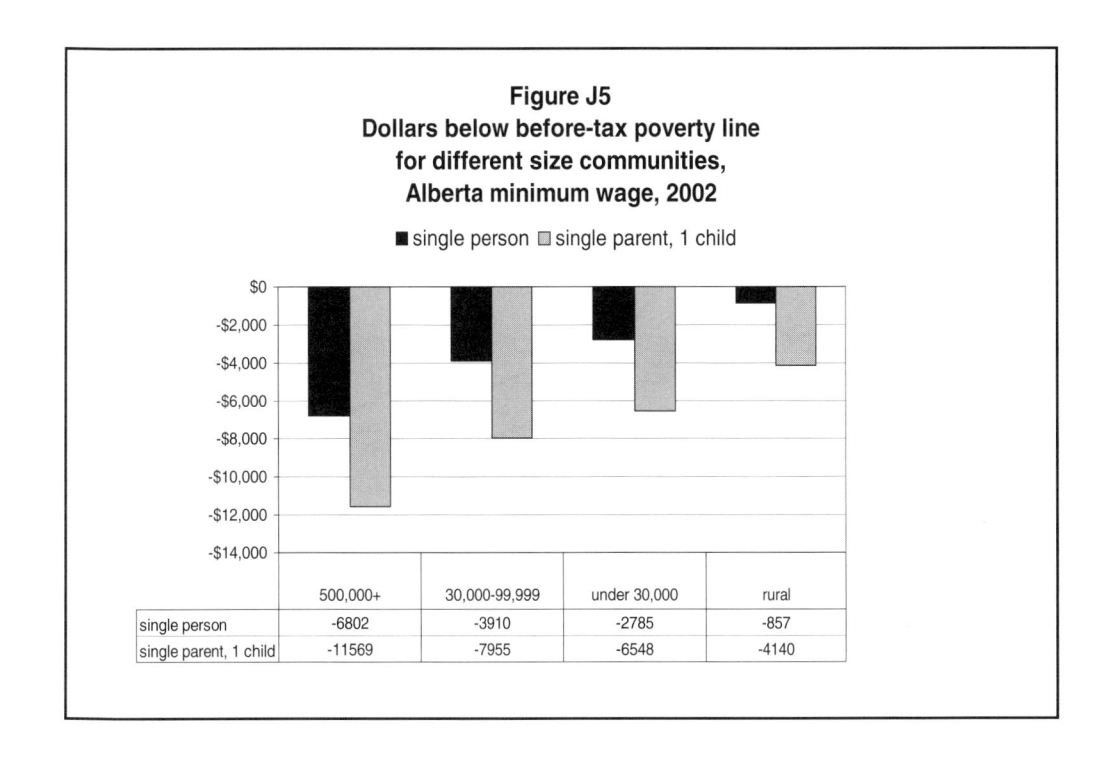

Figure J5
Dollars below before-tax poverty line for different size communities, Alberta minimum wage, 2002

	500,000+	30,000-99,999	under 30,000	rural
single person	-6802	-3910	-2785	-857
single parent, 1 child	-11569	-7955	-6548	-4140

single parent with one child, which falls in the two-person family size category. In 2002, Alberta's minimum wage varied from 51.5 percent of the low income line for a two-person family in Edmonton or Calgary to 60.7 percent for communities between 30,000 and 99,999, 65.2 percent for towns under 30,000 and 74.8 percent for rural areas. Alberta's minimum wage was $11,569 below the before-tax low income cut-off for a family of two in Calgary or Edmonton, $7,955 under for communities between 30,000 and 99,999 inhabitants, $6,548 below the line for towns under 30,000 and $4,140 beneath for rural areas.

Trend in minimum wage as percentage of before-tax poverty line (Figure J6)

The long-term trend when we compare the minimum wage to the poverty line (as measured by Statistics Canada's before-tax low income cut-offs, which vary by size of family and of community) is the same as the trend in dollar value. In 2002, the estimated before-tax low income line for a city the size of Edmonton and Calgary was $19,074 for one person and $23,841 for a family of two. Figure J6 shows the trends.

Alberta's minimum wage increased from 64.0 percent of the before-tax poverty line for one person living in Edmonton or Calgary in 1965 to 95.1 percent in 1977, falling to 58.7 percent by 1991; it then rose somewhat at the end of the decade to 66.9 percent in 2000, though it slipped to 64.3 percent in 2002. For

Contribution of child benefits

Child benefits supplement the incomes of the large majority of Canadian families and are especially important to low- and modest-income families. Increases to the federal Canada Child Tax Benefit, along with Alberta's creation of the Family Employment Tax Credit, are boosting the incomes of minimum wage and other working poor families.

The single-parent minimum wage worker with one child got $2,358 from the Canada Child Tax Benefit and $462 from the Alberta Family Employment Tax Credit – for a combined total of $2,820 or 18.9 percent of disposable income. The one-earner couple with two children received $4,342 from the Canada Child Tax Benefit and $462 from the Alberta Family Employment Tax Credit – for a combined federal-provincial child benefit of $4,804, worth 28.2 percent of disposable income.

The two-earner family in which one parent works full time, all year at the minimum wage and the other parent half that time got $4,342 from the Canada Child Tax Benefit and $953 from the Alberta Family Employment Tax Credit, for a total child benefit payment of $5,295 or a substantial 23.1 percent of disposable income. The two-earner family in which both parents work full time, all year at the minimum wage received $3,647 from the Canada Child Tax Benefit and $1,000 from the Alberta Family Employment Tax Credit, for a total child benefit of $4,647 – the highest among all the provinces and territories for this type of family – or 16.7 percent of disposable income.

Minimum wage versus welfare (Figure J8)

For a single person earning the minimum wage in Alberta, disposable income – i.e., minimum wage earnings plus federal refundable tax credits minus income and payroll taxes – amounted to $11,262 in 2001, which is a sizeable $6,232 more than the $5,030 from welfare and refundable tax credits. Figure J8 shows the comparison.

Minimum wages also pay better than welfare for a single parent with one child age 2, though the advantage is not as great as for single people. Disposable income from after-tax minimum wage earnings, child benefits and refundable tax credits amounted to $14,958 in 2001, or $3,339 more than the $11,619 from welfare, child benefits and refundable tax credits.

However, a one-earner couple earning the minimum wage and supporting two children aged 10 and 15 is worse off financially than if it were on welfare. Total disposable income from minimum wages, child benefits and tax credits came to $17,050 or $1,345 less than the $18,395 from welfare, child benefits and refundable tax credits.

Figure J8
Minimum wage versus welfare in Alberta, by household type, 2001

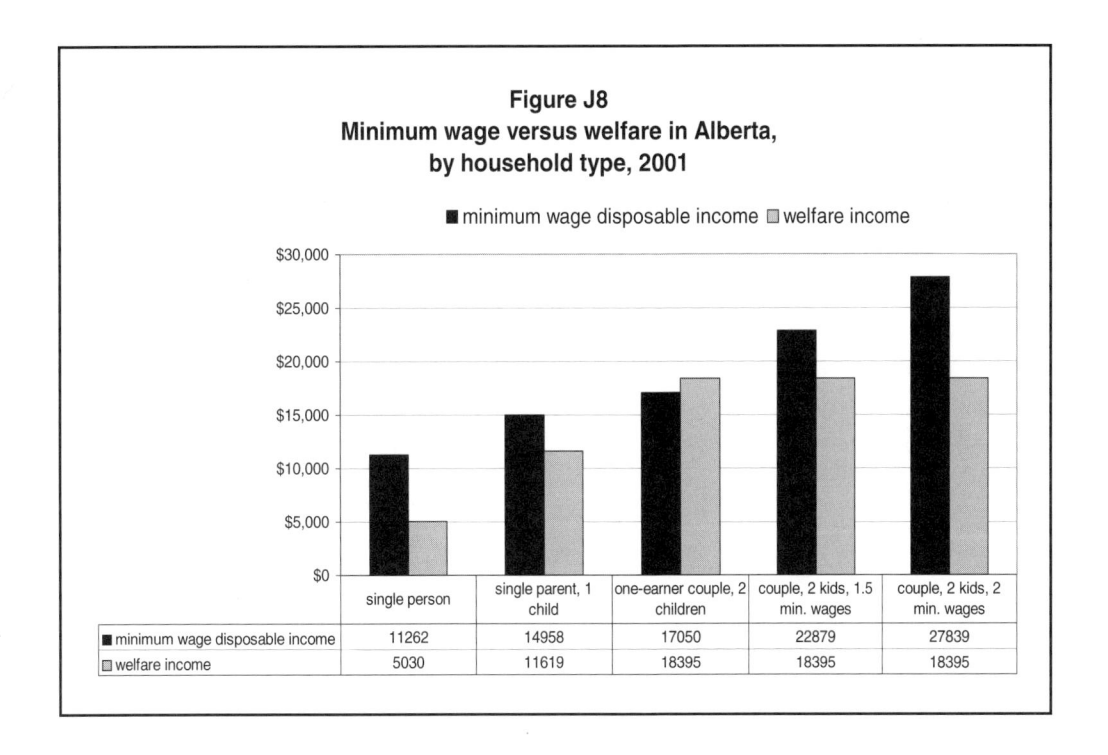

	single person	single parent, 1 child	one-earner couple, 2 children	couple, 2 kids, 1.5 min. wages	couple, 2 kids, 2 min. wages
minimum wage disposable income	11262	14958	17050	22879	27839
welfare income	5030	11619	18395	18395	18395

For a two-parent family to earn more than welfare in Alberta, both parents must work. We look at two examples.

In the first case, one parent works full time, year round at the minimum wage while the other earns half this amount (i.e., works part-time and/or part-year); as above, there are two children aged 10 and 15. This family's disposable income from one-and-a-half minimum wages came to $22,879 in 2001 or $4,484 more than the $18,395 from welfare, child benefits and the refundable GST credit.

The other two-earner family earns double the minimum wage since we assume that both parents work full time, year round at the minimum wage. Total disposable income was $27,839 or $9,444 more than the $18,395 from welfare and other government income programs.

b. Minimum Wage Workers in Alberta

The following text with illustrative graphs analyzes key characteristics of minimum wage workers in Alberta. Appendix 2 provides detailed statistics in tabular form (pages 306-308).

Interprovincial rank: incidence of minimum wage workers (Figure J9)

In 2000, an estimated 26,200 workers in Alberta – just 2.0 percent of the total 1,299,200 employees – worked for the minimum wage. Alberta's 2.0 percent incidence of minimum wage workers is the lowest in Canada, as seen in Figure J9. The national average incidence of minimum wage work is 4.6 percent.

Minimum wage workers are very much underrepresented in Alberta. The province accounts for 4.5 percent of all minimum wage workers in the country but 10.4 percent of all employees, producing an index of 0.43 (the lower the result below 1.00, the more underrepresented are minimum wage workers).

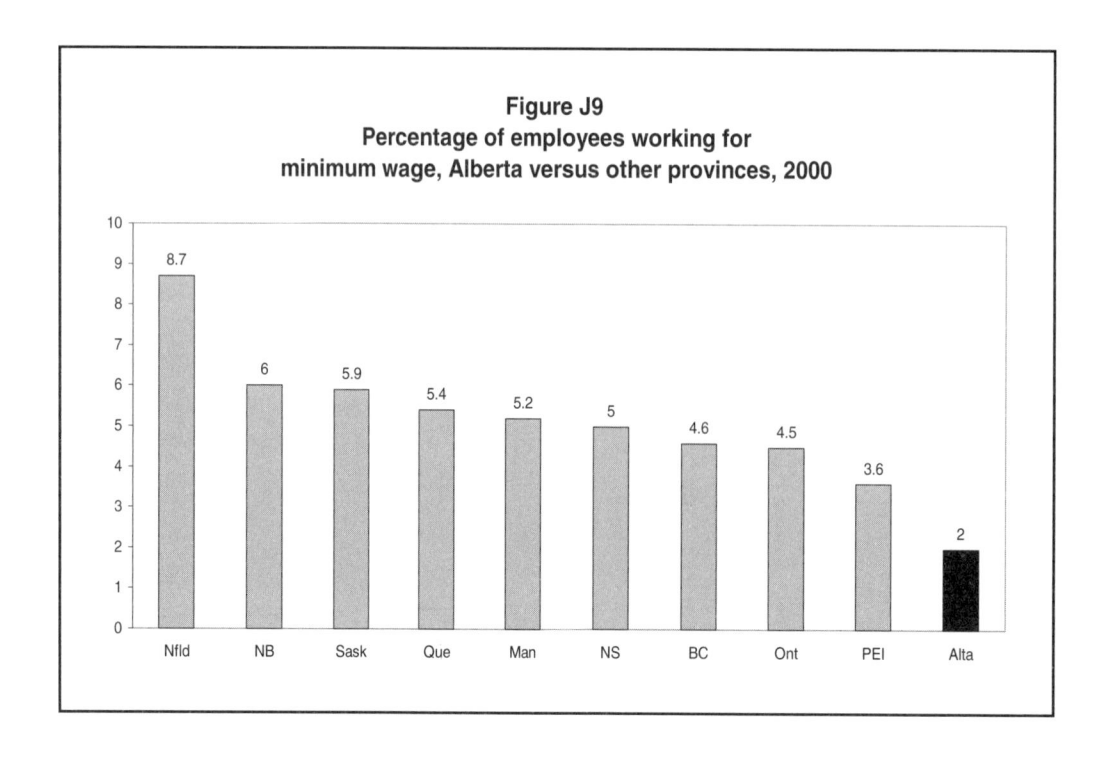

Figure J9
Percentage of employees working for minimum wage, Alberta versus other provinces, 2000

Province	Percentage
Nfld	8.7
NB	6
Sask	5.9
Que	5.4
Man	5.2
NS	5
BC	4.6
Ont	4.5
PEI	3.6
Alta	2

Gender and age (Figures J10-J13)

In Alberta as in the rest of Canada, women run a higher risk of working for minimum wage than men, and women also make up the majority of the minimum wage workforce.

In 2000, 2.4 percent of Alberta's female employees worked for minimum wage compared to 1.7 percent of male workers. Of the total 26,200 minimum wage workers, 14,800 – 56.5 percent – were women and 11,400 – 43.5 percent – were men, as indicated in Figure J10.

Women are overrepresented in Alberta's minimum wage workforce. They constituted 56.5 percent of minimum wage workers but only 47.1 percent of all the province's employees in 2000. Men are underrepresented, accounting for only 43.5 percent of minimum wage workers but 52.9 percent of all employees.

The gender bias among minimum wage workers holds when we control for major age categories. While younger workers of both sexes run a higher risk of working for minimum wage, women still fare worse than men in every age category. Figure J11 illustrates the findings.

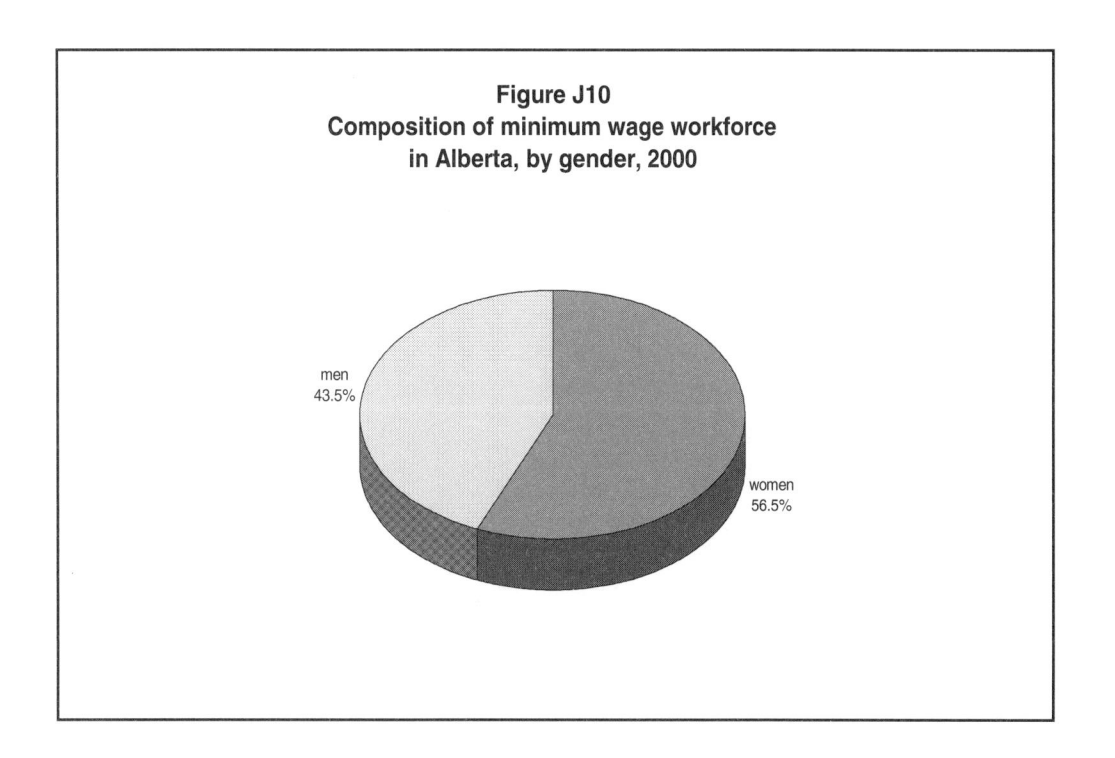

**Figure J10
Composition of minimum wage workforce
in Alberta, by gender, 2000**

men 43.5%
women 56.5%

**Figure J11
Percentage of employees working for
minimum wage in Alberta, by gender and age, 2000**

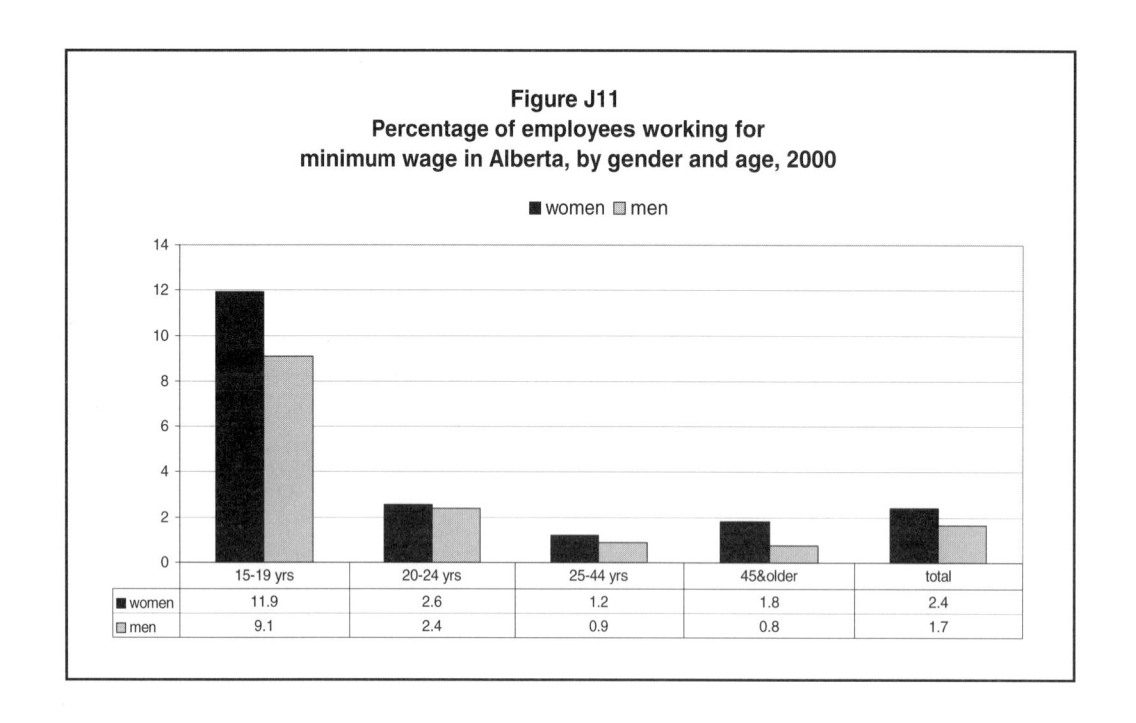

	15-19 yrs	20-24 yrs	25-44 yrs	45&older	total
women	11.9	2.6	1.2	1.8	2.4
men	9.1	2.4	0.9	0.8	1.7

**Figure J12
Share of minimum wage workers versus
share of all employees in Alberta, by age group, 2000**

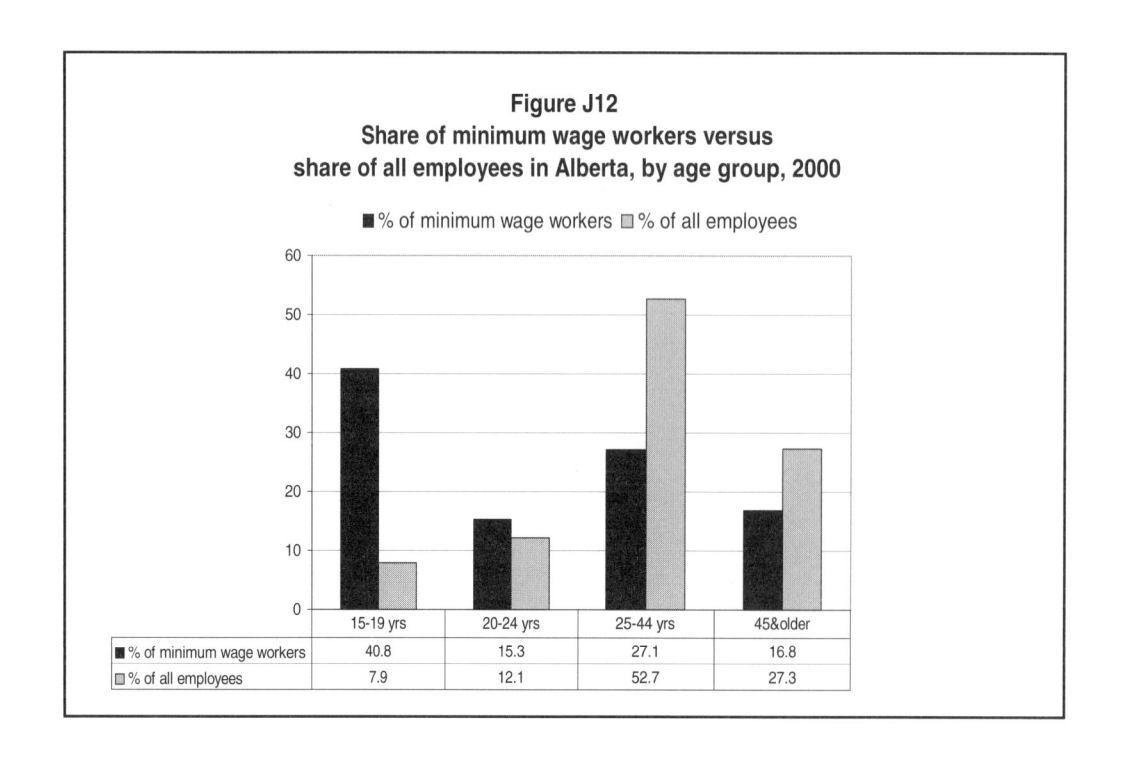

	15-19 yrs	20-24 yrs	25-44 yrs	45&older
% of minimum wage workers	40.8	15.3	27.1	16.8
% of all employees	7.9	12.1	52.7	27.3

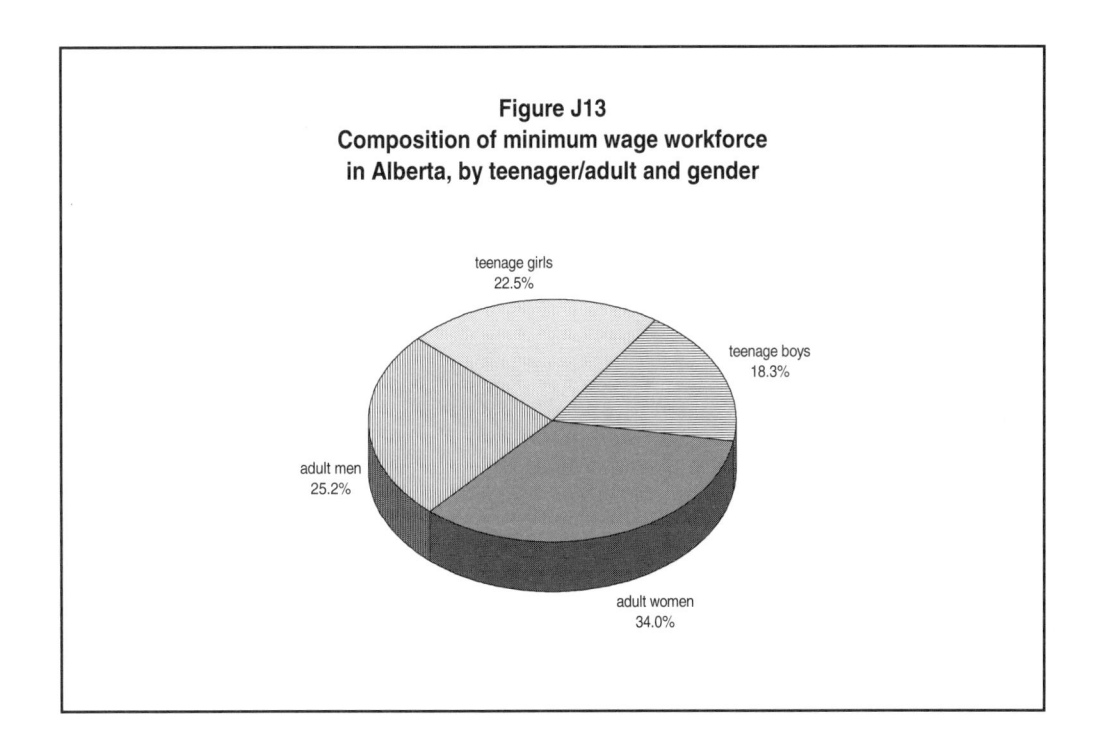

**Figure J13
Composition of minimum wage workforce
in Alberta, by teenager/adult and gender**

- teenage girls 22.5%
- teenage boys 18.3%
- adult men 25.2%
- adult women 34.0%

Among female workers aged 15 to 19, 11.9 percent worked for the minimum wage in 2000 as opposed to 9.1 percent of male minimum wage workers in the same age group. Among those 20-24, 2.6 percent of women compared to 2.4 percent of men worked for the minimum wage. Among workers 25-44, 1.2 percent of women as opposed to just 0.9 percent of men were at the bottom of the wage ladder. Among employees 45 and older, 1.8 percent of women but only 0.8 percent of men worked for the minimum wage in Alberta.

Young people not only are more likely to work for minimum wage than other employees, but the young also make up a large proportion of the minimum wage workforce. Figure J12 compares the age makeup of minimum wage workers and all employees in Alberta. Four in ten (40.8 percent) of minimum wage workers are in the 15-19 age group, as opposed to just 7.9 percent of all employees. Employees aged 20-24 represent 15.3 percent of minimum wage workers as opposed to 12.1 percent of all workers. All told, more than half (56.1 percent) of minimum wage workers in Alberta are under 25 years of age.

The opposite holds for older workers. While a sizeable proportion – 27.1 percent – of minimum wage workers in Alberta are between 25 and 44, that age group constitutes a much larger proportion – 52.7 percent – of all employees. Workers aged 45 and older make up 16.8 percent of minimum wage employees but 27.3 percent all employees.

Figure J13 divides the minimum wage workforce in Alberta into teenage girls and boys and adult women and men. Adult women are the largest group, at 8,900 or 34.0 percent of the total, followed by adult men (6,600 or 25.2 percent), teenage girls (5,900 or 22.5 percent) and teenage boys (4,800 or 18.3 percent). The majority (59.2 percent) of Alberta's minimum wage workers are adults, which is the case in most provinces (the national average is 52.9 percent).

Education (Figures J14 and J15)

Figure J14 shows the incidence of minimum wage workers in Alberta according to level of education.

At first glance, the relationship between level of education and incidence of minimum wage employment does not seem to correspond to common sense: Workers in the lowest educational group (elementary education only) are less likely to work for minimum wage (5.1 percent do) than those with some high school (6.6 percent), while those with some postsecondary education run a higher risk (2.1 percent) than high school graduates (1.5 percent). However, as one would expect, the chances of working for minimum wage are lowest for the two highest education categories – 0.8 percent for those with a postsecondary certificate or diploma (e.g., from a community college or vocational institute) and 1.0 percent for those with a university degree.

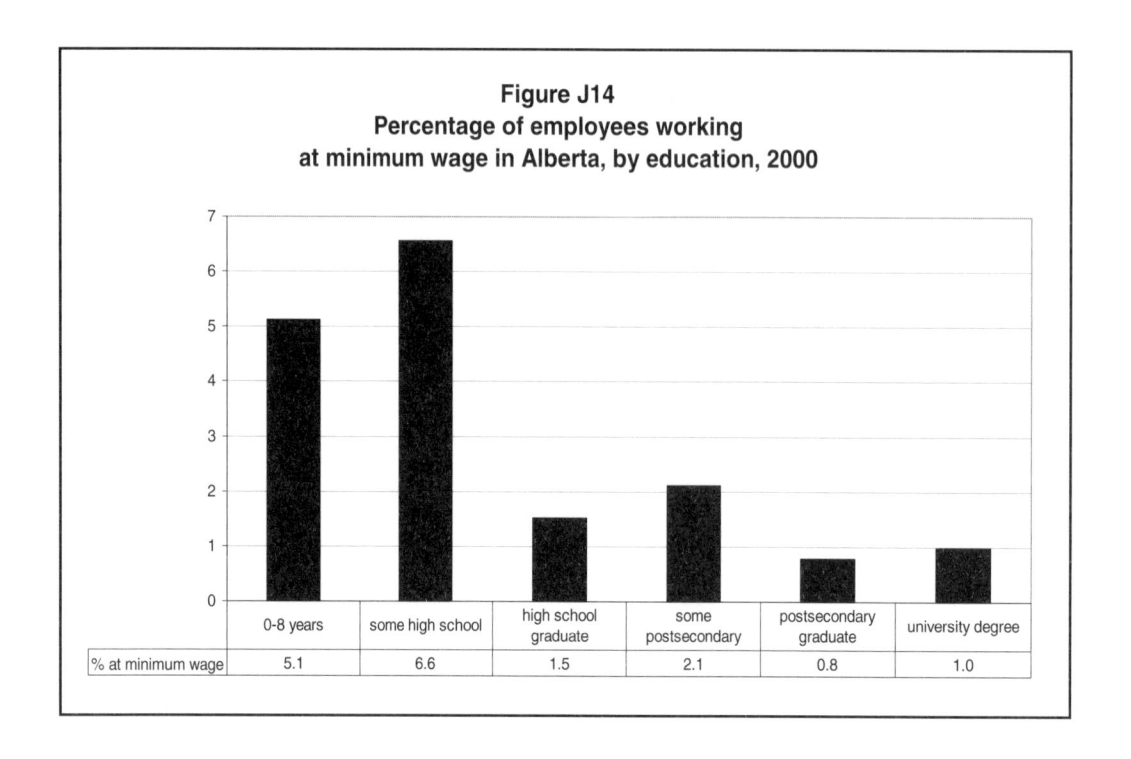

**Figure J14
Percentage of employees working
at minimum wage in Alberta, by education, 2000**

	0-8 years	some high school	high school graduate	some postsecondary	postsecondary graduate	university degree
% at minimum wage	5.1	6.6	1.5	2.1	0.8	1.0

Figure J15
Composition of minimum wage workforce in Alberta, by education, 2000

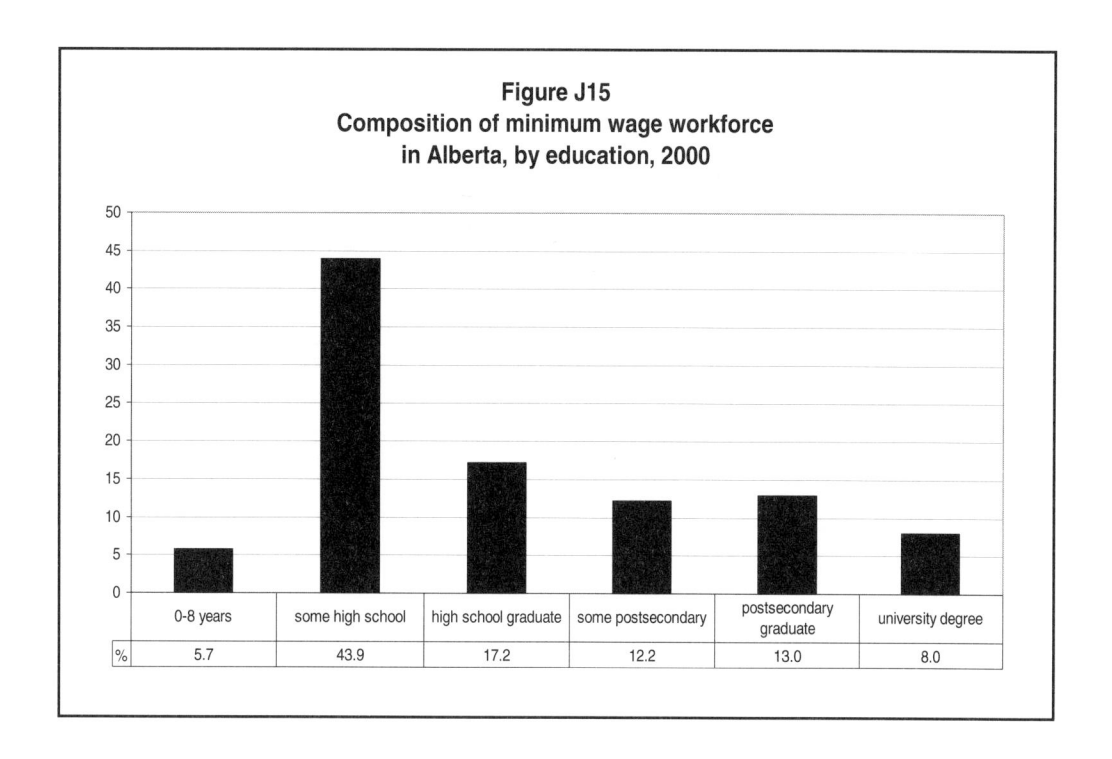

	0-8 years	some high school	high school graduate	some postsecondary	postsecondary graduate	university degree
%	5.7	43.9	17.2	12.2	13.0	8.0

Once we look at the education-minimum wage link for different age groups, the reasons for the apparently inconsistent relationship comes clear: Young people working at part-time or seasonal (i.e., summer) jobs – typically paying the minimum or a low wage – figure prominently in the 'some high school' and 'some postsecondary education' categories; they are still at high school, community college or university, whereas workers in the other educational categories have completed their education.

Figure J15 shows each educational group's share of Alberta's minimum wage workforce in 2000. The largest group of minimum wage workers are those with some high school (43.9 percent), followed by high school graduates (17.2 percent), postsecondary graduates (13.0 percent), those with some postsecondary education (12.2 percent), university graduates (8.0 percent) and workers with 0-8 years of education (5.7 percent). Many minimum wage workers are students (high school or postsecondary) pursuing their education. A significant group of minimum wage workers (33.2 percent) have some form of postsecondary education.

Full-time and part-time work (Figures J16 and J17)

The fact that young people are more likely to work part time helps explain why workers still pursuing their education tend to face a higher risk of minimum wage work than those who have completed

Figure J16
Percentage of employees working at minimum wage in Alberta, by full-time/part-time and gender, 2000

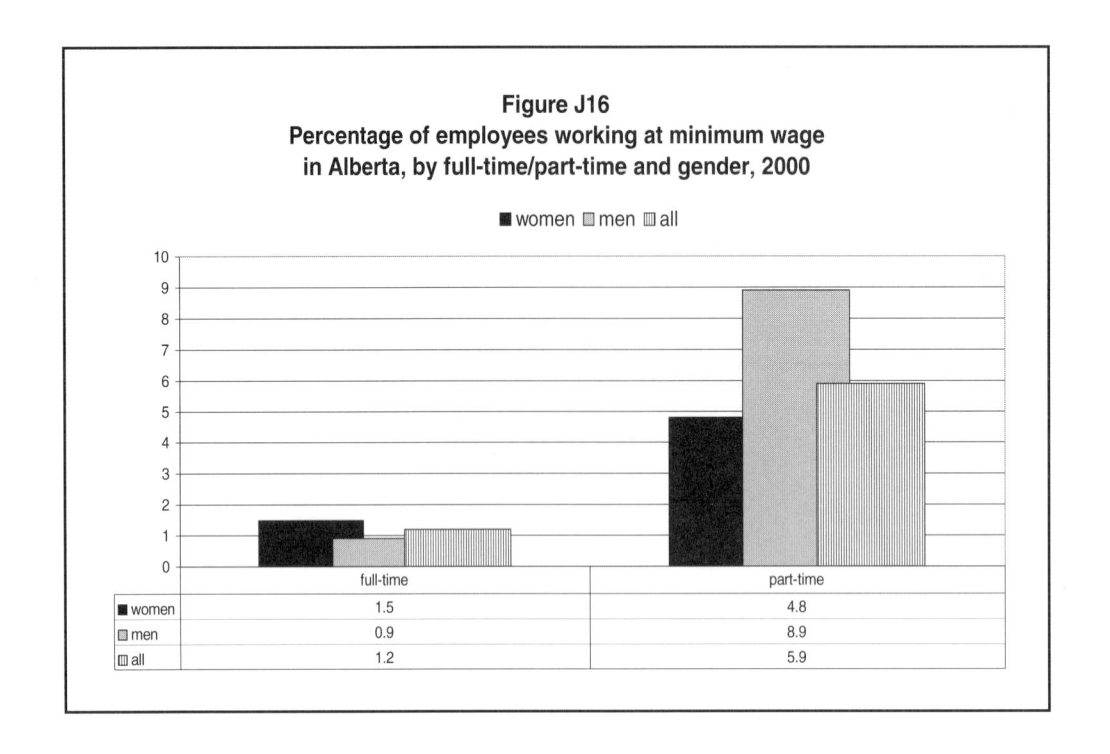

	full-time	part-time
women	1.5	4.8
men	0.9	8.9
all	1.2	5.9

Figure J17
Composition of minimum wage workforce in Alberta, full-time and part-time workers, 2000

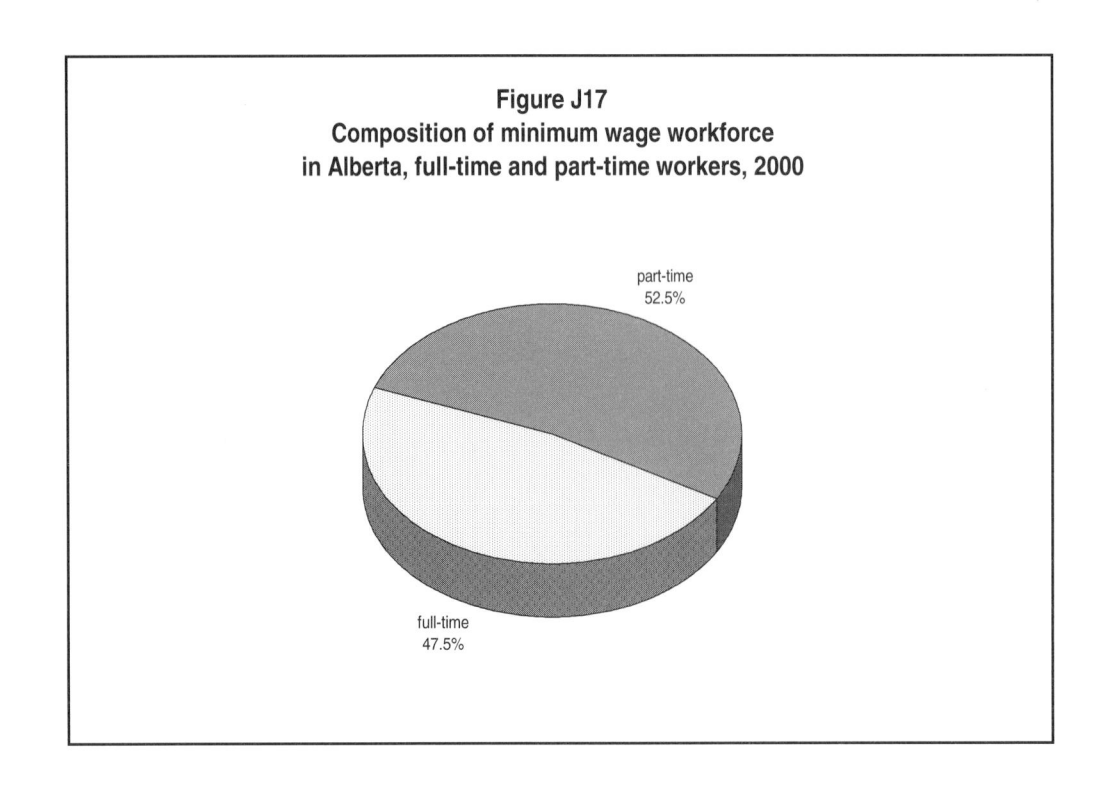

part-time 52.5%
full-time 47.5%

their schooling and are working full time. Figure J16 indicates that 5.9 percent of part-time workers are at the minimum wage compared to only 1.2 percent of those employed full time.

While the majority of minimum wage workers in Alberta (52.5 percent) work part time, a sizeable group (47.5 percent) are employed full time. Figure J17 pictures the figures.

Gender alters the relationship between full-time and part-time work and the minimum wage. Women who work part time in Alberta run a lesser risk of being at the bottom of the wage ladder than do men who work part time (4.8 and 8.9 percent, respectively). However, women employed full time are more likely than men in that group to earn the minimum wage (1.5 and 0.9 percent, respectively).

Women make up the majority of minimum wage employees in the province working both full time (53.2 percent are women) and part time (59.9 percent are women). Among all employees, though, women constitute a minority of full-time workers (41.4 percent) but the bulk of part-time workers (73.4 percent).

Family status (Figure J18)

We noted above that over half of Alberta's minimum wage workers are under 25 years of age. Light on this fundamental fact of the minimum wage workforce is shed by information on family status, shown in Figure J18, which shows that the largest group of minimum wage workers – 14,000 or 53.6 percent of the total 26,200 – are older children living with their parents (or relatives with relatives, as in the case of a niece or nephew living with an aunt and uncle, or grandchildren with grandparents). Of this category, 9,900 or 70.7 percent are aged 15-19, 2,600 or 18.6 percent are 20-24 and the remaining 1,500 or 10.7 percent are 25 or older. More than half (8,000 or 57.1 percent) are still in school and working part-time or part-year (e.g., in summer).

The next largest group of minimum wage workers in Alberta – an estimated 8,000 or 30.7 percent of the total – are members of couples (married or living together). In most cases (6,400 or 80.0 percent of the category total of 8,000), the minimum wage worker's spouse is employed, earning more than the minimum wage. A typical example in this category would be mothers combining (unpaid) childrearing work with part-time minimum wage work. Another 1,600 or 20.0 percent of minimum wage workers living in couples have a spouse who is not employed (most of the latter are not in the labour force).

An estimated 3,100 or 11.9 percent of minimum wage workers in Alberta are unattached individuals. An estimated 1,300 or 41.9 percent of unattached minimum wage workers live alone; of this group, 200 are aged 15-24, 900 are aged 25-54 and 200 are 55 or older. Another 1,800 or 58.1 percent of the province's unattached minimum wage workers live with friends or roommates; in this category, 700 are under 24, 1,000 are 25-44 and 100 are 55 or older.

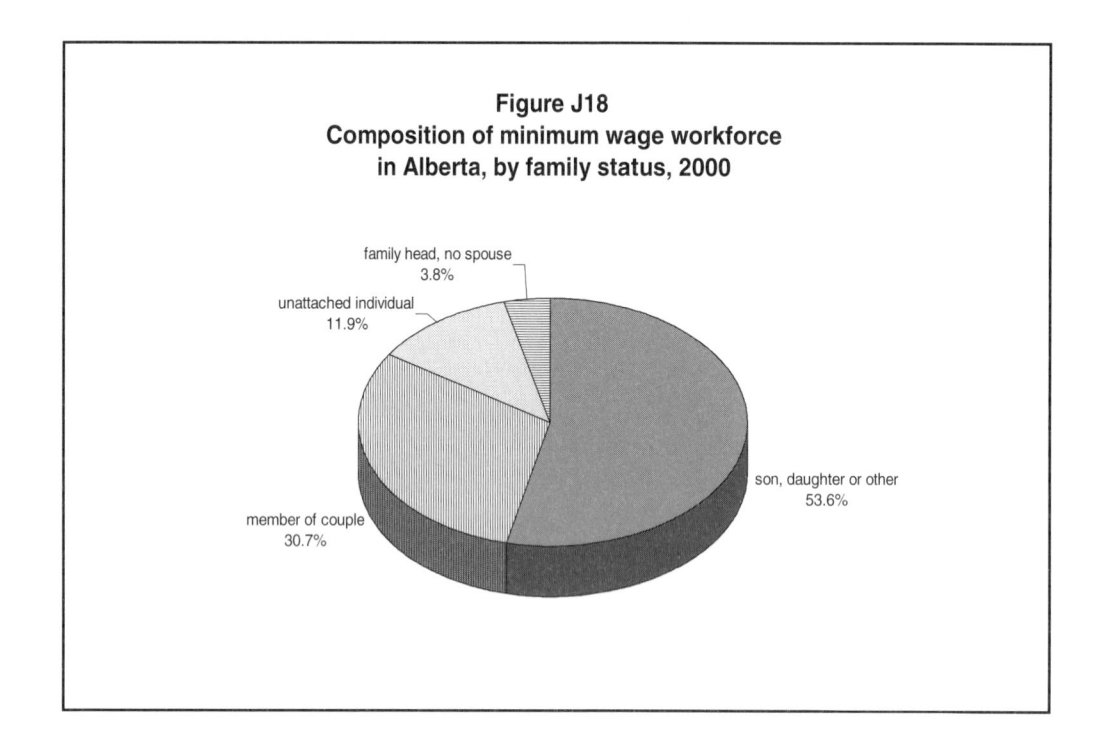

**Figure J18
Composition of minimum wage workforce
in Alberta, by family status, 2000**

- family head, no spouse 3.8%
- unattached individual 11.9%
- member of couple 30.7%
- son, daughter or other 53.6%

Finally, some 1,000 or 3.8 percent of Alberta's minimum wage workers are single parents with children under 18.

Industry

National data show that the incidence and distribution of minimum wage workers varies significantly according to industries. The same applies to Alberta, though sample size constraints permit estimates for only four of the 16 industrial categories. Among the industrial categories for which estimates are available, agriculture tops the list (9.9 percent of employees work for minimum wage), followed by accommodation and food services (6.8 percent), other services (5.2 percent) and trade (2.8 percent).

Estimates are available for the industrial composition of the whole employed workforce in Alberta. Trade tops the list, with an estimated 218,800 or 16.8 percent of all employees. Next comes manufacturing (131,800 or 10.1 percent), followed by health care and social assistance (131,700 or 10.1 percent of all employees), accommodation and food services (106,700 or 8.2 percent), educational services (94,200 or 7.3 percent), construction (89,700 or 6.9 percent), transportation and warehousing (78,100 or 6.0 percent), forestry, fishing, mining, oil and gas (76,100 or 5.9 percent), professional, scientific and technical services (71,900 or 5.5 percent), finance, insurance, real estate and leasing (64,600 or 5.0 percent), public administration (61,900 or 4.8 percent), information, culture and recreation (56,200 or 4.3 percent), other services (52,300 or 4.0 percent), management, administrative and other support (36,500 or 2.8 percent), agriculture (16,200 or 1.2 percent) and utilities (12,500 or 1.0 percent).

BRITISH COLUMBIA

a. Minimum Wages in British Columbia

Interprovincial rank: dollar value of minimum wages (Figure K1)

British Columbia's hourly minimum wage increased from $7.15 to $7.60 on November 1, 2000 and again to $8.00 on November 1, 2001. In 2002, British Columbia's $8.00 minimum wage ranked highest among Canada's ten provinces and three territories, the lowest being Newfoundland ($5.71 average). Figure K1 ranks the jurisdictions.

Trend in dollar value of minimum wage (Figure K2)

Because minimum wages are not indexed, their value changes over time. Figure K2 shows the trend in British Columbia's minimum wage from 1965 to 2002; each year's average minimum wage has been converted to inflation-adjusted (i.e., constant) 2002 dollars to show the real trend, after taking into account the impact of inflation on the dollar.

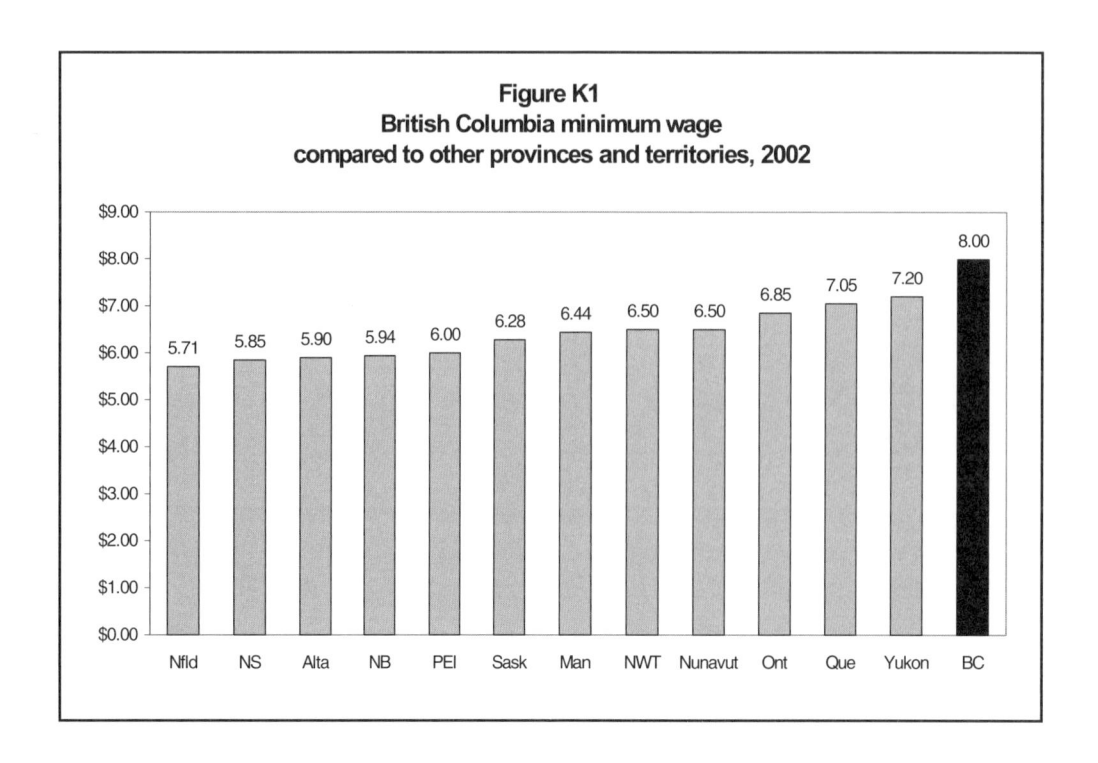

Figure K1
British Columbia minimum wage compared to other provinces and territories, 2002

Jurisdiction	Minimum Wage
Nfld	5.71
NS	5.85
Alta	5.90
NB	5.94
PEI	6.00
Sask	6.28
Man	6.44
NWT	6.50
Nunavut	6.50
Ont	6.85
Que	7.05
Yukon	7.20
BC	8.00

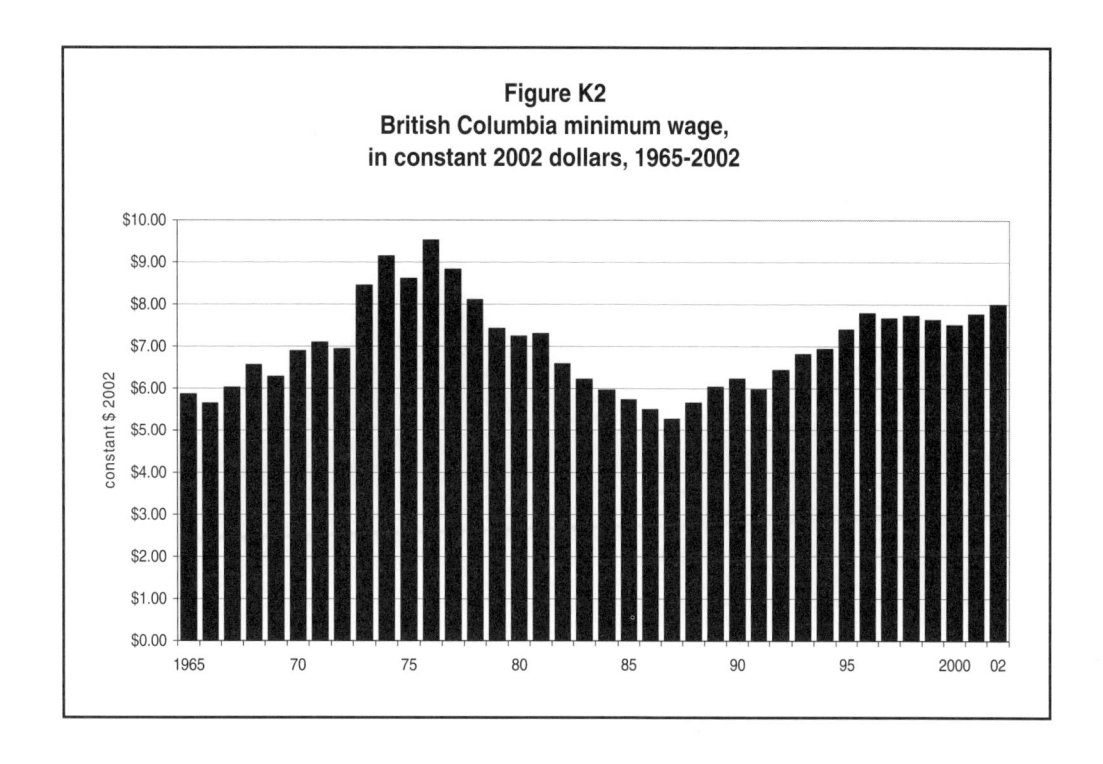

**Figure K2
British Columbia minimum wage,
in constant 2002 dollars, 1965-2002**

British Columbia's minimum wage shows a double-wave pattern, rising and falling between 1965 and 1987, rising again in the latter half of the 1980s and the first half of the 1990s, and then more or less plateauing from 1995 through 2000 (with a small upturn in 2001 and 2002). The province's minimum wage increased from 1965 ($5.87 an hour) to 1976 ($9.53), fell to $5.28 by 1987, and rose again to stand at $8.00 in 2002. Its value in 2002 was $1.53 or 16.0 percent lower than the 1976 high point, though considerably above ($2.13 or 36.3 percent) its 1965 level.

Interprovincial rank: minimum wages as percentage of average earnings (Figure K3)

British Columbia also ranks highest in Canada in terms of how its minimum wage compares to its average wage. In 2001 (the most recent year for which data on average earnings are available), British Columbia's $7.66 minimum wage represented 46.2 percent of its $16.59 hourly average earnings, placing the province top among 13 jurisdictions. The lowest was Northwest Territories at 30.2 percent, while Quebec was second-highest at 44.8 percent. Figure K3 shows the rankings.

**Figure K3
British Columbia minimum wage as % of average earnings, compared to other provinces and territories, 2001**

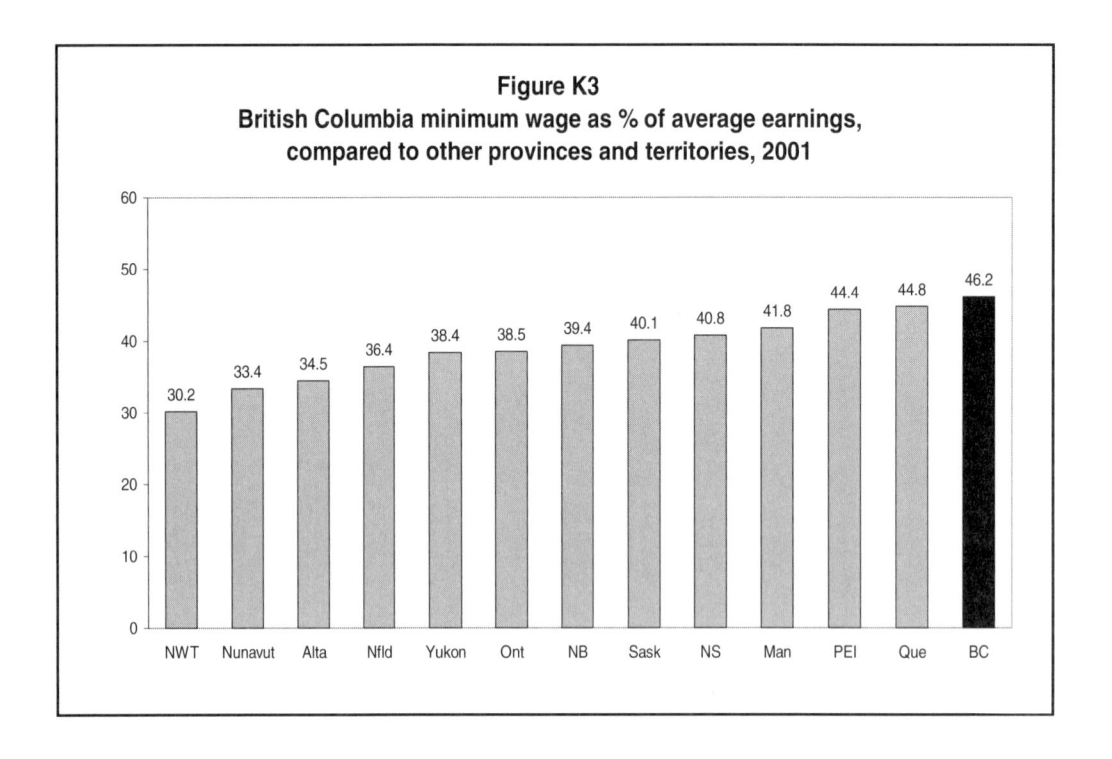

Province/Territory	%
NWT	30.2
Nunavut	33.4
Alta	34.5
Nfld	36.4
Yukon	38.4
Ont	38.5
NB	39.4
Sask	40.1
NS	40.8
Man	41.8
PEI	44.4
Que	44.8
BC	46.2

Trends in minimum wage and average earnings (Figure K4)

The black line in Figure K4 shows the trend in the minimum wage, the gray line the trend in average earnings and the vertical bars the trend in British Columbia's minimum wage as a percentage of average earnings. Read the left-hand axis for the minimum wage and average earnings and the right-hand axis for the minimum wage as a percentage of earnings.

The long-term trend in the minimum wage as a percentage of average earnings is similar to the up-down-up-flat trend in the minimum wage's dollar value. It increased as a percentage of average earnings between 1965 and 1974, fell considerably until the mid-1980s and increased once more in the 1990s, though flattening out in the latter part of the decade (with an upturn in 2001). British Columbia's minimum wage as a percentage of its average earnings went from 43.7 percent in 1965 to 53.1 percent in 1974, declined to a low of 31.0 percent in 1987 and then climbed back up to 46.2 percent by 2001.

Average earnings in British Columbia increased from $27,580 in 1965 to $39,042 in 1977, fell through the 1980s and early 1990s to $33,818 in 1991, recovered somewhat in the first half of the 1990s but slipped a bit after 1997 ($35,861) to stand at $34,511 in 2001. The province's minimum wage followed a similar up-down-up-flat pattern as average earnings, which explains the up-down-up-flat trend in the minimum wage relative to average earnings. On an annual (full-time, all-year) basis, British

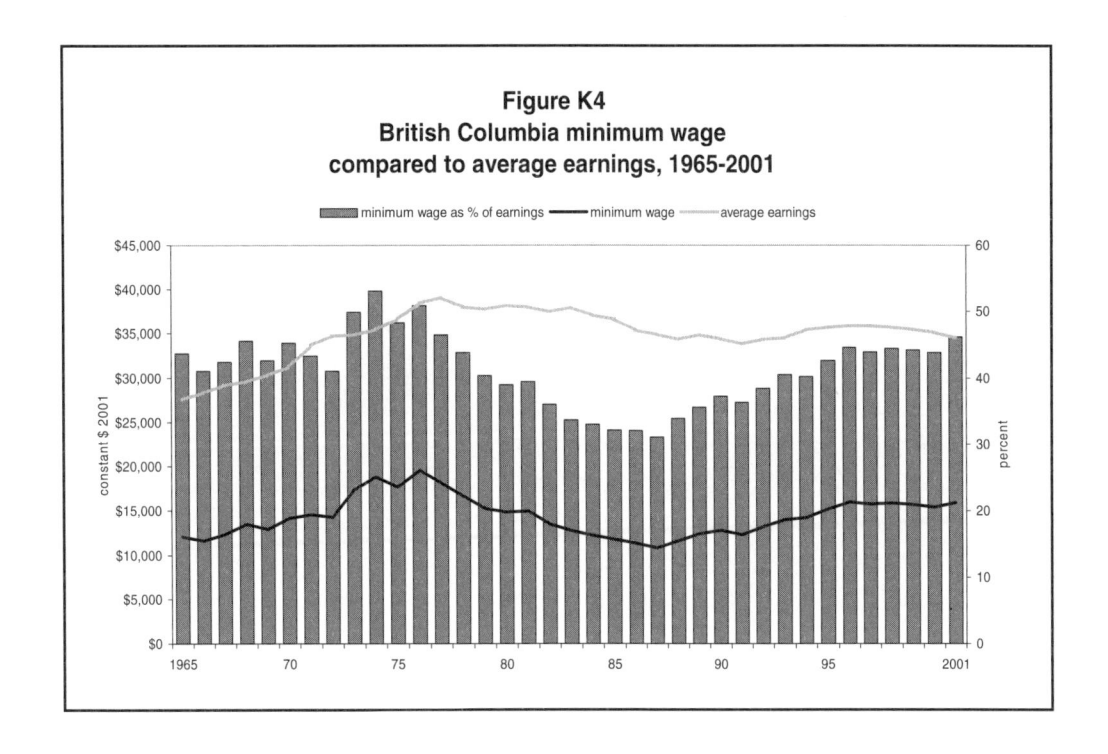

**Figure K4
British Columbia minimum wage
compared to average earnings, 1965-2001**

Columbia's minimum wage went from $12,055 in 1965 to $19,561 in 1976, declined to $10,836 in 1987 and rose to $15,936 in 2001.

Minimum wage compared to before-tax poverty lines (Figure K5)

Statistics Canada publishes two sets of low income cut-offs. The before-tax low income cut-offs are based on gross, pre-tax income (i.e., income from employment, investments, private pensions and other private sources plus income from government programs such as public pensions, Employment Insurance, child benefits and welfare). The after-tax low income cut-offs use the same definition of income but also factor into the picture the federal and provincial income taxes that Canadians pay. We first compare the minimum wage to the before-tax poverty lines

Because the poverty line is lower for smaller communities, the minimum wage represents a larger proportion of the poverty line in smaller communities. In 2002, British Columbia's minimum wage ranged from 87.2 percent of the before-tax low income cut-off for one person in Vancouver (which falls in the 500,000-plus category) to 102.1 percent for Victoria (in the 100,000 and 499,999 category), 102.8 percent for small urban areas between 30,000 and 99,999 inhabitants, 110.5 percent for towns under 30,000 and 126.7 percent for rural residents.

British Columbia's minimum wage in 2002 fell $2,434 short of the before-tax low income line for one person in Vancouver but $345 above the line for Victoria, $458 above for communities between 30,000 and 99,999, $1,583 above the line for towns under 30,000 and $3,511 more than the poverty line for rural residents. Figure K5 shows the dollar difference between the minimum wage and the poverty line for one person in different size communities throughout the province.

Because the poverty line varies by family size, minimum wages (which do not vary by family size) fall farther below the poverty line for families than for single workers. We look at the poverty gap for a single parent with one child, which falls in the two-person family size category. In 2002, British Columbia's minimum wage varied from 69.8 percent of the low income line for a two-person family in Vancouver to 81.7 percent for Victoria, 82.3 percent for communities between 30,000 and 99,999 inhabitants, 88.4 percent for towns under 30,000 and 101.4 percent for rural residents. British Columbia's minimum wage was $7,201 below the before-tax low income line for a family of two in Vancouver, $3,729 under for Victoria, $3,587 lower than the line for communities between 30,000 and 99,999 and $2,180 beneath for towns under 30,000, but $228 above the before-tax poverty line for rural residents.

While there is a sizeable poverty gap for single minimum wage workers living in metropolitan centres and for two-person families in all but rural areas, nonetheless no other province or territory does as well as BC. The reason is simple: Its $8.00 an hour minimum wage goes a lot further in closing the poverty gap.

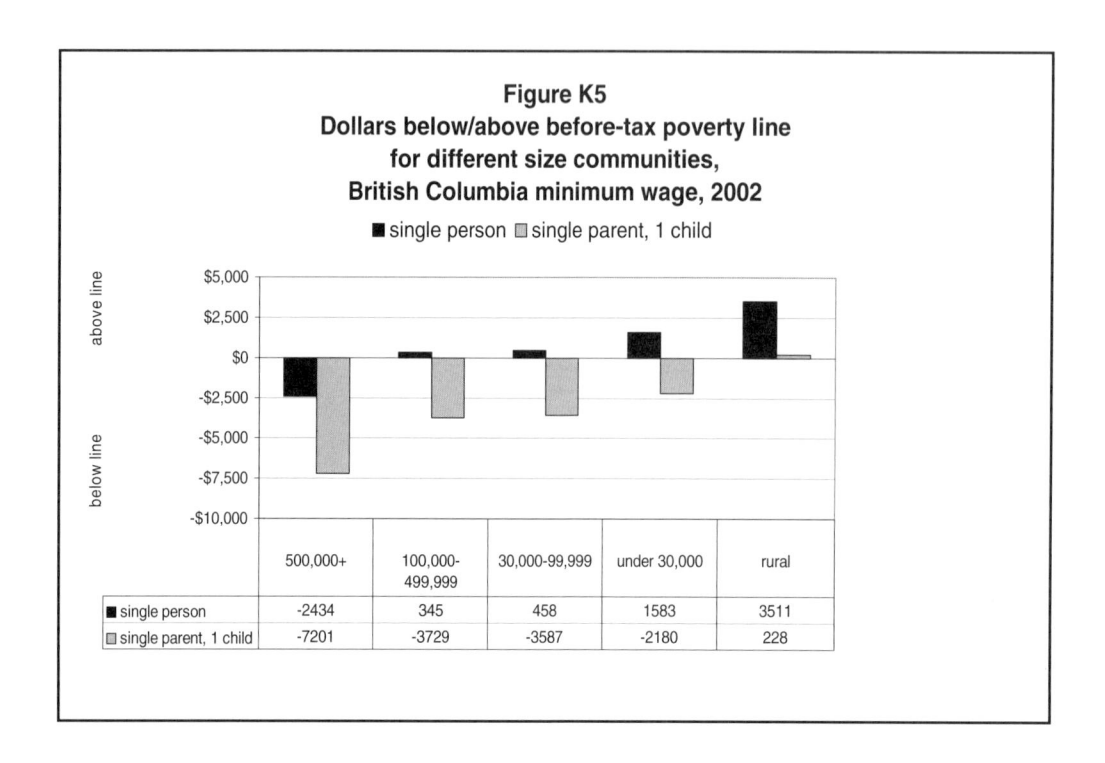

Figure K5
Dollars below/above before-tax poverty line for different size communities, British Columbia minimum wage, 2002

	500,000+	100,000-499,999	30,000-99,999	under 30,000	rural
single person	-2434	345	458	1583	3511
single parent, 1 child	-7201	-3729	-3587	-2180	228

Trend in minimum wage as percentage of before-tax poverty lines (Figure K6)

The long-term trend when we compare the minimum wage to the poverty line (as measured by Statistics Canada's low income cut-offs, which vary by size of family and of community), is the same as the trend in dollar value – up-down-up. In 2002, the estimated before-tax low income line for a metropolitan centre of 500,000 or more (i.e., Vancouver) was $19,074 for one person and $23,841 for a family of two.

British Columbia's minimum wage rose from 64.0 percent of the before-tax poverty line for one person living in Vancouver in 1965 to 103.9 percent in 1976, fell to 57.5 percent in 1987 and then increased to 87.2 percent by 2002. For a two-person family (e.g., a single parent with one child), the minimum wage went from 51.2 percent of the low income line for Vancouver in 1965 to a peak of 83.1 percent in 1976, declined to 46.0 percent in 1987 and climbed back up to 69.8 percent in 2002. Figure K6 shows the trends.

Minimum wage compared to after-tax poverty lines (Figure K7)

Statistics Canada publishes after-tax low income cut-offs as well as before-tax low income cut-offs. We look here at how after-tax minimum wage incomes in British Columbia for five types of household – single persons, single parents with one child, one-earner couples with two children, two-earner couples supporting two children on one-and-a-half minimum wages, and two-earner couples with two children and two full minimum wages – compare to the after-tax poverty lines for different size communities. 'After-tax minimum wage incomes' means incomes from the minimum wage and available federal and provincial income programs minus federal and provincial income taxes.

For a single person earning the minimum wage, after-tax income came to $14,549,[57] which is $1,015 below the after-tax poverty line for Vancouver but $1,439 above the line for Victoria, $1,641 over the line for centres of 30,000-99,999, $2,754 above for towns under 30,000 and $4,345 higher than the poverty line for rural residents. A single parent with one child received $19,525[58] in after-tax income from minimum wage earnings and federal and provincial child benefits and tax credits, which came to $533 above the after-tax poverty line for Vancouver, $3,528 above the line for Victoria, $3,775 over for centres between 30,000 and 99,999, $5,132 higher than the line for towns under 30,000 and $7,074 over for rural residents.

For a one-earner couple with two children, after-tax minimum wage income amounted to $22,319[59] – $7,597 below the after-tax poverty line for Vancouver, $2,881 under the poverty line for Victoria, $2,491 beneath the line for centres between 30,000 and 99,999 and $354 below for towns smaller than 30,000, though $2,704 above the after-tax poverty line for rural residents. For a two-earner couple with two children in which one parent works full time, year round at the minimum wage and the other parent earns half this amount, after-tax minimum wage income amounted to $26,945[60] – $2,971 below the after-tax poverty line for Vancouver but $1,745 above the poverty line for Victoria, $2,135 over

**Figure K6
British Columbia minimum wage as %
of before-tax poverty line for largest city, 1965-2002**

— single person ─■─ single parent, 1 child

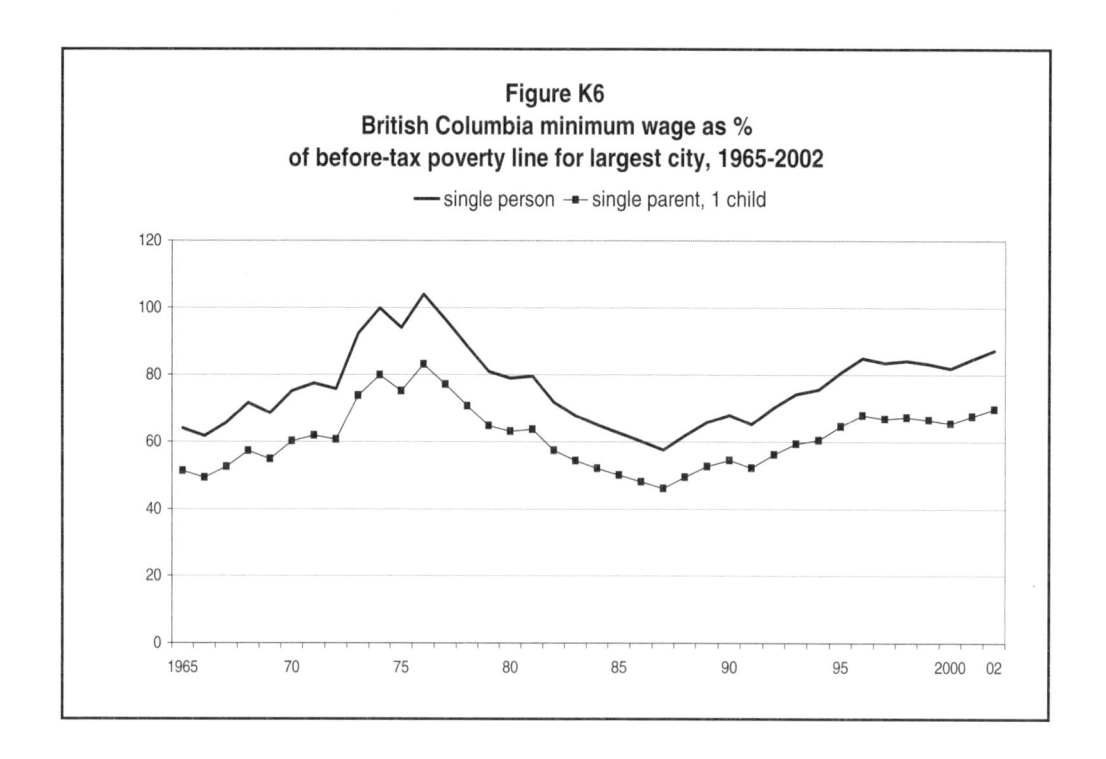

the line for centres between 30,000 and 99,999, $4,272 above the line for towns smaller than 30,000 and $7,330 above the after-tax poverty line for rural residents. In the case of a two-earner family in which both parents work full time, year round at the minimum wage, after-tax minimum wage income came to $30,902[61] – $986 above the after-tax poverty line for Vancouver, $5,702 above the poverty line for Victoria, $6,092 over the line for centres between 30,000 and 99,999, $8,229 above the line for towns smaller than 30,000 and $11,287 above the after-tax poverty line for rural residents.

Income was $31,872 in minimum wages supplemented by $2,190 from the Canada Child Tax Benefit and $310 from the federal GST credit. Federal income tax was $2,442 and provincial income tax amounted to $1,028. CPP contributions were $1,069 and EI premiums came to $717.

Contribution of child benefits

Child benefits supplement the incomes of the large majority of Canadian families and are especially important to low- and modest-income families. Increases to the federal Canada Child Tax Benefit, along with the province's creation of two child benefit programs – the BC Family Bonus and BC Earned Income Benefit – are boosting the incomes of minimum wage and other working poor families.

Figure K7
Dollars below/above after-tax poverty line for different size communities, British Columbia after-tax minimum wage income, 2001

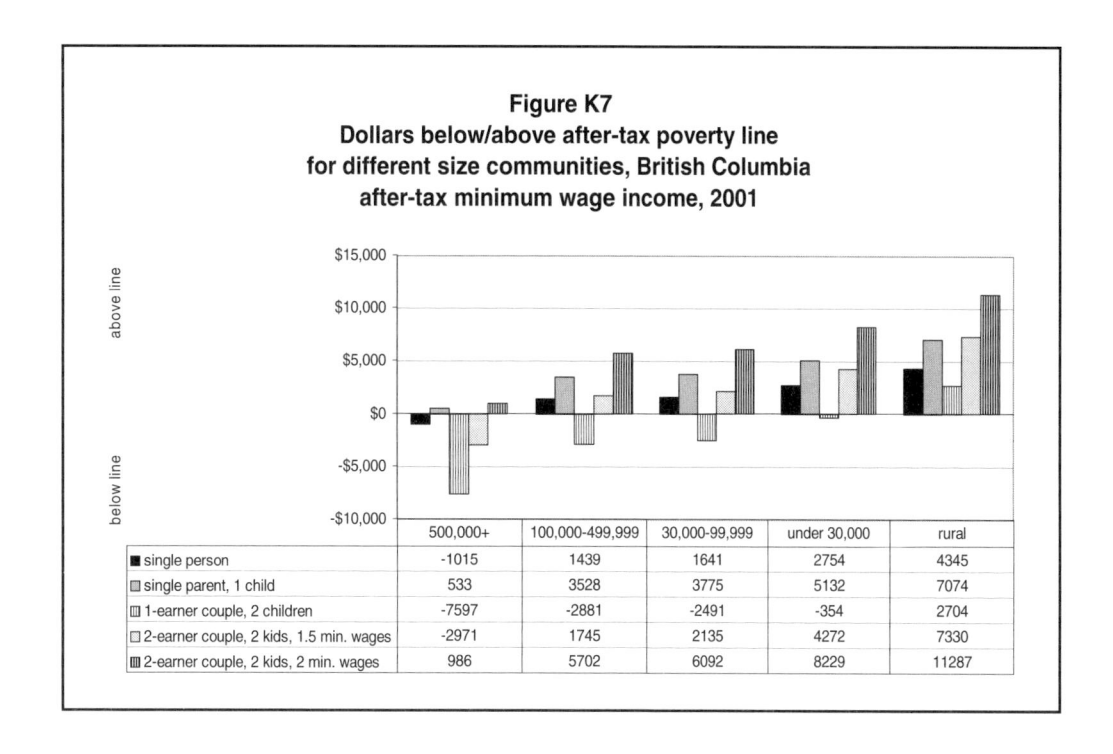

	500,000+	100,000-499,999	30,000-99,999	under 30,000	rural
single person	-1015	1439	1641	2754	4345
single parent, 1 child	533	3528	3775	5132	7074
1-earner couple, 2 children	-7597	-2881	-2491	-354	2704
2-earner couple, 2 kids, 1.5 min. wages	-2971	1745	2135	4272	7330
2-earner couple, 2 kids, 2 min. wages	986	5702	6092	8229	11287

The single-parent minimum wage worker with one child got $2,447 from the Canada Child Tax Benefit and $819 in BC child-related benefits ($214 from the BC Family Bonus and $605 from the BC Earned Income Benefit) – for a combined total of $3,266 or 17.5 percent of disposable income. The one-earner couple with two children received $4,250 from the Canada Child Tax Benefit and $1,633 from provincial child benefits ($623 from the BC Family Bonus and $1,010 from the BC Earned Income Benefit) for a combined federal-provincial child benefit of $5,883, worth 27.5 percent of disposable income.

The two-earner family in which one parent works full time, all year at the minimum wage and the other parent half that time received $3,740 from the Canada Child Tax Benefit and $407 from the BC Earned Income Benefit for a total child benefit payment of $4,147 or 16.1 percent of disposable income. The two-earner family in which both parents work full time, all year at the minimum wage received $2,190 from the Canada Child Tax Benefit, which came to 7.5 percent of disposable income.

Minimum wage versus welfare (Figure K8)

For a single person earning the minimum wage in British Columbia, disposable income – i.e., minimum wage earnings plus federal and provincial refundable tax credits minus income and payroll taxes –

amounted to $13,655 in 2001, which is a sizeable $7,198 more than the $6,457 from welfare and refundable tax credits. Figure K8 shows the comparison.

Minimum wages also pay better than welfare for a single parent with one child age 2, though the advantage is not as great as for single people. Disposable income from after-tax minimum wage earnings, child benefits and refundable tax credits amounted to $18,631 in 2001, or $4,562 more than the $14,069 from welfare, child benefits and refundable tax credits.

A one-earner couple earning the minimum wage and supporting two children aged 10 and 15 is also better off working at the minimum wage, though the advantage over welfare is smaller than for single workers and single parents with one child. Total disposable income from minimum wages, child benefits and tax credits came to $21,425 or $3,013 more than the $18,412 income from welfare, child benefits and refundable tax credits.

Naturally, the minimum wage advantage is greater in the case of two-earner families. We look at two examples.

In the first case, one parent works full time, year round at the minimum wage while the other earns half this amount (i.e., works part-time and/or part-year); as above, there are two children aged 10 and 15.

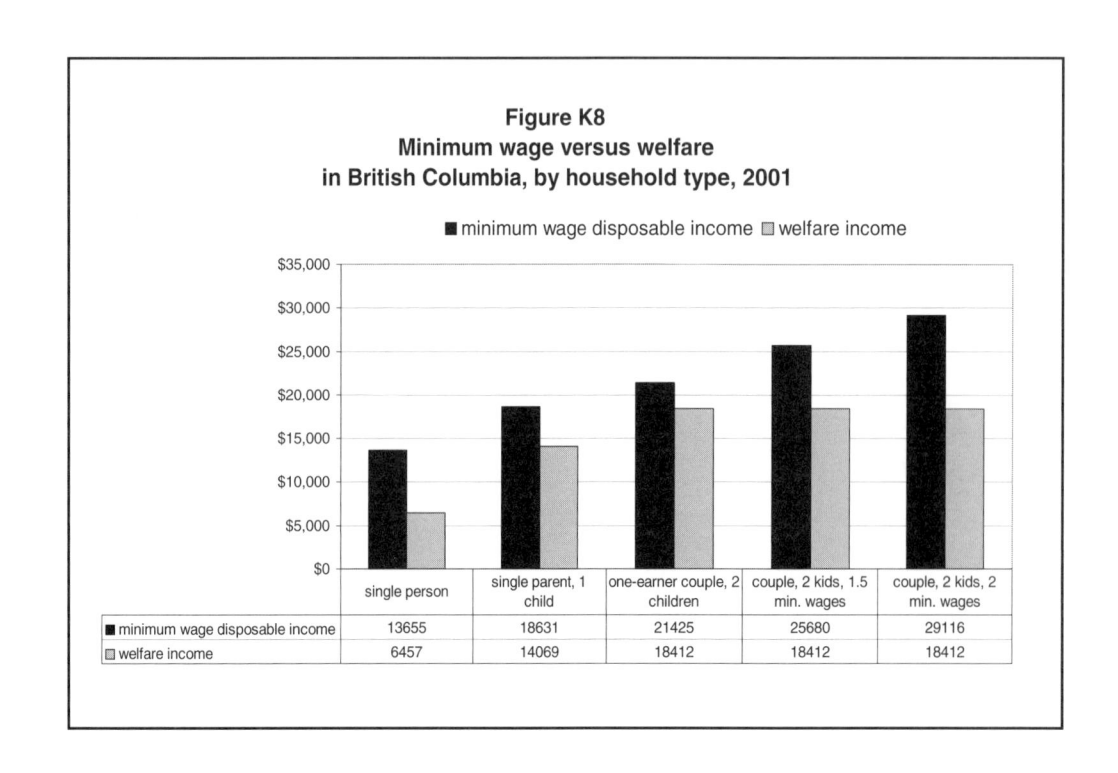

Figure K8
Minimum wage versus welfare in British Columbia, by household type, 2001

	single person	single parent, 1 child	one-earner couple, 2 children	couple, 2 kids, 1.5 min. wages	couple, 2 kids, 2 min. wages
minimum wage disposable income	13655	18631	21425	25680	29116
welfare income	6457	14069	18412	18412	18412

This family's disposable income from one-and-a-half minimum wages came to $25,680 in 2001 or $7,268 more than the $18,412 from welfare, child benefits and the refundable GST credit.

The other two-earner family earns double the minimum wage since we assume that both parents work full time, year round at the minimum wage. Total disposable income was $29,116 or $10,704 more than the $18,412 from welfare and other government income programs.

b. Minimum Wage Workers in British Columbia

The following text with illustrative graphs analyzes key characteristics of minimum wage workers in British Columbia. Appendix 2 provides detailed statistics in tabular form (pages 309-311).

Interprovincial rank: incidence of minimum wage workers (Figure K9)

In 2000, an estimated 72,600 workers in British Columbia – 4.6 percent of the total 1,583,000 employees – worked for the minimum wage. British Columbia's 4.6 figure ranks it fourth-lowest in Canada, after Ontario (4.5 percent), Prince Edward Island (3.6 percent) and Alberta (2.0 percent).

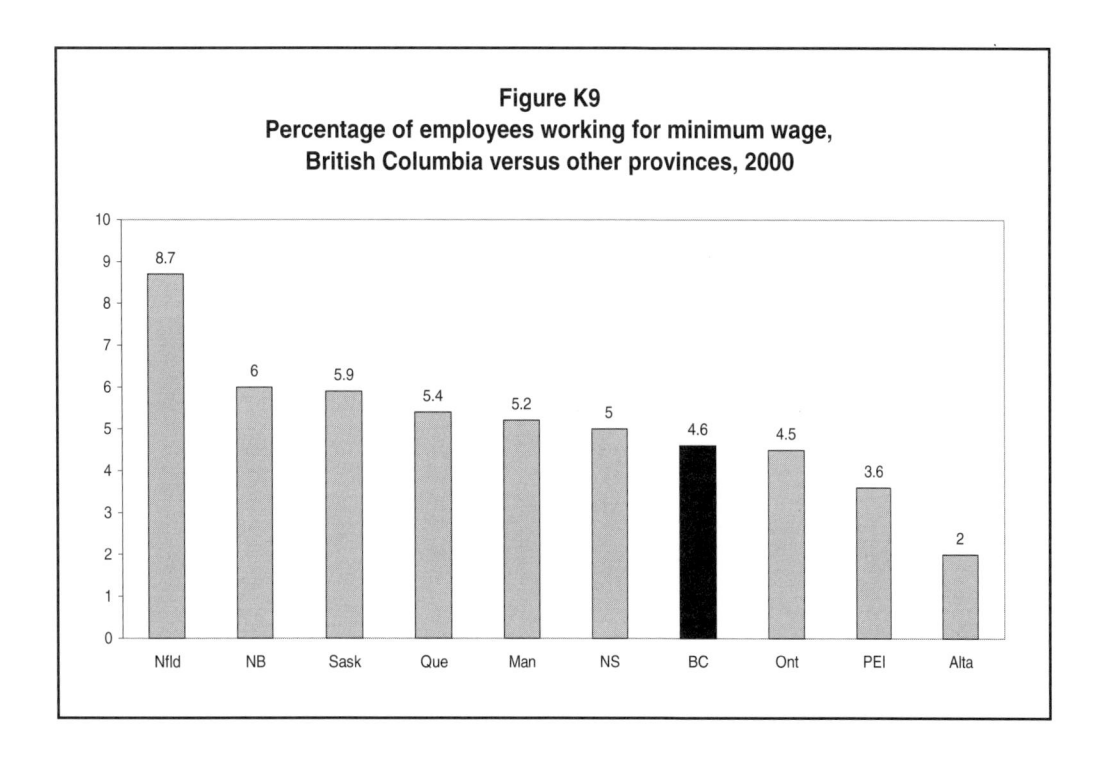

**Figure K9
Percentage of employees working for minimum wage, British Columbia versus other provinces, 2000**

Province	Percentage
Nfld	8.7
NB	6
Sask	5.9
Que	5.4
Man	5.2
NS	5
BC	4.6
Ont	4.5
PEI	3.6
Alta	2

Figure K9 shows the rankings. British Columbia's 4.6 percent incidence of minimum wage workers is identical to the national average.

British Columbia is the only province with virtually the same share of Canada's minimum wage workforce and all employees. British Columbia accounts for 12.5 percent of all minimum wage workers in the country and 12.7 percent of all employees, producing an index of 0.99, which indicates only a tiny underrepresentation of minimum wage workers (the lower the result below 1.00, the more underrepresented are minimum wage workers).

Gender and age (Figures K10-K13)

In British Columbia as in the rest of Canada, women run a higher risk of working for minimum wage than men, and women also make up the majority of the minimum wage workforce.

In 2000, 5.9 percent of British Columbia's female employees worked for minimum wage compared to 3.3 percent of male workers. Of the total 72,600 minimum wage workers, 45,700 – 62.9 percent – were women and 26,900 – 37.1 percent – were men, as illustrated in Figure K10.

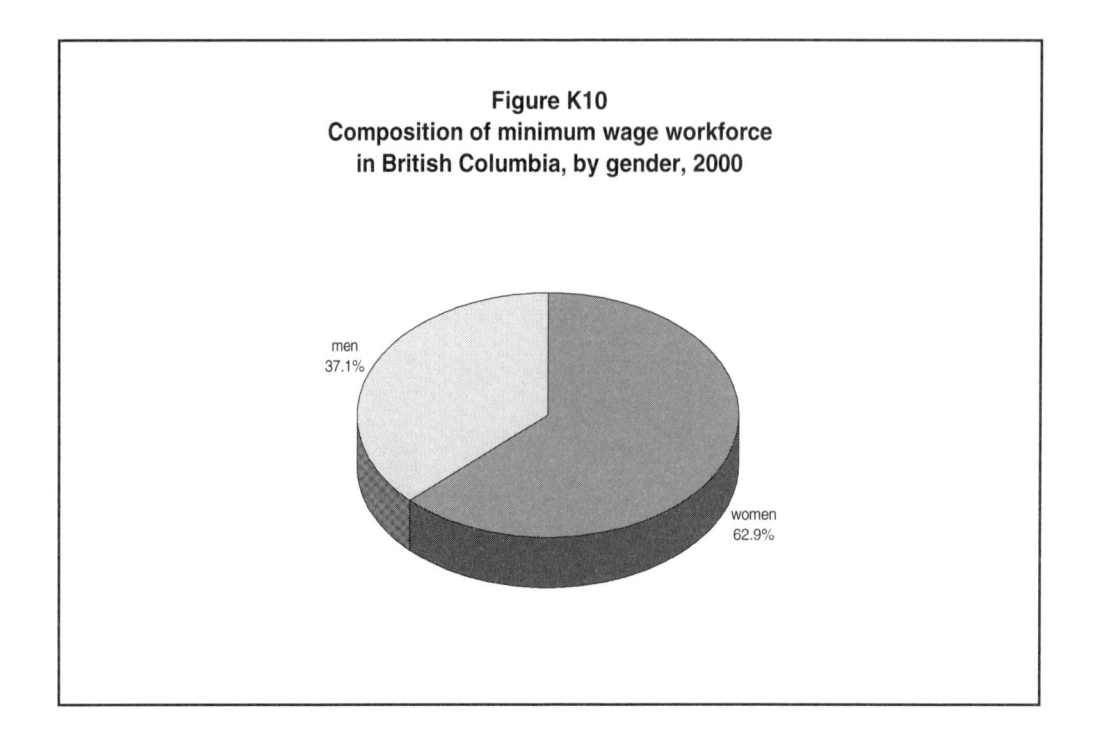

**Figure K10
Composition of minimum wage workforce
in British Columbia, by gender, 2000**

men 37.1%

women 62.9%

Figure K11
Percentage of employees working for minimum wage in British Columbia, by gender and age, 2000

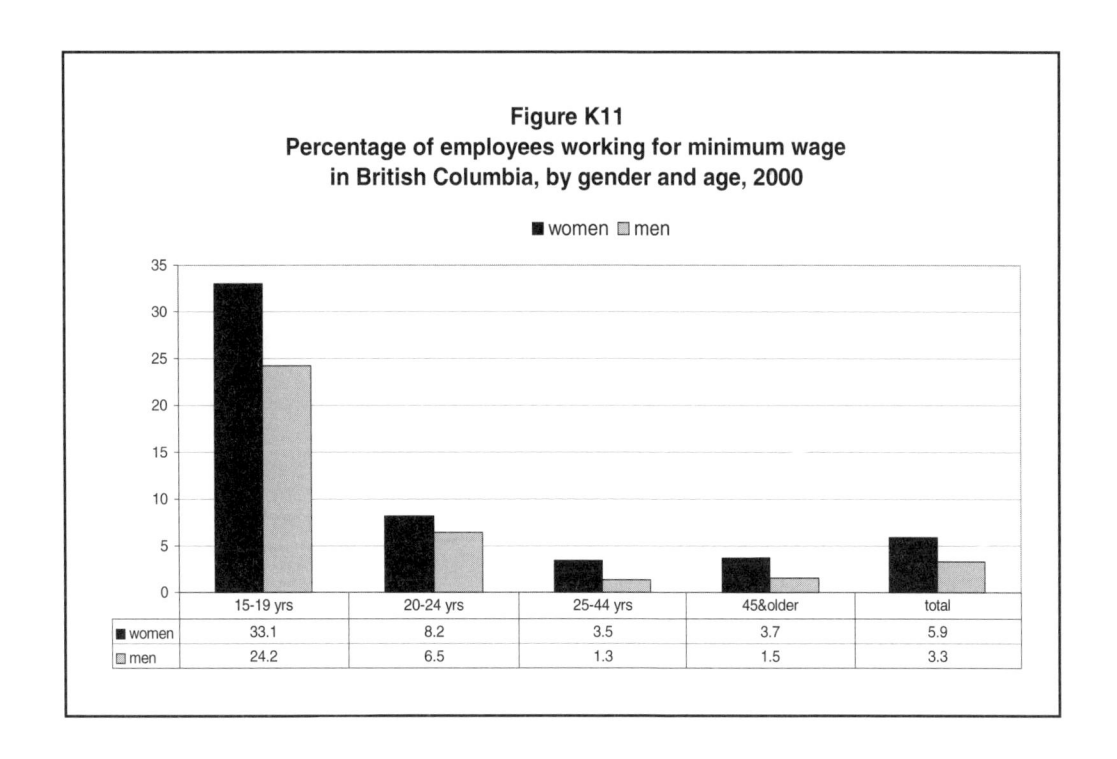

	15-19 yrs	20-24 yrs	25-44 yrs	45&older	total
women	33.1	8.2	3.5	3.7	5.9
men	24.2	6.5	1.3	1.5	3.3

Figure K12
Share of minimum wage workers versus share of all employees in British Columbia, by age group, 2000

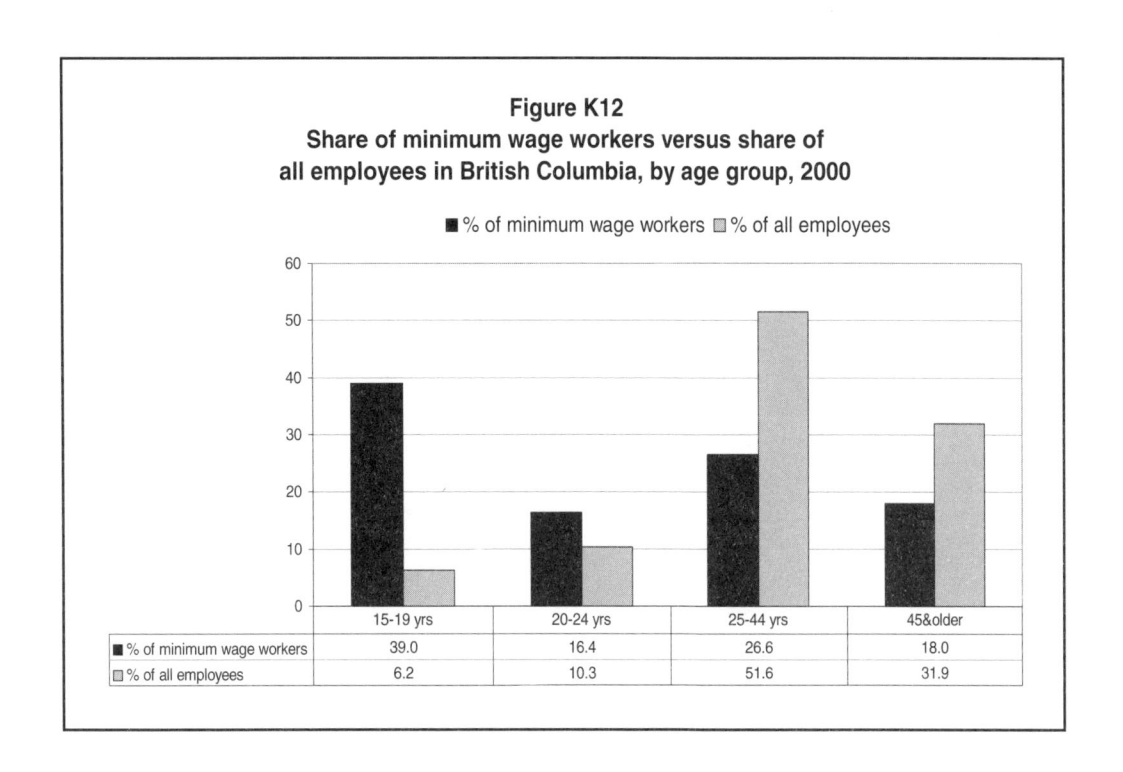

	15-19 yrs	20-24 yrs	25-44 yrs	45&older
% of minimum wage workers	39.0	16.4	26.6	18.0
% of all employees	6.2	10.3	51.6	31.9

Women are overrepresented in British Columbia's minimum wage workforce. They constituted 62.9 percent of minimum wage workers but only 48.6 percent of all the province's employees in 2000. Men are underrepresented, accounting for only 37.1 percent of minimum wage workers but 51.4 percent of all employees.

The gender bias among minimum wage workers holds when we control for major age categories. While younger workers of both sexes run a higher risk of working for minimum wage, women still fare worse than men in every age category. Figure K11 illustrates the results.

Among female workers aged 15 to 19, 33.1 percent worked for the minimum wage in 2000 as opposed to 24.2 percent of male workers in the same age group. Among those 20-24, 8.2 percent of women compared to 6.5 percent of men worked for the minimum wage. Among workers 25-44, 3.5 percent of women as opposed to 1.3 percent of men were at the bottom of the wage ladder. Among employees 45 and older, 3.7 percent of women and 1.5 percent of men worked for the minimum wage in British Columbia.

Young people not only are more likely to work for minimum wage than other employees, but the young also make up a large proportion of the minimum wage workforce. Figure K12 compares the age makeup of minimum wage workers and all employees in British Columbia. Four in ten (39.0 percent) of minimum wage workers are in the 15-19 age group, as opposed to just 6.2 percent of all employees.

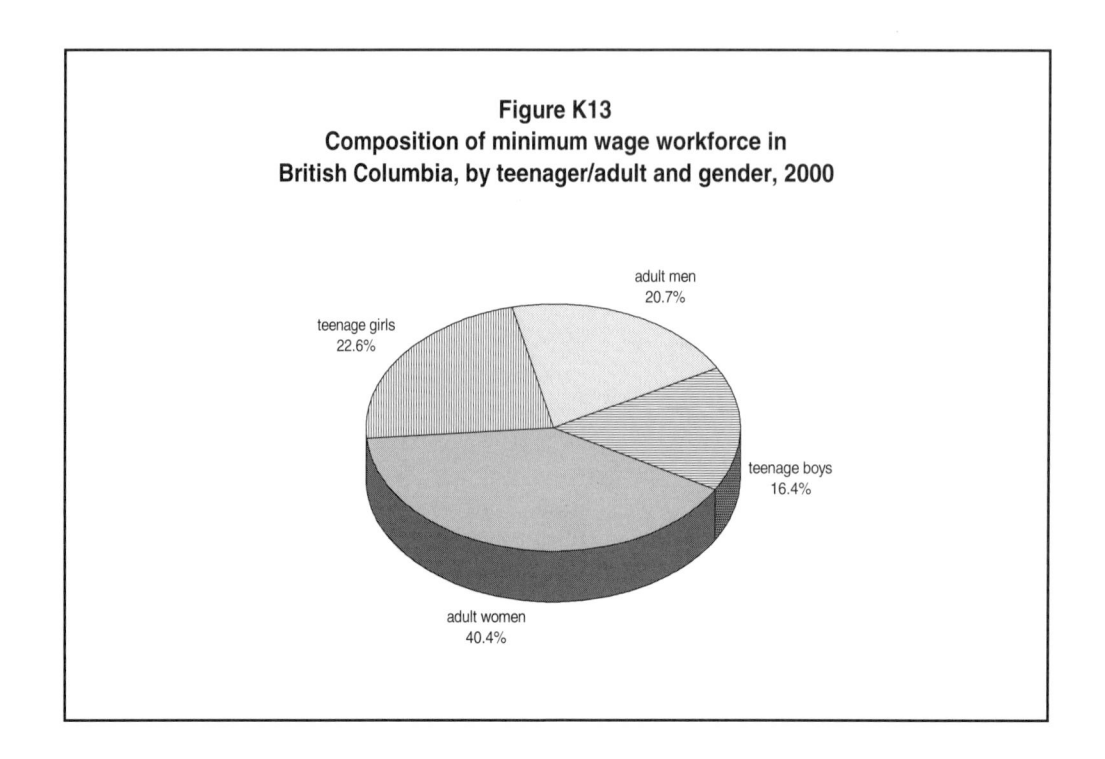

Figure K13
Composition of minimum wage workforce in British Columbia, by teenager/adult and gender, 2000

- adult men 20.7%
- teenage boys 16.4%
- adult women 40.4%
- teenage girls 22.6%

Employees aged 20-24 represent 16.4 percent of minimum wage workers as opposed to 10.3 percent of all workers. All told, more than half (55.4 percent) of minimum wage workers in British Columbia are under 25 years of age.

The opposite holds for older workers. While a sizeable proportion – 26.6 percent – of minimum wage workers in British Columbia are between 25 and 44, that age group constitutes a much larger proportion – 51.6 percent – of all employees. Workers aged 45 and older make up 18.0 percent of minimum wage employees but 31.9 percent all employees.

Figure K13 divides the minimum wage workforce in British Columbia into teenage girls and boys and adult women and men. Adult women are the largest group, at 29,300 or 40.4 percent of the total, followed by teenage girls (16,400 or 22.6 percent), adult men (15,000 or 20.7 percent) and teenage boys (11,900 or 16.4 percent). The majority (61.1 percent) of British Columbia's minimum wage workers are adults, which is the case in most provinces (the national average is 52.9 percent).

Education (Figures K14 and K15)

Figure K14 shows the incidence of minimum wage workers in British Columbia according to level of education.

At first glance, the relationship between level of education and incidence of minimum wage employment does not seem to correspond to common sense: Workers in the lowest educational group (elementary education only) are only slightly more likely to work for minimum wage (14.5 percent do) than those with some high school (13.4 percent), while those with some postsecondary education run a higher risk (6.0 percent) than high school graduates (4.5 percent). However, as one would expect, the chances of working for minimum wage are lowest for the two highest education categories – 2.1 percent for those with a postsecondary certificate or diploma (e.g., from community college) and only 1.9 percent for those with a university degree.

Once we look at the education-minimum wage link for different age groups, the reasons for the apparently inconsistent relationship comes clear: Young people working at part-time or seasonal (i.e., summer) jobs – typically paying the minimum or a low wage – figure prominently in the 'some high school' and 'some postsecondary education' categories; they are still at high school, community college or university, whereas workers in the other educational categories have completed their education.

Figure K15 shows each educational group's share of British Columbia's minimum wage workforce in 2000. The largest group of minimum wage workers are those with some high school (33.5 percent), followed by high school graduates (23.7 percent), those with some postsecondary education (16.3 percent), postsecondary graduates (14.2 percent), university graduates (7.9 percent) and workers with 0-8 years of education (4.7 percent). Many minimum wage workers are students (high school or

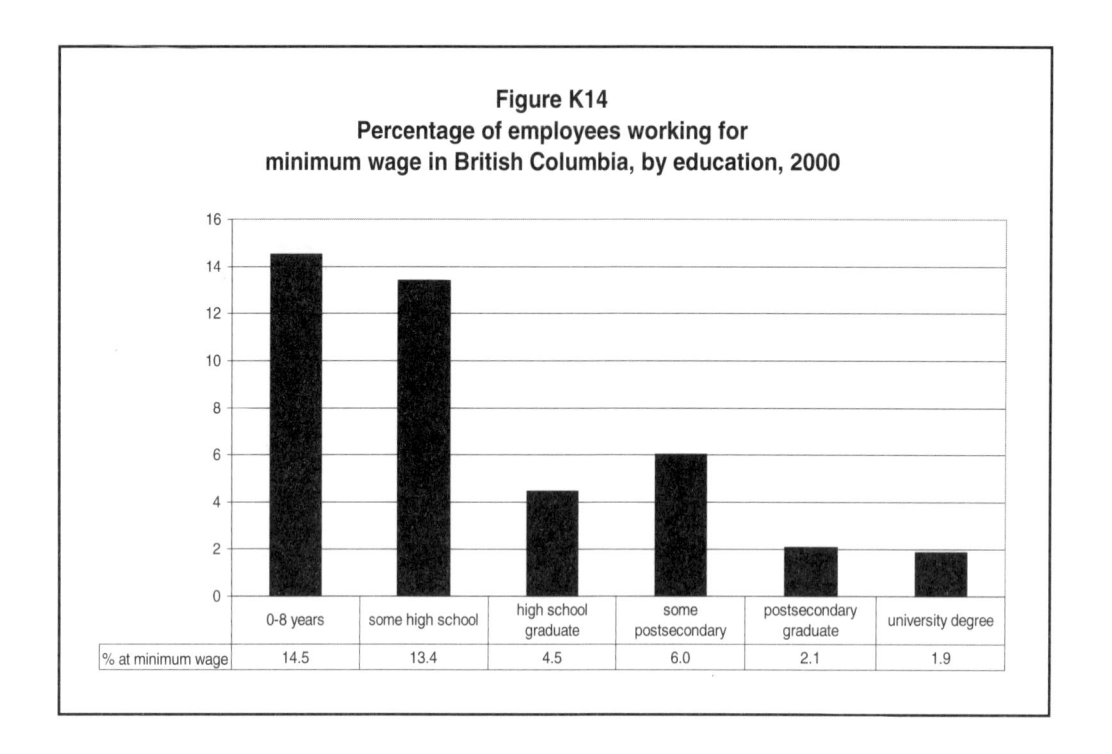

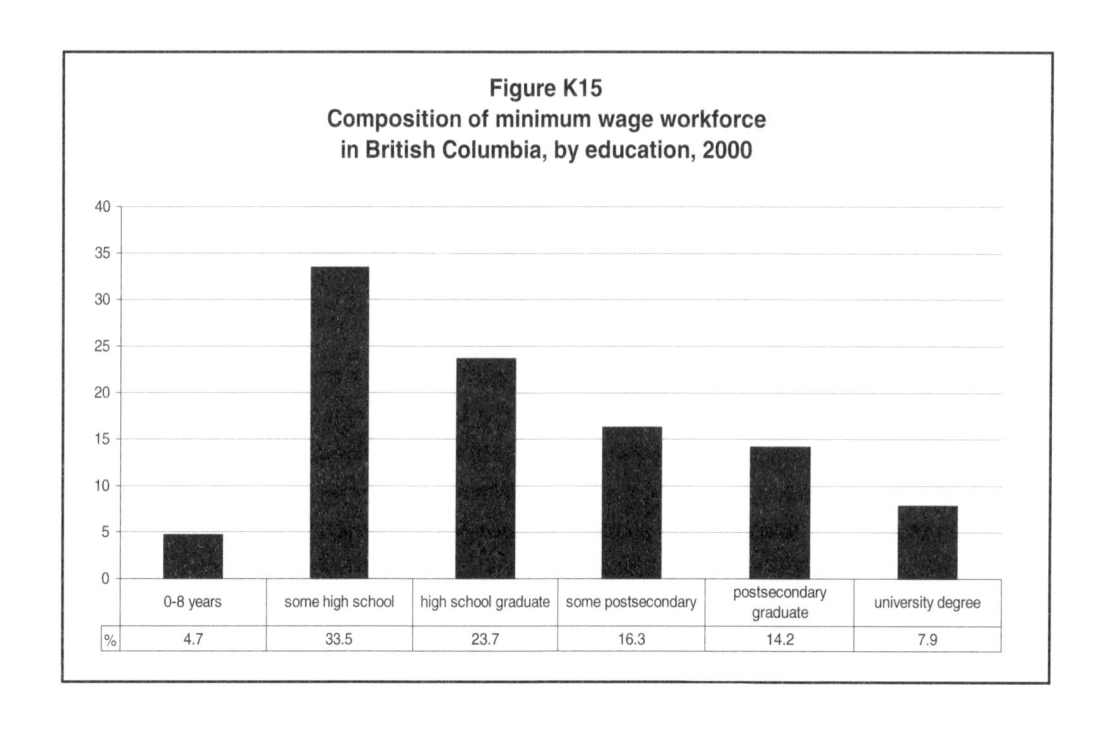

Figure K14
Percentage of employees working for minimum wage in British Columbia, by education, 2000

	0-8 years	some high school	high school graduate	some postsecondary	postsecondary graduate	university degree
% at minimum wage	14.5	13.4	4.5	6.0	2.1	1.9

Figure K15
Composition of minimum wage workforce in British Columbia, by education, 2000

	0-8 years	some high school	high school graduate	some postsecondary	postsecondary graduate	university degree
%	4.7	33.5	23.7	16.3	14.2	7.9

postsecondary) pursuing their education. A significant group of minimum wage workers (33.2 percent) have some form of postsecondary education.

Full-time and part-time work (Figures K16 and K17)

The fact that young people are more likely to work part time helps explain why workers still pursuing their education tend to face a higher risk of minimum wage work than those who have completed their schooling and are working full time. Figure K16 indicates that 12.2 percent of part-time workers are at the minimum wage compared to only 2.7 percent of those employed full time.

While the majority of minimum wage workers in British Columbia (52.9 percent) work part time, a sizeable group (47.1 percent) are employed full time. Figure K17 illustrates the figures.

Gender alters the relationship between full-time and part-time work and the minimum wage. Women who work part time in British Columbia run a lesser risk of being at the bottom of the wage ladder than do men who work part time (10.5 and 16.7 percent, respectively). However, women employed full time are more likely than men in that group to earn the minimum wage (4.0 and 1.7 percent, respectively).

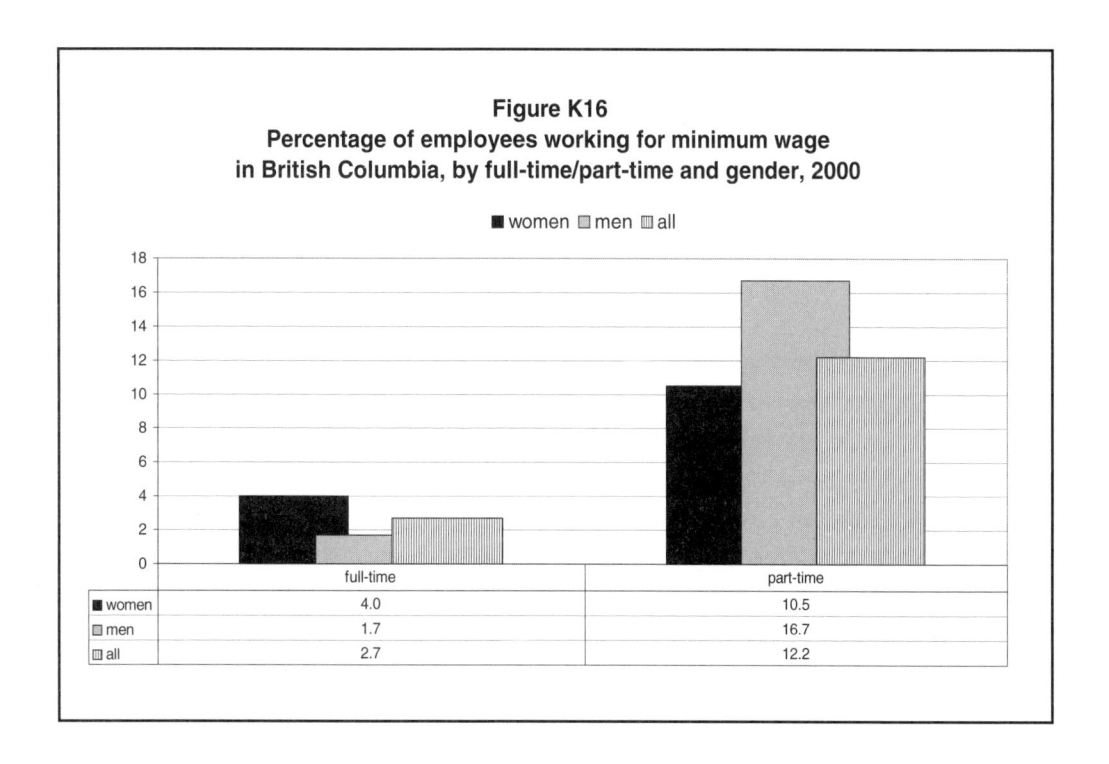

Figure K16
Percentage of employees working for minimum wage in British Columbia, by full-time/part-time and gender, 2000

	full-time	part-time
women	4.0	10.5
men	1.7	16.7
all	2.7	12.2

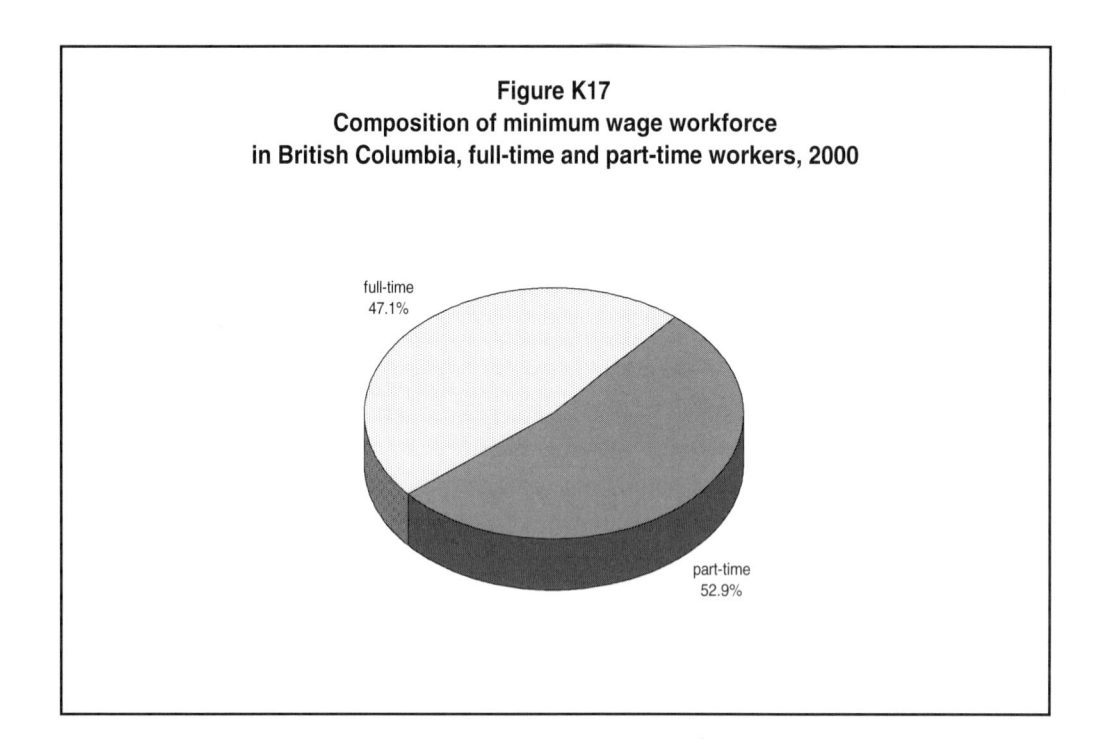

**Figure K17
Composition of minimum wage workforce
in British Columbia, full-time and part-time workers, 2000**

full-time 47.1%
part-time 52.9%

Women make up the majority of minimum wage employees in the province working both full time (63.2 percent are women) and part time (62.8 percent are women). Among all employees, though, women constitute a minority of full-time workers (42.6 percent) but the bulk of part-time workers (72.8 percent).

Family status (Figure K18)

We noted above that over half of British Columbia's minimum wage workers are under 25 years of age. Light on this fundamental fact of the minimum wage workforce is shed by information on family status, depicted in Figure K18, which shows that the largest group of minimum wage workers – an estimated 40,400 or 55.7 percent of the total 72,600 – are older children living with their parents (or relatives with relatives, as in the case of a niece or nephew living with an aunt and uncle, or grandchildren with grandparents). Of this category, 18,400 or 66.3 percent are aged 15-19, 7,900 or 19.5 percent are 20-24 and the remaining 5,800 or 14.2 percent are 25 or older. A bit more than half (21,000 or 52.0 percent) are still in school and working part-time or part-year (e.g., in summer).

**Figure K18
Composition of minimum wage workforce
in British Columbia, by family status, 2000**

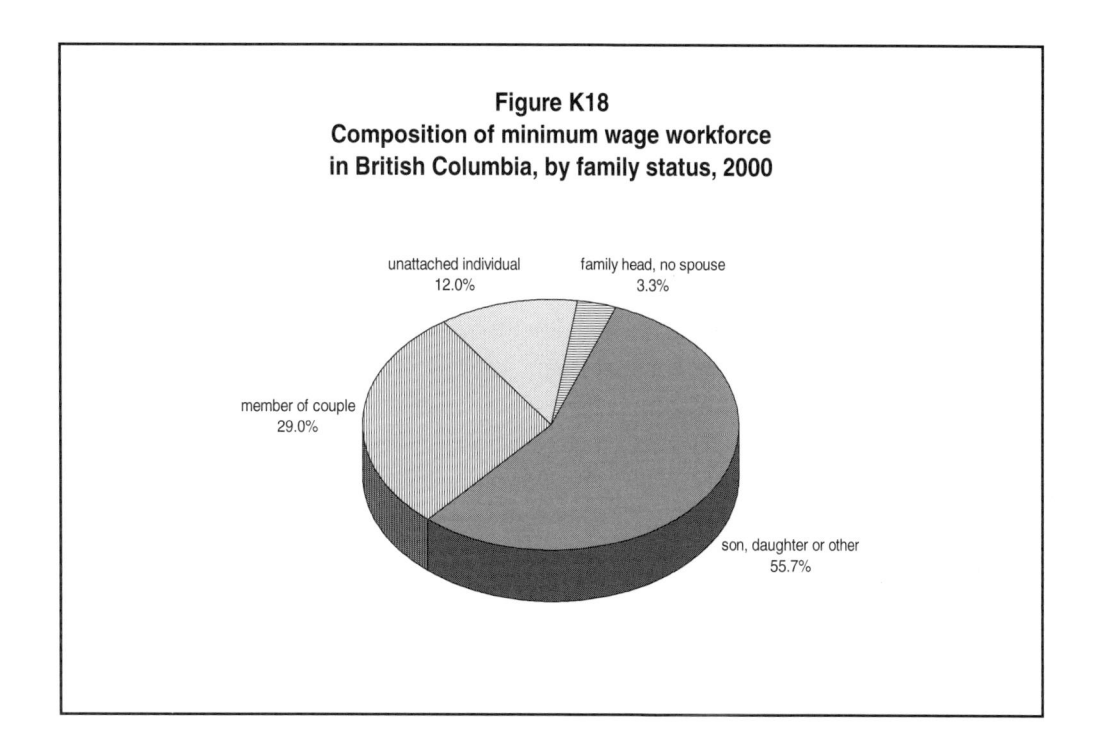

- unattached individual: 12.0%
- family head, no spouse: 3.3%
- member of couple: 29.0%
- son, daughter or other: 55.7%

The next largest group of minimum wage workers in British Columbia – an estimated 21,000 or 29.0 percent of the total – are members of couples (married or living together). In most cases (15,200 or 72.4 percent of the category total of 21,000), the minimum wage worker's spouse is employed, in most cases earning more than the minimum wage. A typical example in this category would be mothers combining (unpaid) childrearing work with part-time minimum wage work. Another 5,800 or 27.6 percent of minimum wage workers living in couples have a spouse who is not employed (most of the latter are not in the labour force).

An estimated 8,700 or 12.0 percent of minimum wage workers in British Columbia are unattached individuals. An estimated 3,900 or 44.8 percent live alone; of this group, 1,000 are 15-24, 2,400 are aged 25-54 and 600 are 55 or older. The remaining 4,800 of the province's unattached minimum wage workers live with friends or roommates; in this category, 2,000 are under 24, 2,600 are 25-44 and 200 are 55 or older.

Finally, some 2,400 or 3.3 percent of British Columbia's minimum wage workers are family heads with no spouse present, mostly (2,300) single parents with children under 18.

Industry

National data show that the incidence and distribution of minimum wage workers varies significantly according to industries. The same applies to British Columbia, though sample size constraints preclude estimates for six of the 16 industrial categories (forestry, fishing, mining, oil and gas; utilities; construction; professional, scientific and technical services; educational services; and public administration). Among the ten industrial categories for which estimates are available, agriculture tops the list (17.9 percent of employees work for minimum wage), followed by accommodation and food services (15.0 percent), other services (8.6 percent), trade (7.2 percent), management, administrative and other support (7.0 percent), information, culture and recreation (5.7 percent), finance, insurance, real estate and leasing (2.7 percent), transportation and warehousing (2.4 percent), manufacturing (2.3 percent) and health care and social assistance (1.5 percent).

Estimates are available for the industrial composition of the whole employed workforce in British Columbia. Trade tops the list, with an estimated 258,100 or 16.3 percent of all employees. Next comes manufacturing (189,700 or 12.0 percent), followed by health care and social assistance (170,100 or 10.7 percent of all employees), accommodation and food services (144,400 or 9.1 percent), educational services (125,400 or 7.9 percent), finance, insurance, real estate and leasing (98,200 or 6.2 percent), transportation and warehousing (95,900 or 6.1 percent), public administration (89,700 or 5.7 percent), information, culture and recreation (82,100 or 5.2 percent), professional, scientific and technical services (81,900 or 5.2 percent), construction (67,900 or 4.3 percent), other services (62,900 or 4.0 percent), management, administrative and other support (45,800 or 2.9 percent), forestry, fishing, mining, gas and oil (44,100 or 2.8 percent), agriculture (15,600 or 1.0 percent) and utilities (11,300 or 0.7 percent).

YUKON

Because Statistics Canada's low income cut-offs do not apply to Yukon (or the Northwest Territories and Nunavut), we cannot provide comparisons between its minimum wage and the before-tax or after-tax poverty lines. Nor are data available on minimum wage workers in Yukon and the other two territories.

Interprovincial rank: dollar value of minimum wages (Figure L1)

Yukon's minimum wage last increased from $7.06 to $7.20 on October 1, 1998. In 2001, Yukon's $7.20 minimum wage ranked the territory second-highest among Canada's ten provinces and three territories, with British Columbia the highest ($8.00) and Newfoundland ($5.71 hourly average) the lowest. Figure L1 pictures the results.

Figure L1
Yukon minimum wage compared to other provinces and territories, 2002

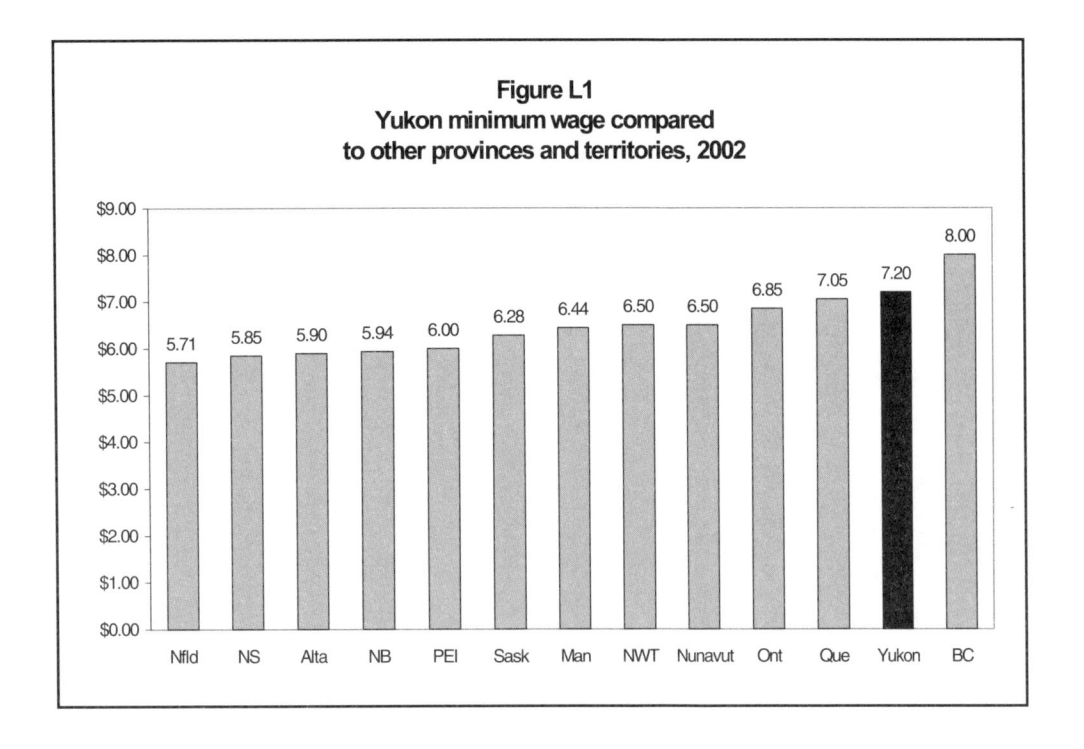

Province/Territory	Minimum Wage
Nfld	5.71
NS	5.85
Alta	5.90
NB	5.94
PEI	6.00
Sask	6.28
Man	6.44
NWT	6.50
Nunavut	6.50
Ont	6.85
Que	7.05
Yukon	7.20
BC	8.00

Trend in dollar value of minimum wage (Figure L2)

Because minimum wages are not indexed, their value changes over time. Figure L2 shows the trend in Yukon's minimum wage from 1968 to 2002; each year's average minimum wage has been converted to inflation-adjusted (i.e., constant) 2002 dollars to show the real trend, after taking into account the impact of inflation on the dollar.

Yukon's minimum wage shows an up-down-up-flat pattern over the long term. It rose significantly between 1968 and 1976, fell to below its 1968 rate by 1984, increased moderately in the latter half of the 1980s and then remained more or less level overall in the 1990s, though slipping a bit after 1999. The territory's minimum wage increased from $6.57 an hour in 1968 to $9.29 in 1976, fell to $5.88 in 1984, rose again to reach $7.69 in 1999 but slipped to $7.20 by 2002. Its value in 2002 was $2.09 or 22.5 percent less than the 1976 high point, though still 63 cents or 9.7 percent higher than in 1968.

Interprovincial rank: minimum wages as percentage of average earnings (Figure L3)

While Yukon scores second-highest of the 13 jurisdictions in terms of the dollar value of its minimum wage, it ranks fifth-lowest in terms of how its minimum wage compares to its average earnings. In

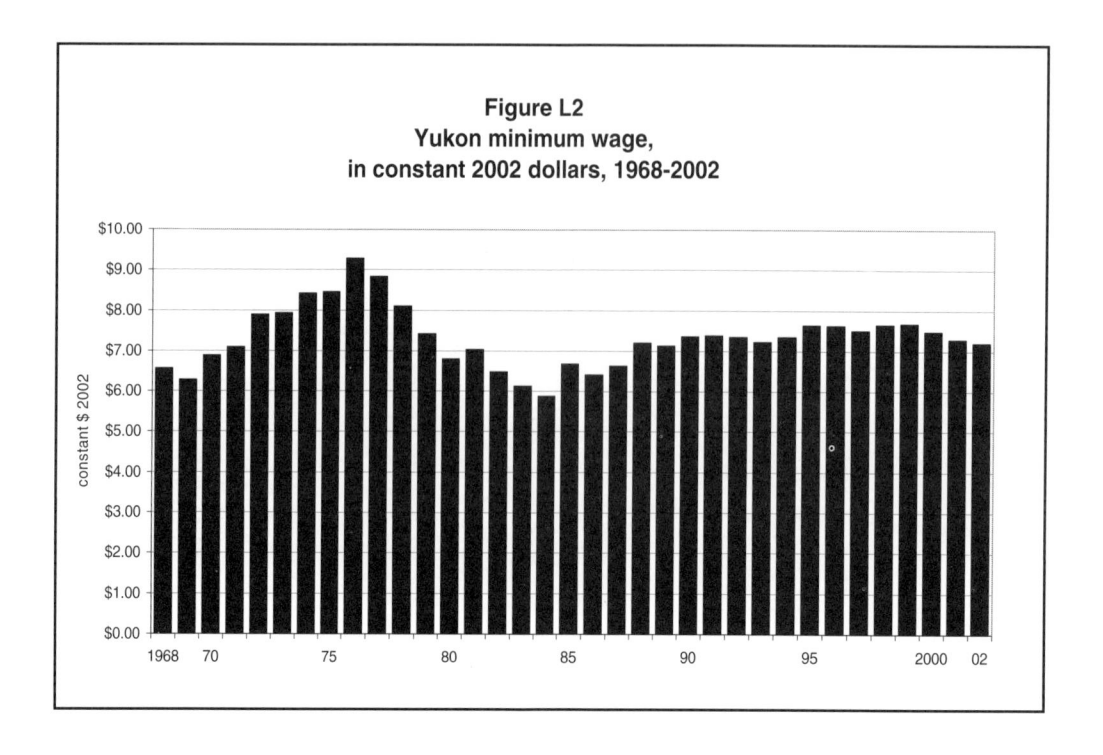

Figure L2
Yukon minimum wage, in constant 2002 dollars, 1968-2002

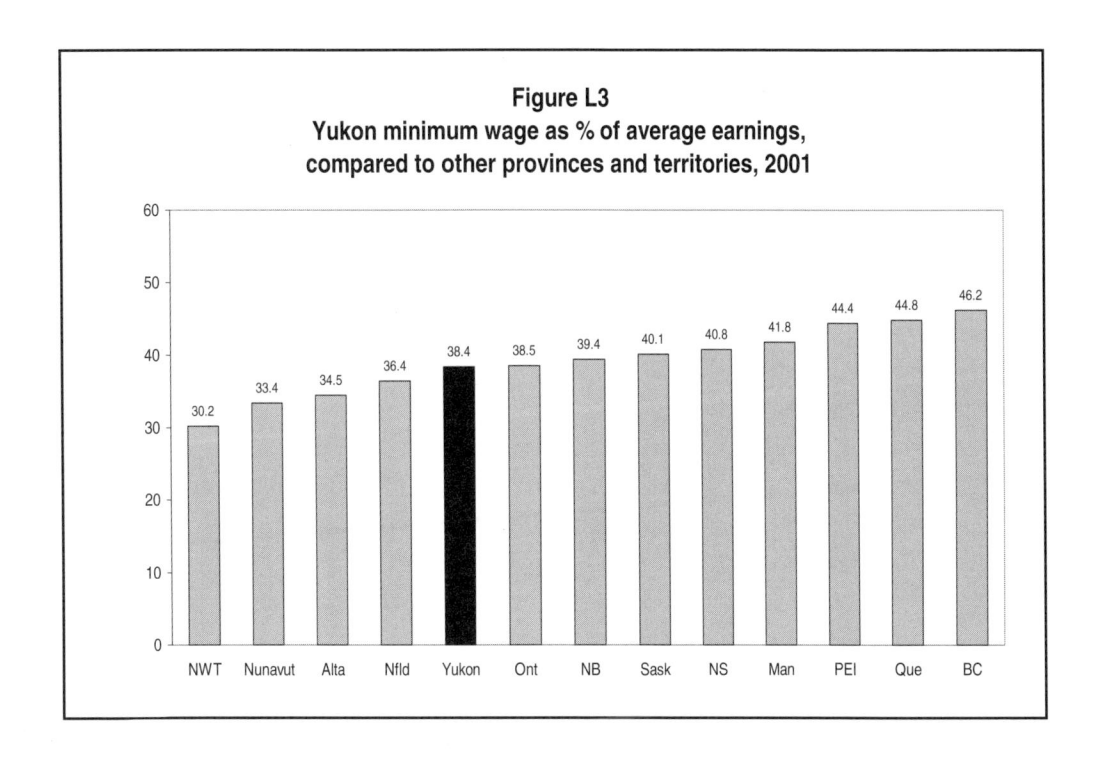

Figure L3
Yukon minimum wage as % of average earnings, compared to other provinces and territories, 2001

Province/Territory	%
NWT	30.2
Nunavut	33.4
Alta	34.5
Nfld	36.4
Yukon	38.4
Ont	38.5
NB	39.4
Sask	40.1
NS	40.8
Man	41.8
PEI	44.4
Que	44.8
BC	46.2

2001 (the most recent year for which data on average earnings are available), Yukon's $7.20 minimum wage represented 38.4 percent of its $18.74 hourly average earnings. The Northwest Territories were lowest at 30.2 percent and British Columbia highest at 46.2 percent. Figure L3 illustrates the results.

The difference between Yukon's second-highest rank in the dollar value of minimum wages and fifth-from-the-bottom score in terms of minimum wages as a percentage of average earnings is explained by the fact that Yukon has Canada's third-highest average earnings ($38,978 in 2001), with Nunavut in second place ($40,538) and the Northwest Territories tops at $44,803.

Trends in minimum wage and average earnings (Figure L4)

The black line in Figure L4 shows the trend in the minimum wage, the gray line the trend in average earnings and the vertical bars the trend in the minimum wage as a percentage of average earnings from 1983 (the earliest available estimate) through 2001. Read the left-hand axis for the minimum wage and average earnings and the right-hand axis for the minimum wage as a percentage of earnings.

**Figure L4
Yukon minimum wage
compared to average earnings, 1983-2001**

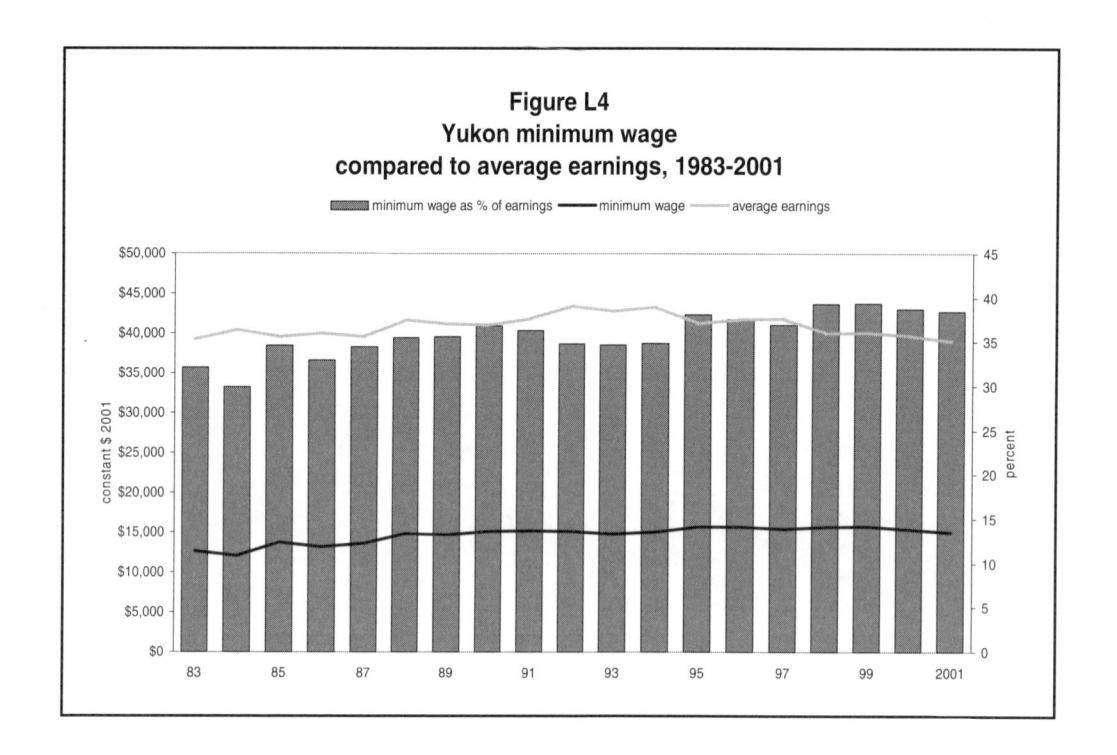

Yukon's minimum wage as a percentage of average earnings ranged from a low of 29.9 percent in 1984 to a high of 39.4 percent in 1999, slipping somewhat to 38.4 percent by 2001. During this period, average earnings in Yukon ranged from a low of $38,978 in 2001 to a high of $43,425 in 1992, while its minimum wage varied between $12,079 in 1984 and $15,780 in 1999.

Contribution of child benefits

Child benefits supplement the incomes of the large majority of Canadian families and are especially important to low- and modest-income families. Increases to the federal Canada Child Tax Benefit, along with Yukon's creation of its own Yukon Child Benefit, are boosting the incomes of minimum wage and other working poor families.

We looked at child benefits for four types of family – single parents supporting one child on the minimum wage, one-earner couples working for the minimum wage and with two children, two-earner couples supporting two children on one-and-a-half minimum wages, and two-earner couples with two children and two full minimum wages.

The single-parent minimum wage worker with one child got $2,447 from the Canada Child Tax Benefit and $300 from the Yukon Child Benefit – for a combined total of $2,747 or 15.9 percent of disposable income. The one-earner couple with two children received $4,250 from the Canada Child Tax Benefit and $600 from the Yukon Child Benefit for a combined federal-territorial child benefit of $4,850, worth 24.8 percent of disposable income.

The two-earner family in which one parent works full time, all year at the minimum wage and the other parent half that time got $4,045 from the Canada Child Tax Benefit and $312 from the Yukon Child Benefit for a total child benefit payment of $4,357 or 17.6 percent of disposable income. The two-earner family in which both parents work full time, all year at the minimum wage received $2,458 from the Canada Child Tax Benefit, which came to 8.8 percent of disposable income.

Minimum wage versus welfare (Figure L5)

For a single person earning the minimum wage in Yukon, disposable income – i.e., minimum wage earnings plus federal and territorial refundable tax credits minus income and payroll taxes – amounted to $13,189[62] in 2001, which is not much more (just $852) than the $12,337 from welfare and the refundable GST credit. Figure L5 shows the comparison.

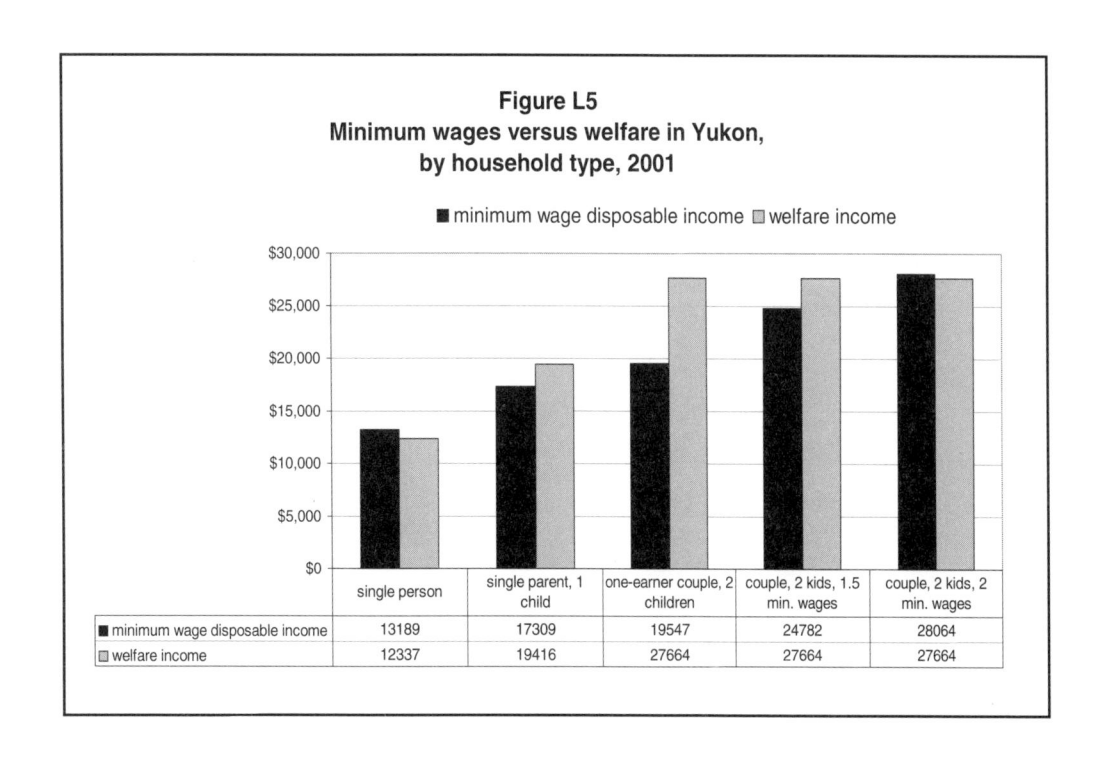

Figure L5
Minimum wages versus welfare in Yukon, by household type, 2001

	single person	single parent, 1 child	one-earner couple, 2 children	couple, 2 kids, 1.5 min. wages	couple, 2 kids, 2 min. wages
minimum wage disposable income	13189	17309	19547	24782	28064
welfare income	12337	19416	27664	27664	27664

The minimum wage pays less than welfare for a single parent with one child age 2. Disposable income from after-tax minimum wage earnings, child benefits and refundable tax credits amounted to $17,309[63] in 2001, or $2,107 less than the $19,416 from welfare, child benefits and the refundable GST credit.

A one-earner couple earning the minimum wage and supporting two children aged 10 and 15 is much worse off working at the minimum wage. Total disposable income from minimum wages, child benefits and tax credits came to $19,547[64] or a substantial $8,117 less than the $27,664 from welfare benefits, child benefits and the refundable GST credit.

Welfare also pays better than minimum wage work in the case of a family with two children in which one parent works full time, year round at the minimum wage while the other earns half this amount (i.e., works part-time and/or part-year). The family's disposable income from one-and-a-half minimum wages came to $24,782[65] in 2001 or $2,882 less than the $27,664 from welfare, child benefits and the refundable GST credit.

For a family with two children in which both parents work full time, year round at the minimum wage, disposable income was $28,064[66] in 2001 or $400 more than the $27,664 from welfare, child benefits and the refundable GST credit. But the minimum wage advantage for two-minimum wage families with two children in Yukon is small indeed.

NORTHWEST TERRITORIES

Because Statistics Canada's low income cut-offs do not apply to the Northwest Territories (or Nunavut and Yukon), we cannot provide comparisons between its minimum wage and the before-tax or after-tax poverty lines. Nor are data available on minimum wage workers in the Northwest Territories and the other two territories.

Interprovincial rank: dollar value of minimum wages (Figure M1)

The Northwest Territories minimum wage last increased from $5.00 to $6.50 on April 1, 1991 and has been frozen ever since. In 2002, as illustrated in Figure M1, the Northwest Territories $6.50 minimum wage ranked the territory fifth-highest (tied with Nunavut) among Canada's ten provinces and three territories – which ranged from a low of $5.71 (annual hourly average) in Newfoundland to a high of $8.00 in British Columbia.

Figure M1
Northwest Territories minimum wage compared to other provinces and territories, 2002

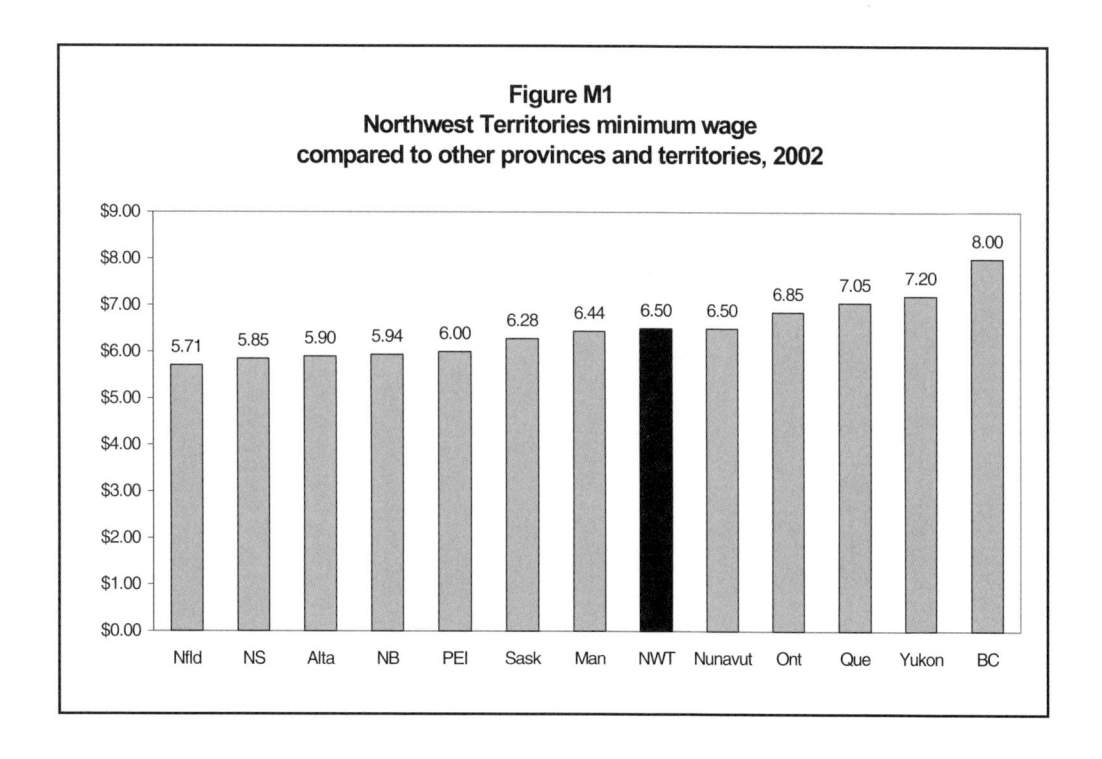

Province/Territory	Minimum Wage
Nfld	5.71
NS	5.85
Alta	5.90
NB	5.94
PEI	6.00
Sask	6.28
Man	6.44
NWT	6.50
Nunavut	6.50
Ont	6.85
Que	7.05
Yukon	7.20
BC	8.00

Trend in dollar value of minimum wage (Figure M2)

Because minimum wages are not indexed, their value changes over time. Figure M2 shows the trend in the Northwest Territories minimum wage from 1968 to 2002; each year's average minimum wage has been converted to inflation-adjusted (i.e., constant) 2002 dollars to show the real trend, after taking into account the impact of inflation on the dollar.

The Northwest Territories minimum wage rose substantially between 1968 ($6.57 an hour) and 1974 ($8.99), fell to $6.32 by 1990, recovered to $7.66 in 1992 but diminished steadily throughout the 1990s and into the new century, reaching $6.50 in 2002. The slide from 1992 through 2002 is due to the fact that the Northwest Territories minimum wage has not been adjusted since April 1991 and so has been eroded steadily by inflation. Its value in 2002 was a hefty $2.49 or 27.7 percent less than the 1974 high point.

Interprovincial rank: minimum wages as % of average earnings (Figure M3)

The Northwest Territories ranks dead last in terms of how its minimum wage compares to its average earnings. In 2001 (the most recent year for which data on average earnings are available), the Northwest Territories $6.50 minimum wage represented 30.2 percent of its $21.54 hourly average earnings, with

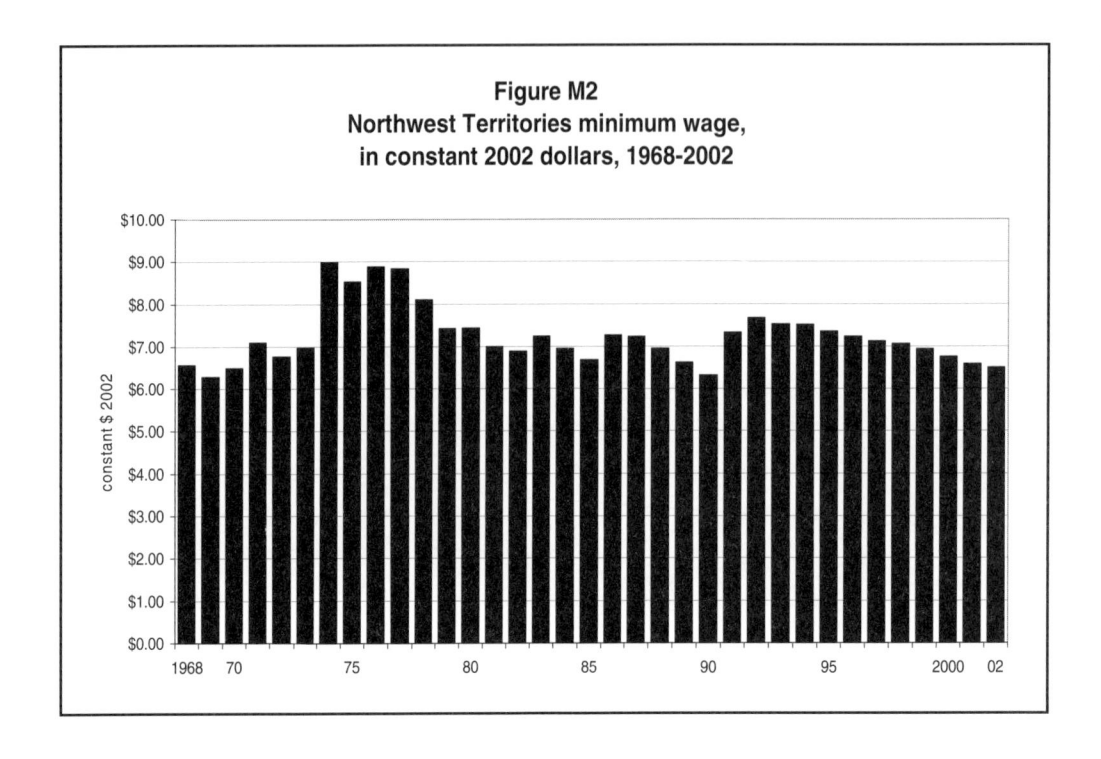

**Figure M2
Northwest Territories minimum wage,
in constant 2002 dollars, 1968-2002**

Minimum Wages in Canada: A Statistical Portrait With Policy Implications

Figure M3
Northwest Territories minimum wage as % of average earnings, compared to other provinces and territories, 2001

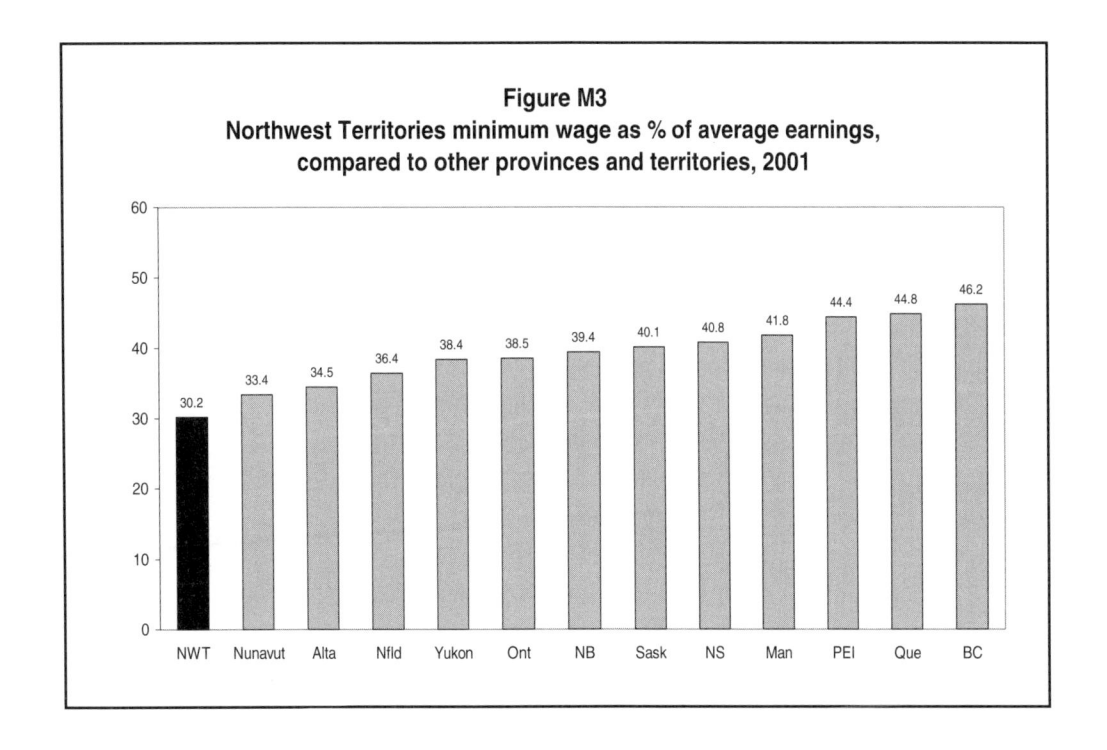

Region	%
NWT	30.2
Nunavut	33.4
Alta	34.5
Nfld	36.4
Yukon	38.4
Ont	38.5
NB	39.4
Sask	40.1
NS	40.8
Man	41.8
PEI	44.4
Que	44.8
BC	46.2

British Columbia ranking tops at 46.2 percent. The Northwest Territories last-place rank can be explained in large part by the fact that it has the country's highest average earnings, at $44,803 in 2001. Figure M3 illustrates the rankings.

Trends in minimum wage and average earnings (Figure M4)

The black line in Figure M4 shows the trend in the minimum wage, the gray line the trend in average earnings and the vertical bars the trend in the minimum wage as a percentage of average earnings from 1983 (the earliest available estimate) through 2001. Read the left-hand axis for the minimum wage and average earnings and the right-hand axis for the minimum wage as a percentage of earnings.

The minimum wage as a percentage of average earnings shows an erratic pattern from 1983 through 1991, ranging from a low of 29.1 percent in 1990 to a high of 35.8 percent in 1993. The ratio has declined steadily since 1993, to 30.2 percent by 2001, due to the steady erosion in the minimum wage.

Average earnings in the Northwest Territories have moved up and down but declined overall from 1983 ($44,708) to 1998 ($41,944); they then increased to $45,403 by 2000 but dipped a bit to $44,803

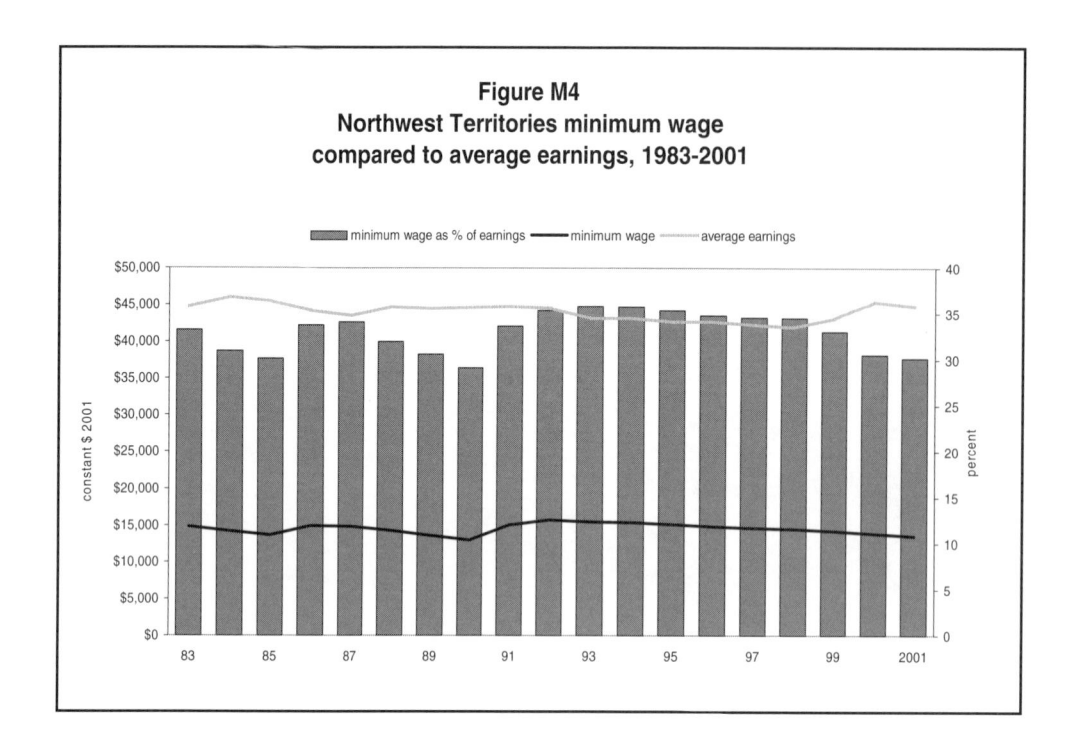

**Figure M4
Northwest Territories minimum wage
compared to average earnings, 1983-2001**

in 2001. The NWT's minimum wage also displays an up-down-up-down pattern, which explains the similar roller-coaster trend in the minimum wage relative to average earnings. Minimum wage earnings ranged from $12,970 in 1990 to $15,731 in 1992. However, whereas average earnings recovered in the late 1990s and early part of the new century, the minimum wage fell steadily after 1992.

Contribution of child benefits

Child benefits supplement the incomes of the large majority of Canadian families and are especially important to low- and modest-income families. Increases to the federal Canada Child Tax Benefit, along with the Northwest Territories' creation of its own Northwest Territories Child Benefit, are boosting the incomes of minimum wage and other working poor families.

We looked at child benefits for four types of family – single parents supporting one child on the minimum wage, one-earner couples working for the minimum wage and with two children, two-earner couples supporting two children on one-and-a-half minimum wages, and two-earner couples with two children and two full minimum wages.

A single-parent minimum wage worker with one child got $2,447 from the Canada Child Tax Benefit and $605 from the Northwest Territories Child Benefit – for a combined total of $3,052 or 18.4 percent of disposable income. A one-earner couple with two children received $4,250 from the Canada Child Tax Benefit and $1,010 from the Northwest Territories Child Benefit for a combined federal-territorial child benefit of $5,260, worth 27.9 percent of disposable income.

A two-earner family in which one parent works full time, all year at the minimum wage and the other parent half that time got $4,250 from the Canada Child Tax Benefit and $1,010 from the Northwest Territories Child Benefit for a total child benefit payment of $5,260 or a substantial 21.8 percent of disposable income. The two-earner family in which both parents work full time, all year at the minimum wage received $3,074 from the Canada Child Tax Benefit and $354 from the Northwest Territories Child Benefit, which came to $3,428 or 12.5 percent of disposable income.

Minimum wage versus welfare (Figure M5)

For a single person earning the minimum wage in the Northwest Territories, disposable income – i.e., minimum wage earnings plus federal and territorial refundable tax credits minus income and payroll

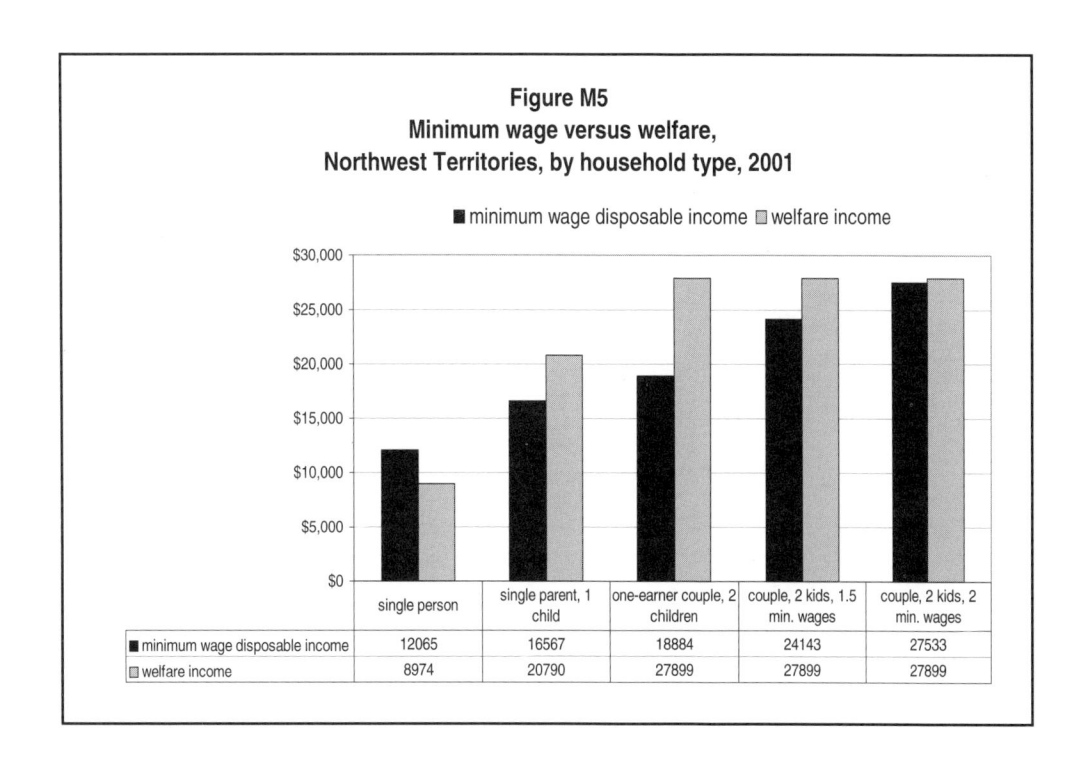

Figure M5
Minimum wage versus welfare,
Northwest Territories, by household type, 2001

	single person	single parent, 1 child	one-earner couple, 2 children	couple, 2 kids, 1.5 min. wages	couple, 2 kids, 2 min. wages
minimum wage disposable income	12065	16567	18884	24143	27533
welfare income	8974	20790	27899	27899	27899

taxes – amounted to $12,065[67] in 2001 or $3,091 more than the $8,974 from welfare and refundable tax credits. Figure M5 shows the comparison.

However, the minimum wage pays less than welfare for a single parent with one child age 2. Disposable income from after-tax minimum wage earnings, child benefits and refundable tax credits amounted to $16,567[68] in 2001, or $4,223 less than the $20,790 from welfare, child benefits and refundable tax credits.

A one-earner couple earning the minimum wage and supporting two children aged 10 and 15 is much worse off working at the minimum wage. Total disposable income from minimum wages, child benefits and tax credits came to $18,884[69] or a substantial $9,015 less than the $27,899 from welfare benefits, child benefits and refundable tax credits.

Welfare also pays better than minimum wage work in the case of a family with two children in which one parent works full time, year round at the minimum wage while the other earns half this amount (i.e., works part-time and/or part-year). The family's disposable income from one-and-a-half minimum wages came to $24,143[70] in 2001 or $3,756 less than the $27,899 from welfare, child benefits and the refundable GST credit.

For a family with two children in which both parents work full time, year round at the minimum wage, disposable income was $27,533[71] in 2001 or $366 less than the $27,899 from welfare, child benefits and the refundable GST credit. Even when both parents work full-time year-long for the minimum wage, they still end up with less income than they could get from welfare and other government income benefits.

NUNAVUT

Because Statistics Canada's low income cut-offs do not apply to Nunavut (or the other two territories), we cannot provide comparisons between its minimum wage and the before-tax or after-tax poverty lines. Nor are average earnings trends or minimum wage workforce estimates available.

Interprovincial rank: dollar value of minimum wages (Figure N1)

When the former Northwest Territories was split into Nunavut and the Northwest Territories in 1999, Nunavut's minimum wage was set the same as the Northwest Territories – $6.50. In 2002, Nunavut and the Northwest Territories tied for fifth-highest place in a spectrum that ranged from Newfoundland ($5.71 annual hourly average) to British Columbia ($8.00). Figure N1 shows the results.

Trend in dollar value of minimum wage (Figure N2)

Because minimum wages are not indexed, their value changes over time. Figure N2 shows the trend in Nunavut's minimum wage from the territory's creation in 1999 to 2002; each year's average

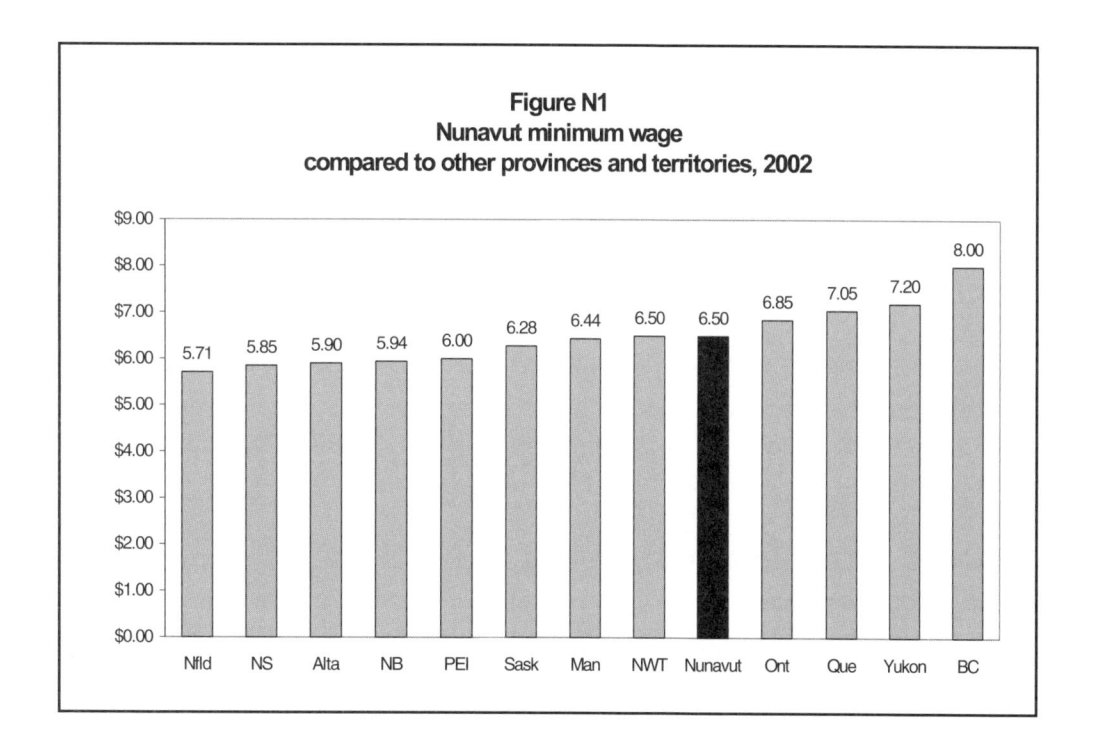

**Figure N1
Nunavut minimum wage
compared to other provinces and territories, 2002**

Nfld	NS	Alta	NB	PEI	Sask	Man	NWT	Nunavut	Ont	Que	Yukon	BC
5.71	5.85	5.90	5.94	6.00	6.28	6.44	6.50	6.50	6.85	7.05	7.20	8.00

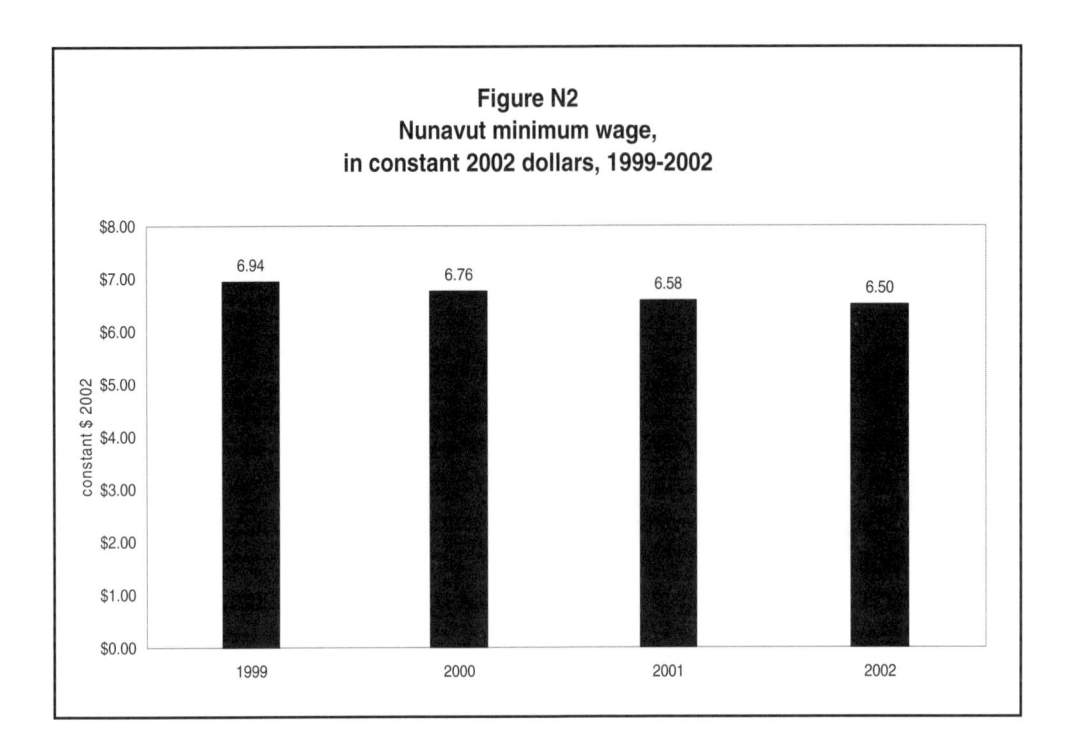

**Figure N2
Nunavut minimum wage,
in constant 2002 dollars, 1999-2002**

Year	constant $ 2002
1999	6.94
2000	6.76
2001	6.58
2002	6.50

minimum wage has been converted to inflation-adjusted (i.e., constant) 2002 dollars to show the real trend, after taking into account the impact of inflation on the dollar.

Because Nunavut's minimum wage has not been adjusted since the territory was established in 1999, it has fallen steadily in value, from $6.94 in 1999 (expressed in inflation-adjusted 2002 dollars) to $6.50 in 2002.

Interprovincial rank: minimum wages as percentage of average earnings (Figure N3)

Nunavut ranks second-last in terms of how its minimum wage compares to its average earnings, after the Northwest Territories. In 2001 (the most recent year for which data on average earnings are available), Nunavut's $6.50 minimum wage represented 33.4 percent of its $19.49 hourly average earnings; British Columbia came first at 46.2 percent. Figure N3 gives the rankings.

Nunavut's low ranking can be explained in large part by the fact that it has Canada's second-highest average earnings – $40,538 in 2001 – next to the Northwest Territories' $44,803 average earnings.

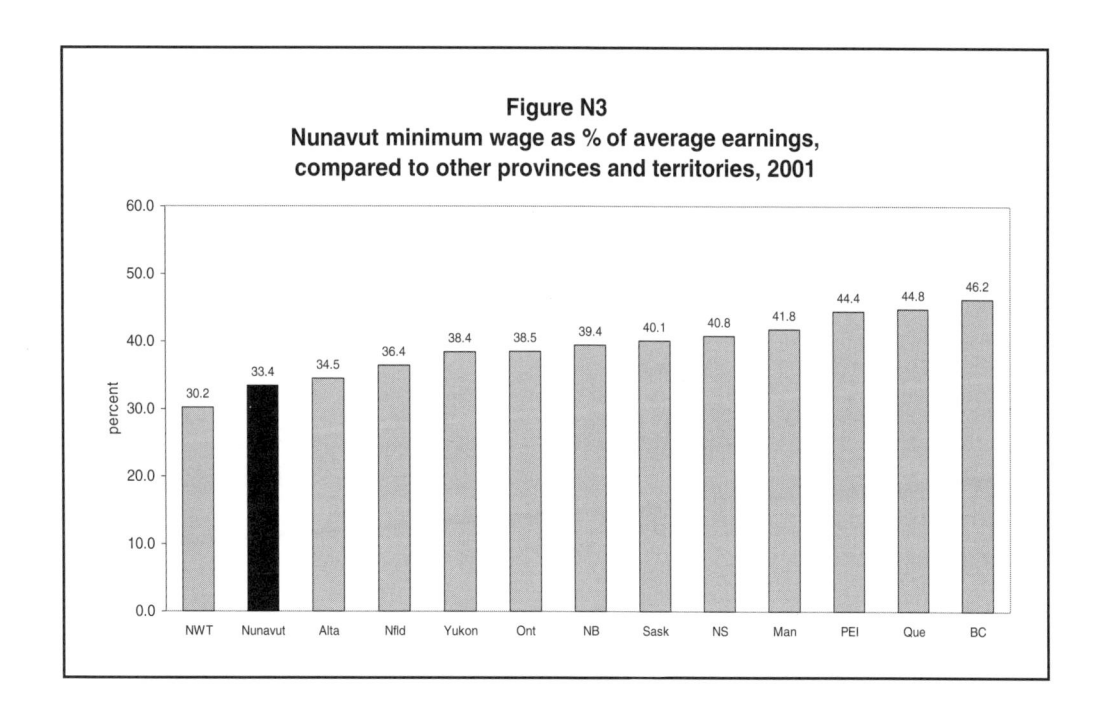

Figure N3
Nunavut minimum wage as % of average earnings, compared to other provinces and territories, 2001

Region	Percent
NWT	30.2
Nunavut	33.4
Alta	34.5
Nfld	36.4
Yukon	38.4
Ont	38.5
NB	39.4
Sask	40.1
NS	40.8
Man	41.8
PEI	44.4
Que	44.8
BC	46.2

Contribution of child benefits

Child benefits supplement the incomes of the large majority of Canadian families and are especially important to low- and modest-income families. Increases to the federal Canada Child Tax Benefit, along with the creation of the Nunavut Child Benefit, are boosting the incomes of minimum wage and other working poor families.

We looked at child benefits for four types of family – single parents supporting one child on the minimum wage, one-earner couples working for the minimum wage and with two children, two-earner couples supporting two children on one-and-a-half minimum wages, and two-earner couples with two children and two full minimum wages.

The single-parent minimum wage worker with one child got $2,447 from the Canada Child Tax Benefit and $605 from the Nunavut Child Benefit, for a combined total of $3,052 or 18.5 percent of disposable income. The one-earner couple with two children received $4,250 from the Canada Child Tax Benefit and $1,010 from the Nunavut Child Benefit for a combined federal-territorial child benefit of $5,260, worth 27.9 percent of disposable income.

Minimum Wages in Canada: A Statistical Portrait With Policy Implications

The two-earner family in which one parent works full time, all year at the minimum wage and the other parent half that time got $4,250 from the Canada Child Tax Benefit and $1,010 from the Nunavut Child Benefit for a total child benefit payment of $5,260 or a substantial 21.8 percent of disposable income. The two-earner family in which both parents work full time, all year at the minimum wage received $3,074 from the Canada Child Tax Benefit and $354 from the Nunavut Child Benefit, which came to $3,428 or 12.5 percent of disposable income.

Minimum wage versus welfare (Figure N4)

For a single person earning the minimum wage in Nunavut, disposable income – i.e., minimum wage earnings plus federal and territorial refundable tax credits minus income and payroll taxes – amounted to $12,020[72] in 2001 or $1,555 more than the $10,465 from welfare and the refundable GST credit. Figure N4 shows the comparison.

However, the minimum wage offers far less than welfare for a single parent with one child age 2. Disposable income from after-tax minimum wage earnings, child benefits and refundable tax credits amounted to $16,522[73] in 2001, or a hefty $11,735 less than the $28,257 from welfare, child benefits and the refundable GST credit.

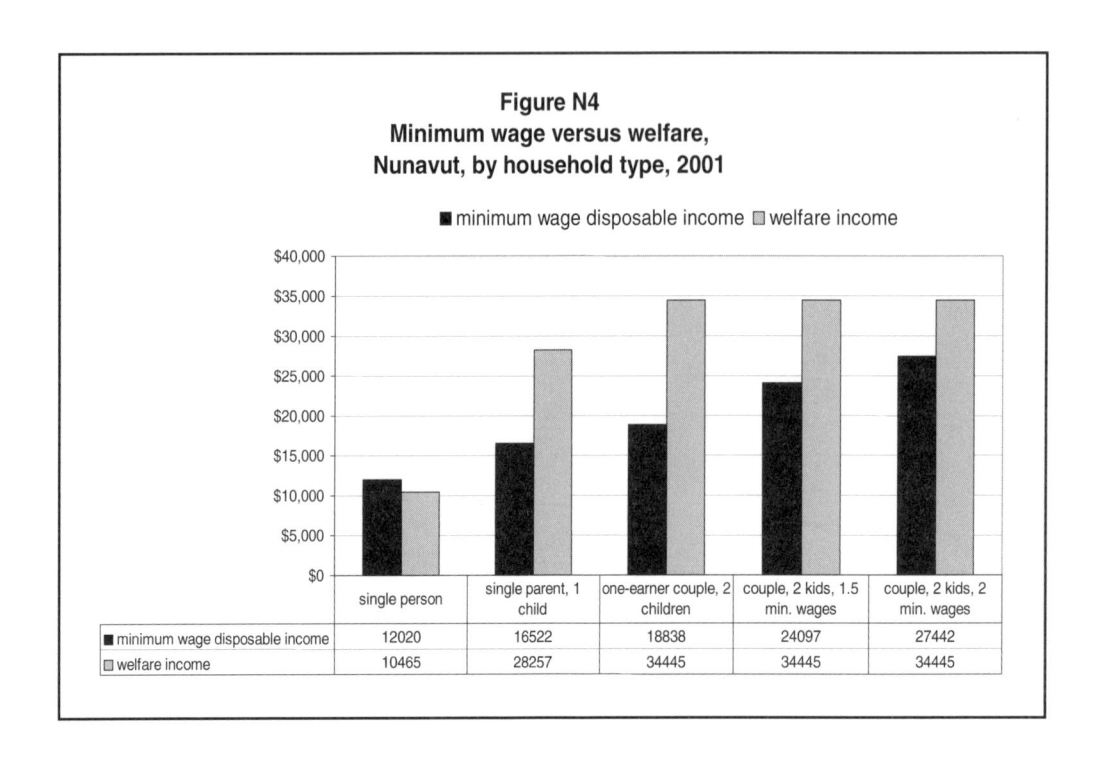

Figure N4
Minimum wage versus welfare, Nunavut, by household type, 2001

	single person	single parent, 1 child	one-earner couple, 2 children	couple, 2 kids, 1.5 min. wages	couple, 2 kids, 2 min. wages
minimum wage disposable income	12020	16522	18838	24097	27442
welfare income	10465	28257	34445	34445	34445

248   Caledon Institute of Social Policy

A one-earner couple earning the minimum wage and supporting two children aged 10 and 15 is much worse off working at the minimum wage. Total disposable income from minimum wages, child benefits and tax credits came to $18,838[74] or a staggering $15,607 less than the maximum $34,445 from welfare benefits, child benefits and the refundable GST credit.

Welfare also pays much more than minimum wage work in the case of a family with two children in which one parent works full time, year round at the minimum wage while the other earns half this amount (i.e., works part-time and/or part-year). The family's disposable income from one-and-a-half minimum wages came to $24,097[75] in 2001 or $10,348 less than the $34,445 from welfare, child benefits and the refundable GST credit.

For a family with two children in which both parents work full time, year round at the minimum wage, disposable income was $27,442[76] in 2001 or $7,003 less than the $34,445 from welfare, child benefits and the refundable GST credit. Even when both parents work full-time, all year for the minimum wage, they still end up with significantly less income than they could get from welfare and other government income benefits.

HOW CANADIAN MINIMUM WAGES COMPARE INTERNATIONALLY

Canadian minimum wages are comparable – indeed, in most provinces lower – than US minimum wages and are relatively low when compared to other advanced industrialized nations.

Canada and the US (Figure O1)

Figure O1 ranks the dollar value of minimum wages in the US and Canada. The American minimum wage rates have been converted to comparable price levels as calculated in terms of purchasing power parity, expressed in Canadian dollars. Purchasing power parity "is the amount of money in each national currency needed to buy a common basket of goods and services" and is a better measure for comparing minimum wages than the exchange rate because the latter "is highly responsive to other influences that have nothing to do with the purchasing power of the currency, such as short-term flows of investment capital" [Battle and Mendelson 2002: 9].

In the US, the federal minimum wage applies under the Fair Labor Standards Act to employees of companies with revenues of $500,000 or more a year and that are engaged in interstate commerce or in the

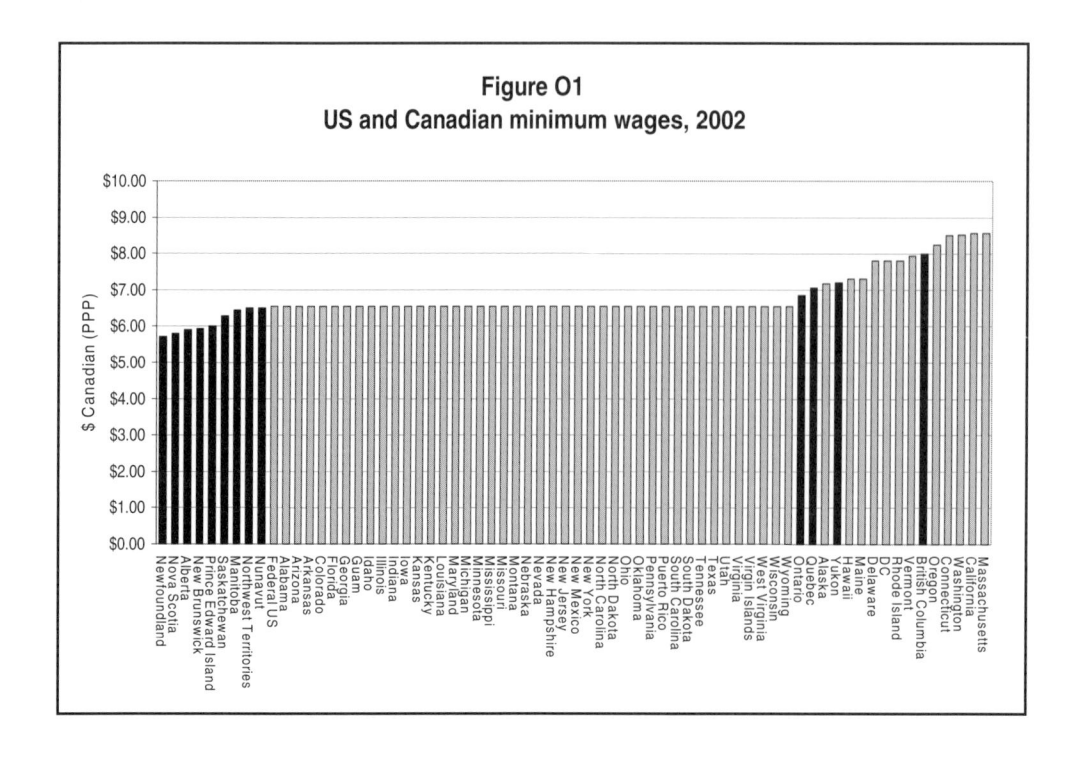

Figure O1
US and Canadian minimum wages, 2002

production of goods for commerce; to workers in construction and laundry/dry cleaning firms with revenues over $500,000; and to employees of federal, state or local government agencies and of hospitals, schools and postsecondary institutions. The federal minimum wage also applies to smaller firms that do not fall under the Fair Labor Standards Act if the workers are engaged in interstate commerce or in the production of goods for commerce, and to domestic workers. Most state minimum wages – which apply to workers not covered by the federal minimum wage – are the same as the federal rate, but 11 states and the District of Columbia have set higher minimum wage rates than the federal level. Seven states – Alabama, Arizona, Florida, Louisiana, Mississippi, South Carolina and Tennessee – have no minimum wages, though of course the federal minimum wage law applies to employees in those states who come under the protection of the federal Fair Labour Standards Act.

In 2002, nine Canadian jurisdictions – Newfoundland ($5.71 annual hourly average), Nova Scotia ($5.85), Alberta ($5.90), New Brunswick ($5.94), Prince Edward Island ($6.00), Saskatchewan ($6.28), Manitoba ($6.44), the Northwest Territories and Nunavut ($6.50 each) – were below the lowest US rate of $6.54 (i.e., the federal minimum wage and the rate in 42 states, districts and other jurisdictions) as expressed in purchasing power parity Canadian dollars. The remaining four Canadian jurisdictions rank in the upper quarter of the minimum wage spectrum, though Ontario ($6.85) is just above the $6.54 US federal and majority state minimum wage rate and Quebec ($7.05) is only 51 cents higher. Yukon ($7.20) ranks just a tick above neighbouring Alaska ($7.18). Only British Columbia ($8.00) ranks in the top ten, below Oregon ($8.26), Connecticut ($8.51), Washington ($8.53), California and Massachusetts ($8.57 each).

Canada and other countries (Figure O2)

Canada ranks low internationally when its minimum wage is compared to average earnings. Our national average minimum wage amounted to 34 percent of the estimated average earnings of full-year full-time workers in 2001. Of 17 advanced industrialized nations listed in Figure O2,[77] Canada comes fourth-lowest, ahead of only the UK, Spain and Japan. Canada even places lower than the US, whose minimum wage represents 37 percent of average full-time full-year earnings.

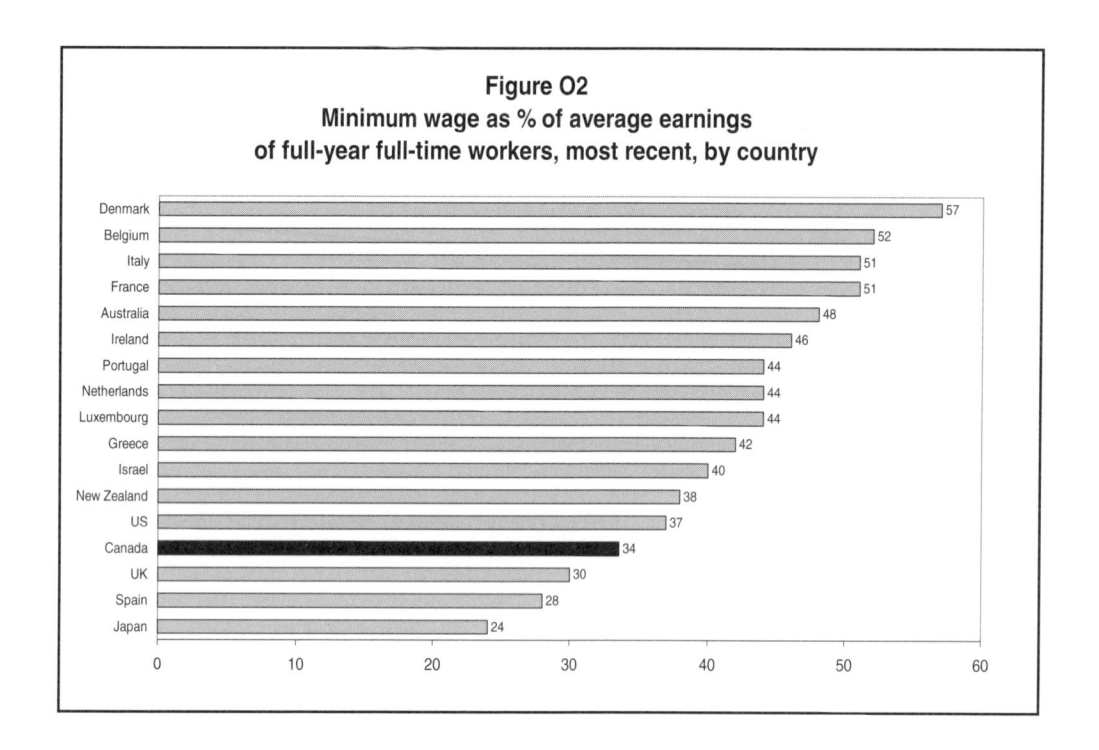

**Figure O2
Minimum wage as % of average earnings
of full-year full-time workers, most recent, by country**

Country	%
Denmark	57
Belgium	52
Italy	51
France	51
Australia	48
Ireland	46
Portugal	44
Netherlands	44
Luxembourg	44
Greece	42
Israel	40
New Zealand	38
US	37
Canada	34
UK	30
Spain	28
Japan	24

POLICY IMPLICATIONS

Our findings shed some light on the policy debate that swirls around the minimum wage – one of Canada's oldest yet still most controversial social policies.

Passport to poverty?

Some people argue that minimum wages in Canada have fallen so low that they amount to a passport to poverty rather than a basic adequate wage and crucial protection from exploitation. They contend that we should boost minimum wages to achieve the long-sought goal of a 'living wage' so that there would be no working poor.

Our results show that minimum wages in Canada lost considerably in value after their peak in the mid-1970s, but the decline has not been steady and relentless. The national average minimum wage rose substantially between 1965 and 1976, fell (but not all the way back) in the late 1970s and first half of the 1980s, levelled off in the second half of the 1980s, gradually recovered somewhat in the first part of the 1990s, flattened between 1997 and 1999, and then fell slightly in 2000 and 2001. This plateau-like pattern of the national average minimum wage over the long term applies generally to almost all provinces and territories: A sharp increase in the value of the minimum wage between 1965 and the peak in the mid-1970s was followed by a similar or smaller decrease until the mid-1980s or early 1990s, then one of three trends throughout the rest of the 1990s and into this first decade of the new century – modest improvements (PEI, Manitoba, Alberta and BC), flattening out (Newfoundland, Nova Scotia, New Brunswick, Saskatchewan and Yukon) or decline (Quebec, Ontario, the Northwest Territories and Nunavut).

Although Canadian minimum wages are not on a relentless downward spiral, they fall far short of the poverty line. The national average minimum wage – $14,061 in 2001 – is considerably below Statistics Canada's before-tax low income cut-offs for all but rural communities, where relatively few people live. In 2001, it fell $4,769 below the before-tax low income cut-off for one person in metropolitan centers (500,000 or larger), $2,026 under for communities with between 100,000 and 499,999 inhabitants, $1,913 beneath the line for small cities between 30,000 and 99,999, and $803 below for communities under 30,000 – though $1,100 above the poverty line for Canada's thinly-populated rural areas.

The poverty gap is deeper for families. For a family of two (e.g., a single parent with one child), the $14,061 national average minimum wage fell $9,474 short of the before-tax low income line for a family of two in metropolitan areas, $6,047 below the line for cities in the 100,000-499,999 category, $5,907 under for communities between 30,000 and 99,999 inhabitants, $4,518 beneath the line for towns under 30,000 and $2,141 under the poverty line for rural areas.

Minimum wages for most household types in most jurisdictions also fall below another definition of poverty – Statistics Canada's after-tax low income cut-offs, which take into account the federal and provincial income taxes that Canadians pay. After-tax income from minimum wages and government benefits (e.g., refundable tax credits) for single minimum wage workers fall short of the after-tax poverty line for the largest city in every province, ranging from $3,649 below the line in Alberta to $2,956 in Manitoba, $2,240 in Newfoundland, $2,015 in Ontario, $1,946 in Quebec, $1,618 in New Brunswick, $1,484 in Nova Scotia, $1,391 in Saskatchewan, $1,316 in Prince Edward Island and $1,015 in British Columbia.

For single parents with one child, after-tax minimum wage incomes are below the after-tax poverty line for the largest city in most (seven of the ten) provinces, though the gap is not as deep as for single people and couples with children because single parents pay little or no income tax and receive the federal Canada Child Tax Benefit and, in virtually all provinces and territories (Prince Edward Island excepted), provincial child benefits. Minimum wage after-tax incomes were $3,381 below the after-tax low income cut-off for a family of two in the largest cities in Alberta, $2,018 below the line in Manitoba, $1,287 below in Newfoundland, $720 below in Prince Edward Island, $543 below in Nova Scotia, $415 under the line in New Brunswick and $80 below the poverty line in Ontario's largest cities.

In only three provinces – British Columbia, Quebec and Saskatchewan – do single parents with one child manage to rise above the poverty line, thanks in large part to relatively generous provincial child benefits and earnings supplements that bolster the incomes of working poor families. Best off are one-parent families with one child and earning the minimum wage in Saskatchewan, which are $2,398 above the after-tax poverty line, followed by Quebec ($1,033 above the line) and British Columbia ($533 over the line). Another plus for British Columbia families is that their province has Canada's highest minimum wage.

The poverty gap is deep for couples with two children that rely upon one parent's minimum wage, despite supplementary income from child benefits and refundable tax credits, and paying little or no income taxes. The after-tax poverty gap ranges from a low of $12,213 in Alberta to $11,051 in Manitoba, $10,205 in Ontario, $8,167 in Newfoundland, $7,869 in Prince Edward Island, $7,597 in British Columbia, $7,456 in New Brunswick, $7,353 in Nova Scotia, $5,811 in Quebec and $3,746 in Saskatchewan.

Having a second earner obviously improves minimum wage families' income prospects, but still leaves them either below or not far above the poverty line.

We found that work pays below the after-tax poverty line for two-earner couples in which one parent works full time, all year at the minimum wage and the other combines part-time minimum wage work with caring for the family's two children. Even with the contribution of the lower-earning parent, this family's income still falls considerably below the after-tax poverty line. The poverty gap for the largest city in each province ranges from $6,132 below the after-tax line in Alberta's largest cities (Calgary and Edmonton) to $5,699 below in Manitoba, $4,207 under in Ontario, $3,259 under in Newfoundland, $2,971 under in British Columbia, $2,741 under in Quebec, $2,246 under in Prince Edward Island, $2,108 under in New Brunswick, $2,205 under in Nova Scotia and $446 below the line in Saskatchewan's largest cities (Regina and Saskatoon).

Minimum wage families need both parents working full time, all year to clear the poverty line, and even then their income is far from adequate. For a two-earner couple with two children 10 and 15 in which both parents work full time, year round for the minimum wage, families manage to place above the after-tax poverty line in seven of the ten provinces, ranging from $180 above the line in Quebec to $442 in Newfoundland, $986 in British Columbia, $1,704 in Nova Scotia, $2,326 in Prince Edward Island, $2,516 in New Brunswick and $2,836 in Saskatchewan. On the other hand, families with two full-time minimum wage workers have a modest income indeed – those in Saskatchewan fare best, but are only $2,836 above the poverty line for Saskatoon and Regina. And families in Manitoba, Alberta and Ontario still end up below the poverty line – by $1,556, $771 and $231, respectively.

Raise the minimum wage? (Figures P1-P6)

We found that Canadian minimum wages are comparable to – indeed, in most provinces and territories, lower than – US minimum wages and are relatively low when compared to other advanced industrialized nations. This revealing evidence may offer some support to those who advocate raising

Canadian minimum wages to an adequate level, though there is no consensus as to what such a standard should be. Suggestions have included setting minimum wages at the poverty line or a percentage of average wages.

Figure P1 compares the average hourly minimum wage in 2002 to the before-tax low income cut-off for a single person living in the largest city in each province. Figure P2 shows how much the minimum wage would have to rise to reach the before-tax poverty line. The amounts range from a low of $1.17 in British Columbia, which has Canada's highest minimum wage, to a high of $3.27 in neighbouring Alberta, which has the third-lowest minimum wage. The increases expressed in percentage terms are considerable – ranging from 14.6 percent in British Columbia to 55.4 percent in Alberta, as illustrated in Figure P3.

Proposals to raise the minimum wage to the poverty line doubtless will be strongly opposed by business and government, given the substantial increases that would be required to close the poverty gap. Alberta, which would face the highest increase of all jurisdictions, would scoff at the notion of boosting its minimum wage to the poverty line, especially since it has Canada's lowest incidence of minimum wage workers (just 2.0 percent or less than half the national average of 4.6 percent). Indeed, the province's Minister of Human Resources and Employment recently stated that there is no chance he will raise the minimum wage any time soon, and he prefers "putting resources into working with [minimum wage Albertans], adding to their skill levels so that the minimum wage actually becomes meaningless to them" [Williamson 2002].

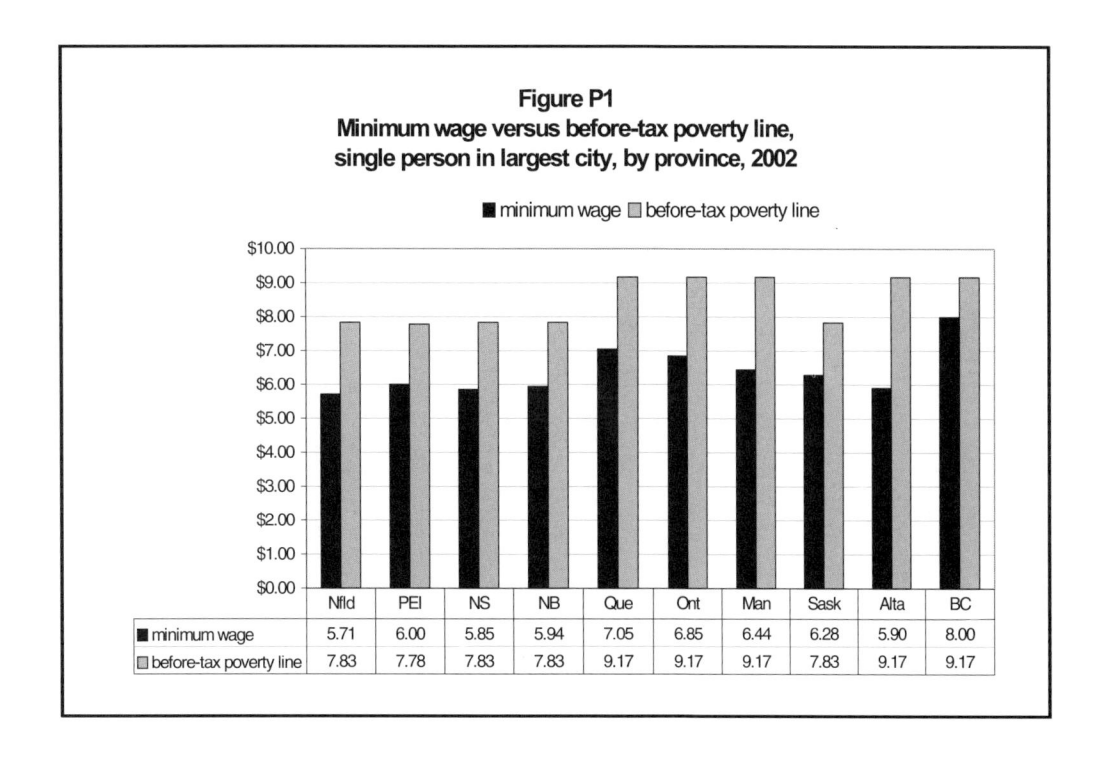

Figure P1
Minimum wage versus before-tax poverty line,
single person in largest city, by province, 2002

	Nfld	PEI	NS	NB	Que	Ont	Man	Sask	Alta	BC
minimum wage	5.71	6.00	5.85	5.94	7.05	6.85	6.44	6.28	5.90	8.00
before-tax poverty line	7.83	7.78	7.83	7.83	9.17	9.17	9.17	7.83	9.17	9.17

Minimum Wages in Canada: A Statistical Portrait With Policy Implications

Figure P2
Dollar increase required to raise minimum wage to before-tax poverty line, single person in largest city, by province, 2002

	Nfld	PEI	NS	NB	Que	Ont	Man	Sask	Alta	BC
$	2.12	1.78	1.98	1.89	2.12	2.32	2.73	1.55	3.27	1.17

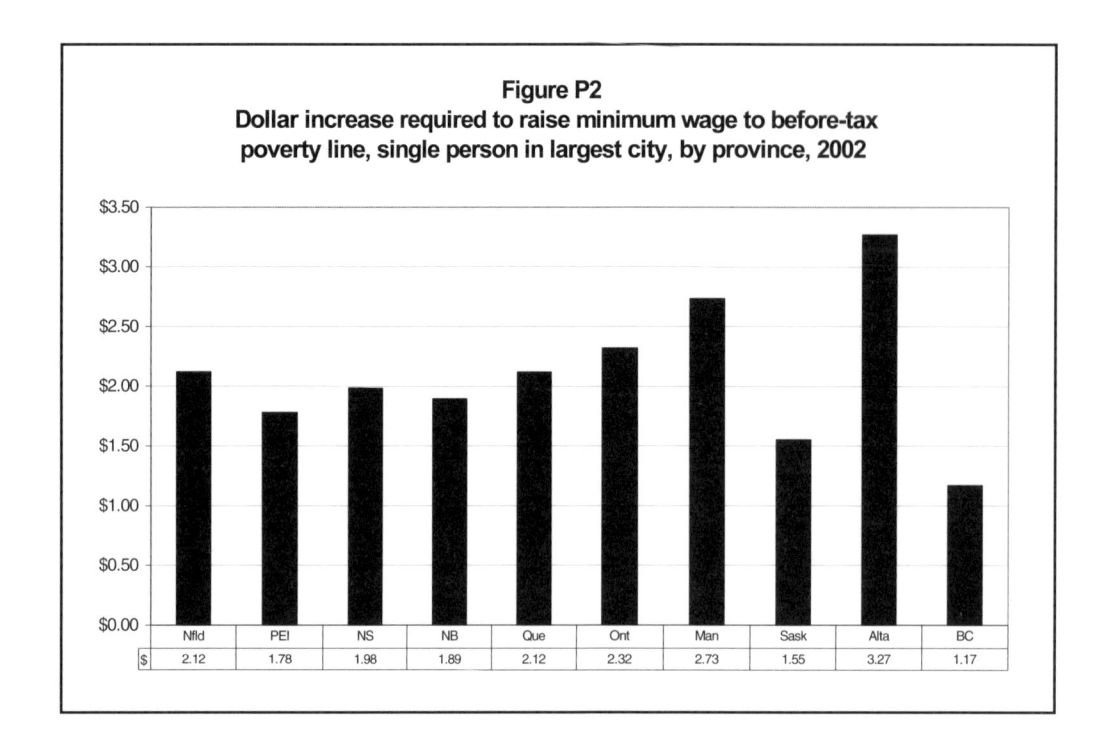

Figure P3
Percentage increase required to raise minimum wage to before-tax poverty line, single person in largest city, by province, 2002

	Nfld	PEI	NS	NB	Que	Ont	Man	Sask	Alta	BC
%	37.2	29.7	33.9	31.9	30.1	33.9	42.4	24.7	55.4	14.6

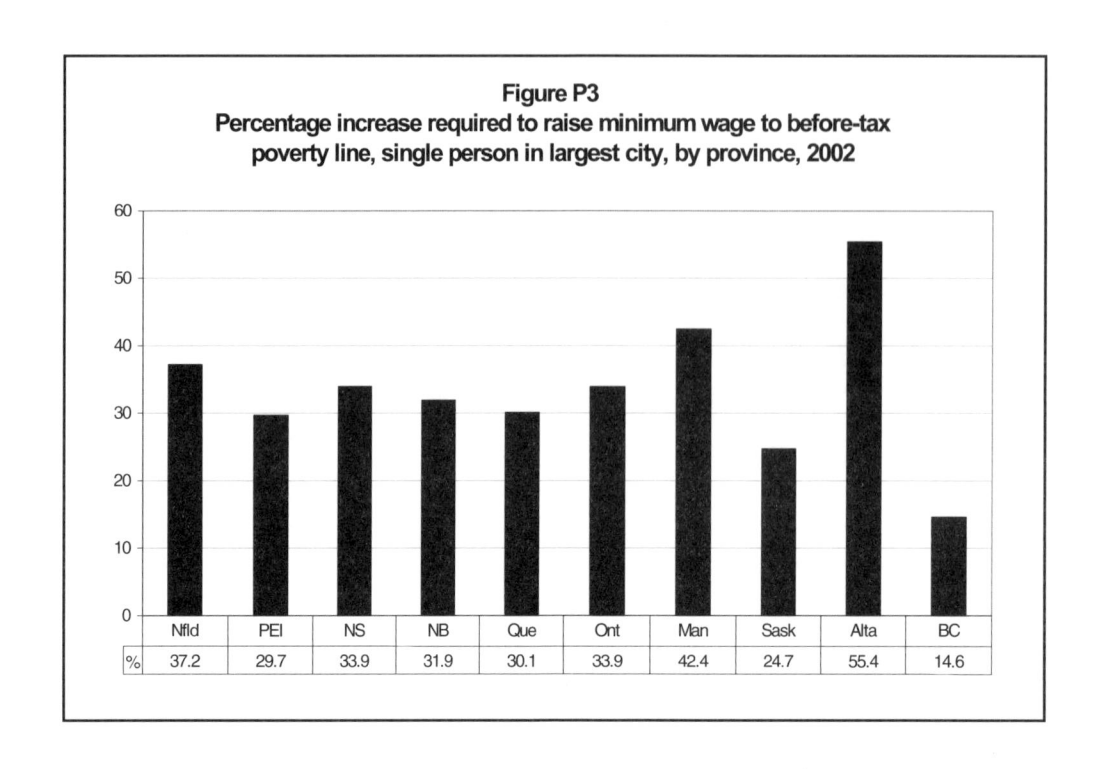

Another approach could be to set the minimum wage as a proportion of average earnings (e.g., one-half) in each province and territory. Figure P4 compares the minimum wage to average earnings in each jurisdiction in 2001 (the most recent data available). Figure P5 shows the dollar increase needed to lift minimum wages to one-half of average earnings, while Figure P6 gives the percentage raise required.

The cash increase required to lift the minimum wage to 50 percent of average earnings ranges from a low of 63 cents in British Columbia (which has the highest minimum wage) to a high of $4.27 in the Northwest Territories (which has the highest average earnings). In percentage terms, setting the minimum wage at one-half of average earnings would necessitate increases ranging from 8.3 percent in British Columbia to 65.7 percent in the Northwest Territories. Again, such increases would be anathema to employers and most if not all governments in Canada.

Index the minimum wage?

A third approach to improving the minimum wage would be to index it – the usual indexation formula being to changes in the cost of living, in average wages, or in a lower part of the wage distribution [Card and Krueger 1995: 395]. Conceivably, a special index could be created.

No province or territory indexes its minimum wage, which our research demonstrates has resulted in significant losses, as well as fluctuations, in value over time. In the US as well, neither the federal minimum wage nor state minimum wages are indexed – with one notable exception: In 1998, voters in the state of Washington approved an initiative to index the state minimum wage to the annual change in the Consumer Price Index for urban wage earners and clerical workers. On January 1, 2002, Washington State's minimum wage was adjusted from $6.72 to $6.90 an hour, to compensate for a 2.658 percent rise in the cost of living [Department of Labor and Industries]. Another way of saying this is that Washington State's minimum wage did not decline in value by 2.658 percent in 2002.

While indexation would not satisfy critics who think the minimum wage is too low, at least it would stabilize the minimum wage and prevent both the large losses that took place in most jurisdictions between the mid-1970s and the 1980s, and the stealthy erosion that has occurred in recent years in the two largest provinces, Ontario and Quebec. Indexation would be the far lesser of two evils (the other being boosting the minimum wage to the poverty line or a percentage of average earnings) for employers and government – though they probably would prefer a third option of the status quo (i.e., low minimum wages and no indexation).

Figure P4
Minimum wage versus one-half average earnings, by province/territory, 2001

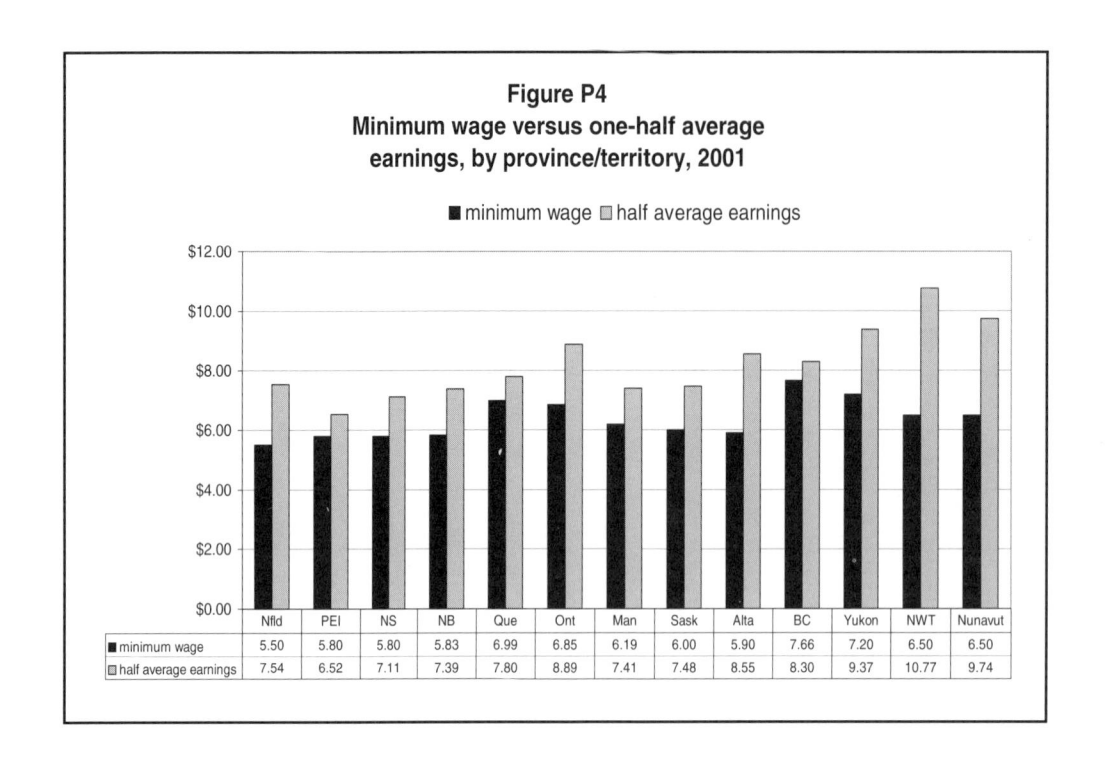

	Nfld	PEI	NS	NB	Que	Ont	Man	Sask	Alta	BC	Yukon	NWT	Nunavut
minimum wage	5.50	5.80	5.80	5.83	6.99	6.85	6.19	6.00	5.90	7.66	7.20	6.50	6.50
half average earnings	7.54	6.52	7.11	7.39	7.80	8.89	7.41	7.48	8.55	8.30	9.37	10.77	9.74

Figure P5
Dollar increase required to raise minimum wage to one-half average earnings, by province/territory, 2001

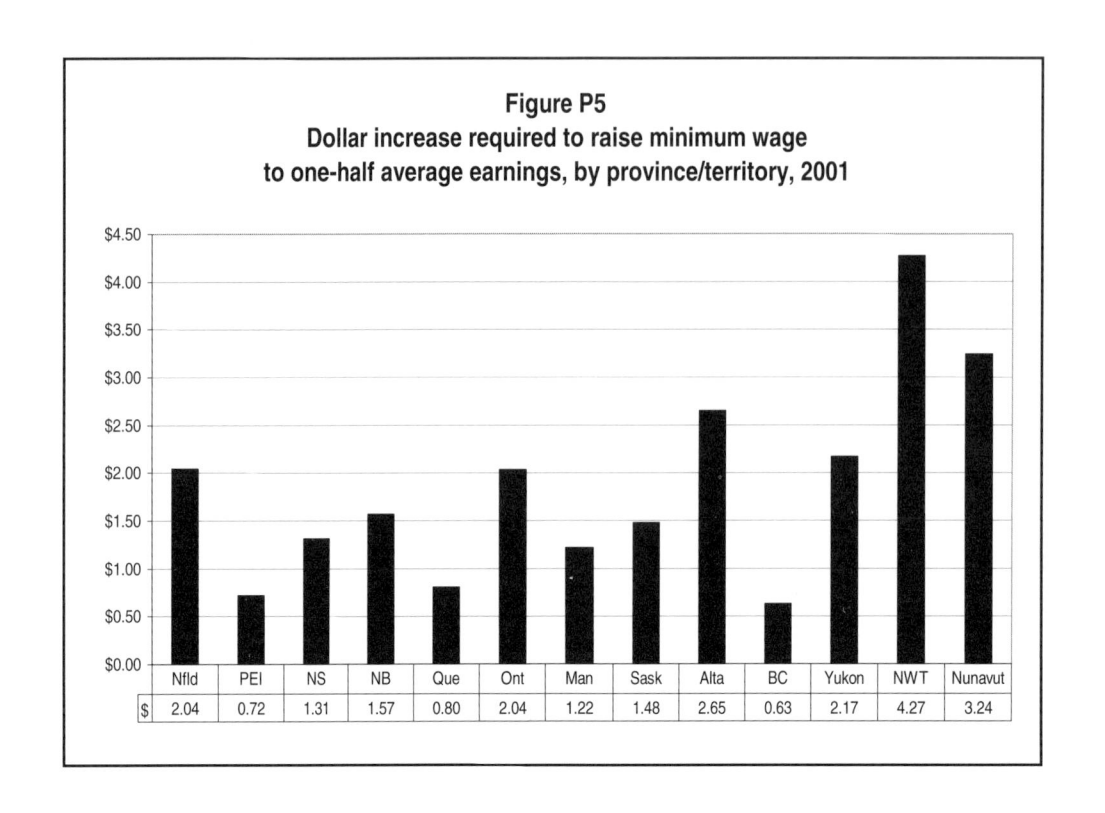

	Nfld	PEI	NS	NB	Que	Ont	Man	Sask	Alta	BC	Yukon	NWT	Nunavut
$	2.04	0.72	1.31	1.57	0.80	2.04	1.22	1.48	2.65	0.63	2.17	4.27	3.24

A Living Wage?

The term 'living wage' is an old one in Canada, going back to the early decades of the 20th century when social reformers were making the case for minimum wages, as well as for child benefits and other forms of income support, to tackle the conundrum that wages do not provide an adequate income for many Canadians, especially workers with families to support. The term has been revived in recent years to dramatize the view that minimum wages at their current levels are inadequate and should be raised to provide a decent income floor: The living wage is still an unrealized dream.

There is yet another use of the term – the Living Wage movement in the US. Under Living Wage ordinances, city and county governments set higher-than-minimum-wage base pay levels for businesses with which they have service contracts or for employers receiving economic development subsidies from local government [Economic Policy Institute 2002b].[78]

The Living Wage movement arose to deal with the problem that privatization of public services often results in large wage cuts for workers who are moved from the public to the private sector. To add insult to injury, some local governments have tried to attract businesses to their community by offering subsidies and tax incentives; research suggests that the jobs created by economic development subsidies pay less than the norm for their industry. Living Wage ordinances are intended to prevent city and county governments from contracting with or subsidizing private sector employers that pay low wages which guarantee working poverty.

The living wage level is typically calculated as the wage a full-time worker would need to support a family above the federal poverty line ($8.20 an hour for a family of four, or $10.41 in Canadian dollars using purchasing power parity conversion), ranging from 100 to 130 percent of the poverty line. Current Living Wage rates range from $6.25 per hour in Milwaukee, Wisconsin ($7.94 Canadian) to $12 ($15.24 Canadian) in Santa Monica, California. By way of comparison, Canadian minimum wages range from $5.80 an hour in Nova Scotia to $8.00 in BC.

It is important to note that living wage ordinances presently cover only a tiny proportion of the workforce – typically less than one percent. Evaluations of Living Wages find that affected employers handle the extra payroll cost through reduced training and recruitment costs or a small reduction in profits. There is no evidence of net job losses, since raising wages lowers employee turnover and attendant recruitment and training costs. As observed below, research into the employment impact of increases to the minimum wage arrives at the same conclusion.

Killer of jobs?

Many economists oppose raising the minimum wage because they claim that would lead employers to trim their payroll costs and so would reduce employment. According to this line of reasoning, boosting the minimum wage would harm, not help, low-wage workers, especially the young and unskilled who are most likely to work for the minimum rate. Not surprisingly, some governments and business organizations cite this 'killer-of-jobs' argument in their opposition to increasing the minimum wage.

This traditional economic orthodoxy has been challenged by revisionist economists who – using the novel approach of empirically investigating the impact of hikes in minimum wages rather than relying on textbook theory – conclude that the modest increases to the low minimum wages paid in the US in the 1990s had no negative impact on employment and, in some cases, showed a modest positive effect [Card and Krueger 1995]. The results of one of their studies – the effect on fast-food workers of an 11 percent increase in the minimum wage in 1992 in New Jersey – have been challenged by another economist, using different data and methods, claiming that employment in fact declined, not increased [*The Economist* 2002]. Both sides in the debate since have rethought their positions and arrived at the conclusion that the raise in the New Jersey minimum wage probably had no effect on employment. Then along came another economist arguing that the higher minimum wage in New Jersey reduced hours of work even though it did

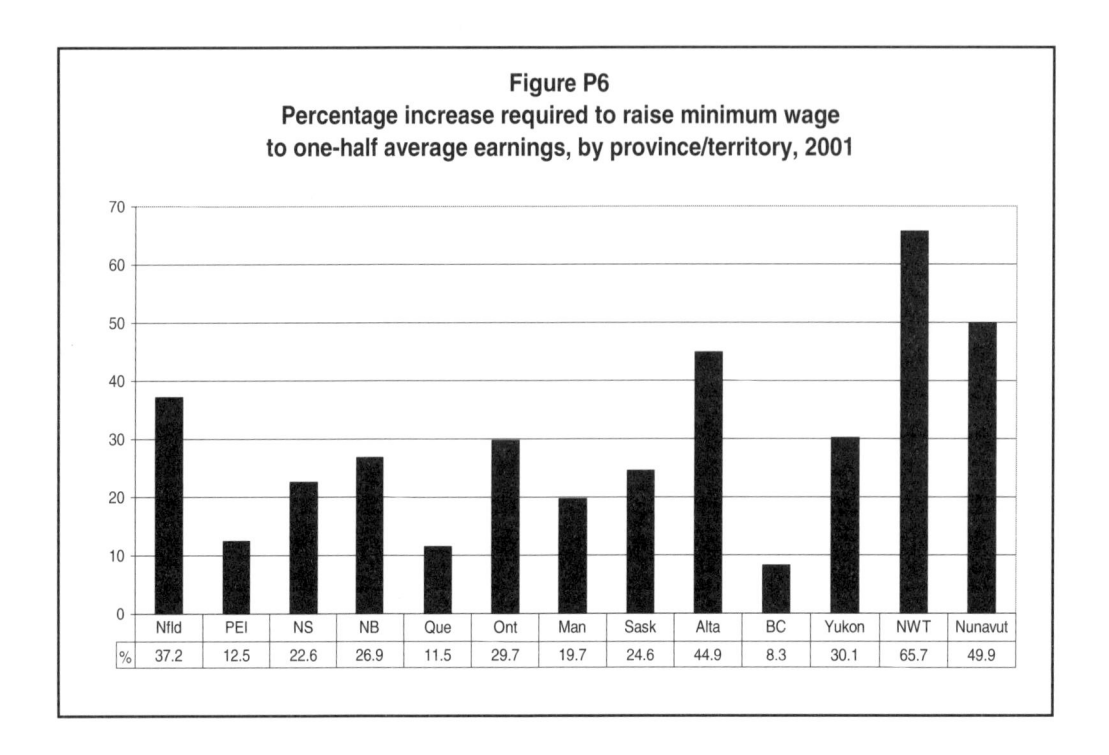

Figure P6
Percentage increase required to raise minimum wage to one-half average earnings, by province/territory, 2001

	Nfld	PEI	NS	NB	Que	Ont	Man	Sask	Alta	BC	Yukon	NWT	Nunavut
%	37.2	12.5	22.6	26.9	11.5	29.7	19.7	24.6	44.9	8.3	30.1	65.7	49.9

not reduce the overall number of minimum wage workers. Yet another economist warns that higher minimum wages could push up wages generally (to maintain differences between levels) and in the process raise inflation, leading to anti-inflation actions that would reduce employment [*The Economist* 2002]. And so the debate rages.

Canadian research corroborates American findings that modest increases to the minimum wage are not the 'job killers' that some critics allege. A study by Michael Goldberg and David Green of minimum wages in four large provinces – British Columbia, Alberta, Ontario and Quebec – concluded that minimum wage hikes had only marginal effects on employment [Goldberg and Green 1999: 21]. The short-term effects were negative but small for male workers (though statistically significant only for those aged 20-24) as well as female workers aged 15-19 and 25-54, and positive but small for females 20-24. Over the longer term, allowing time for employers to react to increases in the minimum wage, the study found a very modest reduction in employment (though statistically significant only for males 20-24 and females 25-54) and concluded that a 10 percent rise in the minimum wage would reduce the employment-to-population ratio (i.e., the percentage of the population employed) by between 1 and 3 percent, depending on age and gender. Other factors – such as the business cycle, economic growth and changes in the supply of labour – are far more important to employment trends.

Proponents of a higher minimum wage not only dismiss its alleged negative effect on employment, but also suggest it would have other, positive economic benefits. They argue that raising the minimum wage would improve the incomes of the low-paid and thus stimulate consumer spending, which is good for the economy. Boosting the minimum wage "can increase labour force participation, bringing new skills and capacities into the workforce and a better skill match vis-à-vis employer need" [CAW-Canada 1998]. A higher minimum wage may benefit employers and employees alike "through increased productivity, lower recruiting and training costs, decreased absenteeism and increased worker morale" [Economic Policy Institute 2002a].

Ineffective anti-poverty weapon?

Social advocates traditionally have placed much store on the importance of the minimum wage. But some people claim that the minimum wage is an ineffective anti-poverty weapon because it covers only a small percentage of the workforce and because many minimum wage workers live in non-poor families.

American research shows that increasing the minimum wage has had a modest but positive distributional impact on the lower-paid labour market, generating wage increases among workers at the bottom of the ladder, reducing the overall dispersion of wages, and offsetting much of the increase in wage inequality that occurred in the 1980s. A Quebec study came to the same conclusion, estimating that the decline in the value of Quebec's minimum wage accounted for between 20 and 30 percent of the increase in wage inequality in the 1980s [DiNardo, Fortin and Lemieux 1994]. While many minimum wage workers are in families whose total income puts them above the poverty line, minimum wage workers still are disproportionately drawn from families with below-average incomes [Card and Krueger 1995: 3; Goldberg and Green 1999: i].

Although only a small fraction of Canada's employees work for the minimum wage – 4.6 percent nationally at last count – increasing the minimum wage would benefit not only the lowest-paid, but also some workers earning higher than the minimum rate. If, for example, the minimum wage were $6.00 and rose to $7.00, then workers just above the old minimum wage, earning $6.01 to $6.99, also would see an increase. Moreover, employers may have to adjust some above-minimum wage rates to maintain existing wage differentials, as noted above, so that a higher minimum wage could have a 'trickle-up' effect.

Contrary to what some people believe, the archetypical minimum wage worker is not a middle class teenager working after school for pocket money. In Canada and the US, the majority of minimum wage workers are adults. Our study also determined that four in ten minimum wage workers in Canada work on a full-time basis.

Postsecondary education is becoming the great divide between haves and have-nots in today's knowledge economy. Our results show that many minimum wage workers are students who rely upon their employment earnings to help pay for their education. At a time when the cost of postsecondary education is increasing substantially, the minimum wage becomes all the more important – especially for low- and modest-income families struggling to finance their children's passport to a better life.

The minimum wage is no magic bullet, and its potency has been diminished by lack of indexation. Nevertheless, the minimum wage is an important weapon in a broader arsenal of measures – income and employment supports, education, health and social services – needed to combat poverty, improve labour market skills and offer learning opportunities for disadvantaged Canadians. The minimum wage is, in the social policy argot of the day, a 'positive' as opposed to 'passive' measure and could be a stronger element of welfare-to-work/make-work-pay policy reforms.

At a minimum ...

The Caledon Institute of Social Policy has proposed that the federal and provincial/territorial governments establish a task force (with provision for public input) to examine the functions and adequacy of minimum wages [Battle and Torjman 2002.] While most if not all governments likely will resist calls to boost the minimum wage, at the very least they could take immediate action and follow the lead of the state of Washington by agreeing to index their minimum wages (e.g., to some measure of cost of living, as Washington has done, or to some measure of average wages). At least the wage safety net would not sag even further.

ENDNOTES

1. See CAW/TCA 1998, Goldberg and Green 1999, Schenk 2001.

2. The Canada Labour Code does not cover federal government employees. However, the federal government in practice applies the federal minimum wage rate to its own employees (which, in turn, is the same as the rate for each province and territory).

3. Information in this section is from Human Resources Development Canada (2002).

4. For employees living distant from the highway system, the youth minimum wage rate is $6.50 and the adult rate is $7.00.

5. In Manitoba, employers of home workers must register with the Minister of Labour and maintain records of wages and deduction from pay. British Columbia does the same. New Brunswick applies a special (weekly) minimum wage rate to employees whose hours of work are unverifiable. Ontario sets a higher minimum wage rate for homeworkers (110 percent of the general adult rate) to take into account the cost of overhead and tools or machinery. Saskatchewan also covers homeworkers.

6. The Northwest Territories and Nunavut use a two-level minimum wage — $7.00 for areas distant from the highway system and $6.50 elsewhere. We have used the lower rates.

7. Minimum wages declined somewhat in the late 1990s and first two years of the new century in Quebec, Ontario, Yukon and Nunavut. The Northwest Territories has seen a steady decline from 1991 through 2002. The reason for these losses is that minimum wage rates either have not been increased in these periods or their adjustments have not fully compensated for losses to inflation. PEI, Manitoba, Alberta and BC enjoyed improvements — mostly modest, while Newfoundland, Nova Scotia, New Brunswick, Saskatchewan and Yukon have had more or less flat minimum wages.

8. British Columbia launched the BC Family Bonus in July of 1996, two years before the National Child Benefit was fully under way; BC's pioneering child benefit program replaced needs-tested social assistance benefits on behalf of children with an income-tested program payable to all low-income families (including minimum wage and other working poor families). Quebec also has created an integrated child benefit system that — though not formally part of the National Child Benefit reform, in which Quebec did not participate — pursues the same objectives and design features as the National Child Benefit. Most provinces have used part of their social assistance savings (welfare benefits for children in most provinces are being reduced by increasing federal payments under the Canada Child Tax Benefit) to help fund their own income-tested child benefits.

9. All welfare income estimates in this study are from the National Council of Welfare's report *Welfare Incomes, 2000 and 2001* (National Council of Welfare 2002). These are the maximum amounts available, though they do not include discretionary special benefits that can increase some recipients' incomes.

10. All estimates of minimum wage workers and total employees in this report were provided to the Caledon Institute of Social Policy by Statistics Canada, based on special runs of the labour force survey. Our analysis of the minimum wage workforce is based upon, though expands and updates, Statistics Canada's 1998 report "A New Perspective on Wages" (Statistics Canada 1998). The Caledon Institute is grateful to Statistics Canada for supplying this data, though of course Caledon alone is responsible for the interpretation and use of the data.

11. In addition to $11,440 from minimum wage earnings, the single worker received $302 from the federal GST (Goods and Services Tax) credit and $40 from the provincial Harmonized Sales Tax credit, and paid $549 in federal income tax and $363 in Newfoundland income tax. Note that the worker also paid $598 in payroll taxes ($341 in Canada Pension Plan contributions and $257 in Employment Insurance premiums), though these are not included in the definition of after-tax income used by Statistics Canada's after-tax low income cut-offs.

12. Income was $11,440 in minimum wages, $2,447 from the federal Canada Child Tax Benefit, $204 from the Newfoundland and Labrador Child Tax Benefit, $520 from the federal GST credit and $100 from the provincial Harmonized Sales Tax credit. No federal or Newfoundland income taxes were owing, thanks mainly to the equivalent-to-married tax credit for the child. See previous footnote concerning payroll taxes.

13. Income was $11,440 in minimum wages supplemented by $4,250 from the Canada Child Tax Benefit, $516 from the Newfoundland and Labrador Child Benefit, $628 from the federal GST credit and $200 from the provincial Harmonized Sales Tax credit. No federal or provincial income taxes were owing. See previous footnote concerning payroll taxes.

14. Income was $17,160 in minimum wages supplemented by $4,250 from the Canada Child Tax Benefit, $431 from the Newfoundland and Labrador Child Benefit, $628 from the federal GST credit and $92 from the provincial Harmonized Sales Tax credit. The family paid $356 in federal income tax and $263 in provincial income tax. CPP contributions were $437 and EI premiums came to $356.

15. Income was $22,880 in minimum wages supplemented by $3,956 from the Canada Child Tax Benefit and $628 from the federal GST credit. The family paid $1,097 in federal income tax and $725 in provincial income tax. CPP contributions were $683 and EI premiums came to $515.

16. The Prince Edward Island government plans to raise its minimum wage to $6.25 on January 1, 2003 and to $6.50 on January 1, 2004.

17. In addition to $12,064 from minimum wage earnings, the single worker received $314 from the federal GST (Goods and Services Tax) credit. Federal income tax came to $642 and provincial income tax were $143. Payroll taxes (not included in Statistics Canada's after-tax low income cut-offs) totalled $639 ($368 in Canada Pension Plan contributions and $271 in Employment Insurance premiums).

18. Income was $12,064 in minimum wages, $2,447 from the federal Canada Child Tax Benefit and $520 from the federal GST credit. No federal or provincial income taxes were owing, thanks mainly to the equivalent-to-married tax credit for the child. See previous footnote regarding payroll taxes.

19. Income was $12,064 in minimum wages supplemented by $4,250 from the Canada Child Tax Benefit and $628 from the federal GST credit. No federal or provincial income taxes were owing. See previous footnote regarding payroll taxes.

20. Income was $18,096 in minimum wages supplemented by $4,250 from the Canada Child Tax Benefit and $628 from the federal GST credit. The family paid $410 in federal income tax but no provincial income tax. CPP contributions were $477 and EI premiums came to $407.

21. Income was $24,128 in minimum wages supplemented by $3,692 from the Canada Child Tax Benefit and $628 from the federal GST credit. The family paid $970 in federal income tax and $343 in provincial income tax. CPP contributions were $737 and EI premiums came to $543.

22. In addition to $12,064 from minimum wage earnings, the single worker received $314 from the federal GST (Goods and Services Tax) credit, but paid $642 in federal income tax and $110 in provincial income tax. Payroll taxes (not included in Statistics Canada' after-tax low income cut-offs) totalled $639 ($368 in Canada Pension Plan contributions and $271 in Employment Insurance premiums).

23. Income was $12,064 in minimum wages, $2,447 from the federal Canada Child Tax Benefit, $424 from the Nova Scotia Child Benefit and $520 from the federal GST credit. No federal or provincial income taxes were owing, thanks mainly to the equivalent-to-married tax credit for the child. See previous footnote concerning payroll taxes.

24. Income was $12,064 in minimum wages supplemented by $4,250 from the Canada Child Tax Benefit, $906 from the Nova Scotia Child Benefit and $628 from the federal GST credit. The family owed neither federal nor provincial income taxes. See previous footnote about payroll taxes.

25. Income was $18,096 in minimum wages supplemented by $4,250 from the Canada Child Tax Benefit, $521 from the Nova Scotia Child Benefit and $628 from the federal GST credit. The family owed $499 in federal income tax but no provincial income tax. CPP contributions were $477 and EI premiums came to $407.

26. Income was $24,128 in minimum wages supplemented by $3,692 from the Canada Child Tax Benefit and $628 from the federal GST credit. The family owed $1,135 in federal income tax and $410 in provincial income tax. CPP contributions were $737 and EI premiums came to $543.

27. In addition to $12,116 from minimum wage earnings, the single worker received $315 from the federal GST (Goods and Services Tax) credit, but paid $681 in federal income tax and $258 in provincial income tax. Payroll taxes (not included in Statistics Canada's after-tax low income cut-offs) came to $643 ($370 in Canada Pension Plan contributions and $273 in Employment Insurance premiums).

28. Income was $12,116 in minimum wages, $2,447 from the federal Canada Child Tax Benefit, $250 from the New Brunswick Child Tax Benefit, $250 from the New Brunswick Working Income Supplement and $520 from the federal GST credit. No federal or provincial income taxes were owing, thanks mainly to the equivalent-to-married tax credit for the child. See previous footnote about payroll taxes.

29. Income was $12,116 in minimum wages supplemented by $4,250 from the Canada Child Tax Benefit, $500 from the New Brunswick Child Tax Benefit, $250 from the New Brunswick Working Income Supplement and $628 from the federal GST credit. Neither federal nor provincial income taxes were owing. See previous footnote about payroll taxes.

30. Income was $18,174 in minimum wages supplemented by $4,250 from the Canada Child Tax Benefit, $500 from the New Brunswick Child Tax Benefit, $250 from the New Brunswick Working Income Supplement and $628 from the federal GST credit. Federal income tax was $511 and provincial income tax came to $198. CPP contributions were $480 and EI premiums amounted to $409.

31. Income was $24,232 in minimum wages supplemented by $3,670 from the Canada Child Tax Benefit, $144 from the New Brunswick Child Tax Benefit, $84 from the New Brunswick Working Income Supplement and $628 from the federal GST credit. The family paid $650 in federal income tax and $393 in provincial income tax. CPP contributions were $741 and EI premiums came to $545.

32. In addition to $14,544 from minimum wage earnings, the single worker received $316 from the federal GST (Goods and Services Tax) credit and $257 from the Quebec Sales Tax Credit, but paid $1,013 in federal income tax and $486 in Quebec income tax. Payroll taxes, not included in Statistics Canada's after-tax low income cut-offs,

amounted to $802 ($475 in Quebec Pension Plan contributions and $327 in Employment Insurance premiums).

33. Income was $14,544 in minimum wages, $2,447 from the federal Canada Child Tax Benefit, $1,925 from Quebec family allowances, $339 from the Parental Wage Assistance Program, $520 from the federal GST credit and $257 from the Quebec Sales Tax Credit. Only $6 in federal income tax was owing, thanks mainly to the equivalent-to-married tax credit for the child. This family paid no Quebec income tax. See previous footnote concerning payroll taxes.

34. Income was $14,544 in minimum wages supplemented by $4,250 from the Canada Child Tax Benefit, $1,250 from Quebec family allowances, $3,131 from the Parental Wage Assistance Program, $628 from the federal GST credit and $308 from the Quebec Sales Tax credit. Just $6 in federal income tax was owed and nothing in Quebec income tax. See previous footnote about payroll taxes.

35. Income was $21,816 in minimum wages supplemented by $4,182 from the Canada Child Tax Benefit, $1,250 from Quebec family allowances, $4 from the Parental Wage Assistance Program (which effectively means that the family likely would not participate in the program, though we include the benefit for this estimate), $628 from the federal GST credit and $308 from the Quebec Sales Tax credit. This family paid $1,013 in federal income tax but no Quebec income tax. QPP contributions were $637 and EI premiums came to $491.

36. Income was $29,088 in minimum wages supplemented by $2,641 from the Canada Child Tax Benefit, $160 from Quebec family allowances, $628 from the federal GST credit and $308 from the Quebec Sales Tax credit. Federal income tax was $2,641 and Quebec income tax amounted to $704. QPP contributions were $950 and EI premiums came to $654.

37. In addition to $14,248 from minimum wage earnings, the single worker received $316 from the federal GST (Goods and Services Tax) credit and $325 in provincial refundable tax credits, but paid $969 in federal income tax and $372 in Ontario income tax. Payroll taxes, not included in Statistics Canada's after-tax low income cut-offs, amounted to $783 ($462 in Canada Pension Plan contributions and $321 in Employment Insurance premiums).

38. Income was $14,248 in minimum wages, $2,447 from the federal Canada Child Tax Benefit, $1,310 from the Ontario Child Care Supplement for Working Families, $520 from the GST credit and $387 from Ontario refundable tax credits. No federal or provincial income tax was owing, thanks mainly to the equivalent-to-married tax credit for the child. See previous footnote concerning payroll taxes.

39. Income was $14,248 in minimum wages supplemented by $4,250 from the Canada Child Tax Benefit, $628 from the federal GST credit and $485 from Ontario refundable tax credits. No federal or Ontario incomes taxes were owing. See previous footnote about payroll taxes.

40. Income was $21,372 in minimum wages supplemented by $4,235 from the Canada Child Tax Benefit, $628 from the federal GST credit and $443 from Ontario refundable tax credits. This family paid $969 in federal income tax but no Ontario income tax. CPP contributions totalled $618 and EI premiums $481.

41. Income was $28,496 in minimum wages supplemented by $2,765 from the Canada Child Tax Benefit, $534 from the federal GST credit and $200 from Ontario refundable tax credits. Federal income tax was $1,937 and Ontario income tax came to $372, while CPP contributions were $924 and EI premiums amounted to $641.

42. In addition to $12,870 from minimum wage earnings, the single worker received $316 from the federal GST (Goods and Services Tax) credit and $608 in provincial refundable tax credits, but paid $762 in federal income tax and $423 in provincial income tax. Payroll taxes, not included in Statistics Canada's after-tax low income cut-offs, amounted to $693 ($403 in Canada Pension Plan contributions and $290 in Employment Insurance premiums).

43. Income was $12,870 in minimum wages, $2,447 from the federal Canada Child Tax Benefit, $120 from the provincial Child Related Income Support Program (CRISP), $520 from the GST credit and $798 from provincial refundable tax credits. No federal or provincial income taxes were owing, thanks mainly to the equivalent-to-married tax credit for the child. See previous footnote concerning payroll taxes.

44. Income was $12,870 in minimum wages supplemented by $4,250 from the Canada Child Tax Benefit, $541 from the provincial Child Related Income Support Program, $628 from the federal GST credit and $848 from provincial refundable tax credits. The family owed neither federal nor Manitoba income taxes. See previous footnote about payroll taxes.

45. Income was $19,305 in minimum wages supplemented by $4,250 from the Canada Child Tax Benefit, $628 from the federal GST credit and $719 from provincial refundable tax credits. The family owed $684 in federal income tax but no Manitoba income tax. CPP contributions totaled $529 and EI premiums were $434.

46. Income was $25,740 in minimum wages supplemented by $3,350 from the Canada Child Tax Benefit, $628 from the federal GST credit and $590 from provincial refundable tax credits. The family paid $1,525 in federal income tax and $423 in provincial income tax, while CPP contributions were $806 and EI premiums came to $579.

47. In addition to $12,480 from minimum wage earnings, the single worker received $316 from the federal GST (Goods and Services Tax) credit and $66 from the Saskatchewan Sales Tax Credit, but paid $704 in federal income tax and $439 in provincial income tax. Payroll taxes, not included in Statistics Canada's after-tax low income cut-offs, amounted to $667 ($386 in Canada Pension Plan contributions and $281 in Employment Insurance premiums).

48. Income was $12,480 in minimum wages, $2,447 from the federal Canada Child Tax Benefit, $389 from the Saskatchewan Child Benefit, $2,428 from the Saskatchewan Employment Supplement, $520 from the federal GST credit and $132 from the Saskatchewan Sales Tax Credit. No federal or provincial income tax was owing, thanks mainly to the equivalent-to-married tax credit for the child. See previous footnote concerning payroll taxes.

49. Income was $12,480 in minimum wages supplemented by $4,250 from the Canada Child Tax Benefit, $985 from the Saskatchewan Child Benefit, $2,870 from the Saskatchewan Employment Supplement, $628 from the federal GST credit and $242 from the Saskatchewan Sales Tax Credit. This family owed neither federal nor provincial income taxes. See previous footnote about payroll taxes.

50. Income was $18,720 in minimum wages supplemented by $4,250 from the Canada Child Tax Benefit, $211 from the Saskatchewan Child Benefit, $1,335 from the Saskatchewan Employment Supplement, $628 from the federal GST credit and $205 from the Saskatchewan Sales Tax Credit. This family paid $595 in federal income tax but no provincial income tax. CPP contributions were $504 and EI premiums $421.

51. Income was $24,960 in minimum wages supplemented by $3,515 from the Canada Child Tax Benefit, $628 from the federal GST credit and $169 from the Saskatchewan Sales Tax Credit. This family paid $704 in federal income tax and $532 in provincial income tax. CPP contributions came to $772 and EI premiums were $562.

52. In addition to $12,272 from minimum wage earnings, the single worker received $316 from the federal GST (Goods and Services Tax) credit, but paid $673 in federal income tax though no Alberta income tax. Payroll taxes, not included in Statistics Canada's after-tax low income cut-offs, amounted to $653 ($377 in Canada Pension Plan contributions and $276 in Employment Insurance premiums).

53. Income was $12,272 in minimum wages, $2,358 from the federal Canada Child Tax Benefit, $462 from the Alberta Family Employment Tax Credit and $520 from the federal refundable GST credit. No federal or provincial income taxes were owing, thanks mainly to the equivalent-to-married tax credit for the child. See previous footnote concerning payroll taxes.

54. Income was $12,272 in minimum wages supplemented by $4,342 from the Canada Child Tax Benefit, $462 from the Alberta Family Employment Tax Credit and $628 from the federal GST credit. No federal or provincial income taxes were owing. See previous footnote about payroll taxes.

55. Income was $18,408 in minimum wages supplemented by $4,342 from the Canada Child Tax Benefit, $953 from the Alberta Family Employment Tax Credit and $628 from the federal GST credit. The family paid $547 in federal income tax but no provincial income tax. CPP contributions came to $491 and EI premiums were $414.

56. Income was $24,544 in minimum wages supplemented by $3,647 from the Canada Child Tax Benefit, $1,000 from the Alberta Family Employment Tax Credit and $628 from the federal GST credit. The family paid $673 in federal income tax but no provincial income tax. CPP contributions were $754 and EI premiums came to $552.

57. In addition to $15,936 from minimum wage earnings, the single worker received $316 from the federal GST (Goods and Services Tax) credit and $31 from the provincial sales tax credit, but paid $1,221 in federal income tax and $514 in provincial income tax. Payroll taxes, not included in Statistics Canada's after-tax low income cut-offs, amounted to $894 ($535 in Canada Pension Plan contributions and $359 in Employment Insurance premiums).

58. Income was $15,936 in minimum wages, $2,447 from the federal Canada Child Tax Benefit, $214 from the BC Family Bonus, $605 from the BC Earned Income Benefit, $520 from the federal GST credit and $31 from the BC sales tax credit. Federal income tax was $214 and provincial income tax was $14. See previous footnote concerning payroll taxes.

59. Income was $15,936 in minimum wages supplemented by $4,250 from the Canada Child Tax Benefit, $623 from the BC Family Bonus, $1,010 from the BC Earned Income Benefit, $628 from the federal GST credit and $100 from the BC sales tax credit. Federal income tax came to $214 and provincial income tax was $14. See previous footnote about payroll taxes.

60. Income was $23,904 in minimum wages supplemented by $3,740 from the Canada Child Tax Benefit, $407 from the BC Earned Income Benefit and $628 from the federal GST credit. Federal income tax came to $1,221 and provincial income tax amounted to $514. CPP contributions were $727 and EI premiums came to $538.

61. Income was $31,872 in minimum wages supplemented by $2,190 from the Canada Child Tax Benefit and $310 from the federal GST credit. Federal income tax was $2,442 and provincial income tax amounted to $1,028. CPP contributions were $1,069 and EI premiums came to $717.

62. Minimum wage earnings of $14,976 were supplemented by $316 from the federal GST credit and $300 from the Yukon Low Income Family Tax Credit. Federal income tax was $1,077 and Yukon income tax came to $496. Payroll taxes totalled $830 ($493 in Canada Pension Plan contributions and $337 in Employment Insurance premiums).

63. Minimum wage earnings of $14,976 were supplemented by $2,447 from the Canada Child Tax Benefit, $300 from the Yukon Child Benefit, $520 from the federal GST credit and $26 from the Yukon Low Income Family Tax Credit.

This family paid $70 in federal income tax, $32 in Yukon income tax, $493 in Canada Pension Plan contributions and $337 in Employment Insurance premiums.

64. Income includes $14,976 from minimum wages, $4,250 from the Canada Child Tax Benefit, $600 from the Yukon Child Benefit, $628 from the federal GST credit and $26 from the Yukon Low Income Family Tax Credit. Federal income tax was $70 and Yukon income tax came to $32. Payroll taxes were $830 — $493 in Canada Pension Plan contributions and $337 in Employment Insurance premiums.

65. Income includes $22,464 from minimum wages, $4,045 from the Canada Child Tax Benefit, $312 from the Yukon Child Benefit, $628 from the federal GST credit and $76 from the Yukon Low Income Family Tax Credit. Federal income tax was $1,077 and Yukon income tax came to $496. Payroll taxes were $1,170 — $665 in Canada Pension Plan contributions and $505 in Employment Insurance premiums.

66. Income includes $29,952 from minimum wages, $2,458 from the Canada Child Tax Benefit and $461 from the federal GST credit. Federal income tax was $2,155 and Yukon income tax came to $991. Payroll taxes were $1,661 — $987 in Canada Pension Plan contributions and $674 in Employment Insurance premiums.

67. Income consists of $13,520 from minimum wage earnings, $316 from the federal refundable GST credit and $211 from the Northwest Territories cost-of-living tax credit. The worker paid $860 in federal and $387 in territorial income tax, as well as $431 in Canada Pension Plan contributions and $304 in Employment Insurance premiums.

68. Minimum wage earnings of $13,520 were supplemented by $2,447 from the federal Canada Child Tax Benefit, $605 from the Northwest Territories Child Tax Benefit, $520 from the federal refundable GST and $211 from the territorial cost-of-living tax credit. The family owed no federal or Northwest Territories income taxes, thanks mainly to the equivalent-to-married credit, but paid $431 in Canada Pension Plan contributions and $304 in Employment Insurance premiums.

69. Income consists of $13,520 in minimum wages, $4,250 from the federal Canada Child Tax Benefit, $1,010 from the Northwest Territories Child Benefit, $628 from the federal GST credit and $211 from the territorial cost-of-living tax credit. The family owed no federal or territorial income taxes, but paid $431 in Canada Pension Plan contributions and $304 in Employment Insurance premiums.

70. Income includes $20,280 from minimum wages, $4,250 from the Canada Child Tax Benefit, $1,010 from the Northwest Territories Child Benefit, $628 from the federal GST credit and $211 from the territorial cost-of-living tax credit. Federal income tax was $834 and Northwest Territories income tax came to $375. Payroll taxes were $1,027 — $571 in Canada Pension Plan contributions and $456 in Employment Insurance premiums.

71. Income includes $27,040 from minimum wages, $3,074 from the Canada Child Tax Benefit, $354 from the Northwest Territories Child Benefit, $607 from the federal GST credit and $422 from the territorial cost-of-living tax credit. Federal income tax was $1,719 and Northwest Territories income tax came to $774. Payroll taxes were $1,470 — $862 in Canada Pension Plan contributions and $608 in Employment Insurance premiums.

72. Minimum wages of $13,520 were augmented by $316 from the federal refundable GST credit and $165 from the Nunavut cost-of-living tax credit. The worker paid $860 in federal income tax, $387 in Nunavut income tax, $431 in Canada Pension Plan contributions and $304 in Employment Insurance premiums.

73. Minimum wages of $13,520 were supplemented by $2,447 from the federal Canada Child Tax Benefit, $605 from the Nunavut Child Benefit, $520 from the federal refundable GST credit and $165 from the Nunavut cost-of-living

tax credit. The family owed no federal or Nunavut income taxes, thanks largely to the equivalent-to-married tax credit, but paid $431 in Canada Pension Plan contributions and $304 in Employment Insurance premiums.

74. Minimum wages of $13,520 were supplemented by $4,250 from the federal Canada Child Tax Benefit, $1,010 from the Nunavut Child Benefit, $628 from the federal refundable GST credit and $165 from the Nunavut cost-of-living tax credit. No federal or territorial income taxes were owing, but payroll taxes came to $735 ($431 in Canada Pension Plan contributions and $304 in Employment Insurance premiums).

75. Income includes $20,280 from minimum wages, $4,250 from the Canada Child Tax Benefit, $1,010 from the Nunavut Child Benefit, $628 from the federal GST credit and $211 from the territorial cost-of-living tax credit. Federal income tax was $834 and Nunavut income tax came to $375. Payroll taxes were $1,027 – $571 in Canada Pension Plan contributions and $456 in Employment Insurance premiums.

76. Income includes $27,040 from minimum wages, $3,074 from the Canada Child Tax Benefit, $354 from the Nunavut Child Benefit, $607 from the federal GST credit and $422 from the territorial cost-of-living tax credit. Federal income tax was $1,719 and Nunavut income tax came to $774. Payroll taxes were $1,470 – $862 in Canada Pension Plan contributions and $608 in Employment Insurance premiums.

77. Data are from *A Comparative Study of Child Benefit Packages in 22 Countries*, led by the Social Policy Research Unit at York University in the UK and sponsored by the UK Department of Social Security and The Treasury. The Caledon Institute of Social Policy is the Canadian investigator in the study.

78. The information in this section comes from the Economic Policy Institute (2002b).

References

Battle, K. and M. Mendelson. (2001). "Benefits for Children: Canada." In K. Battle, M. Mendelson, J. Millar, D. Meyer and P. Whiteford. *Benefits for Children: A Four Country Study.* Ottawa: Caledon Institute of Social Policy and the J. F. Rowntree Foundation.

Battle, K. and S. Torjman. (2002). *Social Policy That Works: An Agenda.* September.

Card. D. and A. Krueger. (1995). *Myth and Measurement: The New Economics of the Minimum Wage.* Princeton, NJ: Princeton University Press.

CAW-Canada. (1998). *Presentation to the Manitoba Minimum Wage Board.* October 20. http://www.caw.ca/whatwedo/pensions&benefits/presentation/index.asp

Department of Finance Canada. (1997). *Working Together Towards a National Child Benefit System in Canada.* Ottawa: Her Majesty the Queen in Right of Canada.

DiNardo, J., N. Fortin and T. Lemieux. (1994). "Labor Market Institutions and the Distribution of Wages, 1973-1992: A Semiparametric Approach." Unpublished paper. Montreal: University of Montreal Department of Economics. (Cited in Card and Krueger).

Department of Labor and Industries, Washington State. *Minimum Wage. Employment Standards.* http://www.lni.wa.gov/scs/workstandards/minwage.htm

Economic Policy Institute. (2002a). *Minimum Wage: Frequently Asked Questions.* http://www.epinet.org/

Economic Policy Institute. (2002b). *Living Wage: Facts at a Glance.* http://www.epinet.org/Issueguides/livingwage/livingwage.html

Federal/provincial/territorial governments. (2002). *The National Child Benefit 2001 Progress Report.* Ottawa: Her Majesty the Queen in Right of Canada.

Goldberg, M. and D. Green. (1999). *Raising the Floor: The Social and Economic Benefits of Minimum Wages in Canada.* Vancouver: Canadian Centre for Policy Alternatives.

Human Resources Development Canada. (2002). *Database on Minimum Wages.* http://labour-travail.hrdc-drhc.gc.ca/psait_spila/lmnec_eslc/eslc/salaire_ minwage/intro/index.cfin.doc

National Council of Welfare. (2002). *Welfare Incomes, 2000 and 2001.* Ottawa: Minister of Public Works and Government Services Canada.

Osberg, L. (1999). "Wages and Unemployment." In K. Battle and S.Torjman eds. *Employment Policy Options.* Ottawa: Caledon Institute of Social Policy.

Schenk, C. (2001). *From Poverty Wages to a Living Wage.* Toronto: Ontario Federation of Labour.

Statistics Canada. (2001). *Income in Canada 1999.* Ottawa: Minister of Industry.

Statistics Canada. (1998). "A New Perspective on Wages." *Labour Force Update.* Vol. 2, No. 3. Ottawa: Minister of Industry, August.

The Economist. (2002). "Debating the minimum wage." February 1.

Williamson, K. (2002). "Welfare groups call for higher minimum wage." *Calgary Herald.* September 12.

SUMMARY OF KEY FINDINGS

Minimum Wages in Canada

dollar value

Contrary to conventional wisdom, minimum wages in Canada are not on a steady decline: The national average minimum wage rose substantially between 1965 and 1976, fell (but not all the way back) in the late 1970s and first half of the 1980s, levelled off in the second half of the 1980s, gradually recovered somewhat in the first part of the 1990s, flattened between 1997 and 1999, and then fell slightly in 2000 and 2001.

The national average minimum wage (expressed in inflation-adjusted 2001 dollars) increased from $5.60 in 1965 to $8.58 in 1976, declined to $5.96 by 1986, rose to $6.98 in 1997 and slipped a bit to $6.76 in 2001. In 2001, the Canadian average minimum wage remained significantly below its 1976 peak – $1.82 an hour less or 21.2 percent smaller in real terms – though it was $1.16 or 20.7 percent higher than in 1965.

The plateau-like pattern of the national average minimum wage over the long term applies generally to almost all provinces and territories: A sharp increase in the value of the minimum wage between 1965 and the peak in the mid-1970s was followed by a similar or smaller decrease until the mid-1980s or early 1990s, then one of three trends throughout the rest of the 1990s and into the first decade of the new century – modest improvements (PEI, Manitoba, Alberta and BC), flattening out (Newfoundland, Nova Scotia, New Brunswick, Saskatchewan and Yukon) or decline (Quebec, Ontario, the Northwest Territories and Nunavut).

Average hourly minimum wages in 2002 ranged widely across Canada, from a low of $5.71 in Newfoundland to $5.85 in Nova Scotia, $5.90 in Alberta, $5.94 in New Brunswick, $6.00 in Prince Edward Island, $6.28 in Saskatchewan, $6.44 in Manitoba, $6.50 in the Northwest Territories and Nunavut, $6.85 in Ontario, $7.05 in Quebec, $7.20 in Yukon and a high of $8.00 in British Columbia.

minimum wage versus average wage

Minimum wages compared to average earnings also vary considerably: They ranged in 2001 from a low of 30.2 percent of average earnings in the Northwest Territories to Nunavut (33.4 percent), Alberta (34.5 percent), Newfoundland (36.4 percent), Yukon (38.4 percent), Ontario (38.5 percent), New Brunswick (39.4 percent), Saskatchewan (40.1 percent), Nova Scotia (40.8 percent), Manitoba (41.8 percent), Prince Edward Island (44.4 percent), Quebec (44.8 percent) and British Columbia (46.2 percent).

At last count (2001), the national average minimum wage was $14,057 – 40.7 percent of the estimated $34,576 in average earnings

The trend in the national average minimum wage expressed as a percentage of earnings is similar to the trend in its dollar value. It rose between 1965 (44.5 percent) and 1976 (50.3 percent), declined slowly until the mid-1980s when it levelled off for the rest of the decade at around 38 percent, increased in the early 1990s (to 41.4 percent in 1997 and 1999) and then slipped to 40.8 percent in 2000 and 40.7 percent in 2001.

Ontario's falling minimum wage

Ontario, with Canada's largest (38.5 percent) share of minimum wage workers, has seen a steady decline in the value of its minimum wage from 1995 through 2002 because the rate has been frozen at $6.85 for seven long years.

In 1995, Ontario had Canada's highest minimum wage – $7.74 expressed in inflation-adjusted 2002 dollars. By 2002, Ontario had slipped from first to fourth place, trailing Quebec ($7.20 as of October, $7.05 annual average), Yukon ($7.20) and British Columbia ($8.00).

In 1995, Ontario's minimum wage amounted to 43.2 percent of its average earnings, ranking the province top in Canada on that measure. By 2001, Ontario's minimum wage had plummeted to 38.5 percent of average earnings, placing the province in sixth-lowest place among the 13 jurisdictions, ahead of only the Northwest Territories, Nunavut, Alberta, Newfoundland and Yukon – and far behind its neighbour Quebec, which took second place with 44.8 percent, and British Columbia at 46.2 percent.

minimum wages versus poverty lines

The national average minimum wage falls considerably below the poverty line in most communities. In 2001, it fell $4,769 below the before-tax low income cut-off for one person in metropolitan centers, $2,026 under for communities with between 100,000 and 499,999 inhabitants, $1,913 beneath the line for small cities between 30,000 and 99,999 and $803 below for communities under 30,000 – though $1,100 above the poverty line for rural areas.

The poverty gap is deeper for families. For a family of two (e.g., a single parent with one child), the national average minimum wage fell $9,474 short of the before-tax low income line for a family of two in metropolitan areas, $6,047 below the line for cities in the 100,000-499,999 category, $5,907 under for communities between 30,000 and 99,999 inhabitants, $4,518 beneath the line for towns under 30,000 and $2,141 under the poverty line for rural areas.

Minimum wages also fall below another definition of poverty – Statistics Canada's after-tax low income cut-offs, which take into account the federal and provincial income taxes that Canadians pay. After-tax income in 2001 from minimum wages and government benefits (e.g., refundable tax credits) for single minimum wage workers fell short of the after-tax poverty line for the largest city in every province, ranging from $3,649 below the line in Alberta to $2,956 in Manitoba, $2,240 in Newfoundland, $2,015 in Ontario, $1,946 in Quebec, $1,618 in New Brunswick, $1,484 in Nova Scotia, $1,391 in Saskatchewan, $1,316 in Prince Edward Island and $1,015 in British Columbia.

For single parents with one child, after-tax minimum wage incomes are below the after-tax poverty line for the largest city in most (seven of the ten) provinces, though the gap is not as deep as for single people and couples with children because single parents pay little or no income tax and receive the federal Canada Child Tax Benefit and, in virtually all provinces and territories (Prince Edward Island excepted), provincial child benefits. Minimum wage after-tax incomes in 2001 were $3,381 below the after-tax low income cut-off for a family of two in the largest cities in Alberta, $2,018 below in Manitoba, $1,287 below in Newfoundland, $720 below in Prince Edward Island, $543 below in Nova Scotia, $415 under the line on New Brunswick and $80 under in Ontario's largest cities.

In only three provinces – Quebec, Saskatchewan and British Columbia – do single parents with one child manage to rise above the poverty line, thanks in large part to relatively generous provincial child benefits and earnings supplements that bolster the incomes of working poor families. Best off are one-parent families earning the minimum wage in Saskatchewan, which in 2001 were $2,398 above the after-tax poverty line, followed by Quebec ($1,033 above the line) and British Columbia ($533 over the line). Another plus for British Columbia families is that their province has Canada's highest minimum wage.

The poverty gap is deep for couples with two children that rely upon one parent's minimum wage, despite supplementary income from child benefits and refundable tax credits, and paying little or no income taxes. The poverty gap in 2001 ranged from a low of $12,213 in Alberta to $11,051 in Manitoba, $10,205 in Ontario, $8,167 in Newfoundland, $7,869 in Prince Edward Island, $7,597 in British Columbia, $7,456 in New Brunswick, $7,353 in Nova Scotia, $5,811 in Quebec and $3,756 in Saskatchewan.

Work pays below the poverty line for two-earner couples in which one parent works full time, all year at the minimum wage and the other combines part-time minimum wage work with caring for the family's two children. Even with the contribution of the lower-earning parent, this family's income still falls considerably below the after-tax poverty line for the largest city in every province. The poverty gap in 2001 ranged from $6,132 below the after-tax line in Alberta's largest cities (Calgary and Edmonton) to $5,699 below in Manitoba, $4,207 under in Ontario, $3,259 under in Newfoundland, $2,971 under in British Columbia, $2,741 under in Quebec, $2,246 under in Prince Edward Island, $2,108 under in New Brunswick, $2,205 under in Nova Scotia and $446 below the line in Saskatchewan's largest cities (Regina and Saskatoon).

Our final example is a two-earner couple with two children in which both parents work full time, year round for the minimum wage. In other words, this assumes the maximum earnings from the minimum wage. The picture improves considerably, since these families manage to place above the after-tax poverty line in seven of the ten provinces, ranging in 2001 from $180 above the line in Quebec to $442 in Newfoundland, $986 in British Columbia, $1,704 in Nova Scotia, $2,326 in Prince Edward Island, $2,516 in New Brunswick and $2,836 in Saskatchewan. On the other hand, families with two full-time minimum wage workers have a modest income indeed – those in Saskatchewan fare best, but are only $2,836 above the poverty line for the largest city. And families in Manitoba, Alberta and Ontario still end up below the poverty line – by $1,556, $771 and $213, respectively.

contribution of child benefits

Improvements in federal and provincial child benefits are contributing substantially to the incomes of minimum wage and other working poor families.

A single parent minimum wage worker with one child age 2 received combined federal-provincial/territorial child benefits in 2001 that ranged from $2,447 in Prince Edward Island to $2,567 in Manitoba, $2,651 in Newfoundland, $2,747 in Yukon, $2,820 in Alberta, $2,871 in Nova Scotia, $2,947 in New Brunswick, $3,052 in the Northwest Territories and Nunavut, $3,266 in British Columbia, $3,757 in Ontario, $4,711 in Quebec and $5,264 in Saskatchewan. As a percentage of disposable income, child benefits for these families ranged from 15.9 percent in Yukon to 16.0 percent in Manitoba, 17.0 percent in Prince Edward Island, 17.5 percent in British Columbia, 18.4 percent in the Northwest Territories, 18.5 percent in Nunavut, 18.8 percent in Newfoundland, 18.9 percent in Alberta, 19.4 percent in Nova Scotia, 19.7 percent in New Brunswick, 20.7 percent in Ontario, 24.5 percent in Quebec and a high of 29.7 percent in Saskatchewan.

For a minimum wage one-earner couple with two children, combined federal-provincial/territorial child benefits ranged from $4,250 in Prince Edward Island and Ontario to $4,519 in Manitoba, $4,766 in Newfoundland, Manitoba, $4,804 in Alberta, $4,850 in Yukon, $5,000 in New Brunswick, $5,156 in Nova Scotia, $5,260 in the Northwest Territories and Nunavut, $5,883 in British Columbia, $8,105 in Saskatchewan and a high of $8,631 in Quebec. As a percentage of disposable income, child benefits for these families varied from 22.5 percent in Ontario to 24.8 percent in Yukon, 24.9 percent in Manitoba, 26.1 percent in Prince Edward Island, 27.5 percent in British Columbia, 27.9 percent in the Northwest Territories and Nunavut, 28.2 percent in Alberta, 29.0 percent in Newfoundland, 29.2 percent in New Brunswick, 30.0 percent in Nova Scotia, 37.0 percent in Quebec and a high of 39.0 percent in Saskatchewan.

Combined federal-provincial/territorial child benefits for a two-earner low-income couple (earning 1.5 times the minimum wage) with two children went from $4,147 in British Columbia to $4,235 in Ontario, $4,250 in Prince Edward Island and Manitoba, $4,357 in Yukon, $4,681 in Newfoundland, $4,771 in Nova Scotia, $5,000 in New Brunswick, $5,260 in the Northwest Territories and Nunavut, $5,295 in Alberta, $5,436 in Quebec and a high of $5,796 in Saskatchewan. Child benefits for these families varied from

16.1 percent of disposable income in British Columbia to 17.2 percent in Ontario, 17.6 percent in Yukon, 18.3 percent in Manitoba, 19.6 percent in Prince Edward Island, 20.9 percent in Quebec, 21.6 percent in Alberta, 21.8 percent in the Northwest Territories and Nunavut, 22.2 percent in Newfoundland, 22.5 percent in New Brunswick, 23.1 percent in Alberta and a high of 24.3 percent in Saskatchewan.

For a two-earner family with two children in which both parents work full time, year round for the minimum wage, total federal-provincial/territorial child benefits in 2001 were $2,190 in British Columbia, $2,458 in Yukon, $2,765 in Ontario, $2,641 in Quebec, $3,350 in Manitoba, $3,074 in the Northwest Territories and Nunavut, $3,515 in Saskatchewan, $3,692 in Prince Edward Island and Nova Scotia, $3,670 in New Brunswick, $3,956 in Newfoundland and a high of $3,647 in Alberta. Child benefits ranged from 7.5 percent of disposable income in British Columbia to 8.8 percent in Yukon, 9.8 percent in Quebec and Ontario, 12.4 percent in Manitoba, 12.5 percent in the Northwest Territories and Nunavut, 13.2 percent in Saskatchewan, 14.3 percent in Prince Edward Island, 14.4 percent in Nova Scotia, 14.7 percent in New Brunswick, 16.2 percent in Newfoundland and 16.7 percent in Alberta.

minimum wages versus welfare

A worker earning the minimum wage cannot provide a living wage for a family, and both parents must work to earn more than welfare. Even if single, minimum wage workers must struggle to get by. However, welfare benefits for employable single people are so low that even the minimum wage – while anything but generous – offers more.

In every province and territory in Canada, single people are better off working for the minimum wage (even after subtracting income and payroll taxes) than on welfare. The 'minimum wage advantage' over welfare ranged in 2001 from just $852 in Yukon – which pays relatively high minimum wages but even higher welfare benefits (the highest in Canada) – to $7,475 in New Brunswick, which has relatively low minimum wages but even lower welfare benefits. In between these extremes, the minimum wage advantage amounted to $1,555 in Nunavut, $3,091 in the Northwest Territories, $5,074 in Saskatchewan, $5,107 in Prince Edward Island, $5,937 in Ontario, $6,170 in Nova Scotia, $6,232 in Alberta, $6,357 in Manitoba, $6,401 in Quebec, $6,996 in Newfoundland and $7,198 in British Columbia.

Welfare pays benefits for other family members (including children), whereas minimum wages do not adjust for family size. However, minimum wage income still exceeds welfare income in nine jurisdictions for a single parent with a child age 2: $1,861 in Prince Edward Island, $2,051 in New Brunswick, $2,565 in Nova Scotia, $3,339 in Alberta, $3,731 in Manitoba, $4,301 in Ontario, $4,562 in British Columbia, $5,361 in Saskatchewan and $5,905 in Quebec. But in four of the 13 jurisdictions – Nunavut, the Northwest Territories, Yukon and Newfoundland — a single mother with a young child gets more from welfare than from working for minimum wage: $11,735 more in Nunavut, $4,223 more in the Northwest Territories, $2,107 more in Yukon and $558 more in Newfoundland.

For a one-earner couple with two children aged 10 and 15, in only six of the 13 jurisdictions – Manitoba, Ontario, New Brunswick, Saskatchewan, British Columbia and Quebec – could a one-earner couple with two children get more income from the minimum wage than welfare, and in most cases the minimum wage advantage is modest – $447 in Manitoba, $598 in Ontario, $895 in New Brunswick, $2,577 in Saskatchewan, $3,013 in British Columbia and $6,384 in Quebec. In four provinces welfare paid only a few thousand dollars more than minimum wage work – $1,039 in Newfoundland, $1,067 in Nova Scotia, $1,345 in Alberta and $3,097 in Prince Edward Island. In the three territories, the 'welfare advantage' is extreme – $8,117 in Yukon, $9,015 in the Northwest Territories and $15,607 in Nunavut.

Our fourth family type is a two-earner couple with two children 10 and 15 in which one parent works full time, all year for minimum wage while the other parent works part-time (half the annual maximum) for minimum wage. These families fare better than those on welfare in all ten provinces, though the minimum wage advantage varies greatly from one province to another – ranging from just $2,281 in Prince Edward Island to a substantial $9,128 in Quebec, which has both a higher minimum wage than PEI (the Quebec family earns $21,816 as opposed to the PEI family's $18,096) and pays $1,254 in provincial family allowances whereas PEI has no provincial child benefit. Despite the fact that the territories' minimum wages are on the higher end of the scale (family earnings from 1.5 minimum wages come to $22,464 in Yukon and $20,280 in the Northwest Territories and Nunavut), their welfare rates are relatively high ($27,664 in Yukon, $27,899 in the Northwest Territories and $34,445 in Nunavut). So welfare still pays better than minimum wages in the three territories – $10,348 more in Nunavut, $3,756 in the Northwest Territories and $2,882 in Yukon.

Our fifth and final family type is a two-earner couple with two children 10 and 15 in which both parents work full time, all year for the minimum wage. The minimum wage advantage is substantial in all ten provinces, ranging from $6,457 in Prince Edward Island to $6,970 in Newfoundland, $7,349 in Nova Scotia, $8,492 in Saskatchewan, $9,250 in Manitoba, $9,444 in Alberta, $9,790 in Ontario, $10,224 in New Brunswick, $10,704 in British Columbia and a high of $11,573 in Quebec. However, two-minimum wage families in Yukon and the Northwest Territories earn about as much from working full-time for the minimum wage as they would get from welfare; minimum wages pay $400 more than welfare in Yukon and $366 less than welfare in the Northwest Territories. In Nunavut, a family with two children would get $7,003 more from welfare than if both parents worked full-time for the minimum wage.

Canada's minimum wages compared to other countries

Canadian minimum wages are comparable – indeed, in most provinces and territories lower – than US minimum wages and are relatively low when compared to other advanced industrialized nations.

In 2002, nine Canadian jurisdictions – Newfoundland ($5.71 annual hourly average), Nova Scotia ($5.85), Alberta ($5.90), New Brunswick ($5.94), Prince Edward Island ($6.00), Saskatchewan ($6.28),

Manitoba ($6.44), the Northwest Territories and Nunavut ($6.50 each) – were below the lowest US rate of $6.54 (i.e., the federal minimum wage and the rate in 42 states, districts and other jurisdictions) as expressed in 'purchasing power parity' Canadian dollars.

The remaining four Canadian jurisdictions rank in the upper quarter of the minimum wage spectrum, though Ontario ($6.85) is just above the $6.54 US federal and majority state minimum wage rate and Quebec ($7.05) is only 51 cents higher. Yukon ($7.20) ranks just a tick above neighbouring Alaska ($7.18). Only British Columbia ($8.00) ranks in the top ten, though below Oregon ($8.26), Connecticut ($8.51), Washington ($8.53) and California and Massachusetts ($8.57 each).

Canada ranks low internationally when its minimum wage is compared to average earnings. Our national average minimum wage amounted to 34 percent of the estimated average earnings of full-year full-time workers in 2001. Of 17 advanced industrialized nations, Canada came fourth-lowest, ahead of the UK, Spain and Japan. Canada even placed lower than the US, whose minimum wage represents 37 percent of average full-time full-year earnings.

Minimum Wage Workers in Canada

incidence and share of minimum wage workers

In 2000, an estimated 580,000 workers – 4.6 percent of the total 12.5 million employees – worked for minimum wages in the ten provinces (data are not available for Yukon, the Northwest Territories and Nunavut).

The 'incidence' of minimum wage workers means the percentage of all employees working for minimum wage. Newfoundland has the highest incidence of minimum wage workers – 8.7 percent of its employees were at the bottom of the province's wage ladder – followed by New Brunswick (6.0 percent), Saskatchewan (5.9 percent), Quebec (5.4 percent), Manitoba (5.2 percent), Nova Scotia (5.0 percent), British Columbia (4.6 percent), Ontario (4.5 percent), Prince Edward Island (3.6 percent) and, last, Alberta (just 2.0 percent).

The 'share' of minimum wage workers means each province's percentage of Canada's minimum wage workforce. Ontario had 38.5 percent of all minimum wage earners in 2000, followed by Quebec at 27.4 percent and British Columbia at 12.5 percent. Thus the large majority of minimum wage employees – 78.4 percent or close to eight in ten – worked in Ontario, Quebec or British Columbia, the three largest provinces that together had three-quarters (75.8 percent) of all employees in 2000.

gender

Women run a higher risk of working for minimum wages than men, and women also constitute the majority of the minimum wage workforce. In 2000, 6.0 percent of female employees worked for minimum wages compared to only 3.4 percent of male workers. Of the total 580,000 minimum wage workforce, 360,400 – 62.1 percent – were women and 219,600 – 37.9 percent – were men.

Women are significantly overrepresented in the minimum wage workforce. They made up 62.1 percent of minimum wage workers but only 48.1 percent of all employees in 2000. Men are underrepresented, constituting only 37.9 percent of minimum wage workers but 51.9 percent of all employees.

The gender bias among minimum wage workers holds when we control for major age categories. While younger workers of both sexes run a higher risk of working for minimum wages, women still fare worse than men within each age category.

The majority of minimum wage workers are adults, not teenagers. More than half (52.9 percent) of minimum wage workers are adults. Adult women are the largest group, at 199,600 (34.4 percent of the total), followed by teenage girls (160,800 or 27.7 percent), teenage boys (112,200 or 19.3 percent) and adult men (107,300 or 18.5 percent).

age

The odds of working for minimum wage are highest for young employees (43.7 percent for those aged 15-16) and decrease sharply and steadily as workers get older (29.9 percent for the 17-19 age group, 7.0 percent for 20-24, 2.6 percent for 25-29, 2.1 percent for 30-34, 1.8 percent for 35-44 and 1.7 percent for 45-54) though the risk begins to rise again among those 55 and older (to 2.6 percent for those 55-64 and 8.2 percent for the 65-and-over age category).

Teenagers (aged 15-19) constitute 47.1 percent of minimum wage workers. Prime age workers (aged 25-44) make up 23.2 percent, followed by young adults (aged 20-24) at 16.4 percent and older workers (45 and older) at 13.4 percent. While teenagers are the largest of the four groups, nonetheless adults aged 20 and older form the majority (52.9 percent) of minimum wage workers.

education

Education and risk of minimum wage work are not smoothly correlated: Workers in the lowest educational group (elementary education only) are less likely to work for minimum wage (7.7 percent do) than those with some high school (13.4 percent), while those with some postsecondary education run a higher risk (7.1 percent) than high school graduates (4.4 percent). The likely reason is that young people working at part-time or seasonal (i.e., summer) jobs – typically paying the minimum or a low wage – figure prominently in the 'some high school' and 'some postsecondary education' categories; they are still at high school, community college or university, whereas workers in the other educational categories have completed their education.

Higher education brings the lowest risk of minimum wage employment – just 2.2 percent for workers with a postsecondary certificate or diploma (e.g., from a community college or vocational institute) and a mere 1.3 percent for those with a university degree.

The largest group of minimum wage workers (37.8 percent) are those with some high school education, followed by high school graduates (20.2 percent), those with some postsecondary education (15.7 percent), postsecondary graduates (15.4 percent), those with university degrees (5.5 percent) and workers with only 0-8 years of education (5.4 percent). Many minimum wage workers are students (high school and postsecondary) pursuing their education. A sizeable group of minimum wage workers (36.6 percent or more than a third) have some form of postsecondary education.

full-time and part-time work

Part-time workers are at a much greater risk of working for minimum wage (15.3 percent) than those employed full time (just 2.4 percent).

Women who work part time are less likely than men who work part time to earn minimum wages (13.7 and 19.2 percent, respectively), whereas women employed full time run a higher risk of working for minimum wages than their male counterparts (3.3 and 1.6 percent, respectively).

The majority of minimum wage workers (58.1 percent) work part time, while 41.9 percent are employed full time. Women make up the majority of minimum wage employees working both full time (60.5 percent are women) and part time (63.3 percent are women).

family status

The largest group of minimum wage workers – 60.2 percent or 349,300 out of the total 580,000 – are older children living with their parents (or relatives with relatives, as in the case of a niece or nephew living with an aunt and uncle, or grandchildren with grandparents). More than half (57.0 percent) are in school and working part time or part year (e.g., in summer).

Next are members of couples (married or living together), who number 144,800 or 25.0 percent of all minimum wage workers in Canada. In most cases (108,000 or 74.6 percent of this category), the minimum wage worker's spouse is employed, usually at more than the minimum wage.

An estimated 62,000 or 10.7 percent of minimum wage workers are what Statistics Canada calls 'unattached individuals' (i.e., living alone or with non-relatives).

Finally, 23,800 or just 4.1 percent of the minimum wage workforce are heads of families with no spouse present. Most of them (21,600) are single parents with children under 18.

industry

The top five industries in terms of their incidence of minimum wage workers are accommodation and food services (19.4 percent of their employees work for minimum wage), agriculture (15.4 percent), trade (8.8 percent), other services (7.7 percent) and information, culture and recreation (6.2 percent).

Next comes management, administrative and other support (5.1 percent), finance, insurance, real estate and leasing (2.5 percent), transportation and warehousing (2.2 percent) and health care and social assistance (2.0 percent).

Industries with relatively few jobs that pay minimum wage include educational services (1.7 percent), forestry, fishing, mining, oil and gas (1.5 percent), manufacturing (1.4 percent), public administration (1.1 percent), professional, scientific and technical services (1.0 percent) and construction (1.0 percent).

The picture is somewhat different in terms of the distribution of minimum wage workers among the various industries. The two largest minimum wage employers are trade (with 30.2 percent of all minimum wage workers) and accommodation and food services (28.9 percent) – for a combined total of 59.1 percent of the minimum wage workforce. Next come other services (6.1 percent), information, culture and recreation (6.1 percent), manufacturing (5.2 percent), health care and social assistance (4.5 percent) and the remaining industry categories.

	minimum wage workers (no.)	all employees (no.)	incidence of minimum wage workers (%)	distribution of minimum wage workers (%)	distribution of all employees (%)
NEWFOUNDLAND	15,500	178,300	8.7	100.0	100.0
Gender and age					
total both sexes	15,500	178,300	8.7	100.0	100.0
15-19	4,300	7,800	55.1	27.7	4.4
20-24	5,000	18,800	26.6	32.3	10.5
15-24	9,200	26,500	34.7	59.4	14.9
25-44	4,100	96,100	4.3	26.5	53.9
45 or older	2,200	55,700	3.9	14.2	31.2
total females	10,600	87,400	12.1	68.4	49.0
15-19	2,500	4,100	61.0	16.1	2.3
20-24	3,200	9,400	34.0	20.6	5.3
15-24	5,700	13,500	42.2	36.8	7.6
25-44	3,100	47,900	6.5	20.0	26.9
45 or older	1,800	25,900	6.9	11.6	14.5
total males	4,900	91,000	5.4	31.6	51.0
15-19	1,800	3,700	48.6	11.6	2.1
20-24	1,800	9,400	19.1	11.6	5.3
15-24	3,500	13,000	26.9	22.6	7.3
25-44	1,000	48,100	2.1	6.5	27.0
45 or older	300	29,800	1.0	1.9	16.7
Education					
all education levels	15,500	178,300	8.7	100.0	100.0
0 - 8 years	700	7,300	9.6	4.5	4.1
some high school	4,000	22,500	17.8	25.8	12.6
high school graduate	3,200	28,100	11.4	20.6	15.8
some post-secondary	3,000	16,000	18.8	19.4	9.0
post-secondary certificate or diploma	4,100	79,300	5.2	26.5	44.5
university degree	500	25,100	2.0	3.2	14.1
Full-time or part-time work					
total both sexes	15,500	178,300	8.7	100.0	100.0
full-time	9,000	151,900	5.9	58.1	85.2
part-time	6,500	26,500	24.5	41.9	14.9
total females	10,600	87,400	12.1	68.4	49.0
full-time	6,100	68,000	9.0	39.4	38.1
part-time	4,600	19,300	23.8	29.7	10.8
total males	4,900	91,000	5.4	31.6	51.0
full-time	2,900	83,900	3.5	18.7	47.1
part-time	2,000	7,100	28.2	12.9	4.0

	minimum wage workers (no.)	all employees (no.)	incidence of minimum wage workers (%)	distribution of minimum wage workers (%)	distribution of all employees (%)
Family status					
member of couple	5,600	125,900	4.4	36.1	70.6
spouse not employed	2,000	38,000	5.3	12.9	21.3
spouse unemployed	800	11,200	7.1	5.2	6.3
spouse not in labour force	1,200	26,800	4.5	7.7	15.0
spouse employed	3,600	87,900	4.1	23.2	49.3
earns minimum wage	400	3,200	12.5	2.6	1.8
earns more than minimum wage	2,800	75,300	3.7	18.1	42.2
spouse self-employed	400	9,400	4.3	2.6	5.3
head of family	400	6,600	6.1	2.6	3.7
youngest child under 18	200	4,800	4.2	1.3	2.7
no children or youngest child over 18	200	1,800	11.1	1.3	1.0
son or daughter	8,100	32,800	24.7	52.3	18.4
15-19 in school	2,000	3,500	57.1	12.9	2.0
15-19 not in school	2,100	4,000	52.5	13.5	2.2
20-24 in school	800	2,400	33.3	5.2	1.3
20-24 not in school	2,500	10,100	24.8	16.1	5.7
25 or older in school	0	700	0.0	0.0	0.4
25 or older not in school	700	12,100	5.8	4.5	6.8
unattached individual	1,400	12,700	11.0	9.0	7.1
living alone	800	8,100	9.9	5.2	4.5
15-24	400	900	44.4	2.6	0.5
25-54	200	6,200	3.2	1.3	3.5
55 or older	200	1,000	20.0	1.3	0.6
living with non-relatives	500	4,600	10.9	3.2	2.6
15-24	500	1,800	27.8	3.2	1.0
25-54	2,600	0.0	0.0		1.5
55 or older	0	0	0.0	0.0	0.0
Industry					
total	15,500	178,300	8.7	100.0	100.0
agriculture	900		0.5		
forestry, fishing, mining, oil and gas	8,600		4.8		
utilities	1,800		1.0		
construction	9,100		5.1		
manufacturing	15,400		8.6		
trade	5,900	32,100	18.4	38.1	18.0
transportation and warehousing	10,000		5.6		
finance, insurance, real estate & leasing	6,400		3.6		
professional, scientific and technical services	5,300		3.0		

	minimum wage workers (no.)	all employees (no.)	incidence of minimum wage workers (%)	distribution of minimum wage workers (%)	distribution of all employees (%)
management, administrative and other support	600	4,200	14.3	3.9	2.4
educational services		15,800			8.9
health care and social assistance	1,100	27,600	4.0	7.1	15.5
information, culture and recreation	800	6,300	12.7	5.2	3.5
accommodation and food services	3,600	10,900	33.0	23.2	6.1
other services	1,500	7,800	19.2	9.7	4.4
public administration		16,100			9.0

	minimum wage workers (no.)	all employees (no.)	incidence of minimum wage workers (%)	distribution minimum wage workers (%)	distribution all employees (%)
PRINCE EDWARD ISLAND	1,900	53,100	3.6	100.0	100.0
Gender and age					
total both sexes	1,900	53,100	3.6	100.0	100.0
15-19	1,200	4,700	25.5	63.2	8.9
20-24	300	6,300	4.8	15.8	11.9
15-24	1,600	11,000	14.5	84.2	20.7
25-44	300	26,300	1.1	15.8	49.5
45 or older	100	15,800	0.6	5.3	29.8
total females	1,000	27,700	3.6	52.6	52.2
15-19	500	2,300	21.7	26.3	4.3
20-24	300	3,200	9.4	15.8	6.0
15-24	800	5,400	14.8	42.1	10.2
25-44	200	14,000	1.4	10.5	26.4
45 or older	100	8,300	1.2	5.3	15.6
total males	900	25,400	3.5	47.4	47.8
15-19	700	2,400	29.2	36.8	4.5
20-24		3,100			5.8
15-24	800	5,500	14.5	42.1	10.4
25-44	100	12,300	0.8	5.3	23.2
45 or older	0	7,600	0.0	0.0	14.3
Education					
all education levels	1,900	53,100	3.6	100.0	100.0
0 - 8 years		2,300			4.3
some high school	100	9,400	1.1	5.3	17.7
high school graduate	400	10,000	4.0	21.1	18.8
some post-secondary	300	4,700	6.4	15.8	8.9
post-secondary certificate or diploma	200	19,200	1.0	10.5	36.2
university degree		7,600			14.3
Full-time or part-time work					
total both sexes	1,900	53,100	3.6	100.0	100.0
full-time	800	44,100	1.8	42.1	83.1
part-time	1,200	9,000	13.3	63.2	16.9
total females	1,000	27,700	3.6	52.6	52.2
full-time	500	21,800	2.3	26.3	41.1
part-time	600	6,000	10.0	31.6	11.3
total males	900	25,400	3.5	47.4	47.8
full-time	300	22,300	1.3	15.8	42.0
part-time	600	3,000	20.0	31.6	5.6

	minimum wage workers (no.)	all employees (no.)	incidence of minimum wage workers (%)	distribution of minimum wage workers (%)	distribution of all employees (%)
Family status					
member of couple	300	33,400	0.9	15.8	62.9
spouse not employed	100	7,000	1.4	5.3	13.2
spouse unemployed	0	2,400		0.0	4.5
spouse not in labour force	100	4,600	2.2	5.3	8.7
spouse employed	200	26,300	0.8	10.5	49.5
earns minimum wage	0	200		0.0	0.4
earns more than minimum wage	200	21,900	0.9	10.5	41.2
spouse self-employed	100	4,300	2.3	5.3	8.1
head of family		2,900			5.5
youngest child under 18		2,500			4.7
no children or youngest child over 18		400			0.8
son or daughter	1,400	11,000	12.7	73.7	20.7
15-19 in school	800	2,200	36.4	42.1	4.1
15-19 not in school	400	2,000	20.0	21.1	3.8
20-24 in school		600			1.1
20-24 not in school	200	3,100	6.5	10.5	5.8
25 or older in school		0			0.0
25 or older not in school		300			0.6
unattached individual					
living alone	200	5,800	3.4	10.5	10.9
15-24	100	3,400	2.9	5.3	6.4
15-24		400			0.8
25-54		2,600			4.9
55 or older		400			0.8
living with non-relatives	100	2,400	4.2	5.3	4.5
15-24	100	1,100	9.1	5.3	2.1
25-54		1,200			2.3
55 or older					
Industry					
total	1,900	53,100	3.6	100.0	100.0
agriculture		2,500			4.7
forestry, fishing, mining, oil and gas utilities		800			
construction		3,000			5.6
manufacturing		6,000			11.3
trade	600	8,900	6.7	31.6	16.8
transportation and warehousing		1,900			3.6
finance, insurance, real estate & leasing		1,900			3.6
professional, scientific and technical services management, administrative and other support		1,500			2.8
		1,600			3.0

	minimum wage workers (no.)	all employees (no.)	incidence of minimum wage workers (%)	distribution of minimum wage workers (%)	distribution of all employees (%)
educational services		4,100			7.7
health care and social assistance		6,500			12.2
information, culture and recreation		2,200			4.1
accommodation and food services	300	4,500	6.7	15.8	8.5
other services		2,100			4.0
public administration		5,600			10.5

	minimum wage workers (no.)	all employees (no.)	incidence of minimum wage workers (%)	distribution of minimum wage workers (%)	distribution of all employees (%)
NOVA SCOTIA	17,900	361,100	5.0	100.0	100.0
Gender and age					
total both sexes	17,900	361,100	5.0	100.0	100.0
15-19	7,700	21,700	35.5	43.0	6.0
20-24	3,400	40,400	8.4	19.0	11.2
15-24	11,200	62,100	18.0	62.6	17.2
25-44	4,100	190,800	2.1	22.9	52.8
45 or older	2,700	108,300	2.5	15.1	30.0
total females	11,200	178,100	6.3	62.6	49.3
15-19	4,600	11,600	39.7	25.7	3.2
20-24	1,600	19,600	8.2	8.9	5.4
15-24	6,200	31,100	19.9	34.6	8.6
25-44	3,000	95,600	3.1	16.8	26.5
45 or older	2,000	51,300	3.9	11.2	14.2
total males	6,700	183,000	3.7	37.4	50.7
15-19	3,100	10,100	30.7	17.3	2.8
20-24	1,800	20,800	8.7	10.1	5.8
15-24	5,000	31,000	16.1	27.9	8.6
25-44	1,100	95,100	1.2	6.1	26.3
45 or older	700	56,900	1.2	3.9	15.8
Education					
all education levels	17,900	361,100	5.0	100.0	100.0
0 - 8 years	500	10,000	5.0	2.8	2.8
some high school	6,800	52,900	12.9	38.0	14.6
high school graduate	3,500	60,800	5.8	19.6	16.8
some post-secondary	2,900	35,000	8.3	16.2	9.7
post-secondary certificate or diploma	3,100	135,900	2.3	17.3	37.6
university degree	1,100	66,600	1.7	6.1	18.4
Full-time or part-time work					
total both sexes	17,900	361,100	5.0	100.0	100.0
full-time	7,700	295,400	2.6	42.8	81.8
part-time	10,300	65,700	15.7	57.2	18.2
total females	11,200	178,100	6.3	62.6	49.3
full-time	4,500	131,300	3.4	25.1	36.4
part-time	6,700	46,800	14.3	37.4	13.0
total males	6,700	183,000	3.7	37.4	50.7
full-time	3,100	164,100	1.9	17.3	45.4
part-time	3,600	19,000	18.9	20.1	5.3

	minimum wage workers (no.)	all employees (no.)	incidence of minimum wage workers (%)	distribution of minimum wage workers (%)	distribution of all employees (%)
Family status					
member of couple	4,800	228,500	2.1	26.8	63.3
spouse not employed	1,200	53,000	2.3	6.7	14.7
spouse unemployed	300	11,600	2.6	1.7	3.2
spouse not in labour force	900	41,400	2.2	5.0	11.5
spouse employed	3,600	175,500	2.1	20.1	48.6
earns minimum wage	200	9,500	2.1	1.1	2.6
earns more than minimum wage	3,000	148,900	2.0	16.8	41.2
spouse self-employed	400	17,100	2.3	2.2	4.7
head of family	500	17,100	2.9	2.8	4.7
youngest child under 18	400	14,200	2.8	2.2	3.9
no children or youngest child over 18	100	2,900	3.4	0.6	0.8
son or daughter	10,800	66,100	16.3	60.3	18.3
15-19 in school	4,800	11,400	42.1	26.8	3.2
15-19 not in school	2,600	9,100	28.6	14.5	2.5
20-24 in school	1,000	6,200	16.1	5.6	1.7
20-24 not in school	1,300	17,200	7.6	7.3	4.8
25 or older in school	100	800	12.5	0.6	0.2
25 or older not in school	800	21,400	3.7	4.5	5.9
unattached individual	1,800	46,500	3.9	10.1	12.9
living alone	900	28,800	3.1	5.0	8.0
15-24	100	2,800	3.6	0.6	0.8
25-54	600	22,200	2.7	3.4	6.1
55 or older	200	3,800	5.3	1.1	1.1
living with non-relatives	900	17,800	5.1	5.0	4.9
15-24	600	6,300	9.5	3.4	1.7
25-54	300	11,100	2.7	1.7	3.1
55 or older	0	0		0.0	0.0
Industry					
total	17,900	361,100	5.0	100.0	100.0
agriculture		4,400			1.2
forestry, fishing, mining, oil and gas		9,400			2.6
utilities		2,800			0.8
construction		18,400			5.1
manufacturing	600	41,500	1.4	3.4	11.5
trade	6,200	67,400	9.2	34.6	18.7
transportation and warehousing		17,500			4.8
finance, insurance, real estate and leasing	1100	18,900	5.8	6.1	5.2
professional, scientific and technical services		1,220			0.3

	minimum wage workers (no.)	all employees (no.)	incidence of minimum wage workers (%)	distribution of minimum wage workers (%)	distribution of all employees (%)
management, administrative and other support	900	13,900	6.5	5.0	3.8
educational services	700	31,100	2.3	3.9	8.6
health care and social assistance	800	45,500	1.8	4.5	12.6
information, culture and recreation	900	14,600	6.2	5.0	4.0
accommodation and food services	4,000	24,600	16.3	22.3	6.8
other services	1,000	13,500	8.1	6.1	3.7
public administration		25,400			7.0

	minimum wage workers (no.)	all employees (no.)	incidence of minimum wage workers (%)	distribution of minimum wage workers (%)	distribution of all employees (%)
NEW BRUNSWICK	17,500	293,100	6.0	100.0	100.0
Gender and age					
total both sexes	17,500	293,100	6.0	100.0	100.0
15-19	7,800	19,200	40.6	44.6	6.6
20-24	2,800	30,700	9.1	16.0	10.5
15-24	10,700	49,900	21.4	61.1	17.0
25-44	4,800	155,500	3.1	27.4	53.1
45 or older	2,100	87,700	2.4	12.0	29.9
total females	11,800	141,300	8.4	67.4	48.2
15-19	4,800	9,900	48.5	27.4	3.4
20-24	1,700	15,300	11.1	9.7	5.2
15-24	6,500	25,200	25.8	37.1	8.6
25-44	3,800	77,100	4.9	21.7	26.3
45 or older	1,600	39,000	4.1	9.1	13.3
total males	5,700	151,800	3.8	32.6	51.8
15-19	3,000	9,300	32.3	17.1	3.2
20-24	1,200	15,400	7.8	6.9	5.3
15-24	4,200	24,700	17.0	24.0	8.4
25-44	1,000	78,500	1.3	5.7	26.8
45 or older	500	48,700	1.0	2.9	16.6
Education					
all education levels	17,500	293,100	6.0	100.0	100.0
0 - 8 years	700	13,500	5.2	4.0	4.6
some high school	7,600	40,800	18.6	43.4	13.9
high school graduate	4,600	68,300	6.7	26.3	23.3
some post-secondary	1,600	23,100	6.9	9.1	7.9
post-secondary certificate or diploma	2,300	102,200	2.3	13.1	34.9
university degree	600	45,200	1.3	3.4	15.4
Full-time or part-time work					
total both sexes	17,500	293,100	6.0	100.0	100.0
full-time	8,300	250,900	3.3	47.4	85.6
part-time	9,200	42,200	21.8	52.6	14.4
total females	11,800	141,300	8.4	67.4	48.2
full-time	5,400	109,900	4.9	30.9	37.5
part-time	6,400	31,400	20.4	36.6	10.7
total males	5,700	151,800	3.8	32.6	51.8
full-time	2,900	141,000	2.1	16.6	48.1
part-time	2,700	10,800	25.0	15.4	3.7

	minimum wage workers (no.)	all employees (no.)	incidence of minimum wage workers (%)	distribution of minimum wage workers (%)	distribution of all employees (%)
Family status					
member of couple	5,300	191,300	2.8	30.6	65.3
spouse not employed	1,200	44,100	2.7	6.9	15.0
spouse unemployed	400	10,600	3.8	2.3	3.6
spouse not in labour force	700	33,500	2.1	4.0	11.4
spouse employed	4,100	147,200	2.8	23.7	50.2
earns minimum wage	200	3,800	5.3	1.2	1.3
earns more than minimum wage	3,600	127,100	2.8	20.8	43.4
spouse self-employed	300	16,300	1.8	1.7	5.6
head of family	500	13,500	3.7	2.9	4.6
youngest child under 18	500	11,600	4.3	2.9	4.0
no children or youngest child over 18	0	1,800		0.0	0.6
son or daughter	10,300	53,700	19.2	59.5	18.3
15-19 in school	4,700	9,600	49.0	27.2	3.3
15-19 not in school	2,800	8,700	32.2	16.2	3.0
20-24 in school	300	2,300	13.0	1.7	0.8
20-24 not in school	1,600	14,500	11.0	9.2	4.9
25 or older in school	0	0			
25 or older not in school	800	18,300	4.4	4.6	6.2
unattached individual	1,200	32,800	3.7	6.9	11.2
living alone	600	19,100	3.1	3.5	6.5
15-24	200	1,900	10.5	1.2	0.6
25-54	300	14,800	2.0	1.7	5.0
55 or older	100	2,400	4.2	0.6	0.8
living with non-relatives	600	13,700	4.4	3.5	4.7
15-24	400	4,200	9.5	2.3	1.4
25-54	200	9,100	2.2	1.2	3.1
55 or older	0	0			
Industry					
total	17,500	293,100	6.0	100.0	100.0
agriculture		4,100			1.4
forestry, fishing, mining, oil and gas		9,700			3.3
utilities		4,300			1.5
construction		15,900			5.4
manufacturing	500	40,000	1.3	2.9	13.6
trade	6,100	48,300	12.6	34.9	16.5
transportation and warehousing		16,300			5.6
finance, insurance, real estate and leasing	1,100	11,400	9.6	6.3	3.9
professional, scientific and technical services		8,000			2.7

	minimum wage workers (no.)	all employees (no.)	incidence of minimum wage workers (%)	distribution of minimum wage workers (%)	distribution of all employees (%)
management, admin. and other support	700	11,000	6.4	4.0	3.8
educational services		22,600			7.7
health care and social assistance	1,000	36,000	2.8	5.7	12.3
information, culture and recreation	800	11,500	7.0	4.6	3.9
accommodation and food services	5,200	20,500	25.4	29.7	7.0
other services	1,100	10,700	10.3	6.3	3.7
public administration		22,900			7.8

Minimum Wages in Canada: A Statistical Portrait With Policy Implications

	minimum wage workers (no.)	all employees (no.)	incidence of minimum wage workers (%)	distribution of minimum wage workers (%)	distribution of all employees (%)
QUEBEC	158,800	2,926,400	5.4	100.0	100.0
Gender and age					
total both sexes	158,800	2,926,400	5.4	100.0	100.0
15-19	63,400	164,700	38.5	39.9	5.6
20-24	31,300	325,300	9.6	19.7	11.1
15-24	94,700	490,000	19.3	59.6	16.7
25-44	41,400	1,541,400	2.7	26.1	52.7
45 or older	22,600	895,000	2.5	14.2	30.6
total females	98,800	1,377,300	7.2	62.2	47.1
15-19	34,800	74,500	46.7	21.9	2.5
20-24	18,500	155,700	11.9	11.6	5.3
15-24	53,300	230,100	23.2	33.6	7.9
25-44	29,600	729,800	4.1	18.6	24.9
45 or older	16,000	417,400	3.8	10.1	14.3
total males	59,900	1,549,100	3.9	37.7	52.9
15-19	28,600	90,300	31.7	18.0	3.1
20-24	12,800	169,600	7.5	8.1	5.8
15-24	41,400	259,900	15.9	26.1	8.9
25-44	11,900	811,600	1.5	7.5	27.7
45 or older	6,600	477,600	1.4	4.2	16.3
Education					
all education levels	158,800	2,926,400	5.4	100.0	100.0
0 - 8 years	13,000	159,200	8.2	8.2	5.4
some high school	38,700	366,900	10.5	24.4	12.5
high school graduate	29,000	520,300	5.6	18.3	17.8
some post-secondary	33,000	249,500	13.2	20.8	8.5
post-secondary certificate or diploma	37,100	1,087,000	3.4	23.4	37.1
university degree	8,000	543,500	1.5	5.0	18.6
Full-time or part-time work					
total both sexes	158,800	2,926,400	5.4	100.0	100.0
full-time	75,300	2,430,500	3.1	47.4	83.1
part-time	83,400	4,596,000	1.8	52.5	157.1
total females	98,800	1,377,300	7.2	62.2	47.1
full-time	46,400	1,034,900	4.5	29.2	35.4
part-time	52,500	342,400	15.3	33.1	11.7
total males	59,900	1,549,100	3.9	37.7	52.9
full-time	28,900	1,395,600	2.1	18.2	47.7
part-time	31,000	153,500	20.2	19.5	5.2

294   Caledon Institute of Social Policy

Minimum Wages in Canada: A Statistical Portrait With Policy Implications

	minimum wage workers (no.)	all employees (no.)	incidence of minimum wage workers (%)	distribution of minimum wage workers (%)	distribution of all employees (%)
Family status					
member of couple	46,200	1,816,500	2.5	29.1	62.1
spouse not employed	11,700	403,700	2.9	7.4	13.8
spouse unemployed	3,700	75,200	4.9	2.3	2.6
spouse not in labour force	8,000	328,500	2.4	5.0	11.2
spouse employed	34,500	1,412,700	2.4	21.8	48.3
earns minimum wage	2,000	27,000	7.4	1.3	0.9
earns more than minimum wage	25,000	1,203,500	2.1	15.8	41.1
spouse self-employed	7,500	182,200	4.1	4.7	6.2
head of family	7,200	163,000	4.4	4.5	5.6
youngest child under 18	6,700	134,500	5.0	4.2	4.6
no children or youngest child over 18	500	28,400	1.8	0.3	1.0
son or daughter	83,500	486,000	17.2	52.7	16.6
15-19 in school	35,500	80,500	44.1	22.4	2.8
15-19 not in school	23,300	69,600	33.5	14.7	2.4
20-24 in school	8,200	51,800	15.8	5.2	1.8
20-24 not in school	10,500	125,700	8.4	6.6	4.3
25 or older in school	200	9,900	2.0	0.1	0.3
25 or older not in school	5,800	148,600	3.9	3.7	5.1
unattached individual	21,700	455,800	4.8	13.7	15.6
living alone	12,100	338,700	3.6	7.6	11.6
15-24	3,900	28,500	13.7	2.5	1.0
25-54	6,300	268,700	2.3	4.0	9.2
55 or older	1,800	41,500	4.3	1.1	1.4
living with non-relatives	9,600	117,000	8.2	6.1	4.0
15-24	6,500	35,900	18.1	4.1	1.2
25-54	3,100	76,200	4.1	2.0	2.6
55 or older	100	4,900	2.0	0.1	0.2
Industry					
total	158,800	2,926,400	5.4	100.0	100.0
agriculture	4600	22,700	20.3	2.9	0.8
forestry, fishing, mining, oil and gas		34,100	0.0	0.0	1.2
utilities		26,800	0.0	0.0	0.9
construction		94,900	0.0	0.0	3.2
manufacturing	13900	600,700	2.3	8.8	20.5
trade	46,800	478,800	9.8	29.5	16.4
transportation and warehousing	4000	144,900	2.8	2.5	5.0
finance, insurance, real estate & leasing	3600	154,300	2.3	2.3	5.3
professional, scientific and technical services		133,200			4.6

	minimum wage workers (no.)	all employees (no.)	incidence of minimum wage workers (%)	distribution of minimum wage workers (%)	distribution of all employees (%)
management, administrative and other support	4,700	76,700	6.1	3.0	2.6
educational services	3,000	214,900	1.4	1.9	7.3
health care and social assistance	9,600	326,300	2.9	6.0	11.2
information, culture and recreation	9,100	122,000	7.5	5.7	4.2
accommodation and food services	42,600	180,800	23.6	26.8	6.2
other services	9,900	109,000	9.1	6.2	3.7
public administration	3,000	206,200	1.5	1.9	7.0

	minimum wage workers (no.)	all employees (no.)	incidence of minimum wage workers (%)	distribution of minimum wage workers (%)	distribution of all employees (%)
ONTARIO	223,500	4,959,500	4.5	100.0	100.0
Gender and age					
total both sexes	223,500	4,959,500	4.5	100.0	100.0
15-19	126,500	337,300	37.5	56.6	6.8
20-24	29,600	505,500	5.9	13.2	10.2
15-24	156,100	842,800	18.5	69.8	17.0
25-44	43,300	2,650,200	1.6	19.4	53.4
45 or older	24,100	1,466,500	1.6	10.8	29.6
total females	139,800	2,403,100	5.8	62.6	48.5
15-19	79,300	171,500	46.2	35.5	3.5
20-24	17,600	245,600	7.2	7.9	5.0
15-24	96,900	417,100	23.2	43.4	8.4
25-44	27,200	1,272,800	2.1	12.2	25.7
45 or older	15,700	713,200	2.2	7.0	14.4
total males	83,700	2,556,500	3.3	37.4	51.5
15-19	47,100	165,800	28.4	21.1	3.3
20-24	12,000	260,000	4.6	5.4	5.2
15-24	59,100	425,800	13.9	26.4	8.6
25-44	16,200	1,377,400	1.2	7.2	27.8
45 or older	8,400	753,300	1.1	3.8	15.2
Education					
all education levels	223,500	4,959,500	4.5	100.0	100.0
0 - 8 years	8,700	139,900	6.2	3.9	2.8
some high school	104,300	656,900	15.9	46.7	13.2
high school graduate	45,400	1,102,400	4.1	20.3	22.2
some post-secondary	30,200	514,700	5.9	13.5	10.4
post-secondary certificate or diploma	23,800	1,488,500	1.6	10.6	30.0
university degree	11,200	1,057,100	1.1	5.0	21.3
Full-time or part-time work					
total both sexes	223,500	4,959,500	4.5	100.0	100.0
full-time	75,800	4,099,200	1.8	33.9	82.7
part-time	147,700	860,400	17.2	66.1	17.3
total females	139,800	2,403,100	5.8	62.6	48.5
full-time	45,000	1,802,500	2.5	20.1	36.3
part-time	94,800	600,600	15.8	42.4	12.1
total males	83,700	2,556,500	3.3	37.4	51.5
full-time	30,800	2,296,700	1.3	13.8	46.3
part-time	52,900	259,800	20.4	23.7	5.2

	minimum wage workers (no.)	all employees (no.)	incidence of minimum wage workers (%)	distribution of minimum wage workers (%)	distribution of all employees (%)
Family status					
member of couple	41,800	2,958,600	1.4	26.3	101.1
spouse not employed	10,800	558,600	1.9	6.8	19.1
spouse unemployed	2,400	98,000	2.4	1.5	3.3
spouse not in labour force	8,500	460,600	1.8	5.4	15.7
spouse employed	31,000	2,400,100	1.3	19.5	82.0
earns minimum wage	1,200	24,200	5.0	0.8	0.8
earns more than minimum wage	23,000	2,057,700	1.1	14.5	70.3
spouse self-employed	6,800	318,200	2.1	4.3	10.9
head of family	9,000	284,900	3.2	5.7	9.7
youngest child under 18	8,100	241,400	3.4	5.1	8.2
no children or youngest child over 18	900	43,400	2.1	0.6	1.5
son or daughter	153,500	1,066,900	14.4	96.7	36.5
15-19 in school	85,500	202,700	42.2	53.8	6.9
15-19 not in school	35,500	119,200	29.8	22.4	4.1
20-24 in school	9,900	90,200	11.0	6.2	3.1
20-24 not in school	12,100	240,200	5.0	7.6	8.2
25 or older in school	900	21,500	4.2	0.6	0.7
25 or older not in school	9,700	393,100	2.5	6.1	13.4
unattached individual	19,100	638,200	3.0	12.0	21.8
living alone	9,300	407,800	2.3	5.9	13.9
15-24	1,700	26,900	6.3	1.1	0.9
25-54	4,800	326,400	1.5	3.0	11.2
55 or older	2,800	54,400	5.1	1.8	1.9
living with non-relatives	9,900	230,400	4.3	6.2	7.9
15-24	4,400	60,600	7.3	2.8	2.1
25-54	4,800	159,700	3.0	3.0	5.5
55 or older	600	10,200	5.9	0.4	0.3
Industry					
total	223,500	4,959,500	4.5	100.0	100.0
agriculture	6800	39,100	17.4	3.0	0.8
forestry, fishing, mining, oil and gas		31,400			0.6
utilities		46,300			0.9
construction	1700	205,600	0.8	0.8	4.1
manufacturing	8400	1,066,100	0.8	3.8	21.5
trade	72,000	750,600	9.6	32.2	15.1
transportation and warehousing	5200	221,700	2.3	2.3	4.5
finance, insurance, real estate & leasing	7800	331,700	2.4	3.5	6.7

	minimum wage workers (no.)	all employees (no.)	incidence of minimum wage workers (%)	distribution of minimum wage workers (%)	distribution of all employees (%)
professional, scientific and technical services management,	2700	279,000		1.2	5.6
administrative and other support	6,500	177,800	3.7	2.9	3.6
educational services	7,400	349,000	2.1	3.3	7.0
health care and social assistance	8,100	472,100	1.7	3.6	9.5
information, culture and recreation	14,400	239,800	6.0	6.4	4.8
accommodation and food services	68,200	308,200	22.1	30.5	6.2
other services	10,900	167,300	6.5	4.9	3.4
public administration	2,700	274,000	1.0	1.2	5.5

Minimum Wages in Canada: A Statistical Portrait With Policy Implications

	minimum wage workers (no.)	all employees (no.)	incidence of minimum wage workers (%)	distribution of minimum wage workers (%)	distribution of all employees (%)
MANITOBA	24,000	462,800	5.2	100.0	100.0
Gender and age					
total both sexes	24,000	462,800	5.2	100.0	100.0
15-19	12,900	36,800	35.1	53.8	8.0
20-24	3,100	53,800	5.8	12.9	11.6
15-24	16,000	90,600	17.7	66.7	19.6
25-44	4,900	233,400	2.1	20.4	50.4
45 or older	3,100	138,900	2.2	12.9	30.0
total females	14,200	226,000	6.3	59.2	48.8
15-19	7,100	18,300	38.8	29.6	4.0
20-24	1,700	26,200	6.5	7.1	5.7
15-24	8,800	44,400	19.8	36.7	9.6
25-44	3,600	112,000	3.2	15.0	24.2
45 or older	1,800	69,600	2.6	7.5	15.0
total males	9,800	236,800	4.1	40.8	51.2
15-19	5,700	18,600	30.6	23.8	4.0
20-24	1,500	27,600	5.4	6.3	6.0
15-24	7,200	46,200	15.6	30.0	10.0
25-44	1,300	121,400	1.1	5.4	26.2
45 or older	1,300	69,200	1.9	5.4	15.0
Education					
all education levels	24,000	462,800	5.2	100.0	100.0
0 - 8 years	1,400	14,000	10.0	5.8	3.0
some high school	11,800	77,000	15.3	49.2	16.6
high school graduate	4,900	111,400	4.4	20.4	24.1
some post-secondary	2,200	45,600	4.8	9.2	9.9
post-secondary certificate or diploma	2,300	135,600	1.7	9.6	29.3
university degree	1,400	79,200	1.8	5.8	17.1
Full-time or part-time work					
total both sexes	24,000	462,800	5.2	100.0	100.0
full-time	9,800	376,600	2.6	40.8	81.4
part-time	14,200	86,200	16.5	59.2	18.6
total females	14,200	226,000	6.3	59.2	48.8
full-time	5,700	163,900	3.5	23.8	35.4
part-time	8,500	62,100	13.7	35.4	13.4
total males	9,800	236,800	4.1	40.8	51.2
full-time	4,100	212,700	1.9	17.1	46.0
part-time	5,700	24,100	23.7	23.8	5.2

	minimum wage workers (no.)	all employees (no.)	incidence of minimum wage workers (%)	distribution of minimum wage workers (%)	distribution of all employees (%)
Family status					
member of couple	5,200	275,500	1.9	21.6	59.5
spouse not employed	1,000	44,600	2.2	4.1	9.6
spouse unemployed	200	7,800	2.6	0.8	1.7
spouse not in labour force	800	36,800	2.2	3.3	8.0
spouse employed	4,200	231,000	1.8	17.4	49.9
earns minimum wage	0	3,600	0.0	0.0	0.8
earns more than minimum wage	3,500	197,200	1.8	14.5	42.6
spouse self-employed	700	30,200	2.3	2.9	6.5
head of family	1,400	26,900	5.2	5.8	5.8
youngest child under 18	1,200	23,700	5.1	5.0	5.1
no children or youngest child over 18	200	3,200	6.3	0.8	0.7
son or daughter	15,000	89,700	16.7	62.2	19.4
15-19 in school	7,800	19,000	41.1	32.4	4.1
15-19 not in school	4,200	14,200	29.6	17.4	3.1
20-24 in school	400	6,100	6.6	1.7	1.3
20-24 not in school	1,500	21,900	6.8	6.2	4.7
25 or older in school	100	1,700	5.9	0.4	0.4
25 or older not in school	1,000	26,800	3.7	4.1	5.8
unattached individual	2,500	69,800	3.6	10.4	15.1
living alone	1,400	45,000	3.1	5.8	9.7
15-24	300	5,400	5.6	1.2	1.2
25-54	700	33,700	2.1	2.9	7.3
55 or older	400	6,000	6.7	1.7	1.3
living with non-relatives	1,100	24,800	4.4	4.6	5.4
15-24	600	8,900	6.7	2.5	1.9
25-54	400	15,200	2.6	1.7	3.3
55 or older	100	800	12.5	0.4	0.2
Industry					
total	24,000	462,800	5.2	100.0	100.0
agriculture	1,200	8,300	14.5	5.0	1.8
forestry, fishing, mining, oil and gas		5,900			1.3
utilities		6,800			1.5
construction		18,700			4.0
manufacturing	1,300	68,600	1.9	5.4	14.8
trade	6,300	71,500	8.8	26.3	15.4
transportation and warehousing	500	29,200	1.7	2.1	6.3
finance, insurance, real estate & leasing	600	25,700	2.3	2.5	5.6
professional, scientific and technical services		14,900			3.2

	minimum wage workers (no.)	all employees (no.)	incidence of minimum wage workers (%)	distribution of minimum wage workers (%)	distribution of all employees (%)
management, administrative and other support	1,300	12,000	10.8	5.4	2.6
educational services	900	37,600	2.4	3.8	8.1
health care and social assistance	900	63,100	1.4	3.8	13.6
information, culture and recreation	1,400	18,200	7.7	5.8	3.9
accommodation and food services	7,800	32,600	23.9	32.5	7.0
other services	1,200	16,500	7.3	5.0	3.6
public administration		33,100			7.2

	minimum wage workers (no.)	all employees (no.)	incidence of minimum wage workers (%)	distribution of minimum wage workers (%)	distribution of all employees (%)
SASKATCHEWAN	22,000	371,700	5.9	100.0	100.0
Gender and age					
total both sexes	22,000	371,700	5.9	100.0	100.0
15-19	10,200	31,200	32.7	46.4	8.4
20-24	3,400	47,200	7.2	15.5	12.7
15-24	13,700	78,400	17.5	62.3	21.1
25-44	5,000	185,900	2.7	22.7	50.0
45 or older	3,300	107,400	3.1	15.0	28.9
total females	12,300	185,200	6.6	55.9	49.8
15-19	4,800	15,100	31.8	21.8	4.1
20-24	1,900	22,400	8.5	8.6	6.0
15-24	6,700	37,500	17.9	30.5	10.1
25-44	3,300	92,100	3.6	15.0	24.8
45 or older	2,200	55,600	4.0	10.0	15.0
total males	9,700	186,500	5.2	44.1	50.2
15-19	5,500	16,100	34.2	25.0	4.3
20-24	1,500	24,800	6.0	6.8	6.7
15-24	7,000	41,000	17.1	31.8	11.0
25-44	1,700	93,800	1.8	7.7	25.2
45 or older	1,100	51,800	2.1	5.0	13.9
Education					
all education levels	22,000	371,700	5.9	100.0	100.0
0 - 8 years	1,400	8,900	15.7	6.4	2.4
some high school	9,200	55,300	16.6	41.8	14.9
high school graduate	4,700	91,400	5.1	21.4	24.6
some post-secondary	2,800	40,800	6.9	12.7	11.0
post-secondary certificate or diploma	2,900	116,800	2.5	13.2	31.4
university degree	1,100	58,300	1.9	5.0	15.7
Full-time or part-time work					
total both sexes	22,000	371,700	5.9	100.0	100.0
full-time	9,800	298,700	3.3	44.5	80.4
part-time	12,200	73,000	16.7	55.5	19.6
total females	12,300	185,200	6.6	55.9	49.8
full-time	5,200	131,400	4.0	23.6	35.4
part-time	7,100	53,800	13.2	32.3	14.5
total males	9,700	186,500	5.2	44.1	50.2
full-time	4,600	167,300	2.7	20.9	45.0
part-time	5,200	19,300	26.9	23.6	5.2

	minimum wage workers (no.)	all employees (no.)	incidence of minimum wage workers (%)	distribution of minimum wage workers (%)	distribution of all employees (%)
Family status					
member of couple	5,900	230,500	2.6	27.1	62.0
spouse not employed	1,300	38,300	3.4	6.0	10.3
spouse unemployed	400	6,500	6.2	1.8	1.7
spouse not in labour force	1,000	31,700	3.2	4.6	8.5
spouse employed	4,600	192,200	2.4	21.1	51.7
earns minimum wage	600	3,500	17.1	2.8	0.9
earns more than minimum wage	2,900	153,200	1.9	13.3	41.2
spouse self-employed	1,000	35,500	2.8	4.6	9.6
head of family	1,400	21,300	6.6	6.4	5.7
youngest child under 18	1,100	18,600	5.9	5.0	5.0
no children or youngest child over 18	300	2,700	11.1	1.4	0.7
son or daughter	12,200	63,700	19.2	56.0	17.1
15-19 in school	6,500	15,600	41.7	29.8	4.2
15-19 not in school	3,200	12,700	25.2	14.7	3.4
20-24 in school	400	4,000	10.0	1.8	1.1
20-24 not in school	1,300	16,200	8.0	6.9	4.4
25 or older in school	100	600	16.7	0.5	0.2
25 or older not in school	700	14,600	4.8	3.2	3.9
unattached individual	2,300	55,400	4.2	10.6	14.9
living alone	1,100	36,100	3.0	5.0	9.7
15-24	300	5,500	5.5	1.4	1.5
25-54	600	25,900	2.3	2.8	7.0
55 or older	200	4,700	4.3	0.9	1.3
living with non-relatives	1,200	19,300	6.2	5.5	5.2
15-24	900	9,900	9.1	4.1	2.7
25-54	300	8,900	3.4	1.4	2.4
55 or older	100	500	20.0	0.5	0.1
Industry					
total	22,000	371,700	5.9	100.0	100.0
agriculture	1,300	9,800	13.3	5.9	2.6
forestry, fishing, mining, oil and gas		14,400			3.9
utilities		3,600			1.0
construction		15,300			4.1
manufacturing	500	27,600	1.8		7.4
trade	6,500	66,300	9.8	29.5	17.8
transportation and warehousing		22,800			6.1
finance, insurance, real estate & leasing		23,100			6.2

	minimum wage workers (no.)	all employees (no.)	incidence of minimum wage workers (%)	distribution of minimum wage workers (%)	distribution of all employees (%)
professional, scientific and technical services		11,300			3.0
management, administrative and other support	800	6,300	12.7	3.6	1.7
educational services	700	34,500	2.0	3.2	9.3
health care and social assistance	900	47,900	1.9	4.1	12.9
information, culture and recreation	1,600	16,500	9.7	7.3	4.4
accommodation and food services	6,700	29,500	22.7	30.5	7.9
other services	1,300	16,000	8.1	5.9	4.3
public administration		26,700			7.2

	minimum wage workers (no.)	all employees (no.)	incidence of minimum wage workers (%)	distribution of minimum wage workers (%)	distribution of all employees (%)
ALBERTA	26,200	1,299,200	2.0	100.0	100.0
Gender and age					
total both sexes	26,200	1,299,200	2.0	100.0	100.0
15-19	10,700	102,300	10.5	40.8	7.9
20-24	4,000	157,600	2.5	15.3	12.1
15-24	14,600	259,800	5.6	55.7	20.0
25-44	7,100	684,600	1.0	27.1	52.7
45 or older	4,400	354,800	1.2	16.8	27.3
total females	14,800	612,000	2.4	56.5	47.1
15-19	5,900	49,500	11.9	22.5	3.8
20-24	1,900	73,900	2.6	7.3	5.7
15-24	7,800	123,300	6.3	29.8	9.5
25-44	3,900	318,800	1.2	14.9	24.5
45 or older	3,100	169,900	1.8	11.8	13.1
total males	11,400	687,100	1.7	43.5	52.9
15-19	4,800	52,800	9.1	18.3	4.1
20-24	2,000	83,700	2.4	7.6	6.4
15-24	6,800	136,500	5.0	26.0	10.5
25-44	3,200	365,800	0.9	12.2	28.2
45 or older	1,400	184,800	0.8	5.3	14.2
Education					
all education levels	26,200	1,299,200	2.0	100.0	100.0
0 - 8 years	1,500	29,300	5.1	5.7	2.3
some high school	11,500	175,400	6.6	43.9	13.5
high school graduate	4,500	297,500	1.5	17.2	22.9
some post-secondary	3,200	151,200	2.1	12.2	11.6
post-secondary certificate or diploma	3,400	431,600	0.8	13.0	33.2
university degree	2,100	214,200	1.0	8.0	16.5
Full-time or part-time work					
total both sexes	26,200	1,299,200	2.0	100.0	100.0
full-time	12,400	1,065,700	1.2	47.5	82.0
part-time	13,700	233,400	5.9	52.5	18.0
total females	14,800	612,000	2.4	56.5	47.1
full-time	6,600	440,700	1.5	25.2	33.9
part-time	8,200	171,300	4.8	31.3	13.2
total males	11,400	687,100	1.7	43.5	52.9
full-time	5,800	625,000	0.9	22.1	48.1
part-time	5,500	62,100	8.9	21.0	4.8

	minimum wage workers (no.)	all employees (no.)	incidence of minimum wage workers (%)	distribution of minimum wage workers (%)	distribution of all employees (%)
Family status					
member of couple	8,000	758,100	1.1	30.7	58.4
spouse not employed	1,600	138,900	1.2	6.1	10.7
spouse unemployed	100	20,800	0.5	0.4	1.6
spouse not in labour force	1,500	118,000	1.3	5.7	9.1
spouse employed	6,400	619,300	1.0	24.5	47.7
earns minimum wage	300	5,200	5.8	1.1	0.4
earns more than minimum wage	4,800	516,600	0.9	18.4	39.8
spouse self-employed	1,300	97,500	1.3	5.0	7.5
head of family	1,000	77,600	1.3	3.8	6.0
youngest child under 18	1,000	68,400	1.5	3.8	5.3
no children or youngest child over 18	0	9,300	0.0	0.0	0.7
son or daughter	14,000	242,000	5.8	53.6	18.6
15-19 in school	7,200	50,600	14.2	27.6	3.9
15-19 not in school	2,700	41,500	6.5	10.3	3.2
20-24 in school	700	16,500	4.2	2.7	1.3
20-24 not in school	1,900	58,100	3.3	7.3	4.5
25 or older in school	100	4,100	2.4	0.4	0.3
25 or older not in school	1,400	71,300	2.0	5.4	5.5
unattached individual	3,100	218,300	1.4	11.9	16.8
living alone	1,300	126,200	1.0	5.0	9.7
15-24	200	12,200	1.6	0.8	0.9
25-54	900	99,500	0.9	3.4	7.7
55 or older	200	14,500	1.4	0.8	1.1
living with non-relatives	1,800	92,000	2.0	6.9	7.1
15-24	700	36,700	1.9	2.7	2.8
25-54	1,000	53,200	1.9	3.8	4.1
55 or older	100	2,200	4.5	0.4	0.2
Industry					
total	26,200	1,299,200	2.0	100.0	100.0
agriculture	1,600	16,200	9.9	6.1	1.2
forestry, fishing, mining, oil and gas		76,100			5.9
utilities		12,500			1.0
construction		89,700			6.9
manufacturing		131,800			10.1
trade	6,200	218,800	2.8	23.7	16.8
transportation and warehousing		78,100			6.0
finance, insurance, real estate & leasing		64,600			5.0

	minimum wage workers (no.)	all employees (no.)	incidence of minimum wage workers (%)	distribution of minimum wage workers (%)	distribution of all employees (%)
professional, scientific and technical services		71,900			5.5
management, administrative and other support		36,500			2.8
educational services		94,200			7.3
health care and social assistance		131,700			10.1
information, culture and recreation		56,200			4.3
accommodation and food services	7,300	106,700	6.8	27.9	8.2
other services	2,700	52,300	5.2	10.3	4.0
public administration		61,900			4.8

	minimum wage workers (no.)	all employees (no.)	incidence of minimum wage workers (%)	distribution of minimum wage workers (%)	distribution of all employees (%)
BRITISH COLUMBIA	72,600	1,583,000	4.6	100.0	100.0
Gender and age					
total both sexes	72,600	1,583,000	4.6	100.0	100.0
15-19	28,300	98,700	28.7	39.0	6.2
20-24	11,900	162,800	7.3	16.4	10.3
15-24	40,200	261,500	15.4	55.4	16.5
25-44	19,300	816,400	2.4	26.6	51.6
45 or older	13,100	505,100	2.6	18.0	31.9
total females	45,700	769,400	5.9	62.9	48.6
15-19	16,400	49,600	33.1	22.6	3.1
20-24	6,500	79,200	8.2	9.0	5.0
15-24	22,900	128,700	17.8	31.5	8.1
25-44	13,600	391,500	3.5	18.7	24.7
45 or older	9,200	249,200	3.7	12.7	15.7
total males	26,900	813,500	3.3	37.1	51.4
15-19	11,900	49,100	24.2	16.4	3.1
20-24	5,400	83,700	6.5	7.4	5.3
15-24	17,300	132,700	13.0	23.8	8.4
25-44	5,700	424,800	1.3	7.9	26.8
45 or older	3,900	256,000	1.5	5.4	16.2
Education					
all education levels	72,600	1,583,000	4.6	100.0	100.0
0 - 8 years	3,400	23,400	14.5	4.7	1.5
some high school	24,300	181,400	13.4	33.5	11.5
high school graduate	17,200	385,600	4.5	23.7	24.4
some post-secondary	11,800	195,900	6.0	16.3	12.4
post-secondary certificate or diploma	10,300	494,100	2.1	14.2	31.2
university degree	5,700	302,500	1.9	7.9	19.1
Full-time or part-time work					
total both sexes	72,600	1,583,000	4.6	100.0	100.0
full-time	34,200	1,268,200	2.7	47.1	80.1
part-time	38,400	314,800	12.2	52.9	19.9
total females	45,700	769,400	5.9	62.9	48.6
full-time	21,600	540,300	4.0	29.8	34.1
part-time	24,100	229,100	10.5	33.2	14.5
total males	26,900	813,500	3.3	37.1	51.4
full-time	12,600	727,800	1.7	17.4	46.0
part-time	14,300	85,700	16.7	19.7	5.4

	minimum wage workers (no.)	all employees (no.)	incidence of minimum wage workers (%)	distribution of minimum wage workers (%)	distribution of all employees (%)
Family status					
member of couple	21,000	905,700	2.3	28.9	57.2
spouse not employed	5,800	184,300	3.1	8.0	11.6
spouse unemployed	1,000	33,000	3.0	1.4	2.1
spouse not in labour force	4,800	151,200	3.2	6.6	9.6
spouse employed	15,200	721,500	2.1	20.9	45.6
earns minimum wage	2,500	31,700	7.9	3.4	2.0
earns more than minimum wage	10,000	590,600	1.7	13.8	37.3
spouse self-employed	2,700	99,200	2.7	3.7	6.3
head of family	2,400	97,300	2.5	3.3	6.1
youngest child under 18	2,300	84,700	2.7	3.2	5.4
no children or youngest child over 18	100	12,700	0.8	0.1	0.8
son or daughter	40,400	285,800	14.1	55.6	18.1
15-19 in school	17,800	50,000	35.6	24.5	3.2
15-19 not in school	9,000	40,200	22.4	12.4	2.5
20-24 in school	2,900	21,200	13.7	4.0	1.3
20-24 not in school	5,000	64,100	7.8	6.9	4.0
25 or older in school	300	6,100	4.9	0.4	0.4
25 or older not in school	5,500	104,100	5.3	7.6	6.6
unattached individual	8,700	291,400	3.0	12.0	18.4
living alone	3,900	159,600	2.4	5.4	10.1
15-24	1,000	10,900	9.2	1.4	0.7
25-54	2,400	126,600	1.9	3.3	8.0
55 or older	600	22,100	2.7	0.8	1.4
living with non-relatives	4,800	131,800	3.6	6.6	8.3
15-24	2,000	35,900	5.6	2.8	2.3
25-54	2,600	90,500	2.9	3.6	5.7
55 or older	200	5,400	3.7	0.3	0.3
Industry					
total	72,600	1,583,000	4.6	100.0	100.0
agriculture	2,800	15,600	17.9	3.9	1.0
forestry, fishing, mining, oil and gas		44,100			2.8
utilities		11,300			0.7
construction		67,900			4.3
manufacturing	4,400	189,700		6.1	12.0
trade	18,500	258,100	7.2	25.5	16.3
transportation and warehousing	2,300	95,900		3.2	6.1
finance, insurance, real estate and leasing	2,700	98,200		3.7	6.2

	minimum wage workers (no.)	all employees (no.)	incidence of minimum wage workers (%)	distribution of minimum wage workers (%)	distribution of all employees (%)
professional, scientific and technical services		81,900			5.2
management, administrative and other support	3,200	45,800		4.4	2.9
educational services		125,400			7.9
health care and social assistance	2,600	170,100		3.6	10.7
information, culture and recreation	4,700	82,100		6.5	5.2
accommodation and food services	21,600	144,400	15.0	29.8	9.1
other services	5,400	62,900	8.6	7.4	4.0
public administration		89,700			5.7

	minimum wage workers (no.)	all employees (no.)	incidence of minimum wage workers (%)	distribution of minimum wage workers (%)	distribution of all employees (%)
CANADA	580,000	12,488,300	4.6	100.0	100.0
Gender and age					
total both sexes	580,000	12,488,300	4.6	100.0	100.0
15-19	273,000	824,300	33.1	47.1	6.6
20-24	94,900	1,348,400	7.0	16.4	10.8
15-24	367,900	2,172,700	16.9	63.4	17.4
25-44	134,400	6,580,500	2.0	23.2	52.7
45 or older	77,700	3,735,100	2.1	13.4	29.9
total females	360,400	6,007,600	6.0	62.1	48.1
15-19	160,800	406,200	39.6	27.7	3.3
20-24	54,800	650,200	8.4	9.4	5.2
15-24	215,600	1,056,400	20.4	37.2	8.5
25-44	91,300	3,151,700	2.9	15.7	25.2
45 or older	53,500	1,799,400	3.0	9.2	14.4
total males	219,600	6,480,700	3.4	37.9	51.9
15-19	112,200	418,100	26.8	19.3	3.3
20-24	40,100	698,200	5.7	6.9	5.6
15-24	152,300	1,116,300	13.6	26.3	8.9
25-44	43,000	3,428,800	1.3	7.4	27.5
45 or older	24,200	1,935,700	1.3	4.2	15.5
Education					
total both sexes					
all education levels	580,000	12,488,300	4.6	100.0	100.0
0 - 8 years	31,400	407,800	7.7	5.4	3.3
some high school	219,100	1,638,600	13.4	37.8	13.1
high school graduate	117,400	2,675,900	4.4	20.2	21.4
some post-secondary	90,800	1,276,500	7.1	15.7	10.2
post-secondary certificate or diploma	89,500	4,090,200	2.2	15.4	32.8
university degree	31,700	2,399,300	1.3	5.5	19.2
total females					
all education levels	360,400	6,007,600	6.0	62.1	48.1
0 - 8 years	18,500	154,400	12.0	3.2	1.2
some high school	127,000	700,400	18.1	21.9	5.6
high school graduate	78,300	1,318,100	5.9	13.5	10.6
some post-secondary	54,700	637,400	8.6	9.4	5.1
post-secondary certificate or diploma	63,800	1,999,500	3.2	11.0	16.0
university degree	18,100	1,197,800	1.5	3.1	9.6

	minimum wage workers (no.)	all employees (no.)	incidence of minimum wage workers (%)	distribution of minimum wage workers (%)	distribution of all employees (%)
total males					
all education levels	219,600	6,480,700	3.4	37.9	51.9
0 - 8 years	13,000	253,400	5.1	2.2	2.0
some high school	92,100	938,200	9.8	15.9	7.5
high school graduate	39,200	1,357,700	2.9	6.8	10.9
some post-secondary	36,100	639,100	5.6	6.2	5.1
post-secondary certificate or diploma	25,700	2,090,700	1.2	4.4	16.7
university degree	13,600	1,201,600	1.1	2.3	9.6
Full-time or part-time work					
total both sexes	580,000	12,488,300	4.6	100.0	100.0
full-time	243,100	10,281,100	2.4	41.9	82.3
part-time	336,900	2,207,200	15.3	58.1	17.7
total females	360,400	6,007,500	6.0	62.1	48.1
full-time	147,000	4,444,600	3.3	25.3	35.6
part-time	213,400	1,562,900	13.7	36.8	12.5
total males	219,600	6,480,800	3.4	37.9	51.9
full-time	96,100	5,836,500	1.6	16.6	46.7
part-time	123,500	644,300	19.2	21.3	5.2
Family status					
member of couple	144,800	7,524,000	1.9	25.0	60.2
spouse not employed	36,800	1,510,500	2.4	6.3	12.1
spouse unemployed	9,300	277,100	3.4	1.6	2.2
spouse not in labour force	27,600	1,233,100	2.2	4.8	9.9
spouse employed	108,000	6,013,700	1.8	18.6	48.2
earns minimum wage	28,800	111,900	25.7	5.0	0.9
earns more than minimum wage	78,700	5,092,000	1.5	13.6	40.8
spouse self-employed	400	809,900	0.0	0.1	6.5
head of family	23,800	711,100	3.3	4.1	5.7
youngest child under 18	21,600	604,400	3.6	3.7	4.8
no children or youngest child over 18	2,300	106,600	2.2	0.4	0.9
son or daughter	349,300	2,397,700	14.6	60.2	19.2
15-19 in school	172,500	445,100	38.8	29.7	3.6
15-19 not in school	85,900	321,200	26.7	14.8	2.6
20-24 in school	24,700	201,300	12.3	4.3	1.6
20-24 not in school	38,000	571,100	6.7	6.6	4.6
25 or older in school	1,800	45,400	4.0	0.3	0.4
25 or older not in school	26,500	810,600	3.3	4.6	6.5

	minimum wage workers (no.)	all employees (no.)	incidence of minimum wage workers (%)	distribution of minimum wage workers (%)	distribution of all employees (%)
unattached individual	62,000	1,826,700	3.4	10.7	14.6
living alone	31,400	1,172,800	2.7	5.4	9.4
15-24	8,000	95,400	8.4	1.4	0.8
25-54	16,900	926,600	1.8	2.9	7.4
55 or older	6,500	150,800	4.3	1.1	1.2
living with non-relatives	30,500	653,800	4.7	5.3	5.2
15-24	16,600	201,300	8.2	2.9	1.6
25-54	12,700	427,700	3.0	2.2	3.4
55 or older	1,200	24,000	5.0	0.2	0.2
Industry					
total	580,000	12,488,300	4.6	100.0	100.0
agriculture	19,000	123,600	15.4	3.3	1.0
forestry, fishing, mining, oil and gas	3,400	234,300	1.5	0.6	1.9
utilities		116,300			0.9
construction	5,200	538,300	1.0	0.9	4.3
manufacturing	30,400	2,187,500	1.4	5.2	17.5
trade	175,200	2,000,800	8.8	30.2	16.0
transportation and warehousing	13,900	638,200	2.2	2.4	5.1
finance, insurance, real estate and leasing	18,300	736,000	2.5	3.2	5.9
professional, scientific and technical services	6,300	619,200	1.0	1.1	5.0
management, administrative and other support	19,600	385,800	5.1	3.4	3.1
educational services	15,600	929,400	1.7	2.7	7.4
health care and social assistance	26,000	1,326,800	2.0	4.5	10.6
information, culture and recreation	35,100	569,500	6.2	6.1	4.6
accommodation and food services	167,600	862,600	19.4	28.9	6.9
other services	35,200	458,200	7.7	6.1	3.7
public administration	8,400	761,700	1.1	1.4	6.1

Shan Fleming Research & Learning Library
Ministry of Education
Ministry of Training, Colleges & Universities
900 Bay St. 13th Floor, Mowat Block
Toronto, ON M7A 1L2